NOW IS THE TIME TO INVENT!
Reports from the Indie-Rock Revolution, 1986–2000

from the pages of *Puncture* magazine

edited by
Katherine Spielmann

with
Steve Connell
Jay Ruttenberg
J Neo Marvin

Verse Chorus Press

CONTRIBUTORS

Alex Abramovich
Tom Adelman
Mike Appelstein
Martin Aston
Patrick Barber
David Berman
Franklin Bruno
Tammy Rae Carland
John Chandler
Liz Clayton
Steve Connell
Merri Cyr
Jean Debbs
Mark Dixon
Jon Dolan
Andrea Feldman
Michael Galinsky
Kate Garner
Kian Goh
David Grad

Matthew Hall
Gina Harp
Dave Haslam
Jeffrey Herrmann
Ken Holt
Johnny Ray Huston
Camden Joy
Alan Korn
David Lowery
Felix Macnee
Lois Maffeo
Sara Manaugh
J Neo Marvin
Mike McGonigal
Bill Meyer
Fred Mills
Joseph Mitchell
Maria Mochnacz
Colin B. Morton
Neil Nehring

David Nichols
Gail O'Hara
Frances Pelzman Liscio
Marty Perez
Bob Pomeroy
Bert Queiroz
Ebet Roberts
Jay Ruttenberg
Dan Schlatter
Brad Searles
Talin Shahinian
Christine Sievanen
Tom Sinclair
Katherine Spielmann
Patty Stirling
Terri Sutton
Judie Tallman
Steve Tignor
Jenny Toomey
Elisabeth Vincentelli
Robert Zieger

Published by Verse Chorus Press, Portland, Oregon | *versechorus.com*

All contributions © the individual authors, photographers, and artists
Full credits may be found on page 320, which constitutes an extension of this page

This collection © 2020 Verse Chorus Press

Book design by Steve Connell / *steveconnell.net*
Interior layout by Liz Pavlovic / *lizpavlovic.com*
Copyediting by Allison Dubinsky

Printed in the United States of America

ISBN 978-1-891241-67-3

Library of Congress Control Number: 2020941464

CONTENTS

FOREWORD

This book collects over fifty profiles of and interviews with musicians, supplemented by reviews of records they released or shows they played, from the years 1986 to 2000. All of the writing, and most of the accompanying photographs, first appeared in the pages of *Puncture*, an independent magazine published in San Francisco and then in Portland, Oregon, during those years. As it happens, these pieces, strung together, yield something like a representative history of the development over that 15-year period of some musical trends that emerged from punk and post-punk and came to be known as indie rock.

It is a partial history, of course. Partial rather than comprehensive—any comprehensive account would need to be a rather more superficial survey in order to encompass in one book all the bands that could be included. Partial, too, in the sense that it focuses on the music that mattered most to *Puncture*'s editors and writers during those years—the artists we were passionate about and in some cases covered repeatedly. There is no single point of origin for indie rock, but two rather different developments in the mid-'80s stood out to us— the brilliant psychodramas that Kristin Hersh conjured up for Throwing Muses at one end of the spectrum, and the deadpan, genre-busting anti-anthems of Camper Van Beethoven at the other. From there we traced an arc that led to the critical triumphs of Sleater-Kinney, Neutral Milk Hotel, Belle and Sebastian, Will Oldham, and others at the end of the '90s.

I'm not going to attempt to define indie rock, but at its best, it was certainly more compelling and heterodox than the "geeks with guitars" stereotype to which retrospective accounts have reduced it on occasion.[1] Yes, there was John Darnielle (Mountain Goats) with his guitar (and, more definingly indie, with the cassette recorder on which he taped his incomparable songs directly after writing them), but there was also Stephin Merritt (Magnetic Fields) with his synthesizers, Elisabeth Esselink (Solex) with her samples and 8-track, and the exhilarating combination of these elements concocted by Stereolab. There was a wealth of striking music, in fact, created with minimal resources and maximal inventiveness, by independent-minded artists who resisted any pressures to conform, either aesthetically or commercially. This was the music we covered and that is presented here.

Like that music, *Puncture* had its roots in earlier punk and post-punk. It began in 1982, a year after Katherine Spielmann moved to San Francisco to start her life over in the aftermath of a family tragedy. She arrived broke, knowing no one, so she got a job as a live-in cook and carer for an elderly alcoholic couple in the Sunset, and saved her wages until she could afford to rent an apartment for herself and her daughter, Paula Keyth. Paula enrolled in art school and was soon immersed in the ferment of the Bay Area music scene. Katherine had worked as a journalist and editor in New York and in the UK, but was now stuck in a secretarial job she'd taken to pay the rent; her creative writing was limited to occasional reviews in local lifestyle magazines. As she watched Paula play in her first band, Black Humor, and went to other shows around town, she realized she wanted to write about this music—on its own terms, and hers. She was introduced (by Paula) to Patty Stirling, who was working as a cook and had similar interests and ambitions—and the two of them started *Puncture*. The first issue appeared in November 1982, a heady mix of typed text with hand-drawn titles and graphics, xeroxed (after hours in the office where Katherine worked) on legal-size paper, folded and stapled. Not much more than a year later, with the help of a few friends, they'd already put out six issues and were looking for a commercial printer to cope with increased demand.

Early *Punctures* had a local flavor and a strong punk element—Flipper, Code of Honor, Dead Kennedys, MDC, and Black Athletes all featured in those first issues. But so did more left-field Bay Area bands like Toiling Midgets and Negativland. And the editors' love of the Virgin Prunes and Crass, as well as icons from an earlier era (Iggy, the Who), meant that *Puncture* was never a strictly local zine.

When *Puncture* #7 came out in the summer of 1984, it had grown to standard magazine format, and sported a glossy (if thin and black-and-white) photo cover depicting Einstürzende Neubauten's Blixa Bargeld. It hadn't turned its back on punk—the next three covers featured Flipper, Hüsker Dü, and Frightwig—but things were changing.

This is about where I came in. I was working in Rough Trade's warehouse in London when I first saw *Puncture* in early 1984. I'd been sent a package of US fanzines, and *Puncture* really stood out.[2] It didn't look quite like the others, even though its mix of type and hand-drawn graphics was hardly unique back then. And the writing was something else: it was wordy, but also bold and punchy; reference was made not just to a range of music but also to the likes of Marx (Karl, not Groucho) and Rilke. More than that, *Puncture* seemed to offer a different way of looking at and valuing music, as J Neo Marvin captures so well in his introduction to this book.

I went to San Francisco on vacation that summer, mostly to visit the folks at Rough Trade's US base, and when I was offered the chance to transfer to a job there only a couple of months later, I grabbed it. Some weeks after I arrived, I met Katherine, we hit it off, and by the end of 1984 I'd moved into *Puncture* HQ, her little apartment at 1674 Filbert Street. And when Patty Stirling decided in 1986 that she wanted to see the world (she later wrote captivating music-themed travelogues for *Puncture* from Zimbabwe, the Philippines, Australia, and New Zealand), I became Katherine's partner in *Puncture*, too. For the next 15 years, we continued working day jobs, but publishing *Puncture* was our real work.

KATHERINE SPIELMANN IN *PUNCTURE*'S "OFFICE," 1985

Puncture was already changing before I got involved, as I said, and it would develop further in the ensuing years. By the final issue (#47) in 2000, it was printed (partly) in color and distributed internationally, and its cover stars had included Yoko Ono, Pavement, Helium, and Royal Trux. I don't want to imply, though, that it had somehow "evolved" to a higher level after an initial primitive stage of existence as a "punk zine"—those later issues weren't better, they were just different. *Puncture* changed because everything around it changed—the independent music scene and the wider commercial culture it was embedded in (and functioned partly in opposition to). The culture industry changed, too; for one thing, corporate magazines saw there was money to be made from writing about "alternative" music. And it changed from a zine into a magazine primarily because of the advent of desktop publishing in the second half of the '80s.

Katherine and I had no fetishistic attachment to the concept of a zine as something that looked a certain way; we were only committed to publishing *Puncture* ourselves. It started out looking the way it did because of the tools available then for a DIY publication—scissors, X-Acto knives, rubber cement, press type (Letraset). When desktop publishing provided a different method, we switched to that, so *Puncture*'s look changed too.

What didn't change was our commitment to covering only the music we wanted to cover—and to covering other stuff in addition to music. Looking back, I think Katherine wanted *Puncture* to be something like a *Harper's* or *New Yorker* for our audience. Serious coverage, but also humor (without the snideness of a certain kind of hormonal boy zine). She wrote a gossip column (as "Doktor Caligari") from the outset, and her use of little "column filler" illustrations betrays her love of the *New Yorker*. *Puncture*'s original subtitle was "the magazine of punk culture"; its first issue contained the ambitiously

titled "How Bands Break Up," and essays would continue to be an essential part of it—Terri Sutton's influential "Women in Rock" and "Women, Sex, and Rock 'n' Roll" and Steve Tignor's "Indie Rock: Dying Breed or Dead Issue," for example—as would interviews with critics Lester Bangs and Greil Marcus (all included in this anthology). *Puncture* published book reviews from the start, too, and many later issues included fiction, from authors such as David Foster Wallace, Susan Compo, William T. Vollmann, R. Zamora Linmark, and Stacey Levine.

Although we had the freedom to cover only what we wanted, we never wrote about simply what we liked; it was also a matter of what we felt needed to be written about and wasn't covered enough (or at all) elsewhere. Sometimes, especially in the early years, this was a matter of geography (West Coast stuff was close to us, but was underrepresented in other zines, the majority of which seemed to be East Coast based/biased[3]). It was also clear that women's contributions to punk and post-punk music, which mattered a lot to us, tended to be ignored or undervalued, even dismissed, by many of those publications.[4]

There were also artists we liked but didn't write about much because they got plenty of ink in mainstream media. As the post-punk music nurtured by zines and college radio divided over the course of the '80s into "alternative" rock, which was assimilated to varying degrees into the commercial mainstream, and indie rock, which (sometimes determinedly) wasn't, the former was granted some space in *Rolling Stone* alongside its coverage of classic rock and pop, and provided the principal fodder for new arrival *Spin*. A lot of fantastic music was marketed as alternative, but we wrote about the artists who produced it only if we had something different to say about them (e.g., PJ Harvey, Beck). The rest of it—the bulk of what those commercially oriented magazines covered, as exemplified by the likes of Jane's Addiction

and Smashing Pumpkins[5]—seemed pretty dire to us.

There was so much happening under those magazines' radar that we felt was far more important. We tracked the careers of bands making wonderful, startling music despite the best efforts of the music industry to chew them up (the Mekons and the Go-Betweens, for instance), as well as those of artists who'd go on to achieve success on their own independent-minded terms (Sleater-Kinney being the shining example).

But what our writers lived for, above all, was the shock of the new—writing about great music that came seemingly out of nowhere—the first Throwing Muses cassette, the Flying Nun/Xpressway bands from New Zealand, Guided by Voices as they first emerged from unfathomable obscurity. *Puncture* was often the first magazine to give wider exposure to new bands.

One or two of our writers were already professionals; they came to us when they wanted to write about music they loved that was too far from the mainstream to be deemed worthy of ink in the publications they worked for. Other *Puncture* writers later became professional journalists and critics, writing about music or something else (tennis and theater, for example); many more—including some of the best writers—went on to do things entirely unrelated to music or writing (see the biographies at the back of this book). The same is true of *Puncture*'s photographers.

This anthology came together very slowly. The initial idea was to put together a collection that reflected the entire range of *Puncture*'s subject matter: the music that was certainly *not* indie rock (e.g., Matthew Shipp, Iris DeMent, MC Lyte, Scott Walker, Kool Keith, Creedence!); the fiction we printed (of which only Camden Joy's Jonathan Richman fantasia appears here); the travelogues that Patty and others contributed; the photo essays (such as Ken Holt's report from Mostar

during the war in Bosnia, or the late Craig Stockfleth's account of visiting Graceland); and the critical coverage of developments in literature and photography.

The mass of potential material defeated our attempts to fit a representative selection of all this in one volume.[6] A separate book reprints the first 6 *Punctures* in their entirety,[7] and from the subsequent 41 issues we've assembled this relatively streamlined account of 15 years of indie rock. Again, though, this anthology is a partial version of that history, and there are obviously omissions. There are many artists we wrote about who would have been included in this book if we'd had more space.[8] Also missing are those whose significance is indisputable, but who never featured in *Puncture* because we didn't care for them that much. But then, there are many possible accounts of this period in music. This is ours.

—*Steve Connell*

1 E.g., Deborah Cohen, "How Indie Rock Changed the World," *The Atlantic*, June 2015.

2 Also the late, lamented *Matter*.

3 The East Bay–based *BraveEar* (1981–87) was great while it lasted. *OP* (1979–84), from Olympia, Washington, had unmatched scope and depth. Two SoCal magazines, *Option* and *Sound Choice*, saw themselves in their different ways (glossily alternative and grimly indie, respectively) as continuing the OP legacy.

4 Terri Sutton cites crass examples of this; see pages 36–37.

5 We did run Lois Maffeo's memorable demolition of the Pumpkins' first album, *Gish*, in #23.

6 Despite J Neo Marvin's fantastic multicolored outline of what such a collection might look like. Maybe that'll be the next book.

7 *Puncture: The First 6 Issues* (Tract Home Publications, 2019).

8 The Aislers Set, American Music Club, Bardo Pond, Broadcast, the Cannanes, the Chills, Come, Bobby Conn, Cornershop, Culturcide, the Ex, feedtime, Freakwater, Gastr del Sol, Lisa Germano, Helium, Low, Matmos, Mecca Normal, Mudwimmin, the Notwist, Joel R.L. Phelps & the Downer Trio, Plush, Quasi, Refrigerator, Sloan, Solex, Sparklehorse, Stereolab, Teenage Fanclub, Tsunami, Unrest, the Verlaines, Versus, the Walkabouts, Bob Wiseman, Yo La Tengo, the Young Gods, and more.

IN THE BEGINNING . . .

EVEN IN ITS FIRST 5x7-inch xeroxed issues, *Puncture* didn't look or read like other zines in the '80s. There was a certain type of voice common to these small publications: a hyperbolic, exaggerated persona testifying that the writer was Right and was determined to show all those other idiots how Wrong they were. Whether you were reading a blatantly political zine like *Maximum Rocknroll*, an irreverently offensive-for-the-sake-of-being-offensive gadfly like *Forced Exposure*, or a pure expression of fandom and youthful enthusiasm like *The Big Takeover*, there was always a sense of reaction, an embattled crusade against an ignorant world that refused to recognize the Truth.

To be fair, that was a pretty accurate assessment of how things were back then. For the mainstream media, punk was a passing fad that had already passed; never mind the thousands of bands forming in every town and the underground infrastructure being built piece by piece to support them and make touring possible. The frustration of seeing your generation's turn at cultural expression being deliberately held back was very real. Zine writers responded with a fierce quasi-evangelistic spirit and, often, overwrought writing.

Those first issues of *Puncture* came in from a different angle. Katherine Spielmann and Patty Stirling approached their subjects from a dry, whimsical perspective, writing about the Toiling Midgets, the Virgin Prunes, or Code of Honor as if they'd just dropped in from another planet and these were the first bands they had ever heard. There was a peculiar sort of innocence in the writing that stood so far apart from the zeitgeist of '80s zine culture that it was almost shocking in a quiet way. At the same time, this innocence was not naiveté; these were educated women who could drop cultural references in such a casual, unpretentious way that you wanted to investigate for yourself what on earth they were talking about. What was mostly absent were all the usual clichés of rock critic–speak and punk rhetoric that clung to other writers like layers of plaque. And when Katherine set her sights on a sacred cow, whether it was Fear, Crass, or Richard Fariña, the results were thought-provoking and often hilarious.

Before long, I was submitting articles myself. At that point, I got an education in what really made the magazine tick. Katherine turned out to be not just a unique writer, but a hands-on editor with strong opinions and non-negotiable high standards. Anyone who walked in expecting their inspired literary brilliance to be embraced without question was in for a surprise. To suddenly have that fierce critical perspective trained on your own work could be jarring to the ego. Contributors would sometimes bristle to see our writing edited: wasn't punk all about free, untrammeled expression?

It could just as easily be argued that punk was also about never taking conventional wisdom for granted, and rejecting all that was lazy and complacent. Katherine would not let anyone get away with substituting attitude for insight, wasting words, or taking too long to get to the point. Plus, while she didn't skimp on praise or support for the writers, she always saw each issue of the magazine as a complete entity in itself, in which everyone's articles had to fit. As a writer, you had to understand and accept that there would likely be parts cut out and rearranged in everything you submitted, and it was your job to make every sentence relevant, yet put your piece together in such a way that the essence of what you had to say would survive the editing process. It could be a daunting challenge, but it was just the sort of pressure that forced you to rise to the occasion. I know I wouldn't be half the writer I am today if I hadn't had to live up to Katherine's expectations, and I suspect most former *Puncture* contributors would agree.

In the early years, it was hard to tell what would become of this small, quixotic project. Even in the lively atmosphere of the proto-indie underground of the mid-1980s, there was little sense that our efforts would be regarded as important anywhere beyond our immediate circle. Other zines were beginning to raise their profiles and gain a reputation as definitive reference works for the era; *Puncture*, meanwhile, grew at its own speed and wrote about what interested us. The early issues constitute a strange alternative history of the '80s in which the major artists include Einstürzende Neubauten, the Violent Femmes, Flipper, and Throwing Muses. There was no attempt to create a unified theory, aesthetic, or scene based on what any of this stuff had in common. It was closer to a series of close-ups of particular anomalies in the wake of a big bang that was expanding and fragmenting faster than anyone could comprehend. The one theme that could be pointed to was something like, "Look at all of these fascinating things being created here and now. Is this not an exciting time to be alive?"

When Steve Connell arrived, bringing along his skills and connections from years at Rough Trade, a long partnership with Katherine began, and the magazine received a much-needed shot in the arm. *Puncture* continued to evolve on its own terms through the years covered in this book, leaving a chronicle of the changing fortunes of what by then was starting to be called "indie rock." But while the covers depicted more famous faces than before, and in glossy color, the magazine retained its smart, quirky identity, and every time a new issue arrived in the mail, I would glow with pride that I was involved with something as cool as this. A steady stream of new contributors kept the pages fresh; I firmly believe that we had the most talented, perceptive, and witty writing staff of any so-called "alternative rock" magazine of the time, and what my peers produced here stands proudly next to any more celebrated piece of music journalism you care to name. For my part, I tried my best to be as interesting as everyone else, and hope I succeeded.

—*J Neo Marvin*

. . . AND AT THE END

In the early 1990s, the story goes, underground rock music somehow took over the mainstream, immediately laying waste to New Kids on the Block, the Sunset Strip, and a dastardly confection known as "hair metal." The music's elevation roughly corresponded with the rise of Bill Clinton. An "alternative nation" was born, and assiduously covered by MTV, *Spin,* and even *Rolling Stone.* Of course, the music that bubbled up represented a small and heavily compromised segment of independent music. Pearl Jam and their ilk seemed akin to Clinton and his Blue Dog Democrats: unquestionably superior to hair metal and George H.W. Bush, but hardly ideal.

In the current age, genres have been conflated into a seamless stream, and "indie" has become programming code for vaguely tasteful rock music. In the '90s, however, two very distinct cliques developed: alternative and indie rock. The former was brash, glossy, and often supported by big record labels; the latter was collegiate, arty, and proudly snotty. With few exceptions, members of the two groups traveled separate paths, like characters from DC and Marvel.

I fell into indie-rock fandom during my first year of college, embracing the genre with a fervor unique to the newly converted. One minute I was listening mostly to the greatest hits CDs of classic-rock stars; the next, I was thumbing my nose at anyone so ignorant as not to have heard the latest Silver Jews B-side. Obnoxious? Perhaps! But it was a glorious time to become obsessed with rock 'n' roll. After all, as a general rule, pop music's golden periods are 1965, 1977, and whatever year it was when the listener in question turned 18.

I was hungry for any scrap of information on the strange new sounds I was obsessing about. But the great '90s indie bands, so fetishized today, received scant coverage at the time, compared to their tacky alternative brethren. These were media footnotes destined for rote, tiny articles and scattered reviews. To read much about, say, the Magnetic Fields or Palace Brothers, one had to

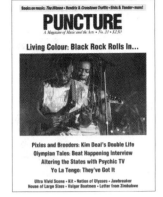

turn to a network of off-the-beaten-path publications. There was *Option*, which was Californian and sleek, with an ear for world music. *The Wire* was esoteric, nerdy, and British—it seemed like you could go bald just leafing through it. Philadelphia's *Magnet* was eager and fannish. All had their merits. But the magazine that grabbed me by the neck was the era's somewhat unsung and utterly uncompromising indie bible, *Puncture*.

By the time I started reading it, *Puncture* had relocated from San Francisco to Portland, Oregon, and had long outgrown its punk-zine roots. It resembled no other magazine. Its pages were non-glossy, with muted black-and-white photographs. The sprawling record reviews section, a precursor to *Pitchfork*, came not at the magazine's end but smack in its middle, printed on the type of colored paper traditionally associated with children's crafts projects. Even more idiosyncratic was the content. The magazine's main section featured erudite articles about artists generally consigned to the margins. Subjects included blue-chip veterans (the Go-Betweens, the Mekons, the Clean) as well as rookie acts of whom I was frequently ignorant. In many cases, this unfamiliarity was because the *Puncture* article represented a band's first interview or real exposure—most significantly, Sleater-Kinney and Guided by Voices.

Musicians were written about as artists, not scenesters. To drive the point home, the magazine often veered away from music to cover art-house film, photography, and, especially, experimental literature. Remarkably, *Puncture* was one of the few publications to excerpt David Foster Wallace's *Infinite Jest*.

Although West Coast–based, the magazine betrayed barely a whiff of regionalism. The focus was on a sensibility splayed across continents. Journalists reported from all corners, writing in highly distinct and often eccentric voices unflattened by any house style or overzealous editing. Stephen Tignor, in New York, spun long and remarkably sturdy pieces, injecting hints of the personal while never slipping into self-indulgence. David Nichols filed from his native Australia, his every profile spiked with offbeat humor. Camden Joy, the novelist and poster artist, and Carlton B. Morgan, the Welsh comic-strip writer, were apparent madmen cut from the cloth of Bangs. It was the only rock'n'roll publication that, while never dry, opted for intelligence over cool at every turn. It perfectly matched the prevailing spirit of the day's indie rock. I wanted nothing more than to write for it.

On New Year's Day, 1996, I moved to London for a semester abroad. I took to attending shows with a regularity bordering on the obsessive-compulsive. Before long, I happened upon a group that, I was convinced, was the greatest band the world had ever known: Broadcast.

Although only one 7-inch into their career, they already had everything a band could hope for, with the possible exception of an audience. The singer resembled a doomed heroine from a John le Carré novel; she sang like a ghost. Concerts were low-budget yet thoroughly stylized, the five musicians appearing as shadows against black-and-white films. The band's sound was immediately familiar yet untraceable, its touchstones being not the Kinks or the Velvets, but hyper-obscure records by the electronic-music pioneer Joseph Byrd and film scores by Krzysztof Komeda. Already, Broadcast seemed stronger than its influences.

Before I left for London, I had mailed college newspaper clips to Katherine Spielmann and Steve Connell, the married couple behind *Puncture*, begging for inclusion. Now, I wrote to them again, raving like a madman about this band Broadcast. There was not a magazine in the world that would agree to a story about an experimental band without an album, fans, or media buzz, to be written by a potentially unhinged college student. Naturally, Katherine and Steve greeted the idea with enthusiasm. Soon, I was on a train to Birmingham to meet with the musicians at a grubby group home where some of them lived. It was Broadcast's first interview. I'm sure my parents appreciated their son using the travel allowance they'd bestowed on him so he could witness the glories of Europe to instead visit Birmingham to meet with pasty-skinned musicians. But I might as well have been flying to a Monaco tax haven to interview Mick Jagger for a *Rolling Stone* cover story, such was my enthusiasm.

Returned to the States, I continued to write for *Puncture*, along with some other publications. But the *Puncture* work was special. Word counts were loose and subjects selected with care; assignments felt like adventures. Gradually, a bona fide underground seemed to uncoil before me. Like Broadcast, a lot of the artists I met for *Puncture* appeared to me as unworldly stars in ways that the better remunerated musicians of the day never could. Their records revealed consummately realized, thoroughly singular visions. Some subjects—Plush, Bobby Conn, Royal Trux—carried themselves and dressed as mythic rock stars of yore, even as they begged for audiences beyond an indie cognoscenti.

After college and some time piddling around Boston, I moved to Portland to work with Steve and Katherine. We set up an office—*Puncture*'s first—but I still spent a lot of time at their house, pestering them. The two editors were like maverick characters from their own magazine. They lived on the far edge of town with a lot of cats and one amiable dog, Bobby. Editorial meetings mainly consisted of breaking up animal fights. They were the only full-fledged adults I knew who maintained the hours and passions of college students; they reminded me of certain professors, albeit with a cooler record collection. They were leftists, aesthetes, rogue intellectuals, and proud contrarians. Steve loathed the Beatles while Katherine had little time for Bob Dylan. In the '60s, Katherine had spent time on a Greek island frequented by Leonard Cohen, and she insisted that the world lost a great novelist when he turned to song. While they had spent lifetimes in music—Steve, an Englishman, had moved to the States while working for Rough Trade—their passions tilted equally to literature. Fittingly, when they first met in the '80s, the editors had bonded over Don DeLillo's *Great Jones Street*.

Puncture was an independent operation in ways that transcended mere finances. Katherine and Steve covered what they pleased, oftentimes from skewed angles, placing a rare trust in their readership to follow. Alas, this autonomy brought with it the freedom to close shop when they saw fit, arguably with the magazine near the top of its game. So in 2000, after 18 years and 47 issues, *Puncture* called it a day, in part so the editors could concentrate on their book imprint, Verse Chorus Press. Sleater-Kinney appeared on the final issue's cover. In many ways, shutting at the turn of the century seemed prescient. The next few years proved punishing for print magazines, and *Puncture* was too fragile a beast for the Internet. Yet at times, I wondered whether the magazine's death was premature. Over the following decade, the music *Puncture* had covered grew exponentially. Bands that once had played to clubs filled with Generation Xers reunited to play theaters and festivals filled with members of the larger millennial bloc. Indie artists began surfacing on network talk shows and commercial soundtracks. Mostly, however, the fashionable new music lacked sting. In the '90s, alternative had supplanted mainstream rock, then was immediately defanged; now, it was indie rock's turn.

As *Puncture* was folding, I left Portland and moved back East. Soon, I took a job as a music critic at *Time Out New York*, working alongside *Puncture* veteran Elisabeth Vincentelli. In the early '00s, I liked to speculate as to which acts du jour would meet the *Puncture* litmus test, were it still publishing. The Strokes? (Not a chance.) The White Stripes? (Probably.) The Moldy Peaches? (Without a doubt.) But as the decade rolled on and indie rock continued its surge, my longing for the magazine abated. After all, *Puncture* was not meant to cover reunited bands playing for Coachella dollars. It was designed to cover those artists who were too smart for their own good— stubborn outsiders destined to get overshadowed and overwhelmed. It was a magazine that few people read about music that few people heard, a small world that made a big noise.

—*Jay Ruttenberg*

THROWING MUSES: DAVID NARCIZO, KRISTIN HERSH, TANYA DONELLY, LESLIE LANGSTON

THROWING MUSES

Throwing Muses were born in the early 1980s, around the same time as *Puncture*. By 1986, both the East Coast band and West Coast publication were outgrowing their respective DIY origins. Following a self-released cassette, the Muses had issued a sparkling debut LP on the prestigious UK indie label 4AD; meanwhile, *Puncture* was pushing past its status as a Bay Area–focused punk zine and incorporating longer interviews. In 1987, **KATHERINE SPIELMANN** and **STEVE CONNELL** interviewed Kristin Hersh, the Muses' chief songwriter and vocalist.

One of last year's most memorable releases was the self-titled debut album of the young New England band Throwing Muses. The record, hailed in these pages and others here and abroad as a masterpiece, had the air of springing out of the blue. As far as any recognizable tradition or style went, the music, with its long, shifting lines and harsh, complex lyrics, was mysterious, if not actually obscure. With every listening, questions formed in our minds.

Throwing Muses were formed some years back, while the original quartet were still in high school together in Rhode Island. They played auditorium gigs and recorded an EP, *Stand Up*. In a change of bassists, Kristin Hersh, Tanya Donelly, and David Narcizo were joined by Leslie Langston. A reggae musician from Santa Cruz, she was until recently the Throwing Muses' only member over 20.

Late in 1985 the band (like so many before and after them) released their own cassette. At this point a few hundred people outside their region got to hear them for the first time (including *Puncture*—see issue 11 for our review [*reprinted here on page 14*]). The head of English label 4AD, Ivo, received one of the tapes. He listened—and promptly signed the band.

Gil Norton (who had worked with the Triffids and Bunnymen) was flown to Boston to produce the Muses' first album, recorded in a barn above the horse stables at Longview Farm, Mass. Then the band took a break while Kristin (the band's principal singer and writer) had a baby, Dylan, at mid-year.

Just a few months later came a trip to England, with the Muses playing a series of shows with the Cocteau Twins. The English press received them with a certain awe—even the usually phlegmatic *Melody Maker*: "It is somewhat bewildering that we should find ourselves having to talk about . . . the finest debut album of the Eighties and a very beautiful, contorted mystery. It makes us want to shout."

The questions included in the interview were planned out by Steve Connell and Katherine Spielmann. In February and March 1987, the questions and answers were exchanged by post (later on supplemented by telephone) with Kristin.

We learned that the new four-song EP, *Chains Changed*, also produced by Gil Norton, has been completed and will shortly be released, and that the band just finished filming "Soul Soldier" for Danger Video. The first weekend in March they went into the studio to record an "extended mix with extra percussion coda." Baby Dylan fattened the mix with rhythmic cries.

The alternative video was made on a $50,000 budget awarded by Mike Nesmith's American Film Institute for the band's earlier "Fish" video. Part of the new video was filmed on a cross-country trip and part in a ruined castle in Newport, Rhode Island.

—*Katherine Spielmann*

Songs and Structures

Your songs often have relatively intricate structures—songs within songs, or evolving into other songs. You've said in previous interviews that you think this reflects more accurately the way people are, that "straight lines" can't tell the truth. Could you expand on this a little? How did the realization come about that straight lines weren't for you? How do your songs tend to get written?

When I say people are not straight lines I refer to linear—the Western way of measuring time—rather than cyclical. In pre-literate societies they don't view a day or a year as a building up of achievements but as a give and take, so that tomorrow may come as it always has.

I couldn't take a song from the Muses, milk it for all it's worth, and then market it. I have to find a piece of what they have and organize it, leaving the whole idea intact somewhere in the sky. I need to take too much, but that's such a tight feeling, that I would have to make up the rest of the song. I wouldn't get any more from the Muses because I wasn't free enough to listen for it.

When I write songs I begin with a piece of lyric, chord, or guitar line, sit with it until I understand it or think it's right, and then, hopefully, the rest of the song will follow.

You've also talked about your music being a network rather than a mass, deriving its strength from the way things connect. Could you go into that a little more? And is it the case, do you think, that women artists tend to find this connectedness easier to tune in to?

Network rather than mass is the little rocks vs. big rocks theory. I've noticed that a lot of women's work and women's functions are made up of small, careful subtleties that don't always carry the "boom-punch" of masculine functioning. Like the Raincoats' stuff— their "drums" are tiny noises that, together, comprise the rhythm. As an example, married men that I know work to lay a sturdy foundation of basic love and security: money, home, car, job, politeness; while their wives seem to concentrate on what they said this morning on their way out. It's dumb, of course, to say *anything* like men do this and women do this, but often there is more yin manifested in the girls and more yang in the boys. And that's why we have girls *and* boys in the band.

"Hate My Way," the song that came out of watching TV coverage of the McDonald's murders,[1] seems to have a savage compassion that extends even to the killer. Is this something that happens when you connect everything up? Was writing that song a way of clarifying in your own mind what the murders signified?

"Hate My Way" was definitely an attempt on my part to figure out how all that stuff fits in the Big Picture. I guess I think that if it does, and I can find out how it does, then I'll be able to deal with it or at least understand it. The lyrics from that song just poured out one afternoon all at once, with no melody or accompaniment. I thought it was a letter rather than a song. I was trying to find out whether I could kill, or my neighbor could kill, or if that could have been my brother, or my little boy, all tangled up . . .

Resources

Without necessarily talking narrowly of "influences," what kinds of music and which musicians do you (a) admire and listen to, and (b) consider to have helped shape the music that you play?

We usually just say that we hate music and don't listen to anyone, because we've been so disappointed lately. But the greats for us are probably just who you'd think: X, the Femmes, Velvet Underground, R.E.M. (only the first few records of all these). Also Hüsker Dü, Mission of Burma, Volcano Suns, some Psychedelic Furs, and the Pixies, here in Boston. I haven't done my homework as far as other people's music is concerned. Camper Van opened for us a few weeks ago at a university gig and they were very swell.

Are there any particular writers you feel have influenced the songs you write?

---

1 On July 18, 1984, James Oliver Huberty entered a McDonald's in San Ysidro, California, and, with no apparent motive, embarked on a shooting spree that killed 21 people.

I started college while I was still in high school, so it's been a while since I've read anything I didn't have to. Jung, maybe.

Britain

Your LP came out on a British label, and you played some shows in the UK late last year, gathering quite a lot of media attention. Do you sense a greater receptivity to your music over there? Do British ears seem to hear you better?

I wish I could say that everybody in England is a pretentious scenester and that we play American roots music that they'd never get, but honestly, they've been great. I had so many preconceived notions of what Brits were like, but I've been far more disappointed by Americans in the big cities we've visited.

The British that I've come in contact with (not overly many) for some reason seem quite open to letting our stuff speak for itself without jamming too many labels down its throat. In big American cities the people and critics don't have any space left in their heads for a new experience, it seems.

America

You've not played very much in the US outside New England. But the album has attracted the attention of critics and radio stations across the country. Will you be touring more in the future? Are there any definite plans yet? Will having a young child to look after affect those plans?

I never know what the band's plans are at any given moment beyond the next weekend. I'm very dumb in that area. The next album we record, probably in the summer, will be with a major label, and we should tour it. We're talking to Capitol, Arista, RCA, MCA, Epic, and some more that I forget.

Having a young child definitely affects everything I do, but I'll let you know.

The picture of today's America that emerges from many of your songs seems to be a pretty somber, even depressing one—a difficult, often traumatic place to live. Would you agree with this interpretation?

America is very special to me. As a new country with barely any culture we seem to embody twentieth-century problems with incredible tenacity. Insomuch as we get sick easily, we're a sort of psychologically honest country. We have no precedent, so we paint our own picture as we go along.

If America can save itself, I think the world can save itself. It's a very special and dangerous country. ◖

THROWING MUSES
(Throwing Muses cassette)

Here's a case history to ponder, especially if you're a good unknown band who find yourselves slumped on the oily concrete of the garage floor wondering will anyone ever hear or care.

This is a three-woman, one-man group from Rhode Island. They released a single that sold locally. Then they recorded a ten-track cassette: they sold some and sent the rest to record companies they hoped might be interested, including the Cocteau Twins' label 4AD in England. It got heard. By the time you read this, Throwing Muses will be recording an LP fo r 4AD.

That's all: there was no gimmick (unless you consider a manager a gimmick).

Throwing Muses are still very young, despite their mature-sounding vocals and their informed eclecticism. Stepsisters Kristin Hersh and Tanya Donelly started the band in 1983 after years of songwriting together. They got a school friend to drum and last summer roped in bass player Leslie Langston, a San Francisco reggae musician who was just visiting.

Kristin, lead guitarist, writer, and singer of most of these songs, has a voice that recalls the cracked folk-rocking throb of Melanie but moves faster and screams readily. The Muses' songs pay quick calls on many styles, with open, ringing, folky harmonies as home base. At times the shifts are quite abrupt (you may think three songs have gone by before the first, "Call Me," is over), but it keeps things fascinating. With repeated hearings, disjunctions disappear and you learn the songs' overall shapes.

Tanya's voice can move from a similar broken, throaty sound through to a fluent soprano (on "Green"). "Raise the Roses" has riffs like "Paint It Black"—and more besides.

There's something rash and headlong in this music, striking considering how well all the drum, percussion, and guitar work is handled. Throwing Muses leave an impression of good clean dangerous intensity.

—*Katherine Spielmann*

Throwing Muses (4AD LP)

Even before you hear it, this is striking. 4AD haven't released a US band before, yet the LP's superb package design tells you (as does producer Gil Norton's name) that the label has total confidence in this 3/4ths-female teenaged band.

Then you hear it. Yes, the Muses are heard: and they threaten a settled and largely predictable scene with greatness: with fierce, unsettling, unpredictable force. Muse music

breaks the expected forms and scatters keening careening twists of music into your mind and into layers you're not usually listening with. The songs in turn contain songs, as a concerto contains movements. Also as in a concerto, all the instruments (acoustic and electric guitars; drums) interact with the lead vocal in such swift unanimity it's as though some discarded discipline had been reclaimed for popular music.

The songs are primarily massive formulations of shame and alienation in America today. "Vicky's Box" joins female domestic musings (whose rigor recalls Sylvia Plath's) with a tale of some youth's sexual and automotive disaster. Tanya Donelly's song "Green" finely shows kinship with Kristin Hersh's songs (the two are stepsisters). "Delicate Cutters," an acoustic song that builds long and hard, using at last a hair-raising undertow of kettledrums, seems to turn on sweatshop labor by women in earlier industrial New England (the Muses live fairly close to the decaying manufacturing centers of Providence and Fall River).

It takes a while to learn the songs' unusual shapes. Playing the LP too many times begins to seem impossible. It's a polymorphic, polyphonic, raving masterpiece.

—Katherine Spielmann

Chains Changed (4AD EP)
The Fat Skier (Sire EP)

The four songs on *Chains Changed* comprise a flawless, four-faceted gem, an almost unbelievable concentration of brilliant energy and fierce intelligence. Throwing Muses produce the most rewarding music I've found in the last few years, and probably the most difficult to write about. Their songs are complex and involved, yet never contrived—the end result is an emotionally charged, joyous, rhythmical flow that challenges the mind while satisfying the heart.

"I found last September in a notebook/It was too much for the book to hold . . ."

Every statement limits the world, boxes it in (a frequent image in Muses songs), overdefines it. Throwing Muses resist this—through shifting forms and melodies within each song, by framing the same lines in different ways to broaden their expressiveness.

As a result, they require a lot from the listener, the way a full life in the real world does; they want to communicate nothing less than that fullness. No shortcuts or easy ways out, just the determined pursuit of understanding and feeling by every means possible. This is brought home by the skilled way in which the band provide strong but varied rhythms across which Kristin's voice skates its path, giving individual shape and force to every word. It is further reinforced by Gil Norton's production, in which every element is distinct and yet an integrated part of the overall impact.

The Fat Skier has seven tracks, including an extended re-working of "Soul Soldier" from their first album, and at least one of the songs ("A Feeling") was written as long ago as 1985. It's also their first record without Gil Norton at the controls. Mark Van Hecke, former Violent Femmes producer, is an intriguing choice to replace him; my only real point of comparison for the Muses' effect has long been the first Femmes album.

Most of the songs take a step back from the heady, passionate rush of *Chains Changed*. They seem deliberately muted, as if taking stock of what has been unleashed until now and listening intently to themselves. "Soap and Water" seems to focus on the danger of attracting too much attention: "If you overrate me I won't talk/If you chain me I can't walk." Most memorable is "And a She-Wolf after the War," an intimate and compelling parable about the need to become dangerous to protect oneself in dangerous circumstances, accentuated by reggae-inflected, edgy chording.—*Steve Connell*

CAMPER VAN BEETHOVEN: DAVID LOWERY, GREG LISHER, JONATHAN SEGEL, CHRIS MOLLA, VICTOR KRUMMENACHER (PHOTO, EDIE WINOGRADE)

CAMPER VAN BEETHOVEN

In 1985, the eclectic Camper Van Beethoven emerged from left field, charming college radio programmers (and *Puncture* critic **ALAN KORN**) with their debut LP, *Telephone Free Landslide Victory*. **KATHERINE SPIELMANN** and **STEVE CONNELL** interviewed Camper's David Lowery and Victor Krummenacher in a South of Market warehouse shortly before the release of the band's second album, *II & III*.

Origins

How did the band get started?

DAVID LOWERY: It was just going to be an acoustic band: a college dorm band playing the pizzeria. We hadn't heard of Violent Femmes. If we had, it probably would have stopped us in our tracks. David McDaniel, a guy named Emerson, and me: we used to make up imitation Russian/Hungarian folk songs. Gibberish, although Emerson came from that background. We developed a feel for the music. We started getting serious. And we all got married.

VICTOR KRUMMENACHER: Jonathan [Segel, violinist] got married three times.

DL: We played a lot. Then Bruce of Independent Projects suggested a record. Thus, *Telephone Free Landslide Victory*.

What music influenced you?

BOTH: A lot of hardcore.

And before punk?

DL: Led Zeppelin. I was into Gary Glitter too. I swear! Rock. Queen. And my dad listens to country, so I know a lot of country. I listened to hippie stuff, which got me into reggae and South American music.

Current bands?

VK: The Fall, though they're going downhill.

DL: The Fall, Meat Puppets, Minutemen.

VK: Blue Orchids.

DL: I've been getting into '60s stuff. I really like Chocolate Watchband.

VK: A great San Jose band.

What about R.E.M.? I know they expressed interest in you.

DL: Actually, I like R.E.M. I just don't want to go that way.

VK: Softening raw edges.

DL: Yeah. And that band going around with them, Three O'Clock, they're becoming bubblegum to match their audience.

VK: R.E.M. are sincere for some reason and better.

DL: They're in a slightly different class from the underground stuff I take more seriously. Some good songs.

"Take the Skinheads Bowling" is sort of the hit single off Telephone . . . *What experience does that song reflect?*

DL: We were reacting against the explosion of hardcore. I went home to Redlands to visit and a huge punk scene had sprung up. Skinheads everywhere . . . breaking windows . . .

VK: Drinking Schlitz on the roof, throwing bottles off.

Some people take the song quite seriously.

VK: Maybe it's pseudoreligious.

DL: I tell people it's a love song.

Directions

What's next?

DL: Our style has changed a lot. We can play a really dark set. We got into taking a sort of Chocolate Watchband psychedelic sound and twisting it, still with our Balkan and Russian and Middle Eastern influences.

Country?

DL: Some people have ruined country. Rank and File . . . Lots are just kids from the suburbs. The Beat Farmers . . . the songs are just urbanites' clichéd notion of what goes on in the country. Only Gun Club—and Meat Puppets—really cross country and punk. The others are sugarcoated imitation.

VK: Cute. Condescending. Exploiting.

DL: Country is actually as diverse as rock 'n' roll. And has a longer history. We are influenced by it, but we make it as authentic and non-modern as possible. Or we twist it.

What about formal music training?

VK: Jonathan and Chris Molla [drummer, guitarist] were music majors. Jonathan got his degree in music from UC Santa Cruz.

DL: But they're not virtuosi. It would be a drag to have someone in the band who's really good on an instrument! They play lots of different instruments, and fuck around: it's perfect.

VK: They play better than I do. They bring in more elements. Through Chris I've listened to 16th-century folk music.

DL: Some creepy stuff.

VK: Really psychedelic. *Real* death rock. With plague in it.

DL: And then we got into Islamic/Moorish influences in European music.

VK: Klezmer music.

DL: We play the more Russian/Czech style of klezmer.

VK: There's also a New York, a Broadway school of klezmer.

DL: Yeah, "big-band" klezmer.

Precursors

What about Box o' Laffs?

DL: Box o' Laffs is a Santa Cruz band I started before CVB. Then Chris joined it. We were in it for a long time. Eventually we bailed. They're definitely a band to check out. They'll be putting out a cassette on Warpt, label of Asbestos Rockpyle, another favorite.

Can you explain your Black Flag cover ["Wasted"]?

DL: It said some things we say, and said them years earlier.

VK: *Maximum Rocknroll* said our version was hippified.

DL: That's okay, man. I'd rather be a hippie than a punk rocker. [*Discussion follows: politics, philosophy*]

The Way We Live Now

DL: But that's not what we really think about. What really happens is, Jonathan comes over and says, "Listen to this!" Sawing away on his violin. "Isn't this dissonant?" "Sure, wow." "I'll play a country riff, no, I'll play a blues riff under it!" *Na-na-na, na-na . . .*

"Yeah, really great. Uh, Jonathan, we're out of beer—"

Afterwards . . . play it over . . . "Hey, notice something?" "Listen to this, man! . . . *Listen to this.*" ◉

CAMPER VAN BEETHOVEN
Telephone Free Landslide Victory
(Independent Projects LP)

Camper Van Beethoven's debut is an absurdist folk-rock travelogue of musics, cultures, situations—equal parts Modern Lovers and Skatalites. Unique is the only way to describe this Tex-Mex border-ska folk-thrash hybrid. With the assistance of mandolins, wheezing Casios, and a violin drone, Camper Van create a unified lunatic sound animating the norteño-ska instrumentals.

Another group of tunes—tall tales like "Take the Skinheads Bowling" and "Where the Hell Is Bill?"—will assure the band's notoriety. The former is a rousing country rocker whose juxtaposition of incongruous subjects treads dangerously close to Dada. The latter song is an epic dismissal of a decade's fickle new-wave fashions, progressively assimilated and discarded by the missing protagonist. Both songs are novelty classics, though they share a certain conviction that helps push a folk rendition of Black Flag's "Wasted" beyond mere parody and into the realm of sublime tribute.

While the surplus irony in CVB's music sometimes overshadows the more carefully crafted rock tunes (especially the brilliant "Oh No" and "I Don't See You"), their sound still has an interesting resemblance to several '60s West Coast bands. Musical antecedents can be found in the work of Kaleidoscope and the Rockets, the former featuring a young David Lindley on violin, the latter escaping obscurity as Neil Young's Crazy Horse. And while the liner notes credit influences like Augustus Pablo, Black Flag, and the Clash (Camper Van's live version of "White Riot" is unfortunately absent from this disk), I'd surmise that they also owe a debt to Prince Buster, Symarip, Clannad, Wire, and the Velvets. Vocalist David Lowery especially recalls a younger, more sinister Jonathan Richman.

It's interesting that CVB deny the folk-punk tag, labeling themselves a reactionary garage band. This music is far from reactionary. Whatever the label, it's clear they genuinely love their ska compilations, their Freddy Fender and Pistols albums. I'd guess that Camper Van's careful assimilation of pop signifiers is essentially a search for musical roots.

The closing "Ambiguity Song," with its rousing chorus of "Everything seems to be up in the air at this time!" could be the band's knowing refusal to choose one side against the other, instead playing all sides against the middle in quest of cultural identity.

The result is folk music from the global village, a new sound both traditional and irreverent. By manipulating this vibrant music lore and infusing it with sensitive though twisted humor, Camper Van Beethoven emerges with a truly exciting alternative to the nationalist trend within the US music scene.

Call them surrealists, absurdists, traditionalists, dabblers, or just plain fools. I'm convinced they're on to something—capable perhaps of establishing a big cult audience both here and abroad.

Everything about *Telephone . . .* , from Independent Project Records' unique hand-fed letterpress cover to the soft, intimate mix, is wonderful. I'm sure this disk will be viewed as a delightful (if puzzling) treasure when studied by future rock historians and ethnomusicologists.—*Alan Korn*

63 DAYS ON THE ROAD

Camper Van Beethoven frontman **DAVID LOWERY** wrote this not-always-factual tour diary for *Puncture* in 1986, chronicling a troubled swing through the era's clubs—including Boston's the Rat, which Lowery later would excoriate in song.

<u>Day 1, SAN FRANCISCO:</u> The tour got off to a shaky start, but I think everything's okay now. When we arrived to pick up Jackson, our road manager, he told us he couldn't go, but not to worry because he'd gotten his uncle Les to replace him. Jackson said we'd find Les at the Mar Vista Country Club. He'd been camped out there since being fired from his job and then kicked out by his wife, Imelda.

So we drove up to the country club. Imelda was chasing Les round the parking lot with a five iron, screaming she was going to kill him. We maneuvered the van between them, pulled Les inside, and took off, but not before Imelda had managed to break two windows. Now, a short while later, we are in high spirits driving northward on Highway 5. Les is teaching us how to make martinis.

<u>Day 2, EUGENE, OREGON:</u> We played our first show tonight. Everything went well, even though we had apparently driven off this morning without Greg, our guitarist. Fortunately he managed to hitch a ride and got here half an hour before show time.

<u>Day 6, BOISE, IDAHO:</u> At a truck stop outside of Boise, Lenny (our sound man) incorrectly identified a poisonous mushroom as the mildly psychedelic Liberty Cap. The entire road crew and half of the Whitespots (our opening band)

are in the hospital tonight having their stomachs pumped. The only person left to run our sound was Les, and he kept turning us down (or even off) so he could talk to the waitresses.

<u>Day 8, LARAMIE, WYOMING:</u> Yesterday was a complete disaster. Fritz (our light man), who was already kind of unbalanced, learned that his girlfriend had left him. He spent the evening screaming in Lapland Finnish dialect about, we can only assume, his ex-girlfriend. Only when Les sedated him with a quarter bottle of Darvon would he sit behind the lightboard. Even then he was four songs behind us by the end of the show.

As if this weren't enough, after the show Les took us down to the bar at the American Legion--his old friend Hank Ferguson is commander of the Laramie post. The locals had forgiven us our appearance and were being downright friendly until the three male dancers for the Whitespots began doing interpretive dances to Elvis Presley songs on the jukebox. Mistaking this for disrespect for the King, the locals took them outside and bloodied their noses. Les and Hank intervened too late. Even Les's promises of golfing in Florida couldn't dissuade the dancers from taking the next Greyhound back to San Francisco.

This morning Les and I got up early

19

and went to Hank's house. Les has worked out a deal to take some antique rifles to Hank's brother-in-law, a gun collector, in Moose Jaw, Saskatchewan. Les explained that since the rifles are so valuable we must take extraordinary measures to keep them from being stolen. When we returned to the motel, the others were still asleep, and Les decided to conceal the rifles inside a speaker cabinet belonging to the Whitespots. Les asked me not to tell them about the rifles because they'll get nervous driving around with something so valuable in their van.

Day 12, SEATTLE, WASHINGTON: Les has asked us to go without per diems for a few days to prevent any cash flow problems. Apparently we haven't been making as much as we expected, and Les says he needs more money for "promotional expenses."

Day 13, VANCOUVER, BC: The Canadian border guards have arrested all the Whitespots on suspicion of smuggling and terrorism. They are accused of trying to smuggle automatic weapons to the ONF (October 19 Faction), a neo-Nazi group based in Moose Jaw, Saskatchewan. Les thinks the Whitespots must have found the antique rifles and traded them for Uzi machine guns. We are also under arrest.

Day 14: Les has persuaded the guards of our innocence, and we have been released. The Whitespots are still in custody, however. The Canadians claim "Whitespots" refers to the band's secret neo-Nazi political philosophy, although none of the Whitespots has confessed to being a neo-Nazi yet. Les says we should leave them to fend for themselves, since they abused our hospitality for their own narrow political interests.

Day 17, CALGARY, ALBERTA: I called our record company, hoping they could find us a new opening band. They have suggested a band called Big Naked. Apparently the leader of the group is a famous underground rock critic, and he won't write a piece on us unless we let his band come on tour with us.

Day 18, EDMONTON, ALBERTA: Tonight we are playing the Ambassador Hotel. Then we have a week off. I feel fine, but some of the band and crew look like they could use a vacation, especially Fritz, who has discovered his ex-girlfriend is now dating a lesbian folksinger. His light shows, which are usually gloomy anyway,

STEVE JENNINGS

have now degenerated into the turning on and off of a single 40-watt black light. Even more disturbing is his adoption of his ancestors' belief in the existence of elves.

Les has decided that during the week off he will drive one of the vans down to Moose Jaw and straighten things out with the gun collector "before things get out of hand."

Day 24: During our week off we went to visit the gigantic Edmonton Mall. Chris Molla, our steel guitarist, got lost and wandered into the plains. Fortunately he was found and cared for by a group of Hutterites, a religious sect that refuses to use modern conveniences like electricity and automobiles. Unfortunately he has adopted their beliefs. Chris now refuses to ride in the van, and we must either leave him behind or cancel the next few shows so he can be deprogrammed.

Day 25, SASKATOON, SASKATCHEWAN: Les has found a temporary solution to the Chris Molla problem. Last night after Chris fell asleep Les carried him out to the van and locked him in a drum case. But some problems still remain. Chris refuses to play electric guitar, and will not allow his acoustic guitar to be miked or amplified in any way.

We have decided that Big Naked will be our opening act for the rest of the tour. They will meet us in Winnipeg in two days.

Day 27, WINNIPEG, MANITOBA: Victor is concerned that the mysterious holes we found in our van after Les's trip to Moose Jaw are bullet holes. Les says Victor is just paranoid from hanging around Fritz too much. He thinks we should send Fritz home, but I'm not sure things are that serious yet, although last night Fritz did drive the van off the road twice--the first time to avoid a band of wood elves, then again when he saw a UFO in the middle of the freeway.

Big Naked have joined the tour. They seem like nice guys, with the possible exception of band leader Michael Albino, who is sort of strange, but probably well intentioned. Yesterday when I introduced myself he told me he only accepted our invitation because he felt sorry for the audience, having to listen to our "pathetic drivel night after night and never getting the chance to hear Big Naked, a band courageous enough to sing about death, destruction, and the rape of the human spirit by the oppressive conventions of society."

Day 29, RAPID CITY, SOUTH DAKOTA: Les has bought a slightly restored Porsche 911. He has also canceled our per diems for the next week. I am beginning to suspect that Les may be embezzling money from us. The Porsche is actually a blessing of sorts, because it keeps Les--and more importantly Ruby, the truckstop waitress Les has invited to tour with us--out of our hair.

Day 31, MINNEAPOLIS, MINNESOTA: The Deadhead members of the crew threatened to quit if we didn't get rid of this Big Naked group. They complain that Big Naked's lyrics are violent and the music gives them "bad vibes." Victor pacified them by explaining that Michael Albino is a music critic and is probably making a statement of some sort, though Victor wasn't sure exactly what.

Day 35, CHICAGO, ILLINOIS: We are now down to a five-piece. Chris Molla, still refusing to play electric guitar, had taken to wandering through the audience as he played, so that at least some of them could hear him. Unfortunately the bouncers at the club last night thought he was some kind of weirdo and threw him out. We haven't seen him since. Another strange thing happened tonight: Big Naked didn't play because Michael Albino disappeared. He'd been seen earlier in the evening getting into the back of a van with three guys who were dressed up like soldiers or something.

Day 38, DETROIT, MICHIGAN: Michael Albino is still missing, and today when we showed up at the club there was a letter for us. It read: "Dear Camper Van Beethoven. You have five days to deliver the goods, or you will never see Mr. Albino again. Sincerely, The ONF." The letter was postmarked Moose Jaw, Saskatchewan. I showed it to Les, but he said it was just a prank, and neither the neo-Nazis nor his gun collector brother-in-law could have anything to do with Michael's disappearance.

It is my belief that Albino has actually been kidnapped by the ONF. I called Homostud Records, Big Naked's label, to explain my suspicions; they told me it was probably a publicity stunt, and that if I happen to see him

I am to tell him to phone Homostud immediately so they can arrange a promotional campaign based on his disappearance.

The remaining members of Big Naked have decided to continue performing, with sound man Lenny as their singer. The only problem with this is that none of them can remember the lyrics to Big Naked songs. In the meantime Lenny is singing from a book of Richard Brautigan poems.

Day 40, COLUMBUS, OHIO: Our show here was canceled at the last minute, but Les got us a gig as Tiny Tim's backing band at a club across town. I had Les take pictures of us together, because I don't think anyone will believe this story without proof.

Day 42, NEW YORK CITY: We played CBGB's last night to a packed house, but we only made $40 because there were 352 people on the guest list.

This morning I got a call from our agency, Indentured Bookings, saying we'd got a real creepy letter with an ear in it. By the time I got down there they were all too stoned to remember what they'd done with it.

We have a few days off. Les, Ruby the waitress, and the road crew are going to Atlantic City--Ruby has a friend there and Les is going to help him buy some property in the Bronx.

Day 45: Indentured Bookings called again. They found the letter and the ear. The ear apparently belongs to Michael Albino. I decided it was time to take this matter to the police. I went to Indentured to get the ear, but someone from Homostud Records had already picked it up and taken it to a press conference.

Day 50, BOSTON, MASS.: Our show at the Rat Cellar was canceled. There was a bomb threat--and the police found a real bomb. They think a disgruntled band planted it because the club is run by the Mafia and has a reputation for not paying groups that play here.

I overheard the road crew talking about going to the Bronx to help Les burn down a building. Alarmed, I asked Les what was going on. It turns out this building is on the property recently purchased by Ruby's Atlantic City friend, and according to Les it is both common and legal to demolish a building in the Bronx by burning it down, as long as it is done between the hours of 2 and 6 a.m.

Day 59, COLUMBIA, SOUTH CAROLINA: Seven of our last eight shows have been canceled due to bomb threats. We are nearly out of money, and Les says we may have to sell one of the vans. But he has kindly offered to let someone ride in his Porsche with him and Ruby.

It is now obvious to everyone (except Les) that the bombings are the work of the group that abducted Michael Albino. So when we heard today that he had been released, we were overjoyed. Apparently his abductors let him go when they found out he is the great-grandson of Benito Mussolini.

Greg and Fritz are no longer with us. Greg quit the band in Norfolk, Virginia, and got a job at a 7-Eleven. Fritz saw a statue of a giant peach outside of Columbia and became convinced it was a secret wood-elf shrine. He could not be persuaded to get back in the van, so we left him there.

Day 63, JACKSONVILLE BEACH, FLORIDA: Four days without a bomb threat. Things were beginning to look up. Then we get to Jacksonville Beach and Les's wife is waiting here for us. She shoots Les. When the police show up they arrest the crew and impound our equipment and van. They claim the crew and van were involved in an arson-for-profit scheme in New York. In the ensuing chaos Ruby splits with the Porsche and what is left of our money.

Les is expected to recover, but is in FBI custody on arson charges. Needless to say, this is the end of the tour. Victor and Jonathan are taking it the hardest. Les had promised he would teach them golf once we got to Florida. They spent most of the morning at the Jacksonville Beach Country Club trying to get someone to take them golfing. Eventually they were told to leave or they would be arrested.

Chrispy, our drummer, has found a job as an exotic male dancer. He says he can get me a job at the same place. I think I'll wait and see if I can sell this diary to SPIN magazine, although when I called the editor he wasn't encouraging. Apparently they have some really important stuff coming up: there's a story on Michael Albino's ear, and Lydia Lunch and Henry Rollins have written a piece about how they like to hang out at Ceiling Fan World in San Diego.

###

THE MEKONS

Where *Rolling Stone* magazine had the Rolling Stones, *Puncture* had the Mekons. Both band and publication had tentacles that stretched from punk to cerebral indie rock, ties to the UK and US, and an undimmed leftist undercurrent. In 1987, fresh into an unlikely renaissance period for the decade-old band, Mekons members Tom Greenhalgh and Rob Worby were interviewed in San Francisco by **STEVE CONNELL** and **TERRI SUTTON**.

The mortality rate for rock bands is high. If they don't break up, their continuing existence is often a living death, a more polished but spiritually impoverished re-creation of past glories. Of the many British bands which began in the late '70s, perhaps only the Fall have come up with the goods year in year out.

The Mekons story is more complicated, but just as satisfying. They began at the end of 1977 with the sardonic 1-2-3-4 abruptness of "Never Been in a Riot," filtering in a barely controlled romantic despair on their next single "Where Were You?" and "After Six" (on their *The Quality of Mercy Is Not Strnen* debut LP). Then they all but disappeared. Isolated, often puzzling records, surfaced only rarely. But in the last four years they have released three albums and two EPs that are among the finest records of the '80s, fusing country and folk idioms into the energetic punk rock that they

helped create, to express a sharp, individual view of the world we all have to live in.

It's often a soberly bleak and despairing vision (it would hardly be realistic if it were otherwise), but against this depression the Mekons offer all they can to create what one of their songs calls "a community centre for the hopeless": positive values of human warmth, friendship, and collective politics (such as their support work for the miners' strike in 1984). Though their lyrics often depict a cruel world, their music (especially when performed live) fills you with passion, optimism, and, simply, joy.

When the Mekons visited San Francisco recently, *Puncture* writers Steve Connell and Terri Sutton took the opportunity to talk to Tom Greenhalgh and Rob Worby in a wide-ranging interview about the band's history and current activity.

Some History

It's been ten years since the whole thing started, and the band's sound has changed quite a lot in that time, although songs like "After Six" and "Where Were You?" still fit in. How do you feel that things have changed, that your music has changed, and to what extent is that related to the way in which things in general have changed in the last ten years?

Tom: I think things have changed more than you'd think in the last ten years, more than a superficial look would reveal . . .

. . . in society in general?

Tom: Yeah, in general. If you cast your mind back to the summer of '76, the political situation with a Labour government, and now you've had eight years of vicious right-wing rule, which is even more entrenched than anyone could possibly have imagined. So just using that as an obvious frame of reference . . . As far as the Mekons are concerned, there are two distinct blocks with a gap in between. The first is from starting up [late 1977] and "Never Been in a Riot" [Jan. 1978] through to "Teeth" and including the second album, on Red Rhino [*Devils, Rats and Piggies*, 1980]. At that point we started to fall to pieces for a while.

In terms of personnel?

Tom: In terms of what we were doing. We did quite a lot of work in 1980, then decided not to play live any more at the beginning of '81.

Then there's another block starting in about April '83. That's when we did *The English Dancing Master* [EP], which I personally consider to be the basis of our new approach. There was a time in '84 when things were quite difficult for us, we didn't have a record company and so on, and felt very isolated. But the basic approach was there.

You and Jon Langford and Kevin Lycett have been there all along?

Tom: Yes.

So what was it that made you decide, in '81, that for now at least you didn't want to go on?

Tom: We were just really pissed off with touring and playing. In '79 we did more gigs than any other band in England apart from the UK Subs. And the atmosphere at gigs was incredibly unpleasant. Not blaming Jimmy Pursey, but that sort of atmosphere . . . We'd play a gig and then find out at the end that someone had been bottled or something, or you'd see it happening and have to stop the gig, all that kind of stuff. That was one of the main reasons. Not even the question of overwork, it was more than that, it was just . . . horrible.

What did you do during the two-year break?

Tom: We did all sorts of things. We did stuff that you couldn't possibly reproduce live, with synthesizers—sound sculptures.

But you were always doing music?

Tom: Oh yeah! I moved to London, which made it a bit difficult, but Jon and Kevin used to meet regularly once a week at this bloke's house who had some recording gear, Paul Griffiths. They met to practice and record. Quite a lot of *The Mekons Story* LP [1982] came out of that.

And Jon was presumably getting with the Three Johns?

Tom: Yeah. And then I used to go up to Leeds or Bridlington, where we did quite a bit of recording.

It seems like you must have spent half your life on trains, judging by some of the songs—trains to Sheffield and to Leeds.

Tom: Yeah, I've done a fair amount of that.

Renaissance

So what brought you back together again in '83? Did you feel like there were different things to say, or different ways of saying it?

Tom: Mainly it was people in Holland, like the Ex, and our friend Kornje, who kept saying we must come over and do some gigs. We didn't really want to, but they kept on at us, so we thought oh it'll be all right. That was just me, Jon, Kevin, and Mark White, who was still in the band at that time.

Was he an original member too?

Tom: Yeah. Andy Corrigan was the other original member. He'd left by the end of 1980.

So we went over there, and it was really good fun to play again. We didn't play a lot, but after that we did play quite a bit. What really got things going again was the Miners' strike. We were being phoned up all the time. I was actually organizing benefits anyway, but we kept getting offers and it seemed a shame to have to refuse them because we couldn't function as a live band. And that's when we met Steve Goulding [current drummer], and asked him to do one gig, and people like Lu Edmonds [bass player]. Suddenly we realized, instantly and overnight, that we'd got this really good band that could play live. It took off from there. And it's been very good since then.

Collective Work

It seems as if a coherent sound emerged very quickly. English Dancing Master *was the start of it, but it seems to have evolved naturally through that despite all the different people involved. You all seem to be on the same wavelength. Is that because there's a basic core of songwriting and singing that holds it together?*

Tom: I suppose to some degree there is that, but I wouldn't like to stress that as opposed to other people's involvement. Certainly Steve and Lu's entrance was immediately a hundred percent their contribution—what they did in terms of providing a really strong rhythm section. Apart from details we've never said, "You've got to play it like this, it's got to sound like this, you do it like this."

That's pretty different to, say, the Jesus and Mary Chain, where when it comes to recording there's only really the two of them there. This idea of a collective of people, even a fairly loose and changing group of people—is that pretty much essential to you, part of what the Mekons is all about?

Tom: Except you shouldn't get too carried away with that. The idea that I've read in a lot of the American press about there having been 73 members of the Mekons . . . it's only because every single person who's played on one track on one album has been credited. And any band you care to think of would have contributions, musical or otherwise, from a large number of people who are involved in producing the final thing. All we're really doing is stating the obvious. But since 1985 we've had a fairly consistent lineup.

How do the songs emerge? Do you write most of the lyrics?

Tom: The lyrics tend mainly to be written by Jon, Kevin, and myself. But generally speaking we'll have a time when we're going to record, and the song will be thrown together on the spot. Or you could have a situation where there are no words whatsoever, just a tune, and words get written in five minutes in the studio.

Does each of you write songs separately?

Tom: I can think of hardly any examples where someone says, "This is a song, it goes like this, the chords are this, the words are this," being entirely responsible for it. That's hardly ever occurred. It's always been a joint effort of two or more people.

Is that why everything is credited to the Mekons?

Tom: Right. The amount of nitpicking that would have to take place if we tried to list individual contributions . . .

Other bands do it.

Tom: I know, but I don't understand how they can, unless you go into definitions of someone being an arranger as opposed to a writer, or something like that.

Politics, Slogans, and the Music Business

It seems to me you could look at the Mekons as a kind of reverse side of the Clash. In the sense that, regardless of their actual political beliefs—which I think were often serious—the Clash had a tendency to sloganize and make large rhetorical gestures. It was important and influential for a while, but it collapsed when a certain hollowness was perceived in it, in relation to some of the things they then actually did. The Mekons, on the other hand, have never gone in for rhetorical gestures, and have been more interested in writing songs not about oppression as seen from the outside but about what it's like to be on the inside of that, trying to see your way out of it,

MEKONS
Fear and Whiskey
(Sin Records)

Fear and Whiskey is what Sun Records might be putting out had the label relocated early on, cartin' the fiddle, harmonica, liquor bottle, and twang o' guitar sound across the ocean to jolly ol' Britain. It's that depressed, broken-hearted, self-condemning thing in country music with the imagination and dramatics of the Celtic mind. It's fiddles chattering and shrieking like man's best friend, falling headfirst into the joy of waltz time, and plucking out a drunken jeer at European classical tradition.

The Mekons are old-timer punks, man, survived all this time without getting famous. It's truly unestimatable the havoc one drop of country-music potion can release from a band that's basically techno-arty Crass-like anarchist minimalists. The Mekons are just enough on the romantic side.

Fear and Whiskey songs are noir ministories about the heartbreak of failure, lost love, and lost war. Only in permanent royal pickle could "Darkness and Doubt" and "Hard to Be Human" be sung and scribed with such hopeless abandon. These are certainly drinking songs to latch onto and belt out the chorus, dance, weepy eye lament, and pain along with. The album couples notoriously with the Pogues' new *Rum, Sodomy, and the Lash* LP. Be careful with two; they're hopelessly addictive. You'll be risking a stumble down that crooked road to wrack, ruin, and the bottle, never to get your life back together once and for all. I grew up with country music and Sir Harry Lauder. The Mekons have done me in.—*Patty Stirling*

THE MEKONS
Honky Tonkin' with the Mekons
(Twin/Tone Records LP)

"When you're a Mekon, confusion is part of your survival kit."—Kickboy Face, *Slash*

The cover of the first Mekons album was a take on the old cliché that if you gave enough chimps enough hours at the typewriter they would eventually reproduce the works of Shakespeare. By the same token, it was implied that if you locked several chimps in a roomful of musical instruments they would someday re-record the entire Hank Williams catalog.

Nowadays, however, we know they fudged on their research. One of the current chimps in the experiment is actually an ex-drummer for Graham Parker and the

Rumour; yet another was a founding member of the Pretty Things and the Rolling Stones. As for the others, it's clear now that they were never chimps at all, but missing links who have since evolved into gods and goddesses of the musical and literary worlds. (Or, if you're a believer in creation "science," they were spawned from the combined rib cages of Percy Shelley and Lefty Frizzell.)

Honky Tonkin' is way slick by Mekons standards. The production cleans up their usual avalanche of guitars, fiddles, accordion, etc., while it highlights the vocals. Fair enough, as this band has *four* excellent lead singers taking turns at a continuous stream of tragicomic/philosophical hard-luck lyrics not equaled since Richard and Linda Thompson's heyday. Tom continues to play the saddest clown in the world, Rico is the romantic tenor, and Sally is again the world-weary crooner with the most appealing way of pronouncing the word "drunk."

This time around, though, it's sly old Jon Langford who steals the show, first dropping his goofy sarcastic front to sing a tongue-in-cheek yet touchingly sincere tribute to his bandmates ("I like my friends / I feel unfit for them"), and then closing the album under the solo spotlight, plunking a Weill-y tune on a tack piano and telling the story of all of us mixed-up folk, lost souls swaying in the Gin Palace. *The quality of mercy is not strnen . . .*
—J Neo Marvin

THE MEKONS
Mekons New York
(ROIR cassette)
So Good It Hurts
(Twin/Tone LP, CD)

Outer space is a really nice place, axle-dragging on the road to Hell. The Mekons' madcap American caravans are caught in a Dada documentary collage. Live tracks, studio outtakes, stage blather, and road fatigue footage add up to a lively portrait of life as a Mekon. The between-song bits are like *Christ—the Album* colliding with *This Is Spinal Tap.*

Sally Timms or someone drawls drunkenly about the day "the Mekons came to towwwnnn . . ." and a Frisco DJ gets hustled for change. Langford snores and introduces his penis while Jim Morrison's "Lament for My Cock" and Crass's "Fold It in Half" disintegrate in a cloud of derisive giggles. Great music too, including a trad tune about skid row, a studio take of "Revenge," and a stark dub of "Chivalry" to lull the revelers to sleep.

The album is the first sign of the departure the Mekons have been hinting at since their last visit. On side 1, they delve heavily

trying to find things you can live with within it, but recognizing that things are pretty fucked up.

Tom: When we started off we didn't pay a lot of attention to lyrics. Songs like "Never Been in a Riot" and "Dan Dare"—it was just anything that was amusing really. But also, of course, we were in each other's pockets with the Gang of Four. They had their very bald, statement-like kind of writing, so perhaps we just thought, we won't do it like this, we'll do the opposite, whatever.

There used to be this bit of graffiti on the door to the Fenton in Leeds which said "Slogans are implicitly reactionary," which is quite good. And also of course there was this "the personal is political" stuff floating about, and I think we found that a way that made sense to write—after a while, not like "we will write songs like this," but as things got going.

I think that's the thing about the Mekons anyway. We were approached by Bob Last after doing one and a half gigs, and he said, "Do you want to make a record?" So we were in the position of being a band with a record out almost overnight, and that kind of thing, which didn't seem that strange at the time, just focused things a lot more.

But things were rather rushed at that time, weren't they? And the majors caught on, and before you know it you've got a major album deal. I don't know how well that worked out, but it meant a lot of things happened very quickly. Do you have any regrets about that?

Tom: The Virgin deal? A lot of regrets, though I don't know how things could have happened any other way. The Virgin thing was very bad—for loads of reasons, which probably aren't worth going on about. Firstly Virgin were signing anything they could get their hands on. And we were signed by Simon Draper against the wishes of his own A&R department, as a sort of pet thing. Thirdly we'd spent about nine months employing, I forget his name now, the same lawyer that McLaren used, to get us this deal that screwed Virgin down to the floor, gave us a high royalty, total control, and a very low advance. This meant that unless by accident we happened to sell a lot of records there was no point in Virgin pushing us because they didn't have anything to recoup. So the whole thing was pretty ill advised. And I think the album came out too late, the songs were stale, blah blah blah.

Now, in the mid-1980s, you're on an independent label. Does that make sense, is that where you want to be?

Tom: I think there was an argument at the time, 1979 or so, that being on an independent label for its own sake was a false idea, like what does it mean? I think that argument still holds true. This idea of some kind of purity because you're smaller and less efficient is just rubbish. But on the other hand I think there'd then be no point in a band like the Mekons signing to a major anyway, unless we just signed for a lot of money and split the band up. Because major record companies release records that are different from the things we're trying to do—especially in England, where it's all intended for the charts. And the charts are in a worse state than they were in 1973 even, when you had good bands like Slade, T Rex, and the Faces.

Rob: I think it's interesting to note that the Mekons were on CNT Records, along with the Newtown Neurotics and also the Redskins, who were sloganizing bands—"Nick Out the Tories," "Unionize!" The Redskins went on to sign a major deal and got completely fucked up, and are now completely split up and screwed up. Chris Moore is in the same kind of situation as Andy Gill [ex–Gang of Four]: at home with an 8-track, trying to write material that's going to sell records. The Redskins signed to a major thinking they were gonna sell more records, or—I don't know what they thought they were gonna do . . .

Tom: Exactly. This idea of reaching a larger audience is . . .

Rob: Well, the Redskins had a top 40 hit.

But to imagine that constitutes subversion.

Tom: Well exactly. What does it actually mean?

Rob: It doesn't mean anything, because of the nature of the medium. I heard Dave Lee Travis playing "Bring It Down (This Insane Thing)," which was about Fleet Street, and it was on during the day—I was at somebody's house—and all the message was there in the words, but nobody actually listens, nobody in the house could tell me what it was about, and then in the gap before they repeat the chorus for the final time, Dave Lee Travis said something like "One more time, boys," and that's all he's got to do to completely undermine all that the Redskins are singing about, everything the Redskins are about is completely fucked up by that.

There is an argument that the economic-political ideological media system, whatever you call it, the whole thing, can absorb more or less anything that's thrown at it. If that's the case, what do you do that has meaning, and how do you give it meaning?

Rob: How is the meaning generated?

Tom: [*after long pause*] Well, I don't know if it is. I think there's very good grounds for being totally pessimistic. To sum up all the arguments you've just mentioned without actually wading through it now, you could probably come to that conclusion.

But you seem to be saying, at least some of the Mekons' songs seem to be saying, that there are places in which you can have fun within it all, that it's not just escapism, although there probably needs to be some of that too, but that there's important things as well.

Tom: I'm sure that's true, yeah. You just throw your

KATHERINE SPIELMANN

into psychedelia, muzak, reggae, glam rock, and general confusion. Very weird, often difficult. They can't bury their hard-won easy way with a tune though, even when they try. A schlocky pop song ridiculing the space program (I have dreams about the Mekons appearing on *Star Trek: The Next Generation*: "What are you feeling, Counselor?") haunts with its Sally vocal. Likewise "Dora," which beautifully skewers Freud and psychoanalytic misogyny. "Foxy Lips" is a rowdy pirate song: "A merry life and a short one shall be my motto."

Side 2 treads more familiar Mekons territory, with some twists. "Sometimes I Feel Like Fletcher Christian" is an anthem and a half, the alienated mutineers adrift on a sea of impossibilities. A fatal joke to clasp to your heart, sung exquisitely by Tom. "Robin Hood" jits and jives Zimbabwe style, retelling the old legend with gay insinuations and anarchist fervor. More dangerous sex here and in "Fantastic Voyage." "Heart of Stone" is torched and lesbianized by Sally while ex–Rolling Stone Dick Taylor gets his git licks in. "Maverick" is a fine Mekons tale of damage and ravage: "Where's my baby face?" howl Langford and company. The set closes with "Vengeance," a zydeco chant of hope for an asshole-free future.

The cover is one to treasure. Diá de los Muertos sculptures of Mekons as historical skelly song protagonists. Improved lyric sheet inside, with literary quotations to clarify the strange stories and explain it all for you, sort of . . . A drifting cowperson's work is never done. —*J Neo Marvin* hands up in horror and try and . . . I don't know. I mean, what can you do? How can you possibly avoid being a part of the power relations that exist?

Rob: The point is you can't.

Tom: So what do you do? You recognize that any kind of product, whatever it is, is an ideological product.

Rob: You can't live in America or England and operate outside the capitalist system. It can't be done.

Country Matters

I remember, the first time the Three Johns toured, I was asking Jon Langford about the country and western stuff between the tracks, and whether it was like a homage or a joke, and he said, "Oh no, we really love that stuff." So I wondered when that started becoming something that you wanted to play.

Tom: Personally I've always liked Cajun and country music since I first heard it on Charlie Gillett—he wrote that book *The Sound of the City.* He used to have a radio show in about 1973 on Radio London, where he played things like "La Porte Dans Arrière" by Dale Menard, mixed in with the Feelgoods, things like that. I heard it, by accident really, and then I used to tape it. So I had these tapes, which I used to play to people, and no one was that interested. And then we used to buy stuff like Freddy Fender albums. So I think we've always been interested in that. Then with the demise of . . . aaargh . . . punk rock or whatever you want to call it, and everyone listening to Spandau Ballet or something, it was quite obvious, or it seemed obvious to me, that something like country music, any type of roots music in a way, would be something that people would look at, turn to. Reggae as well. I think reggae, like Studio One–type reggae, and country music are really close. You find there'll be a reggae cover of a country hit . . .

Like "Islands in the Stream."

Tom: Yeah, great. And also, country music is dead simple. Three chords. Very easy to play.

Has it got anything to do with expressing emotion? I mean, the Spandau Ballet syndrome was this really overblown, romantic, false emotionalism, but it seems important that there is a way of expressing emotions, and country music has always been able to do that, often in a very schlocky and sentimental way, but it gives you the space to do that.

Tom: Oh yeah. I think there's a number of reasons. Certainly that idea of raw emotions feels really good.

When did the violin playing come in?

Tom: Mary was our bass player for a while. She played on the first album, after Ros Allen, who was in Delta 5, left. She was actually a classically trained violin player and had never played bass before, but she started playing bass. When we were recording "Teeth," just messing around, she started playing violin on that. And on "English Dancing Master," John Gill played violin and melodeon. Then when we wanted to play that live and I was asking around for violin players, I was introduced to Susie. So she's been around since '83.

It's interesting, because to an American, a young, alternative music fan or whatever, country and western is the lowest of the low—to anyone on radio or whatever. It's only recently that I've started digging into it some more, and it's really cool, but it's so put down here.

Tom: That's right. I had a letter from a Mekons fan who lived in LA and he was horrified by the turn of events that's taken place in the Mekons. He's from a Tex-Mex background and asked me, "Why are you playing this racist shit?" So I tried to explain why and he never wrote back.

I don't think it's so much a racist thing, it's just dead music.

Tom: But isn't that changing now though, with people like Dwight Yoakam?

It's just part of the New Sincerity thing, isn't it? You've got people who are trying to sound like countrified versions of Springsteen—Steve Earle, for example—that I can't get all that excited about.

The Future

What are the Mekons' plans in the immediate future?

Tom: We want to put out a book, a coffee-table type of object, which is a novel with illustrations which are actual paintings, because a lot of us do paintings or various types of visual art anyway. And then we thought we'd have an art exhibition by the Mekons; we're trying to get something sorted out with an art gallery in New York. The book would be a lavishly illustrated novel with, perhaps, a record in the back of it. That's one idea.

Rob: A soap opera.

Tom: No, it's a serious novel.

What's the novel about?

Tom: It's gonna be a ten-year history of an imaginary band.

A very imaginary band?

Tom: Loosely based on reality, but no characters blah blah blah . . . And musically we want to do more of a . . . I don't know, I'm not sure about this country thing. A lot of people are saying, you're playing country music, and we thought we'd shift it away from that. I won't say to what just now . . . Northern Soul, something like that.

I'm not sure you have to accept what other people say about it.

Tom: Oh no, no.

I think a lot depends on the attitude you take to it, and it seems to me that you're drawing useful things from it, and then taking those further to do what you want to do. It doesn't seem to me that you are writing country songs.

Tom: Right.

Rob: There've been some quite silly reviews, like the *Hi-Fi News* piece last year about country music, that more or less implied, in fact I think it said that the Mekons were the future of country music, along with Dwight Yoakam and someone else and someone else . . .

Tom: Hasil Adkins, George Strait.

Rob: Hasil Adkins opened for the Mekons at Maxwell's last year. We just turned up and there he was. It was great.

Do you think you'll want to keep going for another ten years? How much forward planning goes into it, or do you pretty much take it day by day?

Tom: About a month, two months, however long it takes to organize an American tour, probably. That's like the yardstick.

England and America

I was in England about a month and a half ago, and it seemed that there was more interest in what you're doing here than in England.

Tom: That's true.

Is that a big disappointment to you?

Tom: I wouldn't speak of it like that. I think it's quite interesting, and nice in a way, that people are taking an interest in us over here.

Rob: It's not unusual. The Police became famous by touring America. Miles Copeland organized a tour of American clubs from his phone in England and broke the Police in America. They were zilch in England. And

THE MEKONS
May 4, 1987
I-Beam, San Francisco

I don't go out much anymore. I hate clubs and live bands. In fact it's hardly worthwhile leaving my room for any reason. Ah, but the Mekons tonight made me feel human again. They rekindled the meaning of live performance. I am deeply in love with every member of the band—especially singer/guitarist Tom, the most romantic being ever created.

The violin was so raggedly distorted that it sounded like trumpets. I think this Mekon woman plays a mighty fine fiddle. She knows how to play along with punk guitars.

Their faces and bodies were ravaged and ugly, the feel of youth lost before its time. They were dressed in thrift-shop rags, a perfect impression of how the UK dresses these days, these real dying days. They played with such energy and perfect interaction, such savage normalcy, that you reckon their lives must always have revolved around performing and they were holding on to it as the only thing worth living for.

This was like the past. Like watching the lounge show of what's never going to happen again. The audience was tiny and the Mekons were singing about floating off the edge of the world. I never could live in the UK where the only thing left to be cool about is doomsday. Or in America where it's the apocalypse. Maybe Australia is the edge of the world.

May 6, 1987
Berkeley Square

You know what it was like when Bob Hope

KATHERINE SPIELMANN

I hear that a lot of American bands have to go to England to break.

Right. It just seems that with a lot of bands, there's not any particular relevance in what they're saying to the society they live in. On the other hand, you are saying things that I'd have thought should find a certain resonance in England. Do you think it's the form they find difficult to deal with?

Tom: I don't know really. It's maybe the fashion thing that's very strong in England, and we're just not a particularly fashionable sort of band—and never will be really, unless some gross kind of accident happens. In England it's been really difficult. Recently we were getting reviews where they were reviewing the Mekons as they'd been in 1979 and not what we're doing now, and people are very stuck in that kind of thing.

And also I think the general tone of British rock journalism is just crap. Here you've got people like Greil Marcus, who are writing really imaginative stuff, which is very handy and seems to be really influential. I couldn't imagine someone like Greil Marcus writing in England, I don't see where he gets . . .

Well it's a little hard for him to write in America . . .

Tom: Okay, not even Greil Marcus . . . What's his name, Chuck Eddy—or any of those *Village Voice*–type journalists—the way they write is very serious and intense, and sort of intelligent, supposedly; it's a different approach.

They do have a broader sweep, a wider perspective on things.

Tom: But that's probably just the few . . . Like the *NME*, when they had people like Parsons and Julie Burchill writing, I thought they were really good, but there isn't anyone now who you can read—whatever they're writing about—because you know it'll be an interesting read.

You mean there isn't anyone with some kind of moral authority, where if they advanced seriously the thought that they liked something . . .

Tom: Or even if they hated something, or whatever. Just that it's interesting to read.

What do you like of the music that's going on in England at the moment?

Tom: There are some good bands. There's bands like Gaye Bykers [on Acid] and the Janitors. There's Nyah Fearties, and We Three Kings, punk folky stuff, they're quite interesting. But as I say I hardly bother reading the music press. I can't think of anything that really leaps out. Partly the reason for that is not that I think the bands are all crap, but unless the record is played on John Peel, how are you gonna hear it? Because you can't afford to go out and buy the records. Quite often there will be interesting things happening, but unless someone has given you a word-of-mouth recommendation or you have access to hearing the record or seeing the band, you won't know about it. ✪

used to entertain the troops? I was in that rotten a mood to start with, the fixed dismal state that ruins a show. The electric noise is just part of the depressing irritation, maybe worse because it's why you're there at that moment of your life in a horrible world.

I had always loved the Mekons, and felt foolishly disillusioned and resentful. Maybe they were after all just another rock band trying to make a cool impression so people would give them lots of attention and money.

Less than halfway through the set I broke. I laughed. I was completely in love with the Mekons again and I experienced the ultimate value and meaning of entertainment. The Mekons are so strong they succeed in doing what nothing or no one else can: hack away at the rock of my brain and make me happy. I can't resist.

This is the most vital element of entertainment. People who can really entertain seem to have an immense desire for life. For the Mekons, the desire is so intense that they must make sure they get it . . . They are from that small town where everyone's your mate. You've known them all your life and you can trust and depend on them . . . That's something to achieve in a forty-minute set!

You may think you love your Mekons records. But they're as nothing in comparison with the look of the Mekons' faces as they sing, the movement of their arms slashing guitars in unison, the bouncing buffooning bodies, the poise of the violinist, the keyboardist's smirk, the drummer's popping eyes. More-real-than-you're-used-to humans, onstage in front of you!

—Patty Stirling

LESTER BANGS

In 1979, three years before Lester Bangs died from an accidental drug overdose, **TOM SINCLAIR** interviewed the totemic rock critic for his fanzine. A decade later, when *Puncture* reprinted the interview, Bangs's star had ascended thanks to *Psychotic Reactions and Carburetor Dung*, the posthumous collection of his work published in 1987. In the years that followed, Bangs's inimitable prose would continue to influence musicians and writers alike.

Lester Bangs didn't invent rock criticism, but he was certainly the spiritual godfather of most modern-day rock writers. Bangs died in 1982 at the age of 33 in what may or may not have been a rock 'n' roll suicide. He left behind a massive legacy, in the form of hundreds of thousands of words scattered through the pages of *Village Voice*, *CREEM*, *Rolling Stone*, and numerous other rock journals and fanzines.

It was Bangs's writing that turned me on to Captain Beefheart, Iggy and the Stooges, the Velvet Underground, free jazz, and lots more that helped me make it through adolescence. The publication in November 1987 of a collection of his writings, *Psychotic Reactions and Carburetor Dung*, has helped to consolidate his lasting reputation.

The following interview took place in early summer of 1979 in Bangs's New York apartment on West 14th

Street. It was previously published only in a tiny xeroxed fanzine called *Chaos and Evolution* which I was putting out. I doubt more than twenty people saw it at the time.

At the time, Bangs had just released a single, "Let It Blurt" b/w "Live," on the Spy label, produced by John Cale and featuring Robert Quine on guitar and Jay Dee Daugherty on drums. He had also recently been booted out of the band Birdland for being "too fat."

During the interview, Bangs declined to drink any of the Colt 45 I had brought with me, belying his reputation as a wild-eyed boozer. He drank from a quart of straight orange-pineapple juice instead. Altogether, we hung out and talked for about three hours, only a third or so of which I captured on tape. Before I left, he gave me some of his poems, a rare Pere Ubu single, and an invitation to get together in the future to listen to records. I never took him up on the offer. I was 22 years old and Lester Bangs was as big a hero to me as any rock star. It was the first and last time I ever saw him.

I read somewhere that you used to work as a shoe clerk. How long did you do that?
Let's see, I did that from about March of 1969 to October of 1970. I started out actually in the stock room. I was a stock boy and then worked my way up into women's casuals.
How long has it been since you've had to work that kind of job?
[*Laughs*] Since October 1970. I worked at *CREEM* for five years, but that wasn't the same thing at all. I mean, I used to go into work at four o'clock in the afternoon and stuff like that, just hang around the office until 4 a.m.
Do you find it flattering or disconcerting that so many people look up to you and Christgau as "deans of rock journalism"?
Yeah, flattering . . . and disconcerting in a way. Because . . . the reasons why people look up to me . . . Basically, I think everyone should look up to themselves. I mean, who am I? I'm nobody to say, really, except that I'm very opinionated and I think I've always got something to say, but if someone else disagrees, I'm always happy to listen to 'em. I wish people wouldn't just take what they're handed.

Also, a lot of people, like we were talking before, have this sort of image of me . . . Obviously I encouraged it, but it originally came out of the way I did live and behave—and still do a lot of the time. But I found out at a certain point when I was at *CREEM* that you reach a point where you start sort of imitating yourself. You start doing what you think is expected of you, instead of whatever it is that you might really want to do. And then you just really get fucked up and you start to die. A lot of people, I think, are disappointed because I don't still write like that all the time, or I don't keep up that image, or whatever . . . There was a certain kind of thing that I did at *CREEM* that people liked because it's easy and fun to read—and I'm not saying I wanna shove something real difficult down everyone's throat—but they also liked it because it's kind of cruel, y'know. And really, I think, basically sort of amoral.
I was really impressed by your obituary for Peter Laughner [Cleveland musician, critic, and friend of Bangs, also a founding member of Pere Ubu, who died of a surfeit of drink and dope in 1977].
Thank you.
I wanted to ask you if the song "Live," which was recorded around that time, was inspired by his death in any way?
"Live" was written before Peter died. It was one of the first songs I wrote, in around March of '77, and he died in like July . . . A lot of this punk pose is tough-guy shit. And I hate that kinda crap, like everything's supposed to be a kind of smartass, jive comment, y'know? All that stuff is old. Like in Birdland (Lester's erstwhile band), when they kicked me out they said, like that thing in *New York Rocker*, "Well, Lester is a clown and a buffoon and he makes a fool of himself." And I hate cool people, people who have that pose. It's just so boring. I think people should be open enough to cry or make a fool of themselves or anything.
Do you see it as a good sign that people are dancing again at Hurrah and Club 57?
Not necessarily. I'll tell you, I went to see James Blood Ulmer at Hurrah the other night. And I walked in and it's this big media event. Here's *New York Rocker* in one corner, *Soho News* in another, Christgau, everyone's there, and I started getting nervous the minute I entered the room.

Because it was Ulmer, the DJ was playing nothing but these sort of Contortions-like records, which I like a whole lot. And I was sitting there and I thought, "Well, shit, here's me and John Sinclair—a lifelong dream realized—here's a whole room full of people dancing to free jazz combined with noise guitar. Why am I so miserable that I just want to go home and turn on *Green Acres*?" And then I realized it was because none of those people really liked that music, or most of them didn't. It's just becoming hip . . .

One time I DJ'd at Hurrah, and I did what I always used to do when we had parties in Detroit, which was to go through my record collection and get out every soul and R&B dance record I had: Jackson 5, Martha and the Vandellas, James Brown, Otis Redding, Aretha Franklin, etc., etc. And I lugged this big box of records up there and I was playing all this stuff, interspersed with MC5, Stooges, Richard Hell, the Clash, and the people hated almost every single thing I played.
Anything that was black?
Not just black; they hated the MC5 too. But they really hated the soul stuff. And a whole room full of people, I never thought I'd see the day, that paid six or eight dollars a head to get into this place, and you play "Heat Wave" by Martha and the Vandellas and they sit there lookin' at you, like "What are you, a moron?" And then you put on "Uncontrollable Urge" by Devo, and they all start dancing and jumping around . . .

What I really hate is exclusionariness, like this little group is over here, and there's all these fences and walls, and "we've got our little turf," y'know, and "fuck you." I like cultural pluralism, everybody just gettin' together and sharing stuff, and I thought that was what any kind of avant-garde or alternative or utopian thing was supposed to be about. It turns out the punks are just as bad as the rest of them assholes.

What's your current opinion of Lou Reed and Iggy Pop? Your views on both of them seem to shift a lot.

Well, my opinion of Lou is about like my opinion of Patti [Smith]. They're assholes; I love 'em. They'll be around for a long time. Forever, probably . . . I like Lou, but I think he's one of those heroes who's better loved at a distance. As most heroes are, I guess.

I just heard Iggy's new thing, "Chairman of the Bored," or "I'm Bored" (from the New Values *LP) the other night. That's kinda good . . .*

I haven't heard that. Y'know, every time I go into Bleecker Bob's that goddamn album's sitting on the wall looking at me, saying, "C'mon, you know you're gonna buy me sooner or later." And I know I'm gonna hate it, 'cause I really hated those RCA albums.

FRANCES PELZMAN LISCIO

Just the mere fact that there's a new Iggy album out and I can't decide whether to buy it or not . . . I mean, when *Raw Power* came out, I drove thirty miles just to get my hands on a copy, and I sat there in my car just turning it over and over and looking at it, and raced home and just . . . I mean, God . . .

You were brought up in Detroit, right?

Well, no. I grew up in San Diego. I went to Detroit when I was 22.

How did you get into Iggy?

I was in the *Rolling Stone* office when I was first writing for them, in 1969. The [first Stooges] album had just come out, and they were sitting around and they said, "Listen to this." And they were laughing at it. And I thought it was great, y'know, so I went home and bought it and I just loved it, and so did my friends. We used to sit around and listen to it all the time . . .

This sounds awful, but in a way I almost wish Iggy had OD'd after *Raw Power*, because everything he's done since is . . .

Anticlimax?

Not only anticlimax. It's like Bowie put him in college or something, gave him books to read and stuff. I went to interview him when *The Idiot* came out. He was saying [*Bangs affects a pseudo-scholarly voice*], "Ye-es, have you read Cocteau?" I said no. "Oh ye-es, Proust . . ." [*Bangs proceeds with a description of the interview, contrasting Iggy's* Idiot-*period pretentiousness with another Bangs/ Pop interview of several years earlier, in the course of which the Ig consumed a vial of thirty (!) quaaludes which Lester had scored for him.*]

That's pretty bizarre.

Well that's how people get, I guess. Like lonely egomaniacs. And the thing about it is that people around them will totally encourage them to be even worse, help build the walls up.

You've met the Clash . . .

Yeah, I went on tour with them for six days in England to do a story for *NME*.

That must've been a lot of fun.

Yeah. They're just really nice, y'know. The thing that knocked me out was that everybody was redefining society or behavioral attitudes from the ground up. So everybody was totally straight with everybody else all the time and on all levels. If anybody thought anything someone was doing was wrong, they'd say, "Hey, wait a second, that's bullshit and here's why." And they'd straighten it out.

Admittedly, that's a really hard thing to follow. But I discovered that if you act that way with people, or a whole bunch of people act that way with each other, it simplifies things enormously. Everybody I met was just really nice and really open . . .

Just the attitudinal thing was so different from over here. It was inspiring. Like we'd go and play these little clubs and then big places, and then after the show—instead of whisking off like rock stars—they'd go out in the audience and meet the fans. And they really, actually wanted to get to know these kids. They'd ask, "What's this town like? What do you guys do here?" And some of these kids had hitchhiked like forty miles, and they'd let them sleep on the floor of their hotel room overnight. ◗

WOMEN IN ROCK An Open Letter

Even within the confines of the supposedly enlightened underground, the music scene of the late '80s was an arena of entrenched sexism. In 1988, *Puncture* published a clarion call in the form of **TERRI SUTTON**'s essay, which systematically detailed rock's anti-woman bias while calling for a greater nourishment of female artists. The article was widely hailed—for example, in Greil Marcus's "Real Life Top Ten" column (just below his review of Prince's *Lovesexy* tour)—and helped to spur the nascent Riot Grrrl movement.

I recently experienced one of those confluences of ideas that feminists like to call a "click." I figure it's more like bashing full tilt into a brick wall. Perception shifts, as it must when you're flat on your back with a bruiser comin' up. A couple of years ago, another record salesclerk and I noted the dearth of new female bands expressing badness, sadness, and madness. We'd go through Frightwig and the occasional Kim Gordon (Sonic Youth) number . . . and pull up short. Then we realized how few women's bands there were, period. After moving into the record company side of the business, I was struck by the large number of women in the "industry"—inversely proportional to the tiny group of woman artists.

This year (the last brick in the wall) I watched a female friend join her first band, play her first shows, and prove—by her exception—this rule: that while many women involved in the "alternative" music industry dream of being musicians, few make it into bands, or even reach instrumental competence. Instead a majority of women in music continue to function within and support a mechanism that denies their existence as anything but consumers, advertising ploys, or shitworkers. And so they deny themselves.

Women are to be found as bolts and levers in every part of the music machine: they are heads of record companies, receptionists, bookers, promotion managers, photographers, retail and wholesale buyers and salespeople, owners of distribution companies, band managers, accountants, graphic designers, even engineers. All this effort on behalf of predominantly male bands. As a reward, women get the rock'n'roll equivalents of new kitchen appliances—thanks on a record, a postcard or two, maybe your name gets remembered, you feel part of some "scene." An incredible amount of female energy put toward the end of male artists' security and satisfaction.

Not a situation without historical precedent, of course. It is difficult to break from any tradition, even a short-lived one like rock'n'roll. I grew up on tales of male rock'n'roll heroism: "Shooting Star," "Jukebox Hero," myths of glamorous, guitar slingin' outlaws who sacrificed their emotional health for lonely days on the road, living only to "see a million faces and rock them

all." A guitar has the power to move countless people, and to inspire another young boy to follow the same road. For the woman hearing these songs, the underlying lure is that maybe someday she'll be able to offer the poor, emotionally starved geetar hero lotsa womanly love. And maybe she'll get a song written about her. Pamela Des Barres's autobiography *I'm with the Band* presents a woman who fell for this myth . . . and what, now, is she left with? An out of-print record and a list of men she's fucked.

Half a decade ago, a male friend and I both fell in love with Paul Westerberg of the Replacements. Mainly, I think, because he was unpretentious, approachable, and so self-consciously normal that it seemed we could very easily be in his place. What we loved about him was ourselves in him, and the possibility of us being performers, with the power to move people. In my friend this love was inspiring, causing him to play guitar better, write better, be in a band. To be able to say: look, I've done it as well. In my case, the love was parasitic; I wanted to fuck the guy and get a fallout of power from that position, receive fulfillment and prestige from being Paul's ultimate fan.

Years later, my male friend has his own band, a single released, and a growing audience. I have only the gnawing awareness of time wasted. I didn't fuck Paul, and I'm glad of that: sleeping with him would not have eased the longing to be him, to wield his awkward emotional power. Whatever "prestige" a woman feels in fucking a star is in her own head—it's a myth, ladies, which in the course of rock'n'roll history has acted to keep women like Miss Pamela sewing shirts and minding babies, while allowing men like Chris Hillman the time to write and perform beautiful songs.

False as it is, this pattern of supporting male musicians—body and soul—is a bitch to break. The problem is finding female mentors, musicians with whom you can identify. As Alice Genese of Gut Bank says, "Most boys have their rock'n'roll heroes, but women haven't had many. Y'know—there's Patti Smith, Patti Smith . . . and Patti Smith." In my adolescence, the women I heard on the radio were Ann and Nancy Wilson (Heart), Stevie Nicks, Janis Joplin, Patti Smith, and Pat Benatar. Say

I listened to three hours a day, that's about 45 songs, of which women sang (on a good day) maybe four. Real encouraging. And I haven't seen a lot of progress since the mid-'70s. The latest *College Music Journal* radio airplay chart lists 11 groups involving women in the Top 100. Roughly the same ratio as before.

There certainly are system maintenance features within this business which function to ensure that the number of women musicians remains low, and that most women remain in support roles. One is the already cited tradition of lust and fandom—settling for fucking what you really want to be.

A second maintenance tool is active discouragement, ranging from the subtle to the vicious, from a record company's all-male roster, to advertising that is offensive to women, to flat-out verbal baiting of female bands. Last month I heard a man, ostensibly a friend of the all-female band we were watching, blurt out: "Just think, we could be seeing a good band, with guys, instead of this shit." I don't care if he was drunk, fucked, or joking—that is discouragement.

An afternoon spent skimming through fanzines provided further examples of this attitude:

I usually don't like "rock" bands with female singers . . . (*Blatch* #12)

Let me remind you that metal is mostly attitude and something to back it up. Most women just don't have the necessary balls. (*Your Flesh* #11)

Readymade cunny rock that tries to sponge up the tail trail led by Les Bangles and Les Pandoras. (*Forced Exposure* #13)

Lovely Annette is a more manly version of yesterday's femme fatale Maria McKee, just as pudgy, just as cute (well . . .), but Blood emphasized the punk more than the cow, as in McKee. (*Butt Rag* #3)

The last quote equates "manly" with "punk" and lets us know that loud, angry, obnoxious music is a male domain: a woman becomes more "manly" by singing it. This not-so-subtle shaping of what is and what is not female music goes on all the time in male reviews of female bands. Furthermore, male critics try to define what is acceptable in women's creative expression, and it is often difficult for women to see through the criticism to the prejudices of the scared or witless critic.

It can be intimidating to be attacked on extramusical grounds. To be attacked, for instance, as sexually incorrect. I remember being temporarily duped a couple of years ago by taunts aimed at the Hoboken band Gut Bank in Gerard Cosloy's rag *Conflict*. He led me to imagine the band as some sort of slatternly bull-dyke bitch breed with warts on their noses and no musical talent whatever. (I should have recalled a similarly misrepresented band in my own town—Frightwig had been faced with lesbian baiting for years.) When I actually heard Gut Bank, they turned out to be a three-piece band with an amazing drummer—a band who liked to rock out.

The point is that Cosloy and other biased critics aren't doing music reviewing. They're doing police work. Unless a band of women are "correctly" feminine (not that they'll get equal treatment even then), they are lesbian—and they are outcast. In a business where supporting male dominant standards is a ruling criterion (even at female-run labels), they are also not going to be heard.

But isn't it clear, for starters, that musicians, female or male, are entitled to be gay? A number of highly successfully male musicians are gay, and as far as I can see they aren't subject either to being ignored or to any spectacular media oppression on this account. Even homophobic critics leave the sex choices of gay male musicians pretty much alone. What makes females such a target in contrast? I believe it is that "lesbian" has a far more fearful connotation in our society. Like: identifying with women for one's needs; avoiding a dependence on men; standing outside mainstream culture, whether as a (self-defined) separatist or a (society-defined) outcast. The men who cry "lesbian" seem threatened by any women musicians who obviously believe in and are depending on themselves—writing songs, practicing their musicianship, working with other women toward their musical goals. Such women convey the message: We don't need men in our band. They say: We're not buying into the myth that women must support men in bands. They say: We're doing it ourselves.

Women who identify themselves as lesbian and also women who dress and act and play and sing as though male approval is not first on their list predictably get trashed. My hope is that now, increasingly, women will respond to the lesbian tag without missing a beat. Like, "What's it to you?" Like, "Sure I'm a lesbian, if that means I don't give a flying fuck what you think of me." Scrawl's Marcy Mays remarked, "I was ready to quit over it [baiting] a couple of times . . . Then we just started laughing at it—you have to. Otherwise you quit, and there are no women bands."

The success of many female artists at the moment is severely limited by what male critics think is suitable female expression—poppy/sweet and trancy/slow seem to be the two forms deemed acceptable by men for women. Notice that these are both traditionally feminine types of behavior—saccharine, and mysterious. If you step outta line, you get something like:

Frightwig's first LP *Cat Farm Faboo* was fine by me, but I could never avoid seeing the foreboding finger of feminism pointing in my direction simply because I happened to be born male. (*Your Flesh* #12)

Aside from the fine alliteration, this guy manages to ignore the fact that women have been suffering the foreboding penis of sexism in music for many years. As I remember it, Frightwig's album deals with such topics as saying no and meaning it, enjoying one's sexual partner, making fun of obvious trad male role-playing, love, loss, and loneliness. If this dude considers that threatening, he's got a pretty archaic view of women. Now for a "favorable" review:

Relying on neither crabs in my crotch gutter mentality, or overt superior feminism, this is an '87 dose of norm-raunch. (*Forced Exposure* #13, reviewing Scrawl)

In other words, it's not okay for women artists to be earthy and crass or loudly feminist (what is "superior feminism," for heaven's sake?). In this same issue of *FE*, however, there's plenty of evidence that it's fine for men to be crass sexual dirtballs and raving woman-haters (see Albini's tour diary).

Of course the worst form of discouragement is silence. Look at many prominent fanzines—*Chemical Imbalance, Flipside, Forced Exposure, Non-Stop Banter*—and you'll notice the tiny percentage of articles about women artists. (Aside from *FE*'s obsession with Lydia Lunch, I can't remember them printing an article about a female band.) The prevailing attitude is summed up in *The Next Big Thing*'s review of Frightwig: "On the face of it they mean business but one way or another, who cares?"

A third way of keeping industry women confined to their supporting roles is to limit their decision-making powers. While there are a few women who own or operate record companies and distributors, most women are grouped in lower-status jobs like promo, sales, and reception. At nearly all the best known indie labels—SST, Touch & Go, Homestead, and Twin/Tone, for example—the final decision on who is signed is made by men. Even within their departments, women's decision-making is often undermined: when the head of promo at Twin/Tone, Jill Fonaas, objected to sexist artwork for a Blue Hippos promotional poster, the poster was printed anyway (as a gesture, the quantity was lowered). As promo chief, she should have had the power to reject it. It makes me wonder if perhaps a woman employee at Relativity objected to the Pushtwangers LP jacket that depicted a "seductively" posed woman whose dress peels off.

Unfortunately, too many women in this business don't give a fuck about sexist advertising, it seems—or about seeing more women bands. Both Frontier and Rabid Cat are women-run labels with all-male artist rosters. The reasons for such a bias are numerous. In part, women finding women singers annoying can be traced to culturally induced self-hatred and insecurity. In terms of the market, because male taste has always dominated rock 'n' roll (and Western culture), lots of women have learned to love male voices and to dislike feminine tones. They have become imbued with men's ideas of what is cool. Women music execs who feel this way are convinced, like most of their male counterparts, that female bands won't sell as well as male ones and that there are "no good ones out there anyway." As in other male-dominated industries, a woman in the music business has to do twice the job of a man to be considered successful, to be competitive. By the same token, a woman exec may defensively become twice as idiotic as men on the subject of music by women.

To help other women openly in this—or any—business is seen as subversive (and perhaps it is!). Alternative indie-rock labels seem committed to carrying no more than one (if that!) all-female group. Me, I'm stumped. When I wrote more rock criticism, I used to be made to feel in competition with other women writers; "competitive" was also the word a friend used to describe her band's relationship with other female bands. It's as though, in the minds of men and women, there's room for only so many women critics and bands to exist at any moment.

Such a climate hinders women from talking to and helping each other. It's encouraged by guys like the fanzine editor who threatened to "expose" me as a "lesbian" when I originally wrote about women and music.

Obviously, women's creativity and spunk will hardly develop in such an atmosphere of "foreboding." Just as obviously, those of us who are interested in music by women will have to rock the boat. What I'd like to see is a self-conscious women's network throughout the industry (many women are advantageously placed as I write!) which will nurture—and be nurtured by—a growing number of courageous female artists. Sounds impossibly optimistic, I know. But the basis already exists . . .

Getting information about women bands is the starting point. One good source is *Bitch* newsletter, which covers a huge range of female artists. Record clerks are also a well of knowledge: good clerks listen to most of what comes in, and are excited about sharing their tastes. If anyone had asked me about female bands when I worked at Rough Trade, I'd have overwhelmed them with enthusiasm. Trade tapes with female friends in other towns and states. I wouldn't have heard of Scrawl (from Columbus, Ohio) or Two Nice Girls (from Austin, Texas) without this tactic. Invite a touring female band to stay at your house—they probably need a cheap place to crash. Call up struggling local gals and have 'em play at a party for fifty bucks. It's money, and they need all the shows they can get. Volunteer at a local public or college radio station and work to get a segment or show where you can focus on women. Talk with other women about women's music. Get some cheap equipment (Scrawl started with an eighty-dollar drum kit), gather some friends together, and jam.

For you industry types, how about asking "Michele from Flaming Lips," next time she calls to tell you about the latest male band she's promoting, "Hey, are there any good female bands in Norman, Oklahoma?" Or you hear a hot tape by some women and call up Laura and Stacey at Rabid Cat, or Ruth Schwartz at Mordam Records. Or you track down a fave female group and ask 'em if they'd like to play a show in your town—then bug your local bookers until it happens. Get hold of Laura Fissinger or Carol Schutzbank or Gina Arnold and suggest they write about your band. Warn other women about stupid labels and clubs. If you want to share music and news, write me.

Notice how men do all these things— how they discuss new bands, admire each other's work, encourage and advance other male bands. That's their focus— male bands and their achievements. It is up to us to make female our focus.

I want to be part of a community that gives woman musicians energy, and expects that energy back in the form of honest, self-centered, women-oriented music. And by women-oriented music I mean music that speaks of women's experience, whether it is silly or Butterball or romantic or shrill or mystic or feminist, even. I want to hear the whole spectrum—heck, I've been into Heart pretty hard lately.

A healthy feminist music network already exists. I'd like to see that kind of pride in women's voices and experiences bloom in the alternative rock community as well. Currently the term "all-girl band" carries negative connotations. Says Gut Bank's Genese, "I don't like it when people refer to us as an all-girl band—as if it were a big deal. To me, that's like a cliche." Mays from Scrawl complains, "I think you want to be a band first. Mentally, you feel you're getting cut down if you're labeled an all-girl band . . . A lot of people say [about women bands], 'Well, they wouldn't be anything if they weren't women.'" Personally, I'm a little alarmed by women bands backing off from their identity. I realize that they'd like to be seen as a band and enjoyed in that light. However, I think that denying femaleness, trying to be "one of the guys," hurts women in the long run. As long as "girl band" is a derogatory phrase, women's music will suffer. Until there is pride behind the term, there will be little respect for the musicians themselves. And there'll be a corresponding lack of women willing to buck the pressure not to perform.

Luckily, there are encouraging signs among current groups that women are being inspired by each other. Genese talks of ESG's bassist, her heartening courage and nonchalance. And the flow continues: "I had a woman come up to me and say, 'I've been really wanting to play bass, and I thought my hands were too small . . . But you're tiny!' She went off and learned to play bass," laughs Genese. Mays: "A lot of women are saying to us, 'I really really like you guys.' And that's important to me . . . even sorority girls say they like seeing us onstage." She's run into 17- and 18-year-olds at Scrawl shows who tell her they're starting bands too. That's the growth we all need to see.

To me, rock 'n' roll is about lust, a lust for feeling: the worst I can say about any band is that they're boring. That's why it's so crucial that women get up onstage and impart/inspire some emotion. We've got to prove our existence as creative actors and to portray an emotional reality that is being denied. We can do it alone, if we do it together. So you wanna be a rock 'n' roll star?

Update

I got a letter from Heather Perkins, who's almost a one-woman networking service out of Oregon. Heather releases cassettes of her own music under her Land O' Newts umbrella, ranging from found sound collages all the way to kiddie rhymes and funky Strat-fueled boogie. She trades tapes a lot, and listed 15 or so female-oriented bands I'd never heard of (what a relief).

Heather let me know how difficult it is to find people you'd *like* to play with in a band. I know it's a common enough complaint for musicians of both sexes (it's hard to miss all those "drummer wanted" signs), but the task is complicated further if you're a woman. When I was talking to Marcy Mays from Scrawl, she mentioned that she had played in bands with guys before and had felt too inhibited to write songs and sing.

Journalist Gina Arnold wrote me from San Francisco about a mutual acquaintance: Barbara Manning used to sing and play bass in 28th Day; since that band broke up two years ago, she's been trying to find men and women to play with. Gina says that lots of guys would love to have Barbara play bass in *their* bands, but don't dig the idea of playing *her* songs and being in her band. So she's done a solo record, out now on Heyday Records. I'd guess that's a pretty typical scenario, but I'd like to be proved wrong.

Gina has picked a hard road herself. She's one of the few women writing rock criticism for mass market publications. She's a regular contributor to San Francisco's daily newspaper and also writes for *Musician*. If you want to get some help about writing and getting published, or just want to gripe about, say, the yucky world of rock journalism, drop her a line.

I've got a few views on that subject myself, having spent nine months writing and editing for California's "classic" rock magazine *BAM*, only to find that my (male) editor was taking credit for most of my work. The assistant editor (also male) took me out to lunch and let me know that the (male) publisher and (male) assistant publisher were on my case: what was I doing with my time, why was I working so many hours? The assistant editor advised me to cut back my hours (but do the same amount of work), bide my time (and hang out with the guys, play on the softball team, etc.), and then present the publisher with a list of articles I had instigated and edited. So *don't* say "this editor (your buddy) is a loser—I'm doing his work"; *do* say "look, I've been doing extra work on my own time—won't you appreciate me?" (grovel, grovel).

(TOP) BARBARA MANNING. PHOTO, TOM ERIKSON; (CENTER) SCRAWL. PHOTOGRAPHER UNKNOWN; (BOTTOM) GUT BANK. PHOTOGRAPHER UNKNOWN

Probably good advice, but I wasn't up to the deceit. I also didn't care enough about the club to fight for membership. I *was* hurt, though, that my "friend" the assistant editor couldn't or wouldn't publicly point the finger at the culprit, a fellow member of *BAM*'s old boys' club. Let that be a lesson to us. No one's gonna do it for us.

Now for the good news. Scrawl was in Minneapolis for two weeks in September recording at Paisley Park. We got to peek in at Prince's "personal" recording studio, check out his pet dove, and tour the costume shop while the gals finished mixing. Whooee! The two Scrawl songs I heard sounded full and confident; be sure and check the record out. It's called *He's Drunk* and it'll be released by Rough Trade in mid-October.

Got wind of two bands out of San Francisco. Weenie Roast is a female trio with a rabid sense of humor and a single on Positive Force Records. Yeah, it's Weenie Roast as in "I'm a one-woman weenie roast / Barbecue of desire . . . / Throw that log on the fire." I've also heard about a five-woman band called Ed. Someone please tell me more . . .

The Divas Deray sent me a well-produced tape from Rhode Island: cascades of slippery, colorful vocals, and dramatic guitar. If you enjoy Liz Fraser and Throwing Muses, send the duo a blank cassette and ask for a dupe . . . What's this about an all-woman band from DC on Dischord Records? The name is Fire Party, and if you've heard 'em or seen 'em, please let me know.

One final note. I was looking for old Slits records and noticed that all but one is out of print (I believe Rough Trade's *Typical Girls* is still available). That started me wondering about other women-oriented bands from the late '70s—Kleenex, Au Pairs, Delta 5, Raincoats, Essential Logic—and got me worrying about lost history. Punk went far beyond the Clash, Sex Pistols, and the Jam; its prideful amateurism provided perhaps the first opportunity for a number of women to think seriously about playing rock 'n' roll, and to learn how to play it. For me, their experiments were and are much more adventurous, quirky, and forward-looking than what is remembered as "classic" punk. A lot of female creativity has been lost to us (read up on out-of-print women novelists for some nasty proof)—let's not let it happen in our lifetime. So who's got some extra cash for a couple reissues? ◑

(TOP) THE RAINCOATS; (CENTER) LORA LOGIC AND POLY STYRENE, X-RAY SPEX; (BOTTOM) KLEENEX/LiLiPUT.

SCRAWL

Columbus, Ohio's Scrawl debuted in the mid-'80s, influenced by the (then) unsung greats of British art-school punk but predating Riot Grrrl by years. **J NEO MARVIN** interviewed the trio on the eve of Scrawl's second album and debut for Rough Trade, *He's Drunk*.

You (meaning me—the lamenting rock writer) get sick to death of reading your own excessive hype in your favorite 'zine. You vow to cool it and never get overexcited about anything again. Then along comes another band to blow you away with sheer simple perfection, *demanding* nothing less than your most florid prose. *And you can't explain why.*

The facts then. Scrawl are three young women from Columbus, Ohio, with two albums out: *Plus, Also, Too*, which they released themselves on No Other Records, and the new one on Rough Trade, *He's Drunk*, which was recorded at none other than Prince's Paisley Park Studios in Minneapolis. (Friends of the band say much merriment ensued when Scrawl discovered the costume room.) And you could not have picked three more down-to-earth, unstereotypical gals to invade the regal one's fantasy factory. It seems Prince has to rent out studio time these days to pay the bills for his monstrous

stage shows, so the doors of Paisley Park have opened to unglamorous musical geniuses like Bob Mould and dry-witted, sensible midwestern feminists like Scrawl. Good. *He's Drunk* resonates from the speakers with a full-bodied groove that brings out the best in this band's stream-of-consciousness confessional/garage tone poems. In terms of sound quality, Scrawl have progressed from the rough, K-like charm of their debut to the haunting strum sonics of the best Flying Nun recordings.

The voices of Marcy Mays (guitar) and Sue Harshe (bass) wail in close harmony like backwoods Everly sisters over a backing reminiscent of *Dragnet*-era Fall or something equally jagged and hypnotic. There's something X-like, too, in the way Marcy and Sue trade off lines or harmonize on lyrics that read like random snatches of everyday conversation, or sly observations from a diary. Scrawl's words find the passion, drama, and irony in everyday life, and feast on it. Terri Sutton once wrote that rock 'n' roll was about a "lust for feeling." No wonder she loves Scrawl.

On their first national tour, Scrawl swung through San Francisco in February. Armed with questions compiled by Maati Lyon and myself, I caught them between an in-store performance at Rough Trade (accompanied only by guitar and tambourine) and leaving to play at Gilman Street in Berkeley. We found a small room stocked with pizza and beer, and tried to get serious.

First I asked about their backgrounds. Marcy was born in Charleston, West Virginia; Sue is from Westerville, Ohio (just outside Columbus); and Carolyn O'Leary (drummer, relatively quiet but sarcastic) comes from Chicago.

MARCY MAYS (PHOTO: MARTY PEREZ)

Marcy: I grew up in a very small town. It didn't even have a rock 'n' roll station, just a gospel station. Then when I got to high school there was finally a rock station we could hear—forty miles away. So musically my upbringing was really weird. I listened to Burt Bacharach and Ray Charles a lot, 'cause my mom and dad had the records. I didn't even buy records . . . until TED came along. Somebody gave me a Ted Nugent tape and that changed my life!

Sue: I'm from a small town. One of the fastest-growing suburbs in the United States—that's Westerville's claim to fame.

Carolyn: Plus the town's been dry since Prohibition.

Sue: The Women's Temperance League started in Westerville. At our church.

Carolyn: You can't buy beer inside the city limits.

Sue: You're not supposed to drink it, either.

Marcy: Anyway we have pretty standard midwestern backgrounds with parents who are supportive . . .

Sue: Yeah, every time I call my mom she says, "OK, just don't drive at night, and we'll see you in a couple of weeks!"

Marcy: My dad always wanted to be in a band himself. One day my neighbor asked my dad to buy me a bass guitar so I could play in his heavy metal band. And my dad went out and bought me the guitar!

When the punk rock virus finally hit small-town America, Marcy and Sue responded. Marcy joined "a thrash band . . . not hardcore," while Sue studied classical piano at Ohio State while playing bass in a hardcore band called No America. Then came Skull— "a joke" formed by Marcy and two others. Marcy explained: "None of us knew how to play, we were like maybe a funnier Butthole Surfers. We did a lot of stage antics because we couldn't play."

As the others left, first Sue joined, then Carolyn, whose serious drumming ability inspired the group to

improve instrumentally and aim at making music out of their noise. "We were just doin' what we had to do as college students who were bored. It wasn't anything big. You go from a small town to a university . . . you start seeing all these people doin' their alternative thing and get intrigued."

By the time the present trio came together, the name "Skull" sounded too heavy metal. They sat down and wrote a list of every word they could think of that rhymed with Skull, then decided the new name by playing bingo. The winner got to choose the name from the list. Thus, Scrawl was born. A good choice, actually. It goes with the artwork Marcy Mays puts on the album covers. I asked her if she scrawled with pencils before she scrawled with a guitar.

Marcy: Way before. I went to college as a painting major, if you can believe that! Looking at the covers I know it's hard . . . I went to such a small school that all the art students knew all the people in bands. You always ended up being in a band and doing a show.

How do you approach songwriting? Your songs are all credited to Scrawl; are they actually written that way?

Sue: Musically they are, for the most part.

Marcy: I write most of the lyrics. Usually I write the more ballady songs by myself, the more rock 'n' roll songs we write as a band.

Sue: Marcy had four or five songs ready when we did the first record. But this one was more of a collaboration . . . sitting and playing and coming up with stuff. We're really prolific . . .

Marcy: We just jam. We don't really put pressure on ourselves. If it's gonna happen, it'll happen.

You have two really strong songs, "Breaker, Breaker" and "For Your Sister," that treat the subject of friendship between women with the same amount of intense emotion that most rock 'n' roll reserves for romantic love or male bonding. These songs are unique in the way they deal with basic things that don't often get addressed in music even now. Did you consciously set out to make a statement here?

Marcy: Those are songs we really didn't think about when we wrote them . . .

Sue: But I think that says a lot.

Marcy: People come up to us later and say things like, "Wow, 'For Your Sister,' what's that about?" I write lyrics completely off the top of my head, with whatever comes out. Those are both friendship- and family-oriented songs. It never occurred to us to edit them. We weren't consciously trying to write like that. If you trust your intuition . . . We don't try to figure out what we sing about. We just sing it.

Sue: It's not conscious, it's who we are. And that's the way it is.

Marcy: We do spend a lot of time with each other.

Sue: There is female bonding.

Marcy: People can bond in all kinds of ways.

Sue: Some people in Columbus told us they saw us with a few of our friends and it was the closest thing they'd ever seen to male bonding. [*Lots of laughter*]

Then there's "Small Day" and "I Can't Relax," which are both very good at describing anxiety about relaxing, or guilt about not being driven to accomplish anything.

Sue: It was funny how we wrote this song and Marcy had lyrics for it. About how people come home and say, "You know, I had a big day today." No one ever says, "It was a really small day!"

Marcy: Yeah it was funny . . . but those songs are true, you know. I'm sure everybody knows what I'm talkin' about. Sometimes you think you're doing a whole lot but you never get anything done.

Sue: There's no real game plan going through our minds every time we write a song.

Marcy: Definitely not lyrically. The lyrics are just blurts that we stick together.

Scattered through the two Scrawl albums are some unusual cover versions. One of the most instantly appealing tunes on Plus, Also, Too *is "Sad," which starts as a lazily strummed sort of country doo-wop ballad, then breaks into this chorus: "I'm sad, sad, I'm so fucking sad!" in hearty two-part harmonies. So where did that song come from?*

Marcy: From the first band I was in; it was a thrash song. It was about fifty times faster, basically just the chords and "sadsadsofuknsad" at a hundred miles an

hour. It was a local college thrash band. Then one day when we were goofin' off we slowed it way down and liked it. So I called the guy that wrote it and said, "We do a real slow version of this, is that okay with you?" And he's like, "Suuure!" They don't even do it anymore. Nobody does it but us. It wasn't that great as a thrash song.

Where did you first hear "Rocky Top"?

Marcy: It's always been on records, from the time I was two. They played a lot of bluegrass on the radio where I grew up.

Sue: It's the ultimate traditional song.

Marcy: I've always known it but never quite knew the words; I guess we screwed up the words a bit on the record, but . . . it's always been done real fast before. Very banjo-oriented.

Another cover is the old Hombres hit "Let It All Hang Out"— also covered on the first Micronotz album—which comes out somewhat mutated in Scrawl's hands.

Sue: I have records my brother gave me from when he was 15, around 1965. That was one of them, a 45 by the Hombres! We did it once legitimately . . .

Marcy: And we kept forgetting it, and it kept evolving til . . . the words are now completely different, everything is different.

Sue: The only thing the same is "Let it all hang out!"

Marcy: It just happened. We tried to cover it, we couldn't. I forgot the words and sang whatever came into my head.

The result is that after a halfhearted attempt to mumble through the first verse everything suddenly breaks down and speeds up into a wiseass satirical rap by Marcy about teenage girls buying designer punk outfits in the suburbs: "Girl

where'd you get that thing?/Got it at the shoppin' mall . . .
Black clothes, white tan/That's the way I catch mah man!" So
when did malls start selling "punk" as a look in Columbus?
Sue: Gawd, I don't even know.
Marcy: It probably started in '83 or '84. It was very late,
you can believe.
Carolyn: The Gap, and all that crap.
Marcy: You can well believe it was probably in the mid-
'80s. I mean, we certainly weren't on top of it.
So what do the members of Scrawl do for a living?
Sue: I'm a glorified secretary. I don't have to make coffee
but I do have to type. I work for Ohio State University.
Carolyn: I work for the university too. I'm a "landscape
technician." It takes a lot of skill to . . . cut the grass.
Marcy: And I work for a state anti-hunger organization.
I'm on a government grant to go out and see poverty in
Ohio. It's really . . . fun.
Sue: And there is a lot.
Marcy: Well it's a good job because it's made me realize
a lot of things. But I've seen bureaucracy and it's far
more hideous than I ever dreamed.

The subject of work brought up another subject, a big
one: Can an underground band ever support itself?
Hardcore true believers classify any attempt by a band
to make money from their art as a sellout or rip-off. But
once you start doing it yourself you find rock 'n' roll is
an expensive hobby. One reason people give up playing
music is the amount of money—not to mention time
and energy—required to keep it going: strings, drum
heads, transportation, and practice space don't grow on
trees, Jack. The temptation to have a foolish major label
toss a huge loan at you as you reach some small level of
popularity can be almost too much. Scrawl are as yet a
long way from that temptation, and they are too smart
and skeptical to see a big record deal as the end of the
rainbow. "Even then bands don't make money," Sue
points out.
Marcy: No, and I'm kinda glad because then we'd be
like, "We have to write a song, and we have to do this
gig." Now we still have the luxury of saying no.
Sue: It'd be like writing songs about writing songs! The
only reason you write songs is 'cause you know people
and you do things: you have a job, you deal with people. You don't write songs because you're a "songwriter." You're a songwriter because you need to express
your life in some way. Some people do it through art,
some people end up hitting their kids.
Marcy: Some people do it through Scrawl.
Why did you choose He's Drunk *as an album title?*
Marcy: That's the name of the drawing on the cover. It

was just a picture I drew of a guy falling off a building.
Sue: A portrait. There are lots of people like that at
Ohio State.
Marcy: They have to rope the street off to keep drunk-
en students from falling into the street. I did a whole
series of drawings after I went to a happy hour one Friday night at 6 p.m.—you knew they were gonna be out
for the next two nights . . .
Sue: And drive! It's a real oafy town. Lotsa guys saying,
"Let's party!"
Marcy: They're farmers' sons; no, not even that . . .
more the "medium-sized towns where their dad is the
mayor" kind of students who thought they were big
shit in high school. It's a real business- and fraternity-
oriented university. Those people line up for an hour
and a half to get into one bar.
What's the story behind "Green Beer"?
Marcy: You could get a full-size keg of green beer for
10 to 16 bucks after St. Patrick's Day. They needed to
get rid of it.
Sue: It's about two different parties we went to. One
was the green-beer party, the other one had all these
people . . . it was really weird, and I did steal a six-
pack. And this woman brought her mother . . . it's all
true! And you're hung over, you look in the mirror,
you brush your teeth and you're like, "My tongue is
green!" Everything was green for two days. I can't even
drink beer from a green bottle now.

With two well-received albums behind them, the band
has ventured on their first extended tour. They tell stories about their poor harassed male roadie, and a rock
critic in Portland who wrote that their voices could
"peel wallpaper." All in all, they find the touring lifestyle a lark at this point. But what about the future?
What happens when the thrill is gone? How seriously
do they take the Scrawl project?
Sue: [*laughing*] Well, we're under contract for another
two albums!
Marcy: I really want to make a perfect record. I've been
told it never happens. We wanna make a record that
sounds like Scrawl.
Sue: If I die at 80, they're still gonna find sheet music
in my attic whether it's published, or performed, or put
on vinyl, or not. We're still gonna write. You know, we
all had experience with music before this.
Marcy: I'd find some outlet, if the band ever broke up. It
might not be a similar one. It might be an acoustic thing
or it might be playing rhythm guitar for fuckin' Mudhoney. It's a means of expression, and you're always
gonna need that whether you're in a band or not. ○

THE PIXIES

Perhaps no anti-establishment band flirted as explicitly with pop music as the Pixies, who were ultimately hampered by interpersonal strife, to say nothing of a public mired in the listening habits of the late '80s. **JOHN CHANDLER** interviewed Black Francis in 1989, in the wake of the Pixies' second LP, *Doolittle*. The band would release two more albums before breaking up in 1992, leaving an incalculable influence on a generation of bands and listeners. By the time they reunited in 2004, their fans had become legion.

The Pixies may be this year's model. But they are also genuine originals, with a seemingly casual ability to create one great song after another. Black Francis (aka Charles Thompson) sings and writes most of them, cutting loose with the finest scream this side of Iggy while addressing fractured, acidic open letters to God or whoever is listening. While he works himself into a lather, bassist Kim Deal supplies vocal support and snappy bass lines. Guitarist Joey Santiago performs six-string surgery, cutting through muscle and tendon straight to the bone. Dave Lovering is a percussive overseer with Swiss-watch timing. Together they make some of the strongest, strangest, most consistently interesting music around.

I interviewed mild-mannered Charles at the University of Oregon on Halloween night, shortly before the Pixies—blood capsules in hand (and mouth)—played an incendiary set to an adoring crowd.

Is there any special process involved in composing a Pixies song? Or do you just come up with something basic and bring it to the rest of the band for fine tuning?

Yeah—that's the way most bands do it that have a main songwriter.

Do the other band members bring in particular musical influences?

It's not really that connected. We listen to a lot of music, and we make music ourselves—but we're pretty naive about how we do it. We're into what we're doing and we try to do it well. Our musical influences are kind of vague. We just listen to a lot of basic rock records, even more than actually playing instruments.

One magazine described your lyrics as "guilt-ridden, lapsed Catholic Freudian imagery." Can you elaborate?

That sounds pretty typical rock journalist. I mean, we come up with songs to fill spaces on records and lyrics

PIXIES
Come On Pilgrim
Surfer Rosa
(4AD/Rough Trade)

The Pixies are friends and touring mates of Throwing Muses. One can guess what the Muses like about the Pixies (assuming we like in others those attributes we cannot ourselves supply): the Muses lack nothing essential to great music, but a thing the Pixies have that the Muses lack is their relaxation, their striking ability to seem on an inside track while following their own agenda. In this, the Pixies greatly resemble the Velvet Underground. Like the VU, they seem unanxiously, invincibly cool. Perhaps even cold.

The Muses, meanwhile, would not consider an album cover photograph that highlights private portions of a woman. It wouldn't cross their minds that in some circles it is considered very cool to exploit women. They wouldn't be interested.

Which suggests an important thing to know about the band the Pixies are endlessly compared with. The Pixies lack the stature (probably always will) of their friends. Their friends the Muses I mean—not their friends the morons who assured them this was a good idea for the cover of Surfer Rosa.

In their musical tendencies the Pixies are piquant: willful, madly varied, wonderfully confident, too cool. And they're hard: three men, one woman mixing languages and rock idioms with near-violent abandon.

Their debut eight-song EP and their new LP are both out now, as is the CD that includes all songs from both records. The EP has more of their Spanish-language songs (and rap scraps). These are a fascinating hybrid—rockerriqueño, it might be—not to be missed. The LP features more of the big, airy, eclectic rock numbers. These songs cut an extraordinary swath. They seem to come from some new place in rock—some cultural or tribal otherwhere. Here, the pace, noise, and heat can be effortlessly turned up. Here too, the living is tough and the sentiments sensational. In "Gigantic," Mrs. Murphy's wondrous love song, her chorus repeats mindlessly, comically, cruelly, irresistibly: A big, big love!

All the Pixies songs, with the kind of playground intimacy their voices share in English and Spanish street talk, have this power: a vast appetite combined with a hair-raising don't-care quality. Some day maybe they'll have to care more. For now, everything seems to fall before the rushing advance of the Pixies.—Katherine Spielmann

to fill spaces in songs. It's one of the basic activities of rock 'n' roll, unless you're into instrumental music. You've got to come up with lyrics. You can listen to all the classic rock, the Beatles, the Stones, the Doors, all that stuff—who fucking knows what some of those songs are about? A lot of them are just silly words that may have had some meaning to the songwriter, but as far as the masses are concerned, is there really some deep meaning? Do they have it down? Like [assumes dork rock-critic voice], "George wrote 'Savoy Truffle' about Eric Clapton's cavity-ridden mouth and need for sweets." Your basic famous rock song. It's abstract compared to topical message music, which is pretty damn hard to do. You sit down to write a song on a certain topic and it sounds like shit.

[Assumes dork rock-star voice] "This next song is about nuclear disarmament. It's called 'Stop Building Missiles.'"

Yeah, it's like obvious with the biggest fucking capital O in the universe.

The New Yorker said your lyrics are "manic depressive," that you swing from a nice ditty like "Here Comes Your Man" to something like "Wave of Mutilation."

We get a lot of that. We come into town and local reporters call us up and ask us about song titles. I can picture them reading the titles off the backs of the albums Elektra sent them. It's bulletin board journalism. Rock critics are always looking for an angle. Our music is dark and macabre, but so what? Being dark and macabre is a staple for any art form. A lot of hype comes out about any band that's dark, or gory, or whatever. Anything that isn't light and happy . . .

Plenty of bands have a more specific angle than we do. I don't think you should pigeonhole yourselves unless you come up with the ultimate pigeonhole that's totally amazing.

I think the best a rock critic can do is use colorful and descriptive phrases that have a kind of rhythm. Something like beat poetry, I guess. Lester Bangs is an example.

Yeah, I like Lester Bangs. I like the English rock press too, because of its silly and superficial praise and worship of pop culture and rock music. That's all they concern themselves with.

Your lyrics aren't purposefully vague . . .

I've got nothing to say, basically. At least not in terms of rock 'n' roll music. As a private citizen I could say plenty. But what am I gonna do? I'm playing fucking Eugene, Oregon, on Halloween. I have nothing against Eugene or Halloween. But I'm on this circuit. What can I say or do to change the world? Absolutely nothing. I play rock 'n' roll. If I want to change the world I'll get a haircut, go to law school, become a sleazy politician, and fight my way to the most powerful position I can.

Take someone like Sting. He's so damn world-famous

he can have an audience with the president of Brazil and discuss the problem with the rain forest. Fine. I don't really like Sting, but good for him. I hope he can stop the deforestation of Brazil.

Instead of gathering nice opinions between graduation and two years after graduation, more people should cut their hair, go to law school, and become ruthless politicians if they really believe in what they're doing. That's the way the world works. I have nothing against protests, pickets, and tying yourself to gates and fences while trying to be media-savvy, but there's more to it than that. People need to be a little more ruthless.

Tell me about your contribution to the Neil Young tribute album.

They called me up and asked what song I'd like to do, and I immediately said "Winterlong." I'm a big Neil Young fan, although I don't own a lot of his records. But I do have *Decade* [the compilation featuring "Winterlong," an otherwise unreleased track].

Do you have projects, musical or otherwise, outside of the Pixies?

There's this documentary I'd like to make about the brine shrimp of the Great Salt Lake, but I don't know if it's going to happen.

Sounds like big box office.

I think it's a really good idea. They're the only inhabitant in this supposedly dead lake. They're not microscopic, they're macroscopic. They're the only macroscopic inhabitants of this whole fucking lake. They're sea monkeys. Millions of sea monkeys living in this lake. It's a beautiful locale, lots of natural beauty. It would be a surreal, wacky kind of documentary.

This sea monkey's gone to heaven? How does it feel to be so

MARK DIXON

THE PIXIES
Doolittle
(4AD/Elektra LP)

These Pixies are a natural phenomenon I can liken only to my cat, Lester, on his most hormone-fueled days. They can wind themselves up into a frenzy in a moment, and then unleash and sustain a wave of furious power over the course of a three-minute song, and stop. And start again. And do it over and over. And you get the sense that underneath it all, they're perfectly calm. There's something almost inescapably evil in that kind of self-possession, and when it hits home, as on the opening cuts "Debaser" and "Gouge Away," it's just as inescapably genius.

So where's the Faustian compact? Is it a disavowal of feeling, as the icy passion of their peaks would sometimes seem to suggest? Or is that a misreading of the Pixies' formidable intelligence and their ways of expressing it? A few of the songs here appear to require that they be given the benefit of the doubt, at least this time around.

There's the instant-classic pop song "Here Comes Your Man," for example, with its almost plaintive vocal and irresistible chorus. Also "Wave of Mutilation," a crashing, twisted East Coast response to surf music. And "This Monkey's Gone to Heaven" is one of those rare pieces that alters the musical landscape forever. Like the best Fall songs, it seems like it must always have been there. When Black Francis screams the word "god" (and no one can scream more effectively), the world changes shape.

It's not all this great, of course. There are times when they seem to be coasting—the sly mocking and milking of reggae and blues on "Mr. Grieves," and the deadpan parody of "La La Love You"—and Kim doesn't sing any lead vocals, which is a major disappointment to fans of "Caribou" and "Gigantic" from earlier Pixies records. Furthermore, the production (by Gil Norton), while fuller and more considered than before, and for the most part sympathetic, oddly seems to undermine some of the vocals (like the aforementioned chorus of "Here Comes Your Man"). But the Pixies' collective power throughout most of this album renders these reservations relatively unimportant—and puts the seal on their stunning rise to greatness.—*Jean Debbs*

THROWING MUSES
PIXIES
June 20, 1988
I-Beam, San Francisco

For all the sinister atmosphere they conjure up on vinyl, the Pixies come across onstage as cute, innocent, fun-loving youngsters having the time of their lives. Singer/guitarist Charles, aka Black Francis, is a scruffy cherub striving for maximum naughtiness, while bassist Kim Murphy is giddy with glee, cracking up at every shock lyric and absurd riff. His voice is no great thing (though charming in its whiny way), but her voice is downright beautiful (imagine Ricky Lee Jones's pipes with Lou Reed's phrasing), and when they combine, the resulting harmonies are abrasively spine-tingling. That's one thing that makes them special. The others are Joey Santiago's arsenal of guitar sounds and the whole band's lopsided sense of rhythm and structure: chords and phrases chasing each other around in circles, tripping over their own feet. They seem to have stumbled on this brilliant sound by accident. I hope they can grow with it. One observer called them "sensationalistic." I had to agree, but I also thought they were sensational.

Throwing Muses don't have to try to be scary and bizarre; it comes naturally. Kristin Hersh is like a cross between Sandy Denny and Linda Blair in *The Exorcist*. She comes off as a pleasant-natured, somewhat shy hippie girl—until a song starts and something else takes over. Her eyes glaze up all of a sudden and her head shakes back and forth in an extremely unnerving way. Her guitar and Tanya Donelly's were so meshed it was sometimes hard to tell who was playing what. Leslie Langston was pure grace and fluid bass fingers, and David Narcizo was a raging, obsessive drummer. When he focused on his snare, you almost felt sorry for it.

They may have been slightly agitated and nervous, or maybe this is just the way they perform. The songs were delivered more aggressively than on record, and Tanya even left off the quiet intro and coda from "River" and just plunged into the fast part. Fear of being drowned out by the audience? I don't know. Kristin didn't have that fear, coming out for one encore with a biting solo acoustic "You Cage." Her songs are like half-remembered dreams following their own internal logic, shifting and ending as they please. She and Tanya have been at this since they were children and know exactly what they are after. *Puncture* readers must be immune by now to our over-the-top raving about the Muses. But I have seen them live and they justify it all.

—*J Neo Marvin*

closely associated with college radio? Are you flattered when people say you play college radio rock?

I'm not flattered, but I'm not insulted either. We make records and college radio plays them. They play us, we don't play them. It's not like we're so noble and removed from it all, but we *are* removed from it. We went to college, but so what? We've got a lot of alternative music in our collections, but so do a lot of people. It's a worthwhile circuit for us to sell records and make music and to play gigs where people show up and have a good time. We're not into college radio being the champions of bohemia.

How do you compare the production of Steve Albini on Surfer Rosa *with what Gil Norton did on* Doolittle*?*

It was mainly a question of budgets. Steve had a little money and a little time, Gil had a lot of money and a lot of time. Steve is a harsh guitar guy and Gil is an English pop guy.

Surfer Rosa *seemed really urgent and fast, while* Doolittle *came off as somewhat more sophisticated musically. It sounded like you had more time in the studio.*

Yeah, maybe too much. That's the way it is in the studio sometimes. People think when you're making an album it's always like the Beach Boys meet the Beatles or something. We're actually at the point now where we can record our next album wherever we want to.

What's your favorite movie?

This is a corny, corny fucking answer but . . .

Not The Wizard of Oz*?*

No, *Eraserhead.*

Same thing. What's the last good book you read?

Hmm. It was a long time ago, that's for sure. I don't really read much. I read a lot of comic books, stuff like *Zap, Black Kiss, Reed Fleming: World's Toughest Milkman.*

Any superstitions about playing on Halloween?

Nothing really supernatural has ever happened to me. Though one Halloween I got bit by a dog and electrocuted.

Typical. No history of witchcraft or Satan worship?

One time my cousin and his friend wanted to have a barbecue. They kept a pig for a couple of weeks, then took it into the woods and slaughtered it. When they barbecued it, all this peat caught on fire. The fire marshal showed up, with firemen, but they couldn't find the cause. Everyone in town knew each other, so my cousin sort of sheepishly pointed them in the right direction. After finding burnt animal remains everyone figured my cousin was a Satanist. Now every time he goes into Joe's Coffee Shop for his dollar-fifty breakfast, everyone goes *bzzz . . . bzzz . . . whisper . . . Satan . . . whisper . . . sacrifice . . .* ◗

FUGAZI

LOIS MAFFEO profiled Fugazi in 1990, just after the band released their debut LP, *Repeater*. The DC punk standard-bearers would go on to inspire a wealth of artists both musically and (with their famously strict DIY and straight-edge values) politically.

Record Company: "What kind of a deal are you looking for?"
Ian: "I think we'd settle for five million dollars and complete artistic control."

She doesn't get it. Ian MacKaye is on the phone with a woman from a major label that wants to sign Fugazi. "No, sorry, make that *ten* million dollars."

Repeater, the latest Fugazi record and first full-length LP, has just come out, and things at Dischord are completely insane. Today, alongside the regular crew working and answering mail, are friends and visitors doing homework and recovering from broken hearts. It has all the appearances of a black comedy, and Ian's backwards, artless frankness fits into the day's pattern without effort. "What I'm trying to say is, we already have a record label that we are quite happy with . . .

"Thank you. Bye."

Similar exchanges with Fugazi seem to take place with uncomfortable regularity. Where many other bands see a major-label contract as their final destination, there are still a few who view it as going to work for a media monopoly. But the early-'80s heyday of this sort of refusal has gone the way of all things. Yet it isn't an "us versus the Man" hype against big business that keeps Fugazi and Dischord in their working partnership. It is part of their mutual effort to maintain their rationale for making records in the first place. It has to do with the reasons that, for them, music and community are linked.

"I think we are in a better position than many other bands to deal with the pressures of being popular. External pressures can always be dealt with as long as internal pressures aren't testing the chemistry of the band itself."

FUGAZI
Steady Diet of Nothing
(Dischord)

If you detect a slight note of crowing in some of the recent coverage of Fugazi, consider that their current runaway popularity has vindicated a lot of people who've felt left out ever since the punk scene moved away from the values of community, independence, and social criticism. There's a feeling of being witnesses to a grand experiment: a band trying out all those long-mocked peace-punk tactics on a mass American audience, and still remaining down to earth. If this keeps up, Metallica's impressive chart coup is going to look like music-biz-as-usual in comparison. Certainly, Ian MacKaye's growing maturity and sensitivity show no sign of eroding his legendary hardheadedness, and Guy Picciotto, Brendan Canty, and Joe Lally exhibit the same stubborn honor. At the same time, they've avoided the Crass trap of self-righteousness admirably—you don't hear them dissing other bands that feel the need to compromise; Ian even praises Sonic Youth.

Clichés like "preachy" or "PC" have no place here, unless of course you're one of those whiny knee-jerk critics who squeal in horror at anything that deviates from their tiny, circumscribed definition of "rock 'n' roll." (Hi, *Your Flesh!*) This is music with a special urgency, spark, and inventiveness that's hard

Ian is addressing more than the ability of the band not to hate each other's guts. He is talking about the commitments of friendship and the distortions of traveling and performing. The things that affirm their existence at home, and make them aware of how they got from here to there.

"We took a very deliberate course, as far as becoming a band goes. We went out on two tours without a record. Normally that is considered excessive. But we wanted to learn how to be a band without anyone holding something over us. It would have been easy to push the Minor Threat button. People are much more comfortable entering into something that has already been established. But this way, coming up grassroots was a challenge. None of us knew what was going to happen, and what happened was that we became aware of each other."

There seems to have been a *less* deliberate course in the way that Fugazi came together. At a glance it was: Minor Threat and Rites of Spring get married and have a baby. But the actual courtship had little to do with pedigree. It was more a matter of natural selection. Joe and Ian wanted to work together, Brendan was willing to sit in for a few weeks until they found a permanent drummer, and Guy came in and convinced them that what they needed was a car-crash hybrid of vocal partner and human cannonball.

Viewing it from three years down the line, it seems hard to conceive of a Fugazi other than the present sure-of-itself collaboration. Perhaps this is why Fugazi's bonfire is now burning so brightly. Listening to *Repeater*, you hear both the deliberate step of progress and the delirious thrust of ingenuity. Their previous EPs, *Fugazi* and *Margin Walker*, seem divided not merely into Guy's songs and Ian's songs, but into "this is what I consider right" and "this is what bursts free of me."

In this respect, *Repeater* reaches a full-bore union. It blasts and trembles, often simultaneously. Immediately swinging into effect with the poleaxing guitars and prose fulmination of "Turnover," *Repeater* does not apply the brakes until the fragile closure of "Shut the Door." The album's title song—although it specifically addresses the fear, violence, and decay that jeopardize the District of Columbia—is voice for everyone who is not volunteering to be fucked over.

Fugazi keep their politics in view, not like a placard but like a well from which they draw their inspiration. *Repeater* takes several sidelong glances at the subject of greed, noting its omnipresence not merely in the things they hate, but in the contracts they make with everyday desire. It's a very carefully constructed recording that somehow manages to describe the passage from interior thought to external action.

Kid: "You wouldn't be saying all this shit five years ago."
Ian: "Are you here for a show, or a history lesson?"

Repeater also manages to harness the inspiration and provocative delivery of Fugazi's live shows. It's no rare privilege to be singled out at a Fugazi show. If you open your mouth, be prepared to back up what comes out of it, because more likely than not, someone on the stage is listening to you. Raging sets come to a crashing halt to accommodate the exchanges that fly forth between members of the audience and the band. Ian's responses are stern, Guy's are edgy, and if Brendan comes out from behind the drums, and Joe finds cause to speak up, it's something of a punk-rock symposium. This interruption of the performance format gives you choices as to how you digest the music, scene, and other attributes that give meaning to the rock-show experience.

"Having a response to people is just part of my nature, although I think it freaks some people out. They don't expect to have someone actually respond. Too often, though, it's about the timeline. A kid will want to take me to task about 1982, when he was probably 8 years old. Why does everyone want the timeline to be static? He has obviously done some changing since 1982. And so have I."

A reasonable response, but as an exchange punched out between punk cataclysms, its significance becomes part of the framework of the evening. It certainly gives life to the adage "A little knowledge is a dangerous thing."

In their records and shows, Fugazi express a welcome affirmation of the punk-rock ethic, however mutated, without relinquishing the musical truism that kicking everybody's ass is at least as desirable.

"Punk rock is about doing. Everybody knows that. I'm glad that the steps taken in becoming a band have never changed for me. From my first band on, it has always been the same. We decide we want to look weird. So we try it. We decide to say we're in a band. We try to write a song. And so on.

"And in every band, our highest ambition was to have one show. So I feel pretty good about actually being able to have Fugazi work out in the way it has. Even during the worst show of our last tour in Europe . . . a show in Paris so terrible that Guy wouldn't even turn around and face the crowd, I just had to laugh to myself. 'I'm playing the worst show of my life. But, fuck, I'm in Paris, and these are my friends. How bad could it be?'" ●

to match, and yes, it rocks like a monster. "Graceful" is not a word people often use to describe Fugazi, but get a load of the skankin' reggae groove of "Reclamation," the lyrical bass and agile drum whacks that underpin all the purposeful yelling and clanging. I'm reminded of the way early Gang of Four sounded at the time: like all the components of rock'n'roll, funk, and punk dismantled and welded together in a completely new fashion toward a clear impact and purpose. Jettison the cold, theoretical approach and replace it with the warm passionate rage DC punks have always had; walk a fine line between total precision and a loose, anything-goes approach (the all-bass arrangement of "Long Division" is brilliant), between blunt directness and a newfound love for metaphor and poetry in both Ian and Guy's lyrics; and you're on your way to conquering the universe.

One more thing I don't often hear when people mention Ian MacKaye is "great guitar playing." The sounds he gets out of the instrument are some of the most satisfying noise-and-chord slabs since Bruce Gilbert gave up strumming for sampling. Consider his peers from the hardcore scene; can you imagine Henry or Jello turning around, *learning an instrument*, and taking a back seat to another singer in *their* next band? Seriousness of intent and a total lack of regard for one's own image can take you to interesting places. —*J Neo Marvin*

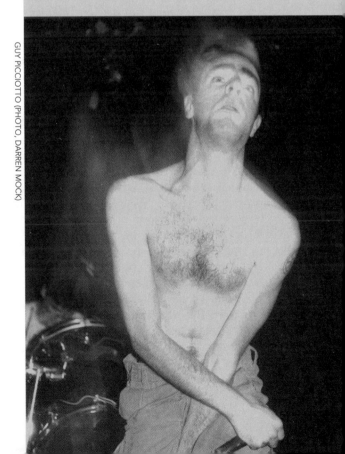

GUY PICCIOTTO (PHOTO, DARREN MOCK)

WOMEN, SEX, AND ROCK 'N' ROLL

In 1989, **TERRI SUTTON** followed up her earlier essay "Women in Rock: An Open Letter" with a piece examining the role of sexuality in feminist rock fans. "Male musicians have trouble seeing that women can understand and appreciate their music," she notes, "without wanting to fuck the dumb guitarist."

I'm sitting here listening to "Foxy Lady," which I consider one of the most erotic songs ever recorded. And I'm thinking about an article in *Rock and Roll Confidential* in which Maggie Haselswerdt defines female sexuality as "slow-building," "diffuse," "buzzing," "melting," and so on, and laments that rock 'n' roll has mostly been a forum for male sexuality, with its "male driving beat, piercing guitar lines, pounding keyboards, and expansive, stage-dominating gestures."

And I'm digging Jimi's punctuating guitar jabs, the rolling drum fills, and the fluid peaks and valleys of the deep bass guitar, and finding that I'm really uncomfortable with Maggie's theory.

Now you know I'd never argue that most rock 'n' roll *does* include and appreciate women. But to say that women shouldn't keep the term "driving" in our female rock 'n' roll vocabulary—well, that's too much to swallow. And to set up the idea that for women, erotic music will necessarily reflect Haselswerdt's model of diffuse, melting, buzzing stuff—that's bunk, sister, or at least only half the picture.

Maggie presents the Ronettes' "Be My Baby" as the best example of what can happen when men (in this case, Phil Spector) take into consideration "female patterns of sexual response" and build a song to fit these patterns. She claims that Spector and the Ronettes "weave a gauzy curtain around the sexual impulse, diffusing and romanticizing it, blurring the focus with walls of vibrating sound," and so on.

Now, have you ever felt like that? It sounds like a Hallmark greeting card view of sexuality. "Be My Baby" always struck me as cloyingly sweet. If we're gonna talk sexy old records by producer-manipulated female puppets, I much prefer the moment when one of the Shangri-Las asks, "Well, how does he dance?" and another answers, "Close . . . very, very close." And they strut right up to the dude and give him a great big kiss. But let's not fuss about '60s tunes. My point is to argue over what is considered acceptable female sexuality, and—as a corollary—what is considered acceptable women's music.

To get started, let's make some massive generalizations and quickly trace the course of female sexuality as seen through the folklore of the last forty years. I was born in the early '60s, and in the '50s—to judge by what I can glean from books and movies—female sexuality as a separate entity from the male variety did not exist. Romance, yes, longing, yes, but when the big bang happened you lay there with your knees spread and took it like a lady. Passivity. I'm not sure if you were even supposed to react.

The mid- to late '60s mythology reads that free-thinking women were out there looking to get laid, actually going after partners, displaying desire as distinct from desire for romance. The problem was, they were *supposed* to. And then, if everyone else was fucking and coming, what was wrong with *them*? Were they frigid?

Then feminism kicked in around the early '70s, and women discovered clitoral orgasms. By the mid-'70s, some feminists were looking to lesbian relationships to define true female sexuality. (You know—when two women have sex together, their sexuality isn't repressed, got it?) I'm sure lesbians then "made love" in as many different ways and with as many different emotions as they do today; still, what surfaced as "correct" sex was categorized as gentle, loving, slow, careful, cyclical, and ultimately based on the clitoris. (Sex was supposed to be focused less on the genitals, but you *were* meant to come.)

Enter the '80s. Buzzing, melting, and diffuse. "Experts" say women don't enjoy intercourse. (You don't come, so why would you enjoy it?) Anti-porn feminists say sex is something forced by men on women, who stupidly lie there and take it. Male sexuality is striving, immediate, pounding; female sexuality is . . . damn near passivity. Cyclical is right. The Ronettes to Janis Joplin to Stevie Nicks to the Bangles. From "Be My Baby" to "In Your Room"; sexual activities are mentioned more often now, but not female sexuality—we'll do what you want, in *your* room. You got a fast car, I guess I'll take a ride. What I am is what I am—just don't let me get too "deep." *The Big Easy* gets tagged as one of the sexiest movies ever—and it's just one long chase by an active male after a protesting, shy, reactive woman.

So what is it? Biology? Is passivity bred in our bones? It's been said. But there's too much evidence against that tired old theory. You've got your friends; let me talk about mine. I move in a pretty small, mostly hetero community based around both music and high school/college connections. Couples come together; fall apart; trade partners; live together for ten years; or they have sex with each other once and never again. It's an intricate dance, done with a lot of humor and some tears. The women I know are not reclining receptacles for revolving male energy, but active partners, with a vocabulary more Shangri-Las than Ronettes. Talk at group gatherings may throw off overlapping commentaries on saucy buns, perky tits, a big basket, nicely rounded arms, the way a pair of boxers peeks out of faded blue jeans, or how appealingly a silky black strap slides down a shoulder.

Moreover, most of us chase down our pleasure pretty actively, whether it's within a long-standing relationship or from the pool of the unattached. Some are more assertive than others, but we're all working on it. After all, we were never encouraged to be aggressive. Harlequin romances and pop radio said let the boy come to you. This is the kind of culture that made sure I didn't even know *how* to masturbate until I was 20. Today we learn from each other.

Within our group, there's a whole range of needs and drives. There are women who wake up their partners at 4 a.m. for sex. There are some who wish their lovers needed it less. Some prefer fucking to clitoral-based sex, some don't. There are women who lust a lot and never do anything about it.

Recently I've been reading erotica written by women from straight, bi, and lesbian perspectives. If one generalization applies to them all, it's that women's sexuality is a varied, changeable force. Sure, a good sexual experience can be slow-building and melting and diffuse; but there're times when driving and thrusting is where you wanna be. Sometimes a chance touch of hands is all it takes to be mindlessly lusting. Sometimes you're so focused on that one nub of skin and blood that the whole world falls away. That variety *is* female sexuality. And that erotic variety is and should be present in the music we make and the music we enjoy.

When I first read Maggie Haselswerdt's description of "Be My Baby," my initial thought was of some friends of mine, three women who play in a band called Babes in Toyland. The Babes are not the Ronettes. They're loud, they scream, they shake their hair around, they sweat. They combine wonderful snaky bass, tumbling heartbeat drums, and shards of ragged, roaring guitar, and come up with this witchy, sonic jungle beat. It's a hard and pounding beat; sensual as hell and very much their own.

Now consider Kim Gordon's songs with Sonic

(TOP) BABES IN TOYLAND. PHOTO, BRAD MILLER; (BOTTOM) KIM GORDON OF SONIC YOUTH. PHOTO, KATHERINE SPIELMANN

Youth. "Pacific Coast Highway," "Shadow of a Doubt," "I Dreamed a Dream"—these are whispered and snarled messages from an ominous, tense, very sexual landscape. You can hear confrontations and compromises of desire, feel fatal disappointment and cagey pleasure. Kim's songs aren't pleasant or melting, but they are female and erotic.

When I saw Sylvia Juncosa play in Minneapolis, I was delighted by her physical presence. She's a big woman, and as a guitarist she uses her space: prancing, strutting, swaying, and spinning. No singer-songwriter tightness, no "feminine" drawing in, no minimalizing. Her playing is as expansive as her stage presence, swooping from quiet melodies filled with space to combustive traffic jams of noise. She says she considers her music to be erotic—certainly, if there's anyone who catches the swing and flow of female sexuality, its sweetness and also its hard, gut-level desire, that person is Juncosa.

My purpose here is not to raise up Babes in Toyland or Gordon or Juncosa as proponents of real female sexuality, as opposed to Toni Childs or Natalie Merchant or the Raincoats or that woman from the Cowboy Junkies. God knows the world needs more of the qualities that have been labeled feminine—an awareness of cycles, of nonlinear thought; the appreciation of slow growth and subtle emotions; the knowledge that time doesn't trudge wearily on but stutters and sidesteps and dances. But to theorize these qualities as naturally and inherently feminine shortchanges both women and men.

To question women's place in rock 'n' roll as both fans and players, we need to ask more than why so many young girls adore U2. We need to ask too why they love Metallica (hey, I was there—every girl around me knew all the words). And we need to know why they love Metallica *despite* (and it's not because of it; I reject that) the fact that Metallica call them sluts. There's a strong love there, and it's too big not to be tangled up in identifying with that crushing roller coaster of sound. I remember seeing the Clash when I was 18 and coming out of the show buoyant and huge, wanting to jump and lunge and keen at the moon and fuck until the sun came up. Feeling rich and strong and full of myself. A joy of loud driving chaotic music is part of me, part of my sexuality, and no one can theorize that away.

Haselswerdt claims women's sexuality is not "catered to" in male rock 'n' roll—which is true. "Too bad," she says. "Girls don't like being ignored." But feeling ignored—being left out—doesn't necessarily follow from not being catered to. As I trace my favorite male bands, from Stones to Petty to Clash to R.E.M. to Replacements to Soul Asylum to, uh, Stones again, I see that I've always included myself—the connection I made was why I enjoyed a band. I get the jokes, musical and otherwise, and know why that guitar solo was the only one that worked; I put my head next to the speakers so I can be enveloped by all the flying sparks of noisy passion; I dance and yell as a fierce answer—yes! this force is in me as well. I feel the same way.

And that's where the ignoring starts, that's where rock 'n' roll is male and doesn't "cater" to my needs. Because most male musicians have trouble seeing that women can understand and appreciate their music on an artistic and emotional level—on an erotic level, even—*without* wanting to fuck the dumb guitarist. Bands that talk about how much they respect their audience are generally talking about their male audience. Not to pick on Metallica, but . . . here's a band that yaps a lot about "the kids," and then leads chants at their shows that go "Cunt! Slut! Fuck your mother!" I mean, I can enjoy Aerosmith and find their music funky and slippery and sexy, certainly—and also find their attitude toward women appalling. Because the phrase "female fan" does not exist in their vocabulary. (For Aerosmith read any number of male bands.)

The more this situation bugs me, the happier I am for women like Babes in Toyland, L7, Girlschool, and Juncosa—for driving, pounding music that looks me in the eye and says hi. For me, the issue is not that male musicians acknowledge some fuzzy view of female sexuality and incorporate (exploit?) it in their music. Guys have the ability to melt and defocus too; I've asked a few. True, it would improve their music to dig into themselves a bit more. But, more importantly, I'd like to see male musicians realize that women "get it," that we can relate to the swing and churn of rock 'n' roll, that it's part of us too.

We're all in it together for another reason as well—one that seems to have escaped the notice of Haselswerdt, who speaks of rock 'n' roll as "the beat of sexual intercourse." Doesn't everyone know that a significant percentage of the sexual activity enjoyed in connection with rock 'n' roll is masturbation? And the boys' basic wanking technique is (wait for it) rubbing. Like girls.

In music, then, male and female sexuality alike can range from idioms of drive and thrust to Haselswerdt's "melting," "blurring" patterns. Women deserve not to be ghettoized at one extreme. And the way women will overcome being ghettoized or ignored is to pick up the instruments and share what's in our hearts (and in our groins), using at last an untrammeled musical vocabulary that knows no gender limitations. ⊘

MEAT PUPPETS

This Arizona trio were true iconoclasts within the parochial walls of '80s and '90s indie rock, their music hinting at a range of influences considered anathema to their contemporaries. **JOSEPH MITCHELL** spoke with the band in 1991 as the Meat Puppets prepared to release their major-label debut following a decade on SST. In sidebars, **PATTY STIRLING** and **LOIS MAFFEO** reflected on the band's early career.

If you remember the '80s at all well, you'll recall the shocked thrill of hearing the out-of-hardcore-into-who-knows-what of *Meat Puppets II*, the confusion and delight of the country-fried *Up on the Sun*, and—if you hung in there long enough—the more robust pleasures of *Monsters*, and a lot more in between.

Since the band's formation in Phoenix, Arizona, at the start of 1980, brothers Curt and Cris Kirkwood (guitar/vocals and bass, respectively) and Derrick Bostrom (drums) have issued a steady stream of often wild, usually wonderful, and always weird records, and have periodically unleashed even wilder live shows. They've thrived, too, although their oddball image and frequent shifts in musical style have kept them from the wider audience now granted to peers such as Sonic Youth or the Replacements. But their recent signing to London Records means the Meat Puppets will have major-label muscle behind them when their next album is released in late spring. Curt Kirkwood, while pleased at this turn of events, is nevertheless not about to lose any sleep over the prospect of fame and success.

It's not something we sit around and hope for, after this long. You can't hope for something like that for longer than about three months. And after you've gone without a pot to piss in for eight or nine years, you think, "Who *gives* a fuck?" Then all of a sudden you get signed! I don't know what to think.

Obviously, it's never been a goal of ours to have anything that could be construed as a normal style of success. We always

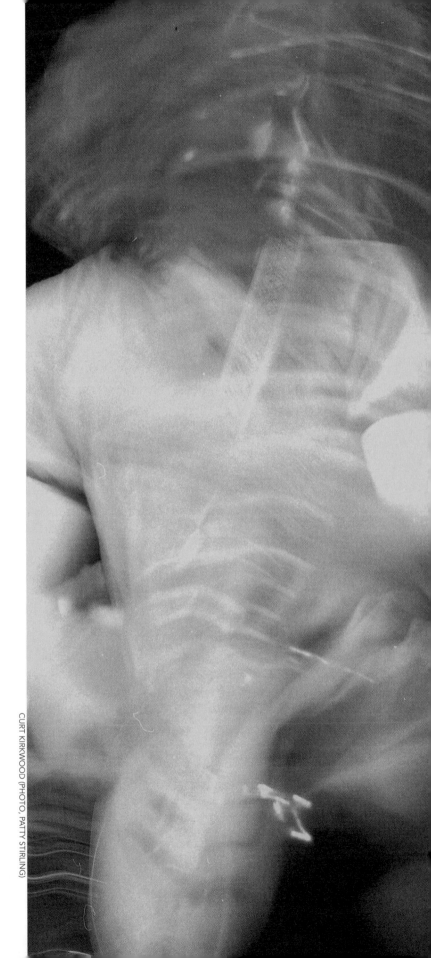

MEAT PUPPETS

It seemed like every five minutes during high school I looked at my watch to see how much time was left before I got out of there. Xavier High. Stupid Catholic school. Nothing going on. And true to everyone else's punk-rock Cinderella story, music came along to sweep me off my feet.

Phoenix didn't have much of a scene, but it was funny and eclectic. Rockabilly and artsy types shared their already dug-in hideouts with the hardcore kids who were suddenly showing up everywhere. Into this doofy scenario, the Meat Puppets arrived and threw everyone for an absolute loop.

They talked about acid and philosophy like hippies; they shared their bills with the most atrocious performance artists (at their own request); they played the weirdest music, faster than anyone could have conceived.

The Kirkwood brothers were a few years ahead of me in the Catholic boys' school, Brophy College Prep—but they were held in high regard in the pot-smoking, chess-playing, Gentle Giant–listening egghead clique I sometimes hung out with.

Through my acquaintance with these brainiacs, I heard about shows and parties where the Meat Puppets would play, and finally I went along to see what the fuss was all about. Egad! I almost died, it was so great.

They screamed so loudly! They sang so incomprehensibly! They played so fast, honest to God, their hands were blurs.

The best thing was that they never seemed to align themselves with a particular look or sound. They always looked sloppy, and played whatever they felt like. I remember how surprised people were when they "went country," but it just seemed to me the big mistake was to call them a hardcore band in the first place. They wanted to freak people out, that's all. —*Lois Maffeo*

wanted it to be a little different, even if it just meant staying in Phoenix.

Hopefully people will like our next record—the people who buy it, that is. The people who don't can go on watching *Twin Peaks* or whatever they do, and we'll keep on making our records.

Flashback to a sultry April night in Houston in 1984. A thousand or so skinheads and spiky-locked, bleached-blond surf-punks have poured themselves into a cavernous makeshift art gallery owned by the University of Houston. They await the arrival of their heroes, macho-anarchist wonder boys Black Flag, who'll soon be playing on the rickety stage hastily thrown up at one end of the room. But before they get the slamarama they're salivating for, they're going to receive a huge slap in the face of their current musical taste.

Three guys in white jumpsuits—the guitarist and bassist both sporting hair that is colored a blinding fluorescent green and is dangerously long for such a setting—gleefully hop on the stage and start to shred forth some of the most mind-whirling music and verge-of-insanity vocals ever to hit the fickle ears of the boys in the throng. Skins, surfs, and everyone else are stunned. This isn't the sludgy, boom-boom thrash-and-kill they've come to hear. Many befuddled looks. No one is exactly hitting it off with these guys. This stuff is alien. This stuff has energy.

Finally, after several songs (including a couple of adrenaline-laden-to-the-point-of-incoherence Hendrix and Grateful Dead covers), some action starts in front of the stage. But not the swirling-down-the-sink, plowing-over-everyone-in-your-path kind of slamming. Sure, a lot of guys are bouncin' around like they're having seizures or something. But they're not hitting each other with any great force; they're kind of popping around like bursting popcorn kernels. It's a pit unlike any I've seen before. The participants are actually looking at the band. They're not slamming for the sake of proving their punkdom. They're doing it because the music is on. The band has sliced into the confined and jaded consciousness of the crowd like Leatherface's chainsaw ripping into the guts of a yuppie, and we're all much happier idiots for it.

Who were those guys who ripped apart all our punk preconceptions? I found out later they were the Meat Puppets—a term often taken to be a penis reference, but which is also a colloquial term in the deepest Southern United States, meaning just plain hard-workin' folk.

Of course, there was—still is—nothing plain about the Meat Puppets. Back in 1984 they transcended every punk convention, and they still baffle the pigeonholers of the musical world today.

Perhaps their musical idiosyncrasy results from the fact that Curt didn't start out with any clearly defined musical agenda, as he confesses when talking about his earlier bands.

> I wanted to play guitar, but I didn't know what kind of music I wanted to do, or how I wanted to do it. I jumped at the opportunity to play with anyone back then, in the late '70s. I was in a funk band, the "Walking in Rhythm" kind, then a heavier rock band, with two lead guitarists. And Cris and I were in a band called Eye, for which I wrote all the material. We had about 14 songs. It lasted a couple of months. The Meat Puppets was my fourth band.

By this time, punk rock had really hit home, and early Meat Puppets recordings, beginning with their "In a Car" single in 1981, show how much they were energized by the music of that time. Their self-titled debut LP followed in 1982; it seemed a little rough and generic, but beneath its of-the-time yowls and guitar fury lay more than a few individual traits (remember "Tumblin' Tumbleweeds"?). And they began to soar off on spirit-liberating, sonic/psychedelic excursions on their next release, *Meat Puppets II*, the LP they were promoting when they supported Black Flag's Damaged tour at the above-mentioned show in 1984.

Meat Puppets II signaled a transition toward a highly distinctive musical identity. Elements of hardcore were still present, but the band's burgeoning new style was represented with equal presence; it also incorporated and transformed some not exactly fashionable influences (Roky Erickson, the Grateful Dead, ZZ Top). Despite some enthusiastic reviews, the band nevertheless remained relatively obscure throughout most of the country, playing to handfuls of cult admirers when they did their own tour to support the LP. About ten people witnessed their Houston show in February 1985 in a small, freezing warehouse space, during which the band remained bundled in their coats and ski masks, nonetheless generating enough musical heat to inspire half the crowd to go topless.

The spring and summer of 1985 not only brought warmer venues for the band, but made it clear that their muse had finally gotten a firm hold on their creative sensibilities. *Up on the Sun* ushered in a more relaxed and meditative Meat Puppets. The tempos were slower. They kept the drums restrained and simple, concentrating on the licks and melodies, while pulling off enough brain-sticking guitar and bass riffs to lull a restless mind into happyland.

The imagery projected in the band's music had changed, too. No longer were jittery, confused

MEAT PUPPETS

At 15 I packed a suitcase and started hitch-hiking down that long lonesome highway. The woods had been bulldozed, leaving me without a future, family gone. So it didn't really matter where the highway led. There's only one logical way for a road to go, and that's toward death.

Hardcore shows at the Mab. I knew I was on the right path with the Meat Puppets. It was obvious they were gonna die soon, because they were the fastest and the craziest. I knew they weren't a San Francisco band; they were from out there somewhere, the suburbs, or out of state. They had long hair and were insane, and it wasn't an act because they weren't political. It wasn't just drugs, either, because their lightning hardcore jazz was dead accurate, precisely synchronized. It seemed like way too much for a mind to handle.

When the Mab became a place for hardcore shows, from Die Kreuzen to the Cheetah Chrome Motherfuckers, the more melodic bands moved upstairs to the On Broadway. Fresh new local trio X-tal opened for the Minutemen and the Meat Puppets. Who still played so manic and fast and crazy I swore they'd soon be dead, or at least institutionalized. No one's allowed to be insane for real like that.

In the summer of '83, Katherine and I rode her motorcycle to Berkeley for *Maximum Rocknroll*'s Day in the Dirt festival, an annual political hardcore event full of positive skinheads and message and stuff. Suicidal Tendencies were headlining. The Meat Puppets played too, but only a very short set. The musical battle lines had been drawn by now, and the hardcore types couldn't deal with the Puppets. A section of the crowd threw bottles and rocks at them. Finally, they were forced to leave the stage. We thought they were great, and went and told them so.

A couple of weeks later they sent us a cassette of the new material they were working on. It included weird slow stuff, and covers of "Billie Jean," "After Loving You," "I Know You Rider," "Mystery Train," and "I Just Want to Make Love to You." And it wasn't done as novelty thrash. At the time I found the tape kind of boring. My skull was thick and I needed to get pounded on to be entertained—the Dead Kennedys, Minor Threat, Flipper.

I always assumed the ones you love fall apart and die. Time and time again I'm proved wrong. Humanity isn't as easily destroyed as grass and coyotes. The Meat Puppets slowed down. It's like you're happily getting bruised and cut all over, until one day you notice it hurts. Gentler things start making you happy. Their next records were country-western music without any cowboys. Just prairie dogs, sunlight, and Indian thinking. There didn't seem to be any white people in their songs, and no bulldozer drivers.

I liked the slow records, because they were like sounds of nature—water, birds, sand. Not New Age of course, rather completely rhythmic the way African music sounds, the way mbiras and marimbas and stuff seem to imitate bird calls. And lead guitars sound like mosquitos anyway.

I had the impression that punk-rock bands had been playing so fast because they were desperately in need of more rhythm to steady their stress, to pace the panic in their hearts, and they didn't know how to distribute and layer rhythms jigsaw-puzzle-style the way other, older cultures do. You don't have to be tense or hyper at all to fit in all those beats; it's a whole bunch of people playing their notes at the proper interval, and fitting perfectly into the melody and rhythm of the whole. It's hard to expect this kind of cooperation and creativity from young Americans; they usually end up in some chaotic mess or state of simple control, like generic MTV rock, generic hardcore, detox, prison, law office, the army, temp work. Maybe the Meat Puppets could do it because Cris and Curt, being brothers, knew each other as well as two people possibly could. The way Chip and Tony Kinman of the Dils/Rank and File/Blackbird could harmonize together. It's a family thing.

So the Meat Puppets moved on. They got played on the increasingly commercialized college-radio stations. But I like to think they still wanted to surprise the folk who bought those records. Because when they played live at more upscale venues like the I-Beam in San Francisco, they still played fast and crazy.—*Patty Stirling*

KATHERINE SPIELMANN

suburbanisms mixed like oil and water with mystical incantations. *Up on the Sun* portrayed the pastoral landscape of a Piscean wet dream, an island with briskly running crystal-clear streams, spring-fed swimming holes, and countless rivers flowing into a big blue ocean.

The band had hooked into something that set them apart from their SST labelmates and fellow forgers of the normal-guys-can-rock-too school, Hüsker Dü and the Minutemen. Instead of relying on beat and tempo to separate themselves from the pack, the Meat Puppets used weird, ear-catching melodies and a sound akin to a country band well acquainted with LSD and amphetamines. And unlike those bands, they weren't urban, politically conscious, or even on the same planet as angry. Their developing sound was born of the sunny deserts of southwest Arizona (maybe the watery images arose from wishful thinking). It didn't hit on an intellectual or even an emotional level. It landed somewhere beyond consciousness. Like a Pueblo Indian peyote powwow with the ancestors, if it was anything, it was spiritual. They continued in this direction with *Out My Way* (1986); though the imagery lacked the awe-inspiring splash of *Up on the Sun*, the sound was just as memorable.

Mirage, in 1987, heralded the start of a second transition for the Meat Puppets. The mysticism took a back seat as the band's image shifted from that of a wondering dreamer to something more like a well-oiled machine. The flavor was still appealing—things were just a lot tighter. This trend has continued on their two most recent albums, *Huevos* and *Monsters*, which have taken the Meat Puppets further toward the status of a rock band with commercial viability. They still retain much of the spice that made them so delectable in the mid-'80s, but they're clearly moving on again.

It's not that common for a band to be able to change so much, and I asked Curt Kirkwood if he could explain how they could do this.

Other people went ahead and carried the flag of their own particular style—like some of my old heroes, they always sound like themselves. But we weren't ready to do that—ever.

I consider it to be integrity on our part always to have done what we wanted to do, and not to have pandered to a style. Even though it often confused people. From the beginning, we've always played to people so that they wouldn't forget the album before. If they got into us with *Up on the Sun*, we wanted them to be able to go back to *II* or the first record and go, "They did that stuff too? Cool." Or whatever.

We've always been into a lot of different kinds

of stuff, and we never wanted to limit ourselves to one style. When people keep playing the same kind of music, they're just doing it to become famous. Or they're stupid, and that's all they can do. Or their record company makes them do it. We just put out what we wanted to. We consider ourselves the ideal—perfect examples of humanity!

With hindsight, it seems obvious that the Meat Puppets' music makes most sense when seen as a distinctive outgrowth of the Southwest, rather than trying to force it into any "post-punk" context. From the heyday of the International Artists label in Houston in the '60s that released Roky Erickson's band the 13th Floor Elevators and Red Krayola, to the present day, there's something that sets the music of the region apart. Kirkwood confirms this.

Though we've lived a big part of our lives in Phoenix, my brother and I were born in Amarillo, at the air force base. I've lived in the Southwest all my life, and most of my favorite music is from Texas. The Butthole Surfers are one of my favorites. And I've always loved ZZ Top—since my teens, my pre-punker days.

Then we got into punk rock and stuff. It's weird—a lot of those bands aren't together anymore, but ZZ Top and the Grateful Dead, which we were into before that, are still together.

Generally I've embraced everything that's been around. I get into it all, and my favorites tend to be the ones that I've seen live. I don't really like to listen to recorded music that much. And I like to see almost anything live. There's not much that really bothers me.

While we're talking about the Southwest, the subject of Arizona voters' narrow rejection of proposals for a Martin Luther King Jr. state holiday comes up. Kirkwood is clearly upset by the outcome, and at a loss to explain it; he also resents the impression it might give about what Arizona is like.

I don't understand why they didn't vote in the holiday. We don't really know who voted against it. We voted for it, and in our town it is a holiday.

If you want to see racism, go to Texas. And it's nothing like as bad here as in the New York City area, or in Boston. I've traveled around enough to see that.

But I have a basic lack of respect for state boundaries—international boundaries too. It's all horseshit. And I don't recognize any racial boundaries. I wasn't brought up that way.

Their involvement in the early days of the punk-rock movement brought the Meat Puppets into contact with

Black Flag, and through them to the SST record label set up by Flag guitarist Greg Ginn and original bassist Chuck Dukowski (Ginn still runs the label). The association does not seem to have been a particularly happy one for the Meat Puppets, even though it lasted until very recently. It's a long story, Kirkwood explains:

Black Flag asked us to open for them on that tour. And we were supposed to go with them to Europe, until we insulted them inadvertently. There's not much to say about that, outside of the fact that they're really thin-skinned. They were always kind of faking it, I think. I liked their music, but I don't know about their commitment. And SST these days . . . They put out a Meat Puppets "best of" compilation [*No Strings Attached*] recently that they didn't even talk to us about.

When they kicked us off that tour, that was our initial falling-out with them. We never got along with them real well after that. There was always a lot of conflict. We just continued using them to put out our records.

They're a bunch of jerks. They pretend to be avant-garde, then they put out compilations to rake in a little extra off the bands. And it's not just us—so many bands who've been on SST have lost respect for them because of the way they did things.

There have always been difficulties to resolve, of course, over the effort to run a label in a way that's different from the prevailing practices, the responsibility to take care of the debts you incur toward the bands who entrust you with their records, and the need to stay financially viable so that you can keep releasing records. Kirkwood is scathing about the way that SST evolved.

The problem is that SST is run by musicians—musicians with a chip on their shoulder because, in their own eyes, they failed. It's kind of a paradox that they'd develop that attitude and see themselves as failures, when the initial goal of the do-it-yourself punk-rock movement was not commercial success. It's made them into typical music-business entrepreneurs and charlatans.

By trying to run a business according to the do-it-yourself ethic, they were doomed from the outset. If they had just admitted they were a business, they could've gone ahead and gotten a little bigger. But they didn't have much business sense. Their biggest problem was that they took and sold what they could and then put the money back into bands that didn't sell. They didn't use their resources first to promote the stuff that would really sell.

Kirkwood does have some good memories, though.

> They had some good bands—us, the Minutemen (one of the best bands that ever was), Bad Brains, and Saccharine Trust, who I always thought were pretty cool. A lot of cool stuff went through there from time to time. And regardless of how things eventually went down the shitter, there were people there who really cared, back around '85. Once those few people went, the label was left to the musicians. And you need a little objectivity in there so as not to let your own frustrations get hold of your business sense.

Curt also makes it clear that he's not calling the SST owners "rip-offs," although the methods of payment have sometimes been a little unusual.

> They've always paid us, pretty much. Whenever they owed us money, we'd say, "Look, just give us the money and we'll make a record with it—whatever it takes to get the money out of you." That's how we made *Monsters*.

He also states that despite the frequent antagonism between the band and their record label, "We never let it affect the way we made records." Nevertheless, it's clear that he's relieved to be out of that situation. But why did it go on so long, if things were so difficult?

> At the time we couldn't get any other label deal happening. We got offers from other independents, but I didn't really see that that could be a whole lot different either.

Now that they're on a major label, they have a new problem to deal with: weird rumors, like the one to the effect that London was forcing the band to drop the "Meat" from their name. "No! They don't care!" Kirkwood exclaims. "We were signed because we've deserved it for years, except nobody could see it." He now thinks that the band's own lack of business expertise may have delayed their progress.

> We've never had a manager—I manage the band—and I think I passed by a lot of opportunities; I just didn't realize when a carrot was being dangled in front of my face. And I didn't really care, either—none of us did. We wanted to wait until we felt comfortable with it. We kept on putting out records and trying to get a little better sense of the business of it.

When I spoke to Curt in January, the band was planning to start recording their next album. One change is that they will be working with a producer, rather than doing the job themselves. The Puppets had been intending to do it themselves again, but after going into the studio in December to cut a few tracks, they found

they were "sick of it." The most likely candidate seems to be Pete Anderson, who once opened for the Meat Puppets with his then equally unknown buddy Dwight Yoakam, but who since has turned to producing the country star (he also produced the most recent Michelle Shocked album). Kirkwood explains the band's thinking on this point.

> We need to get outside ourselves—for this album, anyway. There's a lot of things a producer can do to make it sound . . . different. I can't qualify it, I'm not a producer. Well, I am, but I just produce things a certain way. I wouldn't know how to use all that money, all that equipment. I figure I'll learn a lot here.
>
> I do enjoy production. Maybe I'll learn enough to feel comfortable doing it again, and learn how to use our money the right way. But really, we only started doing our own production because nobody would work with us.

He hopes that the forthcoming record will reflect, as far as possible, what the band does live—and performing live is certainly what the Meat Puppets like to do most.

> Playing live is way more fun than recording. Recording is something you have to do—but it's what you do to document what you actually do. It's like taking a picture of a work in progress. And you have a work in progress continually, because you're a band.
>
> It's been our goal all along to try and record what we do live—except that we'd always get distracted in the studio. We want to pick up that live sound, with no tricks. I think the band sounds good by itself—and we add our own kind of reverberation to it.

Having survived as an independent band for 11 years, of course, the Meat Puppets are still ambivalent about their new status. When asked how they'll be marketed, Kirkwood sarcastically replies, "Sort of like New Kids on the Block." More seriously,

> One reason we were signed is because AOR has opened up more, and alternative has become a commercial thing. We had some college-radio success but nothing big. A lot of our support has been more spread around, more of a cult thing. I think they'd be wise not to target it too much, outside of saying that it's rock. London obviously has some high hopes for us because they're saying everything they do is just as commercially viable as the next. And we've always thought that we're as good as anybody else, too.
>
> And sure, we want to be bigger than God. We're already bigger than God in our own eyes—if we could only have the bank accounts to go along with our imaginations . . . ◗

BEAT HAPPENING

Few bands demonstrated that punk could be played at a whisper like Beat Happening. **KATHERINE SPIELMANN** and **STEVE CONNELL** interviewed the trio in 1990, a couple of years before their final album, *You Turn Me On*. While they are one of the few prominent indie groups to avoid the temptation of reunion tours, their influence remains considerable, as evidenced by a 2019 box set of their entire recorded work, *We Are Beat Happening*. Occasional *Puncture* contributor Calvin Johnson has remained active with his own music and label, K Records.

Listening to a Beat Happening record or seeing them play live tends to induce one of two reactions. To their admirers, they're a brilliant, iconoclastic presence; their detractors, on the other hand, say they can't even sing or play properly.

Beat Happening work—quite consciously—with a handful of elemental forms which are the foundations of rock'n'roll and popular songs—a few riffs, melody lines, and rhythm patterns. In reality, every band works with a very small number of forms (BH actually use more than most)—but usually they are gussied up with electronic tricks and enhancements. What sets Beat Happening apart is that they refuse to pretend that these basic building blocks are more than they are. And they don't even begin to go along with the idea that people playing music on a stage should be objects of veneration—through their manner and onstage patter, they are continually hacking away at the myth of the performer. In all this they're like the kid who pointed out the emperor's nakedness—they strip away the layers of rock'n'roll illusion. But people can get ugly when their illusions are shattered. At the very least, as Bret laughingly recounts in the following interview, people often say Beat Happening shouldn't even be on the stage, that anyone could do what they do. And the band occasionally enrages audiences so much that they throw things—when BH supported Fugazi in Los Angeles earlier this year, Calvin was hit in the face by a glass thrown from the crowd.

Saying that Beat Happening can't play or sing properly is a bit like looking at a late Picasso painting and saying, "I could have done that." Sure, most people could learn easily enough the rudiments of rock 'n' roll—but it's highly unlikely they could exploit them with the subtlety that Beat Happening does; it's even more unlikely that they would succeed in turning them into the perfect songs this band regularly produces. While these songs are in some ways primitive in construction and execution, they're also breathtakingly original, and often highly sophisticated. "Cast a Shadow" (from their 1988 *Black Candy* album) starts out like a yearning, affectionate love song, then unfolds into a vaguely sinister tale of obsession—it does this by wringing a chain of nuances and associations from the word "shadow" in a way that leaves you dizzy. Fairy-tale forms and subject matter (the sandman, trails of bread crumbs) crop up repeatedly in BH lyrics, and—as in the originals—carry overtones of unconscious drives.

This interview took place in Seattle in mid-July, the day after BH had played an unusual show with Mudhoney, in a disused auto garage downtown. Present were the three band members—Bret [Lunsford], Heather [Lewis], and Calvin—plus Calvin's 8-year-old nephew Taylor.

Sixty miles south of Seattle is the town of Olympia and the Evergreen State College, where much of the current Northwest music—including Beat Happening—has its roots. It's home to one of the country's most individual radio stations (KAOS), and it also spawned *OP*, the music magazine which in the early '80s—along with *Sub Pop* (the fanzine that turned into a record label)—helped determine a still-valid agenda for alternative music coverage.—*Steve Connell*

Was it Evergreen College that brought you together?
C: Bret didn't go there a lot, but that's how we met—we had mutual friends there. He and I grew up around here. I've lived in Olympia most of my life.
H: And I'm from Pennsylvania and New York. I came here for the school. It was there or Yale—a natural choice . . .
C: Her family followed her here.
B: It's where all the beatnik punk rockers hung out. Naturally we all gravitated to it.
What's so attractive about it?
H: They don't have grades.
C: I did a radio show there since I was 15, at KAOS. I was at home. I felt it was the only place I'd ever finish college.
Did you all finish?
B: Yes. I'm class of '88—they're both class of '85.
Was there something special about the place, the college, that made the whole Olympia music scene happen?
C: When I started there Evergreen was hippie-dominated. There weren't many great concerts or anything. The

people in charge of the music department were mostly into really bad music. KAOS was the only place I could meet people interested in unusual music—at the time they were divided between punk rock and more experimental stuff, electronic, new music composers.
How did an indigenous music scene develop from that, and how was Beat Happening part of it?
C: When I was in high school there were some bands at Evergreen, but nobody my age knew about punk rock. It wasn't the teenage revolution some people thought it was going to be. It took the '80s and hardcore to get it into high schools. In the late '70s it was just people of college age or older. When I started getting involved with the radio station, I thought I'd do a punk-rock show and it would be new. They'd already been playing it since 1976, but I had no idea. So people doing new music in the area were all in Evergreen and unconnected with Olympia. It's a little isolated—seven miles out of town—and there was little contact then. It wasn't until '81 that things started happening downtown, with people who'd grown up in Olympia.
When hardcore was beginning to make an impact?
C: Yes. But still, if I went to a hardcore show in Seattle at that time I'd be the youngest person there, the only person under 19.

Then around '81 or '82 things started to change. Heather moved downtown and got in a band with some other people, the Supreme Cool Beings. The high-school kids from Olympia would come to their shows.
H: I'd never thought of being in a band before that, but I walked into this apartment one day and sat down and started playing the drums and they said, "Oh do you want to be in the band?"

Something happened that summer, 1982. It was hot. A lot of it had to do with the apartment Gary May [from the Supreme Cool Beings] lived in. He let people party there all the time. Bands played there. People showed up. It was on the main street and it was just like a club. People heard music and walked in the door.
C: It was above a florist's. There were two other apartments. Bruce Pavitt [now head of Sub Pop Records] lived in one. Tim Brock [composer and K recording artist] lived in another. Sometimes they'd open up all three apartments for events. One would be a lounge, one the art gallery, one where the band was playing, and in the laundry room they'd be showing films.

I remember during a party once, the Supreme Cool Beings were playing and Tom Mallon was sitting there with Bruce and Jan Brock and I go, "Hey, don't you guys want to come over and see the Supreme Cool Beings? They're about to play." They looked up and said, "So what else is new?" They had to listen to the Supreme Cool Beings every day of their lives!

B: I was bumming around the country and ended up back here after high school. I met Lois [Maffeo] and Calvin, and others. I decided to go to Evergreen. But I was staying in Tucson when Calvin came to visit with copies of the Supreme Cool Beings tape [*Survival of the Coolest*]. I really liked it. I came up here . . .

So '82 was when the local music scene really started happening?

C: No, there were the bands associated with *OP* magazine in around '80, '81—like John Foster's Pop Philosophers and a band called Tiny Holes, with Steve Fisk and Bruce Pavitt. But they mostly petered out around the middle of '81.

B: When I came back in spring '83 there were bands playing downtown. I saw Laura, Heather, & Calvin play at Smithfield's. That was my introduction to the Olympia band scene.

H: That was pre-Beat Happening. We were just called Laura, Heather, & Calvin. We did it for about eight months before Bret joined.

B: Laura, Heather, & Calvin had a song on *Sub Pop* 9 in '83.

C: They'd been working on the Smithfield Cafe all summer in '82. It had been a beatnik coffee place called the Intermezzo, with poetry readings. But that summer they renovated it and fixed it up for music.

H: At the opening party people danced and ruined their floor. So no more dancing.

B: The show I saw had Rich Jensen's band, the Wild Wild Spoons; John Foster's Pop Philosophers; and Laura, Heather, & Calvin. It was great. I'd been seeing all these hardcore shows around the country—I loved those too—but I was bowled over by the Smithfield show. Everyone was so . . . casual. These guys would just be in the audience first, being real friendly, then they'd get up and do these songs, and all of them were inspired. I have a tape of that show, and it has some of my favorite songs.

C: In Tucson, Bret and I had seen some shows and they confirmed my own thinking. One thing was that shows should be all-ages. There were some really positive things there, but once we went to a bar, this really depressing tavern, to see some hardcore bands. And it was a big hassle, with ID problems and people trying to sneak in. Then the bands played—and it just seemed so depressing. People were sitting way in the back and it seemed like nobody was having a good time. The mood was set by the way people had to grovel to get in the door.

But another show was really great. It was the Seldoms and Rote Kapelle. It was the same kind of atmosphere at first, but the band turned it around; they said, hey, we'll have fun. They got out this parachute and had people dancing under it.

BEAT HAPPENING
Three Tea Breakfast
(K Records cassette)
Beat Happening might have taken a vow to carry minimalism to absurd lengths. Nevertheless there's something attractive about *Three Tea Breakfast*, a wispy little package recorded in Tokyo.

The lyrics have charm. In "The Walk" Calvin Johnson tells how as he walked with his beloved she took the opportunity when he tripped and fell to make an announcement: "Calvin, you're a guy with incredible blue eyes / But I've got to live my own life."

The residence in Japan and the intimate scale of the musical proceedings (voice; acoustic guitar; knuckles on board—at a guess) seem related somehow. You feel like the trio is sitting on mats to do this. Forget about tape quality (Dolby? Wuzzat? At least clean your tape heads first). But the spirit is good.—*Katherine Spielmann*

BEAT HAPPENING
Beat Happening
(K Records LP)
The agonizing and strainful symptoms brought on by being a band seem banished by this trio. I guess I said as much in reviewing their *Three Tea Breakfast* cassette last issue . . . and I'm none the wiser now.

How do they do it? By keeping to themselves in quiet corners? By focusing on how they want to make music, instead of who they want to be like? Bret, Heather, and Calvin themselves probably could not say.

They had Greg Sage (leader of that sometimes superb Northwest band the Wipers) producing here. Maybe Greg did not want to do too much to their music. Who would? Maybe he mainly wanted to be there while they did it. Who wouldn't?

The upshot, still: their aura is unhectically fun and unbelievably relaxed. When you hear Calvin draw a quick, sharp breath in the midst of a rapturous mini-thrasher called "I Love You," you can hardly believe he needs to.
—*Katherine Spielmann*

BEAT HAPPENING
Black Candy
(K Records LP)
Black Candy is white pagan roots—fertility rites and a dance around the maypole—fiendishly bedeviled by Sin Alley feedback rock and blues. Beat Happening, from Olympia, Washington, are cassette label K's international Pacific Northwest stereotypes. Their lyrics are simplistically lush with nature and death, like Wicca spells or children's rhymes about the Red Death—"Cast a shadow over

here/over there," "You see a ghost/I see a halo," "Rub your belly and pat my head," "Build a gate/carry the bride/to the other side"—laden with lead, gold, straw, scarecrow, hay, grass, wood, bonfires, drums, blood, bread, funeral pyres, graves, and cider. Like New Zealand's Chills' pop-rock sound, Beat Happening are often as rhythmic as Druids doing something hypnotic at Stonehenge. Calvin's sluggish bass voice is the impossible envy of many a female singer; his deadpan delivery (and Heather's alto) is childlike, steering away from the danger.

Calvin's words are as bawdy as those of Shakespearean minstrels and American blues singers in their nursery-rhyme lust; his women are jaguar queens, black candy, mustangs, TV girls, with their chicken wire, chastity belts, and beaver pelts.

They pull his hair and suck his blood, the sin dripping down his chin. A naughty boy or a vulgar man, deadpan sans passion? Who wants to end up in the gutter in America. Nothing there but Vietnam vets with one leg, half their sensibilities, and no more paychecks. Heather, on the other hand, casts a Moe Tucker spell: "I leave you/Shoo fly shoo . . ./Count to seven/See you in heaven . . ./Hang up the phone/Throw the dog a bone . . ./Abracadabra/You disappear . . ."

Black Candy is not a bit dismal; it's as fun as age-old children's games in the woods. That's life! —*Patty Stirling*

BEAT HAPPENING
You Turn Me On (Sub Pop)
Humankind can be divided into five types. 1) Those who get all simpery and woofish over BH records and suddenly harken back to a time on the swings when they had a special friend. 2) Those who think "Aw, I wish Heather sang more songs." 3) Those who look out their bedroom window, lazily scratching the paint off the sill with a coin, wishing they could ask a special someone in a print dress/pair of secondhand trousers out, and thinking, "I wish Heather sang more songs." 4) Those who get a tingle in their genitals when Calvin's golden throat trills over their expensive stereo. 5) Those who have lives.

I don't belong to any of the above categories, being something of an individual and a free-thinker. All I want to say is there have been many exceptional pop albums released in the past year (by Vanessa Paradis, for example), and this LP is "up there" with them; it is COOL. The "Sea Hunt" single seemed to be straining at the bit to tell us the best was yet to come—and indeed it was, for *You Turn Me On* must surely be the greatest of all Beat Happening records.
—*David Nichols*

B: There's a definite similarity between those bands and the Olympia thing.

C: Their tapes were inspiring too. The Seldoms tape was unabashedly pop, in the days of hardcore or die. And Rote Kapelle had a rockin' edge—similar to the Supreme Cool Beings or the Milkshakes—a desert rocking feel, American rock 'n' roll. Too bad they came out before cassettes got popular.

So the K label starts with the Supreme Cool Beings cassette in 1982. Did you intend it at that point to be something that would develop and go on for years, or was it just that you wanted originally to release that band?

C: It was at a time when I was working with Bruce on the *Sub Pop* magazine. One of the great things about Bruce was that he would only cover American bands, especially midwestern and northwestern bands, at a time when no other magazines seemed to care about them. You'd pick up *New York Rocker* and they'd have the Buzzcocks on the cover, and they'd be writing about British and New York bands. If they even reviewed an American band it would only be to say they sounded like the Ramones, Patti Smith, the Sex Pistols, or the Clash . . . They seemed to think that no American band that didn't live in New York could possibly stand on its own. They had an Anglophile attitude and looked down their noses at California and the rest of America.

But then *OP* came out and said American independent music was the main thing. It had an effect. Magazines like *New York Rocker* and *Subway News* were definitely affected by *OP*'s attitude toward independent music. It never had occurred to a lot of these people that independent labels were different. They just thought they were a stepping stone on the way to major labels, like many people do again now—not that they could be an end in themselves. *OP* focused on American independent music of all kinds; *Sub Pop* narrowed its focus to rock 'n' roll.

Bruce also believed that just because you didn't have much money didn't mean your fanzine had to be ugly. He made graphics with xeroxes and so on to make the magazine more readable. He was always looking for new formats, new ways of conveying ideas.

Then one day when we were talking he said, "We write about all these bands, and people can read about them—but they hardly ever get to hear them." So I said, "Hey, there's this really great Australian cassette magazine called *Fast Forward*. Why don't we do a cassette fanzine?" At first we were gonna do it like a radio show and say, "Hi, I'm Bruce, and I'm Calvin, and here's this great band . . . " But we decided people wouldn't want to hear us over and over again—and we wouldn't either. So it ended up being a series of compilation tapes, alternating with regular issues of the magazine.

That got me thinking about cassettes a lot. I wanted to do more. So I thought of *K* at first as an umbrella label for whatever projects came up. I didn't really plan for it to end up being such a big undertaking.

What did K stand for?

H: I think it just stood for K.

B: With a shield around it.

Then Beat Happening got together . . .

H: Laura moved away to Seattle. Then so did I. But Laura didn't want to do it anymore.

C: Laura said, "This is great, but there's going to be a point at which you guys are more serious about it than I am"—and so she just faded out of it.

B: The first time I played with you two was the show at the Anacortes train depot. I sat in on drums, unrehearsed.

H: Karen Davidson played drums too.

B: At the same show. Afterwards, Rich Jensen said to me, "Calvin will have to decide whether he wants to do songs that are wildly improvisational or the same song over and over and practice."

C: When we were Laura, Heather, & Calvin, we played three shows before we ever practiced together. The band started because I wanted to be in a band with Laura. Then Laura wanted Heather to be in the band too. So Heather started playing guitar, and Laura played drums. We played at Gary's and at Evergreen, a show on the fourth floor of the library, and somewhere else too, without ever having practiced.

H: I had this guitar part for "I Love You," and you had words, but we'd never played them together. We played it at the college for the first time. You were going crazy.

C: It worked really well. Then we thought maybe we should practice, be a little more formal. But still really improvisational.

At that time Heather was coming off Supreme Cool Beings. And I'd been doing 003-Legion with my friend Stella. We lived in these art studios and I'd play guitar while she beat on drums with high heels. We'd practice for three hours, then go play a show. But the way she worked was not by remembering things. She would play it when it was happening; then it was out of her mind. So all we could plan ahead was the tempos. Like, the first song we'll play fast, then slow, then fast again; on the second, just slow. It ended up we never performed anything we practiced, and we never practiced anything we performed.

After that, I thought the next step would be to work with someone who remembers . . .

H: Kind of . . . I'm one level above Stella at remembering things.

C: Stella's way of doing things was great, though. We'd be preparing to do a show and she'd ask another band,

"Hey, can we borrow your drums?" And they'd say, "Sure, no problem." Then Stella would get out the high heels and they'd go, "Wait a minute . . ."

So which are the first Beat Happening recordings?

B: The ones on the red cassette, just called *Beat Happening*. Five songs. One recorded late at night in the KAOS studio, the other four with Greg Sage.

C: Laura, Heather, & Calvin had opened for Greg and the Wipers in Olympia in '83, and he said, "Hey, your stuff is . . ."

H: ". . . interesting . . ."

C: He came to visit a few times. I asked if he wanted to record us and he said, "Sure." Those weren't the first recordings we ever did, though. The forthcoming compilation CD [*Beat Happening 1983–85*] from Feel Good All Over includes a few songs we recorded at my place before the stuff with Greg.

B: None of us has a copy of that first cassette.

C: I do. We made a hundred. We sold them all. Things were really starting to happen in Olympia. More people were into it than just enough to fill up a party.

Were you able to have shows in halls by then?

C: There had never really been shows in halls, just bars. The Wipers show was the first big all-ages show. It was in a storefront rented for the night. All these kids showed up. After that it took a long time for the person who organized it to find another space, which became the Tropicana Club.

What about the "Our Secret" single and Three Tea Breakfast?

C: The two songs on the single were from that first Greg Sage–produced cassette.

The first songs I heard by you were those on Three Tea Breakfast, *which was done in Tokyo. How did that come about?*

B: When Calvin first approached me about being in the band, it was like, "Hey, do you want to be in this band *and* go to Japan?" It sounded like one of those crazy things you wouldn't ever really do, but you wait to see who backs down first. And nobody does.

H: I was flying separately because I got a free flight through my mom, who worked for the airline. Then I got really sick and was lying in bed for three days while Calvin and Bret were in Tokyo. I was imagining them lost, in Tokyo, sleeping in the street. Then the phone rings and Calvin says, "Where are you? We got an apartment!" They went with just one phone number, for the parents of a girl living in Olympia. That got them completely settled.

B: It was this great apartment, really cheap. They helped us with everything . . . "Here, use this cookstove, here's a broom, here's where to rent futons." Everything.

H: By the time I got there everything was set up.

B: We were there two months. The first month we just looked around and went to rock 'n' roll shows.

C: The first show we went to, we missed because the shows are so early there. We got there at 8:30 and everyone was leaving. It turns out shows start at 7 there. But we talked to the club owners and gave them a tape, and they said we could play there next time. It was a really big place, called Rock Makon, or Rockmaker. We got several shows while we were there.

B: At Rock House Explosion, the Jam Something . . . a few places. We played at a New Wave Night at this heavy metal club.

H: A guy was masturbating onstage. The whole audience was 14-year-old Japanese girls, just sitting there. Applauding.

C: After we did our sound check, I went for a Coke and this guy from another band came up and said, "You radical band-o! Your guitar need tune-ah!"

Is that how you got to know Shonen Knife?

C: A friend took us to a department store one day. I wanted to see the record department because I had a story to write for *OP* about Japanese underground music. I was getting college credit for this trip too.

I was getting a little nervous by then, because we'd been there a couple of weeks and I hadn't seen any underground records. In this store, I saw the usual Japanese generic pop records—bands of 20-year-old women dressed like little girls in sailor suits singing love songs. Then I saw a small section of records labeled "Power Station," with weird punk-rock and new-wave records. I asked the manager what Power Station was and he gave me their address. I also copied band addresses off some records, one of which was Shonen Knife's first record [*Burning Farm*, later released by K in the US]. So I wrote letters, and I met the Power Station guy. He knew Shonen Knife and gave me a tape of their second record. They lived in Osaka. We corresponded but never met them. We found lots of really great records, though.

Did this affect your musical development?

B: The Tokyo trip? Yes. We said, "If we did this, we can do anything."

You've always done things other people haven't. You're not really part of any kind of movement.

H: I have a hard time explaining what it is we do. My boss will say to someone, "Heather's in a band, they have records out." And so they'll ask, "Oh, what kind of music do you play?" And I'm thinking, "Thanks, Laurie." Because if I say punk rock, they'll think loud thrash, or whatever. It's hard to say what it is.

It's out there on its own. It seems to have evolved naturally, and there's a continuity to it. But, after seven years, aren't you sometimes dispirited that you don't really sell that many records? You get good critical responses, ecstatic ones even, like the New York Times *Record of the Week review—but it doesn't translate into a lot of sales.*

H: I never think we're going to sell records.

B: Being a commercial band is just a matter of having the right hype. There are bands no more or less accessible than we are that are some sort of phenomenon because they are made into some sort of phenomenon. I don't think style determines whether a band sells.

Would you want it to happen?

B: I wouldn't mind selling a lot of records. Why not?

But it would affect what you do a lot.

B: How would it affect us?

There are bands who'd do anything with their music to get somewhere. With others, it happens by a slow process of mutation as they go from selling three to ten to twenty thousand records—changes creep in as they start to respond to expectations from the label that's giving them more money to make the next record . . .

It's always seemed like you guys know what you want to do, recognize it might be difficult getting it to a lot of people, and are happy doing it the way you want—you have jobs, you seem to want to do it this way . . .

B: From my perspective, the priority is doing the music that is *our* music, the way it develops, before styling it for anyone else. I'm not worried about pressure of record sales.

H: We're lucky because Calvin does K Records. He doesn't tell us what to do. We don't have to make songs the label will like . . .

B: Or get a bass player . . .

So you have an outlet. And other labels have been interested in releasing Beat Happening records too.

H: I wouldn't want to feel we have to get an album ready by November because it's in our contract. As nice as it would be not to have to work a job to support yourself, it would be worse to be making music and getting paid by a label but have it hanging over your head that if it doesn't work out you have to go back to your stupid job. I'd rather just do the stupid job.

C: There's another side to it, though, that I don't mind. If you have an agreement with someone you like working with that says you have to finish a record by November, you can look at it either as a dreaded obligation, or as a goal to work for. It doesn't bother me. I know we'd never work with anyone who would be an asshole about it.

You avoid advance long-term commitments anyway.

C: We have.

Does that mean you wouldn't always?

C: I don't know if we'll even be a band tomorrow. It's never been very clear.

B: Sure we will.

C: Oh, okay. That's definite then. Tomorrow we will be a band. People always come up after a show in Olympia or Seattle and say, "I heard it's your last show. Too bad."

I don't know where they get this idea . . .

H: Well, we live in different cities. They don't see how it could work . . . Like, "Do you guys practice?"

C: We practice more since we moved apart. And the pace of the releases is speeding up.

H: Now when we practice, it's partly a vacation. We always eat well and see a couple of movies.

What about the tour with Fugazi, and having things thrown at you?

C: I've always got that . . . people pulling the plug, screaming at us . . . ever since Stella and Calvin. It's just part of it. I think it's nice that people can express themselves freely.

But don't you take the hostility personally?

C: Some people are misguided and need straightening out. Others are just assholes, and there's nothing you can do about it.

A friend who likes both you and Fugazi saw the LA shows and told me he didn't think Fugazi worked too well—because Ian and the others try to get these ideas across but nobody in the audience seemed to care. They were basically just being violent.

C: It looks like a lot of people, but really it's a small percentage. People do love Fugazi, and they are paying attention. I walked around during their sets and most of the people in the room were standing there riveted. It's just the ones in the front who are jumping and all the rest. But it seems like I'd be really discouraged if I were doing what they were doing and everywhere I went I got that same reaction.

There was such a difference between the California shows and the ones in the Northwest, like in Eugene. There were still problems, but people were a lot more into having a good time. And in Olympia, Fugazi thought it was amazing that people were dancing between sets. If I hadn't seen the rest of the tour with

everyone struggling and having to deal with assholes, I wouldn't have known what they were so amazed about.

Why is Olympia still so different? Because it has its own culture?

B: It's built itself. There are things that have lasted. People have stayed with it, and more people have come along.

H: There's a majority. Like in between our set and Fugazi, someone put on a disco record—unlike the show last night where they played Soundgarden, just more of the same—and people danced. The few who stroll in who aren't going to dance won't start anything—they're outnumbered.

C: In Seattle we put on the same disco tape and people were yelling, "What is this shit? Take this shit off right now!" I thought we got over that in the '70s.

But the last few years we've seen a resurgence of what used to be called "rockism," with the support given to bands like Mudhoney and Soundgarden. As hardcore fans move back toward that music's roots in the Sabbath and Zeppelin records the kids—and bands—grew up listening to, something's been lost. Fugazi's not like that, but maybe that's a prominent strain here in Seattle.

H: There's an emphasis in Seattle on "you gotta rock." Now I like music that rocks, but I can't hear what these bands are saying, I don't know what they're talking about. Which is fine, but maybe they're not saying anything.

C: It's a sad situation in comparison with 1984, when things were really happening in the Northwest. There was the Metropolis club in Seattle, bands like the U-Men, who were the kings of Seattle then, Green River just starting up, the Fastbacks still playing regularly; and in Olympia we had Girl Trouble, the Melvins, Young Pioneers, the Wimps, Beat Happening.

The idea of putting out a record was secondary for bands then. You wanted to play shows and have a good time. You thought, "Wow—it would be great to make a record," but it was like a dream. Nowadays, you meet kids who've been in a band for two weeks and they talk like lawyers about record deals. The priorities are very different.

The music business seems to be in one of those phases. The majors are signing up bands who would have been independent bands a few years ago. The Northwest is "happening," and they're all looking for the next Soundgarden . . .

C: The most important aspect of that to me is that people who want to do music now seem to have a different reason.

H: Shows aren't so festive anymore. It's just a show. They're no fun. The music is played the same each time.

C: People just don't seem excited.

Would that sum up what you feel is the contribution you'd

like Beat Happening to be remembered for? A festive feeling, a spontaneous feeling, rather than a programmatic thing?

C: We've always been oriented toward events that were special rather than just another rock show. Before the Tropicana, we organized shows in alleys. People played by showing up, and audiences showed up via word of mouth. That was fun. It was different because there were no rules. There was no stage. People didn't know what was expected.

When the Tropicana opened, it was incredible for the first six months. So many interesting people. The shows were really good, and they had poetry and art, too. But after a while, it got to a point where different things didn't happen anymore. People went to Tropicana shows expecting to stand in the audience, look at the stage, and be entertained by the band. It got really standardized. The spontaneity was gone. And it had as much to do with the kinds of events as with the audience's expectations.

After a physical plant has lasted awhile, things are done a certain way. You wear a path through any set space. But you've always liked switching venues, inventing venues.

C: We like shows to be very accessible, financially as well as to people of all ages. In Washington State that is difficult. Most shows take place in bars, and in this state that excludes people under 21.

There does seem to be a sense in which you feel compelled to stir things up. To thwart rules.

C: Personally, I just like to go with the flow.

H: [*laughs hard*] Like with the sound guy last night?

If the flow was to play shows in bars, you still wouldn't do it.

C: Okay. There are some exceptions to that statement I made. Generally, though, I go with the flow.

H: I don't think we intentionally go out there to annoy people. Yet we do. People get upset that we won't play in a bar, or don't have a bass player. They don't get it.

B: Like, "What are you, some sort of snobs?"

H: Like, "Why won't you play in a bar, I don't understand." Like, "How can you not have a bass player?" The sound guy will go, "You're kidding, c'mon, where is he?" And it upsets people we don't practice all the time, and that we switch instruments.

B: It upsets them that we even get up onstage.

H: We still can't find a good enough bass player.

B: What about the guy from the Seldoms?

C: He was good. But why do we need a bass player?

H: To go with the flow.

C: Oh, of course.

There is a sense in which you do like to provoke things.

C: Playing with Fugazi in LA was fine—people hated our guts and they let us know. I enjoyed the shows a lot,

even though they were really emotional and draining. But then we played a Homocore show in San Francisco that was supposedly all about accepting differences. We followed an act as different as anything I've seen since we played in Japan. We were told the audience was open-minded. And the minute we got on people were yelling and throwing stuff. But they weren't strong or passionate about it like in LA. They were lame. Laid-back. I had no respect for those people.

Why do you think some people react against the band so?

C: I really don't know. I don't see us as that different. Other bands that seem radical to me get accepted . . . I think we're really normal, conservative even. Our songs are conservative.

B: People think we don't have the right to be onstage. That can add to the excitement or giddiness in the audience. Like, "Hey, they shouldn't even be up there, and there they are anyway. Isn't it exciting!"

C: In LA, people came up to me and said, "That's the bravest thing I ever saw. I have such respect for you. Who are you guys, now?" [*Laughter*] There were people who knew who we were, but only one or two hundred out of about 1,200. But because a few people hated us, these other people would feel a sense of camaraderie, like, "We were for you guys." This 14-year-old kid came up to me and said, "You really earned my respect up there. I don't know what I would have done if people were doing that to me. But you know . . . don't you think you should be opening for bands like They Might Be Giants?"

The thing about bars. Do you have feelings about alcohol? That it's repulsive?

H: I don't. I go to bars.

B: We have played bars. They can work out great. People who want to drink do, and underage people who want to dance do.

C: I just don't see why bars restrict their premises by age. In states that don't do that, like Montana and DC, then it's fine for us to play bars.

So if a bar has arrangements that they'll let in all ages, you will play a bar.

C: No problem.

You were also implying your experience with all-ages shows made them a different kind of event.

C: Yeah, who wants to play for bored, jaded 27-year-olds? But if they want to come, I say we should let them. People who don't like us are usually in the 18-to-25 age group. When we've played parties, young kids—even as young as 8 or 9—like us; then they get into our records later.

B: We've gotta tap into that market!

KIM DEAL (PHOTO, BRAD SEARLES)

THE BREEDERS

The Pixies and Throwing Muses were between records when Kim Deal and Tanya Donelly, the second-billed members of those respective bands, teamed up with Josephine Wiggs for what was initially a side project, the Breeders. In 1990, **GINA HARP** spoke with Deal about her new gig and the Breeders' debut album, *Pod*. **MATTHEW HALL** followed up with Deal two years later, by which time her twin sister Kelley had joined the band, replacing Donelly on guitar.

Fans of the Pixies and the Throwing Muses were waiting for the Breeders' album with something close enough to wild anticipation. What would the collaboration of Pixies bassist Kim Deal, Muses guitarist Tanya Donelly, and their friends bring forth? Neither Tanya nor Kim fronts her primary band, though each has made important contributions (Kim with "Gigantic" on *Come On Pilgrim*, Tanya a little more frequently, from the debut Muses album's "Green" to "Dragonfly" and "Angel" on last year's *Hunkpapa*). It might be said that in the work of the Muses and the Pixies (who happen to be long-time friends and mutual supporters), these two have been—no doubt for a range of reasons—slightly-to-greatly underrepresented. So something striking was expected for the Breeders' debut. And *Pod* is nothing if not striking.

Its half hour can seem too short, both in actual minutes and in terms of the expectations set up by the music's slowly unfurling suggestions of generation and decay. Like the decadent nature images of the liner art, the songs creep and flash in powerful pulses of dragged-back eroticism. The band seems to work less by calculation than intuition (a feeling borne out by Kim Deal's responses to Gina Harp's questions below).

Yet *Pod* also shows us a band in top form—mature musicians (not excluding the young drummer from Slint) who know their idiom. They toss off instrumental lines from the Beatles to Big Dipper; they impose a clarity of structure on the volatile, instinctive material the songs are crammed with; and they can pile in hard on the big moments.

The Breeders' impressive debut, with Deal's songs often crossing into major status, raises a question about the priority Kim Deal accords her first band, the Pixies.

Deal's music-making was one of the twin pillars of the stunning early Pixies. This time (on *Bossanova*) they left her out of the Pixies songwriting stakes. And it's no small loss. *Bossanova* shows a noticeable falling off in power and originality. If Kim Deal's fellow Pixies are as uninterested in her song input as this interview hints, shouldn't she leave? —*Katherine Spielmann*

The origins of the Breeders collaboration go back some years, when a drunken conversation between Kim Deal and Tanya Donelly led to a vow to create "the ultimate disco album" together. Both women were living in Boston, and would occasionally jam together, but their commitments to the advancing careers of the Pixies and Throwing Muses prevented any sustained work together at that time.

Later, in the course of a grueling Pixies tour, Kim met bassist Josephine Wiggs of British band the Perfect Disaster when that group opened for the Pixies in London. Their paths crossed again last year in Frankfurt, and led to Jo being invited to play bass for the Breeders. (Wiggs has since left the Perfect Disaster, and recently joined Pixies/Muses/Breeders labelmate Ultra Vivid Scene).

After months of planning, Kim, Tanya, and Jo finally found a time when all were free of other obligations, and recording began (with Steve Albini engineering) this past January in Edinburgh. Drummer Shannon Doughton joined the lineup on Albini's recommendation. *Pod*, with 11 original songs written by Kim or co-written by her with either Tanya, Jo, or a certain R. Halliday, plus an impressive cover of the Beatles' "Happiness Is a Warm Gun," was finished in a mere three weeks.

When we did this interview in early July, Kim Deal was at home in Dayton, Ohio, shortly before leaving for Europe to prepare for a Pixies tour. Hadn't I read that Kim and Tanya intended to split the singing and songwriting in the Breeders? "I had no desire to sing every song on the album," Kim replied.

It's fun to share—if you're not singing, you can enjoy hearing someone else sing. It was supposed to be half and half. That's how it started out. I'm a really big fan of Tanya's, I think her voice is really good. And I think the album would have been better if I'd sung half and she'd sung half, but what happened was I had more time.

The idea was, "Okay, Tanya, you write half and I'll write half," and she said, "Okay, Kim." Then it was, "I haven't written my half yet because I had to do this, this, and this with the Muses." And then, "Not yet, 'cause I've had to do this, and this . . ."

I heard a couple of her songs, but at the time when you show the bass player and the drummer what we'll all do, she wasn't there. If you write a song, you want to show it, and be able to say, "The drums go kind of like this." But she's going to have some time off soon, so maybe she'll end up writing all the songs for the next one and I won't have to write any.

I mentioned the recent *Melody Maker* interview in which Kim talked about some of the stories behind the *Pod* songs. She told me they'd got some of it wrong.

Some of those English journalists . . . they write interesting stories, but it's not exactly what you said. Like the one about "Doe" . . . Well, I didn't tell the truth about that one. It is about thorazine and lithium, okay? But the thing it's really about is a blow job—giving somebody a blow job. I was eating a nacho chip one time, and I said, "Jesus, it's so salty!" I thought, cool—wouldn't it be neat if I pretended I was giving Jesus a blow job, and the chorus to the song would be "It's so salty, Jesus." But then, there's just something about that little Christian heart inside me. I couldn't sing it. So I changed it to "It's so salty, Timmy."

The rest of the story is about going with a guy and burning a field down—not a town, a field. And you know, if you've ever given a guy a blow job—sorry—but if you've ever done it, some guys are just so . . . jerky—they're these egotists, and they're just weird, okay? And, well, this one time it was just gross—it was like he was God, he was Jesus. The title "Doe" means like Bambi, a shy little woodsy character like me. That's what I was talking about in the song—how they just pat your head, it's like "doe, doe."

But I couldn't tell the guy that. He was a guy, and you can tell some people some things and not others. There was sex written all over the song anyway. If he could've gotten the point, the point would've been . . . blow job. It's easier to tell a girl about it, if she's ever done it, about what it . . . Especially if you feel like *shit* about premarital sex *anyway*. See, my mom reads those papers.

"Hellhound," the album's rocker, is "about an abortion that lives," Kim explained. "Not a baby on the ground that I just aborted . . . Like if you've ever gone with a guy . . . and you've created this *mess*—it was horrible, just miserable . . . It's about the two of us creating this abortion that lived—not necessarily biological, but emotional."

She thought a moment then asked me one back: "What about 'Iris'—do you like that one?"

I said yes. It had grown on me.

"Oh good," she exclaimed. "The more I listen to it now, the more I think, 'Oh God, why is that one on here.' I used to like it, and I really like Tanya's guitar part on it. I like the drums too, but then I start thinking, 'Ah, *shut up*, Kim!' But that's another one I couldn't tell that guy about . . . *Puncture* magazine . . . how big's the circulation?"

I didn't know the answer—or why she asked the question. Unless she was still thinking about magazines her mother might come across.

She said the "Iris" story, dating from a San Francisco gig, was an interesting one—but not to write about. I said, go on. She said, you won't print it, will you? I said all right. So she told me about Iris. "Okay," I said, "hence the line, 'Sister, sister . . .' I won't ask what happened . . ."

"Good," she said.

That San Francisco show was great. Almost as great as the Halloween show in Eugene.

That was a blast! A weird one. We still talk about the mushrooms in Oregon.

Just a couple of weeks ago I went to a Grateful Dead show in San Francisco. We'd been recording in LA, and I went home via San Francisco. Me and four other girls went to a Dead show and three of us did mushrooms. They were really good. I'd never seen them play, and I didn't know any of their songs. I could barely see the stage—I just sat there on the hill and did mushrooms. It was a good show.

Who was your co-writer on "Doe" and "Glorious"?

There's an acoustic band in Boston called Ed's Redeeming Qualities—the violinist [Carrie Bradley] who plays on *Pod* is from that band, and Ray Halliday, who I wrote those songs with, manages them. We always hung out together 'cause they're from Ohio and I'm from Ohio. Ray used to come over with me and Tanya and Carrie and fill in on bass so we could get a feel of what the songs would sound like with bass. But he's a writer, he's had stories published. And he said, "I've got this great story."

I understand all the songs were recorded in one or two takes. The album has a rawness about it that makes it all the more appealing. Like the lighter flickering and the talking at the end of "Happiness Is a Warm Gun."

Steve Albini had done that before on *Surfer Rosa*. If you've been in a studio, you know they start the tape a little before you start playing, and you get so used to it running that it's no big deal. Somebody'll say, "Okay, now wait—who starts?" or something, but you can always whack that off. So you end up talking while the tape's running. Sometimes you have ten-minute-long conversations, then you suddenly think, we gotta go back, we wasted too much tape. That happens with everybody. And the talking is the drummer asking the bass player, "Josephine, do you think you're going bald?" And her replying, "You asked me that before and the answer is—no way." And Steve thought that was hilarious. So if he got that big a kick out of it, why not keep it in?

Why has so little been said about drummer Shannon Doughton?

You know, Shannon's really a guy. He's 19, he picks his nose and burps, but he's a really good drummer. He's in a band called Slint. [*His real name is Britt Walford; he was formerly the drummer in Squirrel Bait.—Ed.*] Not much has been said about him because he just wants to be in *his* band. He wanted to play drums with us, but he was wary because I'm in the Pixies, and Tanya is in Throwing Muses . . . He's young; I don't think he wanted his face plastered all over with three girls. I don't think he thinks it's cool. So he asked not to be in the publicity shots, and he didn't want his real name mentioned. He probably regrets it now, because it's not a big deal at all.

You've been quoted as saying that you think Pixies stuff is "boy music." What did you mean by that?

You know—boy rock. By boy rock I don't mean only boys like it—it's just that mostly boys play it, not that girls won't listen to it.

Some girls can't do boy rock really good, and if they try they look really stupid doing it. Let me see, who's the epitome of boy rock . . . ? Okay, Iggy Pop. He's lean, right? There's not an ounce of fat on him. He comes off as if he's driven by testosterone and his penis, he's got big balls and he's aggressive, and he's testing the world. Something like that.

If I saw a girl screaming and stuff, a fleshy girl with boobs and long hair like Natalie Merchant, I don't know if I'd believe her. This is just my opinion, of course. And there's stuff that girls can do real good that guys look stupid doing. Like any kind of Dan Fogelberg music, with acoustic guitar—when he sings I want to kill him. I want to seek him out and kill his whiny ass.

A lot of alternative types, especially guys of college age, hate listening to girls playing acoustic guitar. But around Dayton, we've got biker gangs, and I've been in bars when they're there, and if there's a pretty girl playing acoustic guitar by herself, they love it. They're "bad dudes," right? And they're not supposed to be able to take it at all, but they think it's so interesting and special—because it's a girl and she's singing love songs. "Pretty, oh she's pretty." I think they really like that. When guys try to do that stuff, it's like, "Shut up! Quit that whining."

Are you at all surprised by how well Pod *is doing?*

Kind of. I wanted it to be good, but we recorded it in only two weeks, without headphones and stuff. And I thought you'd probably really have to know both the Pixies and the Throwing Muses to get us and to like it at all. I didn't think it would compete too well with albums that had been worked on in the studio for three months. And yet it's done really well so far.

How has your life changed since you became a pop star?

"Pop star"? In America it hasn't changed at all. There's so many bands. In England the Pixies are pretty popular, but it's not like anyone recognizes me in the street. So it's kind of a bummer. No, it's not—but nothing, *nothing* has changed.

I've gone away a lot—thank gosh—from Ohio. That's about it.

But you live in Ohio now.

Yeah. All the Pixies were living in Boston, near one another. Then when we came back from tour this last year, Charles decided he wanted to move to LA. The other two guys stayed in Boston, but I thought, "Fuck—all my family and friends are in Ohio, so I'll move back there." But even though we're living in different states, we're never there for too long . . .

How do the other Pixies feel about your involvement in another project?

They seem fine about it. There's not a problem. There was a little tension when I got back from England, but that was mainly because I'd been working with other people and I hadn't seen them for a while. But now I've been with them for months, and we're touring together again, so it doesn't exist anymore. We're always with each other.

Do they like Pod*?*

The drummer, Dave, likes a few songs on it. Joe hasn't heard it yet. And Charles liked our version of "Happiness Is a Warm Gun," and something else . . . I don't remember which one.

Not a lot of feedback then?

Not a whole lot. When I'm with them we're always talking about Pixies stuff.

You just finished the new Pixies album, Bossanova. *Did you contribute any songs to it?*

There was one that Charles wrote the music to, and then the producer [Gil Norton] asked me to write words. I did, and I sang it, and we recorded it, but it ended up not being on the album. It was really weird—I couldn't see why they didn't want to use it. It's like Doris Day. It starts out, "I deeply enjoyed my life as a beauty," and I'm a beauty queen leading a parade. By the end I'm so desperate to keep my crown, I figure the only way out is up—I'll just blow up the parade. It's just weird. It was good, the producer said we could use it somehow, but Charles said no. And if they don't like it . . . I think even Joe and David were like, "What is this?" So . . .

That's a shame—it sounds really interesting. So what can we expect from Bossanova*?*

Um, let me see . . . more of the same, I guess. Well, it's a little different, actually. It has a theremin player on it. Have you ever seen *My Favorite Martian*? You know that woo-oo sound that plays when his antennae go up? That's a theremin. And the guy who played it on *My Favorite Martian*, Robert F. Brunner, played on our album. It's like an invisible instrument—all you're doing is moving your hands to alter sound frequencies going from one pole to another. It looks like you're waving your hands over a magic hat. And if you shake it, it goes woo-oo. It's really neat. And he plays it on the first single from the album, "Velouria."

It seems to me that the Pixies will either become huge or slowly fade away. What do you think will happen?

I don't know. We're not doing any videos for *Bossanova*, so I think we'll probably just continue. It's hard to become huge if you don't do MTV—it's just about impossible. Which is fine, but we're not going to do any videos. I don't think anyone has a really good idea for one, basically. And there's not a lot of time, either—within a week I'm going to England, and we'll be starting rehearsals for the tour. Our first date is at the Reading Festival. We're headlining one night—I can't believe it. It's like we're gonna own that fairground. I'm just kidding—it's just that we've done so many festivals in the past where we've not even been allowed on stage to see any other bands. This time I'll make sure I can see who I want to see.

What comes after that?

After England, Europe, then back to America. And then hopefully to Japan or Australia—or both.

It's really neat. When we first started out, it was hard, 'cause we had to be there when the crew got there, set up, and then wait around. And of course the clubs we play in are usually in the worst area of town, industrial and whatnot. It's not like you can walk around and see the city you're in. But now we get our own bus, so we'll be able to do some sight-seeing.

Is there any chance the Breeders will do some shows?

We did a couple in England after we finished the recording. But I'll be touring the rest of the year with the Pixies, and Tanya will be playing with the Muses all year. So I don't know if we'll have any time to play together. But the next album, yes. We'll definitely tour that. ◑

THE BREEDERS Two Years On . . .

Dayton, Ohio, is home to Kim Deal and her twin sister, Kelley. One of Dayton's undisputed claims to fame is that it is also home to "the world's largest suburb." It's a town where no one gives an inch, especially when you're in a jock bar. Especially when you win at pool. All this, as Kelley explains, can cause complications.

"We were beating a team of guys at pool," she recalls. "Every time they got the ball in, they were real loud and started bumping into us. It wasn't so bad, but then one of them called me a cunt. He said it to Kim, but he was referring to me. Then he pushed her onto the pool table. It all happened so quickly. She pushed him back, and he came after her. She leaned on the pool-table edge, put her legs up, and kicked him off. There was some scrapping on the ground, and then the whole bar got involved. They ended up shutting it down for the night. 'That's it! Everybody out!' It's really embarrassing when we go back in there."

In between bar brawls and stadium touring with the Pixies in support of U2 ("We didn't fraternize much, so they didn't convert us to Christianity," Kim comments), things are going peachy for the Deal sisters. Their band, the Breeders, have completed a European tour following their *Safari* EP earlier this year, and a new LP is due in the next year. Kelley has thrown in her day job as a computer programmer—"We kidnapped her," says Kim—for a life of rock 'n' roll. In no time, the group are playing a weekend festival in Holland to fifty thousand Dutch kids. And all this is a supposed hobby.

"It all works so well for me," explains Kim. "I spend, like, a year with the Breeders, and by that time the Pixies are back together. By then I'll be so sick of these people I'll be ready for the Pixies."

For Kim, though, perhaps the Breeders have become less of a hobby. With Tanya Donelly retiring to front Belly and a stage-shy Kelley returning to reclaim the band she originally formed and named, the guitar-toting Kim, despite the group's best efforts to be promoted as a band, is seen as the group's figurehead.

But though she may also write most of the band's material, Kim doesn't see it as a desperate grab for center stage. More like a return to familiar haunts.

"I started out playing guitar," she explains. "When I joined the Pixies, Joey was given the choice to play bass or guitar. He picked guitar. So I said, 'Okay, well then, I'll play bass.' And I had to borrow my sister's . . ."

Kim has also been lending her skills to some production work recently. A single released earlier this year by Chris Roberts was instantly named Single of the Week in certain quarters of the salivating English press when it was discovered that Ms. Deal had contributed to the record.

"The song I produced was on the B-side of Chris's last single, 'Catwalk.' The papers went on and on about it. I played rhythm guitar and bass on that as well as producing it. It was really neat. Moose [up-and-coming UK grunge-rockers] asked me to produce their record, too, but I didn't have time. But producing is something I would really like to get into."

Currently, mention a name like the Nymphs, Hole, L7, or Daisy Chainsaw, and cold showers almost have to be installed in the offices of the predominantly male music press. Does Kim see her band as leading a vanguard of female rock?

"It used to be, the girl in the band was some guy's girlfriend. He wants her in the band, so they say, 'Okay, you can play bass. You can't play guitar or drums, you play bass.' She can do that, or be a roadie.

"Still, I don't think there's been a sudden increase in girl bands. They're just getting more press now. It's old stuff to us. After all, we grew up in Scrawl's home state. Then, boom! Everybody gets all this attention. Maybe the press finally caught on and started making a fuss."

Or maybe, with more role models, more sisters are finally doing it for themselves?

—Matthew Hall

THE GO-BETWEENS: ROBERT FORSTER, GRANT MCLENNAN, LINDY MORRISON

THE GO-BETWEENS

The cult Australian band had broken up the year before *Puncture*'s **DAVID NICHOLS** and **JUDIE TALLMAN** interviewed founding members Grant McLennan and Robert Forster in 1991. Both were embarking on solo careers, though they would remain entangled and put together a new version of the band in the late 1990s, recording three more albums before McLennan's death in 2006. Even before that reunion, their first five albums were reissued in 1996, which gave **FRANKLIN BRUNO** the chance to assess the legacy of the original band.

There's a kind of band who turn out to be of lasting significance without ever having been dominant or even very popular when they were putting out records. Such bands almost always operate at a tangent to the typical sounds of their time. They've had passionate supporters, but many more people are uninterested or unaware.

A decade passes and they're still being listened to—and learned from—by another generation of fans and (especially) musicians, while many of their more successful peers are only nostalgic history. The Velvet Underground, Nick Drake, and early Pere Ubu were like this. And I believe the Go-Betweens are, too.

During the 12 years of their existence (1978–90), they wrought a body of breathtakingly fine songs out of themes of hope and loss, anger and betrayal, love and the passage of time, earning themselves a small but intense following with the bittersweet angularity of their music, but never breaking through to a wider audience. In large part this stems from their often oblique relation not only to the mainstream of popular music, but also to what you might call the alternative mainstream. When Robert Forster and Grant McLennan started out in 1978, imbued with an abiding love of Bob Dylan and the Velvets, and inspired to try their hand by the experiments of Jonathan Richman, Television, and Talking Heads, it was at the start of the punk movement in Brisbane, Australia, during the heyday of the Saints. Two rather foppish college kids playing astringent but melodic guitar pop seemed a little weird in that setting, as Grant once explained.

A lot of the Brisbane punk bands were honest-to-God crooks who lived by stealing cars and robbing chemists. It must have looked quite comical, us playing with them! We were friends, but the way we looked and played made them treat us like some sort of odd pet.

The Go-Betweens never did quite get in sync with their times, which was good for their music, but made it hard for them to earn a decent living. They became a trio, with the marvelous Lindy Morrison joining on drums; relocated to England; and released three sensational albums in the first half of the '80s, which received critical raves but didn't shift units. They left Rough Trade after selling only six thousand copies of an album (*Before Hollywood*)

that received rave reviews. Then they were signed by Sire in the brief period of its autonomous British A&R operation—only to be let go (when it was absorbed back into the US company) after the release of the equally impressive (and also low-selling) *Spring Hill Fair*.

In a better world, the Go-Betweens would have been richly rewarded for their efforts to write the Perfect Song. They came as close, more than once, as almost anyone (the strongest contenders, perhaps, being Grant's "Cattle and Cane" and Robert's "Part Company"). They must have known it too, and obviously found it frustrating to carry on in the face of widespread ignorance, overshadowed by this week's big thing. Many interviews from the second half of the '80s bear this out, as they attempt, with jokes and pseudo-rationalizations, to cope with their lack of commercial success. Grant's "explanation" of their brief stay on Sire.

Madonna was signed to Sire with the same pen used to sign us. Then they realized that there was no way that even a company as large as Sire could contend with two artists of our magnitude. There was to be a coin-toss to decide our fates, but being gentlemen we simply stepped down, and let the little girl have her go.

This story dates from what *Puncture* editor Katherine Spielmann called the band's "Ego-Betweens" period, when their interviews verged on the hysterical, piling up one sarcastic, outlandish, megalomaniac claim after another. My favorite is Robert's stating, "There are two people in the world who can dance: James Brown and me." Then there was, "When we walk down the street it must be fantastic just to watch us."

The apparent narcissism of such statements is contradicted by almost everything else about the Go-Betweens: the 1987 video for "Right Here" showed them hell-bent on poking fun at themselves and the whole medium, and the lyrical stance of a typical Forster or McLennan song is self-deprecating introspection.

Another story from this period had them so desperate for cash they were negotiating to write and record jingles for Alcoa Aluminum. Grant confessed:

We started that one. We were without a record label at the time. I was friends with the daughter of one of the company's heads and the idea came to me that maybe a label will think, "If they're good enough for Alcoa, they're good enough for us."

The Go-Betweens, finally achieving label security and support with Beggars Banquet, issued a second trio of albums (as a four-, then five-piece), culminating in 1988's *16 Lovers Lane* (released in the US by Capitol), which edged toward a degree of commercial success with typically fine songwriting and their most sympathetic production yet. A single, "Streets of Your Town," even reached the lower end of the UK charts. But the big breakthrough didn't quite happen, and the band fizzled in 1990 amid rumors McLennan and Forster had fired the rest of the group and would continue as a duo. In the end they split, too, apparently taking their leave of us with only a retrospective, including rare gems, in the form of the double *The Go-Betweens 1978–1990*.

But this isn't the end of the story. Forster moved to Germany and released a solo album, *Danger in the Past* (on Beggars Banquet), in February of this year [1991]. McLennan played some solo shows around Sydney before he too produced a solo record on Beggars Banquet, *Watershed*.

In separate interviews spanning three continents, Forster and McLennan talked about their new records and reminisced a little. There was even a hint from Grant that their separation might not be completely final . . .

—*Steve Connell*

ROBERT FORSTER

Robert Forster's voice and lyrical touches on Danger in the Past, *his first solo album, will instantly ring bells for Go-Betweens fans, but this is a different sort of record. Instrumentation is at a minimum—piano, organ, and bass hold the melody as much as the guitar, and there's a dark country-western influence, evoking a mellowed Lee Hazlewood singing full-moon love songs around a campfire. Or something like that. And though it's billed as a solo work, it certainly benefits greatly from the production and musical involvement of ex-Birthday Party/Bad Seed handyman Mick Harvey. I started out by asking Forster about that.*

The Go-Betweens performed together for so long, it's hard to change your writing habits. The songs are really all Robert Forster, but it's true—I couldn't have made this record without Mick.

I have known Mick for years. He likes my work, and I've always admired his, so it seemed like a good idea to collaborate on making a record. It was done very quickly, in just two weeks, and for the most part it was performed and recorded live. There are a few things that could have been done differently, but I'm really happy with it as it stands.

With the last Go-Betweens album we used a

producer who had a very strong hand in things; we were in the studio forever. I wanted this album to be an enjoyable experience—making a record can be fun! I didn't want to sit outside the room while the bassist records the same note for three hours. I lost my patience with the way we used to make records.

The Go-Betweens' subject matter rarely strayed from loving, longing, and loneliness. Those things don't change much here, but there's a structure to the songs which implies a different way of working. Forster's songs always were a bit stranger than McLennan's, but on Danger *he takes things further:*

I wanted to be more specific and personal. Much of the music I like is based on telling a story, and that's what I wanted to do. If you look at the first lines of songs on the record—"Your sister picked me up at the station" or "I'm a lucky man" or "You say, you want to take a lover"—those are lines that open a scene, draw you in. I started each song with opening lines like those.

The record's opening song (and single), "Baby Stones," is the ultimate romantic loser's lament ("The yellow time of autumn comes / The dying sound of distant drums / The old men that sit on tree stumps know / I am an unfortunate man"). But after a series of dashed hopes and heartbreaks, "Justice," the album's closer, finds a man whose faith in love is restored ("I'm a lucky man / And the best is yet to come / The best is yet to come / And oh to be in times like these / We are not / Hard to please").

The choice and order of songs is very deliberate. Now when I hear the album I realize what the past few years have been about. I listen to it and it surprises me. It's very dark and it's easy to see all the turmoil in the breakup of a band, moving here [to Germany, where he lives with his wife], and a lot of different changes. It's not meant to be depressing. In fact I put "Justice" at the end because I wanted the record to have a happy ending, a "blue sky." Another reason this record is different is because for years I kept writing half an album at a time. That makes it hard to have a clear stream of thought throughout an entire record.

It was clear as far back as the Go-Betweens' 1983 single, "Cattle and Cane," that it was McLennan who possessed the greater commercial sensibilities. Not that Forster didn't have his share of "hits"—"Part Company" and "Spring Rain" being two of the Go-Betweens' best. And not that it matters a whit either, but given the Go-Betweens' cliff-edge existence, it's an inspiring thing that Forster would record an album so far removed from the demands of the marketplace.

I have no idea about commercial viability. I can't figure out how record companies and radio work. Beggars Banquet seemed pretty pleased. I think they thought with Robert Forster and Mick Harvey recording in Berlin, it would be a lot more avant-garde than it actually was. Which is strange—I'm a songwriter, I'm interested in melody and structure. If I'm writing something that sounds commercial I'll follow that. I try to present songs as honestly as possible.

The bad-news postscript to all this is that Danger in the Past has been out long enough for it to be obvious that it's not suddenly going to storm up the college charts or even inspire a great deal of press. It's a real songwriter's album, in a year where the song seems to stand as much chance of surviving as the vinyl LP. Still, Forster will carry on:

I'll come to America probably next year. I'm just not ready for it yet. I only write 10 songs or so a year, so it'll be a while until the next album. I'm writing songs on the piano, I'm learning German. It's very much a period of restoration for me. I've been married a year and I want to spend time here with my wife. America is a place I want to pay a lot of attention to, but now just isn't the right time.—*Judie Tallman*

GRANT MCLENNAN

Talking to Grant McLennan about his new album, Watershed, *I start with the art. The cover shows Grant getting shaved in a barbershop, wearing a San Francisco '49ers cap.* It became a good-luck charm. Peter Blakeley [an indescribable Australian pop singer] gave it to me. In England, where they only have boring soccer, I went through a period of liking American football. I like Joe Montana for his name. It reminded me of what's her name, Kitty Montana from . . . or Montana something from *Slaughterhouse-Five*.[1] A lot of writers I like come from Montana, too. I guess it's a totem.

The photo was taken in summer. It's a still from an imaginary film called *Flag Day in Dogtown*. I haven't got any farther with it. It fitted the idea of being in a barbershop. I wanted a cigar but I don't smoke cigars. I do go to a barber to get shaved. I worry because my barber is getting a little old; a coronary would result in me being sliced. What an end to a brilliant musical career!

---

1 The character from Kurt Vonnegut's novel is Montana Wildhack.

THE GO-BETWEENS
Send Me a Lullaby; Before Hollywood; Spring Hill Fair; Liberty Belle and the Black Diamond Express; Tallulah
(Beggar's Banquet reissues)

I could go on about these five records—the bulk of the Go-Betweens catalog, now reissued en masse—for pages on end, but most of the result would merely be pointing—"Isn't this part wonderful? What about this line?"

The kind of people who love the Go-Betweens are also the kind who don't hear them as an acquired taste, who believe against all evidence that everyone else would hold them dear as well if their attention could only be drawn in the direction of these songs, these sounds. I've probably heard these records too many times, polished their tension into comfort, smoothed their angles into curves, to predict (or recall) what the uninitiated will hear in them. All I can do is try to explain, briefly.

The Go-Betweens were formed by film noir–loving art students Robert Forster and Grant McLennan in 1977 in Brisbane, Australia. They released two singles locally in a Velvets/Jonathan Richman vein, mainly distinguished by youthful energy and Dylanesque sparks of lyric vividness. Joined by drummer Lindy Morrison, they made a thornier single for Glasgow's legendary Postcard Records before recording *Send Me a Lullaby* in 1981 for Australia's Missing Link Records. And here these reissues begin.

Send Me a Lullaby is unjustly maligned by some fans for its dearth of big-chorus moments and its spartan, somewhat monochrome sound, but it has the advantage of revealing the Go-Betweens' still-developing working method at its starkest. Stylistically, their achievement consists in using ideas about space, arrangement, and interplay gleaned from (mostly British) post-punk as a kind of scaling tool, or perhaps an acid bath—a way of scraping clean the tarnished coin of pop-song form, making its features vivid again, returning them to usability as a medium for the exchange of meaning—for communication.

Morrison's irregularly accented rhythm patterns, the counterpoint between Forster's minor-key guitar parts and McLennan's self-taught but precise bass-sense of note placement: these always sound constructed from the ground up, as if no one had ever played these three instruments behind words and melodies before. "It took/you a/week/to say/one day/you were . . ." Robert intones in "The Girls Have Moved," allowing several seconds to elapse before completing the thought in the chorus, ". . . a virtuoso." "I hear sounds so bright they could be stars," Grant sings, and although they're not making such sounds themselves yet, a few songs (the almost drumless, caught-you-cheating "Eight Pictures") are well on their way.

Over the next three albums, the Go-Betweens become more assured and songwriterly, gradually enriching their sonic palette, but the skeleton described above remains in place—rhythm, melody, and the rhythm and melody of language, pressed into service to make the world strange, to hold it up for display, to turn it over in memory. Grant's "Cattle and Cane," "Unkind and Unwise," and "The Ghost and the Black Hat," which seamlessly hook lovely tunes to rhythmic underpinnings in, respectively, 11/4, 7/4, and 14/8, also stand as almost filmic depictions of rural Australian life ("The salt in the wind moves over the mudflats/Sticks to your skin and rusts up the lights," "A hole in the ground spits dirt and the sky") and its attendant losses. Robert, meanwhile, uses slightly more rock-like rhythms to snap the lyric line at its joints ("Me without hindsight/me without," "All that's left/Of me that was/Is a former shadow") while sketching a rogue's gallery of bitter pool-boys, ex-geniuses, and smug casanovas ("Feel so sure about our love/I'll write a song about us breaking up") united— as are the songs—by a self-aware confidence in their own ascetic glamour.

Tallulah, though not their final album, begins to show the Go-Betweens under strain. (The largely acoustic *16 Lovers Lane* is part of this reissue series in England, but not in the US, apparently due to licensing conflicts.) Though each songwriter has some gems ("Bye Bye Pride," "The Clarke Sisters"), Grant is drifting further toward unapologetically pop hooks, with mixed results, while Robert steps well beyond "imagery" into pure language play ("The dull mask of action on circus staff/Mobility the hood of the Hindu scarf.") More of the force of the band, especially with the addition of Amanda Brown on violin and oboe, is placed in the service of the melodic thrust of the songs, while a huge, glossy mix makes for a gorgeous but somewhat one-dimensional listen.

Since these records are reviewed here as reissues, a word should be said about the packaging. Each comes with two CD booklets, one with the original art, photos, and lyrics; another with a partial history of the band corresponding to the period of the album at hand, bits of interviews and reviews, and additional photos. Writing now as a Go-Betweens obsessive, I was slightly disappointed with this apparatus. The history tends toward where-they-were-touring-what-month,

RAY LEGO

We drift on to television.

I watch nature documentaries: I steer clear of all those hokey-pokey Australiana things, but the ones that get to the core of life and why we do things—great. Any show on astronomy I'll look at, because I think the world would be a better place if we were all made to feel like insignificant particles, instead of dominant beings.

Also, shows on writers, artists. Occasional movies. *Twin Peaks* unfortunately has its tentacles round me . . . I wish I had cheekbones like Kyle MacLachlan. *Blackadder* I find hilarious. I used to like *Married . . . with Children.* It's supremely obnoxious and great. Most things are so homogenized and inoffensive, any spark is removed . . . and, ah, Daffy Duck cartoons.

It occurs to me to ask Grant if he's thought of acting a role as himself.

Have you been reading my fucking mail or something? It's funny, a friend of mine who's an actress asked me the same question. I'm actually interested. I want to do a play . . . I used to [act], though not as a career. When I first met Robert Forster we were both trying to impersonate Clint Eastwood, in a Shakespearean setting, rather ridiculous . . .

There was a Go-Betweens movie once, in Brisbane, in the early days of the band. It was called *Heather's Gloves*. I wrote it and a man called Robin Gold filmed it. In 1980, I think, when I got back from America, before Lindy joined. I said I'd love to, but it had to be shot in black and white. My only demand. There was a bath scene. Various things happened, and I never got to see it because I went away. But just a few weeks ago I read the script and it's still good.

When his personal life comes up, Grant turns agitated. He's also run out of cigarettes.

I was 4 when my father died. I was the eldest child.

We moved around a bit and after his death we moved back to where my mother grew up, which is in Cairns. I spent two years there, and then I was sent to boarding school at quite a young age. Then I went on to university; I was 16. During my first year I turned 17; around that time my mother remarried and moved to a cattle station about three hundred miles west of Cairns.

I remark that Grant doesn't seem like a boarding-school type.

That's very tactful of you, yes. Fortunately, I don't have those mannerisms. Yeah, I'm not a lawyer.

My old school asked me to go stand up in front of the boys, but I was never a very good representative of the system, so I declined.

A bit of current gossip . . .

Lindy and Amanda [Brown] are recording an EP, as Cleopatra Wong. Some of the songs are very good. These are the first songs they've written, and when you start, some of your songs aren't as good as others; there are going to be some misses. I don't think it's unfair to say that. Amanda played them to me, and asked me what I thought.

And Club Hoy, the female duo whose debut single Grant produced?

I think they're great. They're two snot-nosed brats with a great ear for melody. All I can say is, don't put your wallet or your purse down in front of them. I love them.

Now that Grant's been back in Australia for a while, I wonder if he'll stay.

After the darkness and desolation of London, it was great to come back here, into light, brightness. But lately I've come to feel it's run its course for me. I'd like to live somewhere different. I'm not sure where. For now Australia's quite good, and I'd like to spend more time in Melbourne. Especially in winter, I could go see football. I went down for a press trip early this year, and to look at some art; I stayed to see my friends and realized I only ever see them on tour. That's really unfair. Not a very nice way to see people: you're busy and you're in tour mode and you're very preoccupied. I love Melbourne, actually. It has something Sydney doesn't . . . grace.

Not every songwriter can talk about the craft. I try asking Grant the shortest time he ever wrote a song in.

Three minutes, thirty-seven seconds. The whole song. And it was "You Can't Have Everything" [from the new album]. How it came out is how you hear it. Sure, I finessed the words a little, but the actual melody and structure came in the time the song takes. "Streets of Your Town" [on the Go-Betweens' *16 Lovers Lane*] took maybe five or ten minutes. And "Easy Come Easy Go" [also on *Watershed*] was written after Amanda Brown said to me as she was going out shopping, "Why don't you write simple songs?" I said, "I thought I did," and

when-was-this-single-released, what-did-the-*NME*-say bluntness; I would have preferred material as specific as their songs: the band's context in the early Brisbane scene, anecdotes about particular songs.

The tone of the newly conducted interviews and surrounding history plays a little too squarely into the party line on the band as critically lauded, commercially ignored. The oft-floated question "why weren't they huge?" is less a mystery than it is a red herring. Their recordings are highly efficient tools, but they don't come with operating instructions. The very fact that the music on *Before Hollywood*, *Spring Hill Fair*, and *Liberty Belle* is slightly disorienting, unfamiliar in ways that extend beyond stylistic window dressing—that its very real insights and pleasures are hidden in nuance, waiting to be unearthed—binds these albums to the listener who expends the effort and attention required to put the songs to work.

Finally: though the Go-Betweens' numerous B-sides were of consistently high quality, these reissues feature no extra tracks. The out-of-print *1978–1990* compilation (which also has wittier notes by Forster and McLennan) includes some of this material, but I hope Beggars Banquet will finish what they've started by compiling the pre-*Lullaby* singles, the Peel sessions (the CD notes refer to several titles that haven't seen official release), and key non-album songs like "Newton Told Me" and "Little Joe" together onto one CD in the near future.—*Franklin Bruno*

THE GO-BETWEENS
Tallulah
(Big Time LP)

In their ungainly rush to sell out, the band may not have buried their talent deep enough. Real fans will glimpse the grinning, sour, abiding bones of Go-Betweens songs under the shroudings and veilings of the vaunted "commercial pop" production. Songs by the band who created the songs on *Spring Hill Fair* and *Before Hollywood*.

They are still that band, conceiving the songs a certain way. Which does not mean this production will not annoy. It's damned annoying. It won't work either—won't send masses hurrying to the record shop. What will the group do when they find out? Turn again to their image? Or back to the real thing: the music?

Image: It's fascinating and even thrilling that a band whose subject and plaything so largely is insincerity should be having the amount of trouble they're having with the scheduled sellout. They give an impression of training at hustlery and rivalry day and night. With each other, even. When Lindy told an interviewer that she and Robert had an occasional "glamorous fuck," it suggested the band try to overwhelm and dazzle each other as they do the rest of the world. It's interesting to study their image phases. Robert and Lindy are now neck and neck in the current competition: a sort of middle-aged English-country-weekend look with worsteds and thin bits of gold and worn, blurry expressions.

The addition of Amanda Brown to the once-trio now five-piece seemed to be viewed by the band themselves as some sort of complex elaboration of their personae (Lindy now had someone around so they could talk about their periods). Whether Brown with her bowing and oboeing suited them in other ways . . . well, who is there but the band, preoccupied as they are with the realization of their personal magic and its manifestation to millions, to attend to their music?

Music: How about that "hit single" track, "Right Here"? Some story, eh? Comforting a lady friend who's been mistreated by another guy . . . really comforting her . . . but true to its source, the sympathy's ambivalent ("You say you're 32 / But you look 55") and the motives are up for grabs. Which didn't stop the producer prying open his tin of golden syrup. Does this mean it's up to a corps of Go-Betweens loyalists to "find the song"? Like, should we dub them up without organ curlicues and Mamas-and-Papas-type backing vocals? Should we re-imagine "The Clarke Sisters" and "Hope Then Strife" from the guitar-figured base of each, before the richly bare lyrics were snared in violin decor?

Alas, we'll just have to wait. *Grant and Robert write great songs. Grant and Robert write great songs.* Close your eyes and repeat till they come to their senses.—*Katherine Spielmann*

she said, "No. Simpler ones." When she came back with the bagful of shopping, I said, "What about this?"

You've got to watch it, though. Sometimes you fall into your own little devices and tricks, and while you always should be pushing yourself to be true to your core, you also have to try and move forward each time. And sometimes, because I think I've got a reasonable grasp of melody and it comes easily to me, I have a tendency to be a little lazy. I go, "Okay, there's one. Now let's do another." Recently, Steve Kilbey and I had a couple of nights when he wasn't busy and I wasn't busy, and we wrote 10 or 12 songs for the next Jack Frost album [Kilbey and McLennan's joint project] . . . some of them aren't bad either. If you're in a rhythm, anything's possible.

That Jack Frost record was so bizarre. We could only take two weeks, and we didn't know if anyone would like it. If we'd had three weeks it would have gone to a double album . . . we could have kept going. We both would have loved to. We'd have been smashing glass.

I didn't think Grant necessarily wanted to talk about the Go-Betweens. But I had to bring up what he said when I interviewed him in 1984. If the band split up, he'd declared, he wouldn't write songs anymore. He would run a filling station and never pick up a guitar again. Now that the Go-Betweens have ended, he must have reconsidered?

Ah . . . have the Go-Betweens ended? They might not have. I'm not throwing a spanner in the works here, but I might still be telling the truth, you know.

At that stage, and for most of my life, the Go-Betweens filled everything I needed to do musically. Then it got to the point, toward the end, where it didn't. Perhaps I went about it in a very savage way by walking, precipitating the avalanche. I think what I meant back then was a vainglorious boast about how great I thought the band was, and how it filled me up . . . that must be why I wanted to run a filling station. Because I would have been empty.

I hope I'll write for the rest of my life, whether it's music or in other ways. I've been working on a sequence of poems for a couple of years, and I'm getting close on that. One of them was published in *Rolling Stone* [the Australian edition] a few months ago. It's called "What the Father Said." But as I've said, "When the teenagers don't want me anymore, I'll move on."

I think a minute and say, "I wonder when that would be, Grant." And he says, "Never."

He could be right. There's something fresh and youthful about Watershed, *which belies its complexity and high-gloss production (no wonder teenagers are clamoring for it). This is an LP with silliness on it—something flimsy, something desperate. You know—something for everyone.*

—*David Nichols*

X-TAL: JIMMY BROUSTIS, ALLISON MOSELEY, MICK FREEMAN, J NEO MARVIN

46 DAYS IN A COKE VAN An X-tal Tour Diary

J NEO MARVIN, a frequent *Puncture* contributor throughout the magazine's run, moonlighted as frontman of X-tal, a politically minded Bay Area indie band. In 1990, the band set out on an ambitious American tour, overlapping with tours by Uncle Tupelo and Redd Kross (with whom X-tal shared bills), as well as Sonic Youth (who drew away their crowds from across town). Throughout, Neo kept a detailed diary.

10/12/90 Portland, OR

Yesterday was a bit of a disaster. We arrived too late for our first gig, a noontime show at Sonoma State, then got caught in a traffic jam on a forced detour from I-5. But our spirits were up. We're on the road. For the next six weeks our only purpose is to play music. Beats working.

Today we find where we're staying for the weekend, a spread an hour south of Portland called the Art Farm, where Cairo (the woman who does a lot of our T-shirts), her girlfriend Cynthia, and Cairo's mother "Spit" (it's

a long story) all live. A gorgeous place, officially dubbed a "tree farm" for tax purposes. We do a funny interview at KLC, a Portland college station, where the DJ asks if "Amateur Alchemist" is about chemistry majors at Reed College.

Tonight we play the Satyricon, opening for UK Subs, Urge Overkill, and a Wisconsin band, Birth DFX. We do a fairly tight, energetic set. People dig us. Our former bassist Mitzi Waltz is here with her husband, Steve. They take me to a Chinese restaurant called Hung Far

Low. The food isn't much, but the bar has to be seen.

Wisdom from Mitzi and Steve: "There are two words you need to know in Portland. If something is good, it's 'sweet.' If something is expensive, it's 'spendy.'"

We miss Urge Overkill's very short set, but get back in time for Birth DFX. Their best moment is a cover of Minor Threat's "Betray" (sung by the drummer with the skinhead singer sitting it out). The UK Subs have become a tired spectacle. Charlie Harper is okay and plays hot blues harp on one song, but the band sounds like the 1982 edition of Chelsea. Jimmy, a fan of the original Subs, is sorely disappointed to hear no early tunes. I fall asleep waiting for the others to say, Let's go. On the bright side, we're offered another gig here tomorrow.

10/13
Our last-minute addition to the bill is a happy accident. Many more people in the audience. We play between Nihilism, a generic thrash-metal outfit, and Napalm Beach, who are a cross between Hendrix, "Raw Power" Stooges, and Blue Cheer, and are absolutely wonderful. I could've danced all night. Crowd likes us too.

The only cause for complaint at Satyricon: over the cool jukebox is suspended the bottom half of a female mannequin sticking her butt in your face as you pick your song. Allison finds this offensive. She's not the only one.

10/15 Vancouver, BC
We had a great stay at the Art Farm, relaxing a little before the tour begins in earnest. We even managed to get in a good practice and work up a few new covers: "I'm So Fed Up," a reggae song our early lineup used to do, and "Winter in America," by Gil Scott-Heron.

Our plan was to make the Canadian border crossing at night, which would presumably cause less hassle, so we aim to hit the north in the early evening. As always, Washington state highway signs are laughably heavy-handed. The best one is "Report Speed Violators." Get a life.

At the border we are polite and honest, so we're sent to Immigration to be treated like the low-grade American slime

we are. We are slapped with a $150 work permit charge (it was $75 until the free-trade agreement was passed last year. No comment), and informed that if we don't have our papers with us onstage, the Mounties will pull us off and deport us.

At Customs we're met by another uniformed brat, who seems to feel that if she's allowed to get off all the lame insults she can think of, she won't conduct a full search. We heard Club Foot Orchestra got hit with a huge fine for not declaring their records and T-shirts, so we show her our stuff and tell her everything is a free promotional item. Of course she wants to see, so the first thing she pulls out is (oh shit) one of Cairo's creations, a T-shirt sporting a line from one of Jimmy's songs (about contaminated

fish in Lake Michigan): "Oh fuck, I ate the fish."

"What's this supposed to mean?"

"It's . . . er . . . an anti-pollution statement," I volunteer.

"I guess you must be a vegetarian, huh?" Jimmy pipes in.

"I'm a meat and potatoes girl," she says huffily. Further poking around. "I guess you're not a jazz band. You must be a rock band..."

"I'm afraid so."

Contemptible as she may find us, she sees no reason to keep us out. The Canadian government is presently more concerned about Americans smuggling guns in than anything else. I can hardly blame them. But I wonder how a band like Lubricated Goat fares at these crossings.

When we make it to our friend Marlene's place in the early morning we are beat. We crash on whatever floor space is available while the sun prods through the curtains. A woefully inadequate nap and then Jimmy, Allison, and I are off to an interview at CITR. Allison and I go up while Jimmy guards the van.

We do a good interview with a cool, articulate DJ who asks interesting questions and inspires us to talk intelligently on the air for once. It's like being on "All Things Considered." There is a subtle difference in Canada. Maybe all the rude people are sent to work the border.

Compared to what we're used to, Vancouver rock clubs are unbelievably clean and well kept. (Though here too, working toilets are a privilege, not a right.) The sound system at the Town Pump is so excellent it's almost surreal. The opening act is a mediocre mainstream rock band. We practice a bit in the basement and knock together enough material for two sets. "Fed Up" is ready but "Winter" still needs work. We do manage to get "Song of the Six Pack" (from our first album) ready. Allison's voice is good, and it sounds great.

A small but enthusiastic audience hides in the shadows where we can't see them. A couple of nice people talk to us after the show. I like coming to Canada, but it gets harder to justify the bullshit and expense. Staying with Dom, Cairo's ex-boyfriend, in a cozy old house, we slumber like babies.

10/16 Seattle, WA

Breakfast at vegetarian restaurant Cherubim has become a Vancouver ritual. No hassle at the border from the Americans, who are usually nastier than the Canadians. Perhaps the budget stalemate has left US Customs understaffed.

Seattle is a hopeless non-event. We arrive too late to get any feel for the town, beyond noticing the most aggressive shoe-shiners I've seen. We're playing a Tuesday-night gig at the Central Tavern, while the whole town is off at some huge Sup Pop to-do elsewhere. I think there were 12 people in our audience. Mick and I get interviewed by a guy from Live 105 back in SF. Odd. The other band on the bill, Supersuckers (just what Seattle needs: another grungy rock band) are nice enough to let us have all the pathetically small door money. We load up and head for Montana. Seattle, we hardly knew ye.

10/17 Bozeman, MT

When I wake up, we're passing through northern Idaho as quickly as we can. Jimmy explains that Coeur D'Alene is a Nazi stronghold. It's beautiful country up here, though. Same for Montana and the I-90 through the Rocky Mountains. But where there are beautiful forests there are thousands of deer hunters. We see carcass after carcass hauled on the backs of trucks.

We'd been trying to get a gig in Bozeman because it's perfectly located on the northern route and the local

college station played our album a lot. But gambling has just been legalized in Montana, and almost all the clubs in town that used to feature live music have converted to casinos. Still, our luck has turned and we got a gig at a place called the Filling Station.

Stop in Missoula for breakfast in a friendly diner with good food. Mick and Andrea are hitting the video blackjack games and computer slot machines. The microchip meets the gaming tables. Count me out.

At the city limits of Bozeman we start to smell burning and can't figure out what it is until the ride gets rough. It's our right rear tire. It was so worn it started smoking. When we get out to change it we learn how cold a fall evening in Montana can be.

The Filling Station is incredible, decorated with old highway and gas station signs (Pegasus lives!), the walls covered with license plates from every state and year. The opening band (whose leader took us to dinner courtesy of radio station KGLT) is called Foil Ball. They're a brilliant, crazed, loose psychedelic mess. Guitar, two bassists (one doubles on lap steel), and drums; nobody plays their instruments the way they're normally played. We do a good long set to an uproarious audience who won't let us go without several encores. An incredible show. Touring bands, make a note. That's Bozeman, Montana.

10/20 Chicago, IL

Thursday afternoon in Bozeman, I got an outrageous pair of shoes, like sawed-off cowboy boots posing as pointy Italian jobs, $8 at a thrift store. With my feet I never expected them to fit, but they did. Another long drive. I had a notion to stop at Little Big Horn and gloat for a spell, but it was dark when we passed through.

Seemed like we'd never get out of South Dakota. We just kept driving nonstop, sleeping in shifts. We got into Libertyville, Illinois, where we're staying with Jimmy's folks, early this morning. Unrolled our bags on the floor and tried to sleep.

Now we're at Edge of the Looking Glass, a nice joint in a remote warehouse area of Chicago, next door to a loud ravin' testifyin' gospel church. We're paired with semipopular locals the Farmers (hasn't somebody used that name before?), but the show doesn't draw a large crowd.

We're adequate tonight if not high-energy—travel burnout—but we entertain a small audience. We get Jimmy's little sister Petra in as a roadie since she's underage. A good time, even if Sonic Youth and Redd Kross stole the audience. Hope this trend doesn't continue. Still, we got free pizza.

The Farmers are on Flying Fish, same as Ed's Redeeming Qualities (they're branching into the "alternative-rock market"). The Farmers are a silly power-pop goof trio with no bass. Songs are simple boy-girl stuff in a Buddy Holly vein with a touch of Cheap Trick. Aging teenage boys, a bit long in the tooth for the innocent act. Oh well, takes all kinds.

10/21 Milwaukee, WI

The Unicorn is made up to look like a cave inside. All the walls are rounded, rocky, and crudely plastered. A subterranean marvel painted garish red and white. Too bad that a) there was a huge party here the night before with tons of local acts and b) Sonic Youth, Redd Kross, and Soul Asylum are all playing Milwaukee tonight. Very few people come to see us, maybe one or two who are not either family or club employees show up. We still have a blast and play well, even gain a couple of rabid new fans. Amazing. We've started doing "Winter" now. Sounds good.

Jimmy's older brother, Danny (a shy technical genius), sadistically drags Don Ubl, an old family friend, to the show. Don is an elderly straight-arrow Old-Style-guzzling Wisconsin farmer type who has enough trouble with vegetarian restaurants and Beck's Light, let alone crazy-ass anarchist folk-noise bands. He gave us a fresh tire for our van, though. Good sport.

10/22 Kalamazoo, MI
It's been convenient playing these dates so close to Chicago, since we can base ourselves in one location for a few days, although we're growing weary of the conservative boring racist suburb of Libertyville. One night Jimmy sneaks out to a neighboring house with black plaster carriage-boys on the lawn and paints their faces white.

In Kalamazoo the proximity of superstar touring bands works to our advantage; we're sharing the bill with Redd Kross at Club Soda (popular name for nightclubs). Loading in, we meet Steve McDonald, a nice guy with no discernible star attitude—nicer than you'd expect a kid in his 20s who started playing at 12 to be.

Redd Kross's sound check is deafening. They seem to be having a helluva time teaching their latest drummer how to play "Deuce." This will provide a convenient excuse for not doing what Woody Allen would call "the earlier, funny ones" later. They have two female backup singers now, one of whom may or may not be a member of the Cowsills. Musically their voices fulfill a similar role to Flo and Eddie's on the T. Rex classics. One of Steve's new songs, a jangly howl called "Where I Am," bears an odd resemblance to vintage Donner Party.

When we set up for our check, we're amused to see that the three front microphones tower over our heads. Redd Kross are one tall bunch. We do an okay sound check and a pretty good set to a mildly enthusiastic crowd.

Redd Kross are a big disappointment, concentrating almost exclusively on their overly serious and blandish new major-label album, while Robert Hecker displays a newfound taste for nauseatingly excessive guitar displays, drowning every song in weedala-weedala wanking and endless Eddie Van Halen hammer-ons. As someone who has seen (and loved) Redd Kross more times than I can remember, I am seriously bummed to see them so lackluster. The brothers are still lovable and funny onstage, but Jeff's rude remarks about the backup singers strike a sour note. Also a woeful lack of Jeff's great Johnny Thunders-style lead guitar, which used to be an essential component of the band. By the end we are ready to slice off a couple of Hecker's fingers. Cease and desist!

10/23 Chicago, IL
We're in a seedy punk-rock dive called Dreamerz, notable for the steepest, flimsiest flight of stairs we've hauled our equipment down yet. It's a two-level establishment with the main bar upstairs and live music in the basement; people could come in and drink all night, never knowing or caring that a band is playing downstairs.

Luckily Jimmy's friends and family arrive in full force along with some other strays, so we have a good-sized audience for our two sets. We watch dumbfounded as Jimmy's estranged, hostile parents actually dance together during "Ragamuffin Girl."

The next set gets pretty wild when a couple of the Dwarves show up, screaming, raving, drunk and disorderly, to egg on their SF homeys.

What a pack of clowns. One of them yells, "Do you know any Sister Double Happiness songs?" and we bluff our way through a spontaneous rendition of "Freight Train," which gives me such a rush I want to actually learn it when we get home.

After we load up we go back for a last drink and a last pinball game (good machines here). The TV over the bar is showing hardcore porno. A culture shock to look up from your Black Russian and see a blow job in progress. I'm amazed the Dwarves could tear themselves away. Allison orders a repulsive drink called Devil's Breath Punch, consisting of grain alcohol, vodka, and Kool-Aid. Let's get the fuck out.

10/25 New York, NY
Two days to get from the Midwest to the East Coast, spending Wednesday night in DuBois, PA.

Crossing the bridge into Manhattan for the first time is quite an experience. It looks tiny from across the river. Once you enter, it's like diving into a pot of boiling water. A surge of adrenaline, a cranked-up existence.

This is our CMJ show. We're first on the bill at the Pyramid, a stone's throw from Tompkins Square. Missing Foundation graffiti everywhere. We watch the other bands' sound checks. One is supposedly Bob Bert's (ex-Sonic Youth, ex-Pussy Galore) new band, but I don't know Bob Bert. Another is Flipperesque with a shy female singer, and the other is like King Crimson throwing up.

Our set is short, concise, and pretty energetic. I think we did okay. I see some old acquaintances with music-biz jobs and meet "Puncture" writer Elisabeth Vincentelli for the first time. She's an interesting character, but our attempts at conversation are derailed by the loud sound system blasting "My Sharona" at top volume. I guess this is an S&M club.

We meet Alias labelmate Milo Binder, a nonstop kinda guy who likes to get into arguments about music. He demands I admit Harry Nilsson is a musical genius. I say, well, he gets points for being John Lennon's drinking buddy. That seems to appease him. A high-strung young folk artiste. His New York showcase is canceled just before showtime for lack of an audience. O fickle nightclub. Good luck, Milo.

10/27 Naugatuck, CT

Unable to make it to our Pittsburgh show, we spent an extra day in New York. We stayed in a snazzy hotel in the World Trade Center, squatting in the room of Giana and Susie of Alias who came here for the CMJ junket (Milo and a friend were there too. It was kinda crowded). Mick, Jim, and Andrea got up early enough to see KRS-One speak downstairs, but the rest of us missed him, emerging bleary-eyed in time to catch Eric Bogosian. Bogosian played it pretty safe, going from a rambling "what rock 'n' roll means to me" sort of speech to an impersonation of a hysterical right-winger (with Southern drawl, of course). I thought poking fun at a Jesse Helms type for an audience of college-radio DJs and music bizzers was a fairly low-risk stunt, particularly after Allison said she'd once seen Bogosian do a devastating parody of a sleazy record-label boss. You should've gone for it, Eric.

We had a lovely day in cold, windy New York. Interracial couples everywhere. Stretches of blocks devoted to lamps. Unbelievably spectacular old buildings. Advertisements

in the subways encouraging people to get on food stamps (you'd never see that in California!). In the course of a long, happily culture-shocked walk around the city, I strain my right heel. Maybe it was the Bozeman boots. Severe pain.

I stayed in the room

while the others went to see Hypnolovewheel (another Alias band) and the Blake Babies, both of whom get good reviews when they return. They also ran into Harm Farm (yet another Alias band) who have played lots of sports bars, all grown beards (with the possible exception of Melanie), and lost a lot of money in Naugatuck, where we are today. We consider combing through the town garbage cans but decide the odds are not in our favor.

This morning we escaped from New York via I-95 thru the Bronx to Westchester County and on to Connecticut. Our very outdated guide to vegetarian restaurants produced a major find: the Bloodroot feminist bookstore and restaurant in Bridgeport. Good food, good attitudes. Bathrooms are labeled Women and Gentlemen.

Here we are in Naugatuck,

playing the Night Shift, located in a huge mall dominated by a Stop & Shop. This is (we hope) the nadir of the tour. No one turns up. We're opening for George Engel & the Wedding Band, post-hippie musos fronted by your basic Michael Franks/ Elvis Costello hybrid with a chip on his shoulder. We play what could be charitably called a sloppy rehearsal. The bands watch each other out of sheer politeness. We blow the joint empty-handed. Should've searched those garbage cans.

10/28 Philadelphia, PA

We arrive in Philly early so we spend the afternoon hanging out on South Street, a trendy post-punk shopping district (the Haight St. of Philadelphia). Tattoo parlors, expensive T-shirts, jewelry, etc. An interesting store run by two Africans, with great Dià de los Muertos stuff; we almost get a wedding calavera for Mick and Andrea. I score a T-shirt with a Posada print.

The Philadelphia Record Exchange is highly recommended, better than any record store in SF. Jimmy goes wild with consumption. We see the new Bedlam Rovers album for the first time... dying to hear it. A couple of bands are playing on the street. The local merchants pay them to do it. It doesn't stop one pretty good punky reggae band from being harassed by cops, while the Hang on Sloopy band three blocks away carry on without incident. The punky reggae band play the best music we hear all night.

The club, J.C. Dobbs, is a comfortable old bar with food served upstairs. While we wait to load in, an atrociously insipid folk singer is whining onstage. He has the nerve to do Dylan's "To Ramona" and screw up all the best lines. Jim and I play pinball as loud as possible.

The bands we're sharing the bill with, Liquid Jesus and the Junk Monkeys, are grebos straight from central casting. The Junk Monkeys are from Detroit and do a decent "No Fun" at their sound check. Liquid Jesus are from LA, freshly signed to MCA, and sound like a puny imitation of Sister Double Happiness. They're all wearing their CMJ badges as prominently as possible. Mick says they remind him of kids at school coming back from ski vacations wearing their lift tickets. We consider auctioning off our CMJ tags after the show for pocket money.

After the sound check we are accosted by a drunk who can't understand why we stopped so soon; why do bands have to sound check; if we were real stars we could just get up and play, man. He keeps asking us if we're from Detroit Rock City, and did we know Iggy was from there, man? Yeah, yeah, he used to be my babysitter, now leave me alone.

My foot is still killing me so I'm hardly in top form onstage. We play an adequate set and split, driving way too long. Allison and I both have friends in Boston, so we're dropped off there. My friends are unreachable, so I crash with her friend, who isn't home; her unsuspecting roommates are decent enough to let us in anyway.

10/29 Boston, MA
Sleep. Do laundry. Eat. Sleep some more while guy in the apartment views "Henry: Portrait of a Serial Killer" in the next room. Blood-curdling screams, weird dreams.

10/30 Boston, MA
I finally locate my friends. Kathleen works for Rounder Records and looks healthy and strong, not like the

inspiration for bad songs by Blue Movie. Steve is head steward at a swank hotel, making money but working too hard and drinking too much. We're no help at all. Allison and I meet him at the B & D Deli in Brookline (not bad) and he takes us to Foley's, a cool Irish bar, where we knock back some Jameson's and play the Wolfe Tones on the juke. (Howzabouta crusade to ban CD jukeboxes? A dollar for three songs!)

Tonight we play Man Ray in Cambridge with our good buddies Ed's Redeeming Qualities, who if you haven't heard you should. Like a smarter Jonathan Richman or a folkier Beat Happening—to know this band is to love them. Mick, Andrea, and Jimmy are late arriving from New Hampshire, where they stayed with Andrea's dad. It transpires they're late because they did a radio interview. Good-o. But sound check is hectic as a result.

The show is an extravaganza. First up are Yukki and Clay from Bullet LaVolta, who we miss while eating, but who'd done a great acoustic version of "Dixie Fried" at sound check. We arrive in time for the Driveways, who do an okay variation on the "Flip Your Wig" blang-blang on an open G-chord thang. Next up is a weirdo named Danny who actually crashed the bill uninvited. His setup is pretty funny, an old TV set showing a video cassette of his mouth upside down doing harmonies while piano chords and drum machines fill in the background as he sings, plays accordion, and acts dopey and arty, like a bastard child of Steve Martin and Laurie Anderson. Initially hilarious, but he wears out his welcome. Poor Steve, die-hard rockist to the end, is visibly pained.

We do a tight half-hour set that kills except when I snap a string on "Zion." Otherwise, the best set we've done in at least a week. I feel proud for the first time in days.

Carrie plays with us on two songs. Ed's do a brilliant set to a huge enthusiastic hometown crowd. Dan Leone is a great comedian and singer/ukelele-ist whose talent and wit put the likes of Carmaig De Forest to shame. Neno Perrotta looks like an old Beat with his bongos and droll songs like "Sad" and "Lawn Dart," and Carrie Bradley is amazing on violin, guitar, and toy xylophone (which she destroys Townshend-style tonight), and writes strange, haunting, ironic songs. "The Boy I Work With" is chillingly funny, like trying to giggle nervously through "Henry: Portrait of a Serial Killer."

10/31 Bard College, Annandale-on-Hudson, NY
Day starts bad, everybody's extremely crabby, we keep getting lost in Boston, a city whose planners seem to have been blindfolded when they laid out the streets. Boston's nice but getting the hell out makes us feel better. Steve says it's the squarest place he's ever seen, but he's a San Francisco native. Poor Jimmy shared some Old Grand-Dad with Steve and tried to match him swig for swig, with tragic results. He's not feeling so hot today. Next thing we know, he's taken some acid and is having a wonderful time. Oh to be young again.

A Halloween party at Bard College with A Subtle Plague. This has the makings of a major blast. A crowd of silly rich youth on psychedelics, having fun fun fun till daddy takes the trust fund away. Slam dancers on ecstasy. About five Flavor Flavs, most of whom are girls. The Plagues are in fine form, though the sound system is not. Bass hell. But A Subtle Plague rock the house, with their wild Minutemen/Agitpop/not-really-fusion punk rave-ups. Two lead singers, three lovable German brothers, bespectacled horn man Jonathan, and the wild and mighty Earl, aka Natty Drunk Locks, on drums. New

86

singer Ana looks like Sissy Spacek in the prom scene from "Carrie," while old singer Patrick looks like a miserable Czech civil servant out of Kafka. Allison finds him hard to watch. A weird, wonderful band. Hope they haven't broken up tonight.

We play a wild, long, loose set that holds together pretty good despite various Plagues waving bottles of Rebel Yell and Jim Beam at us. Dear God. I blow out my voice at this show and feel the effects for days. My foot is fine. Earl is a fucking madman.

11/1 New York, NY
Riding into Manhattan again to the tune of Boogie Down Productions. "I got a hundred guns, two hundred clips, going to New York..." (ragamuffin dance-hall hit of the year, boss; lyrics with a coals-to-Newcastle theme). This time no sight-seeing, we're just here to go. We have a CBGB's show and then we plan to turn around and head back up to Concord, New Hampshire, where beds and friendly folks await us. At CB's, we're smack-dab in the middle of a five-act bill, preceded by a Lithuanian Roxy Music clone and a Finnish trash-rock band (the singer wants to look like Iggy circa "Raw Power," but they sound like the Scorpions). We play okay. My voice is fucked.

11/2 Portland, ME
An afternoon of semi-recuperation and we're on the road again, winding through lovely New England back roads to the Maine Turnpike. We find the radio station we're supposed to be interviewed at and take some poor DJ by surprise in the middle of his industrial music show. We do an interview and he shows us how to get to Geno's, where we're playing tonight. We do an aggressive, fun show (marred only by intense electric shocks from the ungrounded PA) to a small crowd. Met a woman from a band called the Brood, who

had a similar tale of playing in Naugatuck.

11/3 Bennington, VT
The highway from Concord to Bennington is a particularly breathtaking stretch of mountainous back road winding through quaint little towns and some incredible views. Didn't succeed in finding a Ben & Jerry's in Vermont, much to Mick and Andrea's disappointment.

At Bennington College we're stopped at a security checkpoint where they've been instructed to hold our money at their station so we don't party on campus all night. Seems a bit heavy-duty. The campus looks like a Shaker village. A no-alcohol show. My throat is getting better, despite my resorting to coffee to get psyched for playing. We work on "29 Lakewood" from the old "Soul Politics" tape and get it into playable condition.

We do two good sets. Relaxed but tight. Nice kids in the audience. Even the crusty old guy behind the counter likes us. Meet a few cool people including one guy heavily involved in Central America activism. We get an update on events down there, and more dirt on the owner of Domino's Pizza, a prominent figure in one of our tunes.

11/4 Albany, NY
Sunday afternoon in Albany. Because of the blue laws, you can only buy beer in liquor stores. We do a radio interview at the SUNY station. The architecture at this university is a '60s futuristic nightmare or an Ayn Rand wet dream, like something out of a world's fair or Brasilia. Jim, Allison, and I do a mediocre interview.

Tonight is a CISPES benefit at the QE2. We're playing with Begonia and Kuru. Begonia are an interesting trio of women who've been together for 10 years and have absolutely no interest in promoting themselves; they can't be

bothered with music-business bullshit. They live on a farm upstate, play around locally, and seem quite happy with what they do. They're a pretty decent hippie-blues-rock early Bonnie Raitt thing, which I'll take over Liquid Jesus any day. Kuru are sort of King Crimson with Gong and a little Can here and there—progressive/noisy noodling and a swooping female vocalist.

Weird scene with the sound man, who seems to be in a mood to pull rank. He gives us all a schedule for tonight which grants the opening bands about 20 minutes each and X-tal unlimited time. We all take exception to the arbitrary nonsense (all three bands and the CISPES people against one club flunky), and he seems taken aback that a headlining band would object to a club screwing the openers around. In the end there's a compromise and everybody gets 45 minutes.

We do one of our better sets in a while, greatly inspired by a wildly dancing audience. In San Francisco and Albany, at least, CISPES activists know how to have a good time. After the show, Charlene Shortsleeve, the QE2's co-owner, puts us up in her basement. She's cool, seems to be a very together, competent person behind her scattered rock 'n' roller exterior. (The type who has messy piles of papers and tapes all over the place and knows exactly where everything is.) She's totally into the Mekons, too, always a sign of good character. We sink into sleepiness as she pours endless tumblers of Jack Daniel's.

11/5 Philadelphia, PA
Long drive. Hit Philly by early evening. This time it's the Khyber Pass. A letdown gig. Dumb opening band called Blackboard Jungle play wretched Springsteen-punk and do synchronized leg-splits. They all (save black drummer) have big doofy hairtails (what

Killdozer call the "Eastern-seaboard shithead" hairstyle). The peak of their set is a Go-Gos cover for which they apologize profusely. It is much better than their originals. We go on and play lousy to about three people. Drunk guy thinks we sound like the Rolling Stones. Friendly sound man puts us up for the night. Thanks.

11/6 New York, NY
And back the way we came again. Our last New York date is the Space at Chase, where we seem to be sharing the bill with an "open blues jam." Spare me. Untogetherness abounds. Wait forever for the sound man only to be told he left because we "didn't seem to be ready." Well, was he too shy to talk to us or what? The club owner tells us the situation. At first we think he's a psychotic patron. We're half right. We set up and check a bit with Andrea at the board, wait a bit, and go on to play an inspired set to an appreciative smattering of people. We do "29 Lakewood" followed by the entire "Die Monster Die" LP in order including "Goldfish Bowl," which we've never even practiced. Show is marred only by sound man showing up in the middle and trying to "improve" things. Immediately everything starts feeding back and sounding like shit. Maybe the sight of a "chick" at the controls was too much for him.

11/7 Cambridge, MA
We're at the Middle East Cafe (actually only a block from Man Ray in Boston) with three solo acoustic acts. One is a woman who apparently knows Roger Manning personally; the others do lots of questionable covers. The woman in charge adopts the persona of a cranky camp counselor and we all feel like 8-year-olds in her presence. But we get a huge spread of tabouli, hummous, baba ganoush, falafels, and Greek salad, plus beer, cola,

and water. Hot damn. We're very good tonight. "Winter in America" is getting better and better. Even the middle-aged black guy who's been following Gil Scott-Heron for years likes our version.

11/8 Wilmington, DE
We're out of bed early and hit the road by 8:30 or so. Bored by now with the Garden State Parkway and the New Jersey Turnpike. Wilmington is only about 15 miles from Philly, so we take the same route a third time. Mick says this tour sometimes feels like flipping back and forth inside a giant pinball machine.

The show is heavily hyped in the local paper and we are given a huge Mexican meal with margaritas. But very few people show up, and my voice hits its absolute low point of the trip. I'm croaking out every word and my throat is killing me. We get through one long, adequate set. I am depressed. It helps that they pay us well. They sure are nice at this club.

We leave after the show on a long drive to South Carolina. I sleep first and wake up to see Andrea driving all by herself with everyone else crashed out. That's how D. Boon died. I wake up and keep her company.

11/9 Charleston, SC
Drove though North Carolina—what somebody later calls "the buckle of the Baptist belt"—and it's clear we're in Helms country. Looking for a breakfast place, we mostly encounter a franchise called the Waffle House. They tend to have big signs on them shouting "Jesus Is Lord!" which doesn't really entice us into eating there. We wait until we're out of North Carolina.

When we get into South Carolina we feel a sense of accomplishment and celebrate by treating ourselves to breakfast at . . . the Waffle House. (This branch has no blatant fundamentalist signs,

so we think it's safe.) I just don't think I'll ever learn to like grits.

Once we approach Charleston, intermittent super-intense rain starts hammering down, a warm subtropical rain like nothing I've ever experienced. The TV announces a tornado watch. We are on the turf of Hurricane Hugo, which left a wake of destruction that rendered San Francisco's big quake laughable in comparison. [Wait a bit.—Ed.] Fallen trees lying about; freeways appear freshly rebuilt. No tornado tonight however.

At Club Dog Alley, we are briefed on the bizarre local drinking law: bars are required to sell hard liquor in tiny novelty bottles which run 3 or 4 dollars each. So a mixed drink can set you back around 7 dollars. Tonight we are expected to play two sets. We do, and to my astonished joy I discover my voice is back. I can sing!

Andrea's mother, Barbara, and a few of her buddies are getting hammered in the audience. Barbara gets up and dances, breaking hearts throughout the bar. Moderate crowd gets pretty enthusiastic, enough to keep us inspired. The band is mostly in fine form except I fuck up a lot on guitar. A spontaneous, full-band "Goldfish Bowl" holds up. A wild "Captain Plus Four" is greeted with befuddled silence.

11/13 Athens, GA
Our desperately needed three-day break is over. We stayed at Barbara's sumptuous condo in Greenville, South Carolina, doing nothing but taking it easy, watching videos ("Cry-Baby," "Evil Dead 2," "Atomic Cafe," "Shirley Valentine," "Willy Wonka," and more) and letting Barbara cook us delicious food (she won't eat "veggie shit," but she does a good job cooking it). Barbara's pretty funny. She carries a suitcase full of

Dewar's everywhere. The house is drenched with alcohol and I don't care if I ever see a whiskey bottle again.

We have to head out to Athens today but are delayed because a certain member of our posse attempted to fill the van's radiator by putting water in the crankcase. It takes an hour to drain the sludge and get the van roadworthy again. Luckily, Athens is close.

The best show we've had in a good long while! We open for a local band called the Violets, who play the usual college-radio style (R.E.M. meets Replacements) but have good live energy and show good taste in 'Mats influence by covering "Customer" in their encore. Slam jitterbugging is invented tonight.

We get a nice big crowd who dig us with great enthusiasm. One guy says we make the Minutemen look like Republicans (which takes me back to how, when every band used to claim to be anarchists, the Minutemen would say, "No, we're Jeffersonian Democrats.") He loves our Gil Scott-Heron and BDP covers. A rocking night. The Blake Babies played this place (the 40 Watt Club) the week before, and left us a fan letter. Thanks.

11/14 Champaign, IL
A long drive begins immediately after the show. Mick and Jim buy loads of fireworks in Tennessee. Year-round fireworks seem to be a big thing (and legal) down South. I wake up and we're cruising through beautiful Kentucky countryside.

The Blind Pig in Champaign is a very cool club run by a couple of great English people. When we load in, they're playing U Roy and the Gladiators at the bar. We're taken downstairs and fed well. The club owner's amazed when we wash our dishes after eating. The club is new and isn't making a lot of money yet. Mick, Jim, and Andrea

tell tales of the Albion to try and encourage him.

The opening band is called Wonkavision. They have a good style, sort of post-new-wave garage moody nerd funky punk. I am reminded of the Embarrassment, and Allison is reminded of O Positive. We use the same set list as last night. Another good, long set.

After the show we drive directly to Libertyville again. Lo and behold, letters from loved ones and a spanking new issue of Puncture. Looks good, gang.

11/15 Chicago, IL
Chicago is such a huge spread-out city it's kind of hard to get the feel. A lot of the streets look alike, and the city is constantly tearing down its old architecture and rebuilding (worse than San Francisco!), so that even a native like Jimmy can get lost. The street that Dreamerz is on looks a lot like Mission Street, only the signs are in Polish. "The Man with the Golden Arm" could have been written here.

Our third show (hard to fathom that we last played here a month ago!) is at Lounge Ax. Not a bad place, despite the sadly broken pinball machine. After sound check I cross the street to check out Wax Trax. They don't have a lot of what I'm looking for, but I score a Blake Babies tape for the van and an album of S.E. Rogie's "palm wine guitar music" (an African classic that can only be described as holy and sleazy in equal parts) for only $3.50. I'm stoked.

The opening band is called Daddy-o. Some people think they sound like Siouxsie and the Banshees. I think they're a little closer to Bauhaus fronted by Barbra Streisand.

X-tal suck tonight. I break two strings early on. Mick's drumming is not up to par, and I play terribly. But Allison says it's her best gig ever, and plays flawlessly. If only

we could all get in sync. The audience is receptive, though. I'm glad we're the sort of band that concentrates on having good material, so even on a bad night people might still hear something they like. It's the only way to be, unless you're some kind of super god-musician.

11/16 Madison, WI
Sometimes you wonder, why bother? We arrive for a 4 o'clock show at Der Rathskeller lounge at the University of Wisconsin. We set up on a stage beneath an arch, an acoustic nightmare under any circumstances. The situation is aggravated by the fact that the sound man is a moron and an asshole besides. (Allison commented the other day, "How come we have yet to see a single sound woman anywhere we've played?" Perhaps they think women don't possess enough ineptitude and arrogance to do the job properly.)

The impossible happens early on and Allison breaks a bass string in the middle of the first set. We're stuck because she's always ended up giving strings to other bass players when they snap theirs, and now there's nothing when we need it. We muddle through the rest of the set while Andrea runs off to a music store in the Wisconsin cold.

Throughout, the sound man is whining that we're too loud. My amp is on 1, we are all playing at half our usual volume, but he insists on miking everything and running it through the PA at a deafening level and then complains we're playing too loud. At the same time, he can't seem to get the bass at an audible volume. I am fuming. To appease the fool, we switch amps so that I'm playing through a smaller spare. All through the second set I'm standing in front of my amp and can't hear a thing. All any of us can hear is Mick, and Mick can't hear a note. It's amazing we're

able to play together at all.
    The sound man sputters
that we're the loudest band
that's ever played there.
I'm impressed, since that
apparently means we're louder
than the Afghan Whigs or Soul
Asylum. So all you people who
think we're folkie hippie
wimps who can't rock, take
heed. In Madison, we have
revealed ourselves to be the
only true heirs to Blue Cheer.
Where's our Sub Pop contract?

11/17 St. Louis, MO
(University City, actually)
After a couple of bunk shows,
we are bound and determined
to play better and have some
fun for a change. We load in
at Cicero's to find we are
opening for Uncle Tupelo.
What, you mean you've never
heard of Uncle Tupelo? Haven't
you read the new "Rolling
Stone" yet? They are local
heroes who just returned from
a big tour after releasing
an album and getting written
up. They're nice kids, a
country-inflected power trio
with grungy originals and
covers of the Carter Family
and Leadbelly as well as the
more usual Byrds ("Wasn't
Born to Follow") and Neil
Young ("Cortez the Killer").
Lorry Fleming [Alias staffer]
would like them. Anyway, a
good audience is guaranteed
tonight. We have more people
at our sound check than we've
had at most of our shows.
    We do an hour-long set with
complete confidence, playing
great with few horrible
mistakes. For the first time
in days, we get the wonderful
feeling of, "For the next
hour we own this stage and
we belong here" (it beats
feeling, "What am I doing
here, let's go home"). There's
something about going onstage
with an air of authority that
makes the audience like you
more. You don't have this
horrible anxiety about proving
yourself. You're confident
enough to smile, crack jokes,
or give serious intros to
the songs. The huge crowd of
Uncle Tupelo fans likes us.

11/18 St. Louis, MO
Delmar Boulevard in University
City has a "walk of the stars"
similar to Hollywood's, with
names and bios of famous
citizens of St. Louis and
environs. We found stars for
local celebs from Miles Davis,
Betty Grable, and Josephine
Baker to Scott Joplin, Chuck
Berry, Ulysses S. Grant, and
William Burroughs. I indulge
in a record-buying orgy in
Streetside Records' racks
of marked-down imports (as
the vinyl-cide progresses,
watch for more treasures in
"dead product" bins) and an
astounding selection of used
stuff at Vintage Vinyl. I
score a lesser Richard and
Linda Thompson, the infamous
third Big Star album, a good
South African compilation, a
Kaleidoscope retrospective,
and more.
    On the way back to our huge
tiled deco motel (the Coral
Court, check it out, touring
bands), we find ourselves
in this big spendy yup-burb
mall looking for food. We
wind up in a sandwich shop
that serves beer in "yard
glasses" (ridiculously tall,
thin beakers requiring a
wood frame to hold them up)
and "fishbowls." We realize
this is a major frat boy/
sorority girl hangout by the
tunes that come up on the CD
juke. Traveling Wilburys,
Petty, Guns 'n' Roses, Blues
Brothers, soundtracks,
George Michael, Meat Loaf.
You haven't experienced true
horror until you witness a
roomful of youth acting out
the words to "Paradise by
the Dashboard Light." Do we
really live in a nation of
manipulative pinheads who
like to have bad sex in cars?

11/19 Kansas City, MO
We pull into the Grand
Emporium, "Kansas City's oasis
of R&B," and spy our poster
on the door, along with a
good CMJ review we haven't
seen before of our "Old
Colonial" single. It calls
the song "highlife," which
is like saying that Ghanaian

pop music and Soweto township
jive are indistinguishable,
but since the song is really
pseudo-African punk rock
anyhow, nitpicking is hardly
appropriate.
    The club offers us a free
meal, but with only meaty
gumbos and sausagey pizzas on
offer, most of us go wandering
in search of real food. We've
eaten fairly well on this
tour, despite fearing that a
vegetarian could starve in
the heart of America. If you
can stomach cheese and eggs,
you'll do all right. This time
a feminist bookstore (always
a good bet to find out where
the hippie restaurants are!)
directs us to the Corner,
which serves decent cheap
food and hot cider. Close
by is a record store that
actually has our first album
on vinyl and CD. This is the
first time we've found it on
the whole tour.
    Well, the good thing about
tonight's show is the sound
is excellent. This is a real
prestigious club. A lot of
big reggae and blues acts
play here. Mick Taylor was
here last week, though I'm
far more impressed to see the
Mighty Diamonds are due next
week. The sound man's a cool
guy who used to tour with the
Blue Riddim Band doing their
sound. He tells a good story
of going to Jamaica with
these Midwest white boys and
actually getting a Sunsplash
audience on their side.
    Small crowd. We are sharing
the bill with a "cutting-edge
rock jam," which translates
as a bunch of guitar-store
employees doing AC/DC covers.
They play before and after
us, and are deafening. We do
a pretty good set. Susie the
bartender puts us up for the
night, despite the fact that
we didn't play "Dead Flowers."

11/20 Iowa City, IA
Mid-morning and we're off
again, up northern Missouri
to Iowa, where we see our
first Denny's in weeks, a sign
we're going west again. On to
Iowa (Rock) City. A lot of

semipopular bands seem to be emerging from here so there's potential for a crowd.

Gabe's is another club upstairs/bar downstairs combination. We realize we're likely to play two sets to an audience of nearly no one while a crowd whoops it up downstairs drinking cheap beer. Figuring we aren't going to make money anyway, we convince the club to knock down the cover from $3 to $1. This probably saved the show. We got a pretty decent-sized and noisy-as-fuck audience for our two sets. We played well. Looks like we're back on a roll. We give away tons of singles. When it's over, into the van for another overnight drive.

11/21 Boulder, CO

Probably the most boring drive we have made: across Iowa through Nebraska to eastern Colorado. The Rockies are breathtaking, but we don't get anywhere near them until near nightfall.

Boulder is the next-to-last stop on this tour. It feels like we've been out forever. We get into town ahead of schedule and load into the club. We are playing Ground Zero with Laughing Hyenas, a Touch & Go band. Hopefully that will draw a crowd.

The club is pretty loose about set times so both X-tal and the Hyenas get to play as long as we want. We play an energetic hour-long set to a rowdy all-ages crowd. Afterwards, a friend of the people we're staying with accosts me to congratulate me. A big tall guy who looks like what he is, a Green Beret reservist, he tipsily says, "I really like the political edge in your songs. I wish I had a line to offer you but..." Uh, it's okay, I'm

kinda partial to the idea of sleeping tonight anyway. Guy turns out to be fairly cool, bit of a wild man, used to hang out in the Bay Area punk scene circa 1984, then he naively joined the military and applied for the Special Forces, wanting to "learn a skill," as the recruiters have it. First he was shocked to pass the test, then more shocked to see firsthand what the US government is up to. He claims the Special Forcers are full of disillusioned soldiers who hate America's policies as a result of being sent on gruesome secret missions to South America and other places to do questionable tasks. Sounds like a skilled dormant revolutionary guerrilla army, but...

Boulder is pretty cold. We watch the headlining Laughing Hyenas and marvel at their rhythm section. Perfectly brutal, simple bass lines and powerful, skillful drumming. The bass player has a long wispy beard. They're like the Birthday Party the way they attack weird time signatures. A rumpled woman guitarist spews angular Rowland Howardesque riffs. Too bad the singer is something of

a nonentity. Good Lux/Lurch presence, but his screechy monotone gets old fast. Even early Nick Cave had a lot more than a raunchy bellow to offer. Even so, I liked the Hyenas a lot.

We bed down on another floor. Tomorrow is Thanksgiving for most of America, but a long nonstop drive for X-tal.

11/24 Los Angeles, CA

Boulder to LA is a two-day marathon starting off with Thanksgiving brunch at the local Denny's(!). Reconstituted turkey for the carnivores and the usual veggie-melt (i.e., a grilled cheese with extra trimmings) plus garden salad for the rest of us. ("Is there any meat in the garden salad?" "Shut up and have another cigarette!") In the morning, the view is unbelievable. We are on the edge of an endless plain that stretches out indefinitely to the east, while directly to the west, miles-high mountains jut up suddenly like a monstrous snow-covered wall.

We drive to California by way of New Mexico and Arizona, avoiding the gale-force winds of the Rocky Mountain passes, and the unpredictable fascist police of Utah, where Jimmy faces a six-month sentence for an empty pipe.

When I wake up, we're making good time through the last stretches of Arizona, cruising I-40, which follows the old path of Route 66. (London Bridge is said to have been moved to somewhere around here. Mick's English pride forces him to chuckle slightly at this example of American stupidity.) We cross the state line and stop in Needles to have breakfast with the Indians and the rednecks.

The long Mojave stretch from Needles to Barstow always inspires us to put on the tape of Australian folk music Patty Stirling gave me, and we're entertained by tales of macho sheepshearers and hard-boiled bush bastards as the scrub and prickly pear goes whizzing by. Mick has no patience with the aboriginal rock at the end of Patty's tape, though I love the Warumpi Band track that sounds like "Don't Fear the Reaper" in an alien tongue. Mick is not convinced.

Late that afternoon we descend on the land of cush, aka Alias records HQ in North Hollywood, aka the home of Delight Jenkins, label matriarch and goddess of hospitality. Time to do laundry, kick back, settle into the guest house, and check out what music they're listening to lately. This is always my opportunity to practice my skills with a CD player (I'm so backward), bone up on old "new releases" I've missed, and make tapes. Love the new Clean album (Allison doesn't get it; "What do you like about these guys?"; hates the loud drum mix); most of Sonic Youth's "Goo" (amazing how much out-and-out wanky noise they put on their major-label debut; "Daydream Nation" was way slicker. "Tunic" strikes a chord); and Fugazi's "Repeater + 3 Songs" (great; Jimmy goes nuts over this as well as the new Agitpop, which has a nice remake of the Hudson River song). Not enchanted by the new Yo La Tengo, though everybody loves "Speeding Motorcycle," including bike-crash victim Jimmy. Oh yeah, the Embarrassment album gets a big thumbs-up (we all identify

with "get out of my way/I haven't had any sex all day!" Too long away from home?) and King Missile tickles us pink. Dread Zeppelin, however, is a big trendy bore, and will be regarded as tiresome has-beens by the time you read this.

LA is a disaster gig-wise. We had lined up two shows: Friday at Al's Bar, and Saturday at the Gaslight. At the last minute, Al's moves us to Saturday. When we realize it isn't feasible to hop from one show to the other the same night, we have to decide which show to drop. We decide to play Al's and cancel the Gaslight. Then we discover the Gaslight has us advertised everywhere, and Al's has nearly canceled us as a result. Like fools, we elect to play Al's anyway—because we find out the Gaslight's policy is to ask each person who comes in which band they've come to see, and pays each band only a percentage of the patrons that mention their name. Since we see this as an idiotic policy that forces more competition between bands, we reject the Gaslight, only to find out that Al's does the same thing. Only in LA.

So here we are at Al's, and the first band on is a god-awful thing called Mr. Ectomy, a three-guitar Dread/Zappa/Bad Brains hybrid with an overmodulated bass so loud it feels like your teeth are falling out. Next up is a halfway decent funk-punk band called Caustic Monkey who feature a talented cool-jazz alto saxophonist. My old friend Jill Fido (ex-Holy Sisters of the Gaga Dada) shows up, saying she has written a bunch of new songs

and wants to record a couple with X-tal. That'll be fun.

Our set is good but cut short thanks to lengthy sets by other bands. Sound man is a dickhead at the end, singing off-key and babbling idiotically into the microphone in a pathetic attempt to drive everybody out. Sorry, sonny, I've been tossed out of punk clubs by experts; Dirk Dirksen you are not. The Al's employees shove us and our equipment out the door like cops evicting squatters. This is one rude fucking town.

11/26 San Francisco, CA
Home again after a miserable rainy traffic-jammed crawl up I-5 yesterday, stuck for an eternity next to miles of stinking, moaning, penned-up beef cattle ready for slaughter, the smell unbearable for them as much as us, I'm sure. We imagine the gallons of adrenaline being churned up in there to end up in somebody's hamburger. Now we're back home, wondering how long it'll take before everyone tells us, "Oh shut up! No more boring tour stories, please!" Set up one more time at the Albion, playing for a gathering of locals and friends who tell us we're a lot tighter than we were before we left. A modest homecoming, but heartwarming all the same. Earlier tonight I pondered my immediate future over my first burrito in months. An old Minor Threat refrain started up in my mind: "There's no place like home/So where am I?"

###

THROWING MUSES

Throwing Muses released their fourth album, the pop-friendly *The Real Ramona*, in 1991. The album would be the last Muses album to feature Tanya Donelly, who was destined for a snippet of MTV glory with her band Belly. **GINA HARP** interviewed Kristin Hersh at her home base in Rhode Island, finding a musician in transition but confident in her belief that "we're finding that junk food kills us, and it's the same with music."

The release of *The Real Ramona*, their fourth and possibly finest album, amply confirms Throwing Muses' status as one of America's great bands.

After the increased exposure achieved by 1989's *Hunkpapa* album and a year's worth of touring (including support slots with New Order and R.E.M.), the Muses spent the last year working in new bassist Fred Abong, then recording *The Real Ramona*, while also coping with the legal difficulties caused by an acrimonious split with their longtime manager. Kristin Hersh was also under considerable personal strain, as she has explained in several interviews earlier this year, and as the content of her recent lyrics suggests. That the band emerged from all this with their most cohesive and powerful record since their self-titled debut in 1986 seems little short of miraculous.

In addition, Muses guitarist Tanya Donelly, whose two contributions to *The Real Ramona* reveal her most

assured songwriting to date, also has an album's worth of songs ready for the Breeders, her side project with Kim Deal of the Pixies. They'll be recording this summer.

Meanwhile, their recent tour completed, Kristin Hersh is on maternity leave; her second child is due in August. The interview that follows was conducted by phone before the tour, while Kristin was at home in Newport, Rhode Island.

Recording *The Real Ramona*

You guys were in the studio for quite a time.

[*Laughs*] We were in the studio forever! But we knew what we were doing. I'm not used to that: my whole life I've trained myself to be able to give up everything in just a few takes, so that live is pretty much what we are. We've always tried to capture that in the studio. And since the studio process is a lie, to try to work with that instead of around it is kind of a trick.

Tell me about the album's production.

Dennis Herring produced it. I wasn't familiar with any of his work; he'd done Camper Van Beethoven, Timbuk 3—a lot of diverse stuff. After talking to him, we all decided we should be working with somebody like that. We'd been working with Gary Smith for the last couple of albums, and we're very like-minded, which didn't always serve the records well. With Dennis, we had the chance to bounce anything off him, and there were specific recording techniques we wanted to be using this time. It's always gotten in the way for me when a producer or engineer, or even the band, want to record something and get a flat, clean sound, and then manipulate it from the board. I can always tell that it's board manipulation, and it's not the sound that happened in the room at the time. I'm offended by the way that quality dates, it gets old real fast.

But if you can create an incredible sound in an incredible room and mike that really well, then we can manipulate it later and it doesn't take away from the integrity of the original sound. Or, you can leave it as is, and it sounds great. I think this is the first time we've re-created our true live sound on a record without making it flat and small.

What did you do differently?

We didn't do [production on] the drums. We used wonderful rooms and mikes to get the sounds. I tried to stay away from board effects, it's like swinging two bats until it sounds great. We used two mikes with their own pre-amps. You get a real crisp clear sound. It's recorded in the way they would have done in the '50s or early '60s, the way some jazz records are still done.

Did you use a drum machine at all?

No. We did use more click tracks than usual this time, and sometimes that gives the impression of a drum machine. I've always liked the way the band moves in and out of tempos. It's more subtle than anything else; I certainly didn't want to lay a click track over that and have it be like a metronome. It wasn't appropriate—for this material, it needed real solidity to build on, so sometimes that makes it sound like a drum machine, if the sound is manipulated at all.

How did you come up with the title?

We wanted a name that didn't mean anything. David and I had been looking at old postcards in junk shops, cards that were written and sent in the '30s. There was one, a sort of prairie, with a lady down in the corner you didn't notice at first. At the top it said, *The Real Ramona*. We thought it was hilarious that there was no explanation, no reason why she should be more real, or more Ramona . . .

Daily Life

What have you been up to for the last two years? Why so long a break between albums?

We haven't really stopped working yet. We toured *Hunkpapa* for about a year, and then started working with Fred [Abong]. We did a movie title track; then we took him on the road. David and I were working alone with him for a few months; there's a lot of material to go over—he wanted to know the catalog so we'd be able to draw from it in shows. And then time was spent writing and fighting and choosing producers. The work just never stops. I don't know if we've ever had any real time off. Maybe that's just me, because I'm writing all the time.

You must have quite a catalog to draw from yourself. How often do you write?

I write whenever I'm supposed to, and if I'm not writing I'm just practicing. I wouldn't say I'm a real disciplined musician . . . but I've become addicted to practicing the way people are to jogging. If I'm supposed to be writing a song I know it, because it feels like somebody grabs my ears and kicks me in the back of the head and starts shouting at me. Wherever I am, I have to do something about it, or they'll keep kicking me. Practicing doesn't necessarily lead to writing; it's just craft.

Song Lines

I especially liked the guitar work on "Hook in Her Head."

That song is real old, actually. I didn't even want to do it, it didn't seem relevant for now. I wouldn't write it now. I wasn't sure if it would come off as melodramatic. The band talked me into it and we made a sound with it that the album needed; so I'm glad. And I edited the living hell out of it.

I interpret "Two Step" as a sad song. Is it a love song?

It's actually kind of the band's anthem. I'd never written a song without guitar before. But I knew exactly what key this was in and I went with this bass line Fred came up with. When I went in to play it everyone just started playing—and it was finished. In as long as it takes to play, the song was done. It's probably about the band. Your guess is as good as mine [*laughs*].

"Graffiti" sounds like a good driving song.

I haven't been able to figure that one out. I love how the instrumental comes in. It kind of saves it and makes it Velvety—as in Velvet Underground—instead of pretty.

Is "Red Shoes" an older song too?

No, I played it on the *Hunkpapa* tour, along with "Say Goodbye."

When did "Say Goodbye" evolve into a full song?

It went through a lot of metamorphoses. It used to be called "Boy," I think. Dave reminded me of it. It came out this way when I rewrote it. A lot of people preferred the piece of it on *Hunkpapa*. They heard that first and were angry we did anything to it. But it doesn't have to take away from that version to do a different one.

What about "Ellen West"?

That's from a case study by Ludwig Binswanger. Ellen lived around the turn of the century, though she seems very modern. She thought there was a big black bird flying behind her head all her life. She killed herself eventually. That song is one of those that is so honest that it comes out of somewhere other than me. Usually I have no idea what I'm writing about. That's my job, you know: not to know anything about it, so I don't get in the way.

Family Tie-Ins

Is your son, Dylan [4 years old], fond of your music?

He doesn't understand what it is. You can talk to him about anything but he's unsocialized. So he seems out of his mind. He has a logic construct that's not of this planet [*laughs*]. So he doesn't always have the context when things are explained. He assumes everybody's mommy has her own record.

If I were a kid, "Golden Thing" would be one of my favorite songs.

He used to ask for "Busy in My Head," and now he knows there's a song called "Dylan," and that makes him turn red. He bought his first guitar the other day, so I think I should be proud. He thinks if he learns to play soon he'll be able to tour with us! So the pressure is on as far as he's concerned.

You don't take him on tour?

When he was a baby, we traveled in a Winnebago and that was his house. But there was a huge custody battle with his father last year. His father won "physical placement" because I have to travel so much. So now I can't travel with him.

A Solo Tour

You did some solo shows recently.

A couple of months ago. They went well. It wasn't fun but it was romantic. We just drove around in our station wagon, town to town, mall to mall—my boyfriend and I. He's one of our managers, and now he's my husband.

The idea of the acoustic shows was, I needed to figure out why I had written these songs in the first place. I didn't know if I liked them, if they were good; or what they were before the band kind of took them over. The people that came got to hear how the songs were before everything got laid over them. Being technically a rhythm guitarist, your parts tend to get mixed down a lot, and that's how the songs are written, so sometimes it hurts me for them. It's like watching your kids grow up into something you never expected. I just needed to look at some baby pictures of the music.

Lineup Changes

How did it happen that Leslie Langston left the band?

Before we went out on the road with R.E.M. last year, after *Hunkpapa*, she wanted to be back in California. She's in San Francisco right now, living with our old sound man. I think California is more her style, and a break she definitely deserved. There were no hard feelings anywhere. It was the best thing, for no real bad reason.

Freddy Abong, who we picked up here, is a great bassist we've known since we were kids. He's as good a friend as Leslie was, which makes a big difference in a band like ours. If we didn't trust each other we wouldn't be able to write honest parts. You start lying, and then it's hard to stop.

Was there ever any question whether the band would continue?

No. There wasn't.

When did Fred join?

As soon as we knew Leslie wanted to move. We wanted to make sure Fred was very much a part of us before we started any more recording. We took him on the road and did a movie soundtrack with him. If you go into the studio too soon, before the songs can kind of happen by themselves within minutes, you end up working on them for weeks, and you don't know what to make of them. You start making up identities for them and that can get sticky.

Tour Plans: The UK Way

The band's going to England soon?

We usually go there first, because albums happen so quickly there. Their press infiltrates immediately, and it's available all over the country. You get your highest chart position as soon as the record is released. And they die as quickly; it's useless to tour after the first few months. We're going over there, then to Europe, then back here.

With all the material you have now, how do you decide what songs you'll do live?

With lists all over the floor . . . The others had the idea of playing only from the first album and this one—it sounds to me like a good idea that won't work. We've been in this band for about ten years now. The first few albums are pretty much all the material from, oh five years before ever making records. So we feel like we've been playing those songs for years, even though they haven't been heard much, and in the States no one can get our first two albums, three even! We've been playing songs like "Vicky's Box" and "Stand Up" for one

hell of a long time. But I doubt we'll do anything from *Hunkpapa* this tour. We're so sick of that stuff.

I saw you on that tour, opening for New Order in Portland.

I have no idea how we got talked into doing that, it was ridiculous. We'd be backstage after playing a twenty-minute set to a bunch of 15-year-olds and their girl-friends. Leslie had things thrown at her. It was freaky—only Leslie. We'd be backstage and New Order would go on. The crowd would be screaming—their light show was unbelievable—and the music would go on for 10 or 15 minutes. Then we'd walk into the next room and they'd all be sitting there! They like don't need to be onstage at all . . . "Are you guys a band or a machine?"

I read somewhere you said you don't want your music to be "an elitist adventure." How can you maintain that when the folks at 4AD seem to revel in it?

Oh my god. They seem to relish it. No kidding! That has been our biggest argument. And now I see their side of it. In England you are forgiven for that. What is seen as pretentious and dismissible here, is forgiven there.

It's very important to us that we are an American band. I don't know how people who aren't American hear us. They must have this image that we are more from space than we really are.

Yet you've been quite successful over there.

England's a small country. Their music press covers alternative music, and you can buy it anywhere in the country. So you look famous. The same is true in certain regions here. If those were countries we'd be doing really well in those countries!

The Honeymoon

You got married . . .

In December. I wore my mother's wedding dress, because I couldn't afford to buy one. I had to call my grandmother and ask her if it was in good enough shape to wear. She says [*heavy Southern accent*], "Well, it's not white, but I think that's appropriate, don't you?" Like she was saying, you and your bastard son want to try and sell yourselves off that's fine with me, but don't tell anyone you're pure. The gown was ivory, but it was very nice. We got married in the castle here, for free, because it's part of my college. Huge wedding. Safeway cake. Out by the cliffs.

Did you go on a honeymoon?

Kind of. We took a film crew and made a documentary on ostrich farming. We drove to Texas and Oklahoma. The ranchers are pretty much like other ranchers, but they have nine-foot birds on their land. They're raised for their feathers, their hide, their retinas, and their meat. They have red meat that supposedly you can't tell from steak. It's expensive, but they don't market it as a delicacy, they want everyone to eat their ostrich. They cooked us a big ostrich dinner. Since I'm vegetarian my friends would get the meat off my plate so our host wouldn't know. Billy says it tasted like steak.

Do you see yourself as a role model for women?

Boy, I'm not the one to say. I think there are very few women to hold up, at least in music. There are few women who've been allowed to be what they are in real life. They're sex kittens or very ethereal or just leather babes. Most of the roles are directed at men anyway. If they're not imitating a man, they're still aiming at male acceptance.

I don't think we ever knew how to do that. I never took the time to figure it out. I don't know anything about being a sex kitten, and if I did that, how could I honestly be in these songs? If I were acting differently, I couldn't lose myself to the songs.

Feminine Foundation

I think we've been allowed to be masculine and feminine in the music and in our lives. And in the image of a band—that I think is the healthy thing. The feminine foundation that our music has may be alienating to some people, just because music has traditionally had a very masculine foundation. It has a skeletal structure that is easy to follow, it moves with your heartbeat. Whereas a lot of our songs tend to be built on subtleties—along veins, kind of—along tributaries that you can't really follow if you're going to get a grasp of the whole song. That may have been alienating.

Some journalist in Europe was saying, "Did you begin with this all-female band idea?" I said, "We aren't and never have been all-female." He said, "Well it's really marketable." Marketable! Are you out of your mind? The more women there are doing anything, the less marketable it is!

He said, "Think of all the bands that have succeeded with that: the Bangles, the Go-Go's." *Two bands!* Think of all the successful male bands.

I guarantee you, the more women you take out of a band, the more successful it will be. And in order for them to be "marketable," they have to be fucking Bangles, for Christ's sake!

Carrying On

We're extremely poor right now. But it's just lawsuits. Warner Bros. are coming around this time; before, they never really cared what we sold. Now they're seeing what we're doing, why we're doing it, and that it's not a question of we don't know how to write pop songs.

Do you see the band breaking out of alternative mode? Do you mind being marketed for college radio?

We've kind of done all we can on college radio. Isn't it up to radio to change? It does seem to be changing . . . I deeply regret ever releasing "Dizzy," I hate that song . . . "Counting Backwards" is pretty much as pop as I get. I don't think we are all that alternative, and it's such an offensive term anyway. And there's a precious aspect to it, too, which is evil. It's just Top 40 messing everything up, this non-music at the top of everything like frosting, and that's what wins Grammys and sells records. And all the music is underneath it. I'm not going to be a part of it until they're ready for what we do to be a part of it.

Horizons may be broadening a bit.

The Cocteau Twins tour sold out; that's great. I don't know if I should talk about another band . . . Jane's Addiction sells really well. Pixies are doing well. It does seem to be changing, just that much.

Unfortunately, I think MTV has a lot to do with a band's success. They certainly gave a lot of airplay to Jane's Addiction.

The only time I've watched MTV was when Dave and I lived in this hotel room while we were making *Hunkpapa* in Boston. We used to come in about 3 o'clock in the morning and swear to ourselves, *We will not turn on MTV tonight. We won't turn it on because if we do we won't be able to turn it off.* One of us would go take a shower and the other would turn it on . . .

We'd be watching fucking Midnight Oil and INXS and all this stuff. I just can't stomach it anymore. I know that's probably not a very good thing to say. There's so much garbage around, they aren't any big example, it isn't right to single out those bands . . .

I wonder how much we can take? We used to say, "It's good, because it's got to explode someday, this is too bad to exist." There aren't many people in this world who believe as strongly as I do that bad music is evil. I can't shake this feeling so I've stopped trying. It just seems really dangerous to me, and I don't know how anyone is ever going to see that while we have this trash in our ears. You know we're finding that junk food kills us, and it's the same with music. Everybody wants candy in their mouths, but you don't want to die twenty years too young, either. And there's this garbage music that does nothing for you: you just swallow it because it's easy to take. And you never know what beauty is. ✪

HOLE

In late 1991, **DAVID GRAD** interviewed Hole pre-show in a pizzeria next to CBGB, just after Kurt Cobain, during Nirvana's British live TV debut, had announced that "Courtney Love, the lead singer of the sensational pop group Hole, is the best fuck in the world." The band spoke with Grad just as their debut album, *Pretty on the Inside*, was released. Their famous second album, *Live Through This*, was still three years away.

I've seen your repulsion, and it looks good on you
—"Teenage Whore"

While we wait for Courtney Love, I sit in the pizzeria next to CBGB talking to Jill Emery and Caroline Rue, bassist and drummer in Hole. We get off to a good start as they lament the way the lyrics to their single, "Teenage Whore," have been taken to be autobiographical, leading to all kinds of trouble. They tell me that during their tour of England last summer, *Melody Maker* journalist Everett True, delirious over the song, wrote a review implying it was based on events in the life of Courtney Love. Courtney, the band's singer, guitarist, songwriter, and first among equals, took offense. Later on, Thurston Moore, defending her honor, went in pursuit of True backstage at a London gig.

At this point Courtney herself comes exploding into the pizza joint. She asks me to turn the tape recorder off. Giggling, she repeats, "I just can't believe it!" It seems that during a British TV appearance, Nirvana's Kurt Cobain (Courtney's boyfriend) has dedicated a song to the best fuck in the world, Courtney Love. Caroline catches my eye and grimaces.

Following two singles—"Retard Girl" (Sympathy for the Record Industry) and "Dicknail" (Sub Pop)—Hole's album, *Pretty on the Inside* (Caroline), was produced by leading scenesters Don Fleming (Velvet Monkeys) and Kim Gordon. The album features a return-of-the-repressed rage and a sense of mutilated sexuality. I found the Fleming/Gordon imprint heavy-handed, but came to appreciate the recording's lyrical and musical nuances.

Today, Hole is riding the crest of "the next big thing." The album and single got heavy rotation on college radio, and *Spin* rated the LP twentieth in its best-of-the-year survey. Madonna reportedly expressed interest in signing the band to her new label. Courtney has not said no, exactly, but comments, "I don't want Madonna to be my boss."

Hole is clearly Courtney Love's band. She dominates the conversation. I'd been warned she was mercurial and might throw a drink in my face. That doesn't happen, but contradiction rules. Courtney can switch from adolescent giggles to an almost dry academicism in a millisecond.

She describes herself as "one of those poetry girls with a notebook in the corner of the coffee shop" who has always been influenced by extremes. Her inspiration came backstage at a show by Cheap Trick when she was 14. "My whole rock dream was destroyed. I thought, I can fucking do this. This is lame." She got a guitar, "but I really couldn't play. I was posturing." These years were a period of "rock adventures."

She went on to form a band with Kat Bjelland which evolved into Babes in Toyland. Courtney bristles when I note similarities between Hole and the Babes, including identical script for their album song lists. She cuts me off and asks sharply, "Do you know what you're talking about? Do you know the history? We started that band. I wrote that way first. We shared boyfriends."

After parting with Bjelland, Courtney ran an ad for musicians in the *Recycler* and Eric Erlandson answered. He involved Jill.[1] Then Courtney met Caroline at a show, and Hole was born.

Eric is uncomfortable with the view of Hole as a girl group. He dismisses my "How does it feel to be the lone man" question with a disgruntled, "It's just a band. It shouldn't have to do with gender." The others are forceful about the group's female identity. Courtney declares, "We are a girl group. We make girl music. We have a feminine take. I've kicked girls out of bands for playing masculine leads."

Caroline defines the "feminine take" as an attempt "to interpret sounds, embellish them, not run over and dominate them."

Courtney says people mistake her lyrics for her life because their perceptions are molded by a scarcity of good female songwriters. "It's hard for people to conceive that a post-punk female can have feelings in the tradition of Neil Young."

She wants to be taken seriously as a songwriter, but this may conflict with the image she projects. She sees the conflict as based in a perception of "glamour as giving in." She asserts that the quality of glamour is essential to her character. "There is a certain power that you gain from it that validates you like nothing else. If I weren't a woman, I'd be a drag queen in a second."

Given men's ambivalence toward female sexuality,

---

1 Jill has reportedly now left the band, citing religious differences.

HOLE
Pretty on the Inside
(Caroline)

Hole begins "Star Belly" with the intro riff from "Cinnamon Girl," just as Mudhoney, on their latest, begins "Broken Hands" with the closing riff. Something's up here . . . Los Angeles's femme (plus one dude) answer to the Seattle squall finally gets to toss cake at the boys. Heel-tattooed Courtney Love yelps like Joan Jett, moans like Kim Gordon, and acts like a pissed-off debutante whose date threw up on her décolletage. In between expletives aimed at teenage whores, macho bores, and her own perceived powerlessness, she scrapes out unearthly noise from her guitar—Eric Erlandson adding his own monolithic meditations—and the rhythm section registers that Black Sabbath's *Master of Reality* wrote the book 21 years ago. Each song creates a weird vertigo, imparting a primal fear; it's as if the smell of death is near, so desperate is Hole to get the final say. So you won't hear anything startlingly new here, assuming you've plucked your share of Sub Pop and Sympathy singles (Hole has done a 45 for each label), but you will have masochistic fun letting Courtney beat the crap out of you while she purges her angst. "I just get loaded," she confesses, however, in the midst of a Sonic Youth–styled clanging interlude; behind every pissed-off explosion lies a vulnerable psyche.—*Fred Mills*

HOLE
The Off Ramp, Seattle
July 1, 1993

Following worthwhile sets from Pivot, Sourpuss, and Adickdid, Hole appeared to a perfect audience: a not-too-crammed, energetic, and Courtney-friendly crowd. Courtney was willing to discuss the pressure. She also proved that a person doesn't need to be sober (I'd say she wasn't), fully clothed (I'd say that's a slip), or male (I'd say, duh) to put on a hell of a punk-rock show. Of that day's local Kurt-and-Courtney-those-troublemakers story, she said, "Every time we have a beer it makes the news." Makes you wonder what happens when she buys tampons, huh?

Then Hole did what Hole does. They poured out a dark and grimy flood of roaring, rib-cage-heaving, ear-bleeding force. Courtney tickled our spines with her sandpaper-layered vocals through songs from the LP as well as several near-ballads that displayed the cactus-laced smoker's edge of her voice.

I didn't see any muckrakers in the crowd; they must have been up at the house, sifting through the Love and Cobain garbage cans.
—*Christine Sievanen*

this type of assertiveness can be confusing. It can be understood in simplistic and one-dimensional terms, and this is what happened in the case of the aforementioned Everett True. "We had to be white-trash girls from trailer parks, or he just couldn't deal with it. Although I have an academic background, he took the narratives on my record and turned them into reality, foisting on me an image that the English go for: Dark Star Whore. Here I am. A loud American female. There's nothing like it to send them running to the bathroom."

The success of *Pretty on the Inside* leaves Courtney cold. She feels "we don't have a great song on this record. It's not breaking the mold." For her, the guiding lights are Nirvana and the Pixies. The challenge is to write songs "as good and as well constructed as theirs are."

With *Pretty*, Hole has reached the limits of the pop-punk rage-core style. Courtney was surprised by people's reactions. "We thought we made a pop record, and then we're told it's one of the most extreme records people ever heard." She now describes the album as a "catharsis," saying, "We are turning the corner on that rage." She wants to give up the reputation of fronting "the darkest band in the universe." She wants to "create value and light."

Experiencing Hole perform live, one doubts that they have turned any corner on rage. The incredible power of their show is generated by a mix of unstable and volatile elements. Although offstage there is something almost formless about Courtney, onstage she physically transforms herself to something solidly defined. Tremendous energy is expended in the process. In performance, her veins seem to be about to tear through the skin of her arms.

Courtney wails though her material, her voice evoking emotions from isolated despair to manic exhilaration. In her loose-fitting frock she begins to resemble a dangerous mental patient. The band throbs behind her as Caroline throws herself into the drum kit and her pounding leads the guitars. Eric beats the shit out of his instrument. Courtney breaks a string: it is forgotten. She appears almost overcome by self-created frenzy. The band look tense as Courtney leads them like some punk-demon James Brown.

Suddenly, Love throws down her malfunctioning guitar in disgust. The show is over. We reel off wanting more.

A band on the verge of self-destruction: Catch them before they explode. ◑

BRATMOBILE. PHOTO, MICHAEL GALINSKY

INTERNATIONAL POP UNDERGROUND CONVENTION
23 Reasons to Be Cheerful

In 1991, Beat Happening singer and K Records proprietor Calvin Johnson organized the International Pop Underground Convention in Olympia, Washington. The six-day music festival featured sets by Bikini Kill, Built to Spill, and Fugazi, as well as the first public performance by Corin Tucker in her pre–Sleater-Kinney band Heavens to Betsy. It also saw the public unveiling of the Kill Rock Stars label. **ROBERT ZIEGER** reported from the festival.

This past summer, Olympia hosted a six-day orgy of "hangman hipsters, new modrockers, sidestreet walkers, scooter mounted dream girls, punks, teds, the instigators of the Love Rock Explosion, the editors of every angry grrrl zine, the plotters of youth rebellion in every form, the midwestern librarians and Scottish ski instructors who live by night," known as the International Pop Underground Convention. Though not sure where I fitted on the list, I knew I belonged in Washington's capital the third week in August. I'm a skinny, messy white male, 26 when the convention began, 27 by the time it was over, a cynical but cheerful social worker–type who found punk rock in high school and has tried passionately ever since to keep

a world view consistent with what I heard and felt watching the Gang of Four, hearing the first Clash record.

From time to time over the years, I've sensed that the punk-rock flame within me might be flickering out, and the last dozen or so shows I'd been to simply hadn't seemed important to me, much less enjoyable. This led me to wonder if maybe I had finally gotten too old for this medium of youth, or if maybe even— Crass have mercy on my soul—the punk-rock credo had been a pathetic myth all along. Perhaps I had been silly to believe a drunken teenager with a loud guitar could have unique insight into my soul. Perhaps I had been a fool to value D. Boon's thoughts on the

International Pop Underground Convention
August 20-25, 1991, Olympia, Wash., U.S.A.

As the corporate ogre expands it's creeping influence on the minds of industrialized youth, the time has come for the International Rockers of the World to convene in celebration of our grand independence. Because this society is sick and in desperate need of a little blood-letting; sand, sidewalk and punk pop implosion. Because the corporate ogre has infected the creative community with it's black plague of indentured servitude. Because we are the gravediggers who have buried the grey spectre of rock star myth. Because we are the misfits and we will have our day. We won't go away. Hangman hipsters, new modrockers, sidestreet walkers, scooter mounted dream girls, punks, teds, the instigators of the Love Rock Explosion, the editors of every angry grrrl zine, the plotters of youth rebellion in every form, the midwestern librarians and Scottish ski instructors who live by night, all are setting aside August 20-25, 1991 as the time. Olympia, Washington is the place. A double shot of International Hip Swing is the goal. Barbecues, parades, disco dancing, picnics and wild screaming teenage rock'n'roll are the means. Revolution is the end. Revolution is the beginning. No lackeys to the corporate ogre allowed.

political and the personal above those of any president, scholar, or corporate greedfuck.

And so to the International Pop Underground Convention. Five days, eleven shows, thirty-some bands, and hundreds of mostly-swell-and-then-some people later, the adrenaline that kicked in early the first night hasn't left me yet. Many moons had passed since anything filled me with such giddy glee. I loved the crowd, the venues, the atmosphere, and the feeling deep within me. Oh, and, of course, the bands . . . I loved them, too. Even when their music didn't speak to me, these bands were at least doing what they wanted to do without manifesting overblown ego, and they were clearly making others happy by doing it (the one exception being Thee Headcoats, an English three-piece whose pointlessly obnoxious overestimation of their own cleverness earned my contempt).

A few days after this inspirational fun-fest ended, I began emerging from my fog of contented energy to analyze what had happened and why I felt so good. Here are some reasons:

1. Krevace
Tuesday night's show was billed as Love Rock Revolution Girl Style Now, and featured twenty or thirty acts playing from one to seven or eight songs each. Each act was either a woman, some women, or mainly women with an occasional guy. (I was happy to see that we boy types were allowed to play along to support the female acts. Too much rigidity could have dragged this thing down.) The first band of the convention to truly pull me in was Krevace, a Vancouver, BC, ten-piece—a boy-type drummer, a female bassist, and eight more women on guitars, tambourine, or singing. Concept and visual presence alone were enough for a smile and a memory, but damned if these girl rockers didn't belt out some hellaciously fine tunes—snarlin' and catchy the way I like them. And nine guitars make a lot of noise. I must confess that a request for camping space by a totally pretty band member all but sent me out into the warm Olympia night in search of a backyard to rent for the night.

2. I Enjoyed the Evening Immensely without Really Being Impressed by Many of the Bands
This was a good omen: an indication that the environment was right, and that the honesty and integrity of the event would carry me through during the times the music would not be to my liking. Mind you, some of the assembled talent on Night One rocked my world just fine—e.g., the aforementioned Krevace, a solo electric-guitar folk-rocker, Jenny Olay, and a few others. Still, many of the acts seemed to be playing out

for the first time; often, their lack of playing and songwriting ability outweighed their simplicity and sincerity. I seem to recall Beat Happening's Bret once said, "Anyone can start a band—just most people shouldn't." Some participants at the Love Rock night must have made it only halfway through that sentence. My friend Mark summed it up best; as we watched yet another ultra-minimalist band combine simple riffs, steady drumbeat, a heavy-handed affectation of childlike innocence, and half-formed stories of yummy food and being nervous around a really neat boy, he leaned toward my ear and groaned, "Beat Happening have a lot to answer for, don't they?" Talent and vision kinda help, too. But it was a very enjoyable night.

3. Treepeople
Every time I see this band of unlikely punk rockers, I marvel more at the no-frills power, energy, and honesty they pack. They're one of the last bands in the world you'll ever see on MTV, and this seems to be the way they like it. I hear some of them live on my block, and this makes me proud.

4. An Indie-Band Member with a Plan
My pal Rick reported that a friend of his in a band that played Wednesday had spotted spies in the audience from Capitol Records and other evil major labels. Fully and appropriately disdaining these "lackeys of the corporate ogre," she disclosed to him her band's plan to identify the "lackeys" publicly for ridicule and humiliation. This was no New Music Seminar, and her band, like most others at the IPUC, were not there to "get signed." I like it. Go, team!

5. Passing Scrawl on the Highway on the Way Back to Olympia
On Thursday afternoon, I rolled down the I-5 with Heidi (who would be my companion for the rest of the convention), her tape deck blasting Scrawl's *He's Drunk* (a great record, and not only because it has a great title!). As I glanced up, what should I see in front but a tan van with a Scrawl bumper sticker, and—yes!—an Ohio license plate. 'Twas Scrawl themselves! I yelled for Heidi to speed up, so we could pull alongside and wave. (Why this seemed necessary eludes me now, but at the time it was a TFI—Total Fucking Imperative). Them Scrawlrockers are mighty fast women, though, and I could only gaze on in disappointment as they pulled away at close to ninety. But then the Scrawl-mobile became mired in a throng of idiot Washington drivers. Seizing her chance, Heidi sped up on the left and honked her horn as I furiously waved my IPUC badge out the window. The driver—guitarist/vocalist

Marcy—initially looked confused, then returned our waves with fervor. We zoomed on in a trail of giggles, wondering cheekily if Scrawl might be listening to a tape of Heidi and me as they drove.

6. Discovering the Massive Happy Hour at the Spar

Thursday evening, after draining an overpriced glass of juice, I passed through a set of swinging doors at the back of the Spar Cafe and found a room that housed a bar. Looking at a chalkboard over the register, my drunken soul and enlarged liver screamed with joy at the news that well drinks were a buck each from 5 to 7. A sense of destiny settled over me; I had stumbled upon a key weekend feature—a cheap and convenient place to drink. Being the impulsive lad I am, I plopped my ass on a barstool and slammed three doubles. Six shots and nine dollars later (one must always tip well at happy hour), I sauntered off to the North Shore Surf Club, ready to rock and roll like never before.

Being soused at 6 in the evening is fine when it is 6 in the evening; come 11 or 12 o'clock of a prospective all-nighter, it kinda sucks. The euphoria of 6 became the happiness of 7, the indifference of 8, the drowsiness of 9, the crankiness of 10, and the near-desperation that followed as I waged an unwinnable battle to stay awake and enthusiastic. My post-drunken stupor caused me not to enjoy Scrawl and to leave in the middle of the Pastels' set. But damn, it made me happy to discover the happy hour.

7. David Lester's Guitar Freakout

I had missed Mecca Normal several times in the last couple of years, and as their set neared its end I was happy to have been reminded of why I've always liked them. But I wasn't prepared for what came next. Herr Lester loosened a couple of tuning pegs and began hammering on his guitar in a way I'd never seen or heard before. Over the top, he produced a brutal sonic wail—sound enough for half a dozen musicians—while underneath, almost hidden, one could hear a scheme

of ethereal, beautifully subtle notes. A third of the way into this tender maelstrom, I recall thinking "poor Thurston," and sinking into a near-transcendent coma. I emerged from the trance as he tossed the guitar into the air, then caught it and silenced it against his thigh. I whispered a breathy "wow," my innards in a vibrating stew.

8. Watching Heidi Giggle at Jad Fair on Friday at 10 a.m.

To be honest, I kinda found Jad's screeching, often unmiked, always atonal songs of love and friendship and other neat stuff mildly amusing at best and pretty damned annoying at worst. But I enjoyed the hell out of Heidi's nonstop laughter at his antics. His silliness was evidently just the tonic for a tired, hungry, hungover dancer. Her reaction made me like Jad Fair a little, and love Heidi a little more.

9. The Jokes about Sub Pop's Lame Barbecue

Friday afternoon, our local strapped-for-cash heroes sponsored a barbecue at Evergreen State College, a veritable mill for bong-toting hippies. The nifty little convention program promised "salmon, marinated vegetables, and polenta," and even went so far as to state that "vegans will be accommodated." All right, so no one could truly expect Sup Pop to ply four hundred people with vast mounds of salmon. But damn—by the looks of things, they had no intentions of feeding more than thirty or forty. With the exception of Susan Tapert—Ms. Omnipresent Seattle Scene—no one I talked to got so much as a potato chip.

I could drone on for pages about what a crappy thing this was. K Records sold around four hundred passes to the convention, and I reckon a thousand or more people attended some part of it. Sub Pop would have to know that more than a few dozen folks would show up for the free food. True, Sub Pop doesn't owe us a thing, but with a promise they obviously had no intention of keeping, they dragged a couple hundred people to the

LEFT TO RIGHT ACROSS SPREAD: JAD FAIR AND THE PASTELS; SLEEPYHEAD, JAMES CANTY (NATION OF ULYSSES), BEAT HAPPENING (PHOTOS, MICHAEL GALINSKY)

outskirts of Olympia, only to send them grumbling and hungry back to town. If they didn't have the resources to pull it off, they should have canceled the thing, or at least made it clear we'd need to bring our own food. It all showed a total lack of class, and I stop just short of wishing the much-rumored bankruptcy upon them.

Ah, but I still feel so good. So let's look at the positive side of this mostly bogus event. The crummy barbecue did form a bond among us disgruntled masses, and was the source of many witticisms. One wag suggested that there had been plenty of food—until Tad showed up. And Rick from Minneapolis surmised that Sub Pop had offered Limited Edition Food.

10. None of Your Business

If you weren't there—and, with one exception, you weren't—you wouldn't quite understand.

11. The Nap

My nap lasted three hours. It was three hours of muscle death, of open-mouthed, drooling unconsciousness. The nap fully relieved me of the hangover and fatigue that could have dampened the evening, if not the rest of the weekend. I woke energetic and refreshed.

I had tried to fight the urge to nap, since it meant missing some of the early show at the North Shore. And I did miss all but the last couple of songs from an absolutely great-sounding band called Unwound. (Who are they? Where are they from? Anything on vinyl?) Yet I knew even as I reveled in their torrid sound that the trade-off had been necessary to pace myself through the rest of the week. After never quite being able to get Jad Fair in focus that morning and feeling like crap all afternoon, I had sworn off drinking for the rest of the convention. Two or three shows, 8 to 11 bands a day, was too much for anyone—except probably that guitar guy from the Derelicts who's been to every show that you or I or anyone from Seattle has ever been to. From this point on, I let myself take time off and skip a show when I became band-weary. I may have lost out on a

couple of mighty fine groups, but I'm sure I enjoyed what I did see much more.

12. The Fastbacks

An hour of pure and powerful pop/punk that had my head bobbing from beginning to end. I had only seen them before as a three-piece. This time, the presence of on-again off-again guitarist Lulu blew the other shows out of the water. Bet you any amount of money that Kurt Bloch was a real weird guy in high school. But the fucker sure can play guitar.

13. Girl Trouble

Before the show, I approached Kurt (Girl Trouble's singer, who I felt I knew after having seen them play 18 times) to ask whether for my birthday I could get one of tonight's special Girl Trouble prizes. I don't mind grabbing, clawing, and scratching my way to the booty he hurls to the crowd, but tonight there would be more competition than usual, and with my exalted day approaching I hoped for special consideration. Kurt graciously agreed.

Midway through the set, he began sprinkling special prizes onto the audience. He stopped near me and tossed a prize into my waiting hand. It was a cool one, too—liquid ultra-green eye shadow! Imagine my surprise when Kurt later announced that there was a special birthday boy in the house (me! me! me!) and—ignoring the bogus claims of several greedy impostors—presented me with my very own Girl Trouble/Tacoma T-shirt. Never mind that it was an extra-extra large and could fit a family of four with room to spare . . . my life felt complete for the first time since my first orgasm.

Of course Girl Trouble rocked. A couple of years ago, my housemate Monster Brains said to me, "Man, that Kurt sure is a sexpot." Never was it more evident as Kurt pranced, ran in place, and gyrated like all hell in a pair of black, skintight short shorts. Girl Trouble is simply the greatest.

14. Ian Working the Door

At Friday night's show, Fugazi's Ian MacKaye—likely the most widely known of the convention performers—spent several hours ushering at the Capitol Theater. He was polite and pleasant, and I respect his willingness to spend time doing this. It's no big deal, but it's another reason I call this scene my own: Ian and Calvin [Johnson, of convention-sponsoring K Records and the band Beat Happening] are approachable people who live like this. The same cannot be said of Axl Rose or Bruce Springsteen or, for that matter, of Perry Farrell.

15. Half-Price Coffee Day at the Dancing Goat

My birthday coincided with the third anniversary of the Dancing Goat, an outrageously overpriced espresso den in downtown Olympia. For their special day, they cut prices in half, an offer too exceptional to miss. As a birthday treat I had three double lattes in the course of a few hours. Any who know me may find me a little high-strung and irritating under the best of circumstances. Pump a little caffeine into my system and I become damned near intolerable. But hell . . . today was my day to have fun.

16. Getting a Free Record from Some Dude

At the Dancing Goat, some dude walked up to me and asked, "Wanna free record?" He handed me an unidentified white vinyl 7-inch and strolled away. When I played it, I thought it was incredibly cool. But who is it? If anyone knows, tell me.

17. Finding Cheap Food in Olympia

I'd envisioned Olympia as a pristine little hippie community, rife with enormous $2.50 breakfasts and ultracheap vegetarian cafes. After wandering from place to place finding six-dollar sandwiches on menus, Heidi and I began to approach young, hip-looking Oly natives for their advice on cheap eateries. One said no such place existed. Another raved about a place we could not find. A third guy said, "You can get a pretty good lunch at the Urban Onion for about ten dollars." Ten dollars?! Ten fucking dollars?! I have never—never—spent ten bucks on a meal, especially lunch—and if I had, I sure wouldn't recommend a ten-dollar lunch to someone who had just asked about a cheap place to eat.

No one had a helpful answer. We might as well have had hair sprouting from our eyeballs. Most chuckled smugly and threw out something like, "Sounds to me like you're looking for a McDonald's, bud." Hell, someone approaches me on the streets of Seattle with that question, I assume a kindred soul, who, like me, searches only for a cheap meal amid a harsh and uncaring universe. In Olympia, the question seemed to label me a clown or a leper.

Eventually we found a Japanese deli and a falafel joint, both of which offered decent, semi-hearty meals for two or three bucks.

18. Believe It or Not, the Smoke- and Alcohol-Free Environment

I'm not a "Just Say No" kind of dude. I may have given up drugs a decade ago, but it was for personal, not moral reasons; and though I'm a nonsmoker, I'm not usually offended by cigarette smoke. Lord knows, I've ended enough nights facedown on a dance floor not to be mistaken as straight-edge. But eight hours a night in wall-to-wall smoke could have proved pretty oppressive after a day or two. Maybe I'm just getting old and farty, but it was a pleasure to pass five days with no drunken fights, in an atmosphere of congenial and coherent encounters. Some of us drank, sometimes quite a lot—me on Thursday being a case in point. And of course there was the occasional drunken loudmouth and testosterone casualty to contend with. But the pervasive "Let's get fucked up!" attitude was happily lacking, an agreeable change from the usual night at the Off Ramp.

19. Finally Meeting Sean, the Cool Punk-Rock Kid

Over the last year or so, I've noticed this 15- or 16-year-old at the all-ages shows, who has a shaved head, a nifty style of dancing (he does a little chicken-like step that I love), and gives every impression of being a really terrific person. On Saturday night, I finally met him. His name is Sean, and he's every bit as bright, personable, and likeable as I'd envisioned him to be. He's just what punk-rock kids are supposed to be; the sort that gives this embittered old world a little hope.

20. L7

They were so good, it was scary. This was easily the most hard-driving, ferocious set of the convention, and in some ways as flawless an hour of music as I've ever seen. L7 have always been fine live performers, but this was ridiculous—like the hell-bent stage-diving crowd, the band was absolutely out of control. They could obviously be a "success" on a big scale—and we can only hope that when the major-label snake dangles the apple of AOR commercial stardom, L7 will stick to the DIY indie status they seem to love so genuinely. A tough choice, but perhaps the inspirational, integrity-affirming nature of the convention will help keep them on our side. [Word is, L7 have now signed to Slash—Ed.]

21. The Convention Was Well Thought-Out

Enjoying the sound system during L7's set, I began to appreciate how well the convention had been handled. Security, ticket distribution, concessions, and other aspects seemed to be handled with humane intelligence. The IPUC organizers [principally Calvin and Candice of K Records] deserve credit for how quickly potential problems were dealt with. Sound at the Capitol Thursday night had been pretty murky (prompting Calvin to ask the crowd what they expected for five bucks). By Friday night, major bugs had been conquered; by Saturday, the sound approached the impeccable. Elsewhere, if something is fucked up, then fucked up it stays—unless it takes a turn for the more fucked up. In Olympia, organizers and volunteers thought on their feet, with attendees' welfare and enjoyment in mind.

22. The Crowd and My Heroism during Fugazi

Punk-rock crowds, critics, and performers are generally split on the issue of stage-diving. I see the phenomenon as inherently neither good nor bad; sometimes it's great, other times it's a drag. During L7, for example, the action in the pit was fast and furious, and it was clear that band and audience alike would have it no other way. Nearly everyone up front either consented and willed to leap off the stage onto others' bobbing heads and/or consented and willed to have their own heads leapt upon. I fully appreciate this mind-set; the closest I have come to nirvana (the metaphysical state, not the band) has been amid a sweaty heap of punk-rock bodies as noise and feedback rained down on me. (My parents do not understand this.) Such controlled cathartic mayhem can be the best thing in the world if the participants have fun and take personal responsibility to see that no serious injury occurs.

But I thought the situation during Fugazi's set called for different behavior. First, the band has been very clear over the years that it wants no one onstage during their shows, for fear of damaging audience members or equipment. Foes of Fugazi are no doubt leaping to their feet, crying, "Fuck them; what gives them the right to dictate; I paid my money, I'll do whatever the fuck I want, etc.," and to some degree I'd probably agree.

The key factor here was that the crowd echoed the professed desire of the band. My personal estimate is that 90-plus percent of us folk in the pit didn't want two-hundred-pound barrages of bone and boot cascading down on our heads. But a small, small minority of the people in attendance had either a) no grasp of the bleeding obvious, or b) no respect for the wishes and concerns of those around them, and chose to claw, scratch, kick, and pummel their way onto the stage.

One glance at me reveals me to be a totally weak and skinny dude, and my ability to impose physical dominion upon another creature generally begins and ends with Hoarding, my one-pound pet ferret. However, on this evening I discovered that a 130-pound weight wrapped around a would-be stage diver's waist, shoulders, or legs can be enough to discourage that person. This tactic was successful time after time, and by my count I kept up to a dozen people off the stage. The pinnacle of my triumph was a ten-minute battle with a tall, bearded scoundrel who tried repeatedly to use a friend's cupped hand to boost him onto the stage. Although another friend kept asking him to knock it off ("John, no one wants you up there!"), his determination remained fierce and undaunted ("Fuck 'em, man, I'm up there—aaarrrrrgggg . . ."). Each time I was ripe for the challenge, positioning myself between them or reacting with a tug to foil his latest effort. After a dozen tactful interventions I sensed he had caught on to my meddling and was about to smack me one, so I slipped out and watched the rest from the back. My fellow self-appointed heroes apparently took up the challenge, and this probable Viking in a past life never made it onstage.

23. "When I Woke Up, I Had a Tear in My Eye."

Much as I wanted to stay in Olympia the last night for the "disco dancing 'til dawn" and for Sunday's brunch and cakewalk, I had to give them up. Heidi, who had been a trouper all weekend—despite fighting off impending illness—had taken a turn for the worse and was now downright sick. To top things off, the bed we had scammed at a friend's house was reclaimed, and the time had come to put a close to our excellent adventure. We left Olympia after 3 and arrived at Heidi's place at 4:30. She took all of ninety seconds to plunge into a deep sleep. I lay on the bed for over an hour, wired and uplifted, my body tensed with ecstatic punk-rock convulsions, before finally drifting off.

I woke around noon with a case of something akin to post-natal depression. An empty sadness filled me, and a tear rolled from my left eye. The IPUC had been more than just a helluva lot of fun. It had affected me at a deeper level; it was something terribly important, maybe life-changing. I lay there, quiet yet emotionally charged, strangely content in my sadness, yet yearning for so much more. If only I could carry this feeling with me at all times . . . And if only everyone everywhere could feel like this a little more often, I tell you the world would be a so much happier, peaceful, and better place to be.

Never for money, always for love. Oh . . . and fuck Lollapalooza. ✪

THE MEKONS

If you read the coverage they received over the past year, said the Mekons in 1991, "you'd think we were all suicidal." In fact their acrimonious divorce from major label A&M had proved liberating: "We're setting the agenda for ourselves again." **BILL MEYER** spoke to band mainstays Jon Langford and Tom Greenhalgh in Chicago, a city that would soon become home to multiple band members.

The Mekons' story reads like one of their songs—hilarious, tragic, and surreal by turns. A musical force since their first skeptical punk-rock singles of the late 1970s, they emerged during the second half of the 1980s as perhaps the most perceptive, meaningful, and musically inclusive band still at work in rock 'n' roll. From the landmark 1985 *Fear and Whiskey* to 1988's *So Good It Hurts*, the Mekons' independently released albums were what one of their lyrics called "a community center for the hopeless." When the erratic indie distribution system failed to get their records into stores, the Mekons went to A&M, and their disastrous two-year relationship with that label dramatized the consequences for a band that steps out of the rickety independent-music industry and works with a typical major label. This year has seen much ink spilled in the rock press over the Mekons' misfortunes: A&M's failure to adequately promote the band's *Rock 'n' Roll* and *F.U.N. '90* records; their refusal to release the band's excellent 1991 album *The Curse of the Mekons* in America; the precipitous departure of their long-standing rhythm section; and an abortive US summer tour in which the Mekons ended up canceling most of their dates. Yet this past November found the Mekons touring across the United States, full of plans and hopes for the band's future. In separate conversations just before their Chicago performance, Mekons main men Jon Langford and Tom Greenhalgh talked about life after *The Curse of the Mekons*.

The Mekons' story up through last summer has been pretty well documented. What has happened since then?
JL: That's pretty well documented too. So much so that it appears to be totally depressing and boring. If you read [the coverage], you'd think we were all suicidal. Actually it's been a really good year for us. One of the best—we got rid of the whole major-label thing that was preventing us from doing stuff. We're setting the agenda for ourselves again, and we decide what we want to do now, and it makes a lot more sense. Also we've got a new rhythm section and that's changed things quite a lot.
TG: John Langley (ex-Blue Aeroplanes) has been playing drums, and recently Sarah Corina joined us on bass.
JL: Sarah used to be in the Bomb Party, and she was in a band called Die Cheerleader in London as well. I've

known her for a long time so it seemed like an obvious choice. We discovered it was nice having half men, half women onstage, for the chemistry.
Your next record sounds like it will be a concept album. Could you say a bit about it?
JL: It's about LOVE—L-U-V. It's a very loving and sensitive record. No, it's a collection of love songs. Not necessarily quite the same as anyone else would write them. It's just songs, about the subject of love . . . a savage analysis of sexiness.
TG: We've recorded eight new songs, basically just me and John doing stuff, with drums and bass on computers, and with Susie playing violin and Sally singing. And we're quite happy with it.
Is the new material that you and John have done anything like F.U.N. '90 *[the Mekons' 1990 EP of covers done in a dub/dance style]?*
TG: No, it's straight songs, basically. One of the things we thought, after Steve and Lu (Goulding and Edmonds, the band's previous rhythm section) left, was that it would be an opportunity for us to work in a different way, just the two of us . . . We'd had the idea of doing that for quite a long time—just doing stuff without rehearsing a band, and doing it differently. Not necessarily experimental studio stuff, either, because these days it's not just a case of using a drum machine—you can like compute it and store anything. You can fiddle with it until you're blue in the face and it can actually sound quite real, that's the sort of frightening thing. Anyway, that was one thing we sort of wanted to do, and we did it, and it was the right time to do it. Now we're back to having more of a band; we'll do some recording with the band, for an album. We already have a title—*I ❤ Mekons*. The record has a loose theme: all the songs basically are love songs.
JL: We've got four more tracks to record. The ones we've done have gone down very well with people who've heard them, and we've had some surprising offers, after all you may have read about the total despair and despondency, the Mekons-groomed-for-failure sort of thing. I think these tracks are really good, and I'm not going back to the independent treadmill unless it's totally necessary . . . I'm not going to sign to a major unless it's someone we can work with. We gotta get the records out over here.

So you see the indie treadmill as worse than the major-label treadmill?

JL: They're both bad. The indie thing is full of enthusiasts, maybe, but there's no system of distribution here. When Rough Trade went down we lost *The Curse* in England; we've lost so many albums in our career through independent distributors crashing, you know, it's just like banging your head against a wall. I like the people who work for these companies, they've got the best intentions—but they get kind of greedy, you know. Rough Trade in England got really greedy and lost touch with what they were trying to do.

Do you reckon you'll go with a major?

JL: I don't know yet. If they impress us they can get our records where people can buy them, that's all we want. We don't want to sell . . . there was an implication that we were demanding to sell a hundred thousand records at A&M. We just want people to be able to buy the record. A&M couldn't distribute the record, and that was what we had signed with them for—proper distribution. We did everything else—in no way did we ever cause them any difficulties. We actually bent over backwards to do everything they wanted us to do. They prevented us doing things like touring, they were saying "Don't tour," you know. I think we've got a reputation for being difficult out of this, yet I don't think we were difficult. We actually were cringingly nice to A&M. We'd probably have gone in there and been a lot more difficult if we'd known how incompetent and useless they are.

Will the Mekons' back catalog become available again?

JL: I hope everything's going to be re-released. One of the things we're going for now is to try to buy back the trail of albums we've left with companies all over. We want to put it out so you can buy the whole of the Mekons' stuff. People are constantly asking us for it. Maybe it's only a small percentage of the population that wants *The English Dancing Master*, but it would be great if it were available. It's not a big deal to press up a couple of thousand, but we haven't got the resources to do it. We haven't got any resources at all, this tour is like the last stab at . . . it's financially ruining us to do this tour!

There has been talk of a Club Mekons tour, with a group of Mekons past and present taking a Mekons multimedia extravaganza from town to town.

JL: There's no solid plan at the moment, but we want to do it. We want to do a looser thing where we turn up in a town and play a smaller club for three nights, make it a bit more relaxed and do something a bit expansive, get more people involved. That's really all it is at the moment. I don't think we'll do it for the next LP, I think we'll do a full-fledged tour to get to places we can't get to this time.

TG: It's something that has been talked about for three or four years but for practical reasons hasn't happened, partly because we'd need support for it and the support hasn't been there. We don't want to just do tours, the same sort of thing again and again. We want to keep it fresh and try different ideas. It's there, we'll do something with it.

Are you recording tonight's show for radio? [A mobile recording truck was parked in front of the club where the Mekons were to play that night.]

JL: That's just for our own benefit. We're compiling stuff for a Mekons live record. Timothy Powell's got five shows on 24-track. I was out at his warehouse last week where we mixed three tracks from the show at the [Chicago] Exit in 1986. It was weird because the multi-tracks had not been out of the box since that night—we took it off the tape machine and put it in a box. Five years later we come and get it out. It sounded great, like a beautiful recording of a completely fucking mental show. There's some good playing on it, which was surprising. "Sweet Dreams" is on it, and "Hello Cruel World." Basically we're going to mix as many different songs as we can, get the best versions of songs

THE MEKONS
The Curse of the Mekons
(Blast First)

I know it's been said before, but it bears repeating: major labels are scum. Their fairly recent focus on the "alternative" market, and the spate of signings that resulted, have ended up in promising careers almost destroyed; the co-optation of college radio by smarmy middle-aged guys in Nine Inch Nails T-shirts; and a fragmentation into mutually exclusive "scenes" (god forbid a Nirvana fan should be caught buying an album by Eyeless in Gaza). The Mekons' previous album, Rock'n'Roll, didn't sell well enough for A&M, so the company sabotaged their subsequent EP—did you even know there was one?—and dumped the band like a used sock.

Mekons' fans will fork out the $12 for this import, and they'll be right. Though not quite as complex and powerful as Rock'n'Roll, and not following up on the dancey direction taken on the EP, this is still a superior album, from the anthemic "The Curse" down to "100% Song." Sure, there aren't any surprises there, but when it ain't broken, why fix it? —Elisabeth Vincentelli

THE MEKONS
I ♥ Mekons
(Quarterstick)

The ♥ has become very much a riot grrrl thing in recent times (isn't it astonishing, incidentally, how many "alternative" types felt the need to attack Bikini Kill's splendid putdown "Thurston Hearts the Who"?). As it happens, the Mekons had a hand in the origins of RG, as "Millionaire," the satire on sex, money, and power that opens their new album, makes clear. "Lust corrodes my body/I've lost count of my lovers/But I can count my money/ Forever and forever/I love a millionaire," sings Sally Timms in inimitable

from different shows and see how much we can get together, maybe mixing it onto DAT from 24-track, because it's pretty good quality.

Is it all Chicago stuff?

JL: Yeah, maybe because we did that New York thing, we wanted to do something that wasn't just off of cassettes like New York. It should be quite good.

The Mekons, never a jealous band, have often lent musical and producing skills to others. Langford's best known extra-Mekons ventures have been as a member of Leeds politico-punk trio the Three Johns and as producer of the superb Johnny Cash tribute 'Til Things Are Brighter . . ., which benefited the anti-AIDS Terrence Higgins Trust, while Greenhalgh co-produced Michelle Shocked's second album.

You've been producing quite a lot.

JL: Yeah, I'm starting to enjoy it again. I had a bad year in 1990, and I decided not to [produce] anymore. I kept producing things which didn't get released. Or the bands split up, or I didn't get paid. It seemed completely pointless.

You've produced some American bands like Jonestown.

JL: Yeah, that was great. I got to go to Minneapolis and spend some time and work with a band that seem really good.

What will you do next?

JL: After this tour, I'll be working with a band called Wreck, a Chicago band from Wax Trax. I think I'm producing Cud, who are from Leeds. Ironically they've just signed to A&M in England—and A&M in England are really keen for me to produce their LP. It's just upside down, you know, the left arm not knowing what the right toes are doing! In fact they—A&M in the UK—were quite sympathetic . . . they were saying how bad everyone at A&M in America was!

What's the status of the Three Johns?

JL: Sort of dead at the moment. Hibernating, fairly terminally.

What happened?

JL: Well, don't know. Nothing, really, nothing happened; that was the problem. We might do something if we feel like it, but it's a question of time and commitments and I've got other things I'm more interested in.

You did some shows with Tony Maimone [of Pere Ubu, and a guest Mekon on their European spring tour] last month.

JL: Yeah, we did three shows in New York with the Killer Shrews, meaning Tony and Gary Lucas. We started planning it in 1988, when it was really me and Marc Riley (of the Fall and the Creepers) and Tony and Gary and Steve Goulding. We were going to do an album in Chicago with the mobile that's here tonight. Then the company, Red Rhino, went bust. I was actually marooned here for ten days because I couldn't change my ticket to get home. It was a complete fuckup.

[Last month] we did a week in the studio and a week in Gary's flat. We wrote like 12 songs, recorded them on DAT live, did three shows, and recorded each show. Now Gary's quite busy. He's got a lot of contacts, he's busy sending stuff off to people to see if we can't get a deal. I'll just take it as it is, the smoother it goes the better. If somebody says, Yeah, we'll give you some money . . . if they'll put the tracks out we've already recorded live, that's cool, we're happy with 'em. If they want them recorded in the studio, that's slightly more difficult, but manageable.

Do you work outside the Mekons, too, Tom?

TG: Yeah, I've done quite a lot of production and had some interesting experiences, but I began to get a bit disillusioned with it all. I was working with people I didn't particularly want to work with and whose music I didn't particularly like. Since then I've been working with some other people, a much lower-key sort of thing. I also played in a band called Edward the Second and the Red Hot Polkas, a sort of dub/reggae/English country music/dance experimental thing. We did a couple of albums. We worked with the Mad Professor, who is a dub mixer in London. He mixed some tracks on the second album, but then I left the band, along with the guy who founded it, due to band politics. Lately I've been working with John Gill, who was involved in the Mekons over the years. It's difficult because neither of us have any money. John works as an engineer, so we're grabbing time when the studio's free, but it's low-key . . . I'm not much interested in producing stuff to be released tomorrow. If something's good and we're real happy with it, maybe we can persuade somebody to put it out, but at this stage it's kind of in the background. ✪

cool, smooth fashion, while the band powers away in thrash/drone mode behind her.

If the Mekons are an important part of the punk-rock legacy so gleefully appropriated by the riot grrrls, they go way beyond mere historical interest—this is their most focused and powerful set of songs since 1987's *Honky Tonkin'*. Just as it seemed their endless problems with record labels might have worn them down, here they are with another essential chapter in the long-running Mekons story.

It's largely the mixture as before—a masterful stew of punk, folk, and country idioms, coupled with allusive lyrics saturated with wit, intellect, and emotion—though there are shifts in emphasis. Sally sings more songs, including "Love Letter," on which she abandons her usual suavity for a torchy attack; a trio of songs in the middle breathe new life into the forgotten body of punky reggae. Just check out the violin- and harmonica-laden dub of "St. Valentine's Day"); and they've developed the double axis of lead guitar and violin into a formidable aural assault weapon. If you'd begun to think the Mekons could no longer do it for you, that they'd lost the ability to surprise, this album will send you soaring.—*Jean Debbs*

NICK CAVE

When literate Australian goth Nick Cave was interviewed by **MATTHEW HALL** in 1992, he was already almost a decade into a solo career that has lasted far longer than the lifespan of the Birthday Party, the great band in which he made his reputation, and has extended beyond music into books and film. His musical output is characterized by a shifting cast of supporting musicians under the name the Bad Seeds, whose earliest incarnation is captured in a delightful 1984 live review (see sidebar).

Nick Cave and I meet in a London hotel bar. It's a home from home for besuited businessmen discussing their latest acquisitions on the international money market and new ventures into Eastern Europe. The peach- and apricot-colored rooms in this joint cost around £325 per night. That's pounds, guys, English money. Double it for dollars and buy yourself a drink.

Dressed in a red '50s-style cardigan and dapper blue strides, Nick spends the first few minutes rearranging the room to make us more comfy. He opens all the shutters and pulls up the blinds to let the sunlight stream into the darkened basement room. We drink bottled fizzy water with ice and lemon. He smokes Marlboro Lights.

The evidence suggests we've all got to arrive sometime. After a decade or so of global wandering, things are going swimmingly for Nick Cave. He's now a 34-something kinda guy: following a "public" school education, he has a wife, Viviane; a kid; a happy home; a sharp line in apparel; and a multi-pronged career safe from the global-recession blues. He doesn't like people to presume, but we do know he's cut his drug intake. What sets Nick aside from guys of similar station is that he hasn't spent the past decade wheelin' and dealin' in real estate, grafting on the stock exchange, or developing a career in banking. No way, siree. Nick just sang a few songs. His latest collection being his seventh album, *Henry's Dream*. It also features the alternative supergroup known as the Bad Seeds.

"The band is," announces Nick, "Mick Harvey, who plays acoustic and rhythm guitar; Blixa Bargeld, electric guitar; Conway Savage, an Aussie, piano; Martyn Casey, another Aussie, bass; and Thomas Wydler, drums. It is a really strong version of the Bad Seeds. Everybody seems to get on well. Live, it is certainly the most powerful version of the band."

But supergroups being supergroups, things tend to get complicated. "Not only because everyone lives in different parts of the world, but everybody has another band to keep afloat at the same time," he explains. "Martyn (of the Triffids) lives in London, Mick Harvey (Crime and the City Solution) lives in Sydney, Conway (erstwhile Australian piano-plinking celebrity) lives in Melbourne, Blixa Bargeld (from Einstürzende Neubauten) and Thomas Wydler (the only "rock" drummer who should be allowed a solo) live in Berlin. I live in Brazil."

Practicing must be hell. "Hey, Blixa! Can you give us a lift to rehearsal?"

"It's not that difficult to keep them together," suggests Cave. "I just say I want to make a record at a particular point and send my manager off to organize it. For him, it's a logistical nightmare. If in September we say, 'Right, we want to make an album at the start of the year,' then we have to work out how long until it's released. Then we need part of the year free for touring."

It's a matter of finding a window in their respective diaries. *Henry's Dream* was recorded in LA, New York, and Melbourne, helped along by David Briggs, probably best known for welding together Neil Young's records. As far as the dynamics of the band are concerned, it's something of a departure for Cave.

"I write the songs, although it changes from album to album . . . How much the band are allowed to contribute musically and even personality-wise. The record we made before this one, *The Good Son*, was a very definite type of record, and certain elements of the group had to be kept on a fairly short leash. Namely Blixa, for example. He had to tailor his guitar because the music was far more melodic. On *Henry's Dream* everyone was given absolute freedom to do what they wanted."

"One of the things that began to bug me about *The Good Son*," he adds, "was that everything was written before we went into the studio. We knew all the melody lines. It was very much constructed in the studio and it wasn't really a 'band' thing. It didn't have much feel behind it. With *Henry's Dream*, we were all in the studio pounding away at the song at the same time."

Strangely enough, but perhaps not, *Henry's Dream* contains much individual character. The new strategy works: you can distinguish individuals. Listen to the Triffids' tougher moments and you'll recognize Martyn Casey crunching away. One of the album's finest moments, "When I First Came to Town," contains vocal embellishments courtesy of Conway Savage.

"The way the songs eventuate," demonstrates Nick, "is, I come in and have the basic song written on the piano. 'Papa Won't Leave You, Henry' was basically two

NICK CAVE AND THE BAD SEEDS
I-Beam, San Francisco
June 18, 1984

Leaning on the stage, raven-haired girls with crimsoned mouths stretched their arms up toward Nick Cave's pipestem ankles. I thought of what he had said on the radio. "I never thought I'd be alive," he'd told the interviewer that afternoon, "at the end of another American tour." It seemed these rapacious-looking fans would start snapping bits off any minute. But they simply stroked the extremities of their idol as he flung himself about in a wailing lather. They might have been comforting him. At times he did seem worried.

With one exception, the other musicians onstage—caught in what most observers judged an untenable mess—looked beyond comfort. Professionals who presumably expect to earn their keep playing music, they found themselves posted onstage with little to do but be stared at while lending atmospheric support to Nick Cave's poetic vision.

Certainly, the failures of offbeat artists can be more intriguing than the successes of stereotypes. Despite the painful tedium which settled in on that night, I was probably not the only one present who kept listening, later, to past and current recordings by this peculiar, obsessive artist. His post–Birthday Party imagery has by no means lost its fingers-down-the-throat-of-love febrility. What has changed, both at the I-Beam and on *From Her to Eternity*, his current LP with the Bad Seeds, is that music itself has been put on a very tight leash. One might guess that Cave has become less interested in music, more interested in poetry, since the days of those menacingly balanced late Birthday Party EPs *Bad Seed* and *Mutiny!*

If that's the case, he faces a vexing decision. It's no accident that the lead-off song on the new LP is by Leonard Cohen, wizard of both worlds. But even Cohen, veteran of the recurrent choice, might hesitate to advise Nick Cave in this matter. Poets are obscure. Pop stars are the objects of attentions not easily renounced.

The exception to the bad vibes afflicting the Seeds that night was Blixa Bargeld, of world-standard noise band Einstürzende Neubauten. Why an artist of his stature was traveling with this act—like an apparition from still another world—was something of a mystery. A species, perhaps, of visionary folie à deux.

Throughout the set, Blixa stood, nobly intact and perhaps rather blotto, in his customary uniform of bondage, harnessed further by what seemed a genuine dedication to the aims of the tour. Nobody stroked his ankles: an oversight I should like to nominate as historic.—*Katherine Spielmann*

chords; the verses are just hitting away on a G minor, or whatever it is, endlessly. That was all the information the band had: just bang, bang, bang, on the G minor. Everyone sort of looked at each other and said, 'Well, that's it?' And I said, 'Yeah, that's it. You do whatever you want to do.'"

There've been other changes for Nick Cave besides the way the band works. After several years in Berlin, shortly before the fall of the wall, Nick up and left, and relocated to, erm, São Paulo, Brazil. While Brazil is probably a swell place, global goths probably wouldn't have bet their mascara on Nick Cave shifting there. The question had to be asked . . .

"I've always had the freedom to live where I want. I've never had responsibilities to anyone else. Being Australian, I've been cut adrift and allowed to float around the world. I'd been obsessed with going to Brazil for a long time and we managed to organize a tour there. As soon as I got there, I decided I wanted to stay. I met an incredible girl on the second day, which also helped. I was intending to go there for a week or so, but I've been there for a couple of years now. I've got a wife and a 9-month-old child. So I find myself living in Brazil!"

Rain forests, the Amazon, Copacabana, coffee, glamorous soccer teams, Mardi Gras. Shantytowns and death squads. And unlike Berlin, the sun shines.

"It is insane," confirms Cave. "There is no other city in the world quite like Rio. Visually, it's my favorite city I've seen, but I wouldn't live there. The difference between Rio and where I live in São Paulo reminds me of Sydney and Melbourne. Sydney being a beach-type community. It's much more extreme in Rio . . . the sun, bodies, more 'surface' type of things. Then you go to Melbourne which seems to have more of a soul to it, in a way. There's a great difference between the Cariocas, the Rio people, and the people from São Paulo. São Paulo is just huge, the third- or fourth-biggest city in the world. It's massive. You go to some high point and as far as you can see in any direction is solid skyscrapers. There is nothing to see there, it's not a tourist town, it's just a great place—very chaotic."

But don't expect Nick to try conquering the Portuguese-speaking world with deft marketing tactics. There'll be no Gloria Estefan–style release of *Henry* in Portuguese. "Ha! My Portuguese is not as good as it should be," he admits and you hear disappointment in his voice. "I did take lessons, but I'm a moron at languages. But if I stay in Brazil I'm going to have to learn how to play soccer—or I'll be the laughingstock of my street! All dads play and teach their sons how to play football in Brazil!"

And so Nick introduces the other change in his life: Luke, born halfway through 1991. The arrival of his son opened Cave's eyes, launched him on a journey of self-discovery, uncovered neglected traits within himself, and made him think about things many of us take for granted. Like the future.

"Becoming a father has made me take on the role of protector, which I've never ever had anything to do with in my life. In the past, my life was so self-obsessed and self-interested that I went where I wanted to go and fuck everybody else. I never concerned myself with the problems of anyplace I lived: the political and social problems. Now I'm being forced to notice things. It's horrifying to have your eyes opened to the way the world is. I have to make decisions as to where I want the kid to live—where I want to live or where I want to take my family. America, or England, or Australia—or stay in Brazil. It's a difficult decision. We do want to live in an English-speaking country, but do I want my child to be an American? A horrifying thought. Or an English kid? Equally frightening!"

Often, when children mix with the music biz, parents speak of awakenings within during the simultaneous making of record and sproglet. For example, current UK chart-toppers Shakespears Sister recorded their LP while both women in the band were pregnant. The subsequent album was titled *Hormonally Yours*. Does Nick feel any affinity with his sisters-in-rock?

"I didn't have the baby so I didn't suffer hormonal things. The fact that I was a father when I made the record . . . there is one song that is related to that—possibly the most violent and angry song on the record: 'Papa Won't Leave You, Henry.' It's a song of awakening to the horrors of the world."

For those who came in late . . . Nick Cave's first band, the Birthday Party (né the Boys Next Door), trashed the contemporary music scene at the start of the '80s. They picked scraps of punk from the garbage, fried them, put them through the blender, mashed them, beat them, cooked them again, and served them up with double-killer chili. The "establishment" either missed it, or recoiled in horror. Kids loved it, and the group sculpted a new world order while George Bush was still refining his golf.

Things for Australian kids haven't always been easy. Since the dawn of popular culture, geographical isolation and a small population has forced any Australian band wishing to interest more than family and friends to follow the example of '60s pioneers the Easybeats and get passports and plane tickets.

The schlock-rock contingent headed for the United States: Olivia Newton-John, Bee Gees, Peter Allen, Men at Work, INXS, Midnight Oil, and countless others who tragically failed to make their mark. To many Australians, this was justified revenge after America gave them David Cassidy, Van Halen, the Osmonds, and military bases.

For the less commercial-minded, Britain beckoned (its immigration laws, sympathetic to Australians, allowed them to live and work there reasonably unhindered for a few years). And, too, London declared itself the birthplace and center of punk rock and the "new wave." The fact that the "first" punk single was "I'm Stranded" by a Brisbane band called the Saints and that New York was swinging to a new groove a couple of years previously didn't matter to the Brits. Throughout the late '70s and '80s, after a few formative home years, off went Australia's pioneering young talent to spend time in exile: the Go-Betweens, the Moodists, the Triffids, the Apartments, the Scientists, Crime and the City Solution, etc. The Birthday Party were one of the first of the new breed to pack their bags.

Exercising his memory, Nick recalls, "Keith Glass [of Melbourne's Missing Link Records] said, 'Do you want to go to England?' We said, 'Oh yeah, England, oh fuck. Swinging England! When can we go?' Basically he bought us tickets and dumped us.

"We assumed we would never be successful when we were living in Australia," he adds. "We'd been playing the same venues and the same audience for three years before we managed to get out. We didn't have huge hopes, when the group went to England, that the English would suddenly understand us." The real England, not the place in the tourist brochures, can probably claim some sort of responsibility for turning the Birthday Party into what they became.

"I don't think anything we did in Australia except 'The Friend Catcher' and 'Mr. Clarinet,' those two singles, were worth anything at all," he states, and means it. "It was a load of crap basically. It was only after a while that the music became of some importance, that it became great—by some miracle.

"We were enraged by England—we were so pissed off by the place after about a year of living there. We hated the place—we hated English people. That's what the spirit of the Birthday Party was: an intense, blind, boiling hatred for England and English people. I don't feel that way anymore. I actually like England now and I like English people. But it's been years . . .

"It was the right decision to go to London," he adds. "Because everything was so mediocre there when we arrived. The bands were mediocre and no one knew what to do—they were weak and limp-wristed. In that culture the Birthday Party was able to rise up and be what it was—to be at absolute odds to that. If we had gone to New York that might not have happened."

So, love it or leave it, if you don't like the neighborhood, move out. The band headed to Berlin and began what would become a legendary episode in Cave's biography—one which would mean the ultimate demise of the Birthday Party. New things to see, new words to learn, new chums to make.

"When we got to Berlin it seemed like the right place. We instantly had tons of friends, and respect. There was an incredible community of really talented, really interesting people there. It was an incredibly wonderful period of my life. It was my second youth in Berlin. I'd had that happen in Melbourne in the punk-rock days, when we were let loose from school and could rampage around and be as obnoxious as we wanted. Then we went to England and all that was squashed—all our youth had been taken from us. We had to accept basic facts like having no money, living in squats, and the rest of the shit that happens in London: not knowing anybody, not being accepted into the English youth culture, always feeling alien to it. Then going to Berlin and finding we could do anything we wanted again. We could drink all night, we had really good friends, and it was an easygoing, relaxed way of life. And an intense creative scene."

Alongside making music with his Bad Seeds, Nick Cave has also tried his hand in the film world. He helped write the screenplay for the movie *Ghosts . . . of the Civil Dead*, a disturbing account of life in a maximum-security prison under lockdown. He also scored the chilling soundtrack with Blixa Bargeld and Mick Harvey, and acted in the film. He wasn't too bad either.

"Acting is a kind of indulgence," he says. "I don't really think I'm a good actor to begin with. If a role demanded talent or were at all challenging, I couldn't do it. I can do cameos and stuff where I sit around and mumble my lines. But if I had to develop the character, I couldn't. I don't feel confident in that area."

He has made a few other excursions into the film world, like *Dandy*. "It was an experimental film by an Australian/German director called Peter Sempel who paid us large sums of money to sit in front of his camera and play with a gun or a guitar. Me and Blixa were both involved in it. We were very poor at the time." More recently and perhaps significantly, he appears alongside *Thelma & Louise* "hunk" Brad Pitt in *Johnny Suede*, as wasted rock star Freak Storm.

"Blush, cringe!"

Huh?

"It's a light comedy. There are some genuinely funny moments in it, but I wouldn't do a film like that again."

It's a John Waters–style budget flick directed by Tom DiCillo. "Johnny" wants to be like '50s icon Ricky Nelson, and we follow his traipse in search of fame, love, and understanding. Freak Storm offers Johnny advice on chicks and how to get a record deal. In one of the best scenes, Freak donates a song to Johnny: a Cave-esque parody along the lines of "They call me Momma's boy, since my daddy went to the chair two seconds after I was born."

"A lot of my character was cut out," complains Cave. "In the toilet scene for example, I've come out after taking drugs, but the whole conversation where I talk about it has gone. What I liked about it at first was that Freak was a rock 'n' roll joke to begin with, but at the end, particularly in the last scene, he becomes a sinister personality, destroying lives. I liked that element. But overall it's a good-natured comedy."

So perhaps the new domestic reality will cause Nick to tread a little bit more carefully in future?

"This film thing is a risky business. I just saw a film called *First Power*, starring Lou Diamond Phillips. I remember going to an audition in Hollywood to play the bad guy—my one Hollywood audition—and that film is so bad. Lou Diamond Phillips is such a cocksucker! He's the good guy, of course! If I'd been in that film it would have destroyed my career. I can survive *Johnny Suede*, but I would never have survived that film!"

Something Nick does retain control over is his writing. Following the well-received first novel *And the Ass Saw the Angel*, are there any more writing plans?

"I do have a novel in my head, but I haven't sat down to it. I wrote the last one longhand, then typed it—I'd compose the sentence, then tap it out. Every sentence was extremely tailored; I'd write it over and over again to get it right and tap it in . . ."

A decade is a long time in showbiz, and Nick Cave has been kicking around for longer than that. In a business where most people are out to make fast bucks, the turnover of talent is high. Some ascending stars explode after leaving the launchpad; others offer only spasmodic contributions to the book of greatness. After arriving with deserved fanfare, those still held dear often thankfully exploded before they got too chubby: Hüsker Dü, Hendrix, Velvet Underground (well, maybe not, but you get the drift). Meanwhile, for others the difficult second, third, fourth albums rear their heads . . . see Jesus and Mary Chain, the Smiths, the Sugarcubes for recent examples. Who can say that by the turn of the century Teenage Fanclub will have a back catalog that is not only interesting but shows no visible pantyline?

"Just get better and better, you mean?" asks Cave

when questioned about the maintenance of his output. "I don't think I have released a dud. No way.

"As a songwriter, I am so in fear of drying up," he confesses. "I spend days in panic about it when nothing's coming and I'm supposed to have written a record and it's not happening. I wake up in a sweat, I have incredible dreams about it—madman's dreams about creative impotence.

"I just work extremely hard on it. It comes out of that panic over not having anything left to say. Each record becomes tougher to make. It's more and more difficult to squeeze these songs out. I always feel I got there by the skin of my teeth."

When it comes time to lay some tracks, many bands (so the story goes) write a swag of songs, then sift

through fifty or so, deciding which dozen are suitable for inclusion on the new LP. With Cave in a crisis, this approach is out of the question.

"I think about what I want the record to be like, so the songs seem to cross over and link together. It's quite a deliberate thing. What I've done a lot, a certain visual image will repeat on one song and then repeat again in another song and it will have more weight in a way. More depth to it. All the songs link up."

The process is all-enveloping. If you happened be a housemate with Nick Cave you wouldn't see life as a 24-hour rock 'n' roll party.

"I'm thinking about it all the time," he explains. "When I'm sitting in an armchair in a catatonic state, I'm actually thinking. I do become extremely preoccupied for the whole time. It drives my close friends crazy, actually! All the time I'm building up the songs en masse in my mind. There is not a lot of writing that goes on. Eventually I get a verse and stick it in the computer and a week later there is a bit more to add. It's not like endlessly tapping away. It starts off with a few basic ideas, and eventually the album becomes a whole world of characters."

One thing Nick likes to do with his songs is invent characters. *Henry's Dream* seems ripe to be accompanied by a living picture book. In the space of an hour, as in a soap opera, we're introduced to Henry, Joe, Christina, John Finn, and John's wife.

"It's an exciting way to write," explains Cave. "I invent a character in my mind that I like, like John Finn—a skinny, demented guy in a shrunken suit—and place him in a situation and let the story take on life, the characters live out their escapades, whatever they get up to. It's more exciting than to sit down and say, 'Well, I feel this way and that way and this is what happened to me today.'"

Against all odds Nick Cave now has a settled personal life, a convincing collection of musical cohorts, and whether he likes it or not—or whether we like it or not—the chance to pursue a career in any medium he chooses.

Previously, his reputation has gone before him, but with the myths dispelled (remember: the guy is thinking about taking up football!). *Henry's Dream* may announce his arrival. Heavy rotation on MTV, anyone? Perhaps not, but choosing David Briggs for this record may prove to be more than an omen. Roll on the 21st century.

"I'd like to continue to make music and write. I have a feeling that when the music runs out, the novels will run out. All the ideas. They are all very much the same thing. When the music runs out it will mean that I don't have any ideas anymore. If I'm going downhill I'll realize that and stop."

But things just wouldn't be the same around here. ◐

MY BLOODY VALENTINE

My Bloody Valentine's second album, *Loveless*, remains a landmark of early-'90s rock, its lush guitar distortions influencing countless bands and spawning a whole subgenre, shoegazing. **GINA HARP** interviewed the foursome twice for her 1992 story—first in London, then a few months later in San Francisco. After signing to Island Records later that year, the band recorded reams of material without releasing an album, ultimately regrouping in 2008 and issuing the well-regarded *m.b.v.* in 2012.

What follows is a composite of two interviews with Kevin Shields, with contributions from co-founding member/drummer/computer wiz Colm Ó Cíosóig.

London, Winter 1991

What were you aiming for with Loveless*?*

Kevin Shields: There wasn't much preconception. I wanted to have more melodies and instruments than vocals. One big difference is that on the first album, as far as I know, except for one or two songs there're no hook lines or melodies from anything but vocals. We used to do it on purpose. I wanted to start trying to do things with the guitar or sampler over the melodies. Every song on the new album has a melody line that's just as strong and memorable as the vocals. I don't know how many people have picked up on it, but it's a big difference.

There are other differences too, but they're subtle. Like the vocals. On the first album, a song like "All I Need" has six or seven tracks to make up one vocal track. On this album, some of the vocals have as many as 18 tracks at the same time. I didn't plan it, it just wound up like that.

We started using a computer for mundane things when we started the album, and as we used it we realized there were many other things we could do. We went from never using a sampler or sequencer to using them extensively.

And you have complete creative control?

KS: Yeah. Records can't get made unless you make them the way you need to. We don't do demos, nobody hears what the song sounds like until it's nearly finished. No one is allowed to come into the studio. I don't like people hearing stuff that's half-finished, because they go away with weird impressions.

With each record, the band gets a higher profile. How important is success?

KS: It depends. We're less successful than we could be if we'd put our minds to it long ago. It's important to do what we want. No one lets you do what you want unless you've proved you can, so success is important from that point of view. If a record does badly, the next time they'll be like, "Fine, do it your way. But we're not paying for it." Success on someone else's terms is bad. We'd be in big trouble if we did something against our

will and it made us ten times more popular.

But if you sell no records, there's no money, and if there's no money, there's no progress. It's fascinating how bands don't progress if they're left in the middle of nowhere. They do to a degree, but then nothing happens. Rarely do you find a band that's brilliant after ten years of no one taking any notice. You can find bands who've been going for ten years and are really quite good—but they seem to be missing something. Know what I mean? Not that such bands have no guts or are no good—it's just that they're nowhere near as good as they could have been if they'd gotten somewhere. And so much of this has to do with access to equipment. If you're poor and broke you won't get a chance to use samplers and sequencers. Which is really important modern technology.

You mix your vocals so low that they blend in like another instrument.

Colm Ó Cíosóig: Vocals *are* an instrument, basically. They don't seem that quiet to us. What's the point in making them really loud so people who don't listen to music that way can hear them? We hear them fine.

What is your role in the band, Colm?

COC: The computer stuff, samplers.

It seems like a lot of production went into this album.

COC: A lot of recording time. And repeating it. Getting it on tape to re-record and fix . . . a lot of time experimenting.

Creation and Warner Bros. were taking care of the costs?

COC: They're all right. The problem was getting money at certain times. Especially that much. We were riding it through without much money for quite a while. If we'd had loads of money and our own studio it would have taken half the time.

For playing live, do you use prerecorded stuff? It must be hard to re-create certain sounds from the album.

COC: It's just a matter of getting the balance right. We've been running sequencers live, a few weird keyboard riffs. The stuff on the album is quite simple to play, it's just a question of getting the right sounds . . . The guitar sound can be difficult to get sometimes . . . We're still having various problems hearing things during a show, that's the main thing.

You used to be part of a squat scene in the mid to late '80s,

MY BLOODY VALENTINE: DEBBIE GOOGE, KEVIN SHIELDS, BILINDA BUTCHER, COLM Ó CÍOSÓIG (PHOTO, GINA HARP)

along with such groups as the Jesus and Mary Chain and Loop.
KS: Yeah. It's not as easy as it used to be, but it still exists. There are two to three hundred thousand people doing it. Most bands in London have lived or still live in squats. It's the only sensible way to live if you haven't any money and you want a bit of freedom, and you've got the time. If you're not doing much, it's a great way to live.

I find life more stressful in rented apartments, where the quality of life feels doomed. When you squat it's fluid, easygoing, fun. The disadvantages are you have to be around a lot, and if you're busy with a band there's no time. No time to look after the place and do your share.

But we did it for a long time. Most bands have, at least in London. Basically, it's a matter of breaking into a council flat, putting your lock on it, and it's yours.
COC: It's good fun, squatting. That's what brought us to London. You could live somewhere and not have to have a job or pay rent and bills. Scam money off the council. Have a house with friends in it. Do what you want—knock walls down, paint, have parties, a rehearsal room. I first lived in a squat in the mid-'80s. After that I had a year of getting evicted. At the start of this album I was homeless. At the end of each day in the studio, I'd be walking the streets looking for an empty house. It was too much. Things are getting more difficult now, especially if you don't have enough time for it, or an organized group to help. There was no one then to help me. I

was living in a dream world, and at that point everybody has to fend for themselves. We were all in a state of panic trying to get something sorted out. I had to stop squatting, it was too difficult. And if you go on tour, when you come back your place is gone. There was pressure to get a rented place. Fine—I was getting money from the council to pay the rent. If I needed a place for a week I'd rent a really nice flat. It was fun, loads of parties, people coming in and out of our household.

Things were quite nice. Being able to squat or organize a tour and go off on it. Come back, hang around, go into the studio, record. Do another tour, come back, hang out. There was a lot of free time to drink and get stoned. It was fun.
KS: When we first played in London, the gigs we got were squat gigs. There was much more of a scene then than now. But we're not in that scene so much anymore. We're a bit out of touch. If you're not around you can't just go, "Hey, what's happening?" Right now, people are more into surviving than setting up little venues in squats.

How has your life changed since then?
KS: Since *Isn't Anything* came out, it's been busy nonstop. No time off except Christmas and the odd week here and there. We know we have something to do. You can't relax, there's too much on your mind. We've gotten used to it now, after years of being completely busy

MY BLOODY VALENTINE
The Ritz, New York
February 29, 1992

My Bloody Valentine have spawned many imitations of their conjunction of fairly loud guitars and sweet, preferably female, vocals. At best, this results in Lush; at worst, in Curve. But none of their followers have attained MBV's expertise in sound manipulation, or gone so far in sound deconstruction. Lush are above all pop, whereas MBV have strayed farther and farther from pop. "Only Shallow," for instance, is a mind-blowing piece of production, perfectly crafted.

For some, their new album, *Loveless,* may come across as an exercise in style, fascinating but devoid of warmth. The vocals of Bilinda Butcher and Kevin Shields are buried in the mix and become almost irrelevant. Many listeners may find this a problem, but the album's abundance of riches grows on you. The band are smart, very smart, and while that isn't everything—Fugazi are smart and boy, are they tedious—there is much relief in an album that is at the same time emotionally crippled and sonically rich.

Live, MBV amplify the impression. Playing at the Ritz in February, they started with "I Only Said." The volume was deafening, surging at times toward apocalyptic avalanches of noise. Although bassist Debbie Googe moves incessantly, Butcher and Shields possess the stage presence of lampposts. These two noncommittal figures emphasize MBV's brainy asexuality.

An impossibly cerebral band, MBV still expect gut reactions—and get them. Incandescent versions of "Only Shallow" and especially "Soon" drove the crowd into a frenzy. It's amazing to see a band at once so popular and so uncompromising. Their performance lights up the fact that they don't really have songs, don't care about vocals except for the added texture—yet they manage to mesmerize 15-year-olds.—*Elisabeth Vincentelli*

all the time. When you're really busy it fucks up other things, like relationships. So it's quite difficult to live a normal life.

More so on the road than when recording?

COC: I was busy in the studio all the time we were recording. I'd go home, sleep, get up, back to the studio, home to sleep. On the road, you don't know what day it is and you lose track of time. You turn into a bit of a zombie. If everyone is taking care of their job all you have to do is get up and play. Pamper yourself if you can, 'cause you can't go home. You're dealing with people all the time, and it is kind of stressful. I alleviate the stress by just . . . partying, getting drunk. We turn into alcoholics on the road. But when you're drinking every night you only get a bit drunk.

How did your last American tour go?

COC: Good fun, but really hectic. The first week we traveled in a minibus that was horribly uncomfortable to sleep in. We'd spend ten hours driving in the van, then check into a nice hotel. We'd spend a few hours at the hotel, long enough for a shower and maybe two hours' sleep in a real bed. By the time we got to New York we were wrecked. Hunchbacked. It was summer, too, and really hot.

When we arrived there the Mafia was threatening us. The biggest East Coast promoter was doing our gigs, and had set us up to play at a place called the Cat Club, which is really shitty—an uptown club where rock stars hang out and pick up chicks. Friends of ours said they could organize a gig at the Pyramid Club on our night off and we decided to go ahead with that. We were in Canada making our way down, and we started getting frantic phone calls from New York saying, "Don't do that gig or you'll be in trouble." We were like, "What's wrong with doing a gig?" Who were they to tell us not to play?

The next day it got heavier, with the guy's secretary phoning up, really panicky, saying not to do it or we'd never play New York again. There were fliers all over the city for the gig our friend had arranged, but not for

the other one. The guy was mad: it was a pride thing. We arrived in New York not knowing, coming up to the venue to find a bunch of thugs waiting to break our legs. We canceled. We're not used to promoters who threaten to break our legs.

Did that wrap up your American journey?

COC: No. We got rid of the minibus and rented a camper. It hadn't been serviced but we needed it. Everything went wrong: the rear suspension was broken and they hadn't cleaned out all the sewage, so not only were we jostled every time we hit a bump, but the van was filled with a sticky smell of heated summer sewage.

But a lot of the gigs were good. The 9:30 Club in Washington, DC, was really good, a great atmosphere. Maxwell's in Hoboken is really good as well.

What else do you do with your creativity?

KS: I have a pretty big say about how our covers look. The artwork is my idea always. Some I do completely, like the *You Made Me Realise* EP. For *Isn't Anything*, I didn't take the photo but I reproduced it like that. Joe Dilworth was the photographer; the people's positions, the colors, the way it's bleached out, was my idea. For *Loveless*, I picked stills off the video (for "To Here Knows When").

Why is the album called Loveless?

KS: It needed a title. If the record sounded sad and miserable it would be a bit stupid to call it *Loveless*. But because it seems to have a kind of optimism, with chirpy little melodies and stuff, though not really happy-happy, it seems to suit it.

What's it like touring the UK?

COC: At these northern gigs especially, we get to see loads of people we know, and also the bands—the opening bands are people we know. Often when bands go on tour they just have a support band for the whole tour— which is good in one way because it means you get to see them a few times, and apart from that you only have to concentrate on your gig. With us, it's kind of a massive social occasion every night with loads of people we know.

GINA HARP

San Francisco, Feb. 7, 1992

How have the recent shows been?

KS: We did our last two in Los Angeles the same night. They were a lot better. We played a bit worse but they were better because it was rowdier and louder.

Better PA?

KS: Peter, our monitor man, knew some guys in LA who rented us a special PA for the gig. We couldn't do it in San Francisco because we didn't know anyone there. It was really worth it. If it wasn't for that I think we would've been terribly fucked.

The four of you seem to spend a lot of time together. Is it only when you're touring? What about at home?

KS: Occasionally. We go through phases. We don't make a point of it, but if there's something on that's good we might go out together. We'll do it if we feel like it. Sometimes I don't see some of the others for ages.

I read that you and Bilinda [Butcher] are a couple. Is that true?

KS: Sort of.

Do you live together?

KS: Sometimes. We don't live anywhere at the moment. Nowhere, our fixed abode. It's quite nice in a way. I don't like landlords, and the last thing I'm going to do is give them my money when I'm not actually there. It's got good points and bad points: you save money, but you don't have anywhere to go.

Do you party every night like you have when I've met you?

KS: Yes. We try and stop it after a few weeks. After three or four weeks you get into a real weird daze. When you met us in England we were in the weird-daze stage. It had been a few weeks, it was like *Blah!* and falling around. You play at night, and it's boring just to play the gig and go home to bed. Well, it might be appealing—but it doesn't seem to happen, if you know what I mean. Partying is unhealthy—but it's usually the best bit.

How did you like San Francisco?

KS: A lot, actually. It's one of the most laid-back places. There's a nice sense of being able to get around, and it doesn't seem too dangerous. Los Angeles seems a place you could get shot. In San Francisco I didn't think about getting shot. It's pretty, all hilly with quaint little houses.

How did you like the clubs?

KS: I like clubs like that—the people are less self-conscious, more into having a good time. I'm not a jump-around-have-a-great-time person, but I do like that environment as opposed to one where everyone's standing around staring at each other trying to look cool.

What about the "smart drinks" you tried?

KS: Quite nice. I didn't feel any smarter, but it was refreshing.

What about drugs?

KS: Not a lot really. I like feeling in control. I prefer my own inspiration as opposed to being . . . I don't like being conned, if you know what I mean. I'm not really into it.

And I hate regretting something, like drinking too much. If you drink an awful, awful lot you regret it. I usually can't drink for a couple of days afterwards.

What goes through your head while you're playing a gig?

KS: Usually you can see the people at the front who are really into it—who actually bothered to get to the front. The people at the back and the sides are just there, you don't really think about them. Yet you do, you think, This is weird . . . In a club I can generally see everybody right to the very back and outside the door. I often watch people just outside the door, talking to people, and it's like, Why are you here? Especially during "You Made Me Realise," I wait for those people to stop talking and listen up. Because they will. I don't think we have ever done "You Made Me Realise" and not got everyone's attention.

Do you get many groupies?

KS: We don't see it that way. When we were in Japan, there were people who seemed they could be like that—but they weren't. The band has to have that mentality. Or if it's a band like Ride or something, you know, all boys and all looking traditionally kind of good, I suppose you probably get them.

If you asked the Cult if they get groupies, they'd be like, Well, yeah. They get their crew to go out and give backstage passes to the girls they think Billy Duffy's going to like. If you give out enough passes, you're bound to get one or two coming along that will be into that kind of thing. You can make things happen if you want to. If you don't make them happen, they usually don't happen. That whole groupie thing was more of a late-'60s, early-'70s thing. Even then bands had to cultivate it, it's not like it just happened. If you don't think about it, it doesn't exist.

What's it been like touring in America this time?

KS: Seeing a sheriff in Texas is new, whereas a policeman in some English town is nothing. We're seeing a lot of the country we haven't seen before. Like stopping at a truckers' cafe in the middle of the night. They all look at you and you're thinking, They're going to poison our food. Generally they're pretty nice. I think they think we might be famous. I just can't tell.

You are famous.

KS: I mean *really* famous. Most people like that wouldn't have heard of us. The last time we went to a roadside place, people in the shop got our autographs, in case we made it! It's weird when you realize people perceive you as different from them. You don't feel different until you're made to feel different. Or you feel different the way everyone does: everyone has feelings in their head that nobody knows what they're really like. But it's different when you're regarded as special just by being in

a band. Some people love getting off on being a star. I used to think it would be good, but now I really—really genuinely—don't care.

I haven't made out all the lyrics on Loveless. *Do they have similar sexual themes to the previous work?*

KS: It's less direct. We write about similar stuff but it's not as blatant. The bluntness of what we said was refreshing for us before. Now we've done it. Doing it again would probably come across as really bad.

How important is sex to you? I was picking up on things like S&M . . .

KS: The industry side of S&M is stylized and fetishized. The reality is not a big deal to us. It's just another thing to deal with. In Germany, there's a whole movement. I went to a few gigs featuring very experimental bands. There was some extreme S&M stuff onstage. It was quite interesting. We're not really like that. We don't tie people up onstage.

Why not?

KS: It's such a hassle. We have enough problems worrying about bloody effects pedals and stage props. The films are a nightmare, let alone carrying extra people to do it. We like life to be as easy as possible. Because we make life difficult enough just trying to do what we want.

The key to real progress is being really true to yourself, following your instincts, doing what you want. It's very hard to make progress by trying to second-guess the right move and do things to please others.

I understand you are no longer with Creation in the UK.

KS: They didn't want to work with us anymore because we had 100% control and it was unpleasant for them. It wasn't a case of us not wanting to work with them, because we weren't working with them. And that's why we split with them.

We did absolutely everything ourselves. Not every single tiny thing—I didn't organize getting records into shops, or putting the ads in the magazines, or paying for ads, but we did so much it was ridiculous. Jobs other people weren't doing. We didn't like the way they did things, so we did them. They said, We can't handle this anymore. We're not bitter. They were quite honest. I knew it was coming.

Do you think you'll go with a major label, or stay independent?

KS: All in all I don't care. It's just the person. In England, the only difference between a major and an indie is that the major has more cash flow. There's no other difference. In America we'll stay with Warner Bros. because they've been pretty good to us so far. Pretty supportive; and they haven't done anything we didn't want.

The important thing is the people you work with. The majors vs. indies issue has become irrelevant, because nowadays so many independent labels interfere with you more than the majors would. ✪

CRACKER

When Camper Van Beethoven disintegrated at the dawn of the '90s, singer David Lowery moved from California to Virginia and assembled Cracker, a more streamlined unit that cast his songs in a harder-edged rock context. **JEAN DEBBS** interviewed Lowery about the new band as its self-titled debut album was released. In the years to come, Cracker would find a commercial success that eluded CVB. By the early '00s, CVB had reformed, and the two bands started touring together, with overlapping, often virtually identical lineups.

Cracker? With his red hair and freckles, whiter than white skin, and scrawny frame, David Lowery kinda *looks* like a stereotypical cracker, belying the popular image of him and his former cohorts in Camper Van Beethoven as smartass California hippie college kids. And calling his new band Cracker turns out to have something to do with indicating how inaccurate that California stereotype can be. Apparently it also relates to fessing up about your roots—musical roots, that is. But most of all it has to do with "attitude," a word Lowery uses repeatedly during our interview.

Most of the songs on *Cracker* seem far removed from Lowery's songs on the last Camper Van Beethoven album, *Key Lime Pie*, with its brooding, sometimes bitter snapshots of a depressed national psyche: "Sweethearts," "Humid Press of Days," "Come on Darkness." Only the dark, acoustic lament of *Cracker*'s closer, "Dr. Bernice," recalls that material; the songs here seem to

have more in common with the robust, sarcastic ditties of earlier CVB days, although with less musical variation. Musically, Cracker are more unambiguously rockers, as Lowery happily admits: "There's something about the way the whole thing works that's the same as Camper, and the narrative thing is the same—but it's more aggressive, simpler, it's got more attitude, it's more of a rock thing, you know?"

As for the lyrics, you get an idea of what Lowery is (and isn't) going to give you in this new incarnation from the opening cut, "Teen Angst": "What the world needs now is another folk singer / Like I need a hole in my head / What the world needs now is some true words of wisdom / Like la-la-la-la-la-la-la-la-la."

You've probably heard this forceful if rather lightweight song by now, or seen the video; but that isn't the whole Cracker. "Teen Angst" sets the tone for a good chunk of the album, but it's by no means the whole story. There are bittersweet melodies ("Someday," "St. Cajetan") and hook-laden pop songs ("Don't Fuck Me Up (with Peace and Love)," "Happy Birthday to Me"), as well as the aforementioned mournful gem, "Dr. Bernice." And the album is liberally sprinkled with wry humor and truculent wit—a rare commodity in music but one Lowery has always been able to deliver. In several respects, then, Cracker picks up where Camper left off; the main difference is that for the most part they've restricted themselves to a more orthodox musical framework.

Was it a deliberate decision to do something more straightforward in Cracker? "Yeah," Lowery says, "but I think I had been interested in doing something a little more straightforward with the next Camper record, too, though I don't want to deny that Cracker is different.

"I wanted to have a lot of attitude on this record. I knew I needed to do that to satisfy me personally. I wasn't too interested in introspection, at least that kind of sitting-down, "International Coffee Moment" sort of introspection. I wanted something more overt. I was much more extroverted; I was shouting and screaming about a lot of stuff.

"It wasn't something intellectual; it was more my mood at the time. And I ended up finding people to work with who were into that too—once we started, they dragged me off in that direction a lot more than would probably have been the case with Camper. And I let it do that because I wanted it to be different."

The other members of Cracker are guitarist Johnny Hickman, bass player Davey Faragher, and drummer Joey Peters. One thing they have in common is that they've known Lowery a while, either from Southern California childhood days or from the Santa Cruz scene out of which CVB emerged in the mid-'80s. But this familiarity isn't the main reason they're in a band together, says Lowery. Again, it was a matter of attitude.

"I wanted to work with people with a certain attitude. I'd been interviewing all these hardcore alternative rockers and they had an inbuilt attitude . . . I knew that somewhere down the road we'd come into conflict. You see, I don't really care if I play what's viewed as commercial music or if I play underground music. I just want to play music, I don't want to think about how it's going to be perceived by other people, and I don't want anybody in the band thinking about that and that influencing what they're playing.

"One of the great tragedies for me is what happened to the Pixies. I thought they were totally great, but it seems like they're scared of success or something. They've become more esoteric and introverted as they've gone along. But the charm of the band initially was that they were totally noisy, and Black Francis was over the top, yet somehow what came out were these great pop songs. Then I think they read their underground press about them selling out. That was one of the tensions in Camper, too: it was like, we want to be cool. But you can't be cool; somebody else decides that. The only thing you can do is write the songs you want to write.

"So I wanted to get away from strict alternative musicians, people who'd only played that kind of stuff. But I wanted weird people, too, and people who understood . . . just cutting loose, not playing perfect—kind of like the way CVB used to be. So I wanted people who knew how to tap into the raw energy of rock music and go to 11 when it's called for."

Hickman had been in various underground bands, Lowery explains, "but he just wanted to play music, he wasn't interested in being cool." As a guitarist Johnny's not averse to the strong, clear lines Greg Lisher contributed to CVB; his playing on "Someday" and "Satisfy You" perfectly elaborates their first-rate melodies, for example, and he's just as capable of rocking out when it's called for. Hickman also wrote "Mr. Wrong," a honky-tonker with the sardonic wit we've come to associate with Lowery's own lyrics: "I was going to buy you flowers, but I didn't / It's the thought that counts, and I think I'm a bit too broke / But there's some change in my ashtray, maybe just enough to pay / For a half-pint of something that'll probably make us choke."

As for bassist Davey Faragher, Lowery exclaims, "He's so twisted! Musically he can get completely weird, yet he comes from this R&B/soul background." In the '70s Davey and his brothers had a white soul band, the Faragher Brothers. More recently, it turns out, Davey's been making his living as a session musician—singing black female vocal parts. "He can do that falsetto . . . he's this big Scandinavian-looking guy with dreadlocks." And Faragher's ability in this respect clearly influenced some of the arrangements on Cracker: several of the songs have the kind of gospelly backing vocals the Rolling Stones popularized in rock, and which have been appropriated most recently by Primal Scream. (Lowery confesses to liking Screamadelica: "I feel I should hate it, because it's such a rip, but I really enjoy some of the songs.") A certain Jeanie McClain is responsible for harmony vocals on two songs, "but the 'oohs,' that's Davey and Johnny."

The presence of these vocals on Cracker's album points up the influence here of what Lowery calls "all that white-boy soul, that cracker-soul music . . . ZZ Top, Zeppelin, the Stones, Iggy Pop's Kill City." The band's initial demos for the record label were half-jokingly entitled "Cracker Soul," and the name stuck for one of the songs and gave the band its name. Lowery explains:

"When people ask you what kind of music you listen to, especially if you're in some alternative band, you'll name all these cool bands but you sort of neglect all this shit you grew up with, everything you really heard and really played when you first started, and continued listening to secretly. Like I kept all my ZZ Top records, Little Feat, and so on. When I was 15 or 16, in the parking lot at high school, where you went to smoke pot, everyone was blasting their car stereo and what you were listening to was Led Zeppelin, the Stones, ZZ Top, Lynyrd Skynyrd . . .

"And a lot of that stuff you can't get rid of—it's what you grew up with—so you might as well embrace it."

And how does that affect the songs on this record?

"All I'm really saying is that for years I'd blocked those influences, and then I thought, Why should I? And I let them go. Now it's all the things that I've liked coming out, not edited anymore. With some of the songs, in Camper we would have wanted to shift them away from all the things they kinda sound like, whereas here it's . . . It's a fucking good song, just do it. Okay, so it sounds like Led Zeppelin, the Stones, or even that Pixies song on *Doolittle* that goes, 'Hey, I'm dying to meet you . . .'"

I don't altogether go along with Lowery's explanation. Just because you liked something once, when you were young and still relatively unformed, doesn't mean that it's somehow more honest and authentic to make music like that now. It certainly shouldn't imply that it's dishonest to steer away from such music. After all,

creating something significant—in any field of cultural activity—involves not only an awareness of what's gone before but also the determination to avoid whatever has become clichéd and thus impoverished—the desire to break new ground. Nothing comes about from scratch, to be sure: everything borrows selectively from what's already been created, but you have to try and do something new with it, even if that's no more than paraphrasing part of the "tradition" from a certain ironic distance.

Thankfully, at least from my point of view, Cracker's album is by and large not the creature that Lowery's explanation might lead you to believe it is. True, it often relies on more straightforwardly "rock" elements, and for me at least this is the source of its weaker songs (Lowery's "I See the Light" and Hickman's "Another Song about the Rain," for example, which tend to lapse into musical and lyrical cliché). But generally it avoids becoming hackneyed by refusing to take itself too seriously. There's "Can I Take My Gun to Heaven," for example, whose protagonist wants to take his gun with him when he goes ("You know, she's always been by my side") because it's more faithful than a woman. As Lowery admits, tongue in cheek, it's "a sublime tribute" to the cracker-soul genre.

As for the track "Cracker Soul" itself, it's more a parody—musically and lyrically—of a boogie-down good-time song than anything, with its repeated claim that what's best is "what comes easy," veering into bizarrerie when Lowery invites the listener to "come and party with your spirit guide." It's probably the only boogie song that features between-verses yodeling, too. To Lowery it's "the fluffiest song on the record."

"I wrote these lyrics that are kind of a story, and there's all this stuff to it, but it seemed the song didn't want to be about *anything* . . . it wanted to be like the Monkees' theme. Most of the words are just things I heard people say while we were making the record. I was talking to someone at a party, who was telling me "I've just been to see my psychic," and the psychic had told her that your spirit guide guides you, but you also guide your spirit guide, and you need to sit down, light a candle, and have a glass of wine with it. And her response had been, "You mean, I should party with my spirit guide?" It just seemed so funny . . . I like collecting those kinds of things."

The lyrics of several songs on *Cracker* rely on a collage approach—like "Happy Birthday to Me," which is a string of one-liners finally pulled together by the statement "I'm feeling thankful for the small things today." It's the kind of statement that's almost the avoidance of a statement-with-a-capital-*S*, though, and that seems important to Lowery at the moment. When I press him on this he responds with one of his lyrics: "Right, what the world needs now is another folksinger like I need a hole in my head." On the other hand, he points out, "maybe there's something behind all these one-liners, some kind of reason or basic attitude."

At this point I'm getting the feeling there's a lot of reactive thinking going on here. Lowery is obviously determined to reject the labels and interpretations that have been applied to him in the past; both the name Cracker and the repeated emphasis on "attitude" seem to be means of doing this. He gets distinctly testy when he's tagged as an exponent of "college rock":

"Sure, I went to college at Santa Cruz for two and a half years, though the rest of it was at a junior college. But I worked on a farm for two and a half years, and I drove a truck for at least that long too. I also worked in the pressroom of a newspaper for a good three years. But I don't play 'pressman rock'!"

As for "Don't Fuck Me Up (with Peace and Love)," Lowery characterizes it as "kind of an attitude song":

"I had gone on a rant one time about something, like I'm prone to, and the person I was with was being all understanding, trying to see the other side of the argument, and I just came out with "Look, don't fuck me up with that peace and love shit, okay?" I hate it when people say "calm down"; I always think, why?"

But the song is also, he says, "a rejection of a lot of the neo-hippie baggage that Camper got saddled with, which I never felt was deserved . . . Everyone thought we were hippies, just because we were from California!"

The other members of Cracker are also from California too, but as Lowery points out, "what do you have to be to be 'from' California? You go to high school there, then you're from California, because you have the accent." Like so many Californians, Lowery wasn't born there; he saw the light of day in Texas, where his father, originally from Arkansas, was stationed in the air force (Hickman has a similar service background).

Furthermore, the California they grew up in is very different from the prevailing stereotypes, so much so that Lowery argues, "living in California—except for the Bay Area and the coastal cities—is essentially a Southern experience. Go to Bakersfield. Or to the Inland Empire," where three of the band grew up: "Every kid I knew when I was growing up, if they weren't Mexican Americans, their folks were in the air force, and they were from Texas, Oklahoma, Arkansas . . .

"And lots of people migrated out here during the Dust Bowl period and later. My grandparents went back and forth between Arkansas and the Coachella Valley in California as agricultural workers right up to the '60s, then settled in California. My grandfather used to pack dates."

The Inland Empire, Lowery explains, is "an area east of LA. As you go east there's the San Gabriel Valley, which is not hip like LA—they make fun of places like Covina and Glendora. Then you go up some hills and down into another valley, the last valley before you get to the desert, and that area is called the Inland Empire—San Bernardino, Riverside, Redlands. People in LA think of it in the way people in New York tend to think of New Jersey."

Lowery describes the experience of growing up there as "the full-on white-trash Southern California thing, hanging out in the parking lot at the 7-Eleven." Count up the number of references to parking lots in Camper and Cracker songs sometime, and you'll realize he's not likely to forget it.

But he's not trying to pretend he's a real cracker, in the stereotyped sense, even if he does now live in Richmond, Virginia (it's where his girlfriend's from). "I don't feel like I'm Southern or anything like that," he says and then suddenly cracks up. He's talking to me on the phone in the lobby of a hotel in Austin, where Cracker are playing at South by Southwest. A woman walking past overheard what he'd just said and chipped in, "You do, just get with it." It turns out he's wearing his girlfriend's hat, which says AMERICAN BY BIRTH, SOUTHERN BY THE GRACE OF GOD. "Well," he admits, "I do have a certain affinity to all this."

But what Lowery's trying to do by appropriating the name of one stereotype, I think, is to distance himself from other stereotypes that have been forced on him.

"I'm bummed that people think I'm more genteel than I really am. But equally, I didn't grow up in a trailer park, I didn't grow up in the South; I went to college, although perhaps for different reasons than a lot of people. But I'm not a redneck, I'm not a cracker in the traditional sense. I just feel like I'm in the middle somewhere; there's not a good name for it."

And something similar is going on in order to carve out an identity for Cracker separate from Lowery's history in Camper Van Beethoven. But while he points up the differences between CVB and Cracker—perhaps to avoid more lingering stereotypes about "wacky" Californians, Lowery's quite aware of the continuities:

"People have been saying how different this is from Camper, and I suppose I've been playing that up in a way, agreeing with them. But they've been saying how much more straightforward and simple it is, and such a departure from Camper. And I've been thinking, Yeah, it's a lot more like these songs by that band, I can't remember their name, they had that song "Good Guys and Bad Guys," and "Take the Skinheads Bowling" and "Ambiguity Song"—just real simple songs . . . I'm getting to the point of being really argumentative about it. It's different, but it comes from the same place." ✪

SEBADOH

When Lou Barlow was unceremoniously dismissed from Dinosaur Jr., he turned his full attention to Sebadoh. In some quarters, Sebadoh briefly eclipsed Dinosaur: the band's angry confessionals, often captured on bedroom 4-track, were indicative of the lo-fi recording that flourished in the mid-'90s. **DAVID NICHOLS** spoke with Barlow about Sebadoh's *Bubble and Scrape*. In 2005, Barlow rejoined Dinosaur Jr., juggling tours and albums with Dinosaur and Sebadoh.

You have to get excited when a band comes along who (a) play some of the most exciting rock plus the most seamless ballads you've heard in eons, *and* (b) profess a love for Joni Mitchell in interviews. Imagine my surprise when I discover that Lou Barlow, for all his own genius, has no interest in the most recent two decades of Joni's career.

"I was pretty much exclusively into a period of hers," he admits, "from when she started up, to the *Court and Spark* record. Anything after that—I can't listen to it."

Unbelievable! So, you don't even like *Don Juan's Reckless Daughter*?

"No, I never really heard it . . . I don't have her whole career in any kind of grasp. I just know I happened upon a bunch of records I thought were really amazing. Once she started getting jazzy, I eased out. I went through a period where I was listening to her so much I actually . . . stopped."

Okay, Lou, let's say Joni called you up and wanted you to do the kind of thing Billy Idol did for her a few LPs back, would you . . .

"No way, I'd never do that!" he laughs (at least, I *think* he's laughing). "I couldn't even do it with someone who was in another band of our stature. Walking into a studio with someone and deciding to make music because someone has written our names in the same line in a record review! No, that would flip me out, I'd feel like a total idiot."

I always know when it's time to change the topic. So, Lou, what other famous Lou do you most identify with?

"That's a good question . . . Lou Reed, I don't really relate to him, except in that he's not a great guitar player but he plays guitar anyway. That's kind of like what I do! He's always just sort of like gone ahead and done what he wanted and been as pretentious as he

SEBADOH
The Freed Man
(Homestead)

Looking back: the final track on Dinosaur Jr.'s *You're Living All Over Me* LP, "Poledo," was "recorded on 2 crappy tape recorders by Lou Barlow alone in his room," an abrupt mix of sound-noise-static and double-tracked acoustic guitar 'n' vocal folking around. Like Negativland crossed with Tim Buckley—sorta.

Sometime between then and today, Dinosaur bassist Barlow got together with Eric Gaffney to record a couple of cassettes in a similar vein to the aforementioned. Homestead, inclined to lo-fi, demo-ish material, offered them a contract. A little later, Lou split from Dinosaur (acrimoniously, we're told) and began to focus his energies on his and Eric's strums and sonic manipulations.

This LP is culled from the *Sebadoh* and *Freed Man* cassettes, very DIY and underground by design, affecting in the way Daniel Johnston is, yet recalling at times early Tyrannosaurus Rex before Bolan went electric to a T. There's a lot to digest—thirty-plus songs and fragments. It opens with cat screeches and closes with sped-up and slowed-down voices in childish sing-along. In between are snippets of found sound, spoken bits, and tape-machine tomfoolery; but the tunes hold your attention amid the distractions. Nice trumpet in the rollicking sway called "Punch in the Nose," like a cowboy campfire song of another era. It's the odd touches (effects, bursts of fuzz-distortion mania, fractured percussion) that make Sebadoh not a folk duo, and it's the knack for pretty strummage and fragile harmonizing that make Sebadoh worth watching as they develop.—*Fred Mills*

SEBADOH
Weed Forestin'
(Homestead)

If the Residents recorded an album of Simon and Garfunkel songs, it might sound like Sebadoh. As on their debut *Freed Man* LP, Sebadoh have written a set of songs which seem anonymously simple in themselves, yet together form a very cohesive album which is one of the best of 1990. The songs vary greatly in length—some are little more than delicate blurs—but the cumulative effect of hearing all 23 of them is overwhelming.

Dan Fogelberg could sing Sebadoh songs in a Rocky Mountain chalet and be right at home—assuming no one paid attention to the lyrics. Anyone who deciphered these might be a little disturbed. Even your average foul-mouthed rock fan might get

wanted to be. So maybe in that way I relate to him, but I don't want to sound like him and I don't want to sing like him. I *do* think he's pretty pretentious!"

It's worth noting that Lou Barlow *would* go and see the re-formed Velvets—as long as Moe Tucker sticks with 'em.

"I used to listen to my own stuff constantly," he's saying now, "old and new. In the last year or so I've stopped, because it makes me depressed. I feel it's wasting my time. You get too involved in yourself and your own sound, it starts to make me sick. Physically sick."

Physically sick?

"Like, nauseous. It just started happening to me about a year ago when I started re-listening to things. I started feeling like, 'Oh, maybe I don't wanna listen to this, maybe I wanna listen to a bunch of four-track stuff I did last week!' Then, 'no, this is making me feel sick also!' So I slipped out of the habit."

So Lou's been listening to indie-rock contemporaries instead, stuff like Faith Healers and Stereolab, as well as following the changes of My Bloody Valentine. He even co-wrote a Bikini Kill show review for *Melody Maker* last time he was in England ("Their influence will echo like 1977 punk or 1982 hardcore for years to come").

And how come Sebadoh's new album, *Bubble and Scrape* (on Sub Pop), is so rock 'n' roll?

"Our [live] playing has always been pretty rock; up until this one, our recordings haven't reflected that. This is the first time. We've always been electric—mostly electric, anyway."

Dinosaur Jr., Lou's previous band, come up, though I'd rather they didn't. I think it's important to let people be themselves, not tied to more famous signposts. Still, my formal mention of the subject brings a pungent response.

"I believe you left Dinosaur just before they toured Australia?"

"Yeah, right before. They kicked me out."

"Were you annoyed you missed out on that?"

"I would like to get there eventually, because I hear it's completely interesting, and it'd be really cool to go there. But nah, it's not one of the things I was mad at them about, like, 'Ah, fuck! Not only did they kick me out of the band but *I can't go to Australia!*' It was more like, 'Ah, they kicked me out of the band . . . They owe me thousands of dollars . . . They weren't honest . . .'"

"Did you talk to Donna Biddle [bass player who replaced Barlow for the Australian tour, then left] about her Dinosaur experience?"

"No, I heard rumors. I've heard rumors about almost everything to do with that stupid band. They all make me feel, 'Well, they're gonna be fucked up no matter who they have in the band.' For a while, I thought I was the freak. I thought, 'Am I the one who's making this band such a horrible experience? Or is it just like this?' Then the rumors started floating back, and I was like, 'Ah, good, it isn't me.' I met the guy who plays bass in Dinosaur now. I walked into the same room and he was hanging out with some guy in Screaming Trees or something."

What's a creative Lou Barlow day? The muse doesn't seize him at awkward times—he has a deal with his freakative duties.

"Sometimes I wake up and 'Well, I have these things in my notebook that are kind of coming together, I should sit down today and try to meld it onto something . . .' Lately—because I don't have my 4-track, just a Walkman—I sit down and say, 'now I'm gonna make up a song.' I'll rearrange it later: anything I'm gonna

nervous listening to Sebadoh: "It's a joke I play three times a day to sticky magazines/Tired wrist and greasy fist to rotting sister scenes/Bitter, unreal, too worn out to feel/Nulling out my pleasure so I'll never know what's real" ("Three Times a Day").

Sebadoh cope with the seamy side of life by trying to understand it, rather than denying that it exists. Of course, there are facets of life they don't even begin to understand—like love, for instance. But who does understand love? Masturbation and Jesus provide security, while love—at least in its primitive stages—only magnifies insecurity. Sebadoh is idealistic enough to have optimistic fantasies, but honest enough to admit that these often become realities swamped with pessimism.

Few bands are as successful as Sebadoh at entering the netherworld of desire and scraping the stuff off the inside of the walls.—*Jeffrey Herrmann*

SEBADOH
Gimme Indie Rock!
(Homestead 7" EP)

Few people are more qualified than Lou Barlow to pen such a scathing put-down of the rock scene as "Gimme Indie Rock!" Here's a guy who played bass for Dinosaur Jr. (one of the scene's biggest names ever); who ended up being emulated by everyone from Buffalo Tom to latter-day Screaming Trees . . . and who then got kicked out while still being owed thousands of dollars. Next thing you know, his former bandmates are on MTV pitching for a new bass player . . . hard feelings, anyone?

Lou Barlow's two albums with Sebadoh have turned out to be miles more experimental and interesting than anything Dino could come up with. And now we get *Gimme Indie Rock!*, Sebadoh's first effort with a drummer and a recording studio, alternating between Dino/Neil Young grunge and Pussy Galore rave-up. A song for anyone who's fed up with scene gossip, backbiting, and all the other trappings of a "scene" that's looking less "alternative" all the time.

The rest of the songs are the usual Sebadoh timbre, a wonderful brand of acoustic primitivism that starts off sounding pretty good and grows on you. What's the bigger irony: That many folks will focus on the title track and ignore the rest? Or the fact that Homestead is sending out promos to the very people Barlow & Co. despise?
—*Mike Appelstein*

come up with, 80 percent of it will be totally goofy, stupid, and awkward.

"I'm afraid to play stuff to people, because what they tell me really matters. If my girlfriend says she doesn't like a song, that will stick in my head. Recently I put together a 4-track album and played the whole thing for her. She's like, 'Lou, this sucks!' and I was like, 'Oh, man,' and then I just needed to talk to her: 'Why does it suck?' And all of her reasons were really good!

"Why did it suck? She didn't like the lyrics or vocal approach on my 4-track stuff [presumably Lou's solo recordings, which he releases under the name Sentridoh], which has changed to a really intense and meticulously constructed sort of thing; my lyrics have become less confessional, more pointlessly provocative . . . it's hard to describe. It's kind of hard if you're into Sebadoh. It's like 'Oh, Sebadoh's so good because they're confessional and mellow' . . . This stuff is sort of gnarled, still acoustic but overly crafted . . . something like that . . ."

Considering the alarmingly distinctive nature of a lot of Sebadoh records, wouldn't Sebadoh fans, I wonder, understand the need for Jason, Eric, and Lou to move on? I thought it was a punk tenet . . .

This is the stage of our interview where Lou kind of loses it. Not, I believe, for any other reason than that he is extraordinarily passionate about his music. He is extremely sensitive to criticism: whenever he recounts a fan's criticism, it is in the tones of a complete doofus.

"Very few people who are Sebadoh fans move with us through our changes," he says, not stopping to note the impossibility of this claim. "There are people now who don't like us because we don't play Eric's songs, like we used to, 'cause they were 'the only good ones.' But when we used to play those Eric songs live, people would be like [dumb voice], 'Oh god you know, why aren't you guys really acoustic and confessional like you were on the Weed Forestin' record,' but when the Weed Forestin' record came out it was like [whiny cretin voice], 'That's pretty good, but how come you aren't varied and great like you were on The Freed Man?' Each step we take, the fans' first response is disgust.

"Or they're guarded, which is cool. But people come up to me and say, 'Oh, gee, I wish it was more like this or that,' and I'm like, 'Well, fuck you, we recorded over a hundred songs like that, over one hundred. I doubt you know every one of 'em. If you really want us to be that way, we still are."

That "fuck you" was a façade, I feel, fronting a rather more fragile figure . . .

"I even doubt my choice of 'Soul and Fire' as a single. Everyone's like 'Why did you choose that as a single?' and I'm like, 'I don't know! My mom thought it was the best song I ever wrote. What can I say? Whenever we release something, it's like we made the wrong decision. Every record is flawed, totally flawed in its own way, we can't make a record without making mistakes we don't realize till it's way too late."

Lou, it's okay. Change of subject . . . what's the weirdest way anyone's ever said "Sebadoh"?

"The weirdest way? Sehbadowa. There's See-ba-dowah, we also had it written up in a paper once as Sebo. Where did they get that? They must have got it over the phone, 'Sebadoh're-gonna-play.' [Crusty old-man voice] 'Uh? Seba . . . Sebo . . . okay.' It's mellowed out lately, people are learning how to say it, it was chaos before.

"That's another thing. What kind of mistake is that name?! Sebadoh? I kind of forced it on the band: 'It's really great to have a name that doesn't mean anything.' For a while it was like, no one could remember the name . . . I thought I'd fucked up!"

Another fuck-up is Lou's decision to move to Boston from his childhood home of Westfield, Massachusetts.

"Boston is kind of a tense place," he reckons. "For instance, if I'm in a line and there's a bunch of people behind me and I'm paying for something, if I don't collect my change and put it in my wallet instantly, I feel I'm bumming people out, I can hear them complaining about me."

But, I reason, stretching my memory back two years to a rainy evening I spent in Boston trying to find a book with a good bagel recipe, the bookshops are okay there, aren't they?

"The bookshops? I don't read. I haven't made it through a book in years."

The record shops?

"There's Newbury Comics, which is like a chain in Boston, they carry a good amount of imports and 7-inches. And Melody Maker and the NME, so when Sebadoh are featured I can go buy them. I've been going there a lot lately. There's a shop called In Your Ear that's kind of good. But they're not that good. When you go to Pier Platters in New York, you see singles you wouldn't expect to see, compelling-looking singles. Here it's like, their stock is no greater than my knowledge: I hate that. I like stores where they have stuff completely beyond my knowledge."

A revealing thought: this is why Sebadoh themselves are so compelling. As listeners, we don't know what to expect from the next track on any Sebadoh record—and the references, musical debates, and lyricizings could come from any place, any time. Their records—and the new rock one, Bubble and Scrape, is no exception—are a complex rearrangement of rock's most revealing metaphors. If you haven't already been there, you should pick up your ticket. ✪

VIOLENT FEMMES: VICTOR DELORENZO, GORDON GANO, BRIAN RITCHIE (PHOTO, FRANCIS FORD)

VIOLENT FEMMES

Puncture had covered the Violent Femmes from the outset, but **TOM ADELMAN**'s 1994 piece catches them a decade after the thrill of their debut album, facing up to the trickier challenge of moving forward while their audiences just craved the songs they already knew and loved.

The last time I saw Gordon Gano he stood calmly on-stage at the Universal Amphitheatre with his hands over his eyes. "Daaaaaaaaayyyyyyyyyy," he moaned into the microphone and seven thousand fans screamed, congratulating themselves for catching the start of "Add It Up." It was a moment when I was reminded of just how huge the Femmes have become.

At the same time as their audience has mushroomed, though, they've become less and less visible in critical circles—and in general. It's a situation that clearly occasions some puzzlement on Gano's part, and more than a little annoyance, which he's venting over the phone from New York at this moment. "We're always being asked, 'What have you done? We haven't heard of you in a couple of years. Are you guys still together?' And really, we've probably been touring the world most of that time. It's just we have a very under-stated career, where if we haven't played practically on

131

your block, then somebody hasn't heard about us.

"I think we're probably the most successful rock and pop act that's never been on *Saturday Night Live*, never been on *David Letterman*. We have people who open up for us, and then go and do those shows! There's something very unusual about that. I don't know, maybe it will change with this record. Maybe it won't."

This record is *New Times*, the first release of completely new Femmes material in three very long years. Perhaps this gap is part of the reason for their current invisibility. Perhaps too, it's that the Violent Femmes are a hard band to get a handle on. The presence of goofball Brian Ritchie alongside the moody, angst-ridden Gano, for example, sends conflicting signals (their latest promo photo shows Gordon in a characteristic sulk, and Brian almost naked with a golf club); and the strong current of religious fervor and despair that increasingly permeated Gano's tales of adolescent anguish probably put off more than a few listeners. I think it's also that many earlier listeners think the band never again came close to expressing the exalted lust and torment of their 1983 debut album. Or that they feel they outgrew the sentiments it expressed and are embarrassed that Gano apparently didn't.

But perhaps the main reason for the band's absence from critics' discussions—and from *Letterman*—is simply that their now much larger constituency is so heavily concentrated among the young. This increased but altered demographic of the Femmes audience was brought home to me again when I saw the movie *Reality Bites*. Amid the television references and oversimplified slacker/yuppie dichotomies, amid the narrative's calculation and contrivance, along comes the Femmes' song "Add It Up," placed squarely in the film's climax almost as a generational anthem, albeit with its limbs cut off, its momentum skewed, its careful structure pared down to the size of a flippant insult.

I squirmed deeper into my seat. "Add It Up" a Gen X anthem? Is this accurate? Don't today's kids have anything more relevant to their situation than a song improvised by some frustrated, anonymous guy in Wisconsin in the early '80s?

"We kind of have our own version of *Portrait of Dorian Gray*," muses Gano. "As we get older, our fans get younger."

Even if it is not their ticket to a slot on *Letterman*, *New Times* has already fulfilled the promise of its title. It is the Femmes' first album for their new label, Elektra. Their relatively amicable 11 years with Slash Records dissolved last year in bitter legal wrangling and nasty courtroom accusations. Final contractual obligations to their old label were satisfied with the release of *Add It Up (1981-1993)*, a crazy quilt of live material, demos, outtakes, and (apparently) Gen X anthems. A unique greatest hits collection, *Add It Up* was entirely pasted together by the band itself, and as such provides a fascinating seventy-minute survey, pissed-off and vulnerable, of the Violent Femmes.

Having summarized and exhausted their past, they turned to experiment with *New Times*. Then, sometime late last year, drummer Victor DeLorenzo suddenly quit the group in the middle of recording.

As a case of someone simply tiring from the ache of the rock life, it's not at all surprising. People leave bands all the time and it's no big deal; perhaps this was unexpected, perhaps not. But think of the Femmes as three guys who have played together for 13 years, far longer and far more intimately than most any group you can name—who've painstakingly increased their base audience while weathering all sorts of semi-breakups and turmoil and relentless touring (not to mention greatest hits collections and crucial label changes)—and this quiet lineup change can grow to seem rather significant. "Victor just basically wanted to go in a different direction," I was blandly informed by the Femmes' management, "and it was a direction the others did not want to go in."

DeLorenzo, who acts with Theater X of Milwaukee and has a critically acclaimed solo LP to his credit (*Peter Corey Sent Me*, 1990), will not comment on whatever drove him to depart from the Femmes. "It was fun," is all he has told the press, "but now it's done." If that sentiment sounds familiar, that's because it's a quote from a Femmes song; a quote made all the more peculiar when you consider that DeLorenzo, a fine songwriter himself, appears fully capable of writing his own exit lines. "Well," said Gano after hearing DeLorenzo's parting quote, "I mean, I'm flattered he used one of my lyrics."

Gano and bassist/multi-instrumentalist Brian Ritchie acted at once to replace DeLorenzo. "We didn't audition anybody," Gano admitted. "Guy Hoffman was our first thought, so we called him." Hoffman had previously played with many beloved Milwaukee combos, among them the Oil Tasters and the BoDeans. "Guy came out of the same music scene, and it was great because it was the energy of a new member, a new person, and yet there's the roots and connection there as if he had been in the group the whole time."

Still, even with Hoffman in place as the new drummer, it's hard to imagine the Femmes without Victor DeLorenzo. On their last tour, DeLorenzo was the only one who acknowledged the audience—he introduced the band, he introduced the songs, he led the audience in sing-alongs and clap-alongs. Neither of the other members said a word. I mention this to Gano and he is incredulous.

"Victor the bandleader?" he scoffs. "Well I'm glad I haven't eaten anything today, because I would have lost it on that comment. Sometimes in our shows, I would be ready to say something, and then Victor would jump in and say something, and then my timing would be off because I had this different rhythm than he did as far as relating to and speaking with the audience. And Victor probably felt like, 'Hey nothing was happening, I had to jump in and say something.' And now, his not being in the group has actually brought out more talking and communicating from me. Which I think is good."

The biggest change on *New Times* is in the nature of the songs rather than the sound, despite the personnel change (Hoffman's brushes-on-snare rhythms often perfectly mimic DeLorenzo's drumming style). Previous Femmes records were big on tales of teen anguish: the first album in particular was perhaps the most eloquent expression of cosmic high-school doubt ever whined and whimpered onto vinyl. Through the years, hyper-romantic adolescent grief became a Femmes trademark. The only consistent role model seemed to be Jonathan Richman, locked into an 8-year-old's tone-deaf wonderment just as the Femmes were hooked on teenage melancholia. Even on their last album, there was Gordon Gano (getting close to 30 at the time), pleading for a date for his high school prom.

All this has changed with *New Times*, on which Gano never once adopts the voice of a teenager. Gone is the stammering unease, the choking insecurity, the fluid delivery characterizing some of the Femmes' most potent material. The trio's sound is still often spare, the voice is still unmistakably Gano's. But the requisite pledge of Christian belief that traditionally concludes their albums metamorphoses, on *New Times*, into an operatic parable about the 1992 environmental summit in Rio de Janeiro ("Death sits on all our laps / While Christ the Redeemer / Towers high over Rio"). And with several theatrical songs whose complicated lyrics are adapted from the work of Berlin Dadaist Walter Mehring, this is clearly no ordinary exercise in pop music.

I ask Gano to explain about Walter Mehring. "I know very little about Walter Mehring," he begins, then backpedals, "Although I guess if you pulled somebody off the street and said, 'Tell me all you know about Walter Mehring,' and even gave some hints like 'Berlin, 1930s,' most people wouldn't be able to come up with anything." He pauses. "So I guess either I know nothing, or . . . I'm really one of the experts in this country right now.

THE VIOLENT FEMMES
Why Do Birds Sing?
(Slash)

The extraordinarily skillful Violent Femmes can wring hooks out of thin air. Of course, it's a problem when a band gets into the thin-air portion of their career. But let's talk about some of these clever tunes. "Out the Window" is a cheerful ditty about death. "Used to Be" is a pretty, simple, folk-sounding tune aching with nostalgia for lost innocence. "Do You Really Want to Hurt Me?" is the tastiest version of the early-'80s Culture Club megahit I can imagine. It's over the top (dig Brian's bouzouki track), anthemic, and right up the street of Mr. Gordon Gano (or Gorno, to use his music-publishing name). "Yes, I suppose I want to hurt you," he extemporizes, a safe guess. No more surprising is the coda in which he repeats the line *Do you really want to hurt me?* as an invitation, gasping to an accelerated finish. Familiar with Gorno as we now all seem to be, we guess these will be the hottest spots on the record; and they are.

Then there's "Look Like That": a fine and blandly wicked little song which comes closer than anything on *Why Do Birds Sing?* to sounding that first platinum-selling album's note of lush young insouciant decadence.

The Violent Femmes today can craft simple-seeming songs that conceal the ability to sting your mind into repeating them endlessly. What they can't do is believe in the whole fragile business. The fact that Brian Ritchie's work sounds freshest here suggests that he is the one in three still able to enter the spirit. Victor DeLorenzo's sophisticated and impressive solo album is about a hundred years past a teen audience; and Gorno has for a long time been pursuing something to do with the vindication of his ego ("It reminds me of me" is his extraordinary conclusion to "American Music"). But Brian . . . okay, his solo albums are highly avoidable; but the buoyancy of his instrumental lines on *Why Do Birds Sing?* tells us he can go home again.

The fact remains that many of the Violent Femmes' original fans have been replaced by much younger ones, avid for Gorno's sagas of personalized nonpolitical ressentiment. As time passes, the gap in years grows between artist and audience. Without anyone willing it, the persona of a Violent Femmes song now begins to verge on a pose.—*Katherine Spielmann*

"I don't know what else to tell you. A director friend of mine in New York told me about Walter Mehring; I looked at some things and was quite taken by them, and did a staged reading of an English-language translation of one of Walter Mehring's plays, *Simply Classical*. The play concerns the people of Germany in the 1930s, but is based on Greek tragedy. So the original piece was written with these two levels happening all the time, which was very fascinating.

"The thing that got me so motivated about it was that there was a third level—there were things happening in this play which I still find almost impossible to believe. Without changing the script at all, by designating somebody as Clinton, somebody as Bush, and somebody as Perot, these characters were saying all the things that people were saying in our political arena.

"So I did this staged reading for the Clinton inauguration. It was uncanny, incredible, how perfectly it fit everything.

"I believe the play had originally been done as a musical, or parts of it had been sung, and I turned more of it into a song, wrote all the music for it. There were a couple of songs from it which I thought could have a separate life. I played it for the Violent Femmes, and it was fun—I didn't introduce it like, this is something special and different . . . I just played it as one of my songs. Brian congratulated me on the growth in my writing, that I was reaching out and getting better— that it was about time I was getting better with my songwriting, with the lyrics. Later, after we recorded it, I told him, 'By the way, I didn't write that. I know you'll be disappointed, but that's the way it is.'"

I remark that I find the Mehring songs—"New Times" and "Agamemnon"—virtually inscrutable. Gano appears unconcerned. "'Agamemnon' is actually . . . it's abstract and it's surreal; and the difficulty is increased by the fact that there are actually three different characters speaking, to each other or to themselves. But it's part of the dialogue in Mehring's play that I just turned into stream of consciousness."

What makes Gano believe his audience will brave this album? "There's a great variety of songs," Gano explains, adding that the simpler tunes will induce people to study the more complicated ones. "A song like 'Four Seasons,' I think people get the concept of it and what's coming across, and hopefully it's a little bit witty or clever. 'Don't Start Me on the Liquor' and 'Breaking Up' are songs that communicate without a lot of figuring. In fact, there is such contrast in the songs that at one point in the recording process, when Brian was listening to a new batch, he said to me, 'You're losing the common touch.'"

The Femmes are not your average rock band and

VIOLENT FEMMES PLAYING AN IMPROMPTU DAY CONC

Gano is not your average Joe Rock Star. He'll be praising the virtues of unschooled vocalists when his voice will drop unexpectedly and he'll casually laud, of all people, Rex Harrison—for "just talking his way through everything but doing it in such a way that he basically re-created the role, or created it his way, as if that's the only way it could be or should be done."

Perhaps the Rex Harrison reference should not seem surprising. After all, while other pop-music celebrities spend their downtime directing music videos, acting in movies, writing books, or publishing poetry, Gano eschews such typical contemporary career ambitions, preferring to compose old-fashioned musicals. His most recent effort, *Carmen: The First Two Chapters*, was begun after he idly glanced over Prosper Mérimée's 19th-century short story "Carmen," he tells me.

"What excited me was that every musical version I've seen, like Bizet's opera, always starts with chapter three. No one to my knowledge ever dealt with the first two chapters of the original story. And I found them to be extremely entertaining. So I wrote this musical."

The musical was recently presented for a short run at New York's Knitting Factory. Gano accompanied the songs on acoustic guitar and also played the role of guide/commentator. Cast with a small group of singers, the piece was summed up by one critic as "a stage revue of the kind rich college boys in the early part of the century might have put on."

Carmen is Gano's third musical (it was preceded by *Oresteia with a Happy Ending* and *Desire Caught by the Tail*), but the first for which he'd written both music and text. "I had this problem with *Carmen*, in that I had

NEAR SYDNEY OPERA HOUSE, 1990 (PHOTO, CASLIBER / CC-BY-SA-3.0)

Oregon, a university town. Our record had been the number-one thing played on the college station. When we got to this place, we felt we were received like the Rolling Stones, people all singing along to our songs. We were asking each other how somebody out here in this small town in Oregon would know about us. We were just getting started . . . I remember thinking it was wonderful and amazing."

Or maybe he's recalling how he nearly missed the Femmes' first recording session after his parents inadvertently locked him inside the house. This too is documented on *Add It Up*: track five, the answering-machine message Gano left when he called the studio to tell them he'd be late. At the conclusion of the message, Gano promises to call Victor next. He sounds confident that Victor will come let him out. Perhaps, as Gano calls out in front of a mass of delirious California teenagers, his hands over his eyes, he is simply trying to block out the presence of Victor DeLorenzo, that nuisance to his right who is always interrupting, once the dear friend who unlocked his parents' house and released Gordon into the world, now soon to leave the band altogether.

Or maybe Gordon, eyes masked, is thinking about the poor critical reception his work receives, recalling something he's just read in a free local weekly . . . I speak of this because I was one of those critics who was stupidly unimpressed by *Why Do Birds Sing?* On first listening, I thought it sounded too familiar. "Gano is better than this," I wrote at the time, pretending to know. "He used to steer his band through rather unnerving slop that genuinely tested one's faith. Now the most intriguing smashed-up noises with which this group used to thrill us have been muted in favor of an easier feel."

And maybe Gano is savoring the irony, for—after all—the Violent Femmes began as a "critic's band." Nowadays, with their teen audience swelling, you have to really work to find some positive press about them. One could legitimately argue that Gano is being held to an unrealistic standard. While the music world swirls about them in cosmetic revolutions, the Violent Femmes have continued to churn out perfectly timeless, consistently thoughtful albums, while remaining apparently oblivious to outside music trends. And *New Times*, far from evincing a band resting on its laurels, shows the Violent Femmes challenging their audience, both past and present.

Then again, standing before the roaring crowd, his gaze unseeing, Gano may be watching his critics burn, watching us suffer for having the audacity to think we could confidently judge such an unusual artist.

Right, I bet that's it. ✪

written all these songs, and yet there was still the need for quite a lot of connecting dialogue. I kind of balked at that, never having done it before. I thought, maybe I can get someone else to do this. Who do I know who's a writer? So I called up Oscar Hijuelos [author of *The Mambo Kings Play Songs of Love*]. His answering machine had opera music on it, which I took as a great sign. I left a message for him, but I never heard back. Later I was able to thank him, saying, since I never heard from you I had to do it myself, and thank you, thank you, because it really helped push me and I was able to come through in a way that was satisfying for me and was another stretch artistically.

"I told some friends of mine about it. They said, 'So, you need help and you call a Pulitzer Prize–winning novelist to ask if he wants to bail you out with your little project.'" Gano laughs ruefully. "I guess that was pretty cheeky."

"Daaaaaaaaayyyyyyyyyy . . ." I'm back in the crowd at the Universal Amphitheatre, hearing the seven thousand screams. It's a moment of roaring bigness for a band always considered excruciatingly intimate (a similar stadium moment is memorialized as track 21 on the greatest hits CD).

"Af-ter daaaaaaaaayyyyyyyyyy." I don't know what Gano is seeing, with his hands clapped over his eyes. Maybe he's remembering how it all began.

"There's one show that comes to mind on our first cross-country tour, in 1983. I remember one place we got to which at the time we had never even heard of. Of course, now we know it and love it: Corvallis,

THE BREEDERS

By 1993, the Breeders—initially dismissed as a spin-off or side project—had become not only the main vehicle for Kim Deal, but darlings of the flourishing alt-rock world. **DAVID GRAD** met the band at their pinnacle, just after a tour with Nirvana and the release of the second Breeders LP, *Last Splash*. The album remains one of the touchstones of its era.

Confronted by wildly innovative and genre-defying music, we may try to stereotype its creators, boxing them into leaden categories. This phenomenon seems particularly pronounced when women are making the noise and men are writing about it. We don't seem to have a vocabulary that goes much beyond chanteuse, or whore, or one of the boys. I'm reminded of Courtney Love's comment that male journalists couldn't deal with her except by assuming she was white trash and lived in a trailer park. So I approach the Breeders with particular care. Their recent *Last Splash* (4AD/Elektra) is the most estrogen-drenched release of recent times, and it would be easy for me to indulge in a variant of the rocker-as-feminist theme so popular today. That would not only be safe and predictable; it would deny the psychodrama that is the Breeders experience: the hilarity, chaos, randiness, and intelligence constantly exploding around you, the talking in tongues, the breaking into song, the constant interruptions. When you spend time with this band, you talk a lot and you laugh a lot. There's a constant buzz, and stage-managing it all is Kim.

For those of you who just joined us, that's Kim Deal, former bassist for the Pixies, singer and principal songwriter in what was once a side band with Tanya Donelly (ex-Throwing Muses) on guitar, Josephine Wiggs (ex-Perfect Disaster) on bass, and Britt Walford (ex-Slint) on drums. This lineup produced the powerful *Pod* album three years ago. The Breeders also put forth *Safari*, an EP, last year, on which Kim's sister, Kelley, and drummer Mike Hunt played. Since that release, Donelly has been off fronting the commercially successful Belly and the Pixies have become history, while Kim, Kelley, and Josephine, along with new drummer Jim MacPherson, have settled into being full-time Breeders. The recent release of *Last Splash* attests to their fertility and compatibility. How does this compare with Kim's last days in the Pixies, where her talents seemed underemployed?

"Maybe people thought I wasn't having fun because I wasn't singing. But I don't have to sing. I enjoy playing bass. I never said my work was undervalued in the Pixies—that was a journalist thing. I didn't feel that at all. I didn't look around at those three people and go [*adopts a soft submissive tone*], My work is unappreciated. I was on the bus during a Pixies tour once, and a guy who worked for the record company came over to me and said, 'Kim, all you need is confidence.'

"It was so sweet. What was I going to say? 'Get off me, asshole!'? People felt I was so unhappy, trapped in a role . . . that I'd only be happy if I was singing more. I'd rather not sing, even now. It takes so much energy."

Kim calls the demise of the Pixies "a natural evolution." As for frontman Black Francis (aka Frank Black): "It was fine he wanted to go solo, and he's happy. People do musically different things. A keyboard-heavy album, that's great." I hear a veiled but unmistakable sarcasm. Kim may claim otherwise, but she's clearly much happier performing with the Breeders. And she's not alone in this. When they opened for Sonic Youth in July, I was struck by the evident joy with which they tore into their numbers. Even the normally reserved Josephine was smiling, a far cry from her demeanor during a stint touring with Ultra Vivid Scene two years ago. It was apparent then that she didn't want to be there. She tells me, "Someone came up to me after a show and said, 'Are you mad at someone?' I was shocked it was obvious. I thought it was a private thing I was having. Apparently it wasn't."

Hanging out with the Breeders puts you in touch with the classic meaning of a band. Walking into the tiny hotel room where they are sprawled in and around an unmade bed eating burgers and fries, one gets the sense of a particularly dissolute slumber party. The image's classic Americana is complicated by the fact that Kim and Kelley are twins. I ask Kelley how she feels about being in a band with her twin sister.

"Well, we used to do things together in high school. We played a truck stop once." Everyone makes an L with the thumb and forefinger of the left hand, holds it to their foreheads, and screams "Loser!" "Now I think it's great; we tend to get seriously mad at each other, then it will be time to go, and then it's like okay."

And how, amid all this female bonding, does Jim fit in? (Keep in mind that the original drummer was listed as Shannon Doughton, maintaining the fictive all-female identity of the band.)

"I grew up with three sisters," he answers. "This is just a continuation of my growing up. And for a long time I was in a band [the Raging Mantras] that was all-male. There is no difference. Playing live, we're there to rock and have a good time." I expected that answer. It has become a tiresome reflex: a guy in a group that is predominantly female, or a woman in a group

pretty pretty song [*soft purr*]. I used old lyrics, they're really embarrassing—the epitome of everything I hate about songwriting. Like 'the look of love is in your eye.' Everybody knows that, but it doesn't say anything: it's a Hallmark cliché."

Kim seems almost powerless over her drive to redefine the rock heritage in her own image. Summer as an icon of freedom is one of the sacred conventions of pop culture, and *Last Splash* conjures up the sound of a post-punk surf explosion. With its drop-dead Beach Boy harmonies amid broadsides of guitar dissonance, it proclaims "Summer is ready when you are" ("Saints"). Yet it also subverts the purest fantasy of this cultural ideal, the beach movie: the summer of passion and irresponsibility, giving way in the final scene to our heroes stashing their boards and embracing the real world of work and monogamy, a transformation effected by the pure love of a faithful girl. "For the song 'no Aloha,' I got a lyric together that I thought was hilarious: 'no bye / No Aloha.' That's me saying 'You can't count on love . . . honey, it will end in tears.' I'm taking the piss out of myself. I'm telling the guy, 'We're in love now, but next week I'll run off and start fucking a rock promoter. Just wait, just watch, it will happen. Have a happy landing.' It's a self-loathing song. I've been divorced since 1988, and I'm kind of doing the slut scene. When we were recording a demo for this song, I saw something written on the restroom wall: *Motherhood means mental freeze.* I used it as a lyric. Motherhood means responsibility, chasteness, and faithfulness. I can't get my shit together on that, and I'm really sorry about it." The irony of a barren Breeder is not lost.

The tension between Kim's dulcet vocals and the raw, feedback-laden guitars structures these songs and underlies the lyrical expression of a twisted and ambivalent sexuality. The album's single, "Cannonball," was inspired by Kim's reading of the Marquis de Sade. "I was saying, 'Jump into hell, make the biggest splash you can, do a cannonball, we're right behind you.'" Another song, "Hag," is even less straightforward; it has several layers of meaning. "At the beginning, when I say, 'You dirty switch,' it has to do with the fact that maybe not all the people in the band are heterosexual. On my guitar, there's a switch—it's dirty and dusty, and whenever I switch it on, it makes this crackly noise: it's not a clean natural thing. I am making a remark about homosexuality, 'You dirty switch, you're not a clean switch. When you get turned on sexually, you don't get turned on naturally.' It means other things too: about a man who doesn't have a really manly, virile sex drive, I'm saying, 'You're just like a woman, you dirty switch.'

"When we were in San Francisco at our preproduction practice space, we had a Ryder truck we'd used to

dominated by males, never seems to deviate from this happy-sibling paradigm.

Yet there are differences. Like the way this band is openly enthusiastic onstage, without adopting that air of cool detachment, even contempt, affected by most male rock bands. Kim agrees, but points out that this is changing: "A lot of the new indie bands don't pose near as much. It's almost cooler not to pose." Josephine breaks in: "But that kind of self-effacing becomes a pose. The English call it shoegazing." Kim disagrees: "I've heard them say, 'We don't do it as a pose. We do it because we can't play our instruments.'"

The songs on *Last Splash* proclaim their female origins. The unnuanced, one-dimensional treatment of love that is your usual pop artifact gets mutated and transformed in Kim's work. Take "Do You Love Me Now?" "I was trying to expose clichés, and I'm being sarcastic. When I heard 'The Concept' by Teenage Fanclub, I really liked it. So much punk and so much rock takes the male, 'You fucking bitch! Yaah! Gaah! AAAAAH!' [*I told you there would be talking in tongues*] to show impassioned angst. Then I heard this sweet Fanclub song: such a nice attitude toward the girl. It made me wish I was the girl he was talking about. I thought it would be nice if I could make something like that for a guy to listen to and go, Ahhh . . . that's romantic. I thought, drive out from Dayton. One day we came outside and it had *HAGS* written on it. We're like, we're old . . . and this was done by a punk band made up of young guys, very virile and stuff. Later we found out that *HAGS* was everywhere. It was the name of a girl band. We needed a title for the song, and there it was."

On *Pod*, their previous LP, the plan was for Kim and Tanya Donelly to share the songwriting. It didn't work out that way, apparently. According to Kim, "Tanya was hanging out with her boyfriend a lot; she wasn't there a lot." Josephine says, "We were working together really hard at Kim's house, to pull it all together in a short time. We didn't know the songs yet, and she would come breezing in at the last moment." On the new record, Kim may be principal songwriter, but it is clear the songs on *Last Splash* are the product of a close-knit creative unit. Jim describes getting an idea for the drumbeat that would serve as the foundation for "Flipside" and rushing over to Kim's house to see what she could do with it. In turn, Kim describes her songwriting process: "Most of the time, I'll do something on the guitar— a little riff—then drag whoever is around down to the basement. And we'll work it out."

Josephine, something of an ideas person, describes the origins of the song "Mad Lucas": "When they were staying at my house outside London, I had a book called *Mad Lucas*, about a well-known hermit who lived in a nearby town in the last century. People would go to visit him. But Charles Dickens trashed him in the *London Illustrated News* for forsaking his responsibilities as a man of property." Kim goes on: "The song lyrics deal with Dickens. As a social reformer, you'd think he'd be wiser. But he's saying, 'Why do you live like this? You are a pig.' The hermit's line, and I think it's really right on, is, 'I can live however I want to.' Dickens insists, 'You can't do that.' Says who? 'Says eternal providence' is Dickens's answer. What the fuck is that?! In the song, I go 'and I don't like dirt.' Coming from me, that's funny. I have notoriously bad hygiene. Imagine someone like Dickens coming to my house and seeing me living like a pig. Then I got this dumbass guy telling me what I got to fucking do. It's weird how someone like that can be revered."

"Roi" is based on a phrase Josephine overheard in a bar: "She's gagging for it." It's a pretty good example of the sardonic irony which seems to color her world view. On a more somber note, Josephine also wrote the lyrics to "900," which appears on the four-song *Cannonball* CD EP. It is based on the story of a polar expedition at the turn of the century. "It was one of the first expeditions supplied with tinned food. When the ship got blocked in ice, they were poisoned by the lead solder and went crazy. They did ridiculous things. They left the ship and

headed for land carrying everything with them, including tables and chairs. They loaded up sleds and pulled this tremendous weight themselves. They had a thousand miles to go to get beyond the ice. They got nine hundred miles before they were all dead." In the band's outlook, love is like the doomed trek of those explorers: weighed down by useless baggage, doomed to perish in the wilderness.

It is a testament to the power of the ideas behind Riot Grrrl that interviews with women in current bands all touch on the movement. Kim says: "I think it's a really good thing for the girls. I remember being that young." Kelley adds: "Years ago, I was at a show, up on my boyfriend's shoulders, and I felt someone grab my crotch . . . There were these two guys. Do I tell my boyfriend to kick their ass? I feel stupid about this, but I ended up laughing. It was totally my problem: nobody was going to help me with it. And they thought I was laughing with them, damn it."

My time with the Breeders is coming to an end. Another journalist is waiting in the hall. The pressure is on: this band could be the next big thing, and they tell me they're booked through to the end of the year. Doesn't it ever get a little too much? It's then that Kim tells me about the Cringe. "We did a whole day of interviews. Afterwards, I was lying in bed, and I got this overwhelming sense of embarrassment over everything I'd said that day. I just went *Oohhhhhh . . .*"

She buries her head in a pillow. ◗

KELLEY DEAL (PHOTO, BRAD SEARLES)

PJ HARVEY

Polly Harvey was all of 22 when she emerged, fully fledged, seemingly out of nowhere, with her blistering debut album, *Dry*. **MARTIN ASTON** interviewed her upon its release in 1992. **LOIS MAFFEO** and **SARA MANAUGH** reviewed.

Here in England, we've learned to look to North America to taste the cutting edge of female singer/songwriting—the twisting psychodrama of Throwing Muses' Kristin Hersh, the neotraditionalism of Mary Margaret O'Hara, the folk-art weave of Jane Siberry, the currently lauded bedsitter balladry of Tori Amos. Today, from the southwest England town of Yeovil, near the ancient Druid temple of Stonehenge, Polly Jean Harvey redefines sharp.

Like Hersh and Patti Smith, she is part of a group. In PJ Harvey, she punctuates her post-punk guitar grazing with slithers of slide guitar and violin, while bassist Ian Olliver and drummer Rob Ellis retain an almost jazz-trio, pre-punk air of dexterity. Harvey served a brief apprenticeship in the little-known Automatic Dlamini, but otherwise their combined experience is negligible. They emerged from nowhere.

In contrast to Yeovil's bucolic haziness, Harvey's music is raw and confrontational, a jagged hybrid of folk-blues and rock tussle that lurks somewhere between the dynamics of Throwing Muses and the Pixies. In her lyrics for the two UK singles "Dress" and "Sheela-Na-Gig" and for the debut album *Dry*, feminine introspection, vulnerability, and indecision in the face of pressure are taken close to the bone. This may not be new, but contradictions between head and heart have rarely been expressed so forcibly, and no one else (certainly no male) is mapping this terrain in this way. As UK monthly *Select* sums it up: "liberation, devotion, lust, the abyss, tenderness, triumph, trauma."

Harvey has won a reputation for being withdrawn and difficult. An almost insouciant smile can defeat impromptu requests for snapshots, as at this year's Glastonbury Festival. Questions may meet a refusal to explain what she feels is already clear. Harvey won't unravel her psyche.

Select left humor off their list. Both "Dress" and "Sheela-Na-Gig" scan pain and pleasure, devotion and despair, love and lust with a check-out-the-irony grimace—even an outright laugh. "It's hard to walk in a dress / It's not easy / Spinning over like a heavy-loaded fruit tree," Harvey sings in "Dress," a violin mimicking her lament, scraping along like worn-out fingernails as she mocks the perils of costume. "He said, 'Sheela-na-gig, you exhibitionist!'" she sings. "He said, 'Take your dirty pillows away from me!'"

She admits humor is integral. "Things can be much more powerful with it. Otherwise people think you're po-faced." And there is something hysterical about the way Harvey gets red-blooded boys singing along on "You leave me dry."

Her comments on "Sheela-Na-Gig" help explain the music's tension between extremes. "A Sheela-na-gig is a Celtic stone carving, originally from Ireland, of a female figure crouching down, pulling her vagina open and laughing insanely. What I like about it is that she's laughing, and ripping herself apart. Humor and horrificness.

"Extremes are important to me. It's what I'm particularly about and what I'm currently feeling. It's the kind of drive I want to get musically. It didn't always work on *Dry*, but next time will be better. I've done a version of Bob Dylan's "Highway 61 Revisited" for a tribute record (to be released on UK label Imaginary), and it works really well. Dylan's words to that song are amazing. He works with extremes, too, like a film edit from one verse to the next, from almost-Biblical to modern-day imagery."

Another hero is the Pixies' Black Francis, "who can incorporate humor into a serious song. I saw him play solo in London last year. His songs are so strong with just a guitar. I enjoyed them even more than the Pixies, who I already like a lot. It's not for me to say I sound like them, but he's probably been an influence. I admire him."

Harvey is more direct than Francis, who reveals more about his love of space, junk, and Latino culture than about his emotions; or Nick Cave, who uses fictional narrative to explore his feelings. "I think their power comes from the delivery of the words. It's the same with Patti Smith. I heard *Horses* once, and it was brilliant—not so much her music as her delivery, her words, her articulation. Her honesty. When I first heard Nick Cave sing 'From Her to Eternity,' it made me feel physically sick. I found it really frightening, really violent."

But although "honesty is the only way I know of writing," it stops short of explaining. Is the red lipstick on the inside album sleeve a vehicle to promote feminine appeal? A mask for female insecurity? A phallic symbol? Answer: yes, probably. Harvey won't dissect lyrics or discuss issues. Ask her why she sings "ease myself into a body bag" ("Plants and Rags") or the experience that led her to choose for "Water" the dual images of baptizing and drowning, and she'll sit there in this oak-beamed

MARIA MOCHNACZ

olde-worlde Yeovil pub, faintly smiling. Like, I've played this game before. All she'll say is, "I don't feel qualified enough about most things I feel strongly about to draw attention to these issues. I'd rather kick up the dust, as you put it, and let people think about things for themselves."

The refusal to solve ambiguities raised by her work, or to qualify statements, recently created a rare scenario as the UK music press started comparing PJ Harvey features. At the start, she had appeared topless on the cover of *NME* (from the back, showing a small portion of one breast, in the same pose as Siouxsie years ago), and also on the back cover of *Dry*, which got rival sheet *Melody Maker* up in arms. Do women have to take off their clothes to progress in the music business?

The furore surprised her. "To me, it seemed natural to do that cover. I think it's tame, but people have reacted strongly. In my head I imagined the photo would accompany the music. Instead it was treated as a finished product. Which is my own fault. I was actually disappointed with the photo they chose; there were ones that worked better. But it's like with the back of the record. If people listen to the music, the image will make sense."

NME photographer Kevin Cummins claims the idea for the feature was that Harvey would be naked on the cover, and thus vulnerable, while the inside photos around the feature would be more aggressive. Harvey has been called irresponsible for seeming to claim artistic immunity. It's also been said that the line "I've come up man-sized / Got my leather boots on" from the unrecorded "Man-Size," can be construed as feminist commentary.

"I don't spend time thinking about feminism as an issue," she responds. "To me, that's backtracking. You can

141

PJ HARVEY
Dry
(Indigo/Island)

It takes monumental guts to make music in the first place. Ask any frustrated music critic. Putting out a record that exposes the entirety of an experience is an especially heartrending proposition. Polly Harvey has sent out into the world a work about desire that crosscuts the sexual and political, heartbreak and rage, passion and confusion. She's that heavenly mess we saw buzzsawing through Patti Smith's *Horses* and strolling drunkenly in Joni Mitchell's *Blue*. Her desire, although distinctly passionate, is to be understood. She rushes from the need for approval in "Oh My Lover" ("You can love her/You can love me at the same time/It's all right") to the stinging blow-off of the sarcastic hit single "Sheela-Na-Gig" ("Gonna wash that man right outta my hair/Heard it before/No more").

Behind all this soul-searching is *soul*—music that goes down there, makes your heart ache and head hurt. Ian Olliver's bass is like a schoolyard crack-the-whip, stretching and swinging and throwing off those who can't hold on. Rob Ellis punches out windows with the kick drum, serving up the shards via snare. *Dry*'s glory, though, is Harvey's guitar, slide-heavy and distorted, all fury and weariness showing through. A string section on the acoustic "Plants and Rags" is strangely modern, rediscovering the curiosity that electricity is not the only thing that intensifies a stringed instrument.

The basic acoustic skeletons of these songs, which came as a bonus disc with the UK version, are rawboned wonders that feature Harvey's most authentic vocal takes. No doubt about it, *Dry* is a new gospel for our young world. Be baptized.—*Lois Maffeo*

PJ HARVEY
Rid of Me
(Island)

Lucky us, able to pick and choose the best of a good lot. *Rid of Me* comes close on the heels of 1992's *Dry*, praised to the heavens for its outsize raw sound and Harvey's confrontationally personal lyrics. Trying for an even edgier sound this go-round, PJ Harvey solicited eminent noise-monger Steve Albini to spike the punch; and true to form, his big blackened fingerprints are all over the dense, crunchy riffs on these rough-hewn tunes.

Conspicuously absent on *Rid of Me* is the sparse, delicately haunting touch of *Dry*'s "Oh My Lover" and "Plants and Rags," replaced by the jarring chaos of the nervy, rumbling "50ft Queenie" and the primal pavement-scraping punk chordage of "Yuri G." One could argue that the less controlled, coarser sound Albini produces here complements the unfocused vitriol of

talk about things too much and nothing will be done. I prefer to go ahead and do things, not think about them.

I bring up "Sheela-Na-Gig." "The man says, 'You exhibitionist.' Is he saying the female can be powerful and attractive, but mustn't appear willing?" For that, I don't get even a faint smile from Harvey.

Does the question of responsibility to an audience bother her? "I don't know what I think. I never thought of myself in those terms until I saw these things in print. I've talked to close friends who agree with the journalists: I should be more aware, more responsible. But I still think it would be dangerous to express a point of view about things I'm unsure about. People seem to forget I'm only 22. They treat me and the music as if we've been around for years."

I ask if her work is about female desire confronting a world of masculine expectations. "That's someone else's point of view, which isn't important to me," she replies. "What is important is whether I get something out of what I'm doing, and that I'm pushing myself. I don't understand why people have this desire to pinpoint everything. To control. Why not let it speak to you in some way?"

She does say that "Happy and Bleeding" isn't about menstrual periods, and that "Plants and Rags" was inspired by a book of photographs: "Each double-page spread has extreme images, like light and dark; one shows the backs of houses, sheets hanging on clotheslines, sunflowers. It was very simple. I chose it for the sound of the words together."

She also confirms that "Dry" (the first B-side of "Dress," not included on the album) is an ode to sexual dissatisfaction. "A lot of the songs are about dissatisfaction and frustration. Everybody feels those things. I called the album *Dry* because it's a simple, minimal word, and more powerful because of it. It's a word of needing something else, and a lot of the songs are about that. And I think it's funny to sing about dry vaginas."

Not very English, is it?

"No, I suppose not. But people in Europe say it isn't very shocking either. Compared to English reactions."

Polly Harvey, with her huge eyes and short, black hair pulled back tight, looks more like a tiny Spanish ballerina than a typical English rose. "But I am English," she maintains. "My mother's also dark-skinned and dark-haired. No, I haven't traced my family tree."

And are her family atypically English, in that you can be intimate with them?

"Yes, compared to friends' families."

You don't mind revealing yourself to your parents in your lyrics?

"No, they've always been very encouraging. Both my parents love music, which is probably why I'm a musician. My dad got upset when he thought I was going to art college. He thought I should be doing music. I'm very lucky. Dad really loves the music. My mum is shocked sometimes, or maybe just surprised, by what I come out with."

Because nice girls from Yeovil don't?

"I couldn't answer that. Dad wouldn't say if he found something scary. He's quiet about new songs until he's heard them a bit, and then he'll comment. But we don't sit around analyzing lyrics."

Harvey's music walks a tightrope between what is revealed and what is obscured. "I'm very conscious of that tension," she admits. But where does she draw the line? "You learn by mistakes to find the right way of doing things. I know what I want and don't want to show. But I wouldn't talk about that. The *NME* cover was a mistake because it didn't achieve what I wanted. If it had, I wouldn't have to explain."

People want strong, steadfast role models—especially females ones, whose numbers are scarcer. Does Harvey have her own role models? "My mother. That's about it." (Her mother is a sculptor.) Not Patti Smith, another artist whose band used her name? "I'd never heard her stuff until people started mentioning her. You should see my record collection now, full of things I've been told I've got to listen to."

The initial run of five thousand copies of *Dry* in England came with an additional recording of the album in demo form. She explains: "My 4-track demos were what Richard and Paul at Too Pure first heard of my stuff. So we all thought it would be nice to release them with the debut album. It was their suggestion, but for me too, I'd always want to see how things started out if I was really interested in an artist.

"It's the way I work now: when I write a song, I record it, just to document it. Demos are completely different songs—when I record them, they're brand-new, and everything is clear in my head. Later, as the process moves on, things get diluted. You lose the intensity. Afterwards, you're just saying the words instead of the words coming out of you.

"Still, you gain in other ways with the excitement and aggression of a whole band. It's the way that gives me the most excitement: in a band."

We wind up talking about the difficulties of answering questions. She expects to do fewer interviews in future. Is there a difference between female and male interviewers? "Yes. A different atmosphere. With women I probably say a lot of things I wouldn't say to men. Things I'd rather not say."

So does she have more male friends than female? "I have more male friends. The only way I can explain it is, it's to do with how I grew up. I was the only girl in the village." This seems implausible; then I realize she means in her own grouping. "I was a tomboy until I was 14, and played with my brother's friends . . ." Polly Harvey trails off.

She thinks it hasn't been a great conversation. She's feeling sad today. "Actually, I've been feeling like this for three days now."

Yup. She's 22. ⊙

MARIA MOCHNACZ

these songs, emerging in the disturbing lyrics of the obsessive spurned lover on the opening title cut and amplified on "Legs": "I might as well be dead / But I could kill you instead."

Harvey does her manipulator persona one better on the hypnotic careen of "Rub It 'Til It Bleeds": "I'm calling you weak / and you believe me / I wanna stroke it . . . / God's truth / I'm not lying / and you believe me!" This is a different sort of catharsis than we're used to from Harvey, and perhaps it's not for everyone: PJ takes Dylan for a tweaked ride on a revisited "Highway 61 Revisited" that sounds uncannily like a product of the twisted mind and vocal cords of Jesus Lizard's David Yow. Whether or not you think Big Steve shoulda kept his smelly paws out of this pot, *Rid of Me* serves up a brilliant boot-to-the-gut testament to Harvey's ongoing psychic purge. I hope the next phase kicks as hard.—*Sara Manaugh*

GUIDED BY VOICES

In 1993, **JOHN CHANDLER** happened upon a copy of an ultra-obscure album by Guided by Voices and was instantly enraptured. He tracked down the frontman, schoolteacher Robert Pollard, allowing *Puncture* to become the first American magazine to profile the band. "Why would you want to talk to me?" Pollard wondered at the time.

Another workaday morning. The last thing I expected was a musical epiphany. I yawned my way through breakfast, stumbled the three blocks from my modest flop to the office, and feigned meaningful activity until lunchtime, then moseyed over to Green Noise Records.

I was at my usual post, flipping through an alphabet of used albums (Agent Orange, Agitpop, Agnostic Front . . .), when something curious came over the store stereo system. My ears twitched. I sloshed it around in my head a few times as the critic mind kicked in and began to break it down to its essential salts. Let's see: Soft Boys, Neil Finn, XTC, Tall Dwarfs, Paul McCartney. Yikes! Cunningly melodic; the same fragile-gives-way-to-broken ache favored by Sebadoh. A '60s pop sound with noisy distractions. Better add Wire and Mission of Burma to the equation. Low-tech and unpretentious, like something on Flying Nun or Xpressway. Best of all, it's damaged goods! These guys definitely have a skewed version of the universe (whether it came about naturally or chemically isn't important). The firm of Barrett, Chilton & Wilson has hired some junior partners.

But who is it? Mr. Greene, the store owner, looked up from his magazine.

"Some band from Ohio," he said, "called Guided by Voices." The cassette had just arrived in the mail.

"Have you got anything else by them?"

He shook his head. "Apparently they've released six albums and never really tried to sell them. They've got like zero distribution."

My mind raced. I'd borrow money from Mom and start a record label. These guys are too good to languish in limbo. What to call it? Drooling Turnip? How about Dusty Cupcake Records?

"Scat Records in Cleveland signed them." Greene broke into my reverie.

Still, a lot of questions needed answering, starting with: Where have this band been hiding all my life? When I got hold of him, GBV chief songwriter Robert Pollard did his best to explain. He also generously sent me copies of everything the group has done up to now. It's an amazing array of different sounds and styles—feedback psychedelia, fractured folk, bizarro pop, hard-rock din—and all excellent. Getting six overlooked gems like these in the mail is a treat, a rare chance to discover the undiscovered. And the new album, *Vampire on Titus*

(Scat) is much like its predecessors: sincere, vague, and intoxicating.

STUDIO DAYS

"Guided by Voices have been messing around with recording albums since about 1986," Robert began. "Before that we played live for three or four years, but there aren't many places in Dayton to play original music, so we stopped. I think we're perceived as old, weird guys who make their own records. We put out six self-financed albums but didn't try to sell them. We were kind of lazy in that respect.

"Our first recording experience was in a 16-track studio. We didn't know what to do with the stuff when we were done. We just shit-canned everything and decided that in future we'd always put our best songs on record, no matter how they were recorded 4-track in the basement, 8-track, whatever.

"We use different approaches when we record. I can't stand groups making records that all sound the same. We try to incorporate different sounds. We'll plug microphones into our guitar amps and sing through them. Sometimes we record on the spot with the 4-track. We'll rehearse the song later as a band, but then it may not sound as cool as the original demo. We've used everything from low-tech 4-track all the way up to a 24-track studio. About half our last album [*Propeller*] was recorded on 24-track, then remixed to seem like 4-track stuff. It sounds like messed-up arena rock!

"We always made tapes to send to friends—to anyone who was interested. I don't know how so many people ended up with our stuff—tapes being dubbed, I guess. Eventually Robert [Griffin], from the band Prisonshake, who runs Scat Records in Cleveland, decided to sign us on. One of the guys in Pavement got hold of our stuff and played it for Kim Gordon and Thurston Moore. Moore really liked the album we did in 1987, *Devil Between My Toes*."

THE NEW STYLE

"It's great Sebadoh are getting so much attention. We've been doing the same kind of thing as them for years—getting ideas onto tape, no matter how bizarre or fragmented. I think people are starting to get into

the low-tech recording thing. Sure, you can save up a bunch of money and go into a big studio or you can invest in a 4-track or 8-track and do everything yourself. Sometimes ideas flow in the living room: it's nice to have something right there to get it down on. We purposely made the new record fragmented and weird, kind of like an album of Who or Beatles outtakes.

"Maybe bands like Sebadoh, the Grifters, Tall Dwarfs, and us can spearhead a low-tech revolution in the music industry!"

SCHOOL'S OUT
"I teach fourth grade. I've played some of our music for my students, and they seem to like it. Sometimes they dance around, real silly. After a while they get bored. Now we're finally getting reviews. We were interviewed by *Melody Maker* after the New Music Seminar. They did a photo shoot, too! I'm hoping the story appears before school starts, so I can show my fourth-graders something substantial.

"I like teaching, but it has its share of aggravation and pressure. It would be great if I could support myself and my family through music. That goal has always seemed so far away, I haven't thought about it much. Of course, it wouldn't be worth it if a record company tried to make us into something we're not. I don't want to compromise the music. I don't know if a big label would let us keep recording on a 4-track, which I love to do. A lot of strange groups are getting signed, though . . ."

EVERYBODY'S TALKING
"We played at this year's New Music Seminar in New York. It was like the first show we'd played in five years! It was certainly the biggest show we've ever done. I think everyone expected us to be this strange little group, because we're usually pretty weird on vinyl. But we played a straight set of like 18 rocking two-minute songs with hardly a pause in between. It went really well. Afterwards, Mark from Pavement and Mike D. from the Beastie Boys came back and talked with us. I met people from some of my favorite bands!

"It was amazing, since we'd been playing for about ten years and getting very little notice. Most of us are in our mid-30s . . . I mean, we've been kicking around for a while. Before GBV I played Cheap Trick covers in bar bands!

"The most important thing to us has always been 'Are we having fun?' That's why we put out our own albums and do our own cover art. It's fun! We used to do pretend interviews, pretend photo spreads, pretend liner notes, pretend lyric sheets. When we got interviewed by Everett True for *Melody Maker*, it's like we were ready! He said [*English accent*], 'You guys would be huge in England!'"

THE MORAL
There are a million unsigned bands out there. What makes the Guided by Voices story special? Perseverance, for starters. Pollard and company never stopped trying to write their eccentric pop masterpieces, even with six albums gathering dust on their shelves. Many bands fold their tents if they don't get signed after a certain length of time. GBV had no guidelines for success; they kept plugging away, following their instincts. Their music, like the tree falling in the forest in the old conundrum, brought up a question: If no one is around to hear it, does it matter if the sound it makes is any good? Fortunately, a few people with good ears got a grip, and now we all have a chance. ◉

JEFF BUCKLEY

Jeff Buckley's voice and musical gifts—even his looks—eerily recalled those of his long-gone father, Tim Buckley, whom he hardly knew. Those traits may have been in his genes, but the son had his own agenda. **STEVE TIGNOR** interviewed him in 1993, just after the release of his first EP, *Live at Sin-E*. His only studio album, *Grace*, was released the following year; Jeff Buckley drowned while swimming in the Mississippi River in 1997.

Jeff Buckley couldn't be more out of place. Locked in a sleek black publicity room thirty floors up in Manhattan's Sony palace, the artist with the whisper of a voice is trying to stay earnest and low-key amid the show-biz circus. While I trot out my theories about his music, he pulls at his already disheveled hair and picks at the mountain of food the company lackeys have piled in front of him.

But Buckley is forthcoming, his whispers projecting a vulnerable honesty in these surroundings. The conversation comes around to his father, the late singer-songwriter Tim Buckley, who I assumed had been a major influence on Jeff's avant-roots style. But he sounds surprised when I mention the similarities in their singing.

"Do I sound like him? I didn't know my father. He left. He chose another family. I can't help it if I sound like him. My voice has been handed down through the men in my family for generations." I haven't seen any mention of his father in his press. Does he want the connection downplayed? "No, it exists. But he didn't mention me! As a singer, I disagree with some of his vocal choices, but there are songs of his that I think are brilliant."

Jeff's debut release, a solo live EP, has four elaborate, jazz-styled vocal excursions backed with his own guitar. Hints of the blues, mountain folk, scat, and rock guitar come through while Buckley emotes. Two of the four songs are covers, one by Edith Piaf and one by Van Morrison. I've also heard him do Bukka White and Bob Dylan songs in recent performances in New York.

"I'm just trying to slip into other skins," he explains. "I'm doing songs I love, trying to work something out for myself. When I did 'The Way Young Lovers Do,' I was thinking of Van scatting. I just do them and try to forget them. They can be embarrassing. One reviewer hates what I did to that song. I just tried to bring myself to Van's style and stretch it."

Speaking of slipping into other skins, Jeff Buckley sounds like he was exposed to a musician's eclectic tastes from the beginning, even if he didn't grow up with Tim Buckley's record collection. He doesn't seem to have been drawn to roots music by an adolescent or bohemian craving for a foreign sound (like, say, Mick Jagger), but because he always thought: this is music.

And he heard his father's records. He sings a similar space-wrought Cali soul, forsaking rhythm and stretching songs to their tortured limits with his vocals. Like a jazz player riffling through every approach to a phrase, Buckley sings verses from different angles, wringing vocal possibilities from each song.

His musical lineage shows up not just in sounding like Dad but in his habit of phrasing vocals like the originals. John Hammond Jr. (another scion of musical privilege) does the same in his blues playing, executing technically amazing imitations of anything. Buckley and Hammond blow away other musicians but may raise questions for listeners who find the insight of a cover song in its differences from, rather than its similarities to, the original. Inauthenticity is often more exciting (Jagger again), and tells us more about a song and an artist than technical improvement on re-creation would.

I mention Richard Thompson as a possible folk influence. "Thompson's a great player," Buckley agrees. "But to affect me, the music has to be more . . . fucked. Like Dylan, when he puts certain things together and I want to say, 'You can't do that!' but it works. I'm trying to put together everything I've heard and read, the poetry I've written. I've gotten to a point where I need Billie Holiday; but half of what I've always been about is Jimmy Page."

Even for solo appearances, Buckley does accompany himself with an electric guitar, using rock progressions. "Rock 'n' roll has a place in my music. The electric guitar actually has a very warm sound, and there are things you can do with it that you can't do in an acoustic mode. The next album will have a band. I wanted to do live shows to get my ideas together. But I can only get so far

JEFF BUCKLEY
Grace
(Columbia)

Trained to distrust the self-serious and on shaky ground with anything remotely experimental, rock critics are destined to dismiss Jeff Buckley's torturously drawn-out avant-roots songs. His father, Tim, enjoyed critical favor in the early '70s as the LA singer-songwriter who provided an alternative to Cat Stevens—but that was a time when the earnest rather than the absurd reigned. Today's Cat Stevens figure is a big goofy hunk fronting the Lemonheads, and LA folk is currently being revived by Beck, a waif who personifies the '60s as his spaced-out nightmare hippie girl: "She's a self-inflicted obsession . . . she's a science of herself."

So Buckley's earnest '60s connections and science-of-self soul searches won't get him far with new folk hipsters. He doesn't care: he calls his debut album Grace and populates it with song titles like "Eternal Life," "Lilac Wine," "Hallelujah." Buckley's mission is to mix an older tradition of blues and folk with his idiosyncratic solo guitar and vocal arrangements. Gifted with an old mountain-soul voice passed down through his family, he is also an inventive, thoughtful guitar player.

Despite all that, and despite the varied styles he employs on this record, his songs meander in a vain search for center, for melody, for humor, for something to tell an audience. As I listened more and found less to connect with, the simple, clichéd elements—acoustic riff on "Last Goodbye," lilt of "Mojo Pin," and "Hallelujah"—were what I ended up coveting, like beacons in the fog created by Buckley's incessantly soulful voice and amelodic ramblings.

Musicians and singers may sit in awe, but there are too many five-minute vocal escapades here. They're not unoriginal, and not uninteresting, because he stretches his voice so many ways. But this album will take a back seat to Beck's—not so musically accomplished, but funnier—when I need to hear avant-folk.—*Steve Tignor* by myself. For recording, I need ideas from other people."

When he gets rolling about his music, anyone listening to Jeff Buckley can hear his ambition. His voice sputters with frustration: too many thoughts to put into words, too much about his music that he hasn't worked out yet. There's no star trip; he's more poet and craftsman than rocker. His pretensions are inner-directed, visible in a beatnik-like romanticizing of his artistic struggles. Over the course of a thirty-minute conversation, he is mostly serious. I wonder out loud what kind of audience he will have. Is there a place for his songs, none of which have the rhythms or propulsion that rock-fledged ears want to hear, outside of a small crowd of musicians? As he has said, reviewers could prove unfriendly, could dismiss his over-the-top singing as indulgent.

"No, I haven't really thought about an audience. This music isn't just for me, even if it's just a crowd of bridge-and-tunnelers at a show. I can offer stories people can relate to. I'm just like anyone else, with a brain, heart, loves, coffee stains, whatever. Anybody who is into music I hope will want to hear me."

Judging by his choosing to work small clubs in the East Village and to debut with a live record, it seems that Buckley knows his music isn't going to be easy to market to a pop audience. I ask him how his relations have been with Sony/Columbia, and how the company is approaching his career. "It's not a conscious underground thing. I've told them that this is going to be basically me doing a live thing. It wasn't planned to start with a live record, but we had this stuff around. I'm not that happy with any of it. I want to do weirder things with the next one."

On that note, it's time to go. As we get up, Buckley has more on his mind. "I have to be careful at this place [Sony]. They're like a father who buys his daughter everything she wants. It takes me out of reality." We shake hands and I leave him, passing trendy-looking staffers jumping rope in the hallway. My last glance shows Buckley seated again in the shiny room, picking at his cold food as he waits for the publicity rep to bring in the next interviewer. I suspect no matter what they give him, Jeff Buckley will keep to his own path. ◗

GREIL MARCUS

If Lester Bangs represented rock criticism's sweltering conscience, Greil Marcus serves as its intellectual doyen, connecting the dots between artistic movements.
DAVE HASLAM interviewed Marcus—who would later contribute book reviews to *Puncture*—upon the publication of his collection *Ranters & Crowd Pleasers*.

How many critics respond with equal openness and creativity to Bikini Kill and Neil Young, to Robert Altman and Heavens to Betsy? It is the scope of his receptiveness, the sharpness of his attention, and his panoramic awareness of cultural artifacts both mainstream and marginalized that make Greil Marcus such an unusual and valuable observer of contemporary culture. Almost anyone writing about the arts today is to some extent indebted to his work—his overarching books *Mystery Train* (1975) and *Lipstick Traces* (1989), and his regular writing for various magazines, much of which draws attention to things we might otherwise miss, or casts a new and piercing light on what we thought we already understood.

This magazine work has recently been collected in *Ranters & Crowd Pleasers: Punk in Pop Music 1977–92* (Doubleday). Marcus has also assembled a compilation CD, *Lipstick Traces* (Rough Trade UK), which is intended as an aural accessory to his book.

Among the pieces in Ranters & Crowd Pleasers *there are only a couple of interviews—with the Gang of Four and Elvis Costello, for instance. Do you not do many interviews with musicians?*
Almost none, for a whole lot of different reasons. One is, I don't like to do interviews much; I don't think I'm very good at them, and I think the interviews I like to read the most tend to be when the interviewer asks questions that might appear stupid and tend to be provocative, and I'm not very good at doing that.

Another reason is that I work as a critic, and I think I'm not terribly interested most of the time in what the artist thinks he or she is doing. Maybe that's very arrogant—and sometimes I know it's shortsighted, because I've found that out—but I'm more interested in confronting a piece of work, a record, or a concert, and trying to make sense of what's going on there, or to extrapolate out of my own response to what's going on in the music.

The reason I interviewed Gang of Four was that I heard their first album—*Entertainment!*—and it seemed so clear that this music was made by interesting people who I thought I would like to get to know. In fact, they were interesting people, and Jon King and Andy Gill and I have remained friends ever since then—13 years now.

I interviewed Elvis Costello because I was working for

Rolling Stone at the time and they asked me to do it, and I was interested in meeting him. In fact, it was a frustrating thing because we talked for something like six hours, and the only stuff that got printed was just the nuts and bolts of his career, as opposed to him rambling on for hours about Charlie Rich or Billie Holiday or stuff that was actually interesting.

Do you think, though, by not talking through your ideas with more artists, you may have missed out on some good and useful experiences?

I accept that I probably missed out on a lot of situations. On the other hand, the work that I want to do really does come out of a confrontation with the artifact, with the work. The kind of completely—either you could say "liberated" or you could say "irresponsible"—imagination that gets me where I want to go, in terms of writing, would be very cramped if I knew too much about what a given performer thought he or she was doing. So in some ways I'm better off not knowing, though in some ways I might be poorer.

Your relationship to the artifact and the artist, then, is more like that of a fan: standing on the outside, to a degree.

Yes, I hope so. Definitely.

Yet there's sometimes a big gulf between you and other fans. For instance, you write about hearing Springsteen's songs at one of his concerts, and how it "made me think of a story Maxim Gorky told about Lenin's love of Beethoven." At another point, you tell us of Springsteen fans driving around with bumper stickers proclaiming Bruce Is the Rambo of Rock. *There's a massive gulf there, different perspectives, different reactions . . .*

Well, not all fans are alike. You have a crowd of people at a concert and they're all thinking different things.

But are you implying that those fans of Bruce's misunderstand him?

I think a lot of people's fans misunderstand, and in that I would include myself because that's in the nature of art; if there's no possibility of misunderstanding then there's no art.

The fact is, Springsteen plays around with a lot of American patriotic symbols. He's playing a dangerous game and he knows that a lot of people may misunderstand the irony that he's using. But that's a chance he's prepared to take.

But if he's a polemical, oppositional artist—as you seem to see him—surely he's failed if he doesn't communicate his point of view.

I see what you mean, but firstly, I don't think he is a polemical artist, at least at his best. His occasional polemical songs, like his "oh gee, the factory is closing down" songs, are not very interesting, but the songs on

Nebraska, for example, which to me are songs about the complete spiritual desolation of America under Reagan, are not polemical at all, they're very situational. The fact that the album was misunderstood by a lot of people, particularly a lot of critics—because I didn't go out and take a survey among his fans—I think says more about the way Reagan managed to hypnotize the whole country in terms of what was important and what wasn't than Springsteen's ability to say what he wanted to say. There are times when it doesn't matter how brilliant or clever or insistent you are, you're not going to be understood, you're not going to get your message across.

Springsteen is one of the few American artists you write about in Ranters & Crowd Pleasers. *Your main interests are in British bands in the punk and post-punk era, aren't they?*

I found most of the American punk or new-wave bands either very pompous or just good-timey. I know that I was looking at that time for something a lot rougher and a lot more threatening, and as it became clear that Jimmy Carter was a disaster and trouble was on the horizon, the kinds of alarms and warnings the Sex Pistols were sounding really hit home to me.

But the real difference is that there was a frightening seriousness to the British punk bands. I don't mean they all went around frowning, some of them were having a wonderful time—X-Ray Spex were as much fun as any band will ever be—but there was a desperation there too, whereas there was something unserious about almost all the American bands. I mean, "Beat on the brat, beat on the brat, beat on the brat with a baseball bat." Who cares?

Was it a hope of yours that you could turn on the American public to what was happening in Britain?

No. I'm not a crusader. To be a critic you have to be arrogant to a certain degree—you have to trust your own instincts and think they might actually be worth someone else's time to pay attention to—but I'm not so arrogant as to think that if the whole world shared my taste in music the world would be a better place. So when I wrote about Lora Logic, Delta 5, or the Au Pairs, if there was any social component, it was just "hey, you might not know about this and you might want to, this might interest you" as opposed to "you must pay attention to this."

Well, for me that's enough; all music discussion comes back to "you must hear this record."

Exactly, and that's what motivates criticism too. But it's wanting to be part of a conversation more than wanting to make converts.

The Lipstick Traces *CD . . . did you track down the songs and the spoken-word stuff?*

Yes, this compilation is mine. About six years ago, before I finished *Lipstick Traces*, one afternoon I couldn't work, but I was feeling too guilty to take a walk or go see a movie. I had to do something connected with the book, so I got the idea of making a soundtrack for the book.

The first thing I put on it was "Anarchy in the UK" and I began free-associating, running all over the house grabbing this record, this dusty tape, putting things on a master tape. I liked it so much I made copies of it and sent it to lots of my friends. Geoff Travis at Rough Trade was one of the people I sent it to, and he said, "We should put this out."

Ultimately, we couldn't get any Sex Pistols material. I decided that was too bad, but so what? The Sex Pistols material is available anyway. Almost everything else I wanted to use, we got consent for. That means everything from my favorite Slits song, "A Boring Life," to "It's Too Soon to Know," by the Orioles, to Raoul Hausmann's Dada poetry, to Lettrist poetry in the '50s, to Marie Osmond reciting "Karawane."

The book doesn't cover music of the last ten years, so obviously the Lipstick Traces *soundtrack doesn't either. I wonder what stuff from the last ten years you think might have fitted?*

I'd be putting in stuff from [the Mekons'] *Fear and Whiskey*, and that song by Carter the Unstoppable Sex Machine where they sing "Tomorrow I'll be burned as a witch / for playing punk rock" ["While You Were Out," from *1992: The Love Album*]. That could have come straight out of *Lipstick Traces*.

One of the unfortunate effects of the publication of Ranters & Crowd Pleasers *is that it's added to a feeling that the best days of pop are over . . .*

That wasn't my intention.

No, but the establishment are still saying that the great days were the '60s. Richard Branson with his hideous "classic rock" station . . .

It's like "nya-nya-nya—you missed it!"

Exactly. Then the next generation, with Jon Savage's England's Dreaming, *and your books, it's like "nya-nya-nya" all over again, and most of the media heads—people who run the Sunday papers, the BBC—are happy to look backwards.*

That's something I have fought against my whole writing life, this hideous propaganda campaign of whatever generation has suddenly reached power to inflict themselves on the generations behind them: "We're gonna sit here until you forcibly kick us out and we're gonna tell you we had a better life than you. Our values are better than the ones you have, and you're gonna listen to this for the rest of your lives."

If I was a '60s stuck-in-the-mud Deadhead, I'd probably be writing some incredibly dull book about how the Grateful Dead transcend all time and space.

Ranters has two endings. One is, it ends with Bikini Kill, and is saying that what is going on today is just as powerful and just as suggestive as anything and needs no apologies, and all it does is open to the future; we don't know what's coming next. There is also an extra ending, with the brief return of the '60s, which is not my attempt to argue anything, but it's just about my dumbfoundedness at the way the culture of that time has continued to weave its way into the present.

I find it odd that some people see punk as a kind of return to the '60s. In some ways, now, you'd be forgiven for thinking that it actually happened in the '60s!

I was fascinated by the way that for Malcolm McLaren and Jamie Reid, one of the things punk was was an attempt to restage [the student revolts of] May 1968 in Paris in a cultural milieu, but to cause the same kind of disruption with the same sorts of unlimited demands—rather than "we want a more rational school system and better jobs." That was very much on their minds and a great part of their instinct. And I think it's interesting the way John Lydon, in "Albatross," on *Metal Box*, begins to moan "Still the spirit of '68," as if he's never going to escape it.

I mean, there's a way in which making a breach between then and now is absolutely crucial to get anywhere in culture and in history, and there's a way in which the past never goes away; it simply changes shape as time moves on. Because whatever the theories of McLaren and Reid, for the kids on the street—the consumers and, let's face it, the people who were actually making this chaos and disorder—the whole point of punk was that it was a rejection of the '60s. Exactly. They were liberated from a horrible burden.

From the dinosaurs . . .

Yes, but not just from the rich, famous rock stars. They were liberated from the worst thing you can say to anybody in cultural terms, which is, "You can't make your own history." In this new book, I write about the idea that history exists only in the past. Of course, that's how many people see it, but I don't see it that way. History is always waiting to be made. History is the future, history's what we're going to do with our lives. To tell people that you can't make history, that it's already been done for you—that's what the people who were the first punks had been told all their lives. What they were doing with punk was, one way or another, making their own history.

A lot of groups you admire are at their best, you often seem to think, when they're working at the boundaries of rock. I wonder why you bother with rock culture at all, given your delight when Gang of Four or Sonic Youth are breaking preconceptions or denouncing rock 'n' roll? Mainstream rock obviously has no appeal to you: you like groups when they're trying to break out of rock culture.

I don't quite know what you mean. Ultimately—like it or not—the Gang of Four and Sonic Youth are rock 'n' roll; they're not comprehensible as anything else. There are moments of dissolution in the music of both when those labels are the most meaningless things in the world, and there's no way you can put a label on what's happening.

But if there is so much wrong with rock culture—and I think there is—and since those groups were, in part, working to change rock 'n' roll, my question is, why bother with guitars? Why bother with those chords? Why bother with that history? Why bother with going out and playing live? Why?

Well, that's a good question. My answer is probably not a good answer: I like it. I've never found anything that adds so much to my life in terms of pleasure and surprise, and the eliciting of deep emotion. I've never found anything that makes me think as much. I've never found anything that's as good a means to friendship—to meeting people and having something to talk about with them.

What I value so much about the music that was made in Britain in '77, '78, '79, and through the '80s, is that it really is different. It has a spirit of freedom that's irreducible, and it does not sound like other stuff. It's as coherent and as novel as rockabilly from Memphis in the mid-1950s.

Going back to something you said before—that the idea of the Sex Pistols wasn't to talk politics in the sense of "we want jobs," but in that May '68 fashion, I'd like to talk about music and politics. In your introduction to Ranters *you wrote of the Sex Pistols and the groups that followed: "The music made a promise that things did not have to be as they seemed, and some brave people set out to keep that promise for themselves." I wonder how you can describe these people as "brave"? The brave people in our society are the people who may not be rallying about May '68 ideas, but are more concerned with jobs; the people who stand on picket lines; the single parents with low incomes; the people who work in underfunded hospitals. To describe people with guitars and amplifiers playing to a bunch of pissed-up [drunken] people as "brave" seems inappropriate.*

I thought a lot about using that word, about whether it's the right word, because it is a big word to apply to getting up on a stage with a guitar. I decided it was the word I wanted to use. I think that particularly at that time, but at any time when there isn't a formed scene—and there aren't rules and predictable expectations—it takes a lot of courage to get up in front of other people and confront them with what you have to say. Which may, of course, be revealed as nothing. That's what I was talking about; I wasn't just talking about any would-be artist linked to some notable tradition.

What you say about the word "brave" more properly applies to people who are really thrown back on themselves, who have very little or no resources, and yet are persevering in something they think is worth doing, or trying to maintain some sense of autonomy within horribly limited choices. I can't disagree with that. However, I think in many cases what the people I find most inspiring in pop music have done took a lot of bravery to do. I think for Kathleen Hanna of Bikini Kill to get up onstage and make real music out of rape and incest takes a lot of bravery. I think she exposes herself to ridicule and shame and, for that matter, conceivably, physical violence—though not so far—and I think that takes a lot of courage. I don't mean everybody who gets onstage is brave; I've been onstage and it didn't take bravery, it just took a complete lack of scruples.

I think that for someone like Kurt Cobain, who spent his entire childhood being beaten up and called "faggot," to get it into his head that he could stand up in front of other people, utterly exposed, took a lot of courage. So, I'll stick with that; I'll stick with the word. ✪

This interview was first published in the *Independent Catalogue*, no. 6 (July 1993), and is reprinted with their kind permission.

INDIE ROCK Dying Breed or Dead Issue

Does indie rock have a future? Does a great band need the pressure of being on a major label in order to develop its talent and avoid stagnation? Do the new indie/major marriages of convenience restructure old fault lines? In 1994, with the music seemingly at a turning point, **STEVE TIGNOR** pondered these questions and more.

Fed up after countless evenings at CBGBs watching bands moan indecipherably, strum out-of-tune guitars, and trot out pointless root-note bass lines, I took advantage of the third protracted between-song break by Red Red Meat to blurt out the first word that came to mind: "Rock!"

Ten sets of spectacles and white T-shirts turned to see who had interrupted the heavy silence.

This is what indie rock has come to. It derives its name from its status, independent of the multinational corporations that own the major labels, but for me it now tends to mean a sound more than anything—the sound of guitar bands either strumming in a style borrowed from R.E.M., or shambling along like Dinosaur Jr. It's the sound of punk being reduced to the sterile, meaningless word "alternative."

Through the first half of the 1980s, indie labels housed most of America's great punk acts and provided the space for them to experiment and grow. Thereafter, as major labels lured away Hüsker Dü, the Replacements, and others, and with the demise of bands like the Minutemen and Flipper, indie bands increasingly seemed to make their records for a safe college-radio constituency. Indie wisdom had it that their bands were keeping alive the original, non-commercial spirit of rock, but by the early '90s the unambitious anti-anthems of Sebadoh, Superchunk, Seam, Buffalo Tom, and Dinosaur Jr.'s third or fourth remake of *You're Living All Over Me* were hardly subversive—they amounted to a homogenized sound. Indie labels, despite offering some great bands a place to experiment—from early Sonic Youth to groups like Heavens to Betsy today—were putting out more and more of what the majors call product.

Getting up from my candlelit table at CBs (the mecca of punk has a cafe in front of the stage!), I thought for the hundredth time that indie had hurt the development of rock 'n' roll by insulating it from the industry at large. Granted, that insulation kept rock breathing in the early MTV days; and by hitting specific audiences, independents developed more variants on punk than major labels could. But even the great records that came out on early-'80s indies, for example those by the Minutemen (on SST) or Minor Threat (Dischord), were never as realized as the albums of late-'70s punk progenitors such as Pere Ubu. Those earlier bands weren't just addressing a narrowly defined scene as Minor Threat were, or

reducing songs to riffs in some minimalist experiment as the Minutemen did. They were making music they thought the world would hear. If Tom Verlaine hadn't been trying to make a record people west of the Bowery would also want to check out, would *Marquee Moon* have been the enthusiastic, precisely played record it was? Would he have cut his famous guitar solos, which CBGBs regulars must have thought clichéd at the time? I understand the attraction that bands feel towards indie labels—Hüsker Dü got to have a career on SST before moving on, while Television broke up after their second record didn't chart for Elektra—but speaking as a listener, *Marquee Moon* has spent more time on my turntable than the entire output of Black Flag, the Feelies, Big Black, Galaxie 500, and a dozen other indie acts I theoretically liked.

The major/indie divide has become less clear-cut recently—independents with vague major-label financing deals are blurring distinctions both economic and aesthetic. Also, an increasing number of old college-radio bands have signed with majors and made the charts, so the debate about selling out is raging again. I thought it would be interesting to see what's happened to the music of indie bands who have taken the signing plunge, and at least one who has not. What are the effects on the development of a band's music of selling yourself to the big boys, and undergoing the industry's attempts to simulate the "honest" sound of indie rock for the masses?

And I don't mean the effect of having a bigger production budget—that's no guarantee of anything. Much as I like to hear guitar bands reach past amateurish murkiness, *Zen Arcade* and *New Day Rising* sounded like shit—and a decade later I'd still rather listen to them than to the Hüskers' more cleanly produced Warners release *Candy Apple Grey*. A bigger production budget may provide better sound, but a band still has to know what to do with it.

The crucial element that independent labels deny bands is not sound quality. It's the chance for the best rock talents—and most of those have started out on indie labels—to test themselves in front of an audience that won't automatically buy into what they do. Sure, the majors are mostly about milking trends and watering down original ideas to maximize popular consumption (for every Cobain, there's a Vedder, then a Weiland, then . . .), but for the best acts, the pressure a major exerts to reach new listeners can spur them to make the music they can only hint at on independent labels.

Let's start with one of the indie world's original sinners, the Replacements. Here's a band for whom the major-label gamble certainly didn't pay off in musical terms—their records got worse. But while *Tim*, their first Sire release in 1985, was undoubtedly inferior to *Let It Be*, their preceding Twin/Tone release, it wasn't because it aimed too close to the masses. The problem was that it sounded indie. Paul Westerberg, who had screamed ridiculously about answering machines and dentists, was suddenly writing ringingly earnest anthems about generational politics—even about college radio. Where "Tommy Gets His Tonsils Out" careened Heartbreakers-style, "Left of the Dial" was the angst-ridden roar of a thousand college radio stations over the next ten years.

And by 1988 the major-label game had clearly taken a tremendous toll on Westerberg. His chart ambitions eventuated in soft pop with a frigid production. At the same time, he seemed so sick of it all that he had stopped trying to write good songs. Ahead of the market, trampled by Bon Jovi, the Mats split two years later. Since then Westerberg has put out one erratic solo record, its mix of raw rock and overblown pop indicating that the possibility of having hits has brought out the worst in Westerberg, who's a singer-songwriter at heart.

A year after the Replacements withered in major-label obscurity, a band with one awful indie-style album to their credit vaulted past Michael Jackson to number one on the Billboard charts. Seeing "Teen Spirit" on MTV was a pleasant surprise: here was an ex-Sub Pop mediocrity, suddenly on Geffen, cranking out a rock song that simply sounded more important than anything the independents had produced in years.

But it wasn't until Cobain came up with the anti-commercial masterpiece *In Utero* that we saw how recording for a major perversely benefited his music, if not his life. Like an NEA-funded artist creating pornography so as not to appear kept, Cobain set out to prove his non–corporate rocker status by making scabrous, abrasive music. To some extent he succeeded—and in the process he made the best record of 1993. Songs like "Milk It," "Very Ape," and "Scentless Apprentice" united the two sides of Nirvana's work, fusing the straight, simple rock songs with the noise and screeching that dominated some of the material on *Incesticide*. Cobain managed to keep noise under control without writing anything remotely pop.

Part of the excitement of rock'n'roll as purveyed by Elvis Presley or the Rolling Stones was its ability to shock the mainstream, the middle classes. By the '80s, indie had retreated—away from the chance of such engagement and into a college ghetto. Geffen restored to Cobain that broader target for his noise, and in return he dug out his most powerful songs. Would he have dug that deep if he'd known that the songs wouldn't reach beyond the familiar ranks of college-radio listeners?

A band who do it their way, control how they make their records, never cop rock-star attitudes, tour much of the year to sell-out crowds of faithful who imitate the band's dress and lifestyle. Fugazi, right? Or is it the Grateful Dead? Fugazi's DIY process and their attempt to create a self-sufficient scene are punk theory in action, and admirable in many ways. In musical terms, though, it means they end up playing to their own people, preaching to the converted. It's the concept behind latter-day folk music—old folkies like the Dead have played to their cult following for 25 years without having to stretch themselves musically.

As someone who appreciates Fugazi's original sound but finds the records repetitive, I've always thought it likely that direction and production by a major label (unthinkable, I know, and maybe not even smart financially) might get them to shake up their monolithic guitars, to think about playing for people who don't currently know their music—and in this way possibly squeeze out an album that is looser and not so thoroughly guy, one that retains its pleasure over repeated listenings. In their terms, that would be compromise, but to non-cultists it would still be hard enough to still be rock.

Among other larger remaining indie-rock acts, Sebadoh labor over their craft yet stay determinedly lo-fi, ending up with songs that are both fussy and obscure, too abstract for melodies or hard rock. Superchunk still believe that their variation of punk's three chords and lo-fi dust amounts to art or authenticity—and still sell the same records to the same people.

Most of the bands who have moved from indies to majors are not as talented as Fugazi, nor are they as bound by integrity. In aesthetic terms, their results to date have been mixed. Smashing Pumpkins, Soundgarden, and the Breeders have all taken advantage of major-level production to try and create distinctive songs with dynamics of melody and rhythm, rather than producing a slight variation on the well-worn post-punk hard guitar sound, the way the indie ghetto would encourage them to do.

And these bands have all made their best records to date, even if that only means two good songs per album instead of zero. Soundgarden in particular have benefited from the rise of grunge and the demise of metal on the charts. Their latest record is not their major-label debut, but it is their first to reach past the metallic drones they beat to death for metal fans on previous albums. Now they've turned the drummer loose and come up

with grooves that don't involve the same riff pounded out again and again. Even Pearl Jam, the majors' facsimile of an indie band, act punk these days, and on *Vs.* and the newer "This Is Not for You" they move from pop-metal hooks to a hard-rock sound—a sound that, despite the leaden drumming, Neil Young and the Who (the two classic-rock acts closest to punk) would admit was part of their legacy.

The Lemonheads, on the other hand, have gone in the opposite direction since leaving Boston for LA— from two good songs to zero. Evan Dando suffers from the Westerberg syndrome—the singer-songwriter being urged to craft careful, upbeat pop. Like Westerberg, Dando has trouble sounding interested in his latest batch of mushy major chords.

Punk-derived sounds now have a broad enough appeal that it doesn't always seem to matter whether the records originate on a major or an independent label—so much so that indie band the Offspring can reach the Billboard Top 20 just as easily as Green Day. (Who incidentally offer a prime example of major-label watering-down of punk. To anyone who cared about punk in 1977 because its rawness and honesty were not as easily digested as other entertainment, Green Day's songs seem lifeless: fast and simple, but with none of the earlier time's chaotic energy. The edges are rounded off to attract a casual CD-buying public.)

This shift in the market is most obvious in the popularity of L7, Dinosaur Jr., and Sonic Youth. The first two, not known for variety, haven't changed their sound

significantly since signing to majors. Dinosaur may be a little more pop, and L7 more metal, but I doubt either would have gone in a radically different direction if they had stayed indie. Instead, the mainstream has moved toward them, to the point where their old indie styles are now standard hard rock. And they're playing it at Lollapalooza.

Sonic Youth have always been too irony-bound for it to matter whether they're on an indie or not—even in the mid-'80s a song like "Expressway to Yr Skull" blurred the lines between avant-garde art and bombastic rock. But as early as 1988, on *Daydream Nation*, Sonic Youth had advanced the flat rhythms of punk and the Velvet Underground as far as their tunings and hyperspeed could. Their arty, indie No Wave noise had crossed paths with rock; the band had run out of ways to play to their core audience and needed to find listeners who weren't indie connoisseurs to keep from rehashing their last album. In 1990 they signed to Geffen and made *Goo*, a record which didn't water down their noise, but did make the band play it within tighter song structures— three minutes, garage riffs, no breakdowns. Punk/Velvet rhythm and Sonic tunings had successfully broken into the majors—the former helped *Nevermind* reach the top of the charts in 1992, the latter led to the success of the Breeders' *Last Splash* in 1993. Sonic Youth's own return to "art-core," *Experimental Jet Set*, would go Top 50 in 1994.

Four years after *Goo*, the deal between Matador and Atlantic has bound together the aesthetics and economics

155

of majors and indies, leaving the big guys their choice of quality music which happens to sell. If this kind of deal proliferates, the schism between label sensibilities would largely be a thing of the past. It's a bad position for indies—artistic autonomy, their one asset, is being co-opted. Despite that, Matador also puts out Liz Phair and Pavement, two of the best acts around, both of whom make accessible and, by any standards, honest music—which also happens to be the most melodically inventive rock and roll for years.

Pavement in particular are the band that have been able to add another element to punk/Velvet rhythms and Sonic Youth noise: melody. Compare "Trigger Cut" on their first album, *Slanted and Enchanted*, with the song from which it rips off its opening guitar sound, the Velvets' "Coney Island Steeplechase" (on *Another View*). Their respective opening lines (Lou Reed sings, "Would you like to go on a Coney Island steeple"; Steve Malkmus sings, "With your lies and betrayals / Fruit-covered nails / Eeee-lectricity and lust") are enough to show that Pavement are reeling off a sharper, more complicated melody. At the song's coda, Malkmus comes back and imitates with his voice the opening guitar sound ("Aah-ooh, sha-la-la-la . . .") as if making it up on the spot. Such an effortless talent for creating melody has nothing to do with making music in obscurity or with poor sound quality.

Crooked Rain, Crooked Rain, Pavement's second album, fleshes out the melodic potential of "Trigger Cut" and the band's noisier Drag City EPs. "Range Life," their latest laconically mid-tempo pop song, is the finest thing they've done. The events of the song—intro guitar, vocal bridge, etc.—are longer, more assured, never on the verge of art-noise breakdown; Malkmus has time to find melodies in the unlikeliest places (in lines like "Run from the pigs, the fuzz, the cops, the heat" and "Out on tour with the Smashing Pumpkins"), and to punch up the song's essential point, "Don't worry, we're in no hurry" with his most forceful delivery.

Malkmus's gift for singing melodies that don't sound crafted is one that Lou Reed, Thurston Moore, and Paul Westerberg presumably can only envy; it's also a gift that impending mainstream success hasn't impaired. It's even possible that Matador's combination of major distribution and preservation of artistic control for their bands may be the reason that Malkmus has blossomed where Westerberg faded. Whether Pavement (and Liz Phair and Bettie Serveert) can continue to keep their music from being watered down or overproduced, despite Matador's corporate funding and access to WEA's mainstream distribution system, remains to be seen.

If punk-rock bands don't necessarily need indie labels anymore, it seems that talented and unconventional singer-songwriters do. Freedy Johnston's major-label debut, *This Perfect World*, reveals the downside of compromise. The first thing to deplore is the pumped-up drum sound. Then comes his voice—less prairie, smoother. Then you notice the songs heading for obvious hooks more than they used to. It's a decent album, but unlike *Trouble Tree* and *Can You Fly?*, it doesn't reward repeated listenings.

Even if they can't fully develop the potential of a guitar band, independent labels will still be the ones who discover most of the great ones to come, and will release their early records along with all the lesser product. But a much more important role for indies lies in the lifeline they offer to more marginalized forms of music: to singer-songwriters who need to keep their quirks, to new folkies who need to develop a sound (though Beck has already blown past everyone by doing something which pre–indie rock 'n' rollers used to do—engaging black music tradition without simply paying homage to it); and to riot grrrl bands, whose polemics aren't yet co-optable by any of MTV's alternative nations (I doubt Heavens to Betsy could project such a caterwaul if they were being marketed through Atlantic/Matador).

While I make these formulations about indies not coming up with great guitar-band records anymore, I'm taking breaks to listen to the latest album by Guided by Voices. *Bee Thousand* is an old-school, murky, Beatles-esque, sloppy-guitar, college-radio, indie record—it also happens to be the most exciting listening experience I've had in two years, the kind of record that reaches into the future and makes everything else sound old. It has songs I feel I've heard before but in fact have only hoped for so long to hear, songs which rise out of guitar clutter with perfect harmonies, a mix of distortion and pretty acoustic strumming, melodies that aren't overworked, that come and go without announcing themselves, and lyrics which, like all great rock lyrics from Dylan to Patti Smith to Pavement, are not about what the words mean but how they sound. I must have listened to it 25 times the day I got it. And it could only have been made on an independent label (Scat). A major would never have wanted twenty tunes, most under two minutes, and would never have allowed the gorgeous melody from "Awful Bliss" to be thrown away as a filler. If the band were in the situation of being pressed to recoup a major label's investment, I can imagine these songs straining and losing their mystery in the effort to be overnight sensations.

But what do I know? ◗

JONATHAN RICHMAN Liars, Assholes, and Modern Lovers

Jonathan Richman, a patron saint of indie rock, was the inspiration for **CAMDEN JOY**'s short story. Joy's subsequent work—including his postered manifestos and his novel *The Last Rock Star Book, or: Liz Phair, a Rant*—would kick-start a new style of writing about music in fiction and criticism. This piece marked the unveiling of his byline and hybrid style. **FELIX MACNEE** contributed the artwork.

I was born in Boston on May 16, 1951. I started chasing girls from age five onwards. They usually weren't as interested in me as I was in them, and this made me confused and hurt. By the time I was 15 I was pretty lonely. High school and I didn't understand each other. So I heard the Velvet Underground, got inspired, took up guitar and drove into Boston from my suburb of Natick to terrorize Boston audiences with my four-and-a-third note vocal range and crude guitar playing (when I say crude, I mean it). Well I got lonely doing that so I put a band together when I was 19 and called it the Modern Lovers.

> —from Jonathan Richman's official autobiography, released to the media in 1977

The night we eloped, my new wife and I went to see Jonathan Richman for the first time. It wasn't easy for us to get to the concert. We had no car, very little money, and no idea where the show was, other than a street address on the other side of Los Angeles—the rich side where we never went. Our wedding ceremony, conducted in a wedding chapel by a Reverend Garcia (who stood elegant and unfazed beside a plaster wedding cake speckled in grime), had taken thirty seconds and set us back $75. We had no money for rings. We also had an oversimplified view of the other side of Los Angeles. We imagined that over there, on the rich, white, west side, it was different: buildings remained well separated, addresses clearly marked, streets few and easily navigated. From our wedding chapel next door to the La Brea Tar Pits we hopped a city bus, gaily heading for the club.

Rolled up in my hand was our marriage license. The reverend had signed it but the space for a witness's signature was blank, since we'd arrived alone and couldn't locate any witnesses around the chapel. We were one notarization shy of official matrimony—not really married until a witness signed the certificate.

Not that I was worried. Flush with the spontaneity of our deed, caught up in the kind of delirious good cheer you see in Mickey Rooney movies made in the Depression, convinced the bus we had boarded would deposit us at our destination, my bride and I rode happily into a neighborhood we knew nothing about,

while I revealed my plan: we would buttonhole Jonathan Richman before the show and cajole him into signing our license as a witness. What made it fitting was that, for a very short time, her pet nickname for me was "Abdul," from the goofy, amorous sing-along Jonathan Richman had composed a few years before. In some way, though we'd been joined by the power vested in Reverend Garcia, our marriage would not finally be hallowed until witnessed by Jonathan, the sage whose vision of romance rang through our hearts.

Abdul's not seen Cleopatra / It's been almost now a year
How I wonder where she's atra / And I wish the old girl
* were here*
Abdul yearns for Cleopatra / In the early-morning sun
Abdul loves Cleopatra / Thinks she's still the one

Of course, it was the wrong bus. We ended up terribly lost. It took hours of aimless crisscrossing on foot before we accidentally stumbled across the right street. Then we had to hike another few miles, up and down and up and down, to find the right block. By now, thanks to her unaccustomed high heels, Midge's feet were rubbed raw and blistered. Though we were terribly hungry, we could not afford both food and a Jonathan concert. We limped on, no longer talking, blisters growing, stomachs growling, disoriented by this weird glitzy unfamiliar part of town, my arms dangling loosely about her shoulders in a useless display of sympathy. Neither of us had yet turned 20. We felt as square and clueless as people could get. Uppermost in our minds now was the notion of Jonathan Richman as our role model.

I went into this when I was 16. One of the reasons I started was, I knew I had no standard voice. I just wanted to show that anyone could do it. It didn't matter how pretty your face was. All you had to have was feeling. People said it took courage to do what I did when I was performing alone and only knew two chords on the guitar, but it took no courage, it was just something I wanted to do so badly no one could have stopped me. I still have plenty to learn. Like Spanish.

Like how to get along better with dogs and cats, because that would help us get along better with people. I think the group has to learn volume, that the group has to be softer, because at this stage infants wouldn't like us . . . we hurt their little ears and I believe any group that would hurt the ears of infants—this is no joke—sucks. And we have to learn to play with nothing, with our guitars broken, and it's raining.
—from Jonathan Richman's first interview, 1973

Eventually, we found the club. The show was completely sold out.

"Hang out and wait," commanded the lanky fellow guarding the door, whose breath smelled of peanuts. "We can probably squeeze you both in."

We huddled in the darkness of the awning, acting as if this were a normal sort of pilgrimage—wedding chapel to Jonathan Richman concert in less than eight hours. Our courtship had occurred throughout our teen years, in the most hokey places—at schoolbus stops, during pep rallies, in the homeroom. I was captivated by her freckles and flashy 15-year-old eyes, her wry mouth and almost demure manner. We were not only high-school sweethearts: even cornier, we were practically neighbors, our homes a few doors apart. After graduation, all this weird grown-up stuff descended upon us. Reeling from it, unsteady in our ambitions, vague in our values, unskilled at any work, intimidated by grown-up institutions from banks to supermarkets, we ended up in the big city one day, getting married as a way to subvert the dizzying press of things, grabbing the branch of matrimony with both hands to wrench ourselves from the chaotic swirl before the raft bucked from under us and we were swept over the waterfall.

Our giddy, rash decisiveness had thus far served us well, rushing us through secret, spur-of-the-moment nuptials to where we stood now, under a club awning in the nice part of town.

"Here comes Jonathan," Nut Breath muttered. He motioned at a figure approaching from the neighboring motel.

Stepping towards him I extended the wedding certificate and ballpoint pen.

"Oh boy!" my bride giggled. "Oh, this is great!"

I tried to hold my tongue until I could see his face. "Excuse me," I finally blurted out. "But we just got married . . . we wondered if you would sign our license, as our witness? I know it sounds weird—but we really think you're neat."

"Yeah," Midge sighed dreamily.

"If that makes any sense," I concluded lamely.

"Sure, friend," Jonathan Richman told me. "I'm a little busy right now, though. Maybe after the show?"

Nut Breath shrugged at us. "Sorry."

Jonathan performed solo at this time, taking a Greyhound to gigs, packing little more than a rinky-dink Harmony guitar supposedly purchased at Sears for $35. So once we were inside, the first thing we made out onstage was Jonathan, a colorful shirt tied high across his rib cage, Bermuda-style, his belly button bared. "It helps my stage act to wear something I know someone else hates," he once told a reporter. "It makes me stronger. It makes me feel persecuted."

He would set down his guitar mid-song, stepping away from the mike and extending his arms, snapping his fingers and gyrating suggestively and mock-wincing as he improvised one embarrassing rhyme after another. The audience was enraptured with this kind, funny man—except for one guy, a mean, burly asshole with a beard as red and loud as a fire engine. This red-bearded guy kept interrupting Richman, screaming, "You're a liar! You're lying!" Jonathan ignored him ("When he was heckled he put his ridiculers down with ease," noted a critic in the midst of panning a Jonathan Richman show. "It may have been the most talent he displayed all night"). Eventually, Red Beard gave up and stamped out of the club. "Whatever," my wife softly said to the mean guy's back as he departed.

Despite Red Beard, it was a perfect show. Jonathan sang out stories about UFO men who crashed while practicing loop-the-loops, sang out praise for chewing-gum wrappers and Vincent van Gogh and the beach and corner stores, sang out warnings that if you don't celebrate your youth "it will haunt you the rest of your life," sang out very specific directions for a milkshake ("I want two scoops . . . chocolate ice cream . . . No cherries! No nuts! No whipped cream neither . . . no marshmallow . . . but lots of malt!").

He was the perfect ham, three parts Harpo Marx, two parts Jiminy Cricket. He did a song estimating his age at "Just About Seventeen." The next song lowered the estimate to "Not Yet Three" ("Which is it, Jonathan?" Midge whispered). He did an a cappella number about an old-time baseball pitcher who always played fair, and after each verse Jonathan wound up and threw an invisible baseball at the crowd. My bride and I stretched for the baseball as if reaching for his blessing.

Then he sang a song called "Now Is Better Than Before." If we had doubted the wisdom of eloping, Jonathan dissipated our doubts with that song. He transported us to a place free of skepticism and apprehension, where nothing bad could happen anymore. Encore drifted into encore and we could only grin at each other, our hunger and tired feet forgotten, our future beckoning like a magic kingdom. We settled into a joyful hug, my face resting in her knotty hair as I endlessly smooched the top of her adorable little head. That's how we missed our chance to intercept Jonathan for an autograph on our wedding certificate when he dashed out of the club and disappeared into the motel next door.

My wife and I found a cheap apartment in Los Angeles, outfitted it with garage-sale furniture, then got up the nerve to tell our parents what we had done. For a few weeks, they didn't speak to us. We didn't bother to tell them about the Jonathan show. We figured it might somehow upset them more. No one asked to see the license, so no one ever saw the missing signature—or learned that legally, despite what we said, we were not truly married, since in pausing too long to revel in our good fortune we had failed to get Jonathan's autograph.

Around this time, I started learning all I could about Jonathan Richman. I read an essay about him in the *Rolling Stone Illustrated History of Rock & Roll*; it called Jonathan "a grand-nephew of the American New Wave" and claimed he had "uncovered what may have been the last primordial guitar riff" in a song called "Roadrunner" he wrote at 16. I read how in the mid-'70s he formulated a bionic-wave theory he used to review albums; how his pickup musicians would keep time with rolled-up newspapers; how he mounted a crusade to reduce the world's electricity output. I talked with people who'd seen him play street corners, family restaurants, coffee shops, city parks, old folks' homes, wax museums. I met a guitarist who told me Jonathan auditioned him over the phone ("Play a solo over 'Louie Louie'") for a European tour, then rejected him. I came across someone from UCD who said Jonathan had paused during a set in Davis to ask if anyone in the crowd could drum with the band on their current tour.

Most of what I learned was apocryphal: Jonathan despised journalists and seldom spoke to them. I guess it bothered him how rock critics kept talking about "Roadrunner" (which he pretty much refused to perform anymore) and pestering him about the Velvet Underground (he'd spent time as a messenger at Andy Warhol's Factory around the time he was dreaming up "Roadrunner").

The more vague and unreliable clues I collected about Jonathan, the closer I felt to him; he almost held more influence over me than my parents. At times I'd think that he and I were, in fact, related in some way.

It turns out this was mistaken.

One day I was folding laundry in the middle of the apartment, humming along to *Rockin' and Romance*, when there was a knock. It was the next-door neighbor, her cherubic face all appled cheeks and dimples. I could only remember her last name, which was Richman. She asked if she could borrow some sweet white wine for a chicken stew she was preparing.

"My wife and I," I explained to her, "we don't really drink alcohol."

"You don't even have any cooking sherry?"

Coming back from the kitchen with a bottle of something that looked like what she wanted, I noticed her head twisted in an uncommon way. She stood in the doorway on tiptoe, peering towards our turntable.

"Is this Jonathan Richman?" she asked.

"Yeah. It's his latest record. It's good."

She made no other response than a flash of her dimples, so I went on.

"I mean, it's no *Back in Your Life* or anything. It's no *Jonathan Sings!* Those are probably my favorites. I mean, I like him a lot."

She nodded. "You know," she said, "he's my cousin."

My heart sank. Surely he was my cousin. "Yeah?"

"Yeah." And she told me how one day, wandering in Berkeley, she came upon Jonathan skipping rope by himself on the sidewalk. She said, "Howdy" (no doubt in Jonathan's world strangers are forever saying "Howdy"). He stopped jumping and she introduced herself. Struck by their common last name, he told her, "I guess that means we're cousins." They went through generations naming in-laws and half parents, great-uncles and great-aunts, grandparents, birth dates, far-off cities of origin—trying in vain to pin down where their ancestry crossed. When they came up with no names of common kin Jonathan shrugged, hands still gripping the rope ends, and said, "I'm sure we must be cousins." It was silly—there must be thousands of Richmans—but to Jonathan, it was simply a question of figuring out what relatives they shared.

By the time the story was told, my wife had come back from work, the laundry was folded, the record had clicked off.

"It turns out," I filled Midge in, gesturing halfheartedly at our beaming neighbor, "that she's Jonathan's cousin, she says."

"Really?"

Our neighbor nodded happily.

"Wow."

"Yeah," I said without enthusiasm, feeling jealous and left out.

"Maybe she could be our witness," my wife said. "I mean, she's related to him, she's one of the family. She's a Richman."

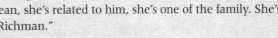

"Yeah," I said. "Guess so." I went to dig out our wedding certificate while Midge explained it all to our neighbor. "What it would mean," she concluded, "is that Camden and I would finally be officially married!"

"That would be absolutely great!" our neighbor cried.

I was digging through our trunkful of papers. "Sweetie-pie," I interrupted, "Where did you say you put the license?"

She checked the dresser while I went through the trunk again. We went on to rifle magazines stacked by the stereo, the pamphlets in the bookcase, the bedstand drawers. We could not find the license.

At some point our cherubic neighbor quietly checked out. The two of us kept searching for hours, then abruptly gave up. We perched on the bed, frowning at the stereo, thinking separate thoughts. Finally I realized neither of us had spoken in a long time. "I just can't believe it," I said. "I just can't believe it."

"Yeah," my wife sniffed, tears magnifying her freckles. "It pisses me off. Can you believe it? I mean, I can't believe she's really, truly related to Jonathan."

You know I love Cleopatra / I'm just grateful I know that old girl
Even though I wonder where she's atra / As I wander through this world
And Abdul yearns for Cleopatra / Abdul takes her or takes none
Abdul loves Cleopatra / She's still the one (Alright Leroy . . . Tell them!)

AROUND THE TIME my wife and I eloped, there was no consistency to Jonathan Richman's recording career. Dropped after one album for Sire (*Jonathan Sings!*), two years later he showed up on Twin/Tone (*Rockin' and Romance*), and two years later on Upside (*It's Time for Jonathan Richman and the Modern Lovers*). It made for shelving problems at my local record store, as some of his earliest demo recordings were also becoming available from Mohawk (*The Original Modern Lovers*) and record-store clerks understandably didn't know how to file it all: which releases came first, whether to file them all under "R" for "Richman" or "M" for "Modern." Filing grew harder when in 1988 Richman found a permanent home at Rounder and a flood of similar-sounding titles appeared (like *Jonathan Richman, Having a Party with Jonathan*, and *I, Jonathan*), followed by Rhino's re-releases of Jonathan's initial Beserkeley late-'70s recordings

with titles like *The Modern Lovers, Jonathan Richman and the Modern Lovers, Rock & Roll with the Modern Lovers*, and *Modern Lovers Live*.

Eventually, despite store-staff puzzlement over uncertain release dates and nearly identical titles, and despite some recordings being out of print for close to a decade, I managed to track down all his records. I had to call stores around the country and blindly send them exorbitant amounts of money. In the end, I had four versions of "Roadrunner" (counting a rarity I purchased on a Beserkeley sampler at great expense), all quite similar. With my set complete, I could piece together the sequence of Richman's career.

First came his experiments with a loud, snotty, Stooges-like band: *The Modern Lovers* (mostly produced by John Cale) and *The Original Modern Lovers* (mostly produced by Kim Fowley). This was the fabled incarnation of the Modern Lovers that everyone still expects to follow the words "Jonathan Richman and," a legendary Velvet Underground–style band that included many Boston musicians later to be famous (notably, keyboardist Jerry Harrison of Talking Heads, drummer David Robinson of the Cars). They played songs of horniness and alienation like "Astral Plane" (in which Jonathan swears he'll "go insane" if the girl he loves won't meet him in his dreams), "Hospital" (in which the girl he loves has gone insane), "Pablo Picasso" (in which Jonathan expresses envy for the title character because "he could walk down the street and girls could not resist his stare and consequently, Pablo Picasso was never called an asshole—not like you"), and of course "Roadrunner." Both records were compiled from major-label demos recorded in 1972 and released after long delays by tiny indie labels—inconveniences that enhanced the storied integrity of each record ("an album so raw with adolescent angst and full-blooded drive that Warner Bros. could never put it out," was how Lester Bangs described *The Modern Lovers*). But Richman never cared for *The Modern Lovers*: "It's OK. It's what I did when I was 20. It never was an album. It's a collection of tapes. That's not quite the same thing."

By the time Beserkeley began to record him, Jonathan had broken up the previous band to set up a new thing altogether: a sweeter, jokier, cozier sound.

"Most of the stuff we do now," he told *Melody Maker* at the time, "I don't see why anyone shouldn't like it. We could play it anywhere. We play for all age groups. I mean all age groups. Once a 7-year-old kid asked me,

'Do you play these same songs for adults?' And I said, 'Yes, I do.'

"When I write songs, I want to feel comfortable singing them for everyone. I don't see why not. They're funny, but there are melodies; people like melodies, and little kids like melodies too."

There is an endearing lack of professionalism to the Beserkeley recordings, as if the musicians have swapped places with the recording engineers and they're all just beginning to learn their job. The songs seem not only written by children and played and sung by children but sometimes even recorded by children. They have a strange, rattling quality, as if recorded live in a dumpster. Richman refuses to stay on-mike; you can guess when he's nodding to people in the sound booth, or making funny faces at his bandmates, or dipping his chin so his vocals disappear. On another pop record, it would force a new take. Here, it's inevitable.

In any case, some people didn't like the new stuff: silly, pared-down rock 'n' roll, nursery rhymes and instrumentals, songs with "little" in their title (the live album featured four: "I'm a Little Airplane," "I'm a Little Dinosaur," "Hey There Little Insect," and "My Little Kookenhaken"). One critic disappointed by Jonathan's turn toward swell-heartedness was Bangs, who now railed, "Richman has succumbed to terminal cutesy-poo, singing twinkster-pieces in his by-now familiar, hopelessly off-key adenoidal drone." CREEM's Billy Altman was harsher still: "The infamous Cale-produced album was a downright masterpiece, and as long as I live, 'Roadrunner' will be in my rock 'n' roll Hall of Fame. But to see someone pervert their own talents for no other reason than simply not giving a hoot or a holler about nothin' no more is a goddamn disgrace . . . Ever run into a gang of drunken sots at a bar who think every word out of their mouths is hilarious and don't seem to know or care that no one else thinks they're funny? That's how I feel about the Modern Lovers. Jonathan, allow me to be not the first, and certainly not the last, to tell you: You are an asshole."

In the '80s, Jonathan altered his approach again, though not quite so dramatically. By now, Beserkeley had gone belly-up and Jonathan had been picked up by a major label. He added two female backup singers, a keyboardist, a new drummer and guitarist. A new producer made sure the sound varied somewhat and the studio didn't echo like a dumpster. *Jonathan Sings!* takes a major-label opportunity to transcend the obnoxious music Richman made as a teenager—to erase the world of "Roadrunner" from people's minds, replacing it with more considered songs. The craftsmanship of *Jonathan Sings!* seems years ahead of his dewy-eyed Beserkeley work. Topics consist of things that delight him—that

summer feeling, those conga drums, this kind of music—and he lets us extend those delights into our own lives. *Jonathan Sings!* showcases a sometimes pushy infant who's grown into a relaxed, charming kid. Richman indicated something of the sort when he told journalist Kristine McKenna, "I think I've become more direct. All my songs come from being in love with life. It's something I've felt since I was a kid, a gift I was born with."

But though Jonathan came through perfectly to meet whatever challenge a contract with Sire Records signified, people failed to notice. Once more, reviewers simply wondered what had happened, asking why he couldn't make rock like he did on *The Modern Lovers*, a record one critic termed "the most influential commercial flop in rock history."

Not long ago a friend told me he gave up on Richman after *Jonathan Sings!* "As far as I'm concerned," he confided, "that's when he became a novelty act, like Pee-wee Herman." Richman drifted to smaller and smaller labels, his songwriting skills solidly under control, his image firmly set, his audiences dwindling.

Most of the rock press and audience still . . . have mistaken ideas about me. I'm so sick of the word eccentric. Pardon my French, but people who call me that are assholes . . . jerks who never knew me in the first place . . . They think I'm eccentric because they're numb. See, society does its work real well on a lot of people. It breaks 'em the day they're born. Chalk up one for society, zero for person.
—from Jonathan Richman's *Rolling Stone* interview, 1980

IT TOOK MY parents about eight months to accept our marriage. Once they did, they tried to make up by offering us a honeymoon. "We'll send you anywhere you want," they offered. But by this time I knew it was too late.

I was coming up against a problem that must confront every poor young married couple: we were seeing so much of each other, so little of the world, we were running out of things to say. Midge was still adorable, but a marriage conceived on the shoals of late adolescence runs like a dialogue loop from a Mickey Rooney–Judy Garland movie. I didn't want the honeymoon because I didn't want the marriage, and I didn't want the marriage because I was sick of the dialogue loop. But I didn't know how to say this. I still hoped the marriage would get better all by itself. I told my wife, "Anywhere you want to go, honey-bunny." Her response was swift—she'd always dreamed of a week at the Disneyland Hotel.

Reservations were made, and soon I found myself inhabiting her dream, checked in for a week at "the happiest place on earth." It was only 45 minutes from our apartment, and our luggage was mostly a boom box and a couple of tapes. My parents, who knew we didn't drink, gave us a celebratory bottle of champagne. It was our anniversary. We'd been married one year. We placed the champagne on the television set in our motel room and stared at it.

THE FIRST DAY at the Disneyland Hotel is easy: you step from lobby to monorail, ride into the amusement park, and tour Disneyland. You stand in line for rides like Pirates of the Caribbean, Haunted House, Tom Sawyer Island, the Matterhorn, It's a Small World. You eat cotton candy and lollipops, wander Main Street USA, ride the railroad, and snicker at animatronic dinosaurs. You get autographs from Disney characters meandering through the park with gleeful grins. At twilight there's the Main Street Electrical Parade; then Tinkerbell flies down from the Matterhorn in a spotlight and there's a magnificent fireworks display. That's day one.

It's harder after that. There's nothing to do you haven't already done, and soon you're back in the dialogue loop. By the third day I'd dug out the cassettes, a couple of Jonathan's Beserkeley releases. I listened to them once, then again. I rubbed my eyes. It seemed the singer's good cheer would never cease. He was off in an other-planetary happiness, like the Disney characters we kept coming across, little people zipped into suffocating plastic suits, smiling and waving merrily. Before I knew what I was doing, I'd opened the champagne and filled the Snow White mug we'd bought that day on Main Street USA.

"How come," I inquired of my wife, who was watching the sun set behind the Matterhorn.

"What."

"How come you didn't pack anything but these tapes?"

"Because, they're happy. They make me happy."

"But haven't we already heard them enough?"

"You're the one who keeps playing them."

I refilled the Snow White mug with bubbly. "I just can't figure . . . Why would you separate these Jonathan records from the rest? They don't make sense that way. If you were gonna bring some, then why didn't you bring them all?"

"I don't know, Camden."

"I just wish I could hear 'Roadrunner' right now, is all." I could listen to it over and over, the hard sounds of discomfort and awkward youth, the anthem of driving alone at night.

Then it came to me. What was wrong with our marriage was Jonathan. At last I grasped that the author of our dialogue loop was not, as I had been thinking, Mickey Rooney; it was Jonathan Richman, an artist who dismissed anguished music, turned his back on loneliness, no longer played "Roadrunner."

"Jonathan," I remembered Billy Altman writing, "You're an asshole."

I saw Midge glance at me, and realized I'd said the last three words aloud. Far below us, the Main Street Electrical Parade was already well under way.

I coughed. "Can we get a little air in here?" Neither of us had tried to open the window since we'd arrived.

The boom box went on playing as the tape ended, clicked over, restarted. It was the first song on *Back in Your Life*: "Abdul & Cleopatra."

"No," I moaned. "Not again." I was wrestling with the window latch and couldn't turn off the music. "Oh god. I really think I'm drunk."

"I'll say."

The window would not open. I saw then, as our theme song started and like clockwork a spotlit miniature ballerina slid down an invisible wire from a huge plastic mountain in the middle of the amusement park and the fireworks began their routine, that ours was not genuine sliding glass but a faux balcony we could not use. I began to bang on the window. "Help! Help!" I screamed. "I'm married!"

I will wait for Cleopatra / for I know my time must come
And I'm getting ready for wherever she'll be atra
Cause I'm getting stronger now I'm not so dumb
Abdul yearns for Cleopatra in the early desert sun
I love Cleopatra / She's still the one

JONATHAN RICHMAN STILL records for Rounder Records. His last album, *¡Jonathan, Te Vas A Emocionar!*, was beautiful. It featured Jonathan singing 11 of his songs in Spanish. He has always been well received in Europe—in England, Holland, and especially Spain. "From those first visits onward," Jonathan writes in the CD's liner notes, "the Spanish public has been the one I get along with the best in Europe." Asa Brebner recalls the audiences' enthusiasm on his last trip to Spain with the Modern Lovers: "They clap in time. They sing harmonies. They add minor sevenths. We did two shows in a huge disco, both nights packed to capacity . . . I almost got writer's cramp signing autographs."

I still hear from my ex-wife. Every year or so she telephones. She often sounds sad. She beseeches me to clarify the reasons our marriage failed, why we stayed together only one year. "Why did we ever break up?" she despondently asks.

"I don't know," I tell her. "I honestly do not know."

Usually then I change the subject and we end up talking about something else, like Jonathan Richman. ◓

THE MAGNETIC FIELDS

Stephin Merritt began releasing albums under the name Magnetic Fields in the late '80s but really found his groove in 1994, when he assumed lead vocal duties on the albums *Holiday* and *Charm of the Highway Strip*. **JOHNNY RAY HUSTON** profiled the songwriter, whose muse and influences offered a radical departure from the prevailing rock orthodoxy.

Fuzzy dice, Chihuahuas, ostrich-feather coats, and other odd details spill from the lyrics of *Holiday*, a 1994 LP by the Magnetic Fields. Metaphors and similes spin topsy-turvy, then shoot off in crazy directions. Three songs in—under a night sky filled with "more stars than there are prostitutes in Thailand"—Stephin Merritt serenades someone with "strange powers." Riding a Coney Island ferris wheel, they kiss, their lips "blue from cotton candy." How does it feel? "Like a flying saucer landing."

Neon gas breaks free from a streetlight and turns into a ghost in the course of *Charm of the Highway Strip*, a second 1994 Magnetic Fields LP. Staring deep into a loved one's eyes, Merritt finds an escape route to distant places: Kansas City, the Mesa Verde, and "long Vermont roads." A collection of traveling tunes, *Charm* is chock-full of train-hopping and alcohol. But its tried-and-true C&W scenarios sport a twist—lonesome cowboys like Jesse James and William Tell appear as lovers, not fighters; Daniel Webster and the Devil are boyfriends, not enemies.

Both albums' sounds are as rich and unique as their imagery. Natural and artificial instruments merge; forlorn strings and horns (cello, tuba) weave in and out of candy-coated Casio tones. Textures are magnified and distilled as feedback buzzes behind carousel synth melodies and the plinkety-plonk of toy piano. Throughout *Charm*'s "Two Characters in Search of a Country Song" a pedal-steel effect whines like a mosquito. Some ditties sport programmed bongos and maracas, while other percussive touches—slamming doors, ticking clocks, pencils hitting desks—are more evocative. And deep in the heart of the whirring machinery lurks Merritt's drowsy baritone, a bottomless well of loneliness.

Merritt's voice isn't featured on the first two full-length Magnetic Fields releases, 1989's *Distant Plastic Trees* and 1991's *The Wayward Bus*; it's Susan Anway who does a choir-girl turn on these. The words she sings are permanently stuck in past tense, an effect heightened by Ronettes-style harmonies and church chimes behind her. Using '50s-era paintings and photos of boy-girl couples for cover art, Merritt subtly tweaks convention, transforming hetero forms of nostalgia—beach songs, road songs—into something queer. Though he publishes his music under the name Gay and Loud, he still has an introvert's preference for private codes. Libraries, desert islands ("We'll develop muscles cracking coconuts / Let our clothing drop off / Feel each other's butts"), and other "secret places" remote from society are the romantic dwellings he's drawn to.

Most of Merritt's lyrics present "I/you" relationships open to any interpretation, but occasionally he'll play with gender, casting Anway as a boy or himself as a girl. Of course, ostensibly straight pop songs are always ripe for playful revision: for instance, it's easy to view the "misunderstood youth" theme of oldies like "A Town without Pity" as a smokescreen for other forms of love. Merritt himself uses this conceit, but on *Holiday*'s most sumptuous cut, "Take Ecstasy with Me," he dispenses with it. "You stuttered like a kaleidoscope / 'Cause you knew too many words," he remembers. Then, as a symphony of flutes grows louder and brighter, his memories turn dark: "A vodka bottle gave you those raccoon eyes / We got beat up just for holding hands."

"How are you?" I ask Stephin Merritt on the Monday night I call him at his Hoboken apartment.

"Never mind that," he replies.

I suggest rescheduling our interview, but he won't hear of it. "I'm depressed enough to be in character. I can pretend my life really is all about the charm of the highway strip, because I've been driving hither and thither all weekend, going to funerals, getting drunk in seedy bars, and having knock-down, drag-out fights with my poor boyfriend."

Merritt has a droll, deadpan manner. He isn't the type of artist who turns an interview into a performance.

Asked if he's a big Phil Spector fan, he answers simply, "Yes." Prodded for memories of listening to pop as a kid, he states blankly, "I grew up on AM radio."

Then, as I babble about a recent obnoxious awards show, he deigns to lob a sound bite in my direction: "Whitney Houston is my choice for this year's artist to assassinate." Why? "She ruined a perfectly wonderful Dolly Parton song."

From there, our conversation roams past Loretta Lynn (favorite song: "You're the Reason Our Kids Are Ugly") before landing on Merritt's prime inspiration: ABBA. For a brief moment, Mr. Glum becomes excited. "I think ABBA are seriously the best thing since Bach," he declares, assuming a professorial air. "They've improved on Bach's extreme simplicity of form. You hear this in 'The Winner Takes It All,' which is one figure in different chords through the whole song." Merritt aims for a deceptive simplicity in his own compositions: "I really think Irving Berlin is better than Cole Porter, and I'm too Cole Porter for myself. Currently, I'm trying to get rid of the clever rhymes and weird imagery." Most of the latter comes, he thinks, from "thinking about the human body."

During the interview, Merritt's boyfriend, Frederick, begins to harmonize notes on a nearby digital 4-track. Merritt can't resist offering advice, stopping mid-answer to tell him things like, "The pitch-tone fuzzer will transpose only one note at a time."

The pair have just moved into the apartment, and are still discovering all the noises to be made in it. By accident and through experiment, Merritt has tested the noise-making properties of many bizarre objects. His current favorite is a Slinky toy: with each end hooked to a guitar pickup, its shape translates to sound, creating a spring-like *doi-oi-oing*.

SOME MAGNETIC FIELDS: JOHN WOO, CLAUDIA GONSON, STEPHIN MERRITT, SAM DAVOL (PHOTO, ALICIA AGUILERA)

While he was growing up, Merritt lived in Hawaii, Germany, Tennessee, and Florida as well as various places in the Northeast, moving in and out of 33 houses in 23 years. Although formally trained as a musician, he didn't start writing pop songs until he "discovered appropriation." He credits an early tutor with teaching him the virtue of simplicity, yet his multiple layers of melody are still complex, especially by indie standards. He has recorded on 4-track since 1978; today, he sabotages the "prefab" fidelity of newer models through tape loops and microphone placement. While he can write a country song in minutes, the recording process is often meticulous: *Charm* was pieced together five different ways before Merritt came up with a version he felt was suitable for release. "I hope I don't have to record it again," he says drily.

To do so would be a waste of time, since Merritt's backlog of over a hundred songs has made side projects a necessity. Under the rubric Future Bible Heroes, he has recorded an album's worth of material with former Boston colleague Chris Ewen. More complicated, and more compelling, is another formation called the 6ths. The first 6ths album, recently completed, features songs with vocals by such illustrious guests as Anna Domino, Lou Barlow, Stuart Moxham, Barbara Manning, Robert Scott of the Bats, Mary Timony of Helium, Amelia of Heavenly, and Dean Wareham of Luna, to name just a handful. A second LP, with contributions by Let's Active's Mitch Easter and Unrest's Mark Robinson, is now under way.

GAIL O'HARA

Always on the lookout for a new voice, Merritt recently set his sights on Broadway: "There's a musical called *Blood Brothers*, starring Petula Clark, Shaun Cassidy, and David Cassidy. I'd love to have any or all of them sing my songs. Anyone who can sell a lot of records and sing is welcome!"

When I ask Merritt if he ever plays live, he hisses out an agonized "Yessss." In concert, the Magnetic Fields' lineup changes from week to week, ranging from two guitars, a cello, and a paper plate for a drum kit, to one guitar, a cello, and a Casio with automatic percussion. One thing remains the same, though: Merritt's disdain for the whole process. "I hate playing live, and I don't care who knows it," he groans. "But I pretend not to while I'm onstage." For the audience? "For the money, yeah."

And what does the typical Magnetic Fields fan look like? "That's the other reason we play live. Our fans are adorable college boys. And some ugly college boys. But they're all straight."

Ah, the world of indie rock—so many cute boys, so few of them (openly, at least) homo. Merritt has recently taken to conducting surveys during shows. "A few weeks ago I asked all the lesbians and all the gay men in the audience to raise their hands," he reports. "There were tons of lesbians, and no gay men. Of course, it could just be that all college-age women think they're

lesbians, and most college-age boys don't think they're gay. Or don't want to admit it yet."

Among the gaggle of queer performers currently on US indie labels, the most notable, found in bands like Team Dresch, Fifth Column, and Heavens to Betsy, are girls with guitars, offering up an emotional intensity and musical flair that seems lacking in boy counterparts like Pansy Division or Mukilteo Faeries. Merritt has next to nothing in common with any of the above—for one thing, he's way more of a romantic. If anything, his voice evokes Lee Hazlewood on a bum trip, his lyrics a more honest American cousin of Smiths-era Morrissey. As Ivan Kreilkamp has noted, the Magnetic Fields sound more like "an aesthete's memory" of early-'80s new wave than it does like early-'90s punk. But even that description doesn't pin them down.

Leaving sexuality out of it, one could lump Merritt together with Stereolab, Saint Etienne, Pulp, and other current outfits who share an interest in "nostalgic futurism," utilizing dated technology and keyboards. Or one could liken him to Aphex Twin, another current figure with unconventional and inventive recording methods. But ultimately, these comparisons fall apart: Merritt's courage and imagination make him an anomaly. At a time when most groups are—to quote a lyric from *The Wayward Bus*—"finding old ways to be young," the Magnetic Fields have turned world-weariness into something fresh. ◑

PJ HARVEY

Back in the mid-'90s, PJ Harvey had a reputation as a tough interview—the words "moody" and "introspective" got thrown around a lot. Undaunted, **COLIN B. MORTON** ventured into deepest Dorset to face the singer—preparing for the release of her now-classic *To Bring You My Love*—only to be ambushed by wit and laughter.

"Asking me what my songs are about is like asking, 'Why do you go to the toilet,'" she laughs.

"A lot of the time what you do is an instinctive thing. You don't stop to think about the process, or why you're having to do it right then, and what you might be passing this time. 'Hmm, what did I eat yesterday?'"

This was not exactly what I'd been led to expect from Polly Harvey. *Hates doing interviews*, they said. *Moody, difficult, taciturn*, they said. And here she is talking to a total stranger about her bodily functions, serious and joking at the same time, deflecting conversation from some subjects, expansive on many more.

Roll Introductory Credits: The PJ Harvey Story, Starring Christina Ricci . . .

When *Puncture* calls me out of the blue to ask me if I'll interview PJ Harvey for them, I'm at a friend's house, a stone's throw from a Welsh pub where hotly tipped new Rough Trade signings the 60ft Dolls are about to play a last local show before their first major tour. At this point, my knowledge of PJ is limited to a borrow of *Rid of Me* from the local library. I taped it but didn't play it awfully much, as it sounded like several people making the same music into different albums. Not in a deliberate, avant-garde sense. There were parts where each seemed to grasp what the others were doing, like in the movie *Wings of Desire* when bits happen in color and Columbo comes in and explains things.

What's more, I have—especially for someone who co-authored a cartoon called "The PJ Harvey Story"—a rather scant knowledge of her history (I remember something about being raised, like Howlin' Wolf, on a chicken farm . . . and some fuss involving riot grrrls . . .).

A Fitting Beginning

My friend's house contains a record collection that jumps abruptly from vinyl trophies of Captain Beefheart, Can, and avant jazz to CDs of Manic Street Preachers, Nirvana, Shellac. Nothing in between. It's somehow not surprising that a friend like this would affably agree to drive me 96 miles to Dorset, England, to visit PJ Harvey . . .

Rid of Me?

In the ensuing week, I am phoned/faxed several times by the folks over the pond at *Puncture*. People have been telling them stories about how PJ is ever so private and moody and difficult to talk to. I ask for the fact that I collaborated on a horrid, sarcastic cartoon of her to be conveyed in advance. I'll have enough on my plate with her sat before me being all private, moody, etc.

I half expect to hear she's blown off the interview: *That *℮^%$#@ cartoonist? I'm not talking to him!*

No Call for It Anymore

Down, down to the pub where a trendy indie disco is in full swing. Elastica, Oasis, the Stone Roses . . . Thinking to seize my chance and educate my companion in the works of our interviewee, I buttonhole the DJ and ask him to play some PJ Harvey.

The DJ, who's called Spit, turns us down. "Haven't got any . . . no call for it anymore."

Express Yourself

Two days before the interview, I'm phoned by someone from U2's management company, who also handle PJ's business affairs. On Thursday I am to be in a hotel named after one of the royal family at 11:45 for 12:15, when I will talk to the Peej about her forthcoming album. A rock vassal with a cellular phone will be watching for me in the foyer.

I tell them I haven't yet received the tape of the new album her record company was supposed to send me.

"Er . . . yes, we can see that would be a problem . . . we'll send one by overnight courier."

So, the day after tomorrow I'll be facing a spoiled, pampered, aristo-rock celeb-in-waiting for whom there is apparently no longer any call, about an album I haven't heard. Why did I ever agree to do this?

What the . . . ?

A tape of *To Bring You My Love* arrives the next morning. I take a listen, and am impressed most of all by the sense of noise, the way that some of it makes me go, "What the fuck is that?"—a sensation I've been missing in popular music for far too long. I hear amid Harvey's songs great rattling noises, spook organ, chiming things, and at one point an extended atonal free feedback passage (replete with what seems to be random radio interference) that transmogrifies into a sketchy blues landscape.

Then there's PJ's voice—or voices, since she has many of them . . .

Beefheart Was My Elvis

As I listen I detect several Captain Beefheart references straight away. Another appears on second listen. It turns out later there are many other things floating through this intriguing mixture, though I'm sure you don't want me filling in your crossword puzzle answers for you. But the music of Mr. Don Van Vliet of Glendale, California, is my specialist subject.* Shit, an exchange teacher from Antelope Valley High School even came to my school in Wales once.

"What was Captain Beefheart like, sir?"

"Rebellious, he was hardly ever there . . ."

"What was Frank Zappa like, sir?"

"Rebellious . . . now get on with your work."

The School Weirdo Theory

Being short of time in which to think up some questions, I listen again, in the company of another friend, a fanzine editor. Maybe he can think up a few smart ones. I tell him of the polite-but-firm call from U2's management, the rumors that the Peej is Moody and Difficult.

"Oh that's probably just with music journalists. She'll be all right with you," he assures me.

How can he be so sure?

My fanzine friend puts forward the theory that this is a classic case of "school weirdo music." He knows this because he was a school weirdo, too. For him, hearing Beefy's *Trout Mask Replica* at an early age caused sensations which . . . well, one could use the expression "hallucinogenic" here, but that would rather be putting the cart before the horse. Listening to all that weird and crazy music caused him to become an outcast among his peers.

He asked if anything like that had happened to me. As a matter of fact, it did.

"Well, there you are, then. She'll be all right with you."

Dangerous Agricultural Machinery Conspires against Us

At the last moment, a few more suggested questions are faxed over. We drive into England, the country to which my race is subject. We pass through villages with pronounceable names. The few pubs we see are named after members of the royal family. We're confused by the road signs being in one language (we are Welsh, and therefore expect bilingual signs).

Here is the county of Dorset: pseudoscience territory, a place aliens come to. Using their advanced technology, they traverse the vast emptiness of space, hover above the cornfields, draw circles in them, then bugger off again. Reg Presley of the Troggs supposedly spends his royalties trying to find out why.

Dangerous agricultural machinery looms out of hedgerows at every turn. Floods flood. We are late. Oh shit. She's probably in a petulant frenzy by now.

I am, in every sense, as seriously off my turf as I have ever been in my life. I wonder: Have they told her about the cartoon? Is this a plot to lure me into a hotel room and publicly humiliate (or privately torture) me? Odd things go through your head when you think you're about to meet a moody introspective etc.

We stop at a roadside cafe, buy a map, call the number the U2 person gave me to tell them we're on the way. It sounds more like a pub than a hotel. I get the landlord, who says he'll find Polly Harvey and relay my message.

Meet Ze Monsta

We arrive forty minutes late. Flustered, I enter the royally named hotel, which turns out to be an unimposing pub. It doesn't even have a foyer. A glance to my left reveals Polly Harvey sat there in black before me, inscrutable, apparently in earnest conversation with a man with a cellular phone.

Shit, I'm in for it now.

I introduce myself, all the while thinking how ludicrous this rock-star cult-of-personality setup is. Fortunately, two things quickly become apparent. Firstly, Ms. PJ is of like opinion. And secondly, in one of life's little bonuses, it turns out me and Polly can crack each other up.

Sorry to disappoint all you fans of moody introspection out there. I think she spoke as much as she cared to about her new record. She's happy to talk, but she does draw the line firmly and politely as to what she will talk about—sometimes almost imperceptibly, sometimes by just saying, "Let's talk about something else."

"Eat Up Your Hair Pie, Polly"

Did they tell you I'd done a horrid cartoon of you in the NME*?*
No. Was it the one where I've got like a vest on, and my hair is done really perfectly right, and my mum's saying, "Eat up your hair pie, Polly"?

Yes. I asked them to tell you . . .
We loved them. Me and my mum, we photocopied them and put them up on the fridge. They were so

---

* Don Van Vliet was called Captain Beefheart when he made music, which he stopped doing about ten years ago (now he makes paintings). He was, is still, the benchmark figure in avant-rock; his epic *Trout Mask Replica* album from 1970 exceeds just about any other record in terms of musically inventive/emotionally poetic impact. His influence far outstrips his fame (and his fame and influence in Europe far outstrips that in his homeland). Some people today think of him merely as a weirdo hanger-on of his high-school buddy Frank Zappa, if they know of him at all, but the Peej is obviously in the know, as were Pere Ubu, the Fall, John Lydon, the Pixies, and many more, even if (Tom Waits) they won't admit it.

spot-on, it was like you knew me and my family. And for her to be giving me a hair pie: that's what she's like . . . into alternative medicines and weird cooking. Me and my mum, we'd never laughed so much . . . do more!

Justine Frischmann, of Elastica, told me off for doing that cartoon.

Really? Why?

She said I'd been very cruel to you. No sooner were we introduced than she sprang to your defense. "You were very cruel to Polly Harvey . . ." Do you know Justine?

No, but I hear she likes the music.

She said she lives in dread of us doing a cartoon of her.

You should do one . . . Go on! Do one of her!

Words cannot express the contrast between this PJ person in person and the moody, intensely serious artist I was led to expect by the phone calls and faxes, and the press kit Island Records sent me, all stark black-and-white pics of Polly staring atcha, chock-full of forbidding words like "menstruation," "melancholy," and "Steve Albini."

She has a mischievous, self-deprecating wit, and a small fund of silly voices: pseudo-serious, thick Dorset, world-weary American (imagine her saying some of the things in the press kit, e.g. "perhaps I should play naked" in the light of this).

She studies the way my borrowed cassette recorder rattles noisily as the tape goes round.

"I like the way the tape has this sort of sound effect. It's a pity it doesn't wobble as well . . ."

MEET ZE MONSTA FEATURES RATTLING PERCUSSION COURTESY OF JOHN PARISH. AT ONE POINT, A WHISTLE BLOWS AND EVERYTHING CLACKS AND SHUDDER-SHAKES. THEN IT BLOWS AGAIN AND STOPS.

Are you fascinated by stuff like that? There's a lot of noise on the record, like you've put microphones up against rattling speakers.

Yes, it was a luxury doing the album over such a long period. I'd only ever spent about two weeks on an album before, and this was six weeks of recording and then another month mixing—so suddenly I had all this time to try things out. What does a guitar sound like if you play it through an amp the size of that tape machine in a shoebox? There were other things too. I did some of the vocals with contact mikes tied to my throat.

Fake Zep II? Polly Rides That Zeitgeist Down, Part the First

LONG SNAKE MOAN CALLS TO MIND BLIND LEMON JEFFERSON AND LED ZEPPELIN IN A HEAD-ON COLLISION NARROWLY AVOIDING THE OSMONDS' "CRAZY HORSES."

Six weeks recording! A month mixing! Compare this with the recent release after five years of the Geffen-millions-funded *Second Coming* of the Stone Roses, which has an exquisitely ill-timed (just as the front half of the real Zep made their comeback bid) sound of fake Zep with indie-pop wuss vocals over the top.

Polly's "Long Snake Moan," on the other hand, casually out-Zeps the Zep, at the same time ironically exorcising the demon cock-rock. (Oh, and note that unlike many pseudo-Zeps, she knows it's Blind Lemon.)

You make references to Blind Lemon Jefferson . . .

Oh, there's bits of everything—Johnny Cash, Ennio Morricone . . .

[Sudden realization] Oh! Yeah!

And I've been listening to lots of salsa . . .

They'll be calling you retro now . . .

Retro Harvey! [*silly voice*] "She's not got an original idea!"

Unlike Oasis!

I don't like the way Oasis do it, where you end up spending the whole time figuring out which song it's come from. Like playing Guess the Song.

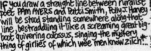

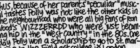

PJ HARVEY
To Bring You My Love
(Island)

Some of you will want more noise, but there's no denying that *To Bring You My Love* is an advance—a methodical deepening of every aspect of PJ Harvey's art.

Her voice. The moans, howls, squeals, and whispers now twist the blues more ways than anyone since Captain Beefheart. But her vocal contortions aren't for shock value or art's sake—they're drama. Her singing makes every role and situation, every encounter with sex and its consequences, frighteningly vivid. To start, she uses the words of the most ancient blues myth, the hoodoo man ("I was born in the desert/Been down for years") to tell her version of the most ancient of literary characters, the fallen woman ("Cast out of heaven/To bring you my love"), the measured hysteria of her voice managing to capture at once the man's sexual aggression and the woman's desperate guilt. For the rest of the record her voice flies from one of those two extremes to the other, from full-throated surrender in "Meet ze Monsta" (Beefheart's Shiny Beast?); to half-crazed pregnancy in "C'mon Billy," a plea in which her growls swing between playful and suicidal; to "The Dancer," a scene from a Western in which a horseman/Messiah rides toward PJ; speechless, she sums up her fluctuating emotions in the most communicative set of squeals in musical history—"Ah?" (voice rising, questioning); "Ah!" (voice high-pitched in anger, hurt); "Aaahhh" (pleasurable sigh). It all works.

The music. Freed from Steve Albini's noise tyranny, she indulges herself, tastefully. Melodies are basic, sturdy enough to lend structure to her vocal flights. Arrangement-wise, there isn't a wasted sound on the record. Acoustic and electric guitars get equal time; bass, drums, and keyboards drop in and out as the mood dictates; the sound is spare but not minimalist.

Despite the album's deliberate quality, it yields surprises: the organ that slowly rises through the title track, surfacing at the end to spooky effect; the siren guitars which push "Meet Ze Monsta" to ecstatic heights; the fat bottom on "Working for the Man"; the chilling click of a wood block (or something) which punctuates her whispered coda to "Down by the Water."

Through all the variety and accomplishment of this record, PJ's métier is still sex. Nothing new for blues or rock'n'roll, except that she sings about it in a way no other performer has. British blues rockers like Led Zeppelin, whose riffs were the source of

Yet they combine really obvious things . . . not like what you're doing here.
And they all just copy each other, which leads to this . . . stagnant pool of music.

Me, I listen to everything!

As I finished writing this, the UK rock press came out with their first estimates of *To Bring You My Love*. "Nick Cave," they said. "Birthday Party," they said. "Oh, and Captain Beefheart . . ."

As if the Birthday Party weren't part Beefheart, part Johnny Cash, garnished with Pere Ubu. At a guess, the glossy monthly music mags will clutch her to their bosoms, while indie kids will think she's betrayed them.

Axe-Wielding Bitch Cat from Hell

In light of the fact that Everything You Know About PJ Harvey Is Wrong, I decided to ask my "leave it till the end" question early.

Why have you got this "difficult to talk to" reputation? I kept hearing that from people, yet we come here and talk about whatever comes into our heads and you don't seem bothered.
I think it's because I say I don't want to talk about my lyrics. They immediately think it's because I'm incredibly moody and difficult. So they do this blanket thing: "Don't talk to her about the music."

I'm sometimes quiet, but that's not moody, is it?
They think it's like Ringo: "I'm not talking about the Beatles."
Yeah, and people end up [*adopts sincere tone*] "let's talk about your childhood . . . tell me about your dreams."

I just don't want to be that specific.
If you did, you could write something on a piece of paper instead of writing a song: "There it is, now go away . . ."
Exactly. I think it's quite amusing in a way that people think I'm some kind of axe-wielding bitch cat from hell. I'm just a gentle country girl.
*Who got hold of an electric guitar and started going [*mimes windmill chord*] "Look, I've got a pubic hair!"*
Yes, moody and difficult upon growing pubic hair: What's this? I'll write a song about it . . .

A Mind Thing

Perhaps people have a vested interest in Polly Jean Harvey being moody. It somehow makes things easier. Like the way they can put people in a box marked "weird" and keep it in a corner of their minds.

It would be more threatening for them to think that a normal girl who's a good laugh in the pub would make these records.

There doesn't have to be any deep explanation. I think she makes a noise because she wants to. She's just been hijacked by all this biographical shit. She's not the first, I'll warrant. But she may be the first who is a girl and is this good and doesn't care.

I Know a School Weirdo When I See One

It's obvious by now that I've been seriously wrong-footed by showbiz mythology, so I decide to float my fanzine friend's theory.

Were you the school weirdo?

Yes, I was very much a misfit. At the time, everyone was going to school discos and listening to Duran Duran, and I didn't like that sort of music.

I went around thinking, "Why has everyone else got a boyfriend and I haven't? I want one!" I couldn't get one because I looked like a boy. I had short hair and was always being told off for being in the girls' toilets, and not wearing a tie in the dinner line. I'd say, "I don't have to wear a tie, I'm a girl!"

And a few years later, it's "Oooh aren't I different, everyone?" time. And you're thinking, "Look here, it's not fun!"?

Yes, I didn't want to be different. I wanted to be the same as everybody else and have boyfriends.

Now what was the rest of the School Weirdo Theory . . . extreme noise fixation?

Are you the sort of person who, if you're walking down the street and see a musical instrument in a shop, you want to have a go on it straightaway?

Yes! Even if it's a child's toy piano! I want to go [*mimes playing a little piano, discusses music sculpture at length*]—

School weirdos of the world unite! A bona fide One of Our Kind has gotten in with the rock-pseudo-rebel-aristocrat U2 management. And she's a girl, with a big sexy voice who looks like the goddamn Mona Lisa. Make way ye hills and mountains, we are coming . . . But there are those of the country of Moody Introspection—whose national anthem is "For Free" by Joni Mitchell—who would claim her for their own.

Riot Grrrl Got Me! Huggy Bear Got Me! Polly Rides That Zeitgeist Down, Part the Second

In the early '90s there was much talk about Strong Women in Pop. Polly Harvey got lumped in with the '90s Women, with Björk and Tori Amos . . . Which is sexist and patronizing—three quite disparate male artists wouldn't get lumped together because they're men.

Then there was riot grrrl, or the British version thereof, which the more faddish end of the UK music press became enamored of for a while back in 1993. A band called Huggy Bear, who weren't very good, tried to be the Sex Pistols for Girls and got it hopelessly wrong (RG may have been a valid artistic statement in the US, but over here it was a scam).

much of *Rid of Me*, reduced sex to macho power and relentless, pounding seduction. Female blues singers like Bessie Smith and Janis Joplin sang about sex and love, but it was either as bawdy entertainment or pure heartbreak. PJ takes elements of Zeppelin and Bessie Smith—of rock seduction and blues consequences—and makes them talk to each other. Nothing in her music is as simple as "want a whole lotta love" or "take another little piece of my heart"—she feels both sides. Thus she conveys what one woman can find in her sexuality, from desperate love to motherhood to God ("man above"); from guilt ("this love my only crime") to ecstasy. She opens rock up to emotions it could not contain in thirty years of macho poses. It's no surprise her music cuts more deeply than anything else around now. Don't listen to this in the car: you may have to pull off the road. Don't put it on at a party: it may startle someone. Save it for later.—*Steve Tignor*

171

I really wanted there to be a Sex Pistols for Girls, and was sorely disappointed when it turned out to be these posh kids just messing it up. It was impossible to say this, though, without being vilified as a "boy-rocker." Partly for populist reasons, and partly because music had got very boring indeed, even normally astute commentators were saying things like "I like their stance" to avoid appearing illiberal.

What made matters worse was that all this came about at a time when there were so many women making good music that it might be possible not to have to remark on their sex when talking about their music. Polly Harvey was an eminent example. Not for her the mealy-mouthed, wet-liberal platitudes, though. Polly didn't like Riot Grrrl—and said so.

Talking as we were about axe-wielding bitch cats from hell . . . the riot grrrls tried to co-opt you, didn't they?

[exaggerated *Dorsetshire* accent with lots of R's] Riot! Grrrl! . . . tried to adopt me . . . co-opt me . . . corrupt me.

Now I know how you write songs!

Yeah, I just keep rhyming. I'm a perpetual rhyming machine . . . I saw Huggy Bear once in London. They were going on about various men/women things. It was so boring.

It seems like you cut the ground from under them by just slamming the hell out of things . . . Did anyone ever tell you, "You can't do that, you're a girl"?

Nobody did say that, but they [Huggy Bear] kind of assumed people were gonna say that before they'd even done anything. It became laughable . . . stupid.

I THINK I'M A MOTHER POLLY JEAN HARVEY VOCALS, MAYBE WITH CONTACT MIKES AS DESCRIBED ABOVE . . . GUITAR, ORGAN . . . MUFFLED DRUMS . . . DEFINITELY A COUSIN OF CAPT. BEEFHEART'S "DROPOUT BOOGIE." YOU COULD JUST ABOUT PUT THE OTHER STUFF DOWN TO COINCIDENCE, BUT THIS, NO SHADOW OF DOUBT . . . SAFE AS MILK.

Under the Influence

You said in one interview that you'd been made ill by being forced to listen to Trout Mask Replica *at mealtimes when you were 11. Now, at that age I had to listen to the worst music in the world at the dinner table, real MOR slop. So I read that and thought, What an ingrate! Which is what sparked our cartoon.*

At Sunday dinner my mum would put on *Trout Mask Replica* really loud while we were trying to eat. It was impossible to eat to. I don't know if you ever tried!

What did you eat?

Not much! You'd just go [*pantomimes eating to* Trout Mask Replica]; in the end you wouldn't want to eat at all.

On the new record I hear things from Safe as Milk. *"Dropout Boogie" . . .*

On "I Think I'm a Mother" . . .

And "Zigzag Wanderer."

It wouldn't surprise me. Which one?

"Down by the Water."

[*Sings lightly for a while*] Yeah, you could be right. I don't deny it, I've been listening to that sort of music since I was so young, I don't feel embarrassed about using it, it's what I grew up with. I'm bound to use it, sometimes I do something like that and I'll spot it later—or someone like you will point it out.

It was the use of the word "holler." I wondered what a person from Dorset was doing using that. Then I noticed it occurs at the same point in the verse. You could sing the words of one to the other, so I thought it was deliberate, especially in the light of "I Think I'm a Mother."

No, it was subconscious. But I won't be embarrassed about it.

Beefheart's really important, more important than Elvis in that he brought more things together. You'll probably get called weird for doing this, yet if you used Elvis no one would bat an eyelid.

And some of the songs are bound to sound familiar because the classic three chords and three lines of melody are the best . . .

But you don't do that, do you?

Yes. What I'm saying is, that's exactly what I do.

But you don't do just that. You put this other stuff in.

Oh, I forgot to tell you. You know who's in my touring band? Eric Drew Feldman! [A member of Captain Beefheart's Magic Band from 1974, and more recently a Pere Ubu collaborator.]

Really?!

Yes, he's playing keyboards and bass. Then there's another keyboard player, Nick Bagnall, a guitarist called John Parish, another one called Joe Gore who's played with Tom Waits a bit, and a drummer called Jean-Marc Butty, who's French. And me, but I'm just singing, not playing guitar . . . And we've got Pere Ubu's sound man.

That's a world-class band.

Yes, I can go on and be rubbish every night and it will still be all right!

Will it be like on the record or will you improvise?

Improvise a little, change things a bit. I'm going to have fun. In the past I was too moody and insular and precise, but I'm older now, I don't care anymore, I'm going to have fun!

Take the world by storm . . .

. . .with my moody introspection.

TO BRING YOU MY LOVE POLLY PLAYS GUITAR, VIBES, AND SPOOKY ORGAN. JOE GORE PLAYS E-BOW, WHATEVER THAT IS. FIRST LINE, "I WAS BORN IN A DESERT," ALMOST THE FIRST LINE OF "SHO' NUFF 'N' YES I DO," FROM *SAFE AS MILK*, WHICH IN TURN DERIVES ITS FIRST LINE, AND TUNE, FROM "NEW MINGLEWOOD BLUES" AS RECORDED BY, AMONG OTHERS, NOAH LEWIS IN 1928.

Don't Mention the Songwriting!
Can I ask you a question about the songwriting? They told me not to.
Like "Which ones have more than three chords?"
No! I wondered if you play about with the lyrics, acting out. You're not from a desert, you're from round here. You don't fool me. This isn't a desert, there were floods on the way over . . .
I don't make it a story. I've always hated that kind of storytelling. But I do adopt a point of view. It's more like . . . imagining how I would be in a certain situation.
There is a spurious notion that all songwriting is autobiographical self-expression. But it seems to me that what you do is somewhere between that and a pictorial kind of a deal. You put obvious imagery in, and then other things that make the listener go "what the hell was that?"
Yeah, it's not like I've thrown myself wholeheartedly into creating a story, but . . .
I suppose if they think you're moody and introspective—
Then they'll take what I'm saying absolutely seriously. If the start of a song says, "I was born in a desert," they go [*bangs table*], "No she wasn't! She's lying! She grew up in Dorset!" Maybe they thought I spelled Dorset wrong . . . I was born in Dorset, no desert . . . [*sings lightly*] "I was born in Dorset . . ." No, it hasn't got the same ring to it.
And it's not angst-ridden enough . . .

Here's a crap question I had from when I thought you were going to be all moody and introspective. These songs have a good bit of imagery about dying and being reborn—Lazarus in one song, the phoenix in another—do these connect to any religious beliefs?
I'm really interested in all the stories, as fascinating stories. But I'm not heavily into religion . . .
I dig out a book called *Blasphemy Ancient and Modern* which I brought with me for light reading along the way, and show the Peej some little-known rude parts from the Bible that are reproduced therein. As I'm putting it away again, she remarks, "That's an Eric Gill picture on the cover." I check the credits and she's right.
Was she an art student then?
I was going to do sculpture, but then this [*I think "this" means her musical career!*] came up. I thought, the chance to do this doesn't happen very often, so I'll do it.

I thought maybe you left because they asked you what one of your sculptures was about . . .
Well, they did. They make you explain everything.

The Polly Harvey Is an Old Cow Myth
How long have we got? An hour? Answer some of those. [throws faxed questions across table]
Do you have to ask those questions? Will they be cross if you don't? I bet they're something about what my first childhood memory is or what record I first heard. [*Reads aloud*] "What state of mind impels you to write music?"

Well, it depends on if I'm having a breakdown or if I'm . . . on course. [*makes rude noise*] Big raspberry from me. I've had all those before.

Can we talk about something else? You can say, "She was incredibly moody and difficult and refused to answer them," perpetuate the Polly Harvey Is an Old Cow myth.

"How do you write a song?" Well, I skip lightly through the fields and allow the sun's rays to inspire me.

In Which the Interviewee Interviews the Interviewer
I ask if I should go on asking questions about the record.
If you think you must.
I think I must . . . No, I won't.
Did you like the record?
Yes. I like the noisy bits more than the bits that sound like Spanish guitar noir, but that's just me . . .
Did you like *Rid of Me*? That's quite a noisy one.
Yeah, but I thought it sounded like several people making different records at once.
I'd agree with that.

Zen and the Art of Being Moody and Insular
If you're such a moody and insular person, why have you surrounded yourself with this vast U2 publicity machine?
Well, we supported them on tour and they really liked the band and they got to hear that we didn't have any management, so they offered. This is just a side project

*I always refer to U2's Bono as Bongo (a character in our comic strip), and PJ did likewise throughout our interview. (*Bongo Fury*, incidentally, is the title of a 1975 album by Capt. Beefheart and Frank Zappa.)

for them . . . I'm quite happy for it to be so.
Oh, I thought it might be a really Zen way of being moody and insular.

Have you met Bongo* [Great Pop Things' pet name for the singer in U2]?
I went to Bongo's *house*. I was *summoned*.
    We had dinner. He had a fish in front of him, this beautiful little fish with mayonnaise stuff . . . and he sat there for two hours, just looked at it, didn't eat it, spoke at me . . . Me, I ate everything on my plate!

We See the Back of Polly

There was this picture, see, on the cover of *NME*. Polly Jean's naked back . . . I thought nothing of it, just "Oh, that's a nice picture of a back," and Polly thought nothing of doing it, apparently, but it triggered a furor of debate: Is the Human Back a Naughty Bit?
So you've made this record now and it's a really world-class album and it's going to be in everyone's house . . .
Oh, I don't know . . .
Bet you a pound. Everyone's going to be sick of the sight of it . . . "Oh no, not that bloody record cover again" . . . What is on the cover, by the way?
It's not done yet.
It's not your back? We don't want a repeat of that sordid episode . . .
No, I'm keeping my clothes on.
Quite right, too.

I'm sorry I wasn't moody enough for you.
I don't mind. But there are some who'll be disappointed . . .

And off goes Polly Harvey round the corner, carrying the herring she's bought for her tea. The hot breath of the cult of personality on her famous back, the teeth of the supposition that all songwriting is autobiographical self-expression snapping sharply at her heels.
    And off I go. To Bristol, where the 60ft Dolls are playing the next-to-last date on their tour. When I get there, I bump into Jeannette Lee, who used to be in PiL, and tell her what I've been up to.
    "What was she like?"
    "She was really nice, really funny . . ."
    "Oh? You must have caught her on a good day."
    Sometimes you just can't win. ●

THE MOUNTAIN GOATS

By 1994 the Mountain Goats had a discography littered with 7-inch and cassette releases, plus a brand-new debut LP. **BILL MEYER** interviewed John Darnielle about his verbose songs and rugged recording style. In the years that followed, Darnielle never stopped writing—the Mountain Goats have remained prolific and gained a much larger following. And two decades after this article ran, Darnielle's novel *Wolf in White Van* was nominated for a National Book Award.

John Darnielle, who sings, writes, and plays all the Mountain Goats' songs, was exhausted, exhilarated, and definitely caffeinated. He'd just finished playing a splendid set at Chicago's Empty Bottle, and was digressing from a discussion of songwriting to give me a warning: "I don't like to do interviews. I say things like, 'my own idiosyncratic notions of the song' . . . That's a pretty academic thing to say."
    Maybe so, but he's a pretty academic guy. He's preparing to be a college professor, and the classical references scattered through his songs betray a fondness for ancient Greek and Roman literature. Darnielle likes to talk about theories and ideas; his conversation includes parenthetical phrases, and he's acutely aware of sounding unlike the usual rock 'n' roll interviewee. As our discussion progressed, he would warn me each time he was about to utter a "pretentious" phrase.
    The Mountain Goats' work is rife with contradictions. The name suggests a band, yet most Mountain Goats recordings feature only one person. The recorded songs betray a concern with songwriting technique, yet their low-tech presentation is the antithesis of conventional notions of craft. Most of the band's work isn't even available on compact disc or vinyl; over half of the hundred-odd Mountain Goats songs are available only on cassette. One thing is certain, though: no one has written and released more good songs in the past three years than the Mountain Goats.
    What are Darnielle's idiosyncratic notions of the song?
    "It ought to be more like earlier English and Irish songs—what are now drinking songs but were folk songs. They managed to touch an emotional chord, yet remain sort of light." His tunes handily meet those criteria. They revel in a near-demented sense of humor, heightened by straight-faced delivery and unusual subject matter; his refusal to play them for laughs lends real weight to his tales of menacing seals, maternal monsters, faithless paramours, superstitious outlaws,

and nostalgic terrorists.

Darnielle is fond of littering his songs with bizarre details and turns of phrase. "Fresh Berries for You" (from the *Chile de Árbol* EP) starts out sounding like a celebration of civic pride, but finishes up vehemently anticipating the arrival of the Easter Bunny. Even odder, "Beach House" (from the *Transmissions to Horace* cassette) is a sung warning to avoid seals, because they are vicious creatures that will bite you if given the chance. John explains the latter song:

> That's an example of a personified narrator. I don't have anything against seals, I happen to like seals. The explanation of the song is, there's a guy who's obsessively in love with some woman and in order to get her to live not far away from him he makes up this thing about seals being dangerous . . . He's an incompetent guy. There are better ways; you can say the crime rate is high, that might dissuade—"Seals will bite you" will not dissuade somebody from living someplace. The same basic character is in other songs. He's neurotic but not psychotic: somebody who gets through the details of daily life, and you wouldn't

really know he's insane unless you were his girlfriend. I never fleshed him out as a guy—he doesn't have a name. The songs are dramatic monologues so the character exists only for the utterance. Hoo boy, you're not going to get much more academic than that! I think songwriting is literary. That's not me singing, generally speaking; most songs are personified narratives, and if you can convince people you are the personified narrator, you've done your job . . . you can get them to feel for you.

Clearly he thinks a lot about what he does, but in song Darnielle doesn't always sound so pedantic. "I have two basic speeches. One is simple and pedestrian, the other is long and complicated. The tendency to use big words and to correct sentences and change fact to tendency is basically how I think."

John balances the relentless craftsmanship of his writing with an extreme audio-verité production aesthetic. The Mountain Goats' recordings are done live to a boom box; tape hiss, tinny distortion, and cassette-machine rumble are omnipresent, and he likes it that way. He usually accompanies himself on acoustic guitar,

THE MOUNTAIN GOATS
The Knitting Factory, New York
August 30, 1996

At a club which typically features the latest and scariest in avant-garde jazz, the presence onstage of John Darnielle ("For purposes of identification, I am the Mountain Goats"), a college-type, buzz-cut white dude in a chair, flailing at an acoustic guitar until his veins popped and singing in a high, flat whine about eating boiled peanuts in Georgia, was odd to say the least. Still, the Knitting Factory was as packed as I'd ever seen it, and the crowd was enthusiastic to the point of cultishness: Darnielle introduced one song by saying, "This is the latest of the Alpha songs, for those of you keeping track," and the couple next to me looked at each other bug-eyed in excitement, like Deadheads I saw at Shoreline in '89 when Jerry croaked the opening line of "Dark Star" for the first time in 37 years.

Well, they weren't that excited, but Darnielle did seem to have touched a nerve in the indie crowd—the earnest, romantic nerve us kids supposedly don't have anymore. Not that he indulges in hippie singer-songwriter earnestness: Darnielle's songs, semi-evoking a wild West (or South) filled by loner characters (not typical folk outlaws, but beings from an ancient, precommunal time), pistols, shacks, and rural settings, have a sense of play that allows him to sing them straight. His deadpan humor cuts his wide-eyed romanticism enough that cynical wretches can swoon, or even sing along. The loudest request was for "Grendel's Mother," his most beautiful song. It goes, "You can, and run some more/From here all the way to Singapore/But I will carry you home, in my teeth." When he sang "teeth," Darnielle jerked his head away from the mike with a performer's knack for wrenching a song's emotions. We cheered like crazy.—*Steve Tignor*

LIZ CLAYTON

although he sometimes uses a toy keyboard, and the other four Mountain Goats (Rachel, Amy, Sarah, and Rosanne), performing as the Bright Mountain Choir, provide occasional backing vocals.

> I don't like production that makes the fact that it's a made thing disappear. I don't like the fact that nobody is playing stuff live onto a record [the way the old] Sun sessions did. You put almost anybody in front of a 4-track and they're going to put in two tracks too many, stuff that does not add, it just thickens. Also, I like to record right after I write. I don't want 4-tracks getting in my way.

Would the Mountain Goats ever work in a regular studio? "In a word, no. I would work direct to a reel-to-reel. I may even do that in somebody's studio, so long as it's being recorded live. [But] that would eliminate some tape hiss, and they [listeners] would miss it in the way that you miss a person, right?"

Unsurprisingly, Darnielle isn't much of a technophile when it comes to musical formats.

> I never liked the CD. It's pretty clearly a device for making money, and I think what's said about its sound quality is a lie—it never sounded better than records. They only have one side if they're an album, which is lame, and I think they play in a really wicked way on a largely American but also worldwide fascination with things they don't quite understand. Once people had the idea of how records worked they weren't quite as thrilled by them anymore. But there's no such thing as an invalid format: a format is something to be worked with. I happen to think vinyl is the most interesting, and it hasn't been used up any more than the book has been perfected. I think there's a million good things you can do with vinyl. I think 7-inches are a good place to work.

He also likes cassettes and has released a number of them on labels like Shrimper, Sonic Enemy, and Car in Car.

> They've been my entire career! I hadn't thought about them much until I put some out on Shrimper. Then I thought, These are good. You consider them differently. You treat them as an article, with less respect than you treat something bigger. The sides on them you consider

MARTY PEREZ

tape hiss or motor sounds when each was mastered.

He can be flexible, though. He has used less basic equipment on two non–Mountain Goats projects. Since this interview he's recorded a single with Alastair Galbraith, New Zealand–based multi-instrumentalist. Explaining his working methods for the project, he said, "I'm going to record as I always record, then I'm going to bump that over to two tracks on a 4-track machine and send him the tape and tell him to use up the extra two." With the Extra Glenns, his side project with Nothing Painted Blue's Franklin Bruno, multi-tracked vocals and even backwards guitars swirl in and out of the mix. "That is 4-tracking," he admits, "but it's not the Mountain Goats. Part of what I'm doing as the Mountain Goats is the aesthetic approach. In different bands I don't dictate like that."

So just what is it that makes the Mountain Goats a band? The records are mostly just him, although Rachel played some bass and sang harmonies at the Chicago show. Why not just be a solo act?

> The Mountains Goats are a group because I wouldn't do it without Amy, Rosanne, Sarah, and Rachel. It's a five-person unit. I tend to do the stuff by myself, but I think of that as the configuration. Rachel is the one who I'm with most of the time, and when the Mountain Goats disband at some point there will be a new band that will be me and Rachel. But I do that also because I don't want what I'm doing to be thought of as singer-songwriter stuff, [which uses] a different set of criteria I never intended to follow. Without those four I'd be completely lost. They have a good idea of what I'm doing and they hold me in check when I'm doing something I oughtn't. It's hard to describe without sinking into hippie terms but I'll do it anyway. There's an energy that works between us. Between various combinations it produces good things; and I don't have that energy by myself.

differently because you can't flip them around as freely, so you have to listen to the whole thing, [get] involved with it. I like them because I'm not entirely sure how they work. Not sonically, but as an object of art to be approached. Oh god, I hate saying things like that!

The Mountain Goats haven't entirely sworn off CDs, though. In fact, they've released two. Their newest album *Zopilote Machine* ("zopilote" is the Mexican word for buzzard), on Ajax, is only available on CD, and the *Beautiful Rat Sunset* mini-album (Shrimper) is also available on disc, but each is distinguished by the Mountain Goats' trademark lo-fi ambience. The latter's eight songs are divided by the sound of a stylus landing heavily on a record, and John forbade the elimination of

The band haven't toured much; they've played three shows outside his LA–area home base. Touring does not attract him: "I don't take a lot of pleasure in not feeling altogether well and not knowing what day it is. And since I don't sleep around there's no appeal in that sort of thing. But I like playing for big audiences that want to see us. We're contemplating something of a mini-tour of places [that have] graduate schools I'm looking into." ◗

THURSTON MOORE (PHOTO, DAN SCHLATTER)

THURSTON MOORE

Somehow the stars never aligned for a Sonic Youth profile in *Puncture*, but in 1995 **STEVE TIGNOR** visited the Manhattan apartment of Thurston Moore and Kim Gordon to interview Moore about his solo album *Psychic Hearts*. Speaking a decade and a half before the band's sudden breakup, the guitarist declared that he enjoyed "that we're nearing 40 and we're called Sonic Youth."

There's a scene in *1991: The Year Punk Broke*, Sonic Youth's documentary of fin de siècle, faux-godless rock 'n' roll on tour, where a European reporter sticks a microphone in Thurston Moore's face and asks him something like, "What are you going to do onstage at the next show?" Thurston, staring straight ahead, not deigning to look at the guy, starts walking and spewing a fantasy story which rapidly descends into non sequitur: "I'm going to take a machine gun and blow away . . . I'm going to defecate and light my shit on fire and kick it into the audience . . ." The reporter keeps up with him, nodding and smiling at every word, as Thurston improvises lines like, "And then the lie, will get caught in my eye . . ."

1991 is a disturbing movie, a docu-Antonioni-style story of rock 'n' roll coming to decadent Europe and withering in tuneless, meaningless noise and bored, self-consciously clichéd star behavior. Kurt Cobain jumps into the drums and the crowd goes nuts; Dinosaur Jr. and Babes in Toyland crank up carbon-copy walls of guitar slop and the crowd goes nuts; elder punk icons Iggy and Joey Ramone are held in neither reverence nor contempt, just kind of mocked, like everything else. The feeling you're left with at the end is a faint disgust that these people are your heroes.

The star of the show, the overbearing personality behind it all, is Thurston Moore. In addition to the scene just mentioned, we see Thurston involved in various banalities: eating catered food, flushing his shit down the toilet, and mooning the MTV playing on his hotel television. He calls himself an over-30 spoiled brat.

Subwaying up to Thurston and Kim Gordon's apartment in SoHo, the movie was haunting me. I knew at some level it was a goof on rock stardom—that Thurston and Sonic Youth in reality have always prided themselves on their level-headedness and normalcy. But I was nervous. This was a rare chance to interview a musician who also possessed a critical/intellectual view of his music—who had the potential to say more than, "We just do what we do." I had the same chance Lester Bangs had with Lou Reed twenty years ago, to do battle with "the one hero left worth battling," or some such. There was also the chance I'd end up like the European journalist in the movie, listening eagerly to how punk rock as rebellion had become a non sequitur. In other words, I might get mooned.

But that didn't happen. The encounter wasn't exactly Lester and Lou: the '90s version of a battle between star and critic is more of an earnest discussion over tea than a struggle between a drunk and a speed freak. My first reaction on meeting Thurston (and Kim, briefly) was amazement that this was the same guy I'd seen rolling around onstage shrieking and bludgeoning his guitars all these years. I couldn't believe this person could put on a rock 'n' roll pose at all.

Thurston was very nice—no attitude, totally cool, the whole nine. He was so lacking in edge that I began to see *1991* and Sonic Youth's recent career in a new light: the bored-star trip hadn't been just mockery or demythologizing, but an attempt to kill off for good the already dying concept of rock 'n' roll as fantasy—putting the music in its place within '90s corporate pop culture, changing the standards of success for rock musicians. But I'll get to that later.

At first I misremembered the address and walked into a building that housed an auto-parts store on its first floor. No "TMoore/KGordon" on the apartment list. Next door, a hip/kitsch accessory shop flashed neon at me. That was it. Had I imagined Sonic Youth would live above anything but a hip/kitsch accessory shop? Thurston was in domestic mode when I walked in: coffee, wet hair, shoes off, his year-old baby, Coco, playing on the floor. I felt stupid remembering my friends and me listening to *EVOL* and *Sister* in high school. On a tree-lined small-town street, that music had frightened us to death. More than just a horror-movie soundtrack, it was American gothic come to life, music to be murdered by. Checking out the Sonic digs, a decent-sized loft with two book-lined studies framing a living room cluttered with baby toys and a big pink doll, I decided the whole Sonic Youth thing wasn't made for 11 a.m. Tuesday. I was disappointed that I wouldn't get to use the description I always thought suited Thurston onstage: John Cage meets Dennis the Menace. He wasn't either of those; more of a gawky big brother with mop top, baritone surfer drawl, a bit of an absent mind, and a willingness to spiel.

We fell into conversation about his recent solo record, *Psychic Hearts* (Geffen). If early Sonic Youth deconstructed punk by spraying it into chaos, this does the opposite, reducing it to riffs without momentum. Thurston didn't seem particularly interested in it. "I don't really care," was his definitive comment.

"I wanted to do something where I called the shots. Sonic Youth is such a democratic process, which is good and bad. I originally thought I would just do these basic tracks in our basement and put it out myself. It wasn't sounding too good down there, just these repetitive riffs. We got some good feedback on a tour of the South, and then Lee [Ranaldo] said I should take the songs to Sear Sound and do them on a 16-track. I talked to the guy at Geffen and said I had some damaged pop tunes I want to put out. He'd seen us do them at CMJ and was like, 'Yeah, we'll do it.' It costs them nothing. I mean, they're used to blowing out huge production budgets for White Zombie or whatever.

"I didn't finesse it too much. I don't like being locked in a studio, I go stir-crazy with the anxiety of having to capture a sound. All the records I've done, half the quality is lost in the studio. At SST, when we would tour, our songs would be amazing . . . We would be so focused every night; then we'd go back and listen to the studio recording and it would be kind of plodding.

"I'm pretty sick of these songs already. Geffen wants me to tour and support it, but I think I'll just play totally different stuff. It's not a career move, anyway. It's not as interesting to me as Sonic Youth, which is mysterious because it can go different ways. This stuff is pretty etched. The best reason for doing the record was probably to get Rita Ackermann's art on the cover."

At this point Kim walks out of a back room and says hello. There's some talk about the baby, who's ready for a nap, then Kim starts making a few phone calls. While I'm talking to Thurston I hear her involved in some gossip—"So what happened last night?" etc. I guess I was expecting a Satanic ritual or something scary, but she too was normal, stopping us to ask Thurston how to spell "savor." They agreed on the Brit "ou" style. Not jet-set exactly, but worldly enough.

Sonic Youth had just finished laying down basic tracks for a new record in Memphis. They stopped to see Al Green preach on Easter Sunday.

"Al was amazing. He ran up to us and asked us where we were from. I said New York City, and he yelled, 'Praise Jesus, New York City is here!' Then he asked my friend, who was like, 'Uh, New Jersey,' and he yelled, 'Praise Jesus, New Jersey's here!' He did spirituals and pop tunes, Burt Bacharach, all that. At the end he collapsed and his deacons had to carry him off like James Brown. I had some shit to say to him, because I saw him on that show *Night Music* once, when he was making fun of Sun Ra. I remember saying, 'Fuck that guy!' So I wanted to walk into the church and say, 'You dissed Sun Ra!' But it didn't happen.

"We went to Memphis so we could make a record outside New York, to try something different. We had never recorded a full album away from here. The studio was a relaxed, homey place where Pavement had recorded, and we just went down for two weeks. I think we're going to call it *Washing Machine*. For a while we thought of changing our band name to Washing Machine, because Sonic Youth had become a brand name. I mean, I like the fact that we're nearing 40 and our band name is Sonic Youth, that's the best thing about the name. It's gotten to carry so much baggage, though. In the end we thought our management wouldn't be too happy with the change [*laughs*].

"The last record we did [*Experimental Jet Set, Trash and No Star*] was pretty conceptual: each of us would bring in an idea and we would elaborate on it, put tracks over it. That can be rewarding musically. This time, we sat down together and improvised organically. We taped these long-ass instrumentals, then went back and rifled through the tapes. *Experimental* had these truncated song structures, which was inspired by people like Guided by Voices, where it's just a great fucking verse and a great fucking chorus and that's it, what else do you want?

"The new record was a product—I guess for the first time—not so much of our influences, but of what each of us had been doing outside the group. We had been on our own for so long last year that it made this recording friendlier in a way, less tense.

"I'd been playing with Japanese noise guitarists and listening to underground cassette labels like Chocolate Monk and Apraxia. They're fascinating—kids throwing away their Pavement records and listening to Blowhole. Punk is like disco to them, like bubblegum. They're into free-form avant-garde jazz and German avant-garde composers, the whole FMP catalog. I went through a heavy period with that stuff, but there wasn't a big scene then, just No Wave really, and now John Zorn. Now it's coming full force, and I'm sitting back wondering what's going to happen with it. Is it going to get big? I saw the

SONIC YOUTH AT CBGB (PHOTOS, MICHAEL GALINSKY)

Clash sell out the Palladium and I thought that was as big as punk would ever get. I thought that was totally nuts, and now Green Day is selling a million records. It's amusing to see this whole avant-garde underground growing up in reaction against punk.

"The new Sonic Youth record takes in some of that stuff, but it'll be weird because most people are unfamiliar with these cassette labels. They'll hear us and say, 'What the fuck is this?' The people who are familiar with it will think we're obnoxious, like we're ripping it off, like we're making it mainstream. They say, 'How much did it cost to put that hiss on there?'

"I guess they have a point, but we're not trying to steal their underground."

I admit I'm one of those who've only heard about the cassette underground through word of mouth. Thurston shows me a copy of *Woolly Bugger*, a paper which documents a scene he has moved to assimilate before it even becomes the new thing. It makes sense, though, that Sonic Youth would need to leave straight punk behind. The current alternative-rock world, from Nirvana to Pavement, is one they essentially created. Keeping on with it would be merely devising new tricks on old themes. It would mean becoming mannered or miniature versions of themselves—something that often happens to artists as they age, and the expansive possibilities of their life and art begin to shrink. At the risk of coming off trendy, the band has to keep its ears open, has to incorporate new sounds. Up to this point, SY have been successful at transforming themselves without sacrificing the gestalt that runs through their work. Their devotion to the new, and their musical egalitarianism, have kept the music consistently open-ended, allowing their work to form a question about the nature of art vs. rock, noise vs. tune, artist vs. star, etc., rather than forcing it to make a definitive, and limiting, statement about any of those paradoxes.

Thurston puts baby Coco to bed, with blues guitarist Tommy Johnson singing her to sleep. Politics comes up in our conversation, and I ask him why the band have retreated somewhat from *Dirty*'s explicitly activist lyrics, and what he thinks of the Gingrich regime and how it could affect rock music.

"Getting more political wasn't really a call to activism as much as it was an artsy thing. I thought using those words could be interesting poetically. I'm intrigued by politics because it's so absurd, but I lean more toward spiritual or social matters. With Gingrich in power it's like Reagan again, which is a nightmare. On the other hand, fascist politics can make for excited liberal art . . . With Reagan you got the hardcore movement. It's hard to figure the '80s musically, because so many great bands never got documented. Now people make cassettes before they even have a band together.

"I don't think the new politics will affect alternative rock's popularity. The stuff that's big now, after Nirvana, is just a more alienated generation coming in. The only thing corporate record companies have done to rock is change perceptions of the creative scene. It hasn't much changed the actual musical product. Yeah, Nirvana were important, because there was this forceful message, and it was sexual. But Green Day aren't like that. They're pretty blank. Billie Joe seems like a nice guy, but . . .

"I guess playing for a major is good and bad. We've always wanted to make money, if only so we can finance other projects. Take a guy like Eddie Vedder. He has millions, but he uses it in a way that's cool. He finances projects without making a big deal out of it. The bad side of a major is obviously that it isn't DIY. There's no shared sensibility. Unless you keep tight control over what's going on, they'll promote your product in a corny way. Geffen's offices have Cher posters up, it's silly. But we have people we trust there—Mark Case, the alternative A&R guy, and Ray Farrell, who was at SST. For us, when we broke with SST, there was nowhere to go unless we did it all ourselves. I think we've carved out a place at

Geffen. At this point, I'm older than most of the workers there anyhow, so I can get my way [*laughs*]."

The niche Sonic Youth have carved at Geffen is an important one, I think. *1991* was not only about how punk's meaning as rebellion had been broken, but also about how punk's insular scene had inherited a rock-star tradition it wanted nothing to do with. Musicians acted bored because the roles they were supposed to be playing were boring. If rock were to keep up its pretense to personal, honest expression (which is what sets it apart from other forms of pop music to start with), yet extend its reach beyond the indie cul-de-sac, it had to forge a middle ground.

Pop culture in the '80s had outgrown rock, overwhelmed it. Michael Jackson's fame made Elvis's seem quaint, almost human by comparison. Madonna's Warholian sense of commerce as art, and the endless ironies that idea produced, made rock's claims to authenticity seem old-fashioned. Sonic Youth were the first to realize that, in their mid-'80s "Madonna, Sean, and Me"/Ciccone Youth phase. I asked Thurston about that time.

"I guess celebrities then had gotten so huge they became like part of your family. We saw Madonna as a big sister, almost; we kind of embraced the human side of the celebrity idea."

That human side is what they've brought to corporate popular music. It's where Matador and Sub Pop, with commitments to marketing quality music with major-label dollars, have followed; it has allowed eccentric artists like Pavement, Beck, Hole, and Liz Phair to have mass impact without necessarily aiming for mass sales; and it has led the most popular rockers, Cobain and Vedder, to call into question the concept of celebrity. That's Sonic Youth's legacy—the stubborn endurance of personal expression despite the efforts of popular music to silence it. Sitting in the domestic calm of Thurston and Kim's apartment, I turn over an idea of them as people who make rock safe for adults. They've scrapped celebrity, taken the music seriously, and turned it once and for all into an art form.

The way they measure success is new for rock 'n' roll: where the classic rock star measured his success by the level of fantasy he could indulge, by the level of privilege he reached or the ease with which he could flaunt middle-class values, Sonic Youth (and Cobain and Vedder) measured it by their work (middle-class value), by the dialogue they hold with other people, by their inclusion. To keep creating, an artist has to live in the world. As Thurston said about Beck, "He's not into making hits so much. He's a middle-class kid who doesn't need to be a millionaire, and he knows it." It's hard to imagine a star ten years ago knowing he didn't need to be a millionaire to be successful.

But the adult artists are also headlining Lollapalooza this year.

"It's funny to me that we're headlining. At first we said no, because this music was so freaky. We were going to do a tour with Pavement and Beck on our own, have fun, lose money. But this was an easy chance; everything is set up for us. I don't really want to be associated with Perry Farrell's company, but basically we just come and play. So what the fuck? I expect when we pull this free-form shit at the end of the day, people will be heading for the gates."

Two final questions: What does he think of the recent Sonic Youth biography [by Alec Foege]? And what does he think of Christgau now?

"I hate panning the book, because [Foege] was so well-meaning, but the whole thing was pretty empty. We wanted Byron Coley to do a book, but this guy was contracted by someone first, so we agreed to do the interviews with him. The book is like bad cocaine to me. I read it and I wondered if there was any soul to our story at all.

"Having Christgau defend our last album when no one else would give us the time of day was great. It made the whole thing worthwhile. I don't know what to think of him, really. I've never met the guy. I do think he started a bad trend by grading records, which is basically what all reviews are about today.

"He's a better writer than most of what I read, though. With us, a lot of younger writers call us cynical, which is too bad. On a song like "Screaming Skull" they thought I was making fun of Superchunk and SST, which I wasn't. I had been over to the SST store in LA, and these ads for Superchunk flashed out at me. It was weird: here was a label and a band I had always connected with something real, something industrious, and now they were just signs, just products in downtown LA. I think younger writers mistake our detached, sort of oblique writing for cynicism."

Kim leaves to buy socks at Bloomingdale's (the banality of evol?), and my tape has run out. Thurston seems willing to talk longer, but I've covered everything I wanted to cover. So I'm out, down into the Village, where I walk into a record shop on First, which has a copy of *EVOL* on the wall for $25. After the easy atmosphere of Thurston and Kim's apartment, the record doesn't hold the old myths for me. I think of it as simply music made by a couple of people who live in SoHo, and listened to by a person in Brooklyn or wherever who relates to it. Underneath the markets, dollars, hype, history, etc., that's what it is. And if people like Sonic Youth had their way, that's all it would ever be. ◗

THE CLEAN, CA. 1994: ROBERT SCOTT, HAMISH KILGOUR, DAVID KILGOUR

THE CLEAN

Of all of indie rock's regional scenes, perhaps the most far-flung and aesthetically consistent thrives in New Zealand. At its center of gravity sit the Clean, a slapdash trio that was born in the late '70s and improbably continues to flourish. On his travels in 1993, **BILL MEYER** visited the Christchurch kitchen of Helen Kilgour to speak with her sons David and Hamish and their fellow Clean conspirator Robert Scott.

It's a rainy late-summer night in Christchurch, New Zealand, and I'm sitting at Mrs. Helen Kilgour's kitchen table. Her sons David and Hamish, along with their friends Robert Scott and Martin Phillipps, are munching on chocolate-chip cookies and talking about their rock band, the Clean. They've just taken a break from thirty straight days of recording to embark on their first tour of New Zealand in four years. This really shouldn't be happening.

Three months ago I'd spoken to Hamish at his New York home and he'd said yes, the Clean would play a show at Big Day Out (South Pacific version of Lollapalooza); but there wouldn't be a tour. "I don't think there's that much interest in one," he'd said with a touch of bitterness, going on to explain that the band had played a couple dates in 1994 after recording their album *Modern Rock*, and the turnout hadn't been that good. He sounded a bit disgusted with New Zealand

apathy, which has variously spurred and dogged the band since it started in the late '70s. Yet here they were once more, slogging north in a rented van. What happened?

"Things change, Bill," Hamish says almost apologetically. Adds David, "It's a bit of a coincidence. We didn't think we'd be recording another LP so soon."

This band—which has changed the face of New Zealand's influential music scene—has broken up and re-formed several times, usually without any plan. Says Hamish, "We don't make conscious decisions. Things just kind of evolve."

The Clean's evolution began in 1978, when punk rock and the Velvet Underground's *1969 Live* record inspired the Kilgours to trade in their surfboards and wet suits for drum kit and guitar. Joined by David's high-school buddy Peter Gutteridge on bass, they set about writing

AN INTRODUCTION TO THE CLEAN (1986)

Say the word: clean. The word is honest. Clear-eyed. Freshly scrubbed. Guileless tunes stripped to their skins. Scratch (acoustic/electric) guitar, basic bass, and snares that snap and crack rather than THUMP THUMP THUMP.

The Clean (brothers David and Hamish Kilgour plus Robert Scott) lasted until 1982 or so. They released "Tally Ho" and *Boodle Boodle Boodle* in '81, followed by "Getting Older" and *Yet Another Clean EP* in '82. The brothers then went on to make an '84 EP as the Great Unwashed with Peter Gutteridge (ex-Chills), who was once a Clean and helped pen a *Boodle* tune.

The Clean were the type of band that gets gleeful about recording on a 4-track ("sometimes only using two or three tracks!") in somebody's dining room or hall. They can come up with a chorus of "Bum ha dada ha dada ha dada" and make it at once sad and sly. They tack on cheesy organ to chanted silly lyrics about hippies and create an irresistible ? and the Mysterians pastiche that's fresher than Monday mornings.

To say they're wondering little kids rubbing sleep out of their eyes gets part of it, but they can be "frantic" and "heavy" (their words)—almost Mark Smith–paranoid.

Coming somewhere out of the void between Big Star #1 and VU #1, the Clean/Unwashed were about spontaneous combustion, about being wide-eyed and open-mouthed in the here and now. And on Clean records, their positive presence still speaks with ungainly honesty and uncertain joy.

—*Terri Sutton*

THE CLEAN
Vehicle
(Rough Trade)

If you draw a diagram of New Zealand's Flying Nun label, many of the bands lead, by membership or influence, back to the Clean. The brilliant records Robert Scott and David and Hamish Kilgour made together in the early '80s were followed by a long hiatus, though the Kilgour brothers resurfaced briefly as the Great Unwashed, and Scott continues making cool, confectionery pop with the Bats.

In joyous contrast to what we have almost come to expect from the recent reunions of punk pioneers, the Clean's new record spares us a rehash of Clean arcana by presenting a mesmerizing blend of Robert Scott's tilt-a-whirl guitar with the spare, spindly David Kilgour sound. "The Blue," a wise child's chant, is quite at home with the lush and vivid "I Can See." The 13-song extravaganza, from the grandeur of "Draw(in)g to a (W)hole" to

their own songs. That was a fairly radical deed at the time: Dunedin had no regular venues for young bands playing original music, so they had to organize their own venues. The first show was pretty rough, recalls Hamish. "We played with the Enemy [the first band led by Chris Knox and Alec Bathgate, now the Tall Dwarfs] at a hall in Dunedin where we used to organize gigs. At our first gig, I was terrified people would throw bottles at me and I built a wall of drums to protect myself."

The Kilgours gigged sporadically for two years with various lineups before settling on bassist Robert Scott as a steady third partner. In early 1981, two things happened. Mrs. Kilgour lent them the money to buy a van for touring. Then a Christchurch record clerk named Roger Shepherd, who wanted to start a label, offered to put out a single. They recorded "Tally Ho," an insanely catchy bit of post–Beach Boys pop leavened by David's ennui-laden singing, for $50 in one night at a studio operated out of someone's home.

Radio stations wouldn't play it, but it sold quite well and peaked at 19 in the national charts. A follow-up EP, *Boodle Boodle Boodle*, did even better. Their success kick-started the Flying Nun label, and drastically changed the New Zealand musical landscape. The band's rough production values (nearly everything the Clean released in the '80s was recorded in somebody's home on a 4-track machine) and their galvanizing live shows were an inspiration to a generation of New Zealanders sick of '70s music and eager to change it.

That inspiration has been manifested in many ways. The band's knack for lacing indelibly chirpy '60s-style melodies with an underlying melancholy and aggressively primitive rhythmic attack, along with their reliance on the primary rock colors of drums, organ, and lots of guitars, was the foundation of the "Flying Nun sound" exemplified by the Chills, Straitjacket Fits, Bird Nest Roys, and dozens of other bands. Others were more influenced by the band's attitude and non-image. Alastair Galbraith, now an established recording artist, saw them play when he was 14. "Their major thing was energy rather than style, a lack of pretension. It made you think you could do what they did." Another aspect that Galbraith and the performers associated with the Xpressway label (Dead C., Peter Jefferies, the Terminals) took to heart was the example of recording at home on low-tech equipment rather than entrusting their music to unsympathetic engineers.

Home recording isn't without cost, though. Laments David, "I don't think we captured what the band were about live." Adds Hamish, "At most the recordings were naive approximations." *Boodle* and its follow-up,

THE CLEAN, EARLY '80S (PHOTO, CAROL TIPPET)

Great Sounds Great, focused on the band's lighter, more acoustic side. But that wasn't the whole story: "In 1980–81, we had a sound David created [live]—a huge sound that was like five guitars—which would have been nice to document," says Hamish. "But we didn't think we had the technology here in New Zealand to do it."

The grind of constant touring wore the band down, and in 1982 they called it quits after releasing a final single, "Getting Older." Everyone kept busy musically, though. Robert Scott formed the Bats, while the Kilgours recorded and toured sporadically from 1983 to '85 as the Great Unwashed. David later played in Stephen, a combo that took its cues from the Clean's poppy side, while Hamish played on the first two Bailter Space records. Fueled by a trickle of posthumous cassette releases (one of them, called *Odditties,* has just been issued on CD by Flying Nun), interest in the Clean never really faded.

When a scheduling coincidence gathered all three members in London in 1988, they got together for two shows, enjoying themselves so much they agreed to resurrect the band. A few rehearsals yielded twenty new songs. Now they toured the world for the first time, and recorded their first-ever album, *Vehicle.* Done nearly live in the studio, it showed that the band hadn't forgotten how to write a perfect two-minute pop song; by now, though, the early-'80s wildness wasn't as evident. The trio took some flack for this in New Zealand, where the record's reception was lukewarm. They toured the country three more times and then, despite talk of another record, in 1991 the band stopped. The Bats were busy touring the world, David was starting a solo career, and Hamish had married and settled in New York City.

In 1994, circumstances once more conspired to

the closing 12-string fragment "Gem," is studded with music and lyrics that make you shiver with their beauty. "Diamond Shine" actually manages to capture the breathless incredulity that the words "I just keep thinking how pretty you are" deserve.

It's such a relief not to have to wish for the decade to start over again so you could buy every Clean record in advance of this one. The only things the Clean rest on their laurels are their guitar cases. Be smitten.—*Lois Maffeo*

THE CLEAN
Unknown Country
(Flying Nun)

The Clean have reappeared on the horizon at intervals—in between the assorted personal projects of David Kilgour, Hamish Kilgour, and Robert Scott—but something special happened a little over a year ago with *Modern Rock.* While performed and recorded quickly and inexpensively, it sounded like the Clean were a band again and not a vacation diversion, jamming as lustily as they had on such early slabs of brilliance as "Billy Two" and "Point That Thing Somewhere Else." With *Unknown Country,* the Clean not only sound like a "real" band, but the Flying Nun prodigal son come home to sit at the head of the dinner table.

For confirmed Kiwi fans, this is a corker. Everything clicks, from the band's fun and chemistry to the material's unique instrumentation and arranging to the expansive cinematic production. There's the patented Clean guitar/organ jam wherein incendiary riffs collide, merge, and slip up the melody stream like so many horny salmon ("Cooking Water"). There's the ethereal folkadelic ballad rife with the sweetest vocal harmonies to be found on either NZ island ("Valley Cab"). There's the oddball experimentation that not only gets your attention but pins it with staples of pleasure ("Wipe Me, I'm Lucky" pits backwards and forwards tracks against one another and the tension turns it into a pop confection; "Balkans" is a quirky ethno/instro featuring mandolin, viola, and thumb piano). Maybe some good-natured self-referential fun, too—it could be my imagination, but I'd swear the scraped-wood-stick percussive squawk at the beginning of "Wall Walk" cheekily nods at an early-'80s track featuring a Donald Duck cameo! Speaking of "Wall Walk," that tune, along with "Changing Your Head," ranks not only as quintessential Clean, but also as some of the most lubricious sound waves ever to emanate from Flying Nun. The former's dark, swirling guitar mantra initially resembles (of all things) the Monkees' epic "Words" before alchemizing inside your ears to a sunshiny piano-and-vocal harmony gem. The latter sports an outrageous neo-surf riff suitable for framing, not to mention a chewy assortment of textural Moog-y squiggles, tambourine/maraca bashing, and something called a crowtheremin (courtesy of Chris Knox, one of numerous guests here).—*Fred Mills* bring the Clean together. The Bats were sidelined while members Paul Kean and Kaye Woodward had their second child, leaving Robert with time on his hands. Hamish wanted to come to New Zealand for a holiday, so they agreed to record an album to kill time and defray his travel costs.

For once the band tried to plan it out. They found a meeting hall at Hoopers Inlet (a remote cove on the Otago Peninsula) and set up a recording studio there. They wanted to take their time recording so they could stretch out and jam, but it didn't quite turn out that way. Hamish and Robert started bringing in loads of tunes; the album's 14 tracks were culled from forty they rehearsed. The resulting album is a big departure from their past recordings, yet it remains very much a Clean record. David, fresh from recording *Sugar Mouth*, his second solo album, did a lot of trippy organ but little lead guitar or singing. Hamish, who usually sang one song a record on the early EPs, did half the vocals. The result was the most layered, crafted thing they'd ever done: "It got a bit controlled," David says. But the old mad energy was still present: in David's wildly echoed keyboard jam "Phluke"; in Robert's driving, primitive bass playing; in Hamish's demented vocal goofing on the B-side "Psychedelic Clown."

The band had so much fun recording *Modern Rock* that when Hamish flew back for Big Day Out in January 1995, they found themselves in a studio once again. The new record is tentatively entitled *Chockablock*, and it's the jamming record they didn't make in 1994. This time, says Robert, "we didn't have any songs written when we went in. We had three practices and put a lot of music down." "It's getting away from the song structures and making bigger sound pictures," says Martin Phillipps. Phillipps, who once roadied for the Clean and played organ on the "Tally Ho" single, is back with the band as a touring utility player and in-studio consultant.

The new record should be out later this year, and the band are already talking about another one. Fourteen years after "Tally Ho," the Clean are recording more than ever, though they still feel like outsiders in their own land. "We're outside of mainstream and alternative music now," observes David. Hamish adds, "We're older, which is funny. I quite like it, because when we were active earlier, kind of pre-1980, we were despised by older people for the music we made. Now it seems it's younger people who despise us. We'll be the angry old men of rock," he says, laughing.

And David confirms, "I heard some kid at Big Day Out say, 'This is old people's music, isn't it?' It was

hilarious. We've always worked best being up against the world."

What they're really up against is New Zealand's stifling sports- and agriculture-dominated social milieu, and the radio stations programmed from abroad to play English and American dance music. The band is heartened by attention from abroad, though: "It helps when you hear from people overseas who like it," Robert notes.

So they soldier on, making the music they like both together and in other bands. David has recorded two albums of light, graceful guitar-pop for Flying Nun, and has compiled an album of 2-track home recordings for Ajax Records. With Martin Phillipps, he's recorded an EP of '60s covers as Pop Art Toasters. The duo enjoyed it so much that they are considering doing another record of early-'70s songs. Robert's looking forward to renewed recording with the Bats, although the group's status as an international touring unit is uncertain. He's also recorded an album of easygoing folk-rock songs with vocalist Jane Sinnott as the Magick Heads, whose debut album *Before We Go Under* was just released by Flying Nun. The Mad Scene, Hamish's band with his wife, Lisa Siegel, has released *Sealight* (on Merge), a diverse new album that encompasses breezy pop and brooding drones.

The band relish moving back and forth between projects, says Hamish. "We have ways to bring in new ideas and redevelop things—it's quite stimulating." Adds David, "For me, it goes back to the thing I create with Robert and Hamish—we create this thing among the three of us. The other things [recording projects] are more me coming up with the goods, so to speak . . ."

At this point, Robert grabs the tape recorder to say, "The journalist now has his hand stuck in the cookie jar."

"Goddamn Americans," David says good-naturedly and goes on, "It's a creative thing to slip into with Hamish and Bob—that's the main reason I do it. I know we create something as a unit that I wouldn't normally create on my own."

After liberating my hand from the cookie jar, we retire to a club where I get to see the Clean chemistry firsthand. Elements of their other projects appear, but there's a percolating excitement—something more aggressive, primitive, spontaneous, and elemental—that doesn't happen in any of their other bands. With luck, says Robert, the rest of the world will witness that chemistry again soon. "It'd be good to come over and play. Meeting people who enjoy what we do makes it all worthwhile." ⊙

SLEATER-KINNEY: CARRIE BROWNSTEIN, CORIN TUCKER, LORA MACFARLANE (PHOTO, SUE P. FOX)

SLEATER-KINNEY

Sleater-Kinney had never been interviewed when *Puncture* profiled the rookie trio in 1995. In the years that followed, Janet Weiss would replace drummer Lora MacFarlane, and Greil Marcus would anoint Sleater-Kinney America's greatest band. The band would fold, Carrie Brownstein would become an unlikely television star, and the musicians would reunite, triumphantly. But back in 1995, early convert **JOHNNY RAY HUSTON** was thrilled to discover "rock reinvented—again."

Offered the love of "A Real Man," Corin Tucker of Sleater-Kinney asks, "Should I buy it?" Her answer—"I don't wanna"—is more than a rejection of one man; her persona struggles against male social control ("no man is gonna rule my life," declares a song by her earlier group, Heavens to Betsy), and will not let a man inside.

The approach to sexual politics on Sleater-Kinney's ten-song mini-album is not a cool one; it runs counter to prevailing notions of ironic, deconstructed identity. Nowadays, sophisticated minds use theory to gloss life's cop-outs and concessions, but Sleater-Kinney refuse both ironic submissiveness and sex-worker rebel poses; their lyrics are simple and true, and resonate in complex, powerful ways. Take "Sold Out," a song that exposes rock's dirty secret: strong women still have to strip to sell records. "Take it, it's my body / Take it, I want money," Tucker shrieks in her greediest, brattiest voice,

conjuring recent female icons—Courtney, Tori, Liz, Alanis, PJ—who have appeared as *Spin* or *Rolling Stone* underwear cover girls.

Sleater-Kinney is full of raw physical/mental metaphors. "You're inside me / I'm your mommy," Tucker shrieks at one point, in a crude yet multifaceted inverse of the predatory real/symbolic Daddys populating the songs on Bikini Kill's first cassette. When she wails, "You hold onto me," it hints at a stranglehold, not a hug. The grain of her voice—high-pitched, choked, trembling—teeters between control and hysteria. "Her Again" shifts from denial of trauma (verse) to erupting rage (chorus); her voice nearly breaks, then clenches tighter.

The whole disc has the sharp spark of a group starting to realize their potential. Few performers have charted emotional and physical boundaries and distances with the precision, urgency, and originality of singer/guitarists

Corin Tucker and Carrie Brownstein and drummer Lora MacFarlane. Accustomed to the duo format of her previous band, Heavens to Betsy, Tucker wrestles with a new collaborative situation, rarely tempering the too-muchness of her voice. On sabbatical from Excuse 17, another trio with a similar lineup, Brownstein is more at ease with countermelodies; her compositions have subtler dynamics. Rejecting a boy who wants to show her "How to Play Dead," she shares Tucker's lyrical concerns, but her conversational vocals (sometimes prone to Waitresses-style ennui) and visceral symbolism (spinning images of anorexia and bulimia) are distinct.

"I'd starve you right out of me / If I knew what else to eat," Brownstein says in "The Last Song"; her clipped strum locks into MacFarlane's drumming as the pace accelerates. (Laced with click sticks, MacFarlane's part matches vocal feeling with rhythmic motion.) In most

SUE P. FOX

of Brownstein's songs, invasive presences are purged, but "The Day I Went Away" highlights empty spaces in even the most intimate relationships. "Please remember me," she whispers, in the record's quietest, most desperate moment.

CORIN: Childhood influences? I really liked new wave: I was into INXS. As a teenager I liked hardcore, but I'm into pop music [now], bands that have melodies.
LORA: When I was little, I liked ABBA—I saw them win the Eurovision Song Contest. I was influenced by a brother who was into mod stuff like the Jam. Then by classical music, which I studied for six years. I was a dork, into Bach and Stravinsky. I had a scholarship to study voice, but I gave it up and started doing percussion. At school, there were more women playing than men. Interesting: women seem to be discouraged more

in pop and punk than in classical music.
CARRIE: When I was really young I liked Fleetwood Mac—still do. I took piano lessons, and wanted to be like Christine McVie, so I played along with—
LORA: "Rhiannon!"
CARRIE: Yeah. And "Don't Stop [Thinkin' about Tomorrow]." In late junior high, I dove into the Ramones, B-52's, Replacements. In high school, I played tennis; I'd take my tennis racket and strum it for the team. I thought, God, I should just play guitar. But no girls at my school were playing, and it wasn't until I saw the Fastbacks play that I took it seriously.
CORIN: I wanted to be a singer. I was in musicals in grade school. In high school, I tried to join my best friend's boy band, and they wouldn't let me. After that, and being inspired by Bratmobile and Bikini Kill, I taught myself guitar and practiced singing. I was 18. Even girls who give themselves self-confidence have to put up with people laughing at them. When Heavens to Betsy first formed, we were harassed onstage.

In the first three songs written and released by Heavens to Betsy, Corin Tucker rejects romantic fantasies of girlhood and zeroes in on the girl's body as a battleground torn by abortion, menstruation, molestation. Though her early songs have the tragic narrative pull of folk weepies like Janice Ian's "At 17," they replace cloying sentiment with bitterness. The baby in the title of back-alley abortion tale "Baby's Gone" isn't a fetus, but a girl killed by the mixed messages she receives about innocence and experience, morality and maturity. The song's lyric is a voice from beyond the grave: "Maybe he loved me / maybe he didn't / . . . it doesn't matter now / because when I needed help I was all alone." In "Baby's Gone," Tucker wrenches notes from her guitar. Greil Marcus rightly compares the song's distortion to Hendrix's "Star-Spangled Banner"; it does what it must to get her words across. Unlike most punk today, Heavens to Betsy's crude primitivism really is primal; the instrumental struggle is both asset and weakness. Rising to overflowing, Tracy Sawyer's distorted bass matches the gathering tension in Tucker's on-the-boil voice; the drums function like commas in verses, exclamation marks in choruses.

Heavens to Betsy fixate on body and soul, the divisions between one's insides and outsides. The group's one LP, *Calculated*, is filled with visceral imagery (a laid-open heart adorns the cover). "You want to diagram my heart! Is it so you will know how to take it apart?" Tucker asks on "Donating My Body to Science."

Calculated is primarily about the struggle to maintain a self. On "Stay Away," one of many H2B songs about sexual assault, Tucker shifts from calm pleading on the title's first word to the shriek of a cornered animal on the second. By the final verse, she's turned the tables on her attacker; her ability to feel is a show of strength, his numbness a form of death.

CORIN: In Heavens to Betsy, my lyrics are sometimes almost childlike. When you're young—which is when I dealt with a lot of abusive junk—you have fewer resources and are most targeted for violence. To stand up in your own defense is crucial for your development as a person. It's important to know you have rights.

Like all the best singers, Corin Tucker can make a single word into a world. In "Decide," a letter to someone imprisoned by a marriage, she attacks the ways marriage is mythologized, depicting it as a fairy tale gone bad, Sleeping Beauty with no wake-up kiss. When she reaches the line "Holding on to nothing else but him," she repeats the word "him" five times, highlighting her friend's obsession with one man.

Calculated's narratives forsake trad rock topics for daily female experience. Many contain fantasies of revenge: "What you do / Comes back to you," Tucker threatens in "Waitress Hell." On the surface, it's a rant about snotty customers, and a funny one ("Miss, I need another glass / This one is smudged! And my lips are too precious for this"). But the comic harangue makes a point on gender and class: "And in the end when I'm covered in your shit / You look at me like I'm the dirty one." As a subject, waitressing lacks the sensational appeal of sex work—a more common feminist rock motif—but Tucker sees it as another realm where women are bought and ripped off.

Righteous anger is a basic punk pleasure, though these days it has degenerated into self-pity; *Calculated*, galvanized by rage, complicates matters by including race in its world view. Audaciously, "Axemen" equates rock shows with pep rallies and the "teenage dream" of a "punk white-privilege scene" with oppressive high-school jock cliques. The song begins like a cheerleader chant, with Tucker naming her school colors. "Hey look around! There's so much white," she sings, suddenly conscious of the segregation she took for granted. Stealing an axe (guitar) from the quarterback (frontman), she tries to chop her way out of the scenario, only to realize she can't cut off her own racism. Throughout "Axemen," Tucker veers between surgical self-mutilation and insanity's release. "I'm going crazy! Do you wanna watch? / Do you wanna come?" implicates the listener in the song's chain of pain.

CORIN: Carrie and I were good friends. Then we became really good friends. We started writing as a joke; we wrote some good songs. Our first single was recorded

SLEATER-KINNEY
Reasons to Say No
(Villa Villakula 10-inch/Chainsaw CD)

Where Heavens to Betsy, Corin Tucker's last band, shattered received ideas about femininity, Sleater-Kinney take on the responsibility of picking those ideas up, living with some, and discarding others. That's not to say the songs are about compromise; the band still have dozens of reasons to say no, and Tucker's screech can still clear a room of beer-swilling guys (I've seen it happen). But this record is remarkable for two other reasons.

The first is its musical economy. Heavens to Betsy backed their rage with a controlled earthquake of noise: the songs rumbled. Sleater-Kinney are terse by comparison, guitars darting, dark holes gaping between instruments, songs kept brief. The cliché "no note is wasted" applies—not so much in a musical sense as in the sense that each note is right because it forms meaning. It's not because of punk ideology that the songs are brief. They do not sound unfinished: they simply last long enough to get a message across. "I Don't Wanna" plays out a psychosexual drama in under a minute, then expires.

The second remarkable feature of this record, to my mind, is its beauty. Not arising from lilting melodies or chiming harmonies or lyrical sentiments, its beauty is in its progress from an early, abrasive "No!" to a thought-out, lived-through, and earned sense of disgust by record's end. The music relaxes, the songs become pensive, the rhythms almost warm, without losing any edge. The singing and playing cut two ways: a rage which refuses everything, and a quiet, tentatively formed wish to live in the world. By "The Last Song," the singer is willing to be vulnerable ("I need you out of me! / Before I turn into you"), but she's also resolved, tough-minded, hellbent on keeping the idea of woman as dependent out of her life.

It was disturbing last year hearing Heavens to Betsy shatter that norm; hearing Sleater-Kinney admit such ideas still haunt them, even as they try to root them out of their daily lives and relationships, is compelling. And beautiful. And even more revolutionary.—*Steve Tignor* with Misty Farrell (from Seattle) drumming. Once we were watching a TV special on kangaroos, and we had the idea of going to Australia. We got the address of every Australian girl who'd written to Kill Rock Stars (Heavens to Betsy and Excuse 17's label), and wrote to them. Iain, a guy who does a fanzine with Lora, wrote back to tell us Lora played drums. We'd never met her, or heard her, but we thought it would be cool.

CARRIE: We do a lot of joint writing—one person has a guitar part and the other works over it, same with vocals. Our new songs are different. They're less straight-forward, they have more dynamics. Lora sings, Lora and Corin together sometimes, all three of us on some songs. We're seeing what we can do. Listening to our first record, we thought, "Wow, that sounds good—but we have three songwriters in our band!"

CORIN: Our new songs are different from anything I've done. Lora's drumming has let Carrie and me develop. We write complex music that still rocks. People are often critical in a stupid way of women rock bands, or they're not critical at all. But a lot of female rock bands are boring—they don't challenge themselves as musicians.

LORA: I agree. I don't like a band just because it has women in it, I like it for the music. The Raincoats are a band who really impressed me and influenced me. They made music in a weird, original way.

The songs on Sleater-Kinney's next record, the full-length album *Call the Doctor* (due from Chainsaw Records in February), are both traditional and wholly original. Most follow verse/chorus patterns, and last less than three minutes. Their choreography—three distinct vocal and instrumental elements that alternately play off one another and lock together—is innovative. Other female Northwest bands (Excuse 17, Team Dresch) have brought similar teamwork to their compositions, but none in music of such fierce beauty. In Heavens to Betsy, Tucker's rudimentary guitar work mirrored her unease; the new band's individual and collective control is the sound of freedom. Momentum becomes mood; sometimes measured, sometimes fluid, MacFarlane's versatile rhythms move in fits and starts. This complex musical push/pull extends to the lyrics. "They want to socialize/dignify/analyze/terrorize you," Tucker sings, high and panicky, over Brownstein's subdued vocal countermelody. Initially, the guitars perform a dueling dance; after a dramatic drum roll, they fuse and accelerate. Wilder than '60s girl-group harmonies, more intricate than '90s grrrl bands' gang shouts, *Call the Doctor*'s entwined vocals resemble sirens and furies, or work like a dialogue between the voice in one's throat and voices in one's head. "Hubcap" starts like something on the Raincoats' debut LP, gradually growing and uncoiling to

Fleetwood Mac "Tusk" proportions. The verse and chorus of "Stay Where You Are" contain some four separate elements shooting in different directions. Brownstein's imagery travels from containment to escape; from inner turmoil to violent action: clawing, scratching, screaming, setting fires.

The body-trouble theme of Tucker and Brownstein's previous bands still dominates. "I'm Not Waiting" shows in one sick snapshot our culture's knack for making little girls into naked women and vice versa. "I'm not waiting / til I grow up / to be a woman," Tucker declares, voice trembling in excitement and terror; "Go out on the lawn / Put your swimsuit on," Brownstein replies with a predatory sneer. Other songs, like Brownstein's "Heart Attack," narrow the focus to a single organ. Although "Little Mouth" is about mute paralysis, it couldn't be harder or faster; Tucker gulps and gasps for air as the song builds speed and volume.

Over and over, "'Little Mouth" refers to "damaged goods," and most of *Call the Doctor* confronts the female body as commodity. An incredibly catchy song about being suspicious of commercialism, "Anonymous" tries to establish a self not defined by words or money. "Not enough for you to know / Not enough for you to own," Tucker's supercharged voice repeats, each statement of opposition shadowed by frustration and ambivalence ("Never on the record / It'll never show up"). Likewise, the things of "Good Things," the stuff of "My Stuff," are internal and external: when Tucker sings, "I will let you own what I have," she's referring to familial scars as much as belongings.

What's the price of love? The title of "Taking Me Home" equates seduction with consumption, pickup with purchase. It's a workplace scenario—Tucker looks to life rather than situationist cryptocodes for her politics. Tired of harassment on the job, the protagonist trades her independence for bows, ribbons, rings, and other trappings. The song's chorus—"Not for sale / Not your girl / Not your thing"—rallies against its verses, where the protagonist is bought, used, discarded.

Call the Doctor's most amazing song, "I Wanna Be Your Joey Ramone," breaks free from constraints of currency, finding liberation in unnamed, untamed currents of energy, the sound + feeling equation at the heart of rock. The chorus is the sonic equivalent of whiplash; its collective catharsis matches Nirvana's "Smells Like Teen Spirit." It travels through private places (the listener's mind, bedroom walls and floors) and public spaces (concerts) of rock, conquering as it enters. Pushing in front of a crowd, Brownstein sings, "It's what I thought / It's rock'n'roll."

In that moment of discovery, rock is reinvented. Again. ◑

NEUTRAL MILK HOTEL

When Jeff Mangum introduced Neutral Milk Hotel with *On Avery Island*, he received warm reviews but little attention outside of artsy enclaves. Yet for *Puncture*, this alluring new voice was big news. **STEVE TIGNOR** interviewed Mangum in early 1996 about what was still essentially an under-the-radar, one-man recording project.

"Yeah, I've been around since 1983!" says Jeff Mangum in a husky drawl, and with the slightest hint of a Southern accent. He is joking about his earliest teenage recordings in small-town Louisiana.

"My first songs were about the kinds of things you talk about when you're 13—running away from home, defecating. I'm going to get those tapes out someday . . .

"When you grow up where I did, in the South, there's not many people who share your viewpoint. You seek out freaks. You see someone walking down the street with green hair, and you're like, 'Hey! Come back here!'

"Will Hart [now of Olivia Tremor Control] also lived in my town, Ruston. We were into punk and put on a few shows—Calamity Jane, the Supreme Dicks, Sebadoh. I went to college in town. But since it was just down the road, it was kind of like being back in high school. I tried pretty hard to fail out, and finally quit after two years.

"I went to Athens [Georgia] because Will had gone there. I was in a band called Synthetic Flying Machine. I liked it more in Athens, because of the music and lifestyle. But I wouldn't want to live there forever. Too many crazy people. Like my roommates—I had to watch out they didn't kill me. I went out west for a while, lived in LA and Denver. I had to find something new.

"I was always doing Neutral Milk Hotel on my own," Jeff explains. "It was kind of a side thing, away from being in a band. I never thought it would become my main thing. It was always sort of just for me—to get extra songs on tape, ones that I didn't think fit with the band."

I ask if Neutral Milk Hotel became a bigger deal for him after the early-'90s spate of home recordings on indie labels.

"Well, sort of. But it wasn't like I was thinking, 'Wow, now I can do that stuff and people will listen.' That never really entered my mind. The music I did on my own was special because it was my music, at its most basic, not trying to fit someplace.

"I sent out a few tapes and got a call from Cher Doll in Seattle. They were like, 'Do you want to do a record?' I said 'Sure.' That was it. We did singles and a few other things leading up to the album. It's not just me in Neutral Milk Hotel, though. I wrote all the songs and sang and played, but I still think of the records as more filled out—more like a band—than my original idea of the music was."

At a time when indie bands are branching out from pop-song forms, the Neutral Milk Hotel album, *On Avery Island* (Merge)—despite its dalliances with noise

and with bleating, marching-style horns—is pretty traditional. With a layer of fuzz on top, these are melancholy indie tunes filtered through a '90s-style lo-fi lens. Moving past the limits of collective playing, Mangum downplays rhythm and lingers over his vocals, freelancing the melody.

In fact, the record could be said to be a vocal improv on a mini song suite. But that doesn't imply conceptual pretentiousness or enforced repetition. There are enough strange noises and breakdowns to keep you guessing, and the tunes he rings variations on come across as catchy rather than as vocal improvisation for its own sake. Nothing falls apart.

The word "suite" in rock is usually reserved for prog-style motifs which get developed (or not) inside a larger idea. But Mangum's songs rise up whole again, the emphasis not on any extended work but on the tune itself refocused, extended, given to us one piece at a time. And why not? The tunes are beautiful, and it's a pleasure to hear them return with new additions. The lyrics, spewed rapid-fire, concern those moments during a person's 20s when relationship and freedom are tested together, when everything but fun is tentative, before commitments turn into battles. All is loose and a bit mysterious.

"I'll probably do a couple more records like this one. But I want to do noise, something weirder, too. I've always listened to jazz guys like [Eric] Dolphy and Pharaoh Sanders. I saw him last week; I'd heard him for so long . . . to see him live blew me away. I'm in New York for a bit, then we'll probably move out to some small town in Arizona. We're going to tour later this year. It'll be a band, and we'll probably do folky songs, and some noisier stuff."

Jeff Mangum's presence on a prominent indie label like Merge is a healthy development, I think. Whether his music fits into a lo-fi movement or not, his songs are a way for indie-style pop to continue developing after the four-person-band ideas of first-generation acts like R.E.M. have either played themselves out or moved into a rock context. Stuff like *On Avery Island*, too delicate for any alternative market, would not have been released with such a high profile ten years ago. But it's just that reputation preceding them that has gotten a 4-tracker like Jeff Mangum to fill out his bedroom recordings—to play them without obscure indulgences and squeeze them into a big, uniquely personal statement. The effect is a music that doesn't forsake tune, or attempt to leave rock behind; at the same time, it is too personal to fit with a band's need for variety. This record benefits from its single-mindedness. Its sharply honed ambition doesn't leave out pop-wise roots. And it still delivers plenty of surprises. ◗

GUIDED BY VOICES

When *Puncture* first covered Guided by Voices, the band were still enigmatic and obscure. By 1995, the world had caught on. **JOHN CHANDLER** returned to interview the band in the thick of its golden period.

It's 4:30 and our trusty bucket has chosen rush hour on the Seattle freeway to call it quits. Cars whiz by on both sides, missing the tiny Chevy Spectrum by nervous centimeters. Guided by Voices #1 fan Stan McMahon and I are supposed to catch up with the band two hours from now at the Crocodile Cafe. We toss a coin to see who's going to walk a lonely mile to the nearest gas station. It's starting to hail. This is not the way I was hoping to start my big story.

In 1993, I'd chanced on a copy of *Vampire on Titus* and soon after was compelled to force myself into the life of Dayton, Ohio, schoolteacher Robert Pollard, GBV's chief tunesmith and singer. I wanted an interview; I was curious about such a blazingly talented songwriter keeping his light under a bushel for so long. His attitude during our initial conversation was quizzical: "Why do you want to talk to me?" *Puncture* was the first American magazine to profile Guided by Voices. Only that

rascal Everett True from English weekly *Melody Maker* scooped us.

Robert mailed me the previous GBV albums, and I made so many tapes for friends that my vinyl was worn nearly smooth. GBV graduated from being a band I liked into a cause . . . this was MY band.

In the months that followed, I watched the name Guided by Voices pop up all over the place, from the tiniest zine to the halls of mammon (*MTV, Spin, Rolling Stone*, etc.). Not too shabby for a bunch of greying duffers who for the past seven years had been churning out maddeningly insistent British Invasion–smacked pop collages heard by a fortunate few. Music flowed from their creative tap like frothy brew at a Senior Keg, and the buzz kept getting louder. Pollard is one of the most prolific songwriters on the planet. "I could write five songs while taking a shit," he once quipped. "And three would be really good," added a nearby wag.

In June 1994, Guided by Voices came to Eugene,

Oregon, where I was living at the time. I collared Robert at the show and introduced him to my pal Stan McMahon, who fanatically plays no fewer than fifty Guided by Voices songs on acoustic guitar. Robert was impressed enough to ask him to open the show. Stan has subsequently toured with the band as sound man and low-rent opening act, soaking up attention and anecdotes along the way.

The Eugene gig, played in the rain under a tiny shelter, was one of the best shows I've seen. Nirvana biographer and *Rolling Stone* writer Michael Azerrad was in the crowd, bouncing up and down, joyfully digging this elemental rock greatness. GBV are grubby scruffs who look like your older brother's car-obsessed chums. Their love of the cool chord and snaky melody was evident on every face as they skipped from song to song with barely a pause while Robert cued them up like human tone arms. "This one is 'Striped White Jets.' 1-2-3 . . ."

Afterwards, we took the band to a microbrew pub, where they enjoyed the food, but were confused by the expensive and exotic beer. The next few hours were spent discussing the merits of Jerry Lee Lewis (Robert loves him) and the art of songwriting. "I write songs I want to hear," Robert tells me. "'No one else is writing songs like Lennon/McCartney or Pete Townshend, so I guess it's up to me." We laugh and order too much beer.

We arrive frazzled at the Crocodile, near Pike Street Market in downtown Seattle. Guided by Voices are sound-checking, and something about them looks different. Either guitarist Tobin Sprout has had a dramatic facelift, or some kid has taken his place. "Toby's wife is having a baby, so he had to fly home last night," Robert explains. "We were going to cancel the West Coast leg, but Nate bailed us out."

When all seemed lost, cocky roadie Nathan Barlow stepped forward to learn forty-plus songs in a single day. The sound check is close to two hours, and the band runs through the whole set, coaching young Nate on older material like "Quality of Armor" and "Shocker in Gloomtown." When Robert runs off to eat a hamburger, Stan sings four or five tunes. Assorted music bugs wander in and smile. We kidnap Robert and settle him in for serious interrogation.

The Devo Discovery

The beginning of the GBV odyssey goes back to the dazed and confused '70s, with Robert and guitarist Mitch Mitchell playing Slade and Thin Lizzy covers in a Dayton pop-metal band. Robert remembers when things changed:

"One day, Mitch played me the first Devo album, *Are We Not Men*. I found it completely repulsive on first

listen. I couldn't believe anyone would put out an album that sucked that bad. But then, since I was into that theatrical prog-rock stuff, I kept listening to it and reading the lyrics, and decided, 'This shit's amazing!'

"The two greatest periods in rock for me were 1966 to 1969, later British Invasion, psychedelia and stuff like that, and 1978 to 1981 punk and post-punk," says Robert. "That's why we might go from something soft and Beatles-y to something snotty and noisy like Wire. It's also why we might do something inspired by the Who; or twisted and trippy like Soft Boys; or big, anthemic shit like the Skids; or heavy like Killing Joke. It's all there."

Back in Dayton, Robert and Mitch found their love of new music running counter to popular opinion. The boys were soon bandless.

"Mitch and I decided to get radical. We shaved our heads—well, burred them anyway. Everyone thought we were fucked up and crazy. Then we started to incorporate Bram Tchaikovsky songs into our set. The band played them; then they had a secret meeting without me and Mitch. They came and said, 'You guys are going to have to leave. We'd like to keep you, Rob, but Mitch has to go . . . he's influencing you in a bad way.'" [*laughter*]

Suddenly released from their comrades, Robert recruited Kevin Fennell to play drums (he still does) and a new band began. Toby came later, but an ebb-and-flow lineup that usually included brother Jim Pollard as well as Kevin and Mitch began wrestling with Robert's unconventional compositions.

"I always wrote songs. Even as a kid I'd write these a cappella melodies. Some of the things we do were actually written in the '60s! You can't call us retro!

"We fucked around in the basement a long time recording our stuff. We weren't really good enough to play anywhere. I think there are snippets of things we recorded at that time [the early '80s] still popping up on our albums [see "Return to Saturn X Radio Report" on the *Propeller* album]."

"I was writing complicated songs. I'd write songs we couldn't actually play. I was listening to Jethro Tull and Sparks: it was like Ian Anderson and Ron Mael were writing songs that purposely fucked up their bands; it sort of appealed to me."

Of course, a band isn't a band without a name. Or a gig for that matter. "About a year before we played live," Robert recounts, "I started going around, trying to get us a gig. We weren't actually ready to play, but I figured if someone would give us a show, we could get our shit together. I'd hang around and talk to these guys at the Thousand and One Club [in Dayton] and say 'I've got a band!' They'd ask what my band was called, and the name I came up with was Instant Love-lies. We didn't get a gig.

"The second name was even worse! I said we were called Beethoven & the American Flag. We still didn't get a gig. But they were starting to know my face, and it was just a matter of time. Funny thing is, we never got a gig there . . .

"Guided by Voices was a name I'd written in a note-book, and I thought it was cool. I pictured a record bin and the names: 'Genesis . . . Gentle Giant . . . Grate-ful Dead . . . Guided by Voices . . .' We started playing our weird pop at these seedy redneck bars. For our first show I dressed in black with a string tie to look like Johnny Cash. It didn't help. Everyone was like, 'What the fuck is this shit?'

Despite constantly recording, the album parade didn't get into high gear until 1986, when GBV hit the studio to record the R.E.M.-inspired EP *Forever Since Breakfast*. This also marked the end of live performance for a few years. Robert decided concentrating on re-cording was more fun and rewarding than playing to indifferent audiences.

"I didn't like *Forever Since Breakfast*. It's so obvious I was a huge R.E.M. fan. We didn't know what we were doing in the studio," Robert confesses. "So then I came up with my recording philosophy: whatever I like goes on the album."

Early Album Round-Up

"*Devil Between My Toes* is a quirky, experimental album full of improvised jam stuff. I told Kevin to use only snare, high-hat, and kick drum. He'd play these rhyth-mic, Devo-like patterns we'd jam over. It's a hodge-podge but still one of my favorites. I was listening to a lot of Wire around that time.

"We rented some nice equipment for the next one, *Sandbox* (1988), as a Big Star/Cheap Trick/Dwight Twil-ley power-pop stab. I think we succeeded in getting a big sound, but I'm not crazy about that one. After three records, I was still bashful about our music. We only pressed a few hundred copies.

"After *Sandbox*, I got closer to my psychedelic roots on *Self-Inflicted Aerial Nostalgia* (1988), though there's still plenty of pop on it. Then we started hitting the deep, dark depression of *Same Place the Fly Got Smashed* (1990)."

After satisfying his psych-pop sweet tooth for a while, Robert and crew stumbled into a part-brilliant part-dreary concept album about an alcoholic.

"It didn't begin as a concept album. We finished the songs and I sequenced them, and then we realized it told a story. We were like, 'Wow, it's linear!'

"The album starts out with a series of things that nauseate this guy—they're the same things that suf-focate me—stuff like air shows, carnivals, bars, strip-pers . . . The second part has the guy sitting in his room drunk, pissed, and sick of everything. The shit going on in the streets leads to "Local Mix-Up." The guy goes out and does something bad, I'm not sure what, and it goes into "Murder Charge." Then this poor fucker gets the chair: "Blatant Doom Trip." And last this David Lynch everything's-all-right-in-heaven ending: "How Loft I Am."

With their fifth album in the can and no payoff in sight, Robert figured the end was near.

"After *Same Place*, everything started to get to me. We were still having fun, but people kept asking when I would quit fucking around with this band shit, if we weren't actually going to play anywhere. We recorded off and on for two more years and put the best left-over stuff on *Propeller* [1992]. The name was a joke. We were going to shut it down after that. I told people it was going to propel us to success . . . In a way it did, because it led to us getting signed to Scat."

It remains mysterious how Guided by Voices got out of Dayton if no one tried to market their albums. Rob-ert isn't sure, though he offers some clues.

"We met a band called New Creatures . . . they heard our albums and sent them out without permission. We ended up with some nice reviews. We also somehow ended up with a fan base in New York. Thurston Moore and people like that were passing around tapes of our stuff."

One question I keep asking is why the band didn't try harder to get their music to the outside world. It's mind-boggling that Robert would be so shy about such strong material. His explanation: "I told the band if we were any good, [the music industry] would come to us. I didn't know if we were any good. I loved the music, but I thought it was kind of a rip-off; awfully close to a lot of other things.

"Only recently have we tried to figure out what it is we're ripping off, but we can't. There are familiar things in the songs, but it's all mix and match. You can tell what kind of stuff I listen to, but you can't place it exactly. That's why I sing with a British accent . . . I grew up listening to British pop songs—it's where my sense of melody and vocal style came from. If I didn't sing with a British accent, it wouldn't sound like me."

"So why do you record your pure power-pop in such an offhand, lo-fi way?" I persist. "Why don't you go into a big studio with Steve Lillywhite or someone, and record as best you can?"

Robert's fielded this one before. "If we had money, and only one fucking song, we would have. But we had no money and a hundred songs. Do the math. I couldn't spend that meticulous time on all the songs, and I want them all released.

"We've got a big suitcase full of song tapes going back to the beginning. I was thinking of selling the suitcase lock, stock, and barrel to some fucked-up major label, to do with whatever they wanted. Or we were thinking that we might release it all under about 25 different band names. But there's some pretty corny shit in there. We've got enough back material for Volumes 1 to 10 of *King Shit and the Golden Boys* [the name of the collection of previously unavailable material included in GBV's box set, *Box*].

"Lately, I've been going back, looking at old songs that didn't make it, and analyzing them. What was good about them? What wasn't? I might add something from another song that didn't quite work, give it a new title, and there you go. I'll never run out of songs." I ask him about the scarcity of early songs in the live set. There've been so many lineup changes in the band over the years, he explains, that relearning old songs would be like doing covers. They'd rather move forward. Pollard loses interest in better songs than most bands are capable of writing . . .

The Seattle show is flawless, even with New Guy Nathan on guitar. The place is stuffed to bursting, and eventually the fire department show up to clear us out, but not before some memorable displays. Young Fresh Fellow and R.E.M. hired gun Scott McCaughey (who tells me R.E.M. have been covering Chris Isaak's "Wicked Game" on tour) gets up, with the ubiquitous Stan, and delivers dead-on harmonies for "Echos Myron." Robert is his usual Roger Daltrey–meets–Stiv Bators geeky frontman, and we are blessed with crystal-perfect sound. The walls drip adulation. While taking a piss, the guy one urinal over is beaming happily: "I came all the way from Tucson for this!" he gushes. "They'll probably get down your way pretty soon," I answer, trying not to mess my shoes. He just keeps shaking his head and smiling. "I don't care. I don't care."

The next night I sit down with a revolving cast of characters who enter and leave like soldiers summoned for guard duty. Robert was present, along with road manager Pete Jamison, drummer Kevin Fennell, and new bassist Jim Greer (who, I might add, is quite a good player, and was not selected to replace Greg Demos because he is a *Spin* editor or the significant other of Kim Deal). I've brought fellow *Puncture* scribe Scott Nasburg, photographer Kristi Holden, and our inscrutable friend Jim Stirling, who dutifully passes out beer. I love them one and all. The good news is, there's input from different sources. The bad news is, things get weirder, more fragmented, less cohesive (much like a GBV song).

I start out asking Robert about his other projects, which include a solo album due early next year, as well as Freedom Cruise, GBV's groove-oriented alter-ego band. The solo album is tentatively titled (Robert has a tendency to rename things at the drop of a hat) *Panic on Landlord Street*.

"It's going to have me, Greg Demos, Don Thrasher [an ex-GBV rhythm section], and my brother Jim on amp noise," Robert says.

"So no smooth pop product?" I ask. "It doesn't sound that different from any other GBV album." It isn't. It's simply a case of Robert having too many songs on too many burners. The next GBV album, *The Flying Party Is Here*, is scheduled for October release, and three months is too short an interval for another. The solo album, Robert tells me later, will come out under the group name Instant Lovelies (see above).

The Freedom Cruise side band has released a single and will have a cut on an upcoming release from Red Hot (charitable organization that funnels money from music toward AIDS research). The song is called "Sensational Gravity Boy" and features Robert, Toby, Jim Pollard, Jim Greer, and Kim and Kelley Deal. "Anytime we come up with a song that's primarily one groove without too many changes, I save it for Freedom Cruise," notes Robert.

"Tell him about MTV," Jim Greer puts in.

"They asked me to host *120 Minutes*," Robert admits. "I told them we'd be happy to go on and play, but I didn't want to sit there and read off the monitor and talk about videos by a bunch of goofy bands I don't even like. I saw Matthew Sweet do the show a few weeks back. I could tell he wasn't having any fun."

Strike a Match

I ask the group about "Ex-Supermodel" on *Alien Lanes*; yes, that is snoring that makes a distorted chord running through an otherwise harmless song. Robert fills in the details. "This three-hundred-pound friend of ours was drunk and asleep in a chair in the middle of Toby's basement where we were recording. So we put a mike on him, equalized it, and recorded him for half an hour."

The song is interesting and annoying. It's been said that GBV often sabotage a nice song by throwing a monkey-wrench noise in the works.

"'Ex-Supermodel' was a little too wimpy, and the snoring gave it some edge," says Jim Greer. "Enough to keep people guessing."

"You're right. It is annoying. I don't care if people think it's ugly," Robert says, getting warmed up to the topic. "I like people to dig for the goods."

I bring out my hypothesis that if you strive for perfection every time out, you end up with lots of overly similar variations, like an artist who only paints bowls of fruit. Photographer Kristi Holden says she often "takes a match to the negative" of a picture for wild, unpredictable results.

"The snoring in 'Ex-Supermodel' is just us putting a match to the negative," Robert confirms. "I'm as interested as anyone to see what'll happen."

Straight Dope

"We wanted to make sure *Alien Lanes* was a gatefold album so people could clean pot on it," Robert informs me.

"You're living in the past," I tell him. "It's all tiny amounts of killer bud these days. Nobody buys bags of pot that need to be cleaned anymore."

Robert smashes my lob. "They do in Dayton." Laughter ensues.

Fasten Your Seat Belts

After Robert runs a critique of GBV's last three albums (*Vampire on Titus*: "A beautiful album buried under a lot of noise. One of my favorites." *Bee Thousand*: "At least seven songs from *Bee Thousand* will probably never leave our live set. Side one is the best side we've done." *Alien Lanes*: "I like it a lot, but it takes a year or two to tell if it's one of my favorites") the talk turns to the album in progress, *The Flying Party Is Here*. The GBV boys are giddy and optimistic about its possibilities.

About three-quarters of the album was produced by Kim Deal at Easley Studios in Memphis (home of their buddies the Grifters) and, with longer and somewhat cleaner songs, will answer those who peg GBV as lo-fi sketch artists. In lieu of a producer's fee, Ms. Deal copped a song from the sessions called "I Am Decided," which will probably see the light of day under the Breeders moniker down the road a piece. Another couple of songs were produced by Steve Albini in Chicago, with instrumental support supplied by various Grifters.

"Steve doesn't like a band to mess around and change what he produces," Robert says. "I heard his original mixes of Nirvana's *In Utero*, and frankly, it was a much better record than the version that got released."

Kings, Queens, and Airplanes

I went fishing for the lyrical motifs that spring up so often in Robert's songs. "What's with all the songs about flying, kings, queens, knives, kids?"

Kevin fires the first retort: "Dayton was the home of the Wright Brothers."

"Yeah, Dayton is big on aviation," Robert continues. "Those songs ["Air Show '88," "Blimps Go '90," "We Have Airplanes," "Striped White Jets," etc.] are a product of my environment."

"What about the rest?"

"For the past 14 years I've been teaching school," Robert says with a sigh. "Every year I read Grimms' Fairy Tales to my class. Kings, queens, knives, things like that are a big part of the literature."

"So you are influenced by 11- and 12-year-olds," *Puncture* writer Scott Nasburg puts in. "How could I not be?" Robert replies. "I've got two kids of my own." (One of the best songs on *Alien Lanes* is called "My Son Cool.")

Robert, Jim, and Kevin go on to talk nostalgically about other songs based on Daytonian exploits: "A Salty Salute": war veterans drink in a local bar and get ticketed driving home; "Wished I Was a Giant": a crazy woman interrupts a game of basketball; "14 Cheerleader Cold Front": a group of aloof rally gals from a rival high school. Sheer profundity . . .

When Scott asks what they'll be doing in five years, Jim Greer says, in a word, "Detox." Robert amplifies: "I'm just going to keep writing songs. I don't know how long we'll keep playing live, though. We're not going to be like the Stones, playing into retirement age. Shit, my hip already hurts."

"My back is killing me," Kevin complains, stretching uncomfortably.

"Maybe I'll be one of those songwriter-for-hire guys who contribute songs to singers and groups who can't write their own," Robert says.

"Like Neil Diamond with the Monkees?"

"Sure. Everyone needs good songs."

Final Exam

The hour grows late, and the lads must put on their game faces for tonight's performance at Reed College. (The show is rather sloppy compared to the Seattle triumph. Robert and company are a bit tired, the power keeps going out, the sound is pretty bad. Still, the GBV show is all anyone in Portland can talk about for weeks after.) As I review my notes and some of the tape I recorded, I worry that my high opinion of GBV sounds too damn gushy. While we're packing to leave, I ask Jim Greer a question about journalistic integrity.

"How do you avoid sounding like an idiot fanboy when you're writing about your favorite band?" I ask.

Jim thinks it over.

"I joined the band."

PALACE

Following in a venerable tradition in American folk music, Will Oldham began his career burnishing his own myth. When he recorded and performed under various versions of the Palace name, the singer cast his every move in an enigmatic fog—even requesting, for a time, that interviewers call him "Push." In this 1995 essay, **PATRICK BARBER** used an Oldham interview as a springboard to explore false memory, the interview process, and rock journalism.

I first heard the Palace Brothers when I was 12 years old. Of course, I didn't know it was them; this happened ten or more years before they released their first album. I was lying on my bed in a sort of afternoon adolescent stupor, trying to space myself out by staring at the ceiling until the whole room started to get bluish-hazy and wobbly. I was listening to the radio, the big band show on the college radio station. It was on pretty quiet and as I spaced myself out the radio got quieter and quieter until it was just a grey burble and my head filled with the thick absence of sound.

It was then I heard some words in my head. No, not heard. It wasn't like voices in your head. It was more like having an idea, like when I get an idea for a story, but these words were a string of repetitive, simple rhymes. Words that stumbled through my head, changing a syllable here and there, as if guiding themselves through a very limited narrative. It became a game I could play with myself: first I'd get in that hazy blue headspace and then the words would come along, different ones but mostly simple, repetitive mutations of a phrase—"I send my love to you, I send my shades to you, I send my hose to you, I send my nose to you." Silly stuff like that. The words weren't exactly the ones I would hear years later on a Palace Brothers record, but the form and cadence were the same.

I realized later that hearing these words was sort of a premonition, a habit of mine that would follow me through adolescence. At 14, lying spaced out on my bed, I suddenly got the idea that my mother would die of cancer within a year or two. I didn't tell this to anyone, naturally, but I wrote it in my journal, and I believed it, and it was like a terrible secret I kept to myself until she did indeed die, not of cancer but in a car wreck in a blizzard on Rabbit Ears Pass, coming home from a ski weekend with her sister. And it's still a secret. I never told anyone that I knew she would die, just as I've never told anyone about the words I heard as a 12-year-old. I'd rather just keep my job, and my life the way it is, and continue, as I always have, to tell my secrets to my notebooks.

The first time I heard the Palace Brothers record that had those words on it—the words I'd received that day—it blew me away. I loved that record anyway—it was their second one—and when I recognized those words it was as if a prayer, a forgotten one, was finally being answered. I cried, I really did, when I identified the words to "I Send My Love to You" as the ones I'd daydreamed into my head years before. It was like a message from my mom, or a message I'd sent to my mom.

As I grew up, I ached to be able to feel or see beyond this world, fantasized about it always, was crazy in love with Tabitha from *Bewitched*, all that. But these scattered premonitions I got weren't as exciting as I'd hoped, and after Mom died (I thought it was my fault, of course, even though if I'd told her—or anyone—it wouldn't have changed anything), I tried to avoid having those kinds of thoughts. Then I got to be about 15 or 16 and found that drinking beer made it so I wouldn't have many thoughts at all, especially the kind I got in that trancelike state.

I forgot about what-was-to-be-the-Palace-Brothers for a while. I got through school, got my degree, and moved here to Seattle and got haphazardly going on what appears to be my "career"—music, I guess. Playing it, writing it, writing about it, selling it in record stores. Anything to keep me around music, all the time. It must be pure luck, or more likely the work of whatever body governs premonitions and clairvoyance, that I never wrote a song with those Palace Brothers lyrics. What the hell kind of copyright laws would come into play there?

Then, in my late 20s, I actually got to interview the Palace Brothers. Specifically the singer, who called himself Push, although according to every article I'd read his name was Will Oldham. But he really wanted to be called Push. The editor I was writing the piece for was really bugged by that, and also by the fact he kept changing the name of the band—on the first two records it was Palace Brothers, then the third record and one of the singles were credited to Palace Songs, and right around when I interviewed him, things were just starting to say Palace. In fact, they even changed the title of the second LP. The first copies said simply *Palace Brothers*, but later editions were titled *Days in the Wake*. Will explained in the interview that he didn't figure out the title until after the record was released. I liked that, because even though they kept changing everything slightly, it was obvious that it was the same band or at least the same project: Will's songs were so strong,

and his voice and style so recognizable, that it was almost pointless to give them a name at all. The Palace Brothers' music drew on a rich tradition of storytelling song, like Leonard Cohen, the Byrds, Kris Kristofferson. Funny how the hippest "indie rock" band of the day reminded me mostly of stuff my dad used to listen to. There wasn't anything particularly amazing about it, except the pervasiveness of the feeling the music gave me, and also Will's voice, which was pale and crackly, decorating his melodic delivery with reedlike overtones.

I had been warned by other writers and editors that Will didn't like to talk about his music in any specific way. He also didn't like to be called "Will," and insistently denied any connection with Slint, an entirely forgettable mood-rock band that he or someone else in the band had been involved with, or indeed his earlier movie acting career, which, again, I had only heard about, and in which I didn't have much interest. Since I enjoyed the idea of having a pleasant conversation with the guy, I resolved to follow all of his rules, and to keep to myself what I knew about his words in my head.

When I saw him come into the club that afternoon, I got up to introduce myself. I walked up to him and said, "Are you Push?" He looked at me with the most curious blend of relief and disgust I've ever seen—like while he was happy that people were following his little preferences about his pseudonym, it also repulsed him that actual human beings, in order to get their day's work done, had to make decisions like this: I will call him Push. I will avoid Slint questions. Even though I knew he was doing this to make people focus on the music instead of the usual laundry list of questions about previous bands and other bullshit, it still seemed

199

to perpetuate the myth of the rock star vs. the critic, a dichotomy which, as a musician and a writer, I found particularly tiresome.

At that point, though, I didn't really care; I was pretty much finished with rock journalism. I was tired of the self-perpetuating repetition that seemed to prohibit any kind of creativity or expansion in a medium which you would think might actually foster such creativity. But rock journalism relies on the ever-renewed innocence of the reader, the writer, and the subject—and as a writer, either you succumb to writing the same piece over and over again or you constantly attempt to find new ways to write about music. I found the former impossible, while the latter entailed a lot of work for almost no pay—and then no one liked it anyway except the occasional adventurous editor. The readers, the bands, and of course the publicists, they all wanted to know what I was on about. How the hell were they supposed to use my literary experiments to sell more records—which is, in the last resort, the function of rock writing, like it or not.

I could accept that my work was ultimately used as advertisement, but I couldn't write it that way, and it ended up burning me out, to no one's dismay. There were plenty of young writers ready to take my place, willing to say: "From a myriad of influences, they carve out a niche all their own" and all those inflated pleasantries that punctuate the raging tide of mediocre rock journalism like so many B7–Emaj resolutions in an endless, self-congratulatory white-boy blues jam.

Rock journalism. That term baffles me, as do the writers who actually think they're "reporting" something. Here's the big story: Band Makes Music. Releases Record. All the rest is ephemera, detail, and creative writing. But hardly anyone seems to realize this, and the rare writer who turns the art of writing about music into a process as powerful as music itself (or writing itself) is often frustrated, overlooked, and quickly forgotten.

So my attitude at the time I interviewed the Palace Brothers was problematic. It helped, I think, that Will had the same feelings about the whole thing. He was better at being vague than anyone I'd ever met. When

I asked him where the band usually played, he replied (and I quote from my transcription): "The only time we play is when we go out somewhere. We've gone to different parts of . . . uh, different parts of the country." Beautiful. An empty answer to an empty question.

And on top of our merging disinterest in the process in which we were engaged, I was also dealing with the déjà-vu-like euphoria mixed with discomfort of talking to a guy whose songs had inhabited my head for as long as I could remember. I wished more than anything that I could tell him somehow, that maybe he had an answer or a clue as to how such a thing could happen. But here's the rub: these people don't have answers. In fact, they don't know a goddamn thing that could help you. It's utter coincidence that a song someone wrote manages to make you feel something powerful, and if it has to do with anything specific it is musical structure, tradition, and your personal, ingrained musical background. The creator of the music could be anyone, and

expecting that they'll know the answers to your troubles simply because they've moved you with notes and words is a fatal mistake.

Will and I did have a pretty nice interview, after all, even though I answered as many questions as I asked and didn't get much to use in any kind of article, at least not one that anyone would print. At one point, I asked him vaguely about influences—another empty question— and he countered by going into a discussion about artists' previous work and the way it reflects off their current work.

"Like, Cat Stevens," he said. "He is a different thing now from when he was 35 or 36, and up until he was 19 or 20, he was a different thing as well, and then there was a middle time when he made music, and luckily there's no information available about him from before or after, I don't know what he is now . . ."

"He's sort of . . ." I mumbled, trying to remember exactly what Cat Stevens had turned into.

"You know a little bit," said Will, "But do you admire him, or not admire him?"

"But do you allow his present circumstance to affect your appreciation of his music that he made previously?"

"It's almost nice because he so cleanly cut it off," Will said. "He doesn't allow you to compare or relate the two."

DIANNE BELLINO

"He himself rejected it."

"He rejected it, but almost rejected it in a way that supports the songs. He didn't reject the songs so much, because they're still there. It's more like he's not them anymore, so his actions can't affect what they were."

I realized afterwards that it may have seemed to him that I was trying to lead him into a discussion of his pointedly unacknowledged previous work. I wasn't, and in fact it was he who started up that discussion, so maybe, I thought later, he was trying to see how close we could get to the subject without actually involving his own music, the supposed subject of our conversation. I understood his resistance to the usual interview style; we agreed, I assumed, that most of the information usually passed along in a rock interview was useless, tangential detailing that only served to construct a false, handily chronological narrative convenient for magazine readers and press releases. I remember hearing interviews with two fiction writers at the time who both expressed it very well. One of them was Martin Amis, who I usually thought was a bit of a pompous ass. In a radio interview, he explained how he regarded the literary biography as a "dead medium"; that it only served to inject cause-and-effect where there was none. Then there was Russell Banks, who in a similar radio interview described his efforts as a writing instructor to give his students (most of whom were incarcerated young men) power to inform their own narrative of their lives, instead of being forced or tempted into accepting one of the "standard narratives" that people seem so eager to fall into.

Look at what I am doing now: attempting to connect events in my adolescent life—my druggy little "premonitions"—with the artistic work of someone with whom I have literally no relation. Is this any more ludicrous than the usual rock interview, which attempts to comment on musical style by attaching previous events and bands to tired comparisons and buzzwords?

There was me, sick of interviews and not looking forward to try and turn this vague, slumbrous exchange of words into a coherent piece of prose. And there was him, bored, tired from driving and touring, uninterested in interviews, doing all he could to politely derail my questions. On top of it was my unspoken secret about my premonitions of his lyrics, a situation which seemed simultaneously trivialized and deified, right there in the air above us, as we sat at that table outside the café on East Pike, watching the boys and girls amble by in their spring finery. It was an exercise in futility, and I was glad to be a part of it; it sealed the deal. My last interview.

That was so long ago. It was the last I ever heard of the Palace Brothers, because when I quit writing rock criticism and went back to just writing stories and just playing music, I stopped getting free records from the labels. I was so determined to escape the churning engines of the music business that I stayed away from record stores, whose purpose sometimes seemed to be to make you believe that you were hopelessly without music, that there was so much to be heard that you could probably never catch up.

But even now, decades later, I still listen to Palace, especially that second LP, which, I am convinced, is somehow my elegy to my mother, even though it was created without my input, in another part of the country; most of it written, Will said, while he was in Russia for a few months. It could not be further from my hand; yet I feel that I have touched it, and that it has touched me. I could not explain that to anyone, ever. I have never tried. What meaning would it have? Whose beliefs would it strengthen?

Nothing. No one's. ✪

CAT POWER

Cat Power's Chan Marshall made her recording debut in 1995 and, by the end of 1996, had three albums to her discography—including her debut for Matador, *What Would the Community Think*. **STEVE TIGNOR** received an advance tape of that album as he was finishing up this feature and presciently thought, "Better and better."

The first time I heard Chan Marshall (aka Cat Power) was at the Cooler in New York. The dim, low-ceilinged, blue-stainless-steel space was split in two. Up front, people were sitting, spread out, staring up at the stage; most seemed to have come alone. In back were people huddling around candlelit wood tables, chatting loudly. Onstage was Chan, shoulders slumped a bit, playing guitar now and then, getting drowned out. Her straight brown hair was cut short in back but fell forward to nose level; she wore a brown-checked shirt loose and untucked, over sagging blue jeans; her black shoes protruded almost clown-like. Her vocals were half-enunciated, ethereal, fading out just as her voice reached the mike.

In the middle of the first song, a woman stood up near the stage and shouted back over the audience, "If you people want to talk, why don't you go in the other room?" That got a few grumbled replies from the tables: "Play some Skynyrd." I turned and saw two guys in rugby shirts smiling sheepishly, embarrassment dragging down their stab at bad taste. Marshall, cradling the guitar face-up and giving it a puzzled "how does this thing work?" look, snapped to attention, looked out at the crowd for the first time, and smiled. She was the least obtrusive presence in the club.

From our spot, my friend and I could hear her singing about as well as we could hear conversations at the tables behind us. Chan (it's pronounced "Shawn") kept coming back to the names "Jesse" and "Jackson" with increasing melancholy. The song seemed to be about someone having a baby. She didn't narrate the story explicitly; her words circled the events, wrapping an aura of ambivalence and sadness around them.

Her public, up front, allowed her their languid attention. In one corner, a big guy with bushy black hair, wearing gigantic black boots, leaned back in his chair and seemed to doze. Across the room, a girl in a brown print dress sat at the edge of the stage, hypnotized, her mouth open, staring upward. The music—narco-slow, rising and falling in impressionistic waves, guitar lines crunched, then crumbling in her hands—was not played to them, but left to hover in the air.

The best moment for me came when she began singing, out of the blue, the line "James Carr isn't insane."

"Check it out, James Carr," I said. Lately, I'd been playing James Carr, a '50s Memphis soul singer, for this friend ad nauseam.

"Yeah, so? I still think he's insane."

But at that point I was ready to make some kind of connection between Chan Marshall's singing style and James Carr's. Despite the indie trappings of her show, her voice—the way she flung it up and out, the lines she bent, the scary beauty it conjured, the nerves it bared, and struck—sounded like soul to me.

So when I talked to Marshall a couple of months later, I asked her about James Carr, whether she was a fan.

"Do I listen to James Carr? No."

"So what was that whole 'James Carr isn't insane' thing about?"

"Oh, that! Yeah, when we were recording in Memphis, we took a break during mixing—we were sitting around a table and I was drinking a beer. Suddenly this huge shadow moved across the table and I look up and there's this big guy who's black, looking down at me. He had on a red satin shirt and a pinkie ring. He said, 'I heard y'all are doing some recordin'.' I said, 'Yeah, we're doing the mixing.' His eyes got real narrow and he looked right at me and said, 'Well, how do you feel about doing the mixin'?' I started laughing and we talked for a long time. We got along. I went back into the other room and someone said, 'God, isn't James Carr insane?'

"I said, 'no!'"

That pretty much explained that. So much for my theory.

The first time I heard Cat Power on record was in my apartment. I had bought her early single "Headlights/Darling Said Sir" (on the Making of Americans label) and was listening to it on headphones at about 3 a.m. in bed alone. Guitars clanged in like a cross between Lou Reed and the sound of an assembly line. Marshall's voice slid into the middle, traumatized and conversational, repeating the line "Last thing I remember . . ." a couple of times without bringing herself to finish it. From there, the guitars stayed clamped, VU with the groove wrenched out, 100% tension. Chan's voice hovered in near-whispered asides, shot itself upwards, and unraveled a first-person story of a woman lying in the road after a car accident. The most frightening moment came when, without any break, she moved from the present back to the normal, conversational words

CAT POWER
Moon Pix (Matador)

Starting with a feedback drone, fading into backwards drum thwacks like sudden intakes of breath, followed by clusters of resonant guitar tones . . . you realize at once that this fourth Cat Power record won't be like its predecessors. Then Chan Marshall's clear, bold vocal dives in and you know it will be essentially the same—only, it turns out, on a whole other level, one that could make a very intriguing singer accessible to a wider audience than she's reached before.

The aching, blurry strum and half-murmured, half-yelled plaints of early records *Dear Sir* and *Myra Lee* felt great, but they didn't always sound great. Guitarist Tim Foljahn and drummer Steve Shelley provided valuable support in helping Marshall make those albums, but the foursquare rock style that is their stock in trade often acted like a straitjacket on songs whose genius lay primarily in her daring, idiosyncratic vocal lines. Even on 1996's *What Would the Community Think*, with a wider palette of sounds and rhythms, the arrangements don't really fit the songs. There seemed no way to swell and flow the way a Cat Power song needs to do—without forcing the instrumental parts toward conventional rock thrust, or the voice toward an overcompensatory yell. (The latter was the only option when she played one of her fascinating but maddeningly inconsistent solo shows.)

That Marshall's work has nevertheless always mattered so much is a testament to that voice and the offhand intensity (sometimes bordering on desperation) of her delivery. She needed to move forward, though, and in Mick Turner and Jim White of Australian trio the Dirty Three she's found the musicians to help her realize her songs in more potent form. It's White's arsenal of subtle percussion, and the plangent clang of Turner's Gretsch hollow-body guitar, that provide the memorable intro to *Moon Pix* opener "American Flag." The duo supply a warm, texturally rich yet never overbearing framework so Marshall

someone was speaking into her ear just before the accident: "Get up around eight / Let's make some coffee and get real stoned / Hey, let's play a record or two." Those words would have been banal and overdramatic ("see what can happen just when you least expect it") if they didn't sound like so much fun. They grounded the story and at the same time told the truth that we deny every day: death exists on the same banal plane as the rest of our lives.

At the end of the song I sat up and pulled off the headphones, scared of the dark, as creeped out as I'd been one night when I was 13, listening in bed to Blue Öyster Cult's "Joan Crawford Has Risen from the Dead."

"Is your father a musician?"

"Yeah, he plays the piano in Atlanta. He used to be a singer and one of his bands in the '70s recorded a single. But now he works on his own music—I'm not sure what to call it—blues, or roots music, I guess. I lived with my mother in North Carolina, mostly. Except I went back to live with my father after I dropped out of school, when I was 16. I really got my act together for a while and almost finished high school.

"But then I had to leave my dad's place, and I never finished.

"I didn't really play music until I came to New York later, when I was 20, I think. An old boyfriend had a guitar and I started making up songs. I think I played a show in Brooklyn where people saw me.

"Mainly, I was alone in New York, except for a close friend. It could be such a weird, silent place, really. Everyone with their eyes down. It almost reminded me of the South, the stillness of everything. My main memory of the South, growing up, is visual: a still landscape, very beautiful. We had this old run-down graveyard behind our house. I remember running over a mud bridge through a tobacco patch in bare feet. God, now that's pretty Southern.

"I came to New York to get away from things that were happening there with me. I had a friend pass

away, and other people were just so crazy. I still love going back . . . it's that visual image I have of the South. It's part of me, and I don't even realize it when I'm gone."

Ben and Lauren and I were sitting around drinking and listening to Cat Power's LP *Myra Lee* on an extremely hot, humid spring night in Brooklyn. In the haze, the record's half-collapsed flirtations with songs, its constant fade to black, and the sound of Chan's voice twisting itself free of the warmth it naturally projects seemed like the perfect soundtrack to our inertia, our lapsed conversations. Lines hung in the air: "I am not what you are." "Where are the dreams of babies going?" "My heart fell at your feet." "I'm not made of successful things." And most relevant that night: "I think you need ice water." The music, and the evening, were getting downright lugubrious.

Compared to the first single, her two albums to date, *Myra Lee* (on Smells Like Records) and *Dear Sir* (on Italian label Runt), suffer a bit from the attempt to fit Marshall's songs into an indie-band format. Guitarist Tim Foljahn and Sonic Youth drummer Steve Shelley play with her, and though they provide solid accompaniment, they can't help making her sound more conventional. It's not really their fault. Marshall, like the best soul singers, seems to write her songs via her unpredictable vocalizing. Check out the end of "Rockets," where Shelley and Foljahn briefly settle into a groove that Sonic Youth would have stretched and built on. Here, it's too straightforward, too rock 'n' roll for the song Chan has written. They're forced to abandon building the groove so they can slow it back down.

Listening to *Myra Lee* that night, I couldn't help wondering what Chan Marshall's music would have been like if she hadn't begun within the confines of the indie-rock world—if she had lived thirty years ago, stayed in the South, and become the most eccentric soul or country singer of her day. Even if she's never heard James Carr, I think the connection exists, and I hope she pursues the rootsier possibilities in her can relax into her singing, more engaged with it than ever before, confident that a song won't collapse around her or be short-circuited by rock rhythms.

The varied intervals, the shapes and stresses she gets into the delivery of "It is so nice to meet you" (in "He Turns Down") give the words a musical complexity that perfectly catches the contradictory emotions being played out in the song, while her cover of the traditional "Moonshiner" shows a mastery of phrasing and emotionally weighted delivery—here, fury at a bleak and wasted life—found only in great singers (not surprisingly, it makes Uncle Tupelo's version seem insipid; more impressively, it outmatches Dylan's).

There are three songs Marshall recorded solo, and while "You May Know Him" is too muddy and strummy to maximize its potential, "Back of Your Head" is wonderful—angry, rueful, depressed, funny: "You hold the big picture so well / Can't you see that we're going to hell," she asks, then goes on to despair: "Couldn't park that fucking car / Couldn't part from you." Despair also permeates "Colors and the Kids," which Marshall sings to her own piano accompaniment.

But it's on the tracks with the band that Marshall's songs sound most complete. Without Turner's edgy, country-blue guitar and White's deadpan shuffle on "Moonshiner," it's doubtful Marshall could have so successfully reimagined a classic and created something thrilling and new out of it. Her own songs, too, are often transmuted. Turner's arpeggiated playing, cracking the chords into resonant flurries of sound, makes the quiet elegy of "No Sense" more heartbreaking still, while they frame "Metal Heart" (which used to drift out of focus when Marshall played it live, partly because its lyric attempts the tricky task of reproducing a rambling emotional outburst) with fractured notes and broken rhythms that respect the song's character—and reveal its greatness.

—*Jean Debbs*

singing. It may be a corny idea, but I'd like to hear her sing more standard, foursquare songs, letting her voice take off on interpretations of traditional American music. I'd like to hear this talented woman take control of all aspects of her music, and try to make a more ambitious record—in part because popular female singers in the past (Aretha, Etta James, even PJ Harvey) have often been at the mercy of Svengali-like male producers; and also because I think Marshall's music is too soulful for this era's ironic, broken-down style of rock.

Still, both LPs retain a dark atmosphere. Dark enough to annoy my neighbor, a 35-year-old ex-junkie who plays drums in a Johnny Thunders cover band. I could almost see him next door—skintight black jeans, punky black hair thinning, purple elevator shoes—flicking his cigarette around in anger: "Fucking alternative-rock kids." He must have decided to give us some real rock (not that they'll appreciate it, I imagine him thinking): through the wall, guitars suddenly came thundering. Chan's slow-motion vocal twists were engulfed.

"Hey, that's the Undertones," Ben said, coming

to life. And it was. Their best song, in fact, "Teenage Kicks," and it sounded good. I turned off *Myra Lee* and we got up to dance and stumble around to the music coming from behind the wall. By song's end Ben was doing a handstand, quarters and nickels dropping from his pockets to the floor.

"I guess I'm happy with the two albums. We recorded them in one day. Most of the time, though, Steve and Tim ended up looking at each other like, 'What do we do?' I wasn't sure what to tell them, since I had never really written songs with a band in mind . . . it was hard to fit the whole thing together. Those guys just, kind of . . ."

"Fucked things up," I prompted jokingly.

"Listen to you! No, they were just kind of left hanging. Really, the only song I'd say I like right now is 'Ice Water.' I think that's a good one. 'Rockets' was just a hymn . . . like, stay in school, don't do drugs.

"Mostly I just make up lyrics while I'm playing guitar on the couch. I take things from my life, things that

206

happen to my friends or whatever, lines I'll remember. The first single . . . a friend and I just got some beer and went in the studio. I had no idea what I was doing, and I'm not really happy with how it came out. It sounds too trapped.

"The third album [*What Would the Community Think*, due on Matador in August] is more technological. I've learned how to work in a studio and control things. I'm doing the cover art for it, and I have these tech-type things in mind . . . it makes me think of squares.

"I just fell into this indie-music scene or whatever it is. I don't like to think of it as a career. There's so many other things I'd like to do . . . go work on a boat in Alaska or teach kids their A to Z. I want to move back to New York, but everyone I know there is part of music. It keeps me on one track and away from other things I'd like to do . . . Is there a song, 'All my friends are rock critics?'"

Sometimes before work I find myself giddy for no reason at all and the only thing I want to do is play records. Just one more, I tell myself. But it never is, and I'm inevitably late for work. These days, there is a regular rotation of songs I play, changing from week to week; they're typically catchier songs, songs with a rush, songs I want to hear over and over. This week's heavy rotation includes "If This World Were Mine" by Marvin Gaye and Tammi Terrell; "That's When I Reach for My Revolver" by Mission of Burma; "Ark of the Covenant" by the Congos; and "Pretty" from the new Raincoats album, among others.

One I can't do without right now, though, is Cat Power's cover of Hank Williams's "I Can't Help It (If I'm Still in Love with You)." Williams sings the original like he's sobbing publicly, moaning to anyone who will listen; he's speaking to his old woman, who's got a new man. Chan, stopping and starting, breaking up lines, mumbling one verse and calling out the next, sings the song to herself. Hank is embarrassed but can't control himself; Chan is alone with her thoughts, and resigned to this private lament. Where Hank floats on the surface of the song, singing it to commiserate with the other lonely guys in the bar, Chan dives inside it and tests every simple, painful line before letting it go. She commiserates with herself, and doesn't ask for your pity.

Anyway, the song sounds great between Marvin Gaye and Mission of Burma. Is there any higher praise?

The week before this story went to press, I got an advance tape of *What Would the Community Think*. I played it and immediately thought: better. Better and better. The songs get beyond simple chord repetitions; Shelley and Foljahn have learned now to play around her. And, needless to say, Chan can still sing.

On the other two albums, everything sounded ad hoc, an extended demo; Marshall just sang, and the songs happened around her voice. Here Foljahn takes more control, doing what a guitarist does, fashioning rhythm, swelling it, filling in, getting the music from one place to another. While I still wish the songs were a little less vague, Chan's voice, vibrating and quavering against the sparse background, more than makes up for their tentativeness. Is there such a thing as anti-soul? She could be its pioneer. Rather than taking painful emotions and stylizing them like most classic soul singers, she cuts through any phony fluency and gets to the naked truth of a song's premise.

The situations she creates seem to me akin to how painters describe the way they see the world. Not in facts or insights, but colors and atmosphere. She never pretends to understand anything, but instead sets down lines and obscure stories ("I've got a son in me / And he's related to you"; "You look so impressive"; "If I was a photographer / Taking pictures of beautiful people / I might make a mistake and take a picture of you"; "Whatever happened to home?") that, somehow, she doesn't distance herself from. She refuses to comment, yet retains emotional contact. What it all means I'm not sure, but there's a dark beauty to this music which will only strike deeper as she learns to fill out her songs.

A very good record; a great artist in the bud. The next PJ Harvey? Nah. She's more the Carson McCullers type. ◗

BECK

Beck's second major-label LP, *Odelay*, may be the definitive album of the mid-'90s. The pop savant scrambled sounds, cultures, eras, and sensibilities with an élan that seemed a perfect match for the century's end. **STEVE TIGNOR** profiled him for a 1996 cover story.

An hour had gone by, but Beck wasn't done with the interview.

"I wanted to say something about how I've been tagged with the whole slacker thing and misrepresented."

"I remember you said somewhere that once you were driving and you heard 'Loser' and thought, Oh shit, that's such a slacker thing."

"Actually, after the song I heard the DJ go, 'And there's the new slacker anthem by Beck'—and I just froze. I wasn't even plugged into the media at that point; it hadn't even entered my head that I would be thought of that way. The term 'slacker' has faded, which I thought it would, because it was all hype anyway; but it's been frustrating to make music because you love it— and then to have it boiled down like that. I don't come from a world where you could be a slacker.

"The term has to do with middle-class privilege, which is not what I come from at all. Not that those people piss me off—I always envied people with that kind of comfort, who went to college or whatever.

"I did 'Loser' when I was 20. I was trying to rap like Chuck D and I was so bad that's what I called myself as a joke. If it ended up meaning anything, it was more about the difference between the '80s and '90s; that was just becoming clear when the song came out. In some ways, the music that was out then—grunge and gangsta—was part of a death knell for the '80s. It was music by people who were left out of the '80s, when everything was materialistic. Tom Cruise, you know? Phony. And I think 'Loser' happened to come along right as that was going on. But people writing about me didn't seem to want to talk about that: they wanted to make it some kind of generational conflict."

Russell Banks's novel *Rule of the Bone* is about a 14-year-old runaway from a working-class family in a small town in upstate New York. The boy watches MTV: "Beck this singer with one name like me was standing in this orange and purple haze with silhouettes of the leafless trees of death against a pink sky and singing about how no one understands him either . . ."

While Beck may be peeved about the media's portrayal of him as a privileged goofball, I think the lines from Banks's novel tell another story about why Beck's appeal has been so broad. On *Mellow Gold*, his Geffen album from '94, which led off with "Loser," he wrote songs that addressed, in a mythically roundabout, jokey way, the topic that dares not speak its name in America today: class. Mixing hip-hop with folk, blues with urban wasteland imagery, Chicano with black with white, Beck brought stories back from a largely silent new underclass. Grunge, which came from a similar suburban/ trailer-park jungle, spoke in the language of the bohemian (Kurt Cobain's ultimate insult was "redneck"); gangsta rap was all about race. It took Beck, a white kid from downtown LA who grew up in a predominantly Mexican/Salvadoran neighborhood, to connect the dots among all three cultures (white working-class, bohemian, and urban minority), seeing more similarities than differences, and speaking for them as one large group.

He may seem a sort of surf-style Beastie Boy, but if Beck reminds me of anyone, it's Bruce Springsteen. Not that his music is in any way similar—but that's part of the point. In the early '80s, Springsteen spoke for a dying small-town, white-focused idea of America. His songs personalized the decline of one working class and its reliance on a manufacturing economy; his songwriting came out of those people's folk-rock tradition. Beck's songs personalize the rise of a '90s class which is urban, polyglot, and mired in the service industry. Postmodern, sui generis, he's got no tradition to back him up because no one tradition rules anymore. He appropriates hip-hop the way the last generation of white musicians appropriated the blues. He's been tagged as slack only because he's versed in the now-dominant language of irony. Maybe it's his sense of humor that gets in the way, but no one seems to notice that his songs have little to do with Gen X pop culture. Rather, they talk about some pretty horrible situations.

"I can't think out lyrics. They come out best when they're made up as I go along, when they just go with the groove and the words sound good together."

The lyrics on *Mellow Gold*, from the opening line ("In the time of chimpanzees / I was a monkey"), more than went together. At times they did sound made up on the spot, but even the non sequiturs told stories. The difference between these stories and the ones told by old folkies like Springsteen was Beck's lack of an overriding moral. His narratives are driven by detail. In fact, Beck's lyrics, in contrast with the indecipherable anger of someone like Kurt Cobain, or Dr. Dre's monolithic attitude, were all details.

In "Truck-Driving Neighbors Downstairs" we get the picture quickly: "Acid casualty with a repossessed

car / Vietnam vet playing air guitar." In "Soul-Suckin' Jerk," he quits his job at a chicken stand: "Puke-green uniform on my back / Had to set it on fire in a vat of chicken fat / I leaped on the counter like a bird with no hair / Running through the mini-mall in my underwear." "Pay No Mind (Snoozer)" describes mass-music culture in terms of real-life debris: "Sales climb high / Through the garbage-pail sky / Like a giant dildo crushing the sun." Not that Beck doesn't find a perverse joy in the mass culture: "Talking on a walkie-talkie / Credit card glued to my hand / Feels good" (from "Fuckin' with My Head").

More than anything, those details accounted for the platinum success of *Mellow Gold*, I suspect. The album's grounding in cheesy reality hit home. It was a breath of fresh air blowing between the angst of the white and black American musical cultures of the time. And Beck was funny. Who else had Death appear (in the "Loser" video) as a squeegee guy? Who else could punch a hole

in rap's decade of tedious boasts by answering their age-old question (in "Beercan"), "How ya like me now?" with "Pretty good"?

"When I met Cypress Hill at Lollapalooza, I found out we grew up not far from each other. I said I was from Pico Hill, and they were like, 'Shit, that's right next door. We thought you from Europe or something.' I didn't hang with them too much, they had their own posse going. But yeah, I was known as the white kid on the block by the Mexicans where I grew up, though half my family is Mexican. Even now I feel more comfortable being around Mexican people than anyone else; it's just the way of life that was around me growing up. It's very natural with them. I can feel out of place with other people, but not with them.

"I went to high school until about tenth grade, then dropped out. It was a downtown LA public school, and it sucked. It wasn't education at all, more like mass day care, a sort of unorganized way of killing time.

"After that I was just working—as a messenger, as a clerk at the Video Hut, next to the Pizza Hut. I was doing mowing jobs, making IDs at the YMCA. Nothing too exciting.

"I was doing music that whole time, too, but I never, ever thought I would make money at it. I was like a side act in bars. I would come on between bands, with my guitar, and play to please the inebriated. That's why I have a lot of songs with the devil in them; it was the only way to get the attention of people who were drunk. That's how to get people's attention anytime, in fact—just bring the devil in.

"I guess I first got into old music when I was a teenager and saw a cover of a Mississippi John Hurt album at a friend's house. He was sweating so bad on the cover . . . it just looked so twisted it got my attention. Then I heard it. I was in another world. The sound was so antique, especially after the pop music I had been listening to.

"I started doing folk songs, and did them pretty exclusively for a long time. I came to New York and was part of the 'anti-folk' scene. I was doing a lot of Woody Guthrie songs. I was more into him than Bob Dylan. I always felt some need to get to the source of a piece of work or a style. When I was playing in bars, I'd be doing a blues song and people would say, 'Oh, a Led Zeppelin song.' It would be a song Zeppelin had done, but I'd never heard their version. There are still gaping holes in my musical knowledge, stuff from the '70s. I was never a heavy indie-rock listener, either. I was aware of the stuff and went to see Sonic Youth and Firehose, but I wasn't interested in doing that music.

"With the folk stuff, I wasn't trying to do anything like what Dylan did with the original music. That was part of the anti-folk idea, to keep the basic style but not to write typically, you know . . . singer-songwriter songs. I was trying to keep my songs cut down, tight, not like Dylan's half-poetic style.

"The K record [One Foot in the Grave, 1994] had some of those old songs on it. I'd been trying to make that record for about four years, but I could never get up to Olympia to do it. Either I didn't have the money or I was working or something. It was strange, that record was my main style, really—what I had always done. The Geffen record, the hip-hop stuff, was like a side project that took over.

"It's part of my contract with Geffen to be able to do albums for other labels like that. I wanted the freedom. I even turned down a couple of better offers because Geffen was willing to give me that. I just want to be able to make a record without having to make concessions or feel like I'm limiting myself. Geffen has never put

pressure on me to make a certain type of record. They said they would have been happy if I had done another record like the K record for them. I wouldn't know how to make a record designed for them, anyway."

One Foot in the Grave, released at the peak of Beck's "Loser" fame, seemed to me at the time to be Beck's way of finding a level of success, and an audience (underground rather than mainstream) he could be comfortable with. The record is an exercise in updating roots music. It has the feel of a demo; the songs mostly seem like one-takes, Beck with guitar and minimal accompaniment. It was the lyrics—mostly a series of funny little aphorisms—that made the record interesting, that made straight folk and blues music compatible with '90s-style irony and absurdist humor.

Beck's vocal delivery sounded at once ancient (he could have been 50 rather than 23 when he made it) and deadpan. Like *Mellow Gold*, the songs told stories of out-of-the-way places and fringe-dwellers. In their sense of final resignation toward outside forces, the lyrical attitude was similar to that of the original roots artists from the earlier part of the century. What is different, perhaps, is that Beck's characters—not farmers or travelers or failed artists or even bohemians, just some people living on their own—are beyond fighting those outside forces. They relate—in small, personal detail—the underside of the American success story: what everyday life is like when ambition has faded.

There's no Gen X bitterness and little hippie celebration of this lifestyle; just stray moments strung together: "Let's try to make it last / The past is still the past / And tomorrow's just another crazy scam"; "Gettin' fat on your own fear / Bring that beer over here"; "Definitely, this is the wrong place to be / There's blood on the futon / And a kid drinking fire"; "17 years in the city / Static clinging to the ceiling / . . . Outcome is different than I expected"; and my favorite, "Take off your sweats / Cool off your jets / I got a funny feeling they've got plastic in the afterlife."

When the record first came out in fall '94, I was unemployed, not seeing many people, and pretty bored. I played *One Foot in the Grave* a lot. It didn't inspire me, or make me feel better, really. I just played it; it fit.

"Becoming well known was a pretty unreal experience. Meaningless, really. It's disturbing to be focused on suddenly. I would see articles devoted to saying terrible things about me. But what you do every day isn't that much different. You're still working with people. Instead of working with some guy in a retail store, you're working with a producer at a studio, you know? You're around different people, but what you do and how you act aren't much different. The media part is just a haze,

to change the songs to play them live to a big audience, so they'd fit the atmosphere of that kind of show. The songs on the new record I put together with a live show in mind, so the arrangements would hit an audience a little harder."

That record is *Odelay*. Released in June, the Geffen follow-up to *Mellow Gold* has a similar mix of hip-hop and funky-beat rock. I first listened to it on a Manhattan subway returning from work in the evening. In the guts of the city, as a soundtrack to young couples styled up for a night out—hipsters and black 20-year-olds heading downtown—it didn't quite fit. I had been listening to Tricky's new record in the same way the day before, and its long, spooky, turned-down grooves seemed more appropriate to the setting. Somehow *Odelay*, with its energetic, varied set of songs, its big beats and blasts of guitar, struck me as a bit old-fashioned in comparison—almost too tight and centered for the dreamy, anonymous rhythms of the nighttime subway.

My favorite moments were the least songful: the little stretched-out, ambient-style keyboard groove tacked onto the end of "Hotwax"; the improv-sounding guitar vamp at the end of "Lord Only Knows" where Beck fades out while telling us, apropos of nothing, he's "Going back to Houston / Do the hot dog dance / Going back to Houston / To get me some pants"; the Eastern-style polyrhythmic drone in the middle of "Derelict." I found myself wishing he allowed himself more of those between-song riffs. I wanted something along the lines of what his fellow LA Mexicans, the Latin Playboys (a spin-off of Los Lobos), had done on their album in '95, when they left songs behind, broke their ideas down to a series of musical moments, and kept them that way.

Still, I did like most of *Odelay*'s real songs, and found all of them pretty memorable. There's a song called "Readymade," and that was the word that kept coming to mind. I thought of these tracks as ready-mades: beats and grooves and melodies and declamations that I thought I had heard before somewhere in hip-hop's past. That's not to suggest these are rip-offs. It isn't even a criticism, just an early observation made in the context of Manhattan. Great artists from T. Rex to George Clinton to Bikini Kill have taken basic formulas and built brilliant music with them.

"I got together with the Dust Brothers (producers of the album and, in the past, of the Beastie Boys' *Paul's Boutique*, among other records), first because I wanted to get going on the record and not waste time. They lived in the area, and we had mutual friends, so it seemed like the best way to get the thing done. I liked working with them. A reporter asked me whether they were my Burt

because it isn't part of your life. Nothing stands out from the fame aspect of life. I try to sidestep that part, anyway. I try my best not to take the whole thing too seriously, to take the piss out of it whenever I can.

"Lollapalooza was a pleasant experience, but a non-experience, too. We went on pretty early in the day, before most people even got there. We would play to a lot of plastic seats or an open field, which made it a non-experience, and gave the whole thing a generic quality after a while. The main thing I remember is heat. I kind of liked it as sort of a Desert Storm, though, traveling out to face the country. The best thing about it was getting to hang out with the other acts. All the guys in Pavement were really sweet, and I hung out with Steve Shelley a lot, he's a great guy. I don't know what Cypress Hill thought of my rap shit, they probably thought it was a joke. But in some ways, that's the way I look at it, too.

"When it came to the songs from the last album, it was hard to re-create them live. They were all kind of slow—even 'Motherfucker,' which seems rocking, but is really pretty slow. I had made most of them on my own, so they didn't have a bigger audience in mind. We had

Bacharach and I was their Dionne Warwick, like I was just the product or something. That's not the case at all, even though they were good enough at what they did to have an effect on everything.

"But these songs are my babies. I wrote the music and came up with the ideas, and they got the best sounds for me. Which was really nice, because I like to write and play more than anything, and I was able to concentrate on that. They're really good at turntable stuff, too, so we were able to collaborate. 'Hi-Five' was all of us just going in and messing around together.

"The recording process was a bit different, because I had more time and studio space to use. The approach was similar, because with hip-hop stuff I'm really just improvising and realizing a song as it's being recorded. What goes on the record is a document of that process.

"Hip-hop is more exciting for me right now. It's newer to me. I've been doing folk stuff for ten years, so I feel freer to try different things with hip-hop. It's a wide-open field, I think, especially the lyrics. A lot of things haven't been said in raps, because there's only been one basic style of rapping. Self-aggrandizement, I guess. That was what made 'Loser' funny to me, to turn that style around. I mean, as a joke. But I also take it seriously now, I want to make it as good and interesting as I can.

"It's like the blues to me, it comes out of blues, and I play it with that in mind. I've always been turned off by differences, or anything that splits things apart. It's all music, and I don't think about not being able to play anything because of who I am or who is supposed to play a style. Every person is different, and putting them in groups is impossible. I tend to look at things in a longer view. I'm not interested in what's trendy. The 1930s seem as real to me as anything now. The past still seems relevant, because most parts of life haven't really changed. We're locked into our TVs now, that's probably the main difference, and we go along with what TV tells us is hip, but that has nothing to do with my life. I have a deeper appreciation for rap that makes me want to keep doing it.

"Nowadays, since you can't sample as much, you have to come up with music yourself. No one can say it's just stealing now. I'm into the Wu-Tang Clan, which is getting back to rap's original idea. Hard. Ol' Dirty Bastard is great. They do so many things with the production. They have to cut the shit up so much, to avoid sampling for too long, that the sound is strange and harsh. We [Dust Bros. and Beck] did a remix for 'Where It's At' [the first single] with all these samples, and it's like a different world—like the old style, pretty cool."

Memorial Day weekend a friend and I took a trip to the Jersey shore. Driving out of New York onto the highway,

I put *Odelay* on. The heat bouncing off the concrete suffocated us. Traffic lurched forward, then ground to a stop. Everywhere we looked there were kids hitting each other in back seats and parents staring glaze-eyed in front seats, everyone restless and annoyed. The Garden State Parkway loomed in front of us, a sea of concrete blocking any other possible scenery. The record started to kick in for me.

The beats busted out, bigger than I remembered them. The guitar was pleasantly scuzzy. The little touches—keyboard swooshes, harp snippets, sounds dropping out and reappearing—flew through the car. Beck's voice—controlled, opiated, grooving—serenaded me past Atlantic City tour buses in style. The tunes—though I felt like I knew them from somewhere—stood out from one another and flowed into a whole which made sense. When we came to a rest stop in South Jersey, we walked into a Burger King and were immediately hit with a mass of people crowding forward, lots of black and white teenagers with sideways caps and enormous sneakers swinging everywhere. My friend and I found ourselves for some reason harmonizing on *Odelay*'s first song, "I got a devil's haircut in my mind."

This isn't to say I suddenly loved every minute of the album. Some of the hooks and vocal moves still struck me as formulaic. And while many of the trademark non-sequitur details flitted through my mind, I couldn't make out the full-fledged characters that populated his first record. These lyrics seemed to skate along on the surface, flicking cryptic tropes and images to either side.

Yet away from the pretentious reserve and pseudo-European musical cool of New York City, Beck's music had found its setting. That doesn't mean his music is cheesy, or only relates to the mainstream. Not at all. But in its outgoing mix of styles, it fits with a Middle American/suburban youth culture that can appropriate black styles more freely than many people feel able to do in a city like New York, where lines of race and class are so clearly marked. Beck plays the music these kids like: unpretentious, funny, loud, with an edge of mysterious cool. He has the guts to play whatever he likes.

"Yeah, I've read *Puncture*."

"It's nice to write for a magazine that music fans read. Where you don't have to spell everything out."

"People who can think for themselves? That's all that matters."

"This is going to be a cover story, I think."

"Really? You're going to need something juicier. Something more controversial about me, to get people interested. How about 'Beck Eats Raw Meat'? You can say that if you want." ◐

THE GRIFTERS

Memphis quartet the Grifters was profiled in *Puncture*'s spring 1996 issue—which featured Yoko Ono on the cover and an excerpt from *Infinite Jest* in its fiction section. The Grifters were shining examples of their age's indie rock, with scuzzy recordings celebrating a proud underdog existence. **FRED MILLS** interviewed the musicians about their album *Ain't My Lookout.*

Over seven years and four albums, the Grifters have suffered the repeated pigeonholing efforts of us "experts." The Memphis foursome have been variously labeled lo-fi white-trash rock, deconstructed Beefhearty blues, cinematic noise-pop—and just plain messy. Well-intentioned stabs all of these (except the last), but as the band have a penchant for placing 4-track (sometimes 2- or 3-track) red herrings along the path, frequently off the mark. Maybe that's not too important, really—most have at least agreed that the Grifters have a rare ability to wing provocative, intelligent, and altogether hookish rock 'n' roll.

All this since 1989, when guitarists/vocalists Dave Shouse and Scott Taylor, guitarist/bassist Tripp Lamkins, and drummer Stan Gallimore began squeezing out sparks within strict financial and technical limits. In retrospect, it was coincidental that their band emerged during the lo-fi ascendancy of Guided by Voices, Sebadoh, et al. A listen to the Grifters' substantial back

catalog now suggests a band pushing back creative and mechanical boundaries to reveal unique, crafty twists on traditional song styles. Last year's *Eureka* EP (on the Shangri-La label) was certainly testimony to how, as Shouse puts it, "you overcome the lo-fi scruffiness of the 4-track, labor over it, forget it has drawbacks, and really use it, in an environment where it's comfortable and cost-efficient."

By signing with Sub Pop for their new album *Ain't My Lookout*, the Grifters got to work in a more comfortable environment still (Easley Studios in Memphis), with a budget sizable enough that they could spend time harnessing the potential of a 24-track studio.

The new record clearly showcases the Grifters' formidable skills as songwriters. Tunes range from the infectious surf-flavored pop of "Mysterious Friends"; to the riff-laden, pulse-quickening Stones raunch of "Return to Cinder"; to the moody, suite-like Chris Bell (Big Star) homage, "Radio City Suicide"; to the Brian

MICHAEL GALINSKY

THE GRIFTERS
Full Blown Possession
(Sub Pop)

Best known for being underappreciated, the Grifters have been quietly crafting masterpieces of subtly tweaked pop noise for eight years now. After four critically acclaimed, commercially snubbed LPs comes *Full Blown Possession*, a 12-song exercise in restraint that's almost like a sideways joke on the rock excess they seem constantly to be citing.

Try the blissed-out Beatles-esque psychedelicized vocals on "Happy" as they degenerate into a grim repetition of the song's title on the chorus; or "Re-entry Blues," a raveled, dissipated mess that reads like an acid trip gone south to the middle of the desert, and swaggers around self-consciously like the Velvet Underground might've if they'd spent more time on the Southern California coast: "Check out this place: ladies have horns," wonders our narrator. "Truth has become martinis and toast—and look at me now: I'm the most," he brags, before working his way into an incongruous indie-pop chorus.

With every song, the Grifters seem to launch into a very slightly damaged version of a rock signature sound and then, just as any other band would have launched themselves over the edge into the abyss of a raunchy guitar solo, indulgent crashing refrain, or obvious pop figure, they pull themselves up, shake it off, and nonchalantly wander down another path entirely. Whether it's the Cheap Trick chordage and tossed-off glamour-puss vocals on "Contact Me Now" that spin out into a discordant guitar scuffle; or the sidling spacewalk of "Fireflies" that shifts into a desultory swamp-rock ramble, *Possession* remains gratifyingly unenmeshed in the expected.

Better still, the Grifters never get caught with their irony showing. They're not making fun, they're having fun—and it's a joy to behold.
—*Sara Manaugh*

Wilson-meets-"Suffragette City" boogie of "Last Man Alive"—which has been tagged, and wisely so, for the commercial FM push.

But more than anything, *Ain't My Lookout* is a document of a band in full creative flow. One which announces: (a) it's our studio time, so anything goes; (b) there are four of us, and everyone has total input; and (c) our bottom line is: serve the material, not the ego. This kind of approach—unlike others currently foisted upon the record-buying public, either in the fan underground or the alterna-mainstream—places the Grifters in a realm we critical eggheads like to call art rock.

That's my take on the Grifters, so when I interviewed Dave Shouse and Scott Taylor recently, I got my chance to test it out on them.

DAVE SHOUSE: "Art rock" can have negative connotations. I'm thinking of some '70s bands, Keith Emerson clones . . . But we're not talking about prog-rock bands, right?

No, I'm thinking Roxy Music and Eno, Bowie, the Velvet Underground, Red Krayola, Pere Ubu, Patti Smith, Destroy All Monsters, your fellow Memphis band Panther Burns, Pavement, Gibson Bros, even Giant Sand. Groups who're isolated geographically or alienated culturally. Who use musical—and, when they're available, visual—signifiers to suggest other musics and to embrace the entire spectrum instead of just burrowing into a stylistic cul de sac. Definitely not Keith Emerson.

SCOTT TAYLOR: Emerson, Lake and Palmer is not art rock, anyway, it's masturbation. Not that I'm putting down masturbation! But one of our bylines has always been, "Play for the song." Whatever the song calls for. Not what the band or the audience call for. It may be moody and slow, it may not need any distortion on it. Or it may be angry and need to be that way. Instead of creating a sound—"this is the Grifters sound"—we're interested in songs as individual things.

SHOUSE: You mentioned Roxy Music and David Bowie: there are certainly snippets of those things on this record. I don't know if this is correct, but I think some of those people thought, It's only a bunch of pompous fuckers who get onstage anyway, so why not take it to the hilt! This is pompous, this is me acting out! And that's so far removed from the smug nonchalance the indie-underground scene is mired in now. In a way it's like everyone's the same right now. Everyone would love to be Steve Malkmus: clever, witty, distant. Steve gets away with it because—that's Steve, boy genius guitar-pop songwriter! That's why Pavement have had such success. But the wannabes sound so sterile.

You also mentioned Panther Burns. Tav Falco is very conscious of presentation. He was like an archivist; he'd say, "Here's my interpretation." His visuals were so elaborate; his posters were great.

TAYLOR: Tav Falco used to organize the annual Counter-Fest here; we played some of those. We were musically isolated, growing up in Memphis. There wasn't a college radio station to speak of; radio was classical, Kenny G–type jazz, or Top 40. So in Memphis, you sort of turned to yourself. The first punk-rock bands I saw live were local bands, and that made an impression. I didn't know there was anything else going on; I thought Panther Burns was about the coolest thing in the world! I think when you really have to look for it, your taste gets better. Isolated bands get their own identities. In some cities you've got twenty bands that sound like White Zombie, because that's the cool thing. What are they gonna do later, with all those holes in their bodies?

One thing that interests me about the Grifters is that you seem to put a lot of deliberation into the material's impact. Your records have overlapping vocal parts, odd effects, instruments colliding in the songs to give things an unusual degree of depth and texture. How far would you go, finances permitting, to make a full-blown presentation?

SHOUSE: There's a division within the band about this. I don't want to call it pro and con. But there are definitely elements of artiness and elements of casualness. We're actually thinking about taking lighting on tour with us now. With foot pedals to change the lights. We're also talking to a video guy, a projectionist, because he has some neat things. We want to give people something new—they've paid money to see you, and "see" is a word we maybe forget sometimes. So, try and enhance the package a bit. We don't want to go overboard; in each of us there's an element of, "Ah, let's just rock." We don't want to lose the ability when we play live to astound each other now and then as people make stuff up—and astound the crowd, too!

The best art-rock bands, like jazz ensembles, seem to be composed of strong-willed players who've developed the grace and good sense to know when to hold back and leave a space for someone else to pop in.

TAYLOR: "It's not the notes, but the spaces between them." Yeah. I think one of our strong points is that we play really well together. Over the years we've gotten intuitive about what each person plays, and we go to each other's strengths. We still play stuff from back when Dave and I first started playing together, but they're different. now. When you create these things, it's almost organic: you play them, and they're alive. When they can live as you play them, things change and things grow. I don't think of the band as like a jukebox, with places for the hits.

You know, Dave will put out chord sheets. A few of our songs have real open-ended bridges; the recorded version just happens to be what we played that day.

Live, anything can happen. We can change keys with these chord sheets, develop different patterns to bounce off of and go into space.

SHOUSE: We look at a set list and see how we want to start and how we want to end. But we change things every night, and we want to see how it can metamorphose into somewhere we're not. Everyone's paranoid about stagnation, about treading water.

The new album reflects what you just said. It has a specific flow; I could imagine it being played as a piece—Lookout: the Rock Opera! Yet it's loaded with surprises, especially pop references—to Bowie, the Stones, Big Star—that catch the listener off guard and give it a "happy accident" feel, too.

SHOUSE: When we went in, we didn't know what we were going to do. We had two songs finished, one song completely rehearsed—that was it. But everybody just came in, and it's amazing how relaxed we were. We surprised ourselves, making a pop record with a bit of humor in it. When people were always saying, "Oh, the Grifters, they're dark and murky."

TAYLOR: The album's cathartic as hell. If you look at the others, too, you'll see we give a lot of thought to sequencing. We think of a vinyl record, and try to split it into even sides, so if you played side two of the vinyl, it wouldn't be like starting in the middle of a CD. "Last Man Alive" would be the end of side one.

Sometimes we think too much! In both directions—"It needs something else" and "We need to get rid of something else." The true art of mixing is not so much putting together what you've got, as trying to find what to take out. It's where to put the holes, more than filling them up. And that's hard! You get ego clashes, because these songs and guitar hooks are our art, our babies. The way we write songs is collaborative. Tripp describes it as a sculpture: when a guy's about to make sculpture out of a rock, it's inside the rock, and you just have to chip away all the stuff that's not the sculpture. You have to find it in there. Our songs take a lot of chipping and hammering and arguing, in order to bring the song alive.

That sounds like an artist talking: the joy and excitement of having something appear before your eyes.

SHOUSE: The luxury of having a little more time made it possible. It was fun sitting back watching someone—like Tripp, who plays bass but is good on everything else—lay down a second drum track, or put an organ on something. Or Scott put down a harmonica part, or pick up a wah-wah pedal when he's never played through one. People would go, "Ooh, what's that thing over there?" Easley Studios has a mellotron, and we were thinking, What if you used that but mixed it with a guitar, so you'd hear the overtones and couldn't tell which instrument was which? Things like that. It's all Brian Wilson anyway, his thing—taking an oboe or bassoon and a Fender bass and mixing them together so you couldn't tell what you were listening to. We even dragged the 4-track in this time, but used it in different ways. Like this random loop you can make; a lot of the backwards stuff is 4-track looping, run through an amp, and us playing to it.

Amid all the experiments, you've still managed to come up with a song that screams radio hit in "Last Man Alive."

SHOUSE: That actually came out of a side project, a faux-band I created to pay tribute to a lot of my favorite bands: the Stones, Roxy Music, Sparks, Bowie. We were all freaked out and I was self-conscious about it [because] our songwriting is collaborative and "Last Man Alive" pretty much came from the demo tape. Then the Sub Pop people decided, "This will be the single!" For the radio and video version, we remixed the bridge and added a vocal to the mix in the style of the Jordanaires [the '40s/'50s Missouri vocal quartet who backed Elvis Presley].

TAYLOR: The funny thing is, "Last Man Alive" is not really representative of the rest of the album. It does stand out! We got great college radio-play before we were on Sub Pop; I think we got to as high a level as we could. Getting onto Sub Pop, the intention was to move up a rung. And if commercial radio is the next rung, hey, we'd already decided on that when we signed.

SHOUSE: We just hope the curve of the graph crosses us at some point in the direction we're going. We don't want to change too much. All kinds of things go through your head: Is this punk? Is this cool? Is this rock? What do we do now? And you don't know, so you finally arrive at, "We signed a deal. Let's work together." It's a Southern thing. Trusting, committing to something you didn't think you'd commit to. It'll be interesting to see what happens.

I'm hoping I didn't flog my art-rock angle too much here. Shouse and Taylor, at least, seemed glad to be considered within a broader context, rather than being saddled with the usual post-Nirvana approach (and that damn lo-fi question).

Tacitly suggesting that Sub Pop might not realize what kind of band it was getting, Shouse quips, "Well, they pitched Supersuckers really hard, but it didn't take off. And Sebadoh . . . I'm sure they're looking at Folk Implosion and thinking, 'What did we do wrong?'" And Taylor concludes, "Most people who see the term 'art rock' forget that it includes the word 'rock.'" ◓

THROWING MUSES

Puncture's third Throwing Muses feature came over a decade after their debut. **JOHNNY RAY HUSTON** interviewed Kristin Hersh in 1997, as she began the transition into a solo career. Soon afterward the Muses would be placed on hold, although they regrouped in 2003 and have recorded and played live together intermittently since then.

ANDREA FELDMAN

The third time I talk to her on the phone it's August 1996. She and Throwing Muses have just finished playing a show in what she calls "Ew Nork"; I'm in my apartment, stressed about a rapidly approaching newspaper deadline. For a while the conversation isn't an interview. Kristin Hersh mentions she turned 30 two days earlier. I say I'm 28 and babble something about losing the spirit of my youth. "You're much smarter once your spirit goes," she kids. "I was stupid all through my 20s—just last week I was stupid. Now I'm going to be crotchety . . . *I don't like anything!*"

We talk about places to live in America. I'm in San Francisco; Kristin has just spent time in Southern California. "It feels like you're on TV in LA, like you're in a human habitat. The bad things about LA are funny, and when they stop being funny, it's time to go. It's a kooky place. It was made by people recently, so you can see what they decided to do—sociologically it's fascinating."

The above quote contains one of Kristin's favorite conversational words: kooky. Most of her favorite words end with the letter *y*. Her voice is an affectionate growl. She laughs a lot and has reason to—she's funny. Our chat's next thrilling subject, weather, inspires this proclamation: "If you're not a fur-bearing mammal, you should wear a sweater sometimes." From there, we move on to healthy eating habits and vegetarianism. "If you don't take care of yourself you get ugly and stupid," Hersh remarks.

I hear a high-pitched voice in the background, and Kristin stops for a moment to talk to her 5-year-old son, Ryder. When she returns, I ask about touring. Her tone gets a bit weary. "Moving onto the tour bus is like moving into an old apartment. Ryder was really worried this year that the Easter Bunny wouldn't find him in our apartment because we weren't on a bus. Isn't that sad?" She laughs.

What bands do the children—Hersh also has a 10-year-old, Dylan—of a rock mom listen to? "The Ramones make them so happy—they start pogoing like they have the pogo gene. And they like Nirvana, Vic Chesnutt, and Robert Johnson. But Hank Williams makes them weird and twitchy."

For the third time, Kristin is pregnant, and for the third time she's touring while pregnant. This time she's demanding some basics. Her previous beer-and-coffee road diet ("At the start of a tour, the reviews say 'power trio' and talk about how muscular we are as a band. At the end, they say, 'Kristin Hersh is so frail I can't believe she can lift a guitar'") has been replaced by a soy-milk regimen. "And we're asking people not to smoke in the clubs," she adds. "It's weird not having a haze around—it can be disconcerting."

Still, anyone who has seen Hersh perform knows that she's not really there during her songs. Her eyes stare, transfixed by a vision only she can see. Her solo acoustic shows of 1994 were startling for many reasons—name another alt-rocker who can hypnotize a crowd for over an hour with just a voice and a guitar—but mainly due to a stark contradiction: first off, she'd be possessed by a scary song; next, she'd be telling a three-minute goofy story.

"I know performers who look at the people while they play," she says. "I don't know, I guess I'm not cut out for many facets of this job. But the songs do have to happen between me and the audience. As goofy as that sounds, it does seem to be the truth." When I mention her acoustic shows, she groans. "[Playing solo] was like taking an exam. Everyone was silent. No one was drunk. But it was a good thing to learn, because if I made the songs happen in the room—if I really did disappear instead of leaning on craft—everyone liked it. They didn't even mind that they were paying 25 bucks."

The next time I see the Muses play, a few weeks later, the songs don't really seem to "happen in the room." It's a hot night in Portland. The club is half-full, the crowd is half-interested, and the sound is small and leaden. Kristin seems detached between songs, like the show is a chore she wants to finish quickly. I move from spot to spot trying to find the best place to meet the music. I never find it.

The following evening, I see the Muses in San Francisco. The club is packed with devoted fans. The sound leaps from the speakers. At one point, during "Hazing," Kristin's eyes get wider and darker, as if she's going further and further into the song. Up front, I think about my favorite concert metaphor: the musician's and audience's souls mixing into an electric, invisible cloud specific to that particular time and place. That may sound goofy, but it's happening here.

The first time I talked to Kristin Hersh on the phone was in 1987. The Muses' second album and American debut, *House Tornado,* had yet to be released. I was writing about them for a fanzine some pals and I put together. I don't have a tape of the interview. My main memory is of the ugly blue shag carpet in my bedroom, which I used as a desk while transcribing it—by hand.

The finished article was rife with keen observations by my teenage critical mind. Confusing hyperbole with profundity, I favored adjectives like "amazing" and phrases like "searingly emotional and individual." But Kristin managed to put a few good quotes in amid the goddess worship. About songwriting: "It's a good thing there's a place for it in society or it would be really strange. I mean, to bang on a stringed box and move your vocal cords and put words together is odd."

Playing the Muses' 1986 debut album at the record store where I worked, I used to feel exposed and embarrassed when "Hate My Way" and "Vicky's Box" blared over the speakers. They were the most nakedly honest songs about teen identity trouble I'd heard, and I was a teenager with identity trouble. Also, in sheer terms of sound, they were a shock. The chord and tempo changes were sudden and severe. The words were disjunctive. And Kristin's voice—simultaneously old and young, weak and strong—rejected "prettiness" for a more untamed, personal beauty.

I remember sending a tape of *Throwing Muses* to my best friend Tracey. The first few times she played the album, she didn't connect with it. Then one day in her bedroom she truly heard "Hate My Way" and burst into tears. From that point on, talks about Muses' songs that signified on "so many different levels" (our favorite phrase of the time) were a central part of our bond. An aspect of the Muses both of us intuitively responded to was the volatile sense of self in their songs. During "Hate My Way," as Kristin travels a traumatized interior landscape, identifying with broken things and people, victims and victimizers, each word takes on a new, radical vocal/verbal meaning. One of the song's many object-metaphors ("I'm TV") uncannily articulated what Tracey and I both, individually, were struggling with at the time—an inability to draw boundaries between our insides and the outer American societal garbage.

"A home is your body, a home is your parent's home, it's your married home, it's your country, it's life itself," Kristin said in that interview, when I asked about her lyrical references to boxes, cages, and homes.

"But if you're young, if you're a teenager, you have no self-concept, no idea of where you're supposed to belong. Things come very readily to you—you just feel what's happening in the world and it happens in you, and it's hard to tell the difference."

Though Kristin was only a little older than me, she was far wiser. Her maturity may have stemmed from the fact that she was already a mother (not yet 2 then, Dylan knew a few words, including "surfboard" and "Dave"). But it also seemed like part of her being. As for me, back then, I felt like the opening character in "Vicky's Box," an unhappy, closeted "queer" trapped and numbed by the cyclical repetitions of everyday life. And "Vicky's Box" did what my all-time favorite songs have done: it hit me like a revelation, showing me something about my life that I didn't know.

The next time I talked to Kristin Hersh on the phone was in 1992. In less than half an hour, conversation ranged from music to strange crimes in Providence,

Rhode Island (where she grew up). "Rich people are always doing crazy things," Kristin said, after I asked if she'd lived near infamous alleged poisoner Claus von Bülow. "No one locks their doors or bikes in Providence, but these bizarre things happen. A friend of mine's sister was flayed alive. And this guy was taped to death not long ago—he taped his head until he died."

In the five years between the first two interviews, Kristin had separated from Dylan's father and lost a custody battle, had surgery to remove a tumor from her sinus cavity, and been diagnosed with bipolar disorder after years of seizures. She'd also gotten married and had another child. But the only Kristin I knew was the one on the Muses records. On 1989's *Hunkpapa*, she tried—and failed—to work successfully within traditional song structures and commercial production; on 1991's *The Real Ramona*, she tried again and succeeded. During this time, I had love affairs with other bands—in my rock writing, I used My Bloody Valentine and Morrissey to wrestle (pretentiously) with gender and sexuality, my (unoriginal) obsessions. But the Muses remained the main soundtrack to my life, the music that was me.

While Kristin was making records and having children, I was wrapped in typical early-20s behavior: studying and substance abuse. College-damaged, I tried to intellectualize her music during the interview, drawing comparisons between her songs and the ideas certain authors (Julia Kristeva, Kathy Acker) had developed about fragmented female identity. "I think daily life teaches more [than books]," she replied. "You don't have to tear it apart, it's visceral rather than analytical, it goes right into all of your senses and comes out of your heart and mouth."

Kristin's creative approach remained practical: "Three different notes vibrating against each other—that's what I've based my career on," she noted with a laugh. When I said her compositions weren't statements so much as states of being, she drew a series of less critical, more practical analogies. She likened songwriting to "meeting someone," and songs to "people, gods, ghosts" that "happen in my hands and face." As she put it, instead of telling stories, "the songs take everybody on their ride. They use sweaty words, color words, words your mind jumps at. By the time I get to screaming, you're ready to scream, too, because the song's doing it, not because you're thinking, 'Wow, I really care that her boyfriend walks all over her, so I guess I feel like screaming, too.'"

My favorite Muses song of the time, *The Real Ramona*'s "Red Shoes," showcased a marked change in Kristin's perspective. This is a love song, albeit one that digs beneath rote gestures and declarations of affection to interior ties and rifts. Midway through, the lines

"Eyes closed / You close them in the dark / What do you think you can see?" nail the psychological (rather than merely sexual) intimacy that comes from sleeping with someone. But it's the final line—"I become you"—that pushes "Red Shoes" beyond the tidy longing of romantic convention into total identification with another. Double entendre doesn't capture the meaning/feeling Kristin gives those three words: they are a vow, a threat, and more.

The same month I talked to Kristin the second time, the Muses released *Red Heaven*, their first album without Tanya Donelly. The transition to trio was somewhat awkward, Kristin compensating for lost dynamics with increased distortion. As usual, I was drawn to the most dramatic moments, particularly "Furious," where Kristin's singing, once fractured, was powerful and defiant. ("Every time I go live life for a while, then come back to the music, my voice is doing something different," she said.) More impressive than *Red Heaven* was the live, limited-edition, solo acoustic disc accompanying it, a recording that forecast the brilliance of Hersh's 1994 official solo debut, *Hips and Makers*.

The third time I talk to Kristin Hersh on the phone I want to ask about the changing nature of her love songs. Tracks on *The Real Ramona* and *Red Heaven* address a male figure with bitter detachment—not as "you," but as "him" or "it." But from *Hips and Makers* onward, Kristin's music has a newfound trust. While hardly restful, it is content, built from a belief that someone is willing to ride alongside through the emotional peaks and valleys. "Thank you for chaining me to the bed / That was sweet," Kristin sings to a "sad brother" and "sunny lover" on "Tango," one of many recent compositions that render a relationship through dance imagery.

Limbo's choreography is surreal: Kristin and her loved one shift shapes and leap into new surroundings with each line. The settings are still domestic, but Kristin has largely traded the kitchen-sink drama of early Muses records for another part of the house: the bedroom, site of dreams and sex. Though lines like "I wanna wake with your weight on me / Arms around / My favorite sound / You make" (from "Mr. Bones") have a tone of familiarity that comes from a shared history, the main constant of *Limbo* is change.

But instead of talking about her new music, Kristin tells me about Throwing Music, the label she and husband/manager Billy O'Connell have started in conjunction with Rykodisc. "At the outset," she says, "we [the Muses] told everyone we weren't a major-label band, including the majors. When we signed with Warner Bros., I don't know what we were thinking." I remind her she was young at the time. "And stupid. I didn't

even know what a producer was—they'd come in and talk about the songs, we'd ignore them and make the record, and then we'd give them thirty grand." Now, commercially at the height of what she calls "success with a small *s*," Kristin has seized control. "We own our own masters," she notes. "We want jobs—to work as musicians without playing the [hit-making] game."

Though she hopes to work with other bands, Kristin will initially use Throwing Music to "flush the pipes" with her own projects. Nearly a decade after their celebrated UK debut on 4AD, *Throwing Muses* and the *Chains Changed* EP will get official American releases on the label. In addition, five songs from the group's pre-4AD period—which included an ultra-rare 7-inch in a 10-inch sleeve with cover art that looks like a high-school yearbook/scrapbook—will be part of the package. Though Kristin is far from excited about her juvenilia ("Those songs deserve no more than to disappear forever"), the enthusiasm of fan/Muses drummer David Narcizo motivated her. "He actually forced me into the studio to record songs we played when we were 15, that were stolen out of his bedroom," she says. "I told him, 'You're the producer, this will end in tears.'"

Kristin also hopes to record a second solo album soon at Stable Sound, the same barnlike studio where she created *Hips and Makers* ("there are little horse girls there with hats and jodhpurs"). One thing could get in the way of this plan: her belly. "When we get back from this tour, I might be too fat to make an acoustic record," she worries. "You can sling an electric guitar around your side Chuck Berry–style, but you can't do that with an acoustic guitar."

Much has changed in the ten years since I bought my first Throwing Muses album from a goth clerk who scoffed that the band sounded like the B-52's. Back then, Kristin was almost alone as a woman in rock, save for a few Bangles and baubles. "I guarantee you, the more women you take out of a band, the more successful it will be," she told *Puncture* in 1991, going on to argue forcefully that "bad music is evil." Today, bad music often stems from the magical marketing genre "alternative," once used to dismiss the Muses. And much of this bad music is made by women: as one of them says in a chart-topping song, "Isn't it ironic?"

Kristin has a right to be irritated, and she is. Of female performers she says, "Most are one-dimensional. Maybe it's just impossible to see women in 3-D, because it's men who we're used to seeing as having lots of different aspects. But they choose these ridiculous stereotypes, like 'angry young woman' and 'art poetess' and 'ethereal.' As far as I'm concerned it's just 'bimbo'—if you yourself don't present yourself as a three-dimensional person, then you're a bimbo." ◑

SMOG

Throughout the '90s and early '00s, Bill Callahan performed as Smog, recording spare, increasingly sophisticated songs. Callahan eventually became celebrated for his unsettling and often darkly funny poetics, but for much of his early career critics mostly seemed to focus on his lo-fi recording quality. **FRANKLIN BRUNO** dug deeper in this 1996 profile, revealing a figure who transformed a distinctly male disgust into a compulsive body of work.

The last time Smog—that is, Bill Callahan—played in Los Angeles, it was on one of those unfortunate (but probably unavoidable) evenings when many in the crowd have come to drink and say they were there, rather than to listen. At Spaceland, a perfectly acceptable club recently hyped as the center of the "Silverlake scene," opening for Gastr del Sol (in their starkest, two-man acoustic form) and legendary guitarist/composer John Fahey, Callahan seated himself alone onstage ("I've been playing alone, but that was the first time sitting down"), saying little or nothing to the restive hipsters, playing largely unfamiliar material from his then-upcoming album *The Doctor Came at Dawn* (Drag City). Quiet, deliberative renderings of these new songs seemed to get across to more of the crowd than Gastr, who were all but drowned out by chatter through most of the by-then packed club. (Fahey's sphinxlike presence and set-long ruminating though thirty-plus years of material chased the unprepared from the scene.) All this is a far cry from the previous LA Smog show, when Callahan and then-member Cynthia Dall diffidently faced a crowd of 10 or 15 while Refrigerator's Chris Jones gradually settled on a drum pattern behind them over the course of a song. Typically reticent, Callahan's only comment when we meet for coffee the next morning is that "the audience in San Francisco was quieter—I've heard that Fahey talks more sometimes, but I haven't seen it."

Later, wondering what made the show so discomfiting, I decided it wasn't the noise of the crowd, but their bare presence—a perfectly quiet, perfectly attentive audience would have been just as disorienting. All three of the artists involved make music almost expressly designed for solitary listening: Fahey in the iconoclastic American Transcendentalist strain in his work; Gastr del Sol by virtue of their sheer compositional intricacy; and Smog, the closest to a "singer-songwriter" of the three, both in the one-man-band character of most of his recordings and in many songs' explicit tension between a desire for isolation and a need to connect.

Both these long-standing Smog trademarks are developed in fresh directions on the new album. "I wanted it to sound like it was all recorded in one . . . very quickly, and with a similar feel, almost like it's all one song. My other records differ a lot from song to song." *The Doctor Came at Dawn* ("The narrator dies at the end of the record; so the title is sort of like the last line of the album") is a grim little autopsy of a record, as if Burroughs's Dr. Benway were examining a human soul with a rusty set of tools. The guests of *Burning Kingdom* and *Wild Love* are gone (Dall sings on one track) in favor of the acoustic spareness of Smog's previous release, 1995's four-song *Kicking a Couple Around*, supplemented by more (all-Callahan) layering than that stark EP employs.

The step taken on the new album is to combine the fully drawn but sometimes too-straightforward narratives of that batch of songs, the spontaneity and hermetic imagery of early records, and *Wild Love*'s sonic confidence.

"The strings are me—it's a keyboard, a very expensive sampler. I did all the vocal and guitar parts live in one or two days in a studio in Sacramento—I just picked it out of the phone book. It was about sixty dollars an hour—for the kind of studio it is, that's cheap. Tesla recorded something there, their acoustic record I think."

And how did the engineers of *Five Man Acoustical Jam* take to Callahan's non-band-based approach? "They thought it was pretty weird at first, but they came around a little." Results range from the pizzicato glitter of "Spread Your Bloody Wings" to the ramshackle clatter of piano and slack-strung acoustic on "Everything You Touch . . . ," but the album's centerpiece sound is that of three lengthy, achingly slow tracks: opener "You Moved In," "Lize," and "All Your Women Things."

"To me, the new record is really still—like a ship that's on the water, like a ghost ship. The waves are crashing around it, and there's wind blowing, but it's not affected by what's going on around it." Indeed, all three proceed by alternating between two chords in waltz meter for up to six minutes, creating a sense of a great, static expanse, upon which Callahan (or the character he portrays) compulsively turns over the details of failed relationships, resigned to the fact that it's too late for much to be salvaged. In "You Moved In," a typical Smog narrator finds his solitude interrupted ("You moved in / To my hotel / You could have

SMOG
Red Apple Falls
(Drag City)

Listening to an earlier recording like 1990's *Sewn to the Sky*, it's obvious that Bill Callahan, who records as Smog, is on a mission to refine his songwriting down to its purest essence. The sound quality may have gotten cleaner compared to the ultra lo-fi beginnings, but only to underline the classical elegance of the songwriting.

Although he's often described as a doom-and-gloom bard, Callahan is much smarter than that. Beyond his sparse eloquence, his sense of humor is his saving grace—gallows humor, more often than not, but humor, anyway: he has the lucidity to inject a little self-deprecation into what would otherwise be unbearably masochistic tales of loss and deprivation.

On *Red Apple Falls*, coming hot on the heels of last year's *The Doctor Came at Dawn*, Callahan's humor is on typically understated display: "And why do you women in this town / Let me look at you so bold / When you should have seen what I was / In the last town / You should have seen what I was / If I was a stranger / I was worse than a stranger / I was well-known" ("I Was a Stranger").

And I'd like to read the lines "Whenever I get dressed up / I feel like an ex-con / Trying to make good" in "Ex-Con" as Smog's way to explain the simple arrangements he prefers for his songs. Away from the limelight (he never got a tenth of the ink spilled on, say, Mark Eitzel or even Palace), Smog is slowly but surely building a body of work that is unique in the American musical landscape.—*Elisabeth Vincentelli*

SMOG
Knock Knock
(Drag City)

Perhaps a press release should not stress the fact that half the songs on a record were written in one eight-hour drive—at least not until after the release has been deemed an overwhelming success by someone other than the artist and his promo department.

Braggadocio aside, *Knock Knock* is more success than failure. Dark and catchy numbers like "Held," "No Dancing," and "Cold Blooded Old Times" prove that the production/collaboration relationship with Jim O'Rourke continues to be a fertile one. And sonically, Smog have spread out here to include horns, a string quartet, and even a children's chorus. It's the record's content, however, that doesn't always measure up.

Smog releases are characterized by

done better/ . . . But, oh well") only to find himself grasping at too much intimacy ("I tapped your phone / I read your mail"). In "Lize," he complains to a deceptive partner, "You don't make lies like you used to . . . You used to pay more attention to details." It's not that the singer doesn't want to be lied to, it seems, but that he can retain his self-respect only if the lies are nominally consistent: "It used to be I could live off your lies."

The ugliest moment in this postmortem is "All Your Women Things." Seven years after the breakup, the singer takes out all the "frilly things" his ex-lover left behind ("All your bridges and bras / All your cotton and gauze") and arranges them into a "spread-eagled dolly." Mercifully, we are left to imagine what he does with this tableau before he asks, "Why couldn't I have loved you as tenderly? / How could I ignore your left breast, your right breast?" This song, though clearly fictionalized, is genuinely upsetting when performed live, and is the clearest expression of a creeping, uniquely male disgust present in Smog's work at least since 1993's *Julius Caesar* ("She said I could do it without protection / That's not a woman at all / She said she's an angel / What kind of angel is that? / An angel of death").

The aquatic claustrophobia of *Wild Love*'s "Bathysphere" and "Goldfish Bowl" is explicitly linked with this troubling attitude (to call it "misogyny" would be to shove it off into an easy category) on *Doctor*'s "Spread Your Bloody Wings," where a certain woman is explicitly compared to a sea on which "a thousand men" have attempted to sail, only to have "the icy waves drive them back again."

Even on this front, there's been some growth. "Whistling Teapot (Rag)" rehearses a love triangle much like that of *Kicking*'s "Your New Friend," which has the singer hiding behind his Chinese screen as his girlfriend sets up her next affair on the phone in the other room. In the current variation, though accusations fly ("Between the two of you / Could not come up with / Enough compassion / Not to screw"), they are followed by joyless "whoo-hoo-hoos" that undercut the self-righteousness. This wordless vocalizing, a contrast to Callahan's intimate, conversational singing style, shows up on several songs.

"Depending on what the song's about, there might be different reasons for that. On that song, I guess I'm mocking the narrator—or maybe just making him sound like a wimp."

Eventually, the "two of you" mutates to the "three of us," as the singer accepts his role in creating the situation he's trapped in. (Strangely, the lyric sheet contains a final line—"And why did you have to take my only friend"—that's inaudible on the recording I was sent. Asked about this, Callahan said, "There's something at the end of the song—maybe you didn't want to hear it. You blocked it out." I don't know what to make of this: repeated listening reveals no trace of the line.)

Emotional nuance aside, the achievement of *Doctor* lies largely in its ability to create and sustain the moods and tensions described above over longer durations. Early Smog records tend to throw a couple of interesting sounds together with a snatch of lyric—a suggestive tinkering, the lack of interest in completion expressed on 1993's "A Hit" single: "It's not gonna be a hit . . . Just lay it down and forget about it." Oddly, each release from that single onward becomes more musically accomplished, culminating in the clean recording values, varied instrumentation, and small-scale lyrical cohesion of 1995's *Wild Love*, and the more sweeping ambitions of the current record.

"I think all the records are pretty much the same, but there's always a different little goal I'll have. On 'Your New Friend,' I just wanted to make something sort of conversational. On the new record, I don't know, it's there, but it's hard to put into words. I do keep goals in mind. I already have the whole next record written." ◉

meticulous self-analysis. This tendency, coupled with singer-smogwriter Bill Callahan's prolific release schedule, has afforded attentive fans ample access to the minutiae of Callahan's mind. On previous releases, this is expressed as a refreshingly unretouched distillation of a generation's sublimated pessimism. While indie rockers sing about DIY, Callahan sings "It's not going to be a hit . . . so why record it?" While alterna-rockers whine about boredom, Callahan resignedly documents "Forty-seven push-ups in a winter-rate seaside hotel." A Romeo-like frontman "can't forget the girl," while Bill arranges an ex-girlfriend's underthings into a lingerie "dolly." His is unique, potent music that finds its inspiration in isolation. So while I'm disappointed, I'm not exactly surprised to see that Callahan is now struggling with his waning obscurity.

Like *Red Apple Falls*, its predecessor, *Knock Knock* wastes almost half its content documenting the adventures of the increasingly encroached-upon bubble boy. This is not a new trap for the introspective songwriter, nor is it uncommon subject matter in the media-obsessed alterna-underground. Still, it is far less interesting territory than his daring first releases explored.

On "Teenage Spaceship," Callahan waxes nostalgic about simpler days as a "teenage smog," and it's easy to sympathize. If it weren't for the sheer creepiness of the songs produced with the children's chorus (remember, a song on *Red Apple Falls* explored fantasies of child-kidnapping in the supermarket), and the surprising joy of "Held," this album would amount to little more than a few steps in place.

—*Jenny Toomey*

PAVEMENT

Pavement, the defining indie-rock band of the '90s, were profiled by **STEVE TIGNOR** on the release of their fourth album, 1997's *Brighten the Corners*. The band would release only one more LP before breaking up at the end of the decade. In 2000, frontman Stephen Malkmus contributed a short article to *Puncture* about Creedence Clearwater Revival; the band reunited as a touring entity in 2010.

I worked at a record store in the first half of '92. A few days before I quit, another record by a no-name indie band came in. It bore the ridiculous title *Slanted and Enchanted*. Manager Mike said, "Oh, yeah," grabbed it out of my hands, and put it on. About six songs in, he looked up at me. "What do you think?"

I said, "I feel like I've been waiting about ten years to hear this." He smiled, like I was exaggerating. I could tell he was thinking the same thing.

"Stephen and I have known each other since third grade. We played soccer together," Scott Kannberg, down-to-earth college type and co-creator, with Stephen Malkmus, of the aforementioned no-name indie band Pavement, says. "Stephen was in a punk band in high school called Straw Dogs, who were well-known in the area. I was never in a band, really. I was a high-school kid going to Dead Kennedys shows.

"In Stockton, the West Coast punk scene seemed really dangerous to us at the time. There was a Fall of Christianity show where a riot started, the local aggies versus the punks. Those punk bands were like a glimpse of some other world, some underground world from the city. At that point, Stockton was a pretty nice family-type place, where people had come and settled in the late '60s and '70s. It's changed quite a bit now—stopped growing and kind of reverted to the past, this bleak, industrial town.

"But Stephen and I didn't start playing together until college. He'd come back over breaks from Virginia and we would jam. He was involved in college radio, so he knew anyone could put out a single. We wrote some things together and went to a studio run by a guy named Gary Young. We were doing a little tribute to our favorite bands at the time—Can, Swell Maps, the Clean. It was our first single. We pressed a thousand, and some people who were hip to that sort of stuff picked up on it. Drag City ended up starting their label with it."

I saw Pavement play a show at Maxwell's in Hoboken in '92. The place was packed and very hot. When the band went on I noticed the drummer was a bearded, stringy-haired homeless guy who'd been barking at people as they came into the club. He spent large portions of the show stalking the stage, shouting. He wasn't homeless, though. It was Gary Young. When he played, he played loud.

The rest of them were darling boys in comparison—short-brown-haired and skinny, in T-shirts and jeans, smiling like angels at nothing in particular. They shambled around the stage with lazy grace, screwing up songs I loved, falling apart as they played. Malkmus, the storky, David Byrne–like frontman, changed all the words and seemed to play his guitar solos backwards. Any momentum the band built up was frittered away as they coaxed Young, like a drunken uncle, back to his chair. As "Summer Babe" reached its crescendo, Malkmus bobbed his head in a mini–rock star gesture and knocked his mike off the stand. He played a solo, stepped back up for the final scream, and saw the mike wasn't there. "Oh shit." He got on his knees and sang the rest into the mike on the floor, playing guitar with one hand. The woman I was with summed the show up: "Magic."

"I guess Straw Dogs were like a joke-core band. We had a slight leftist streak and acted Marxist; or we thought so, even though we had no idea what Marx said," says Stephen Malkmus, a blank-voiced, hard-to-read University of Virginia grad, his humor so deadpan it seems accidental. "I played bass and wrote a few songs. We had no plans for music in our future, though—no concept of developing. You'd dream of being on SST, but you never thought it was possible. You were the audience, and they were the musicians, and that's the way it was. We would listen to people on Homestead or whatever and think those people were such a big deal. We didn't see how we could get to be making music on a label like that.

"I was always listening to punk when I was younger, Black Flag, the Sex Pistols, the B-52's . . . Scott made a jump before I did into R.E.M. and British stuff like the Smiths. When we did our first single, it was for the fun of the ritual of making a single. I'd been to England and seen these old Rough Trade singles by bands we loved. Just to do that seemed part of carrying on some tradition.

"Scott and I played during college, but it was nothing permanent. I came to New York after I graduated. I was 22, had no idea what I wanted to do . . . I was just going to live. I answered an ad for a publisher of Judaica, and got a job re-editing their stuff on computer. It was tedious, and I had no interest in publishing. You couldn't make any money. I was hardly getting anything. It seemed like a job for Ivy League girls who were going to become housewives. After I left, the place went bankrupt, anyway. I got a job working as a security guard at the Whitney Museum. That's when our first album came out."

When John Lennon heard Elton John's "Your Song" in pre–rock aesthetic 1970, he purportedly said something like, "Okay, somebody's finally moved past the Beatles, taken pop the next step." I don't mean to suggest that Pavement are in any way related to Elton John, but when I heard *Slanted and Enchanted* in '92, I had the same reaction. The late '80s and early '90s weren't rock's most progressive years. With few exceptions, indie rock's trajectory had flattened out: R.E.M.'s rhythms were strummed to death, Sonic Youth's noise was beaten into the ground. Pavement left all that behind.

Their early EPs do sound of a piece with Brit post-punkers like Swell Maps and the Fall. Fuzzy bits of melody get tangled and thrown in a heap on the floor. But *Slanted* came from somewhere else. Full-blown, self-assured, waves of melody tweaked but not undermined by noise, accessibility masking dozens of tricks and surprises, this was punk rock well adjusted and shedding its outsider status. If Kurt Cobain took punk to the marketplace, Stephen Malkmus, his voice moving from laconic to shrill in no time flat, his melodies and vocal moves spun out with appalling ease and invention, his lyrics pulling the rug out from under their own ennui, gave it a higher education. This had nothing to do with rebellion; it wasn't something anybody could do: it was pure talent.

Pavement were branded slacker music. Having started during the youth-culture wave that washed up over the first years of the '90s, they've been lumped in as Gen X cynics, grunge for grad students, etc. They do share with someone like Cobain a distrust of rock-star power and easy pleasure, a feeling of white-boy disinheritance. But while Nirvana raged against immovable forces, against their own commercial success, Pavement have mused, obscurely, over what artistic (rather than commercial) success means. Malkmus has deliberately sabotaged his melodic talent with his quirks; the band, avoiding classic rock at all costs, have cut their hard rock with aimlessness; the lyrics question the value of pleasure, and the answers are ambivalent.

Listen to "Frontwards," the second song on their '92 EP *Watery, Domestic*. One of their more conventional mid-tempo rockers, it's a lyrical keynote for much of what the band has done. Over a sustained guitar ring and heavy, steady beat, Malkmus strolls in, jaded and breathy, with the lines, "I am the only one searching for you / And if I get caught / Then the search is through." He stops singing and speaks the last word, as if he's given up. I've heard the song described as a "What price fame?" indie lament. But that's only part of what Pavement are after. Malkmus, his voice dropping in mock seriousness, then laboring to rise in emotion, goes on to detail the trivialities of daily existence: "I hear the natives fussin' at the data chart / Be quiet, the weather's on the night news"; "Empty homes, plastic combs, stolen rims, were they alloy or chrome?" He contrasts those with scenes of European decadence: "She's the only one who always inhales / Paris is stale"; "In the Magritte [?] hotels they never sleep, they never will / Their souls are crumbling . . . / Your cigarette's cupped to the inside." Malkmus finishes the song: "I've got style / Miles and miles / So much style that's it's wastin'." He's got all the talent in the world, but can't figure out how to make it mean anything or to bridge the trivial day-to-day and the static, stuffy museum of art.

There's the dilemma Pavement constantly revisit. Their songs are filled with signs of the good life: transcendence, in one form or another, is always within reach. But whether it's art ("Frontwards," "Gold Soundz"), the road and simpler living ("Box Elder," "Range Life," "Western Homes"), stardom ("Silent Kids," "Elevate Me Later," "AT & T"), material wealth ("Unfair"), or just a summer babe, they always see through the good life, find it somehow stale. Not phony, which is the clichéd complaint. More like confining: they don't know how to breathe there. ("They never sleep / They never will"; "I wouldn't want to shake their hands / Cause they're in such a high-protein land," he says of the stars in "Elevate Me Later.") They don't rage at their inability to get these things. They're caught wanting them, even knowing they can have them, but they are false utopias, trade-offs like anything else.

Not only do Pavement have trouble with success in the world's eyes ("A career, career, Korea, Korea"); they, unlike other starving artists, have trouble with success in their own eyes. They go back and forth about whether their artistic achievement is another false utopia. Nobody deliberately fucks up as many golden (but perhaps confining) tunes as Pavement do.

On their second full-length, *Crooked Rain, Crooked Rain*, where punk-rock drive was sacrificed to meticulous crafting of melody, they lamented the fact that the beauty they carved would be heard only through the forum of a pop-culture image business. To begin, the singer in "Silent Kids" leaves the ecstasy of the stage behind and ends the night alone, spilling himself; in the end, with "Fillmore Jive," Malkmus says "goodbye to the rock'n'roll era" and wanders lost through a land of fragmenting, disconnected youth scenes he can't join.

Malkmus: "I appreciate pop fans, but I guess I like smaller music, where you can control what you do and how people react. I've been influenced by the spirit of bands like Royal Trux, Sleater-Kinney, My Bloody Valentine, Silkworm . . . and lately this band Bis from Scotland who use Riot Grrrl iconography, and Ghost, a Japanese psychedelic band. I like being in the band just to hang out, make jokes with the other guys. That's really what it's about, the fun of touring with those guys. I'm into the work of it, putting in our time, getting better, seeing what we can do with it. I guess it's become a career, but it's still so much of a social thing for me that I don't have to think of it that way.

"Pop like Oasis is good in a way, but it's like pornography. You might want to look, but you don't want to marry it. Or maybe you do, I don't know. I'd like to do a more elaborate show next time, I'm getting tired of the boys-in-T-shirts thing. But I'm not doing this so I can hang out at the Viper Room with the cast of *Friends*. I'm not a rock-star type. I'm not some primal guy up there, like Iggy or something.

"I like words a lot. Without words, the world would be a duller place. But I don't have any urge to be literate when I write lyrics. I'll read somebody like John Ashbery because a friend of mine who's a grad student says, 'You gotta check this guy out.' But it's pretty vague to me. You have to be in the poetry scene to get it. For me, it's more like something you should read when you're stoned. It's different than what I do. I read forty-something novelists like Thom Jones and Thomas Mc-Guane, and I like them—they're sort of complexly into what they do, the craft of writing, the way I am with music. I used to try to develop a nice, compact theory for journalists about how we make music, but I can't do it anymore, there's nothing definite enough about it for me to describe. I want to make a nice, warm-sounding record, I guess, with some heart to it, so that it's not purely clever. Sometimes it ends up being that—just clever—because I try to approach lyrics spontaneously. They're not really written beforehand."

Wowee Zowee (1995) went further than *Crooked Rain*. The rockers became throwaway filler while Malkmus indulged his talent for melodic invention in a series of lugubrious, delicate, dragged-out gems. He provided brilliant vocal moments on command: the falsetto "makes me" (I think) cutting through a deadpan chorus at the end of "Rattled by the Rush"; the gently unfolding "Black Out"; the almost-cracked harmony at the end of "Motion Suggests"; the elaborate "Grounded" and "Graaaaaave architecture." It was music that left rock transcendence and a driving rhythm section behind. It tried, painstakingly, to manufacture beauty at every turn. Pavement's old fans hated it.

The lyrics acknowledged this in advance. *Crooked Rain* was about the cross-purposes of making music and getting involved in showbiz; *Wowee Zowee*, right from the opening song's paradox, "Maybe we can dance, together / . . . But no one will dance with us," was more despairing. They wanted optimism, thought that was what art was for; they wanted beauty, too. But they knew no one, from indie kids to major labels marketing rebellion, had any use for either. What was a bored teenager, or a trangression-seeking intellectual, supposed to do with a sentiment like, "I'm too much, I'm too much comforted here"? Malkmus, caught, had to stutter during the ridiculously brilliant "AT&T" just to sound punk.

That brings us to Pavement's new record, *Brighten the Corners*, the closest thing to an Event in indie-rock culture.

Kannberg: "Yeah, we worked with Mitch Easter (producer of early R.E.M., member of Let's Active, etc). We found out about Mitch from a guy named Brian Paulson. Mitch had renovated his house in North Carolina and set it up as a studio. He's a pretty cool guy, we went down there for a while and recorded a lot of songs. We hung out in the town he lives in, and saw some local color, went to some weird bars. All very laid-back. Mitch is a shy guy—he wouldn't come out and say that much, but his house was like a museum of rock. We would be trying to get different sounds, or talking about old-style sounds and records, and he would be like, 'I've got that exact guitar!' He's a historian of the music. We were exposed to a lot we didn't know.

"Bryce Goggin—he's done Chavez and Band of Susans—also helped. He mixed the last record. Now he does all the biggies. In the past, our records were mainly just Stephen and I telling each other parts and putting it together. Overdub city. *Slanted* was a band playing in some ways; me, Stephen, and Gary pretty much played that one. But this is the first one where the whole new band put in their contributions and we played it together. We practiced at Steve West's [the drummer who replaced Young] house in West Virginia. I think this is our best record. It's more refined and groove-y. Playing it the way we did gave it more life."

Malkmus: "Yeah, Mitch was a gentleman, really. I enjoyed the time down there. But I wouldn't know how to compare this record to the others. It is more 'band'; I guess that'll be the journalists' hook. We tried to record some blatant pop for this one, but it didn't end up sounding like our music. I guess the only goal was to make a record we feel comfortable with, and that people want to listen to."

No doubt Malkmus has succeeded with the first two songs. "Stereo," the band's best rocker since "Unfair," makes the art/life trade-off explicit. In the middle of a free-associated decline-of-the-US lyric ("Hi-ho Silver, ride" becomes "The infrastructure rots / And the owners hate the jocks"), Malkmus screams out, "Listen to me! I'm on the stereo / Give me malaria / Hysteria." Like everything else in the culture around him, his music has been reduced to a cry for attention.

Next is "Shady Lane," a plea for peace. They're fed up with cultural politics, amused by attempts at significance, ready to junk the whole thing—"The worlds collide, but all that I want is a shady lane." The band have shaken off *Wowee*'s moroseness and given their detachment a funny, exasperated edge.

By the fourth tune, "Transport Is Arranged," things have begun to bog down. It's a slow, breathy song, reminiscent of the last album minus the strange twists and indulgences. It is more refined, pared down a bit; but it was *Wowee*'s decadence that yielded so many delights. Here, Malkmus's vocal is less elaborate. He follows a tune that could have been written down.

For the rest of the album, the scope is narrowed slightly, the execution more straightforward. For me, its pleasures are also fewer. "Type Slowly" (a power ballad for grad students?) is probably their first outright failure; the rocker "Embassy Row" is tangled between '70s flash guitar and Malkmus's stab at a scabrous punk rescue; "We Are Underused," another big slow one, crosses the line between delicate and dull, its sentiment and music both a bit tired. The new guitar rave-ups meander timidly, like the band aren't sure how to incorporate them.

It may have been the tension between desire and skepticism that made their old music so exciting. Perhaps their ambitions have been reined in and, as Malkmus says, they're going about their business in workmanlike fashion. Maybe the possibility of transcendence—via rock 'n' roll or otherwise—has finally been seen through. Whichever, this album never really follows through on the reckless bemusement, the snobbery made fun, of its first two songs.

Kannberg: "This one will have the Capitol logo on it, which is okay. I wouldn't mind hearing our songs on the radio. We should be on there, right? I'm managing the band, so I have to schmooze the Capitol people. They seem to have a compatible sensibility. I wouldn't work with them if they didn't. But Matador handles most of that, anyway.

"We're making a video for 'Stereo,' the first single. Videos are hard—it isn't really what we do. But they get played in Europe! They play a lot more stuff. Here you're lucky to get it played more than once. We'll be happy to do bigger shows. We don't have that much concern for staying small and indie or whatever. We played some stadium shows in Europe in the past, and it's addictive. We felt invincible for about half an hour."

A friend and I were sitting near Stephen Malkmus in a bar in Brooklyn a couple of years ago, watching a college football game. Malkmus's alma mater, UVA, was playing. Two girls in their early 20s came up to him, blushing, and said, "We want to thank you for the pleasure you have given us with your music."

And that's really all that needs to be said for Pavement. Their new record may be a bit of a comedown, but what wouldn't be after their last three classics? If they haven't given us a fully formed world view (à la Velvet Underground, Clash, X), or forced a new formal style on rock music (Sonic Youth), or brought the world together (Nirvana), they have written insightfully and stylishly about how the promised good life of their suburban American youth has turned out to be a complicated, even elusive, proposition.

More importantly, while they may see through music's transcendence, they haven't given up on its pleasures. When I'm listening to "Debris Slide" run amok, or the simple strummed-guitar break in "Gold Soundz," or Malkmus singing with genuine warmth in "AT&T" ("Open up your hands / And let me see the things you keep in there"), I can't think of any pop music that yields as much surprising, affirming, and ultimately pure pleasure. Pavement—optimistic and snotty, arch and royally tuneful—give me the elusive good life, distilled to its contradictory essence. ◐

ROBERT SCHNEIDER (THIRD FROM LEFT) WITH WILL CULLEN HART, JOHN FERNANDES, AND BILL DOSS OF THE OLIVIA TREMOR CONTROL, RECORDING AT PET SOUNDS STUDIO
(PHOTO, HILARIE SIDNEY)

ELEPHANT 6

The music collective Elephant Six Recording Company starred the bands Neutral Milk Hotel, Olivia Tremor Control, and Apples in Stereo. In the mid-'90s, all three released acclaimed debut albums, offering three distinct interpretations of home-recorded psychedelic pop music. **JAY RUTTENBERG** interviewed the de facto leaders of each band.

Ask three core members of the three core bands who make up the Elephant 6 Recording Company about their recording collective, and you'll get three different responses.

Apples in Stereo's Robert Schneider: "We believe in homespun devices, in ingenious ways of coming up with stuff, and in writing songs that communicate with people. We want to make classic records that can stand up out of their time and that people of all ages can listen to."

Olivia Tremor Control's Will Hart: "It's just similar ideals about music [as a] tangible thing; a belief that it can take you somewhere and it's not just fluff."

Neutral Milk Hotel's Jeff Mangum: "We're just all friends . . . it just sort of is."

That Elephant 6 lacks a congruent manifesto somehow makes sense. The "artistic collective" approach is

a relatively foreign concept to pop music, bringing to mind the visual-arts movements of pretentious Europeans rather than college-radio aficionados from Ruston, Louisiana. What's more, the "collective" aspect is a bit less formal than press reports make out—even the E6 participants themselves give conflicting answers as to what peripheral acts are included on the roster.

But they all concur on this: Elephant 6 was formally conceived in 1992, when Robert Schneider, Will Cullen Hart, Bill Doss, Jeff Mangum, Hilarie Sidney, and Jim McIntyre decided to pursue a musical project that transcended traditional band or geographic barriers. The project's true inception extends back to tiny Ruston, where Schneider, Mangum, and Hart had been close friends since childhood; Schneider and the somewhat older Doss became musical collaborators in

229

high school, as did Mangum and Hart.

Schneider had since relocated to Denver, where he launched the Apples with Sidney and McIntyre; Doss and Hart joined forces with Olivia Tremor Control; Neutral Milk Hotel guy Mangum hopped around the country with a 4-track and guitar. What began as a record label morphed into something larger, until anything artistically produced by the six conspirators falls under the Elephant 6 umbrella.

This loose collective approach allows the six to have their cake and eat it, as the musicians are liberated to chase similar themes down different alleys: the Apples shoot for the heart, the summer, and tight perfection; the Olivias shoot for the subconscious, the spring, and loose dreaminess; Neutral Milk shoot for the soul, the fall, and an emotional feast. Each band released an endearing full-length debut in the past couple of years, recorded at various home studios with Apple Robert Schneider's technical aid and cameos from the other bands. Each album represents the next logical step for DIY recording, borrowing the methods so slothfully employed by Sebadoh and Guided by Voices, but striving for something sonically grander if just as autonomous. Perhaps the answering machine at the Apples' studio best sums up this juxtaposition of lofty goals vs. crude means: "You've reached Pet Sounds Recording Studios and also Jim's house . . ."

THE APPLES IN STEREO

Apples' quarterback Robert Schneider is Elephant 6's technical maestro, playing pivotal roles in the production of all three albums and also helping his drummer and girlfriend, Hilarie Sidney, run E6's record label (which at this point is a separate entity from the Elephant 6 Recording Co., since the Apples, Olivias, and Neutral Milk now record for SpinART, Flydaddy, and Merge, respectively).

A conversation with Schneider can be an intense affair. Talking with the rapidity of a post-espresso-shots auctioneer in a voice that reflects a modicum of his South African birthright and Louisiana youth, he is consummately garrulous and consummately sweet, pausing only for the occasional bong hit or self-deprecation ("I'm gonna be really embarrassed when I hang up the phone," he worries. "You're gonna say I'm the most self-indulgent guy you ever talked to").

His personal hyperactivity and saccharine soul bleed liberally into the Apples' sound. Checking in at the pop end of the Elephant 6 spectrum, their perky 1995 debut *Fun Trick Noisemaker* seems like the most accessible of the collective's works; somewhat ironically, it also took the most listens for me to fully appreciate. What appears as typical contemporary fuzz-pop extends

THE APPLES IN STEREO: ERIC ALLEN, JOHN HILL, ROBERT SCHNEIDER, HILARIE SIDNEY (PHOTO, TAMEE EALOM)

beyond its cuddle-core exterior, with splendid harmonies and spastic interplay between Sidney's drums and Schneider's and John Hill's guitars, all of it cradled in gingerly designed 8-track production.

An examination of the trio's earlier 4-track work (collected on the less enjoyable *Science Faire* LP) neatly traces the progression of mid-'90s basement recording. The same learn-as-you-go autonomy traditionally employed in creating the music eventually carries over to recording—you can practically hear the pages of Mark Lewisohn's *Beatles Recording Sessions* being turned behind *Fun Trick*'s idiosyncratic cymbal crashes and vocal harmonies. The Elephant 6 albums consequently boast the rare combination of wide eyes and technical adroitness. Where the class of 1992 struggles between stagnation on the rock and slick conformity in the hard place, E6 hog the sacred middle ground.

"I really love *Wowee Zowee*, I think it's amazing," Schneider says of the last Pavement album. "The songs are as good as anything they've done, but I think the recording is really slick. That's not what I'm after. I don't think Pavement have fine enough ears, technically, to hear that. To them it just sounds like a recording of them—because they weren't listening to stuff like the click of the bass drum. I'm listening to the warmth in the recording: that's what I like to hear.

"I've always had an antipathy for recording studios—ever since I started doing music. No modern album recorded in a nice recording studio has ever come out sounding good to me. It always sounds too posh."

After this, I'm taken aback when Schneider announces his recent decision to record the Apples' follow-up in a professional studio—an anomaly for an E6 band. After struggling to capture the band's live sound in the space he shares with former bandmate McIntyre, he opted to record the group's basic tracks at a Connecticut studio notorious for its mid-'60s propensities, then embellish the album at home. "In my head, I hear a drum sound better than any drum sound anyone's ever done. I hear records in my head that are perfect. Then when I get to the eight-track, they don't quite come out that way."

Schneider records at home neither from politics nor necessity—it's simply a way to reach a vintage sound typically swallowed by modern engineers. He begins telling me again how the best records are home-cooked, then corrects himself: "Most of my favorite records were done in studios. In the 1960s."

OLIVIA TREMOR CONTROL

This flexibility applies only in part to his cohorts. "Whether it's a 4-track or a 42-track, if it's sitting in your house, it's always your house," says Olivia Tremor Control's Will Hart. "You can have the right pictures hanging and the right light. You feel comfortable, and free to experiment." He gets downright giddy when I broach the legend of the Stones recording *Exile on Main St.* at the supper table, lauding the "field recording" aesthetics of Captain Beefheart's *Trout Mask Replica* and Bob Dylan and the Band's *Basement Tapes*.

More so than the others, the OTC's *Music from the Unrealized Film Script "Dusk at Cubist Castle"* is an undeniable product of home-recording experimentation. Pampering the epic album's 27 cuts over a three-year period on various home 4-tracks, co-leaders Hart and Bill Doss do not shrink from overindulgence, embroidering the mammoth recording with the "Elephant 6 Orchestra" at Schneider's.

Olivia Tremor Control are Elephant 6's artsy extreme. While Schneider informally functions as the collective's producer, Hart is E6's resident visual artist, and this vibe is embraced by the Olivias. Audaciously debuting with a 74-minute monster based on their "as-yet-unrealized conceptual film script" *Dusk at Cubist Castle*, the quartet's expansive pop stems more from loopy surrealism than scary psychedelia. Despite its outlandishness, the record is more in the vein of ascetic surrealists Magritte and Ernst than

ostentatious Dalí. It rarely forsakes a traditional pop sensibility. "It's about balance," says Magritte/Ernst fan Hart. "We could do a totally instrumental, experimental record—and we will do a bunch of records of all varieties, because it's about both. Sound and pop songs work well together."

Revolving in true surrealist fashion around a mystical dreamworld (the press kit mentions C.S. Lewis), the *Cubist Castle* album specializes in goofy, interconnected melodies bouncing off an addlepated freak-out. As in a dream, the listener is urged to drift during less focused segments, leap to attention for more concentrated ones, and at album's end recall only the general theme and a few volatile details.

I'm repeatedly surprised that *Dusk at Cubist Castle* works—that OTC are able to tame their chaos. It's such a ramshackle, flaky album, sonically stuffed to the rim with quirky effects, and melodically refusing to sit still. But this very basement-bred indulgence removes the Olivias from '60s knock-off status, while their prolific knack for melodies sets them apart from contemporaries like Home and Gorky's Zygotic Mynci.

The looseness also affirms Olivia Tremor Control's role as Elephant 6's resident wackos. While the Apples' CD halts precisely at an anal forty minutes, the Olivias' casually meanders along until the theremin shuts down and there's no more space—at which point listeners can slot in their complimentary bonus disc of ambient wanking. As Schneider explains, where his own choir and band training and Jeff Mangum's background as a drummer may frequently prevent off-kilteredness in the Apples and Neutral Milk Hotel, the

THE OLIVIA TREMOR CONTROL

Olivias "don't even hear rhythms that are on or off. They just hear a good song. And that's really cool."

NEUTRAL MILK HOTEL

Schneider spoke about 240 words per minute during our conversation, becoming the first person I've interviewed who I eventually had to hang up on (with deadline rapidly approaching and no more tape).

Jeff Mangum, his best friend since second grade, logged 120 words per minute and became the first person I've interviewed to prematurely hang up on me (allegedly due to a 1-year-old's interference). "People always think they woke me up," he's forced to explain seconds into the interview, after the Olivias relinquish the Georgia-based telephone.

"Your singing has a really lethargic vibe," I offer.

"Cool."

"That's a good thing, then?"

"Well, if it's good to you, ya know," he responds in the first of several answers that seem swiped from a Palace interview, minus the smugness ("I'm sorry," Mangum says more than once, "I'm not trying to be difficult").

His polite reticence fits the bill: where the techie Apples expound on production and the arty Olivias on surrealism, Neutral Milk Hotel songs just sort of gush out naturally. Bedroom-recording extracurricularly from his usual band activities for over a decade, the 26-year-old Mangum has honed an artful faux-slackerdom. Much like the cool student who feigns languor yet consistently sets the curve, Neutral Milk Hotel's *On Avery Island*, despite its beauty, carries that I-don't-give-a-shit attitude. It's an amazing trick to lay down untouchable melodies and evocative lyrics over a carefully planted background, and still manage to sound listless—a trick that cuts straight to the heart of every college kid in a faded Superchunk T-shirt.

And it can be attributed in part to the fact that with *Avery Island* Mangum doesn't have to try: he's free to sit back and play boy genius while Schneider sweats the production details. Although the Neutral Milk entity is essentially Mangum's one-man project, for his first full-length the peripatetic songwriter stopped by his friend's Denver bedroom for four months, in a recording arrangement similar to the Cardinal duo's. Mangum sings, drums, and plays guitar; Schneider handles the 4-track and takes care of horns, organs, and arrangements—a role that's been almost completely overlooked in reviews of the album.

"It was Jeff's concept, but I was the person who had to work it out," says Schneider. "The reason he asked me to do it was that he wanted to do something more enticing than anything he'd done before, but at the same time he wanted to retain the same spirit" as in his previous self-recorded work.

So as Mangum's spat-out phrases tend to carry the songs, Schneider's garnishes help him realize NMH's vintage aura, an element rarely aimed for by mid-'90s one-man bands. "I'm not as influenced by the '60s as people think," Mangum explains in a sober voice that seems to take coffee breaks between words. "My retro is a 1930s and '40s influence. I'm more interested in big band and swing and Thomas Edison and the olden times. I think the '60s are cool, but I don't care to relive them. At the same time, I make pop music, and a lot of pop music began in that period. But I don't think I'm emulating '60s heroes. I'm not into that."

Although Mangum has probably been compared to every white folk and rock hero who recorded between 1965 and 1973, his album is far more inclusive, being both timeless and timely. Aside from the predominant "fuzz-folk," *Avery Island*'s inhabitants include grinding '90s guitars, budget Casio samples, prominent horns, and a drone send-off consuming a quarter of the recording. "That took us two or three times longer than anything else on the album," Schneider says of the little-noted "Pree-Sisters Swallowing a Donkey's Eye." The producer goes on to elaborate extensively on this brush with experimentation, which replicates monks chants by toying with a skipping banjo loop, a Denver neighbor's gamelan orchestra, and tape-speed manipulation that renders previously inaudible octaves audible. Generally skeptical of such experimentation, here Schneider realized the spirit of "what the 1950s composers were going after—trying to make these sounds mesh in an organized way.

"I want to make things sound novel and kind of odd, to project the sounds we conceive. One common denominator in Elephant 6 is that we're very much focused on songs, but at the same time we're all involved in different ways with experimenting. My experimentation's much more technical. If you ask Jeff [about 'Pree-Sisters'] it would be a totally different explanation."

"What does your album's conclusion mean?" I ask Jeff, who currently seems more concerned with entertaining the 1-year-old crawling around Hart's house than with the umpteenth interviewer asking pretentious questions about his record's place in indie rock. "It's supposed to be sort of going off into—oh god! The baby just smashed its head into the wall!"

ELEPHANT 6

Many have noted the peculiarity of this deluge of trendy pop experimentation emanating from Ruston, a Baptist town where the necks are as red as the Bible.

WILL WESTBROOK

they discovered the virtues of the aberrant setup.

Now I'd like to see the musicians take the Elephant 6 Recording Co. a step further and not shy away from the pretentious implications of an "artistic collective": complete the incomplete *Dusk at Cubist Castle* film; be more specific about their tacit manifesto; even invite more bands to the party, which already includes Schneider's occasional Marbles solo project, Hilarie Sidney's and Lisa Janssen's Secret Square, Jim McIntyre's Von Hemmling, Olivia Tremor Control's electronic alter ego the Black Swan Network, plus second-generation E6ers like Chocolate USA and the Minders.

The non-musical aspects of indie rock (and there are many) are fast turning dull. Many regret the phenomenon of independent labels and bands being engulfed by the biggies, but that seems to be beside the point: the whole indie thing itself has become a trite buzzword. People are afraid to take sincere chances—are often afraid to even try, effortlessly retreading similar themes of lackadaisical sarcasm. Creative experimentation is being suffocated by a fear of pretension. Elephant 6 can go beyond this. The collective approach does

But it makes sense. While a non-heavy-metal rock show was indeed a rarity for the Four Lads from Louisiana, the town did have an accessible college-radio station and an inspirational guitar teacher. In the '60s, budding small-town rockers would relocate in search of a place to play out; in the '80s, all they had to do was buy cheap recorders and play in. "We'd just see each other in school, go home at night, plug into the tape recorder and try to play two or three instruments at once—to make a really interesting tape for Jeff, then give it to Bill or Robert," Will Hart says about Elephant 6's informal genesis.

Elephant 6, Schneider explains, was not conceived for the outside world's interest. I get the feeling that it began more as a stoner in-joke, then gradually blossomed as their recordings became more poignant and

more than make for good press—it offers a fresh way of viewing pop trends, one that circumvents the current, rather stale categories by resorting to independent businesses. It also affirms an incipient move away from concerts (which more often than not seem mere traveling advertisements) and toward the art of recording. I have little urge to see any of these bands play live: that seems extraneous (the Apples were the only E6 group to form as a conventional band rather than a taping unit).

The Elephant 6ers already seem to be on the right track for avoiding a critical backlash, as they plan to augment their pop with musique concrète and to keep their feet planted somewhere between home and studio-recording camps. It'll be rewarding to see how much longer they can keep straddling the fence. ◖

VIC CHESNUTT

Cranky but caring, earthy and unexpectedly funny Southern songcrafter Vic Chesnutt talked up a storm in his interview with **JON DOLAN** for this 1997 article. It was a busy period for Chesnutt: he had just been the subject of a star-studded tribute album, and Capitol Records had released *About to Choke*. It would be the lone major-label release in a prolific career that ended in 2009, when Chesnutt died of suicide.

A few hours before show time at the 400 Bar, Vic Chesnutt sits in his wheelchair in front of the bar piano, chillin' in his brand-new green Vans and a shirt that's about three sizes too big, while Christmas lights on the wall behind him make a broken halo for a sad Peter Pan. Bundled in oversized clothes, he'd still be a little guy even if he got up out of his chair and stood. Yet his curmudgeony casualness owns the room; it helps him maintain a sort of benign dictatorship over what goes on around him.

A slew of guests stop by to greet him, including his A&R guy, an interview crew from a local TV station, some dopey local musicians, and one jittery rock critic (me). Vic extends his disabled right hand and politely talks trash with each of us. A few feet off, his wife and onstage sidekick and bassist, Tina, minds her own business and tunes her guitar. Her shyness nicely foils Chesnutt's porch chat. When I ask her if she'd like to do a short interview, she acts surprised. "You wanna talk to me? Nah, I'd probably just say the opposite of what Vic says."

Vic says plenty for both of them. Yet, despite his sprawling spiel of non sequiturs and my exposure to the American Original myth the middle-class rock press has arranged for him (Vic the cranky New Dylan sitting in his wheelchair on a kudzu-covered Georgia porch strumming a blue guitar and singing in his chalky drawl to the rambling wind), the true Vic is not that hard to read.

He's a neo-hippie, an ex-drunk, an ex–garage rocker turned earthy Southern songcrafter. In conversation he trumpets the virtues of agrarian socialism and talks earnestly of the benefits LSD confers on the creative process. In writing songs he indulges his love of wordplay ("Images, images—that's all I want!") the way his pals in Phishy country band Widespread Panic indulge musicality. He's even turning into an admitted guitar-god dweeb. "When I was a teenager, I didn't want any space without lyrics," he tells me. "Now I'm like, fuckin' wank. Go forth and wank!"

"New Town" is a song on the new Vic Chesnutt record. In it, the partially paralyzed and idiosyncratically miserable Georgia singer-songwriter who unapologetically berates the political careerism of his friend Michael Stipe as "kissin' Bill Clinton's ass" while describing his own life's endeavors as "one big regret," transmogrifies into a tender political folk singer. He's a believer in togetherness through prosperity, a Clinton liberal greeting the American new day: "New Town, beat the crowd . . ."

Later he paints a vivid picture of a place where "kittens discover that the birds scrape the ground / And even the loneliest old ladies get social calls . . . And the grassroots effort to incorporate elects a smilin' mayor."

He breathes out the word "Americana" and the phrase "elects a smilin' mayor" with a gentleness that begs you to believe not just the words themselves but the fact that someone else believes them too. Listening to "New Town" on an advance cassette of *About to Choke* a week before election day, I amuse myself imagining it in a Clinton campaign commercial the same way Reagan used "Born in the USA." The idea becomes less funny when I realize it would probably work.

That's why the song's so brilliant. It never really lets you know which side it's on. "New Town" is where irony comes full circle and bites itself in the ass, where the prick becomes preacher, where cynicism and optimism effortlessly do the deed over a net so flimsy you're sure they're doomed to topple into the bottomless well of rote irony. But Chesnutt is no ironist, even if he has constantly marked his career by being one of the more obviously misanthropic writers of pretty songs. He is not a hater of life; in fact, he's sort of a believer.

"I care about politics," he says firmly when I ask about "New Town."

"I'm kinda frustrated with it, you know? but I'm a liberal Democrat. I'm embarrassed, but what else are you gonna do? I'm a bleedin'-fuckin'-heart liberal." Despite an utter conviction that people who know his records and read his interviews think he's a "fuckin' prick," Chesnutt insists he isn't. And when I talk to him on the fourth consecutive snowiest night of the year in Minneapolis, he does nothing to suggest otherwise. He has flown in just for the night to play a show for the grand reopening of a friend's club, the 400 Bar.

It's a pretty exciting season for Vic. His major-label debut has marked his move out of the underground and into pop life. Though he's been going around telling journalists he titled the album *About to Choke* because "I kept thinkin' I was gonna fail," it is his most confident work yet.

It may lack the literary depth of his brilliant Stipe-produced 1992 album *West of Rome*, and the dressy production that made *Is the Actor Happy?* in 1995 such a nice departure from the demo quality of *Drunk and Little*. *About to Choke* finds the perfect middle ground between lo-fi and big time; the man and the studio; and most importantly for Vic, explicit misery and faith in self.

The realization from the album's first song, "Myrtle," that he "felt like a sick child dragged through the myrtle" until he "worked it out and destroyed his selfish cocoon," gets triumphantly expanded on by "See You Around," a Dylanesque salvo at record's end. In between are the gingerly jaded acoustic songs "Tarragon" and "Degenerate"; the murky trip-hop of "It's No Secret Satisfaction"; and the buoyant cheese-jazz of "Little Vacation." And then there's "New Town," goading the cynics and reminding the optimists not to get too cocky.

It's been a long road for Vic: four very great, very different, utterly fucked and unmistakably beautiful neo-country albums for tiny label Texas Hotel, plus years of touring and critical scrutiny. Now at last he's joined his pals in Cracker, Sparklehorse, and country-rock supergroup Golden Smog on the fringe of the winners' circle. "I like it. It's exciting to be on a major. To other people it means big things: I like Capitol because it was started by a Georgian, Johnny Mercer, one of the greatest songwriters. The Beatles were on Capitol, and that's pretty fuckin' cool. We'll see what kinda hate we get goin' between us over the years—but for now, the honeymoon continues."

Chesnutt, now 31, grew up Southern, the adopted son of born-again Christians James and Marian Chesnutt, the former an Eastern Airlines baggage-handler, the latter a clerk at the Immigration office in Atlanta. He spent his childhood hunting and fishing in the woods round his home a few miles outside Zebulon, Georgia. At age 4, Vic's favorite song was "Kaw-Liga" (Charley Pride's version, not Hank Williams's). "It had a story to it," he says, recalling the country-music primal scene, "and I liked the idea of a doll movin'." At roughly the same time he wrote his own first song, which he renders for me in a patchy, childish yowl: "God is our creator / God is our fuckin' savior."

At 14, his imagination pushed him beyond his parents' Protestantism. "I had a religious breakthrough. I was sittin' in church and they were talkin' about the blood of the lamb, and it struck me as queer to transfer your sins onto a lamb . . ." Music filled any spiritual void left by his newfound atheism. At first it was country (Dolly, Loretta Lynn, Tom T. Hall); later it was rock 'n' roll. In his teens he took classes at the community college in Griffin (pop. 5,432), a few miles from Zebulon, and played guitar and keyboards in bands he formed with any remotely hip rock fans he could find who shared his love for Dylan and the Velvets and his disdain for the racist hicks who kicked his ass for saying the KKK sucked.

He also worked on cultivating an acute passion for something he's called in songs the "chemical buzz."

"Some people are like that. When I first tasted alcohol I thought, 'Mmm, I'm gonna like this . . .' When I first smoked pot, I thought, 'I'm gonna be doin' a lot of this . . .' First time I injected heroin and cocaine into my system, I thought, 'Hmm, well, something to say about this kinda feelin' . . .' First time I took LSD, I thought, 'This is special . . .'"

Fortunately, he hit the brakes after acid, but the personal narrative continues. "I'm fascinated with certain chemicals and what they do to my brain. I like artificial inspiration."

Which was all good and fine for an 18-year-old pre-college stoner. But then he fucked up. One night in 1983, while driving drunk, he crashed his car, paralyzing himself from the waist down. He speaks of the event in the tone you might expect from someone talking about a divorce or some everyday lapse. "I was just kind of like calm and accepting. I thought, 'Well, I really fucked up this time. I overheard people sayin' 'paralyzed for life' and 'quadriplegic.' I heard these terms and thought, 'Well, damn, I can't believe I did that. What an idiot.'

"But I wasn't really angry. I wanted to get on with life. I wrote songs in the hospital. Some of my friends thought I'd tried suicide, because I was kinda suicidal as a teenager. It was very interesting, and exciting for a while."

If Vic has handled his disability with dignity, the star-making machinery hasn't. Nothing has contributed more to the Vic myth than the fact that he can't stand up. More than one of my semi-sensitive friends who've seen him live have referred to him in passing as "that dude in a wheelchair who opened for Bob Mould." THE PARAPLEGIC TROUBADOUR ran the headline of a *GQ* profile. Those are the terms on which people first confront him.

Even several of the authenticity-craving post-alt musicians who covered his songs on *Sweet Relief II*, a benefit compilation for disabled musicians, seemed to love the music only insofar as they coveted his myth. "Vic Chesnutt is a hero of mythological proportions," reads the opening of Live's Ed Kowalczyk's entry in the *Sweet Relief II* liner notes. "Red clay on the wheels of a wheelchair," Amy Ray of Indigo Girls writes in the pathetic poem that accompanies her group's contribution: "if Vic can't show what it's like to be a Southerner, nobody can."

Chesnutt has gone on record as disdaining the over-special treatment people offer the disabled, but in a sense he's received a version of it whether he wants it or not. He reacts to the mythmaking by pretending there is no myth. When I asked about it, he flatly denied its existence.

He informs me without irony that he wants his "every song to be a Wallace Stevens poem." He drafts and redrafts the lyrics to certain songs, and gets the most pleasure when people are impressed by his use of phrases like "load haulage," odd words like "sharpies," and references to obscure and/or weird cultural figures like Stryper, Deborah Norville, or publishing mogul Bill Lowery. "I think, 'Oh, I gotta write a song about Charlemagne,' or some shit like that, ya know? It happens all the time."

But if Chesnutt's a neo-hippie, he's a damn interesting one. He's certainly funnier, more irreverent, and meaner than any hippie I've ever met. He's also cool and smart enough to know when he's full of shit. "It's pretentious white-bread bullshit to write a song in the first place," he declares. "I try not to repeat. Maybe that's pretentious. I don't really care."

Plus he has short hair that's not even that messy. As we talk more, he gets misty over the Specials. A minute later he pours disdain on "those bastards," the Dutch, for inventing capitalism. (Did the Dutch invent capitalism?) Five minutes after that he starts getting damn ornery about his newfound sobriety: "I think I'm gonna start drinkin' again," he says with salivating resolve. "I think I'm gonna be a ravin' drunk. If I wanna sneak a shot a liquor tonight, I might sneak a shot a fuckin' liquor."

And maybe he did. The show that night is characterized by a boozer's disregard for anything remotely coherent. Playing with a gang of backing musicians that includes the drummer from now-defunct alt-country band the Jayhawks and an anonymous but great fiddle player, Chesnutt runs through a sort of greatest hits set that's disjointed and a bit labored.

It opens with Vic scraping out a timorous version of "New Town" on his miserably out-of-tune acoustic guitar, and ends forty minutes later with a fairly funny one-off version of "Hang On Sloopy." Vic wrangles his way around his guitar, hacking out chords and leads with a pick attached to a glove he wears on his crippled hand. And as recorded versions of Vic's singing suggest, his voice is about as comely as a made-for-TV *Book of Virtues* narrated by Stephen Hawking would be. Still, between his lyrics and labor, the fiddle player's gorgeous augmentation, and Tina's wry looks and dry leads, something beautiful slouches out of the dust: the end product works.

Even if there are dreary moments, execution really isn't the object here. As is the case at most Vic Chesnutt shows, the emphasis is on persona rather than performance. If it's not exactly Tamburlaine in terms of massive over-the-top-ness, it is convincing. Vic is funny and feisty; the lyrics come across; the set goes over great. The crowd is split between the converted and the curious, but everyone is sympathetic, except for a woman to my left who spends most of the show jabbing at her boyfriend: "I've seen enough, lemme go home!" Apart from her, we all leave happy.

It hasn't always been this way. Chesnutt learned how to create this unstable synergy back when he was "that dude in a wheelchair" opening for Bob Mould. "It took a lot of nights to figure out how to connect with them," he remembers. "At first, I was depressed because they wouldn't shut up and sit down and listen to everything I said and worship me.

"Then I realized that was, ya know, ridiculous. They owe me not one damn thing. I'm ruinin' their night, probably in more ways than one. Once I realized that, they started likin' me . . ." ●

THE PASTELS

Active since 1981, by the late '90s the Pastels were elder statesmen, their records being discovered by a new generation of fans via younger acts who bore their mark, particularly Belle & Sebastian. **DAVID BERMAN** (poet, singer, Silver Jew) interviewed the indie lifers in 1998. By fax.

It's a sad reflection on critics' knowledge that the singing of Belle and Sebastian's Stuart Murdoch is so monotonously compared to Donovan's; it should be clear to anyone who's heard longtime Glasgow legends the Pastels that Murdoch's biggest debt is to Stephen McRobbie, aka Stephen Pastel. He would tell you as much himself if he'd sit still long enough to be interviewed. He did, however, contribute the following testimonial for the recent Pastels album *Illumination*:

When I was a boy, and when Stephen was a boy too, my friends and I went to Greenock to see the Pastels play. I was drawn to all the shambly people I saw around, even though I was quite sporty. They knocked about Hillhead and

listened to strange music. I had a notion that the Pastels were kings of this strange music, but I don't know why.

The Pastels came on. People took quite a few steps forward. They embraced the punky sound, they listened to the tender words. The possibilities seemed endless.

Nothing much has changed, even though that was ages ago. They're still punk, and the songs are just as tender. But they are still learning about music. Every unexpected note in their new record sounds like a fresh discovery. And who else manages to pull that off every time? Nobody. That's why they are the kings.

Not long ago, a flurry of transatlantic faxes between David Berman and Stephen Pastel, Aggi Wright, and Katrina Mitchell yielded the following interview.

In the first one minute and 12 seconds of "Cycle," before you start to sing, did you know when you were going to come in? Did you know your lips were going to unstick and then you were going to say "sticking"? What were you thinking about while you were waiting?
Aggi: I knew, but not in terms of time. I didn't know my lips would unstick so audibly. I was dreaming about cycling up a mountainside of hairpins, stopping halfway up to eat goat's cheese, collecting hazelnuts in the woods.

Could you describe the most significant weakness you ever identified in your team, and how you remedied it?
Stephen: To be honest our team wasn't a team at one point—in 1989. That's the reason the original Pastels lineup split. We reconvened in a more solid way, based on the friendship between myself, Aggi, and Katrina.

How do you turn an occasional Pastels fan into a permanent Pastels fan?
S: That's impossible to answer, but I suppose I hope people will find things about our music that's exclusive to us, that they will be drawn in or intrigued and find us contrasting and slightly complex.

William Carlos Williams famously said, "no ideas but in things." Can you think of a Pastels song idea that started with a simple object?
Katrina: I'm sure modern lighthouses are quite sophisticated really, but the idea of a tower built on rocks with a bright shining light on top seems simple and romantic. One of the Seven Wonders of the World was a lighthouse. They're so lonely and romantic, especially since they've been mechanised. "Mechanised" is a Pastels song I wrote.

Tell me about the piano playing on Illumination.
S: For "The Hits Hurt," we asked our friend Bill Wells to go in and improvise over the outro. What he did seemed kind of random but also melodic. We asked him, out of respect, if he wanted a second go at it. Happily, he didn't. No one in our band is too precious about playing the keyboard parts, although we're all intent listeners. Katrina played most of the keyboards on our last two records.

My uncle handwrote a 24-volume history of June 18, 1984. I can't find your names in the index, so I wondered where you were and what you were doing on that day.

A: Happy to be packing my bags after my first year at art school in London to go home to Clackmannanshire. That may have been the first night all year that I didn't go to Alan McGee's club, and so I missed the Jesus & Mary Chain's first London (or ever?) concert.

Glad to be getting out of that flat that smelled of cabbage, where you'd stick to the kitchen floor because the Legend had spray-mounted his fanzine there, and perishing foam sprayed out of the plastic chairs, and the landlord kept you waiting to pay the rent while he buckled up his trousers.

In my luggage were two unfinished plaster sculptures—a head and a spine—life-size. That was also the year when the first Pastels Peel Session happened, and we didn't get asked back again till this year.

I realized recently why I have a hard time with classical music. The orchestrations seem completely out of scale with the environments I hear them in. Such epic music—with themes like marching armies, mountain ranges, and stratospheric ideals—played by a hundred people—sound absurd in a strip-mall bookstore or a coffee shop.

Then there's Journey or Asia, whose grandiose arrangements illustrate another problem of scale: the lyrics are about relationships, yet seem comically tossed around in a whirlwind of heroic keyboards.

How does your music address the proportion of components in a song, the proportion of the music to the environments it will be played in? And what kind of room/architecture does Illumination *most comfortably fit into?*
A: Our music is compact, for modern urban living, but it expands where necessary. Could be an old building, but we're not afraid to rip out old Victorian cornices. If it's a tidy modern loft you might open a secret cupboard and find all the junk the owner left behind. Either way it has a good view to the sky to watch clouds rushing by. Also good in tents.
S: I think we try to make music that sounds close. Close to each other and to the listener. So we're striving to make music that's stylish and slightly grandiose, without the bombast that often goes with that.

Does the Pastels' music look like Aggi's paintings, or do Aggi's paintings look like the Pastels' music?
A: At first my paintings looked like the music, but now the music also looks like my paintings . . . I think.
S: I think there's a strong correlation between Pastel music and Aggi art. There is a similarity of approach—maybe the core of this is almost a twisted folkiness. Some people have said Aggi's art is naive—a comment that recurs with regard to our music—but I don't think it's exactly true in either case. Although both demonstrate a certain rawness, I'd say it's more a matter of

choice and a preference for understating more sophisticated ideas.

But Aggi's art is completely fluid; it seems like she has an intrinsic grasp of the atmosphere of the music, and she'll often amaze us by visualizing it. On *Illumination*, I think we all felt the music was slightly more minimalist, and probably more European than on *Mobile Safari*. Aggi started taking out-of-focus photographs of her artwork. When she showed us them, we knew they implied a three-dimensionalism we felt we'd found with the music. Katrina spotted the shot that should be the cover, and it seemed so natural.

What other artists' paintings look like the Pastels' music?
S: I think "Yoga" or "Remote Climbs" is maybe like one of Tinguely's sculptures, or some other kinetic art. Katrina thinks some of our music is like her mother's paintings.

Do you have lions in your house?
A: Lions? I thought I had aliens, but it was Stephen making a funny noise. Actually he is a Leo.

What is your favorite Scottish cliché?
A: That Scottish people are friendly.

What part of the US is most like Scotland?
A: New York, except there are no drumlins.
S: In terms of its landscape and climate, probably the Northwest.

You said the new album sounds more European. I agree but can't explain why. Maybe it's the sound of cosmopolitan Poland—a more sensual vision of Poland than we're normally granted. Is this what you meant or am I off track?
S: If you think it's the sound of cosmopolitan Poland, then that's what it is. And I'm flattered.

What do you think is the legacy of the Butthole Surfers?
S: Bombast is okay. Sometimes.

I have a black eye, insomnia, and am in the early stages of gum disease. What physical problems do you suffer from?
S: I think I mainly suffer from a lack of sleep. It makes me look ill and feel irritable, unfocused, and hyper.

Who do you love?
S: Katrina. Aggi. My parents. ◗

WILL OLDHAM

By 1997 Will Oldham had made a career out of alternately delighting, tormenting, and baffling his audience—not to mention getting under the skin of journalists. But **ALEX ABRAMOVICH** caught Oldham fresh from jettisoning his Palace moniker and willing to talk about his past and present. Oldham gradually became less tight-lipped over the years, but at the time this was an unprecedentedly illuminating interview.

To me, "Palace" has always been a misleading name. Less a palace than a weird mansion on a hill, Will Oldham's music is full of false surfaces, semi-obscure passages, and sudden eruptions of violence. Since first hearing it a few winters ago, I've wandered through its halls somewhat obsessively, seeing traces of its architect everywhere, never catching a glimpse of the man himself. Throughout six albums and numerous singles, Will Oldham has worked to maintain his status as a cipher—afraid of nothing so much as having his own persona—or anyone else's—intrude on our perceptions of the structure he's built. By and large, he's succeeded.

In many ways Oldham's recalcitrance is absurd; this is a man who's connected to Kevin Bacon six different ways, in three easy steps, and who came to music only after turning away from a promising career in movies. Oldham's first love was theater; as a teenager, he studied playwriting at the Walden Theatre in his hometown of Louisville, Kentucky, and had a play produced at Washington DC's Kennedy Center. By the age of 16, he'd acquired a reputation as a promising if idiosyncratic young actor. His hangdog looks landed him a lead role in John Sayles's 1987 coal miner/union epic *Matewan*, playing a child preacher whose sermons are infused with an intensity that would later surface in Oldham's music.

Though he passed up subsequent opportunities in favor of returning to school, after a semester at Brown University Oldham dropped out and returned to LA. There, he played Jessica McClure's father in the 1989 TV movie *Everybody's Baby*, a melodrama about a little girl who fell down a well. His performance was generally praised (though Jessica's real father was quoted saying, "I didn't look that scruffy"), but his next role, as Miles in *Thousand Pieces of Gold* (1991), turned out to be his last. Disenchanted with acting, Will used the money he'd earned in movies to travel the country—sometimes working, sometimes not—back to Louisville, then on to Brooklyn, Rhode Island, and Cape Cod, where he suffered a breakdown (in our conversation Oldham refers to it as "fantastic internal trouble") that led him to

JOE OLDHAM

return to Kentucky. He alludes to this period repeatedly in songs like "Riding," "More Brother Rides," "We All, Us Three, Will Ride," "(End of) Traveling," and "I Am a Cinematographer."

I am a cinematographer / Oh I am a cinematographer / And I walked away from New York City / And I walked away from everything that's good / And I walked away from everything I leaned on / Only to find / It's made of wood

And I walked away from California / And I walked away from everything that shone / And I walked away from everything I lived for / Only to find / Everything had grown

Oldham had played in a band called Box of Chocolates during his brief time at Brown, but his somewhat lukewarm contributions to *Fearful Symmetry* (1990), their one album, gave little idea of what was to come. Re-settling in Louisville, Oldham, then 20, began making music with his older brother Ned and Ned's friend Brian McMahan, who had played in Squirrel Bait and Slint (he now fronts the For Carnation and plays in Eleventh

Dream Day). Some of what he'd learned in Hollywood proved useful, it turned out.

"The things I imagined acting could be but weren't are things I've been able to work with in music. They have to do with starting something at the beginning and carrying it through," Oldham told me. "It's a craft that takes practice and lots of work; you can't externalize it: it's part of everything. There's no difference between any activity of the day and a song, though the song is what gives activity meaning."

Together with McMahan and a fourth member—King Kong's Rich Schuler—the Oldham brothers formed a band they called Palace Flophouse to play shows around Louisville. Their sets consisted mainly of covers: Will remembers them playing traditional Irish songs such as "Carrickfergus" and a cover of Bob Dylan's "New Pony"—and a few songs that made their way into the recorded Palace repertory, among them "Valentine's Day" and "Riding." The latter is particularly interesting, as it embodies, even at this early stage, so many qualities found in Palace:

241

Who you gonna ride with, boy? / All dressed up and with that look of joy / Who you gonna ride with, boy? / I'm gonna bring my sister Lisa

Because I love my sister Lisa / I love my sister Lisa / I love my sister Lisa most of all

Don't you know that that's sinful boy? / God is what I make of him / I'm long since dead and I live in hell / She's the only girl that I love well / We were raised together and together we fell / God is what I make of him

This note of dark sexuality reappears later, now coupled with an emotional severity all but unparalleled in popular music. Thankfully (for Oldham no less than his fans), the severity is tempered by songs of painfully emphatic tenderness, as in "All Gone, All Gone" (from the *Hope* EP):

Oh I see you can shake that thing / Let's have some of it over here / It's tragic that your love is long crossed / But we can fix it up with some beer / It's a dream to just be here with you / One in the morning, just going on two / With nothing, nothing but . . . snuggle and coo / It's a good thing, a really cool thing to do

Once you hear Oldham's thin, cracking voice intone lyrics like these, it's a struggle to reconcile his gentle tone with the violent acts he describes in songs like "A Sucker's Evening," and even harder to understand the brutally stark language he frames them in ("make a noise, crack a glass / I'll hold his arms, you fuck him / fuck him with something / the fuck—he deserves it"), or "You Have Cum in Your Hair and Your Dick Is Sticking Out" (with its refrain of "she won't come; I'll be gone").

Looking back, what initially drew me to Palace was the sheer range of Oldham's songwriting. That his songs could accommodate such violently different emotional worlds seemed strange—almost paradoxical. But if Oldham's scope is remarkable, what songs like "A Sucker's Evening" and "All Gone, All Gone" have in common is their unapologetic intimacy. If the first pushes the form of the pop song deep into Flannery O'Connor territory, the second captures the simplicity and directness of words that might pass a lover's lips in the middle of the night. It's an intimacy Oldham is acutely aware of, and goes to great lengths to protect, even to the point of accepting his reputation as a brat, a pain, an enfant terrible.

How to Win Friends . . .

Having ditched the name "Palace" in favor of a billing as "Will Oldham, formerly of Palace," he is playing Tramps—a sizable and rather dismal club in New York City which tonight looks something like a lumberjacks convention. The vast majority of Oldham's fans,

EDIE VEE

it turns out, have beards, as do half the people in his band—not chic, Gen-X-facial-hair-type beards, but full-grown, Walton family–type fuckers. Oldham himself is clean-shaven, relatively short, and absurdly skinny. He's wearing old black dress shoes, black jeans, and a black T-shirt; he looks like a scarecrow in a SoHo storefront. A fluorescent orange baseball cap with "Vermont" inscribed on it is perched on his head; before going on-stage, Oldham will pull it low over his eyes, and trade his wing tips for a pair of dime-store flip-flops. When he pulls up a chair to talk to me, he pulls it up close. He leans forward, adopting a position he'll hold for most of an hour, maintaining direct eye contact through each question and answer.

He speaks slowly, allowing for long, uncomfortable pauses on my part, and long, comfortable pauses on his own. He's clearly anxious to be understood, a concern that carries over to his music.

"I hate playing live," he tells me. "That's not what it's about. It's about songs the audience can listen to at their leisure, at any volume, as many times as they want. It's about them getting something that becomes theirs, that they can use for whatever they want."

"So why are you playing this show?"

"Why?" He looks at me the way you'd look at a dim-witted child. "Because Drag City asked."

"But if it was solely up to you, you'd never play out?"

"Exactly. Though I also depend on it financially."

"Say you didn't, and no one else needed you to perform. Would you still play for people?"

"I only present the songs in a recording situation, or in a practice situation, or on a tour. I think maybe once, or possibly two times, I played songs on a guitar for the woman I live with . . .

"I write a song in order that I may record it and it can

become a record. Because that's what I feel like I do, make records. That's what I value. I don't like to go see music I have the records of. I'd rather see a live band—like the Jesus Lizard or a mariachi band or a band who exist to play live and don't ever make an effort to make a record that's different from what they do live."

When I read my transcription of this at home, I think about things Oldham's done in public over the years—things that have driven at least one major journalist, and one of his press agents, to tears—and it occurs to me they might be simply a way of maintaining the music's integrity. Oldham may protect his songs the way a bird hops around feigning a broken wing to distract a predator from its nest.

"His Oldship"

Do I really buy all that? Not fully. I understand there must be something in Oldham's nature predisposing him toward being an asshole. Interviews make him uncomfortable, and his natural reaction is to evade the media's glare. But it's also obvious that Oldham is fiercely protective of his music, and if he's sitting down and talking now, it may be because he feels that the reputation he has been building as a difficult interview, and the ensuing lack of sympathy that many journalists have for him, is beginning to cloud the perceptions of his listeners and potential listeners.

He must wonder what readers think when they see stories like the one entitled "Thrillbilly" in the *Dallas Morning News*, which remarked, "Oldham's got the duds and deportment, but his Palace is miles away from Appalachia." Referring to the subject as "His Oldship," it questioned "the sincerity of Palace's hillbilly routine."

This is a persistent line in Oldham's press. A reviewer in these pages thought that the first Palace album "came off phony," and a fanzine review of the recent singles compilation *Lost Blues and Other Songs* saw Oldham's "fake backwoods illiteracy" as deeply problematical: "Here we have a very articulate, literate cat trying to pose as a backwoods hick."

Mr. Popularity

What is it about Oldham that elicits such strong reactions, casting such shadows on the authenticity of both his songs and the mythology which has arisen around them? Certainly, his behavior in interviews, which has ranged from mere flippancy to outright fabrication, has hardly encouraged confidence in his sincerity. To cite just a few examples, he used to deny that he had ever had an acting career; when asked about it, he would claim his interviewer was deluded, even though *Matewan* is available at almost any video store. There was a period when he would only allow journalists to talk to

him if they'd agree to address him as "Push." Complaining that "reviewers are lazy," he's refused at times to allow review copies of his albums to be sent out.

Meanwhile, his live performances have become so well known for being erratic and difficult that it almost appears he's out to willfully try the patience of his audiences. Jason Loewenstein (Sebadoh, Sparkalepsy), who played drums on the third Palace album, *Viva Last Blues*, seems to think so: "With his live stuff, I do wonder what Will's trying to do by never playing with anyone long enough, or with anyone competent enough to be anything but a terrible distraction to his songs. His talent and abilities are immense, and he is really great at something very difficult, but I wonder why he adds all the distraction."

A number of musicians and industry people I spoke to went further, suggesting that Oldham is playing a game with his listeners' responses. Still, his shows are often brilliant, and the stunts he's pulled on journalists are just the sorts of things most rock writers (an often sycophantic bunch) would normally take as evidence of the romantically contrarian, individualistic streak it takes to convert adolescent misfits into nascent rock stars. Why, then, is Oldham's case peculiar?

It may have something to do with the discordancy between how intimate Oldham's songs are—the visceral responses they elicit in his fans—and his unwillingness to provide those same fans with a correlative to that intimacy outside the music itself. In an ideal world, perhaps the songs alone would be enough, but as Don DeLillo noted in his novel *Mao II*, "When a writer doesn't show his face, he becomes a local symptom of God's famous reluctance to appear . . . People may be intrigued by this figure but they also resent him and mock him and want to dirty him up and watch his face distort in shock and fear when the concealed photographer leaps out of the trees."

DeLillo is speaking of a character based on J. D. Salinger, but the words apply equally well to Will Oldham. We live in a consumer culture, where emotional investments should pay dividends. Conversely, we hate to have our emotional attachments mocked. Thus we may be secretly happy, or relieved, when the poet sticks her head in the oven, or the rock star blows his brains out, or the guitarist dies with a needle stuck in her arm. In the unspoken contract between artist and audience, giving one's life is the ultimate way artists prove their unfeigned sincerity. Yet not only doesn't Will Oldham have the decency to die for us—he doesn't even give good interviews. In his refusal to put out emotionally outside the context of his music, he violates the contract, fails to validate our emotional investment, and makes us feel he's mocking our attachment to his songs.

JOE OLDHAM

Expect the Worst

Of course, our attachments are misplaced in the first place. Ideally, it should be enough that the song has meaning for us, whatever Oldham's intentions. (Therein lies the tragedy, and irony, inherent in the cults of Sylvia Plath or Kurt Cobain—the cultists find the affirmation of their hero's work in their deaths, while the true goal of art can only be an affirmation of life.)

What makes Oldham's case more frustrating is that his reluctance to give forthright answers to a reporter's questions, or aim for consistency in live performance, has little to do with his being a contrarian or rugged individualist. It's that aforementioned reluctance to cloud the listener's mind with facts that are beside the point, plus a certain tendency to infantilism that seems inherent in his personality—this comes up again and again when I talk with those who have dealt with Oldham personally and professionally.

Before I met with him, I spoke with another writer who'd once been assigned to write about Palace; she told me to expect the worst.

"All through writing my article," she said, "I found myself calling Will things like 'precocious little shit.' During our interview, he displayed an unnerving concentration, and seemed to treat the enterprise with utter seriousness. But the follow-up interviews we'd agreed on quickly dropped to the level of farce. It was as if part of him wanted desperately to connect, to use me as a mouthpiece, while another part did everything

possible to derail the project. One minute he was demanding to see my notes and complaining no one had written a serious article about him—the next, he was blowing off a scheduled interview for an unscheduled road trip, without so much as a call or forwarding coordinates. One minute he was a thoughtful, articulate artist; the next, a little boy."

It's typical of the way Oldham presents himself in public. Onstage at Tramps, he looks like a child channeling a force that lies wholly outside him. His body twists out of time with the music. His flip-flop-clad feet writhe around each other like those of a gunshot victim, or someone in the throes of passion. Often as not, he concludes a song by throwing his hands high in the air—a gesture at once comical, endearing, and grand within the confines of an indie-rock show.

Yet for all his dismissals of playing live, Oldham at his best is not at all self-conscious before an audience. Not only does he have it in him to be a consummate performer, he's the sort of performer who doesn't enter the fantasies of his audience: he enters his own private world and draws his fans into it. To see it is beautiful.

Songwriting, Part 1

The irony in all this is that where Oldham stumbles in performance and interviews is precisely where his music soars. The very qualities that make him frustrating to follow, and have alienated many of his fans and supporters in the media—the strange, contradictory stabs at creating a personal mythology, the tendency toward being willfully obtuse and willfully vague—are the same qualities that make him so effective as a musician. In songwriting, he knows just how much to hold on to and how much should be given away. His lyrics almost add up, but never quite, and you get the feeling that's exactly how Oldham wants it: he stops short of meaning something, making you think it means that much more. His elliptical music and spare, sometimes skeletal, arrangements do the same.

Still, he writes brilliant, evocative songs that are unlike any others. Their biggest debt is to Neil Young, but it's a debt Oldham repays in an odd way. Despite his fondness for waltz time, his country inflections, and a voice so paper-thin that when it cracks (as it often does) it feels more like a rip, his songs are ironic in a way Young's could never be—in a way no other songs are. Pavement, the Pharcyde, the Feelings—all have realized the irony inherent in making music today, but in each case, the epiphany was short-lived. Following after postmodern writers, and making the same pratfalls, these bands ended up writing commentaries on the state of music itself. Their songs were interesting, and often brilliant. They were smart, and funny, and we could pat ourselves on the back for getting the joke, but if they were affecting, it was in spite of themselves. At their worst, they betrayed a deep forgetfulness of why music means something in the first place.

Will Oldham, on the other hand, is unique in that, while he understands irony as well as Steven Malkmus or Robert Pollard, he uses irony against itself, as a shortcut to sincerity. This, to my mind, is Oldham's peculiar genius as a songwriter and lyricist—to adopt an emphatically ironic approach to an emphatically sincere genre; it has enabled him to take a tired music that had fallen prey to clichés and sentimentality, and restore it to its former glory.

Take a song like the aforementioned "All Gone, All Gone," whose power derives from the tug between sincerity and ironic distance; part joke, part love poem, part just plain weird, each verse alienates the listener just enough so that when the chorus kicks in—pure Neil Young, "hey heys" sung over and over again, with female harmonies so sincere they bring tears—you're reminded of the music's power to infuse simple syllables with a power out of proportion to what they signify. A graduate student would probably call what Oldham is doing an application of Brechtian principles to popular songwriting. Anyone else would call it beautiful.

For a better example, look at the last, best, and least accessible Palace album, *Arise, Therefore*. By the time it was released in 1996, Oldham had taken Palace through so many changes—the lo-fi anachronisms and self-conscious Appalachianisms of *There Is No-One What Will Take Care of You*, the one man/one guitar folk of *Days in the Wake*, the relatively straightforward country-rock of *Viva Last Blues*, and the gorgeously lush, synth-drenched songs on the *Mountain* EP—that it was hard to imagine what direction the next album would take. As it turned out, *Arise, Therefore* was a violent departure from anything Oldham had done before—in some ways, from what anyone had done before.

Arise is a deeply unsettling album—personal, naked, stark. If Oldham's previous records came close to the bone, this one cuts right through. Melodies are stripped to a scattering of notes. The same two-note lick is repeated over and over, with Gastr del Sol's David Grubbs, at a distant-sounding piano, sounding out subtle variations on the same accent while Oldham's thin, weightless voice floats above it all like a balloon hovering over a fire. Underneath, however, is the steady, unyielding clank of a hopelessly archaic drum machine Oldham picked up somewhere and used on every track of the album. Jason Loewenstein, who saw Oldham perform live with the contraption, describes it as an "awful-sounding sequencer/drum machine thing." On the album, it is ever-present. Unabashedly mechanical, its effect—so against the grain of everything else Oldham and his band are doing—is disconcerting and disorienting.

Ultimately, though, the machine anchors the album in a way a drummer couldn't. Its beat is so unyielding, so inhuman and severe, that the personal and musical struggles Oldham is working through on the album are thrown into high relief. After a while, the machine's indifference begins to resemble the indifference of fate. Its effect is disconcerting enough to make us pull back from the songs, allowing their impact to be evenly distributed. One gets the sense that without the machine the music would crack under its own weight—too unsettling to play, too unsettling to absorb, so our first instinct would be to recoil from it as if from a dangerous animal. But Oldham pulls back enough to let the songs slip under our defenses, and under our skins. His restraint allows the music to rise above the genre's usual melodrama, to acquire a dignity beyond what we've come to expect.

Songwriting, Part 2

To pull off something like this requires a degree of craftsmanship, a sense of balance, and a real talent for manipulating the listener's responses. It explains, to some extent, Oldham's preference for keeping his music within the confines of the studio, where he has the highest level of control, and his aversion to playing live, where the wiles and whims of the audience can't help affecting the quality of the performance. Most of all, it

explains the nature of Oldham's relationship with the press; why he is reluctant to explain what his music means, or enter into a relationship where the balance of power is shifted inexorably away from Will—away from the music.

In fact, Oldham does spend an almost inordinate amount of time honing and shaping his songs. Listening to him describe his manner of composing, one can imagine the speaker as a sculptor rather than a songwriter. Here's Will's description of the genesis of one of his songs: "A song like 'The Weaker Soldier'—the last song on *Arise, Therefore*. Which started off as a chord—the opening chord. Then, it had a line, I think, which was 'I once was a lonely soldier.' Then it took six or eight months to put the verses together. At one point it was a 12-chord song—now it's a four-chord song. And it had this supercomplicated melody . . . it was getting more and more complicated, and then some of the verses I took away, and I'd go to another set of notes, get parts for a new verse.

"Probably a month before recording, I simplified the melody, simplified the chords, got the drum machine, started working with it and taking it into the studio with Grubbs and my brother Ned to work out the final arrangement."

The song that emerged is so simple one would scarcely recognize it from Oldham's description. Look carefully, though, and you see how forcefully the lines have been shaped, how much has been left out, and how much the song gains from it:

I once was a weaker soldier hanging in the war / But I left, like an ape, folded neatly in four / And silently played for a moment slow, and bled / On a sandalwood bust I had / Where was the field where I had pressed another down / Where I had revealed myself by crying and shouting? / I turned away from that and into this / Black kettle of one-ness

What is left is almost surreal—all allusion, so vague you have no clear sense what Oldham is singing about, so perfect you can't imagine it being another way. Hearing it is not knowing what hit you, but knowing you've been hit. And when Ned Oldham's voice comes in on the chorus, echoing Will's, who now pulls ahead, now lags behind his brother, Ned's lines begin to sound like an inverted hallelujah:

I have not been feeling the same / I am not fit to carry your name / I am not fit and I am not willing / To go on

The words are simple, but as the Oldham brothers shuttle them back and forth, like some just-found precious truth, they are transformed into something resembling a myth: you don't know quite what it means, but that it means, and means a lot, is inescapable. "The facts?" Oldham says when I ask why he used the drum machine on *Arise*. "Do you really want them? Facts just float on top of everything that's important."

A New Man?

The general response to last year's announcement that Palace had broken up was a scratching of heads. After all, Palace had changed so much over the years, both musically and in terms of personnel; Oldham's presence seemed to be the only constant throughout the band's career. Rumors abounded as to what would come next. I heard people at parties claim that Oldham was taking the drum machine from *Arise*, adding a Casio, and forming some weird, Folk Implosion-y techno band. A guy in a Manhattan record store told me Oldham aimed to abandon the softer side of Palace in favor of the straight-ahead rock songs that had cropped up on *Viva Last Blues*. Most likely, it seemed, the man would simply climb more and more into himself—get more and more obscure, more and more vague—taking off in weird directions, leaving his fans ever farther behind.

Oldham stopped playing under the name Palace, he claims, out of a sense of pride in what the musicians he played with accomplished, and a desire to seal those achievements off and preserve them, closing the narrative to go on to the next. "I felt really bad over the past couple of years," he says, "even playing under the name Palace. It was fine because it was supporting a record that was made before, but I don't see the connection between live music and recorded music."

"All the records are the property of all the musicians. They demonstrate the ability and originality and brilliance of everyone who plays on all the recordings. Their ability to interpret music, to play. When I listen to the records, I'm blown away by the musicians. So part of it is out of respect for those records and for the efforts of everybody, to let those stand forever as they are. Because who knows what will happen, and now those are an enclosed unit nobody can touch. And I can't fuck it up.

"I could fuck it up if I played as Palace. I didn't want the show—whatever the show was like—to affect how people heard the records."

Given the way Oldham has consciously shaped the Palace narrative over the years, it's a generous and fitting end. Longtime fans, however, can draw solace from his first solo record, *Joya*. As it happens, *Joya* (Oldham tells me the name pays homage to a favorite Minutemen single, "Joy") is not the radical departure one might have expected. The production's a little fuller on certain songs (though some are as spare as anything Palace did), the sound's a bit warmer, but elliptical lyrics, dragging waltzes, familiar sidemen, all put in an appearance. True, *Joya* doesn't sound quite like any Palace record—but then, no Palace record sounds quite like another. If there's a difference between *Joya* and what came before, it's one of temperament, less a clean break, more a tying up of the loose ends that trailed those records. *Joya* is more settled, more stable, than earlier recordings. Oldham's vocabulary hasn't necessarily changed, but the voice is steadier, more certain. The recurring references to folk and country traditions, held over from Palace, have acquired a weight and validity they lacked before.

If the last Palace albums were searching, unsettling shots in the dark, *Joya* is the sound of someone who's come into a light place, found some small truths there, and returned to share them. Oldham's voice has matured, and now possesses a confidence missing from any Palace release (Oldham tells me he's actually come to enjoy singing in public).

While Palace songs were interrogative, new songs like "O Let It Be," "Open Your Heart," and "Be Still and Know God (Don't Be Shy)" are framed as gentle imperatives. Moreover, Oldham's acquired a wryness, a playful self-awareness, rarely hinted at in earlier releases.

"I Am Still What I Meant to Be" (which contains the lines "I know I lied to you / But when did I ever say I'd tell the truth") may be a love song; but it could just as well be directed to Oldham's fans.

I'm Set Free

Jason Loewenstein's experience of playing with and listening to Will Oldham gave rise to some interesting observations:

"Will called me out of the blue one day and said his brother Paul had mentioned me as something of a drummer, and that he was going into the studio three days later to make a record. He sent me a plane ticket and I went to Birmingham, Alabama, for three or four days . . . there, I kept thinking about Bob Dylan's album *Desire*. It's one of my favorites, and I was thinking about similarities I saw between Will and Dylan. The clever lyrical twisting, the self-made working-class image, the insanely confident, laid-back attitude, and the way no two versions of his songs had exactly the same thing going on vocally: there didn't really seem to be a 'best' way to do it . . . Dylan was able to do that real well.

"I also thought about Will's acting background and wondered if he used it in everyday life. Whatever it was, it was clever, and he was making songs on a par with the best.

"A mystique this thick wasn't really worth figuring out—but I thought about it anyway."

As I sit listening to *Joya* one more time, I think back over Oldham's career to date—the years of concerted effort put into protecting and manipulating the Palace narrative, and how the parts of that narrative segue into one another, the limits that must impose on Oldham . . . and I get a sense of new vistas opening up for him. I'm reminded of Lou Reed singing, "I'm set free / To find a new illusion," and I feel sad and happy for where Oldham's been, and for where he's going. ☻

BELLE AND SEBASTIAN

Belle and Sebastian emerged in 1996 and, by the following year, had charmed their way onto stereos far from their native Glasgow. The band shunned most press, a fact that played no small role in their becoming one of the era's most talked-about indie acts. In a three-part article about the then still-mysterious band, **JENNY TOOMEY** explored the band's burgeoning myth, while **FRANKLIN BRUNO** and **ELISABETH VINCENTELLI** checked in with reports from New York after the group's first Stateside appearances.

SEPTEMBER 1, 1997. The Tsunami tour van is speeding westward, and every night, in every town we play, I meet kids playing bootleg tapes of Belle and Sebastian records, trading thirdhand anecdotes about the band, and figuring out how to get back East for the band's first (and so far only) US shows at this year's CMJ Convention in New York City.

Clearly, the buzz is on for the Scottish band, and for them it's an exciting—and dangerous—place to be. Exciting because Belle's success up to now is almost completely a reflection of this kind of grassroots, word-of-mouth support. Dangerous because they're now attracting the attention of scenesters and music-industry types who sense the next big thing. The transition from grassroots support and indie buzz to mainstream critical acclaim and commercial success is one that happens with the rarity of visiting comets, and with the same force of combustion.

Despite B&S's well-earned position in the hearts of tape-trading music fans, they are also the latest lure in a tornado hipster underground whose ability to identify new talent, kiss ass, and wield superlatives is matched only by the speed with which they amnesiate, raise anchor, and wax pejorative.

Furthermore, such accelerated fame lends itself to the worst kind of hyperbole and misinformation. Young artists promoted like this are almost always promoted superficially, while critics fall over one another to plagiarize press kits. Most often, this brings undeserved good fortune to a mediocre and unprepared artist, lucky to be puffed into 15 minutes more fame than they would otherwise receive, circumstances of climate/romantic association/drug addiction notwithstanding. So flavor-of-the-minute artists find themselves catapulted into a mainstream spotlight with lots of hype and no sticking power. Take an unseasoned singer-songwriter like Hayden—not untalented, but manifestly incapable of living up to the magnified expectations generated by the bombastic gush put forth by his handlers. Every year yields so many examples, it's easiest to reference Darwin and move on.

Belle and Sebastian are a different story, being very successful before they are truly well known, and much, much better than their flattering, two-dimensional write-ups so far would have you believe. Word count aside, most journalists haven't gotten near their genius. The forty pages of press I've read for the most part boil down to three points, at best insignificant, at worst misleading and wrong: (1) they sound like Donovan; (2) they put themselves down in a familiar indie-rock "loser" way (most noted in US press, quoting weak lines like "We're not photogenic / We don't stand a chance"); (3) they are arrogant, literary, and clever—"a new Morrissey" (common in the UK press, where these killer couplets are oft-quoted: "You liberated / A boy I never rated / Now he's throwing discus / For Liverpool and Widnes").

Based on these shallow observations, Donovan + Morrissey + grunge add up to genius and musical success. Huh? Belle and Sebastian's principal singer and songwriter, Stuart Murdoch, may or may not owe something to Donovan, Morrissey, and Cobain, but dropping those names doesn't explain why B&S are heating up dubbing decks across the nation. Clearly it's time to step past the press kit, ignore the lazy copy, listen to the band's songs and their fans' reactions, and begin piecing together a more accurate representation of Belle and Sebastian's singular strengths.

A fourth point often mentioned, which does have a bearing on the band, is that they're extremely reluctant to engage in self-promotion. The members have done very few interviews; they don't encourage photos of themselves (recruiting friends to pose for their press photos); and they avoid playing standard commercial shows, preferring to play awkward venues, frequently churches. Their two New York shows are set in a former synagogue.

Several months ago I fell into the favored, if now apparently extinct, category of "chosen interviewer." What it amounted to was half an hour of polite conversation and cagey one-sentence answers from Stuart David, the band's bassist and the author of *Ink Polaroids* (a tiny book of "photographs with a cheap old pen"—stick-figure drawings with anecdotes representing significant moments in the band's history). David was absolutely charming, but he revealed even less about the band than their press kit, which weaves a tale so steeped in luck, fate, and general "hey kids let's put on a show"-ness as to give the Commitments a run for their money.

The story goes something like this: The band's other Stuart, Stuart Murdoch, picks up a guitar at age 24 in Glasgow and starts writing songs in his bedroom. He gets the name Belle and Sebastian from a French children's TV show that was popular in the UK in the early 1970s. He falls in with a talented bunch of students, dole recipients, and cheap laborers/musicians. In early 1996, they scrounge some time in a state-subsidized recording studio and record an album's worth of songs. As luck would have it, the resulting tape lands in a local college's music-business course, taught by Alan Rankine, formerly of Scottish duo the Associates. One thousand copies of an LP, *Tigermilk*, are released as part of a course project on how to put out a record. The records sell out in 15 minutes and the masters are destroyed, elevating the band to near-legendary status. They then accept a couple of record deals, first with ultra-cool UK indie Jeepster, later with the ambitious, ill-defined, and now-defunct EMI boutique label the Enclave in the US. They release another, even better album, *If You're Feeling Sinister*, on those two labels, plus a couple of UK-only EPs; this time, the records stay in print long enough to fuel the buzz that makes their CMJ showcase so sought after. All sheer happenstance, you see.

Since my first attempt at an interview netted little more than Stuart David's muffled voice saying yes and no into my tape recorder and explaining how the best thing about being in Belle and Sebastian was seeing salmon jump from a lake on a recent band excursion, I try to schedule a follow-up call. It never materializes.

Stuart D. had warned me that B&S were already tired of doing press. Stuart Murdoch—as Belle's chief singer-songwriter, the most prized target of every hipster journalist—had already ceased doing interviews the month before. This move confirmed his repeated statement that he and the others were "anxious to make this band a reflection of our lives, rather than life itself." Shortly after, the other members followed his lead.

That's a shame, because Murdoch's few published interviews reveal him to be even more sophisticated, sincere, and hysterical than his lyrics (and dense, Faulknerian liner notes) suggest. In them, he devotes equal time to emphasizing the importance of the group as a whole ("I'd been hoping for some sort of band for a long time before. That was what I wanted to achieve"), and making fun of his newfound fame: "I have a list of desert-island discs sewn into the lining of my underpants, just in case I get run over and they have to read it out posthumously."

It doesn't surprise me that Belle and Sebastian have escaped adequate description, and not just because they refuse to lend us writers much assistance in our quest. Though any journalist with a thesaurus would be reluctant to admit it, a band can defy characterization.

I'm not going to avoid band comparisons myself, but I think I can do better than Donovan, whose only point of comparison to Stuart Murdoch is a slight similarity of vocal timbre. When I first heard B&S, before fascination really took hold, they reminded me of the Velvet Underground. Of course, so many bands get compared to the Velvet Underground that the comparison may seem worthless, but I don't mean it the usual way. B&S are not like the Velvet Underground because they play the stripped-down, psychedelic, schlocky, frat-party jam-rock of open-mic nights and talent shows (they don't). Nor are they like VU because they have a slightly flat, poetic, beshaded, lipless frontman (which they also don't). Nor have they a trash-can-battering androgyne or a viola-wielding Fluxist in the band, though they do run to two art degrees and a modicum of strings. They do owe a musical debt to the Velvets—from gentle yet barbed ballads like "Fox in the Snow" to the organ swirl propelling "Lazy Line Painter Jane"; and they've been known to encore with a cover of "What Goes On," too. But the most striking parallel is that they're the first band since VU to capture consistently a sort of song I associate with early Velvets, which I'll call "story song."

The most obvious VU story songs are the "Says" songs ("Lisa Says," "Candy Says," "Stephanie Says"). Remarkable for their amoral, clinical detail and economy of language, these songs paint broad, three-dimensional character sketches in short expository sentences that are not exploitative. By expository I mean that they quote or describe a character in a way that represents their complexity. For example, "Candy says I've come to hate my body and all that it requires in this world." Or "Stephanie says, she wants to know, why she's given half her life to people she hates now." By contrast, exploitative lyrics will use character for metaphoric or associative potential, without allowing them human complexity (personality, voice, etc.). A clear example of an exploitative lyric is the chorus of the Counting Crows hit "Mrs. Jones." (This song so saturated commercial radio you'll probably have heard it no matter what your musical tastes.) In "Mrs. Jones," the singer refers to a Spanish dancer. We learn she is "Spanish" only for the exotic associations to that stereotype, not to develop her personality or character. Ultimately she is only in the song to respond to the narrator/singer as reflected in the hook and punch line of the chorus, which repeats "She's looking at you / No, she's looking at me" ad nauseam.

In a less obvious form, the great majority of pop/ rock/rap lyrics are exploitative. The "you" in Kiss's "I was made for loving you" only exists in relation to the narrator's affection, for example. The "Stone Temple Pilots" in Pavement's "Range Life" are only described as "elegant bachelors" to imply something specific about the narrator's relationship to rock stars . . . and so on. Whether it's a function of the narcissism built into rock's bombastic history or a "desire to influence" that has carried over from rock's origins in religious music and folk protest music, it's undeniable that most contemporary rock musicians write songs whose lyrics talk exclusively about themselves and express their own beliefs, with characters who are rarely more than two-dimensional figures, appearing as if labeled with their function. The reverse is true of the characters in Belle and Sebastian's songs; maybe that's why Stuart Murdoch's songwriting stands apart from the navel-gazing, punch-line moralizing of most contemporary rock.

The opening lines of "Stars of Track and Field" (the epic first track of *If You're Feeling Sinister*) perfectly introduce his brilliant expository writing. "Make a new cult every day to suit your affairs / Kissing girls in English, at the back of the stairs / You're a honey, with a following of innocent boys / They never know it / Because you never show it / You always get your way." There's

no clear punch line to this lyric. "She" isn't produced for a specific moral or narrative end, to prove a point. She just is: sitting in the middle of the song in her ambiguous complexity, a complexity she retains over the course of the song, whether she is "on her back," "in college," or "liberating a boy."

The only characters presented in two-dimensional, "exploitative" terms in B&S songs (as in VU songs) are authority figures. It isn't just the Vince Guaraldi-ish piano part in "Seeing Other People" that brings the TV version of *Peanuts* to mind. The "major" who "doesn't understand and doesn't try" and the "nobleman" who "looks down on me like I was never born" (in "Me and the Major"), or the employers and teachers in "You're on Top of the World Again," are cut from the same cloth as the gibberish-wielding parents and teachers who hover offstage, heard but not seen, in those old Charlie Brown specials. In both cases the adults and authority figures are outside the central story lines; sometimes speaking at the main characters, but never to or with them. No wonder story songs often open a window into an obscured, sometimes seamy, always private "young insider" space.

In Velvet Underground songs, Lou Reed talked about heroin, S&M, cross-dressing, and self-destruction with the casualness of one who lives in that world. When I

251

BELLE AND SEBASTIAN
If You're Feeling Sinister
(Enclave)

Morning, and I still haven't slept, having spent the night nursing a bleeding right nostril while packing my belongings for the afternoon's 18-hour train ride. I'm in the midst of an all-American low point—returning home from college with a hot-off-the-press sheepskin in one hand and zero prospects in the other. It feels worse than I anticipated. All that's left in my room is my stereo, and all that it plays is Belle and Sebastian's *If You're Feeling Sinister*.

Packing for summer breaks in the recent past, I always played Pavement's "Box Elder." Triumphant, cocky, brazen, the song snarls about ditching town, the world ripe for tackling, etc. . . . It was ideal when I could tell strangers "I'm a university student" rather than "I live with my parents, teach kids tennis, and hack my way through articles about rock music." Packing up for good, now that loserdom has officially struck, I can't stop playing *If You're Feeling Sinister*'s centerpiece: "Ooh! Get me away from here I'm dying/Play me a song to set me free/Nobody writes them like they used to/ . . . You could either be successful or be us . . . we don't stand a chance." Granted, most of the record avoids such overt, slightly cheap self-deprecation, but a sentiment of defeat hovers over all the band's work, perhaps most prominently displayed in Stuart Murdoch's pretty-as-patter sigh. On their sophomore full-length, Belle and Sebastian never wallow in pain; instead the Scottish band rip your heart out, smile at it, buffer it in lush arrangements, and wait for the Nick Drake tags to roll in.

Belle and Sebastian's soft charm also points to Donovan ("Like Dylan in the Movies" even taking its cue from the Donovan-via-Dylan *Don't Look Back* documentary), an influence reflecting the band's national heritage and tender aura. With seven musicians forming around Murdoch's vision and vocals, the group's delicate approach hardly meets current conventions. The pianos, strings, and horns (brass via a keyboard, it sometimes seems) floating through the album are neither padding nor pageantry. They help the band give off a honed, urban-folkie timelessness, making the project a kind of wimp Neutral Milk Hotel UK.

Belle and Sebastian's commercial approach, or lack thereof, furthers the anomaly. On record, Murdoch never cowers from a pop leader's forwardness, but publicly the band duck promo shots, interviews, and big-money ambition—their debut album being released by a music-as-business class taught by a former member of the Associates. This one was

heard those records in junior high, I sensed, even without understanding the lingo, their danger. The songs channeled the same hedonism and flat, amoral images I was decoding from graffiti, passed notes, and first sexual fumblings. Belle and Sebastian's *If You're Feeling Sinister*, with its matter-of-fact references to homosexuality, drugs, sexual/physical abuse, and suicide was the first record in 15 years that gave me that feeling of insider access again.

Writing songs on controversial subjects is hardly new; what makes Belle and Sebastian songs unusual is their juxtaposition of difference and transgression with lines about bike rides, dancing, lovesickness, aspirations. "Taboo" subjects are neither sensationalized nor brought up to prove a point. In *Tigermilk*'s "She's Losing It," an irrepressibly joyful tune is paired with disturbing opening lines: "Lisa knows a girl who's been abused/It changed her philosophy in '82/She's always looking for a fight/She keeps the neighbors up all night." When the trumpets (half Herb Alpert, half Mexican-restaurant band) kick in a second later, I can't help tapping my feet to the improbable chorus: "She's losing it, oh yeah she's losing it." Nothing in the song leads the listener to an obvious conclusion about the girl, her abuse, or her response to it. The song simply presents its story with a sort of intimate tact.

The moral ambiguity in B&S songs is heightened by deliberately non-specific mentions of sexuality and age. Murdoch is an equal-opportunity-romantic raw nerve, singing with intimacy about both boys ("We lay on the bed there/Kissing just for practice/Could we please be objective/'Cause the other boys are queuing up behind us," in "Seeing Other People") and girls ("On a beech tree, rudely carved NC loved me. Why did she do it?/Was she scared?/Was she bored?" in "Do Something Pretty").

Murdoch is 28 now, but he still sings with frightening accuracy about the horrors of school. And his lyrics are lifelike in their matter-of-fact detail and unresolved story lines. Joy and loss coexist casually and without irony; at the same time, they spare us the moralizing.

Music writers frequently compare Belle and Sebastian to lo-fi bands, and as regards the best aspects of basement music, that's absolutely correct. Belle aren't slick, perhaps aren't even especially skilled players—certainly, they prefer evocative takes to note-perfect ones. But they avoid the crude sameness of many lo-fi bands, producing instead a rare combination of immediacy and sophistication.

Although the rest of the band are mainly overlooked by the press, it is not false modesty that drives Murdoch to declare, "Each individual is equally important to our sound. When I take the songs to the band, they come alive."

The contributions of the other members may become more apparent with future releases and tours. The recent *Lazy Line Painter Jane* EP features Isobel Campbell's fine alto trading verses with Stuart M. on the title track (though typically she's credited under an assumed name); another Belle boy (unidentified in the liner notes) steps to the mike for a spoken-word-ish story piece. It's great to see them trading roles and sharing the spotlight and it makes perfect sense, given the band's egalitarian philosophy. As Isobel explained in a French interview this summer, "The groups we've admired seemed to function as a family . . . they always gave the impression that powerful things were happening inside the group . . . that it wasn't just a singer accompanied by musicians." The camaraderie and collaborative environment she refers to are clear from the few group interviews there have been, and from their live performances, too. I hope they stick to it, even though Murdoch's lyrics, melodies, and singing—which far outshine those of most current songwriters—suggest that barring drastic change he'll continue to get the lion's share of the attention.

In an always misquoted lyric from "Get Me Away from Here I'm Dying," Murdoch sings: "Play me a song to set me free / Nobody writes them like they used to / So it may as well be me." Many critics have lazily used this line as a blunt tool with which to pound him squarely into the round hole of the self-deprecating loser as cool, cynical post-grunge songwriter. It might be more interesting to ask who he's referring to as "they"? Whose work do Belle aspire to match? Perhaps the critics would point to Donovan, though he was little more than a voice. There are other contenders, most obviously Nick Drake, whose music is distilled/tender and raw/sad like B&S's: but despite vocal similarities between Drake and Murdoch, Drake is less emotionally and musically expansive—and he's far less accessible. Morrissey, another contender, writes songs as witty and well crafted as B&S's, but his muse is a deliciously selfish, myopic, whiny one. (Even a somewhat generous Morrissey song like "Sing Your Life" presents a clear ultimatum: be more like him.)

Belle's songs, on the other hand, project outward. They want "to sing the saddest song" ("Boy Done Wrong Again") so that others can sing with them. And they want others to sing a song so they can sing along ("You're on Top of the World Again"). They urge the listener "Do something pretty while you can" ("We Rule the School"). In a recent BBC radio broadcast, they dedicated that song "to Nadia from Colsen, because life

first released on a label called Jeepster, also the title of T. Rex's most touching song. In the US, *If You're Feeling Sinister* is on EMI boutique label Enclave—a word for a distinct cultural force enclosed in foreign territory. Both monikers apply perfectly.

—*Jay Ruttenberg*

BELLE AND SEBASTIAN
The Boy with the Arab Strap
(Matador)

Last year's *If You're Feeling Sinister* was a remarkably complete record. While it wasn't officially the Glasgow band's debut (that was the limited-edition *Tigermilk* from 1996), *Sinister* was the first thing most people heard. It was a grand entrance. A pocket orchestra—eight people playing guitars, bass, drums, piano, trumpet, cello, organ, and various exotic instruments—shaped careful and momentous folk-pop. Stuart Murdoch's singing was boldly fey and he wrote with a literary edge. At once breezy, catty, and realist, rummaging through influences, then pushing them out of the way, this was catchy pop at its most sophisticated and nimble. It was not indie potential: it was a world fully formed.

So now what? How can they surprise us again?

They don't, of course, and that will be a slight disappointment the first time through this record. But you'll love it the second time. The arrangements and musicianship are still intricate, natural, deceptively gutsy. Murdoch continues to find variations on pure tunefulness. And his lyrics are always surprising.

As Murdoch swells melodies with his soft, lispy voice, he doesn't tell stories so much as describe his people: delicate, arty outsiders trying to keep their individuality as they function in the world. There's sadness in the struggle—the sham artist who has a stroke at 24, the woman who gives her "time and insanity to people," the girl "too frumpy for the teenage population." He finds freedom in indolence—wasting away the summer, he remembers the sky as "blue beyond compare." He's not a moralist or a meticulous observer; his songs are rarely straight narratives. Rather, they flow between sharp-tongued commentary, deadpan raciness, and religious and sexual ambivalence. He's literary, but he's not trying to be a poet; just someone who can spout long runs of verbiage and mold them into unforgettable melodies. You could never hum "The Asian man with his love-hate affair with his racist clientele"? You can now.

The music hasn't changed. It's built around acoustic strumming; bouncing soul-style bass; flat, quick rhythms; and various keyboard/ horn/string colorings that weave in and out.

GAIL O'HARA

All is done with utter cohesion and economy. The effect is sunny and pleasing, and the band are rhythmically strong, too, a fact that often goes unremarked. They give Murdoch's hooks real punch; and when asked, they can rock with professional abandon. Listen to the way a tight, buzzing lead guitar pushes "Simple Things" to an unusual pitch of emotional intensity; or the way electro-pop synths bubble quiet and weird through "Sleep around the Clock," eventually rising to a strong, controlled instrumental break.

The arrangements also save a couple of these songs from turning into formulaic strum-pop. "Ease Your Feet into the Sea" and "Dirty Dream #2" have no exceptional hooks. But the former is deepened by strings, bells, and piano popping gently around each other. The latter's Motown beat is lifted high by a horn/string duet folding seamlessly into a sawing solo violin, then returning to float through the outro.

It's too soon to guess how this record will measure up over time. I am amazed by the band's balance of energy and polish, their ability to combine musical variables without sounding self-consciously eclectic. There's room for Murdoch to focus his eye more sharply, but I can wait for that. Belle and Sebastian have achieved something rare: bored in their Northern town, idling on the fringes, they've imagined and created an original music. I hear moments of antecedent—a horn part from Love, a guitar progression from Nick Drake, some of that dreamy Felt sound—but I never think of them in terms of influence or history. They're friends playing for themselves. And we can't stop listening.

—*Steve Tignor*

isn't easy for a 16-year-old in the middle of nowhere." Compared to most rockers whose emotional palette rarely strays from the cynical or narcissistic, Murdoch is an oasis (no pun intended) of passion, enthusiasm, and hope. These idealist themes contribute as much to Belle's "out of time" quality as any '60s musical aesthetic could—maybe that's why their music seems to have more in common with figures like Bob Dylan and Patti Smith than with the superficial psychedelic-folk ghetto to which the press keeps consigning them.

Belle and Sebastian's lyrics evince a greater thematic range than I've indicated here. Work themes, for example, run through many of the songs. I'm often reminded of Patti Smith's "Piss Factory"—not only because of the acid disgust she directs at the workweek, but because she speaks from a place of innocence, betrayal, and ultimate transcendence. Her character doesn't hate her factory job just because it's boring or beneath her. She rages at the work for dulling her drive, obscuring hope, quashing ambition—and, in the song's pivotal gesture, she vows to do something about it. Several B&S songs, especially on *Tigermilk*, have a similar impetus, and while Belle are less aggressive in reaching for transcendence, they're also coming from a different historical perspective. Their recurrent themes of aspiration, enthusiasm, and quiet persistence in economically depressed, disenfranchised, isolated Scotland might well be the '90s equivalent to '70s punk rock and a more flamboyant, confrontational US sensibility. In "My Wandering Days Are Over" Murdoch exposes conflicts between work and art, sympathizing with a friend: "I saw you in a Japanese restaurant / You were doing it for businessmen on the piano bar / You said it was a living hell." And the album's liner notes explain how guitarist Stevie was "chain-ganged by employment training," but "still sang Negro Spirituals as he built footbridges over the Dumbartonshire marshes."

There are also religious themes in Belle and Sebastian songs, whose expression evokes Bob Dylan at his best (*Blonde on Blonde*, *Blood on the Tracks*), avoiding both the folk proselytizing of his early work and the later religious proselytizing. Critics tend to miss these, and even a (simmering) lapsed Catholic like me didn't pick them up at first. This isn't surprising, given the understandable mistrust of religion within much of the rock world, the counterculture at large, and the intellectual community. But, like it or not, there are repeated religious references (even C. S. Lewis quotes!) in B&S songs. In everyday life, Murdoch sings in a choir and has a job as superintendent of a church; in return, he gets a place to live and a place for the band to practice. But even though B&S state in an early interview that "a lot of [the songs] try to be quite spiritual" and a

Murdoch line advises "lowly youth and bankers alike" to "get back to the Church!" we tend to think they only play churches for the acoustics.

It's hard to say why the religious element is so ignored. B&S's representations of faith should be seen as an alternative to the paltry spiritual platform of contemporary rock. This music offers a spicy alternative to spiritual absence; to bland, antiquated fundamentalism; and to the new macho-hip religious underground with its modern-relic baby-tees and straight-edge, abstinent, two-dimensional morality.

However one assesses the religious element in Belle and Sebastian's songs, it's clear that they never proselytize or pontificate. Questions of faith take their place among descriptions of discos, high school, underwear, weddings, crushes, arguments, bus journeys . . . And after all, Murdoch isn't saying faith is the answer, since elsewhere he also sings: "If you are feeling sinister / Go off and see a minister / Chances are you'd probably feel better / If you stayed and played with yourself."

All this is Belle and Sebastian—plus passion, humor, good looks, and the catchiest melodies in town. But I'll leave it to others to throw laudatory adjectives in those directions. I'm giddy with the power of their language. If the critics could move on from their favorite self-deprecating "we're not photogenic" line in "Get Me Away from Here I'm Dying," they might notice that the key to Belle and Sebastian's gift is the pregnant confidence of the song's final lines: "'Good-bye,' said the hero in the story / 'It is mightier than swords / I could kill you, sure / But I could only make you cry with these words.'"

—*Jenny Toomey*

LIVE FROM NEW YORK

Dear Jenny,
The venue was great, a former synagogue that's now a Jewish arts center. I didn't quite get the story on what usually goes on there, but it wasn't this. Nice big stage for the eight of them (including a trumpet player who would walk onstage for his parts and go off somewhere the rest of the time), and a disco ball in whatever the recessed part at the back of a synagogue is called.

You quickly get a strong sense of their individual personalities. Stuart Murdoch is skinny, a bit jug-eared, confident while singing/staring out but otherwise diffident—when he switched to acoustic guitar or piano he'd forget to turn his electric guitar down, resulting in feedback the bassist would have to go fix. He did this several times, as if oblivious to the equipment aspect of things.

The other guitarist seems like the anal musical-director guy, and you can definitely sense already a tension (mostly on his side) between him and Stuart—jealous that everyone focuses on the singer. He was the one likely to shoot someone a look if they fucked up, and the only one who acted onstage as if he cared whether anyone thought he was cool. The bassist just seems a geeky student type who fell in with a talented crowd—he was fine but didn't seem like a great musician or anything. The keyboardist is geeky too, but is probably the best player (save the drummer) in the band—surrounded by electric piano, a Moog, and a couple of organs. He seemed as excited as anyone about playing.

The two women switched off a lot—cello and violin, recorders on "Judy and the Dream of Horses," bass on one song, various keyboards. The stockier one seemed very nervous, and the Edie Sedgwick/Jean Seberg one (who also sang a little) seemed bored and disdainful, especially when she had to play tambourine—she just went and sat on an amp. My traveling companion, Daniel, who was over on their side of the stage, reckoned they weren't very confident players, mostly adding texture.

The trumpeter, as I said, came and went as if he had no particular stake in being onstage. The drummer is older, and a bit of a ringer—very solid, seems like he's played a lot longer than anyone else. He is Scottish, though. I listened to the records again and tried to figure out if it's him playing or if they hired him for live stuff, but I can't tell—the drumming on the record isn't obviously sloppy. Without him, I suspect a lot of the songs would fall apart live.

The players, switching off, would often show each other parts right before they played a song. There's a synth riff on "I Could Be Dreaming" that "Edie" (I guess her name is Isobel) was learning from the keyboardist and never got right through the whole song, and when Sarah (the violinist) played bass, the other guitarist nodded or shook his head every other note until he was sure she knew the song (a new one). In another context, I'd find this annoying, but it didn't seem like calculated incompetence (given that the arrangements are so elaborate), and I was charmed by the fact that even though this was a hugely anticipated, industry-crowded show, the band had not overprepared. Most songs ended with long, building vamps—Stuart would say "last time" as loud as his singing (i.e., not very loud) into the mic and everyone would stop, usually pretty tightly.

They opened with two unrecorded songs, one with another chorus about buses, the other long and Dylanish. They did another two later, one called "Seymour Stein" and one I can't recall. (Reportedly, between this show, the one the next night, and their PBS taping the previous day, they didn't repeat any recorded material and did at least ten new songs, and I believe they've done yet others for Peel Sessions.) Their set here included "Fox in the Snow," "Get Me Away from Here, I'm Dying," "I Could Be Dreaming," "My Wandering Days Are Over." There was at least one other from *Tigermilk*—I can't remember which.

They did a slower version of "Seeing Other People" with Murdoch, the guitarist, and Isobel singing a verse each, then doing the last chorus in rough harmony. Isobel changed "You're going to have to go with girls, at least they know what they're doing" to "at least they know where to put it," while giving the audience a withering stare. On "The State I'm In," Stuart changed the line about Marks & Spencer to Sears & Roebuck for us Americans, except he said "Rosebuck," which I found endearing. Otherwise, the arrangements were very close to the records.

Before the last song, the guitarist said something about always wanting to do this song, but it was like bringing coals to Newcastle to play in New York: then they closed with a tight, energetic "What Goes On," for most of which Stuart just danced, joining in on the chorus. This was the one where Isobel played tambourine, looking around at the others as if to say, Boys . . . It didn't get sloppy, didn't go on too long, and as Daniel said, "stopped on a fucking dime."

Obviously, the above is just descriptive, but in case there's any doubt, it was a wonderful show, with more sense of event than I've seen in a while, making my hassle in getting to New York and playing a crappy showcase the previous night, paying too much for parking over the three days we were there, worth it. They were excited to be there, but they weren't obnoxiously ingratiating. Of course, the pop-maven audience was in rapture . . . lots of lyric-mouthing. I do suspect the band have a limited lifespan—either they'll get too slick after a couple of records, or the guitarist will leave. Murdoch is obviously wildly talented; I get a sense these subtle narrative songs pour out of him. He's imagining and describing little moments in the lives of characters, and grander themes, if any, fall out of that.

See you in November,
fjb

Note: The above is a slightly revised e-mail (based on notes from my tour diary) I sent to Jenny Toomey a few weeks after seeing Belle and Sebastian in New York at CMJ in September. As such, it isn't a formal review, but an attempt to convey some information about an exciting event to an interested friend.

—*Franklin Bruno*

I MEAN, WHAT'S THE DEAL?

No small part of Belle and Sebastian's allure derives from their mysteriousness. Not only do they not appear in their promo photos; not only is their first album now impossibly rare, but the band hardly ever play live and when they do, it's in non-traditional venues—their two New York shows were in a Lower East Side synagogue. They were the most anticipated performers at this year's CMJ convention, with people wandering around trying to get tickets to the sold-out events. Even more surprisingly, the band were invited to record a set for the PBS television show *Sessions at West 54th Street*, whose guests are usually more musically mainstream, and better known.

Live (or as live as you can get in the frigid Sony Studios where the show is taped), Belle and Sebastian focused on their guitar-driven songs, and turned out to be, well, a jangly-pop band—albeit with better-than-average lyrics, a wonderful singer, and good arrangements. (My neighbor described them as being like Felt with a Scottish accent.) The only time they didn't sound like the records was when singer Stuart Murdoch forgot the lyrics to "Mayfly" and ground to a halt. Upon which someone sitting in the first row whipped a copy of *If You're Feeling Sinister* out of his bag and obligingly loaned it to Murdoch so he could read out the remaining lyrics. That was when it all became clear: not so much Belle and Sebastian themselves—they remain blessedly opaque—but why they have suddenly acquired quasi-mythical status.

Belle and Sebastian's appeal, in addition to their admittedly good music, may be partly explained by a certain desire—or need—to create an event out of a mostly acoustic band in a year when acts such as Prodigy and the Chemical Brothers got most of the attention. In 1997, nobody really thought about guitars, unless to compare them unfavorably to electronics. For many, idolizing Belle and Sebastian is an offensive move—a way to say that traditional bands are still worthy of debate and attention, and that their traditionally structured songs and sense of narrative are still relevant at a time when these very notions are being messed with by electronic music. It's also a way to reclaim a certain grassroots directness in contrast to the perceived hyping of electronica by major labels and the press: Belle and Sebastian's popularity is fan-based, and spread through word of mouth, not as the result of heavy rotation on MTV or articles in *Details*. Did I mention that the copy of *If You're Feeling Sinister* proffered by that helpful fan was vinyl?—*Elisabeth Vincentelli*

THE MEKONS

Two decades after forming, the Mekons—improbably—were thriving. Their long game—as an art collective that reached beyond punk, and beyond music itself—was coming into focus. **NEIL NEHRING** reported on the band's mid-'90s outpouring of records, writing, and art. Meanwhile, **BOB POMEROY** examined Jon Langford's flourishing career as a painter and comic-book artist.

LAST YEAR, the Mekons released their most challenging, most experimental album yet. Simply entitled *Me*, it's a dive into the muck of cultural narcissism, inspired in part by the legacy of former Prime Minister Margaret Thatcher's creed of greed. Guitar-less, country-less—in fact quite urban, sonically ("We went and got some of those young people's records," jokes Jon Langford), *Me* wasn't easy for longtime fans: no anthems, few sing-alongs, but it just might prove to be the Mekons' *Exile on Main St.*, as mature artists at the height of their powers throw everything they've absorbed into one dense pottage that takes a while to absorb. And with the reissue of their 1980 album, *Devils, Rats, and Piggies*, on Quarterstick, virtually the entire Mekons catalog is now on CD—an unlikely prospect not long ago, when a number of the band's recordings were collector's items.

This musical activity comes on the heels of three adventurous and strikingly varied projects: the *Mekons United* book and CD, an endlessly stimulating retrospective collection of the band members' painting, fiction, criticism, and music based on an exhibit unveiled at the Polk Museum in Florida, that has since traveled to New York and England; *Pussy, King of the Pirates*, an obscene paean to grrrl power composed and recorded with the late novelist Kathy Acker, who performed it onstage with them, heroically, just two months before her death; and the *Theater Piece for Rock Band* show organized in New York by performance artist Vito Acconci. The ambitiousness of these multidisciplinary projects indicates the Mekons' continuing vitality, however much the first two were reviled by a parochial, largely conservative rock press who wanted, as Langford puts it, "a normal album with 12 songs on it, like we needed to be shepherded back into the fold."

Langford, probably the band's most visible member in the US (he lives in Chicago), also released *Skull*

THE MEKONS
Me
(Quarterstick)

"There's a kind of standard Mekons-type lyric, which is very personal . . . We wanted to attempt a different kind of song, that would be incredibly impersonal . . . A title like *Me* [is about] the creation of Self in a modern capitalist culture where Self isn't a whole, organic thing but fragmented, dislocated. A person's Self is as much created by advertising, pornography [etc.], which bite into what a person is." —*Tom Greenhalgh*
(*interviewed in* Rebel Route)

What was it about this band that made you love them in the first place? Was it their drunken, melancholy abandon? Emotionally eloquent lyrics hitting home on subjects like romantic agony or late capitalism or existential angst ("you have the right/to lie awake at night")? A sense of strength found in weakness, a realization that imminent failure is no reason to give up? Or maybe just a whole lot of really great tunes?

Whatever you love most about the Mekons, you'll find little of it here. *Me* is a concept album on fragmented identity and alienation, topics you'd expect this bunch to work wonders with. But concept overwhelms content, and the results are . . . well, fragmented and alienating.

The Mekons, one of the great bands of all time, occasionally yield to a "self-deconstructive" urge that really screws up a good thing. It happened once before, in the early '80s, when they put out crappy sub-PiL noise records like *Devils, Rats and Piggies* or *This Sporting Life*—just before the brilliant run of focused masterpieces that extended from 1985's *Fear and Whiskey* to *Curse of the Mekons* in 1991. This tendency resurfaced with *Pussy, King of the Pirates* (1996) and has continued into *Me*: an arty avoidance of anything coherent, seemingly motivated by boredom and a notion that their best work is too conventional.

From a band known for triumphant mastery of the song form, *Me* has no real songs. In their place are rhythmic word/sound collages with layered grooves under spoken-and-sung lyric bits apparently assembled via ye olde cut-up technique; plus a lot of goofing on pornography and consumerism, recitations of shopping lists, dildo catalogs, etc., with mostly dirgy tempos reminiscent of the *Fun '90* EP—minus the fun.

Many of the tracks seem deliberately unfinished, as if they shied away from

Orchard in 1998, an album of highly personal songs, at once angry and evocative, that call on his South Wales roots; and published *Great Pop Things: The Real History of Rock and Roll from Elvis to Oasis*, a collection of comic strips he co-created (under the name "Chuck Death") with satirist Colin B. Morton.

In addition—besides playing in hard country band the Waco Brothers, releasing a collection of Johnny Cash covers (*Misery Loves Company*), and producing records by Welsh punk band 60ft Dolls and fellow Mekons Eric Bellis and Sally Timms—Langford attracted considerable attention with his paintings—darkly gorgeous yet defaced depictions of country-music icons. A show at the Yard Dog gallery in Austin during the South by Southwest music conference even had Sire Records' Seymour Stein pledging to bring Langford's work to the attention of the Rock and Roll Hall of Fame (the Mekons—in there?!).

Hall of Fame or not (as Langford notes, "It's still tough at the bottom"), this blooming of his own projects and those of the Mekons leads him to agree that the general trajectory of the Mekons' twenty-year career has been upward: "It's been jumpy, but we didn't see any reason to stop if we were still interested; after all, we didn't have corporate jobs to go to!"

Certainly this world-class raconteur has reflected a good deal lately on the Mekons' improbable longevity—so unlikely considering, as he sardonically puts it, "We're not really very popular." The group's persistence even occasions cynicism: "The curse of the Mekons is that the Mekons ever existed in the first place. We bear the curse of the Mekons by actually being in it. You realize you've spent your entire adult life doing something 95 percent of the people on the planet would consider completely futile: 'Are you still doing that?'"

The band's twentieth anniversary, however, most often roused a sense of pride based not only on past accomplishments, but also on the burgeoning projects of the present. In explaining two works—a painting and a song on *Skull Orchard*—entitled "Tom Jones Levitation," inspired by a fellow native of Wales who remains an icon there, Langford acknowledges that his band's perseverance has a good deal to do with the subjects of the music (and of his paintings). Jones is "someone I'm interested in in the same way as Bob Wills: they weren't people who have this amazing 15 minutes of fame, and then just drop dead, [leaving] a beautiful memory you can idolize. It's like Johnny Cash: you have to make sense of an entire life, rather than just a little career. I don't want to be like a basketball player. The message I was getting in England in the late '80s, after the Mekons and the Three Johns, was: 'You should stop doing this—dismantle the first 15 years of your adult life you've spent playing music, and stop, you're too old now.' And I thought, 'Wait a minute, that doesn't make sense.'"

The Mekons' refusal to give up the good fight has something to do with the way every album is "a big social thing," Langford says. "I get to see all those people when we work, and they're some of my best friends." That conviviality is captured in a tribute to the group by critic Greil Marcus: "In a world ruled by a language one refuses to speak, they are a reminder there are still people one might want to meet."

With band members dispersed between Chicago and Leeds, the collaborative process has become harder, and *Me* required a more intensive approach. Langford went to England in order to spend a weekend in Leeds just working on lyrics. "It was a total party . . . We wheeled out people from our past and got them to talk about what they liked about the band, and we wrote down what they said." A couple of Langford's cousins arrived and were "egging us on; we were sitting around a computer drinking as much as we could, shouting stuff out; they were laughing and going, 'Hey, you've got to put that in!' So all the things we'd normally say 'That's too ridiculous,' we kept."

The rawest lyrics on *Me* (like the entirety of "Come and Have a Go If You Think You're Hard Enough") bear witness to this process. Some songs were written in the studio, when Sally Timms brought in her own material "and insisted on reading it all over everything. It's perfectly pornographic rubbish, but it kind of made sense of it."

Was it an issue to break from the band's collaborative mode with *Skull Orchard*? Langford shoots back: "You mean I fucked it all up by doing an album on my own?"

But he agrees "it's a bit weird. Everything else I've done, even the Waco Brothers, has been a big collaboration." Yet having already written several songs about South Wales, based on his own experiences, "it didn't seem to make sense to do anything with those but put them out under my name." Making a solo album also reflects the fact that "moving from Europe to live in America has had an isolating effect on me. It gave me a lot of time on my hands, at first."

More importantly, perhaps, becoming an exile "changed who I am; I'm a different person since I came here." Hence the interest in Tom Jones: there is a parallel in his and Jones's leaving Wales, and in their periodic returns to a homeland that's suffered a decline all the more noticeable from a more detached perspective: "I go back over there and go 'Aaah! What's going on here?' For the people who were there all along, family and friends, it's crept up on them. But I left Wales in 1976, and it's very different now; it's as

MARTY PEREZ

completing a thought lest they wind up too normal. At best, this approach can be enigmatically evocative, but on a song like "Come and Have a Go If You Think You're Hard Enough," it sounds lazy, pointless, and a waste of a good idea. And the less said about little-more-than-their-titles space fillers like "Whiskey Sex Shack," and "Back to Back"/"Belly to Belly" the better.

I'd like to think the band are acquiring new ideas through experimentation that they can later execute in another run of masterpieces. But even if that turns out not to be the case, while they may squander their talents, they can't deny them, and they're simply too good by now to go back to their early-'80s nadir. The abstract landscapes of *Me* are strewn with tuneful bits and richly textured with folk instruments (much Honeyman-style fiddle, and the most ubiquitous use of sax since Kaleidoscope broke up) and the occasional undeniable dance beat.

Personally, I'll hang on to *Me* just for "Tourettes," a stellar track that caps the album's ambitions and flaws with a driving reggae riddim, spooky electronic sounds, a ludicrous Greenhalgh rap, and Sally Timms hilariously reciting bits of some bad porno story alternating with the aforementioned dildo ad. Somehow it all works: it's both eerie and funny, it stomps all over the Nirvana song by the same name, and you will never, ever hear it on the radio.—*J Neo Marvin*

if someone kicked the shit out of it."

During their 18 years in power, Britain's Conservatives dismantled social services that dated back to the election of a Labour government in 1945, and essentially tore the country apart, offering Wales only what Langford calls "phony investment," involving massive tax breaks for Far East electronics companies and the like "to get people off the dole. They say, 'keep the labor cheap; Wales is booming'—but it's made Wales like a Third World country."

The actual subject of "Tom Jones Levitation" is a disaster that occurred in 1960, when a coal mine's slagheap collapsed onto the school in Aberfan, killing many of the village's children. The tragedy left a deep personal mark on Langford, one that makes it clear why a solo album was necessary to deal with Wales: "I heard it on the radio, on the way home from school. I was the same age. If I'd been born twenty miles away, it would have happened to me." A "hideous piece of negligence on the part of the Coal Board," Aberfan always reminds him that the "people who allowed that to happen are the same sorts of people still in control. The level of neglect is still there, the lack of caring."

The social aspect of the Mekons' collaborations involves much more than their famously inebriated camaraderie—a carry-on that tends to obscure what is, in fact, a serious theory of artistic production derived from an academic grounding in the European avant-garde. Langford, Tom Greenhalgh, and Kevin Lycett (who has returned to the Mekons after a long absence, and played a crucial role in the *Mekons United* project) acquired their commitment to collective collaboration at Leeds University in the mid-1970s. (Later, Greenhalgh and Langford went back to Leeds to complete their degrees in art after the release of the Mekons' second album in 1980, when the band seemed moribund. The next album, *The Mekons Story*, though a retrospective collection, marked a renewal and a preparation for the subsequent *English Dancing Master* EP, a first step toward the immortal *Fear and Whiskey*.)

Along with future members of the Gang of Four, the soon-to-be Mekons studied at Leeds with T.J. Clark, once a member of the Situationist International, who would move on to Harvard and Berkeley on the strength of putting the history into art history. (Marcus, in *Lipstick Traces*, cites Clark's *The Painting of Modern Life* for its Situationist-inspired defense of the continuing subversive potential of popular music, however much some critics might claim the genre has now been commercially co-opted.) Another important influence at Leeds was

Terry Atkinson, whose long-standing collective Art & Language has recorded with Red Krayola, and inspired the Elvis painting (credited, typically, to the Mekons as a whole) on the cover of the great rave-up *Mekons Rock 'n' Roll*.

Atkinson and Clark stressed, in essence, the integration of art and social life that defines (or ought to) the avant-garde past and present. In Clark's conception of "theory-practice," as Atkinson describes it in *Mekons United*, theory was not a lofty academic abstraction, but a matter of how artists talked and what they talked about regarding both art in general and specific artistic practices. They "placed a little more responsibility on the artist," Langford recalls, than just "paint paint paint, don't talk, then some critic turns up and tells you what it is" that you've done. Instead language—including critical reflection—and art practice should be closely related: Atkinson refers to a closely linked trio of "talk/ practice/writing." The Mekons have adhered to the whole model, not just fraternizing and making music, but also collectively authoring *Living in Sin*, the novel about their experiences as a band (included in *Mekons United*). In this light, the *Pussy* project with Kathy Acker seems an obvious development rather than the sidetrack condemned by rock critics.

Langford says he was once told by a record-company executive to "dumb it down" in interviews because the "average listener" doesn't care about "intellectual stuff." In fact he makes a subject like the relation of theory and practice in art sound as lively as some ribald anecdote. "For me," he says, "the theory's got to be in the practice, got to be implicit in what you're doing," not something separate from the work of art, whether an album or a painting. "I think that's a lot of what Tim Clark was talking about, and Terry Atkinson as well. You fail to some extent if your work doesn't explain itself." Theory means "using all the tools you have. If you study Marxism in the 1990s, not everything Marx said will apply, but it gives you a series of tools to help you analyze the world. They're not at the front of your mind, but they're part of what you are. You become geared to thinking in certain ways about things. Sometimes your quick and immediate responses to problems or ideas can be very useful" because of this underlying knowledge.

"For the Mekons, it's like looking and seeing the possibilities of things. We certainly don't wait around for the muse to hit us, but we don't plan everything in advance either, like 'the next album should be something that illustrates the theories of da-da-da.' What we do is more like trying to raise questions." In practice, he explains, the Mekons build albums starting from a title, or an initial concept on which everyone agrees, such as "Me" or "The Curse."

The Leeds background, stressing give-and-take as the basis of "theory-practice," makes it clear why the Mekons have taken pains at all times to present themselves as a collective artistic entity, "a negation of ego," as Tom Greenhalgh once put it. The intention here is to refute the idea of the isolated individual genius, whose originality makes him superior to the crowd and to cultural forms contaminated by commerce—an anti-democratic conception at heart, and one that at times (in the earlier part of this century, for example, at the height of modernism) has taken on distinctly right-wing, even fascist overtones. This conception of the artist, which originated with late 18th-century Romanticism, remains largely unchanged, thanks to the worshipful way art and literature are still commonly taught: just try free-associating to the word "artist" with most people you know.

In keeping with their rejection of romantic notions of originality or authenticity, and their emphasis on collective creation instead, Mekons songs and paintings alike have long been credited to the group. There is no central figure in the band, Langford insists: "Name a Mekons album and I'll tell you who's central on it—it's always changing. People have said to me, 'Ah, that song you wrote is really great,' and I'm like: 'Which one? I wrote some of it.'"

If you know anything about the Mekons, of course, you'll know that they're hardly meek characters. They push each other a lot. Langford admits: "I live in constant fear of Tom's intellectual rigor, or Kevin's vicious sarcasm, or Eric's sexual capacities, or Sally's fierce . . . everything." As a result, their method is far from any bland, lowest-common-denominator, consensus-seeking procedure; among other things, it represents an attempt to enrich the creative process by getting past the limitations of any individual's ego and abilities. The group's emphasis on the social over the individual thus combines artistic and political commitment: in this light one understands clearly why Langford would single out former Conservative leader Margaret Thatcher's statement that "'society doesn't exist, we are all individuals'" as her most malevolent moment.

An artist, whether a painter or a punk musician, does not "exist in a vacuum," says Langford. "Notions of 'genius' reinforce this myth of originality—when there's actually a history to everything. Anything I do, there's millions of decisions that've been made before me, and have nothing to do with me," that affect the outcome. It is never the case, he reiterates, that "the muse comes out and touches you" and inspires an original vision: "If we write a song, how could we write a song no one else has thought of? There's never a song that's never been sung."

In fact, a primary reason for his interest in Bob Wills

and His Texas Playboys (he recently assembled an album of covers, *The Pine Valley Cosmonauts Salute the Majesty of Bob Wills*, for Bloodshot) is that "they more or less covered everything—if they'd had a rapper they would have covered everything."

Langford declares he's not dismissing artistic efforts to break new ground, but suggests that claims to innovation are largely posturing, though the desire to distinguish new sounds from what's come before is understandable, even legitimate: "There's always a Year Zero mentality. Techno has that now. It's absolutely fine—there's a point where you have to feel that. When punk rock happened we thought we were tearing it up, and writing the book from new. In my mind, time still falls into before '77 and after '77. I'm sure it happens with every generation, and right now with kids doing techno." But "when you get a bit older, you get past that tear-everything-up attitude."

Romanticism also shows up in popular music in an obsession with authenticity, or freedom from commercial taint, exemplified by the puritanical preference of some music fans for independent labels. Langford doesn't entirely disagree with that stance: "Christ, two of the biggest crises of my life have occurred when I've been on major labels, when I've actually signed a contract, when I've suddenly found myself in impossible situations. I don't think I could do it again." Yet despite his traumatic experiences while signed to major labels, and although he praises Touch & Go/Quarterstick, his current indie label, for fairly lavishly funding a break-even (at best) project like *Mekons United*, Langford believes that you can't make an absolute distinction: in the final analysis "there's no real difference between independent and major labels—you can get a crook running any of 'em."

In general, he says, he's not interested in notions of authenticity. "When is country music authentic and when does it cease to be authentic? That's a blind alley. What's inauthentic about the Spice Girls? For me, they're completely 'authentic' as a very interesting reflection of the power structure that's involved in what they do." The Mekons took up country music in the 1980s, he explains, not because it seemed authentic, but because it seemed to offer a more direct response to circumstances at the time. He finds the same social realism in much reggae, blues, and some folk music, with the notable exception of Irish music oblivious to Belfast "or anything that's happened in the last hundred years."

"There's a directness in honky-tonk music, in its attempt to deal with reality. That's why I like Merle Haggard. Here's an American artist using the word 'class' in his songs. Everyone slags him off as a right-winger.

Maybe he is, but he's possessed with a need to deal with things head on."

For Langford, the most interesting music is made "where cultures rub together," and he believes this hybridity (whether in Welsh punk bands like the 60ft Dolls or in the Mekons pillaging everything from country to urban dance music) is where the health of popular music lies now. "My exile" and the resulting music, he jokes, "are much more authentic. I authentically fucking don't know who I am."

Issues of authenticity are also the crux of Langford's paintings, and a source of their power. Commenting on his depictions of country musicians signing their first contracts, he says, "A lot of the paintings have the theme Optimism vs. Nostalgia: I show the people looking out optimistically at the start of their careers. And then we look back nostalgically . . . an equally naive thing to do."

The medium is the message, too, in that Langford makes the paintings look "deliberately fake-old," part of the nostalgic effect.

His technique is also a reminder of the commercial status, from the start, of the hallowed heroes and heroines of country music: "That's why I use fake gold paint. It's cheap, bottled acrylic paint, meant to look like gold, and then I fake-age the painting—I rub dirt on it. It's actually a cathartic thing, destroying a nice picture, 'cause that's what happened [to the musicians]."

The intention is not "some damning critique of these stupid people," though; it's to suggest "that what they did is quite amazing," given the music-industry juggernaut they were up against. "One of the reasons I came to America is that it's a treasure trove of neglected culture. And my paintings are like little adverts for American culture—the good things about America."

For all his reflections on the politics of theory and practice in art, Langford stresses, finally, that in live performance the Mekons have resisted contriving a confrontation or engaging the audience in intellectual exchange. "I've seen bands try to do that; it seems to me much better" to treat a gig "like a Friday night out with the band playing. The very act of doing it this way is an attempt to break down the barriers"—the classic punk project, plus not talking down to the audience.

But, once again, he's being ironic: the Mekons, far from being "cursed," have clearly chosen to accept the modest commercial success entailed in sticking to their principles. Without being romantics about it, they've never sought to be big stars ("Why does everyone have to buy the same record?" asks Langford). When the band signed a deal with A&M in the late 1980s, he explains, it was understood that the sales objective lay in the twenty- to thirty-thousand range, which *Mekons Rock 'n' Roll* did in fact achieve. The problem was, the executive who signed the band left the label, and his replacement decreed that the Mekons "were not doing too well; we've only done twenty-five thousand on this record."

To Langford, it did sound good: "I pictured twenty-five thousand people—each with a copy of our album. It would be like going to see Leeds United play and each person in the stadium holding a copy of our album!"

He's totally clear-eyed, though, when he says: "It's not missionary work, what we do; it's not preaching; it's a business."

Far from lamenting the relatively limited size of the Mekons' audience by the standards of huge corporations, Langford's ultimate conclusion about the band's business is that besides each other the Mekons have met "a whole bunch of people who, if you can be bothered to find them, are in it for love, fun, and thrills—like us."—*Neil Nehring*

JON LANGFORD

Shortly before his final exit, Hank Williams stopped to pose for one more publicity shot. Standing by some fairground hay, he smiled over his shoulder at the camera as he shook hands with a grinning Fan. The Fan guffawed and reared back, his arm extended in electrified delight while the camera caught the thousandth back-slapping yuk of Hank's career. Not long after that, both Hank and Fan faded away. Only a black-and-white photo remained to mark the occasion.

Forty years later, Jon Langford sees the photo and bases a portrait of Hank and the Fan on it. He adds some color but avoids the gaudy pastels of a Nudie suit, opting instead to fill in the black-and-white gradations with dull, earth-tone acrylics. Langford's brush lends a certain depth to the figures' features, animating their tics and twitches with finely etched black lines. The Fan's western shirt is emblazoned with serpents, a third eye opens on his forehead. These words adorn the picture frame: "There is no end I can't pretend that dreams will still come true / A slave to a heart of stone I can't escape from you." The original publicity shot's suggestion that somewhere there's a heaven built on the rock of fame gets reversed, and Langford charges it with a sense of mortality as funny as it is grim. The Fan's grin, the look in Hank's eye, the secret joke they seem to share: Hank's made his deal with the devil, and the Fan has come to collect his due.

Over the past few years, Langford has painted roughly thirty portraits of honky-tonk heroes from the golden days of country music. For the most part, these figures now lie in their graves. Following the same approach he used in the Hank Williams portrait, Langford draws from old publicity shots to render the images of Ernest Tubb, Bob Wills, Hank "Sugarfoot" Garland, and others. He fills the negative space around them with red, orange, and gold ponies, skulls, guitars, and other cowboy iconography. He finishes the surface in dim lacquer, taking a razor blade to many of them at last, lending a time-worn

MARTY PEREZ

effect to the paintings that makes them appear to have hung in some dingy bar for the last fifty years.

They seem to hang in one particular bar, as a matter of fact: Tootsie's Orchid Lounge in Nashville, where the walls are lined with ghostly promo shots of Opry stars who used to drink there. "When I first came to the States in 1988, I went to Tootsie's and saw all those pictures—photos of singers I knew and others I'd never heard of, staring out of layers of historic snot and nicotine juice," Langford has recounted. "They were all torn—but all smiling out hopefully."

If Langford had settled for reproducing old promo shots, these paintings might depict a sort of quaint country-music hero worship; but he almost always pushes the paintings into thematic leaps, often inscribing the frame with fragments of song lyrics or found

phrases. Throughout his work, two themes persist: cowboys and death.

The pictures may look like folk art, but Langford's painting is neither "primitive" nor "naive," to use the terms that come up in descriptions of the work of pure folk painters like Joe Light, Mose Tolliver, or Howard Finster. Those painters are mostly self-taught, but Langford's work, for better or worse, betrays more technical skill. Much folk art looks depthless as a road sign (often a source of its charm); but Langford has picked up the methods of two-point perspective.

He also dabbles in printmaking and etching—processes that seem to maintain a dialogue with his painting. "The one-off paintings are kind of perverse . . . they're so informed by the process of reproduction," he says, adding, "perverse is good."

A fairly extensive reading of pop-culture figures (in this case C&W) also informs Langford's images. Folk art offers many common media images, from blues legends to basketball stars. Howard Finster has Elvises. Artist Chuckie is completely obsessed with the Jacksons. But their paintings tend to look like sincere tributes. Langford brings more literacy to bear, launching more detached, ironic responses to the public images and popular myths surrounding his cowboys.

One of his portraits of Ernest Tubb, *Sleeping on the Bus*, depicts a Texas troubadour cracking a faded smile somewhere in country-music heaven. In the surrounding negative space, a tiny woman, the color of flame, "dances with death in her dollar dress," while a second death angel, clad in western wear, strums his guitar. The inscription at the top of the frame hints at old-time religion's classic struggle between serving the devil and serving the Lord. It reads "Saturday Satan Sunday Saint."

Whose image and art embodies this conflict better than Jerry Lee Lewis'? Langford bases his portrait on the sleeve photo from his first Sun EP from 1957, *Whole*

Lotta Shakin' Goin' On. Here, Jerry Lee's head is engulfed in hellfire, a golden lock of hair hanging over a face full of Holy Ghost violence and joy. Once again, Langford replicates the original shot in acrylic, but surrounds the floating head with four skulls, their foreheads tattooed with the words *Yes! No! Now! Never!* By now, the story of Jerry Lee's personal apocalypse deserves its own Revelations-style chapter: it could be named after the inscription at the top of the portrait: "The Church of the Almost Here End."

As far as the music goes, that "almost here end" may have already come to pass, at least in Langford's view. Travel to the outskirts of his vision, out beyond Hank Williams's grave, and walk on past the spot where Ernest Tubb lies all but forgotten, and you'll reach the spot where country music is buried. Lest we forget what has come and gone, that spot is marked by a 135-pound pink-granite gravestone, designed by Langford, sandblasted, frosted, polished, and sprayed by a real Cincinnati monument maker.

Whose image should appear on the gravestone? Hank's, to be sure, shirtless but not hatless, ribs sticking out of a rail-thin frame pierced with arrows: the St. Sebastian of honky-tonk. The chiseled inscription reads: *And the bones of Country Music lie there in their casket beneath the towers of Nashville in a deep black pool of neglect.*

Langford's stones, saluting a deceased music, number around a dozen, and can be mass-produced. "The gravestones came about," says Langford, "because my friend David Lusenhop from Cincinnati wanted to do a book of my work. But when we sat down to talk about it, it seemed like a lot of hard work. We decided to do something more hands-on and pithy.

"Walking down Milwaukee Avenue, we glanced into a Polish funeral director's window and saw these headstones. It seemed to fit with the Death of Country Music theme on the last Waco Brothers CD."

One of the monumental designs seems to unite many themes that arise in Langford's visual art, ranging from references to methods of production, the death of country music, and its neglect by the modern Nashville assembly line.

In it, an image from his painting appears again: a woman who dances with death. At first the image suggests a personal and metaphysical notion of death—the death we all face. But combined with the stone's inscriptions (phrases like "Late 20th Century Music Wars" and "Functionalism vs. The Star System") and the dollar sign on the woman's dress, the meaning becomes more specific. The woman dancing with death in the dollar dress is Country Music—and she's not getting out of this world alive. —*Bob Pomeroy*

NEUTRAL MILK HOTEL

Neutral Milk Hotel's songs seemed to offer a way out of the era's dead-end irony and rock recycling. For *Puncture*'s spring 1998 cover story, **MIKE McGONIGAL** went down to Georgia to search out the source of the sounds, specifically the band's startling new album, *In the Aeroplane over the Sea*. His two-day visit led to the definitive interview with the media-shy Jeff Mangum. The next year, Mangum entered a period of public seclusion during which the band's legend grew exponentially. Neutral Milk Hotel reunited as a touring act in 2013.

No other band puts songs together like Neutral Milk Hotel. Their marching-band-from-slumberland sound captivated hearers of their joyful 1996 debut, *On Avery Island*. Let's begin where NMH are most discernibly different: with their words, forged by Jeff Mangum, who also does the initial songwriting. It's hard to imagine anyone else singing lyrics like these ("Two-headed boy, she is all you could need / She will feed you tomatoes and radio wires"), at least not convincingly. One set of imagistic word clusters connects to another, leaving the listener pondering the song—and the new album, *In the Aeroplane over the Sea*.

The short, folky, plaintive "King of Carrot Flowers Pt. One" opens the album with Mangum's multi-tracked voice sweetly nasal-singing, "When you were young you were the king of carrot flowers / And how you built a tower tumbling through the trees / In holy rattlesnakes that fell all around your feet." Jeff uses phrases like "and how you," "as we would," or "and this is the room" to link scenes and images together, making them whole—a smart, speechlike device.

Mangum's magic realism is striking, too, not just in the convulsive beauty of its juxtapositions, but in the way it so imagistically conjures a scene. Real-life detail makes the scene authentic—Mom and Dad weren't just fighting, "she would stick a fork right into Daddy's shoulder." If you ever listen to music for any of the emotionally cathartic or romantic reasons that are curiously out of style these days, Mangum's songs are likely to resonate for you.

Early one morning, my wife, Paige La Grone, and I drive the five hours to Athens. Nowadays, a decade and a half after the initial music-community hype about the place has died down, it seems genuinely groovy and fun again. Before Austin or Seattle, after all, there was Athens—Pylon, the B-52's, Love Tractor, R.E.M. . . . And today, once more, it is a booming music town.

Mangum lives in a house with busy, arty roommates who include his old friend Julian Koster (besides playing in NMH, he has solo project the Music Tapes, whose new, pop-up-packaged single is a collectible; and he contributes to the Black Swan Orchestra—a sort of ambient/found-sound outfit featuring members of off-kilter psych-pop act Olivia Tremor Control) and Jeff's girlfriend Laura Carter (she sings and plays keyboards in the big-sounding yet frisky Elf Power, whose album *When the Red King Comes* is out on Arena Rock; she's also in Dadaist performance group Dixie Blood Mustache, for whom she plays a discontinued-model sax-synthesizer that sounds curiously warped). Their house is a sloppy, brilliant mess—pretty much what I'd imagined.

CDs and melodicas are strewn about. I spot discs by bizarre, genre-hopping '70s Brazilian rock act Os Mutantes; jazz bassist/bandleader Charlie Haden; and musique concrète composer Pierre Henry. By the fridge there's a stack of gig flyers in psychedelic watercolors.

Old keyboards and reel-to-reel machines clutter the house. The walls are covered in artwork by friends and residents. A door is postered with photocopied images from turn-of-the-century editions of the *New York Times*, and in a corner there's a beautiful old organ a friend of Jeff's bought for 15 bucks and gave to him.

Next to the organ there's a physics book by Einstein, and another by John Cage on nothing. Part of the hallway is lined with tinfoil; big and elaborate puppet props from an Elf Power show are strewn about the living room. There are clothes in the corners, and a stack of vinyl records by Moondog, Minutemen, and Monk, among others. As she's showing us around, Laura gives a sneak preview of a string instrument she's making out of a gourd as a present for Jeff.

And there are two dogs—one looks almost like a big greyhound, the other's the ultimate Muppet mutt. The mutt, which looks way more like a stuffed animal than any living creature I've seen, was rescued from an animal-testing laboratory. The dogs are happy. They have a yard out back, but they clearly want to hang out with Laura and Jeff and their visitors.

Jeff Mangum smiles easily. Nevertheless, he's a bit shy, or guarded, at first. When he finally loosens up, the words trip over themselves, syllables smashing into one another as they scramble to get out. Jeff is a real good listener, too, and a pretty good storyteller. He's describing a cult headquarters in Georgia where some UFO conspiracy theorists are building pyramids. He and his pals went there to take photos . . .

Mangum mostly looks like he spends his time hunched over a guitar or keyboard or mixing console. His hair is mid-length, swept back, doesn't look like it's been washed today but still looks good . . . his pants have holes, but who cares? He has the authentic look of cool—the look a serious artist or heavy-duty absentminded scientist has, and he seems to be one of those people who lives healthy and looks good without trying. You can tell he doesn't think about the way he looks—except when he's going home to see his folks. Speaking of a trip there with Laura, he mutters, "I should try and find some clothes that don't have holes in them."

Mangum is charismatic in a low-key way, and clearly no egomaniac. While he doesn't seem oblivious to his talent, or embarrassed by it, he does downplay it (typical line: "I just write pop songs, you know?") while enthusing about others' work. (In this he reminds me of the genuinely humble Jim O'Rourke, the experimental Chicago guitarist/producer/engineer who's fairly recently discovered the delights of pop-based sound.)

Jeff and I settle down to talk in the living room, focusing first on the songwriting process.

Are you conducting experiments on how many words can be said in one breath, in one song?

Ha ha. The songs sort of come out spontaneously; it'll take me a while to figure out what exactly is happening lyrically, what kind of story I'm telling. Then I start building little bridges—word-bridges—to make everything go from one point to the next to the next, till it reaches the end. A stream of words keeps coming out like little blobs, in some sort of order. Like with "Two-Headed Boy," each section sort of came out at a different time, so many I've forgotten most of them by now. None of the editing happens on paper: it goes on in my little computer-storage brain.

How often do you write songs?

All the time. There's at least four records' worth of stuff that's not out and may never come out ever . . .

Is it because these haven't fit in with the concepts of On Avery Island *and* Aeroplane? *Because your records are concept records . . .*

No. They're stories. But I guess a story is a concept, huh?

When you're walking around doing whatever, do you have melodies happening in your head?

All the time. My songs pretty much revolve in my brain most of the time. It's usually whatever's coming next. Right now I have a lot of Hawaiian music in my head.

Are you on a slack-key kick?

It's not real Hawaiian music—that's the closest thing to what it is that I can call it. For some reason I hear the ukulele in my head lately . . . It's like everything I've done, just intuition.

I know you're into French musique concrète composers like Ferrari and Henry, and I guess that's part of why NMH sounds so great—those dissonant touches in the background. The mixture of ethnic-influenced droning sound, carnival music, and total noise that you put in these pop songs seasons them and makes them instantly recognizable as Neutral Milk Hotel . . . But why don't you make out-and-out experimental stuff yourself, too?

Oh, I do. I do music like that. [Jeff later shows me boxes full of tapes of his experimental music that hardly anyone's heard.] But with songwriting, there's a place I've reached where I'm comfortable expressing it openly. [Mangum made songs for ten years before unleashing them on the public; since he's only been making experimental music for three and a half years, we might have to wait a while to get to hear it.]

The kind of music Ferrari and Henry make is part of the same angelic, otherworldly music that's in my head, and that a lot of the jazz guys seem to inhabit. It's amazing music, and it really has nothing to do with rock 'n' roll.

How much of an influence are the sounds of the circus?

I'm very influenced by the circus. And by my dreams. In a lot of dreams I have, I'm in the circus. I'll dream there's a Ferris wheel in flames, and I'm walking through the crowd.

Do you think of different records as like different places in your head? Places that exist, but only you can see or hear them?

Oh, definitely.

And the record is sort of a document of that?

You're right. There's a certain feeling the songs come from, and the songs can't come into being unless the feeling comes to me. It's kind of an uncomfortable, lonely feeling I get in my stomach. And I get freaked out so I have to go play and sing; sometimes a song evolves, sometimes not. The songs are all sort of in the same place for sure.

"Song Against Sex," and the one on the new album that goes, "Your father made fetuses with flesh-licking ladies"—these seem to be visceral reactions against copulating bodies. Does sex gross you out?

I'm grossed out about sex being used as a tool for power; about people not giving a shit about who they're putting their dick into. I've known a lot of people who have been badly damaged by some asshole's drunken hardon. That really upsets me.

Your work has elements of the way a 6-year-old, looking at a car going by, might find it weird that such a thing exists. I hear this in Aeroplane, *in the line that goes, "How strange it is to be anything at all." Is that your philosophy?*

I usually wake with a shock. Whatever dream I'm having has something to do with being freaked out that I'm in my body. Then I relax, forget it, go have a cup of coffee.

Do you reconnect with that first-wake-up feeling in your music?
Yeah. It's also about the crazy sleepwalking dreams I have.

You sleepwalk?
Incredibly, yeah. I have all kinds of crazy hallucinations. I open my eyes and see things. I've seen, like, spirits moving through the walls. I've seen a vortex coming through the wall. I've seen amorphous balls of light bouncing around the front yard. I've seen giant bugs on the floor. I was in a hotel room in Amarillo, Texas, and all I remember is standing on the bed, seeing the wall in front of me filled with lights popping like popcorn out of the wall.

I like how the word "sober" appears in your songs: it goes against the grain of the hippie "underground" mentality still prevalent in many music scenes. There are magazines where you can't read a review without anything interesting or droney being compared to a drug. Yet doing a lot of drugs, it's much more difficult to make interesting art. Think how much better it'd be not to be fucked-up.
I had the typical drug experiences in high school, but I don't do anything now. Other people can do what they want, I don't preach. Plenty of rock people have made great records while totally fried!

When I started writing "Ghost," the song that goes [*he sings*] "Ghost ghost I know you live within me," we thought we had a ghost living in the house, in the bathroom. So I locked the door and started to sing to the ghost in the bathroom. But that was sort of like singing about the ghost who we thought was whistling in the other room, and that kept waking me up, and then also a ghost that may or may not live within me. And it ended up being a reference to Anne Frank, too. A lot of the songs on this record are about Anne Frank.

> *It's so sad to see the world agree / That they'd rather see their faces fill with flies / All when I'd want to keep white roses in their eyes.*
> —*"Holland, 1945"*

Art that refers to World War II and the Holocaust . . . I don't hear a lot of records doing that in 1998. Yet that was only a generation or two ago. What compelled this? You read The Diary of Anne Frank?

NEUTRAL MILK HOTEL: JEREMY BARNES, JEFF MANGUM, JULIAN KOSTER, SCOTT SPILLANE (PHOTO, WILL WESTBROOK)

Yeah. I know it might sound kind of cheesy . . . Right before recording *On Avery Island* I was walking around in Ruston waiting to go to Denver to record. I don't consider myself to be a very educated person, 'cause I've spent a lot of my life in dreams.

And I was walking around wondering, would everything make more sense to me if I knew the history of the world, or would I just lose my mind? I came to the conclusion I'd probably just lose my mind. Next day I walked into a bookstore, and there was *The Diary of Anne Frank*. I'd never given it any thought before. Then I spent two days reading it and completely flipped out . . . spent about three days crying . . . It stuck with me for a long, long time.

I'm not sure I could allow myself to connect with a book that much.

While I was reading the book, she was completely alive to me. I pretty much knew what was going to happen. But that's the thing: you love people because you know their story. You have sympathy for people even when they do stupid things because you know where they're coming from, you understand where they're at in their head. So here I am as deep as you can go in someone's head, in some ways deeper than you can go with someone you know in the flesh. And then at the end, she gets disposed of like a piece of trash.

I would go to bed every night and have dreams about having a time machine, having the ability to move through time and space freely, and save Anne Frank. Do you think that's embarrassing?

Wanting to go back in time to save Frodo the Hobbit . . . that would be embarrassing. But feeling intense empathy over a real and shocking narrative—no.

The record doesn't necessarily take place in that time period so much. It's a reflection of how I see that time. I'm not even sure anyway if time is linear, if it's all going in one direction. The world is an incredibly blurry, crazy dream I'm sort of stumbling through. Science has pretty much figured out that the reality we live in isn't necessarily reality.

A lot of the songs on *Aeroplane* freaked me out, and it took other people to make me be comfortable with them, and to see it was okay to sing about this stuff, not shut the songs inside. 'Cause it was too intense. I would ask a friend, "What the fuck am I doing?" It took a while to figure out the songs were positive, they were okay, not just fucked-up nightmares I was throwing up.

And now a song for Jesus Christ
and since this seems to confuse people I'd like to
simply say that I mean what I sing although the
theme of endless endless on this album is not based
on any religion but more in the belief that all

things seem to contain a white light within them
that I see as eternal

—a note to the lyrics

Do you think this record's lyrics are gonna weird people out? When you sing "I love you Jesus Christ" rather than "I love you Peggy Sue," people might think of you completely differently, because of that line . . .

For a lot of these songs I was able to lock myself in a room and allow my mind to let out what it wanted without worrying too much about what others would think. A song about God was inevitable, because of my upbringing and the intense experiences I had, growing up, going to these crazy church camps where everything was very open. We talked about sexuality freely, we talked about . . .

How old were you?

From 11 to 17.

Where were the camps?

In central Louisiana, out in the boonies.

Was it a hippie kind of Christianity?

It wasn't really hippie, it was just weird. You could spill your guts all over the place. People were leaping and freaking out. It wasn't so much a God trip as an emotional trip. Even if you were an atheist, if your parents shipped you down there, you could talk about it. You could talk openly about your atheist beliefs and there would be debates; and being an atheist was as beautiful as anything else.

A few weeks ago in Athens, we played a show with Vic Chesnutt. He sat on the stage and played for thirty minutes, singing songs about how action and reaction are the closest things to truth in the universe, how he's had out-of-body experiences but they weren't supernatural. I thought it was the most beautiful thing I'd ever heard. My love for Christ has more to do with what Christ said and believed in. Then the Church put this fucked-up bullshit around it and made it this at-times really evil thing. If you attach man to anything, he's gonna fuck it up somehow. You think that's too cynical?

No, we all fuck up. My church is my records.

Right. With *Aeroplane*, I feel it's spiritual—but not religious.

On your first disc, you thanked your hometown of Ruston, Louisiana.

It was a way of thanking the whole town, and the community there, but also it's where I grew up, so there were a lot of intense experiences there.

You don't particularly have a Southern accent. How come?

In school I was surrounded by racist, sexist jocks. From an early age, my friends and I all felt we didn't belong there. We all kind of saved ourselves from that place.

The little world we had there was beautiful. But when we saw some guy going, "Hey may-an whah don' we lahk git drunk and lahk fuck that whore over thair mahn," we wanted to be as different as possible. When I was young I must have made a conscious effort to stop talking that way, 'cause that's how those motherfuckers I hate talk. My lack of accent stems from that early rebellion.

The Elephant 6 people carry on from there. We sort of record for each other and write songs for each other. Anytime I'm in here recording, if I'm going places I don't understand, I'll know my friend Will's gonna listen to it. I give him a tape and he'll really dig it. So that gives me a certain gratification, to put something on a tape, walk down the street and hand it to him.

Which bands is Will in?

[*laughs*] Will Westbrook, he's in the Gerbils, and he also does a solo thing called Wet Host. He's a sax player. There's about 25 people who live here now, who all came here from Ruston. We gravitate toward each other. We've always played together, our whole lives. But we're not a closed club or something. There are people showing up all the time and they go, "Well, I sort of bow this thing and it makes a squeaky sound!" Then we go, "Waaaa! Cool, man! Come squeak on this thing over here!" If anyone wants to play, they just have to show up and want to play.

The curious thing about *In the Aeroplane over the Sea* is that it's a more folky, guitar/vocals–centered effort than *On Avery Island*, while it's the first record Mangum's done with a fixed lineup. NMH used to be Jeff and whatever friends were around at the moment. He's ping-ponged across North America under the moniker. But this group came together roughly two years ago, not long after the release of *Avery*. Julian Koster was a catalyst; he was the first E6'er to release records on an established label—doing two albums as leader of Chocolate USA in the early '90s for Bar/None. Not long after that group ceased to exist, he arranged for NMH to stay in the basement of his grandmother's apartment on Long Island, in New York. Imaginative horn player/arranger Scott Spillane (also in the Gerbils, who make slightly skewed pop—closer to the Apples in Stereo, exceptional and distinct, sloppy but great—like the better songs by Fly Ashtray or Uncle Wiggly but maybe even more obscure at this point; their record *Are You Sleepy* is due on Hidden Agenda) had been working in a pizza joint in Austin and living in a van. At Julian's urging, Scott got on a Greyhound in Austin and rode all the way to Long Island. He credits Julian's vivacious personality as the reason he joined. Scott is not as introspective as Jeff; he's more of a relaxed groover.

NEUTRAL MILK HOTEL
In the Aeroplane over the Sea (Merge)

Indie rock got no reason to live, right? Its time-honored specialties aren't so special anymore. Irony stinks up everything on TV; the latest in antisocial noise comes out of a beat machine, not a guitar.

Then again, those are just tools, easily discarded. As the name suggests, indie rock's real specialty is *difference*, and the search for that continues. Arty experiment has been one route; bent melody another. Neutral Milk Hotel, keeping the experiments loose and the melodies radiantly idiosyncratic, have gone both ways.

They represent a fresh injection of the genre's roots—the next wave of misfits. Along with Olivia Tremor Control and Apples in Stereo, NMH are part of the Elephant 6 collective, a group of friends who grew up in the boondock outpost of Ruston, in Louisiana. Without many cultural outlets, it's the kind of place where bohemianism is not a role to try on, but a way to survive. Art-minded types have no choice but to band together and play for each other. In Neutral Milk Hotel, that small-town insularity has produced uncannily fresh music: folk-pop rooted in, rather than deconstructed by a backwoods musical circus.

Their 1995 debut, *On Avery Island*, featured singer-songwriter Jeff Mangum spouting stream-of-consciousness lyrics and moaning melodies as pretty as Brian Wilson's. Trombones, xylophones, air organs, and various exotic or cheesy instruments (many played by Mangum himself) blurted woozy acid-march music around his voice. Far-flung as these elements sound, they were channeled by producer Robert Schneider (of

Apples in Stereo) into a fuzz-heavy, delicately tuneful song cycle.

With *In the Aeroplane over the Sea*, some of the fuzz has been cleared, leaving room for Mangum to fly solo more often with his speed-freak acoustic surrealism. Other songs retain the first record's bizarre style of accompaniment, even finding space for euphonium, zanzithophone, musical saw, and "one-note piano"—so the credits say. The band—Schneider again producing—march, honk, and trill. They go down-home here and punk out there. They conjure a spacey textural hum to counter the singer's naked emotion.

But NMH is still Mangum's vehicle, and he's made this record a starker, more urgent affair. In many spots he dispenses with hooks, letting songs follow the shifting outlines of his own intensely expressive vocal style. He breaks from indie tune-making, offering instead an instinctive and madly personal musical vision, where "outsider" pop (Wilson, Syd Barrett, Daniel Johnston, etc.) is wedded to what sounds like an archaic social music. Voiced in lyrics that venture from spiritual yearning to raw sexuality and World War II, the recording that emerges seems to stand oddly apart from its time.

It begins ambitiously, with three-part medley "The King of Carrot Flowers." A quick acoustic strum figure is filled out with gently rolling accordion. Mangum, his voice flat and double-tracked, sings long melodic lines to fit the words tumbling out of his mouth. The lyrics fall into a recurring NMH theme: innocence seeking refuge. "Mom would stick a fork right into Daddy's shoulder/...As we would lay and learn what each other's bodies were for." The kids lying together in secret have courage: "From above you how I sank into your soul/Into that place where no one dares to go." The parents don't: "Dad would dream of all the different ways to die/Each one a little more than he could dare to try."

There is a sense that the young will become the old, the dream will meet hard reality. But the rapturous physical descriptions of youth overwhelm all other perspectives. Mangum, who is 27, can't speak about youth from any distance; but he doesn't sound naive. Rushing headlong, he's determined to make a fleeting moment into an eternal one; to make "reality" sound surreal and a young person's dream the only way to live.

Headlong rush and willful belief have largely defined Neutral Milk Hotel thus far. Their first record flew on lines like, "We ride roller coasters into the ocean/We feel no emotion as we spiral down into the world." It shocked with a lack of irony: "Kids in their

Jeff had been in a bad funk before all this, not knowing if he really wanted to tour after the release of *On Avery Island*. Julian made Jeff get on a train to Chicago to visit a drummer called Jeremy Barnes (never got the names of his other bands). According to Jeremy, Jeff only played half of one song with him the whole time he was there, 'cause he was freaked at how expensive the studio time was, and was happy enough with the way they sounded together. Nevertheless he asked Jeremy to drop out of school and meet the group in Long Island in three months. To the chagrin of his folks, Jeremy agreed, because he "loved *Avery* so much." He's been in the band ever since.

Jeremy is quick to point out he's not a Ruston guy: "Oh no no no, God no." He'd been in a free-jazz band in Chicago who'd played with Chocolate USA, and dug them. He stayed in touch with Julian, hoping to work with him in the future.

The newly assembled Neutral Milk Hotel group stayed in the New York area for several months, playing a lot of shows (including a celebrated turn at the Terrastock festival) and touring as well. They now all live in Athens, where Will Hart from Olivia Tremor Control landed and settled seven years ago.

While we're in Athens we meet the extended family of Elephant 6 people. They all seem very busy amusing themselves: making art, making sound, talking about art and music, telling stories, smiling, listening to each other's new mixes. I feel like I'm in a bohemian coffee commercial—I don't meet a single jerk. Everyone's music is at the very least pretty good.

I know we were only there two days, but someone could at least have been rude . . . Then I wouldn't have felt these twinges of envy and awe, and this article might have more of an edge to it.

It seems like sort of a commune you have here in Athens, one that works. And you've talked about getting land and building your own dwellings out in the woods, and all living together, right?
Yes. Pete from Olivia Tremor Control is really into geodesic domes, and Scott and Laura have ideas about how to maintain a community . . . giant waterwheels that would create electricity, things like that.
What makes Athens so great?
'Cause everybody's here!

I'm not like these other people who like it so much—not that I dislike it. See, I've never been particularly comfortable anywhere I've lived. And Athens is a nice, easy town to live in.

When he is asked the same question, Jeremy replies, "One really good thing about Athens is how

cheap it is. We tried to live in New York and you just cannot do what we do there unless you're independently wealthy. Here, I pay like a hundred dollars rent for a beautiful house, and I have enough space, and live with people I really love.

"I live with Will and Pete from Olivia; our house used to be a boardinghouse. We painted it, and the inside looks like something out of Dr. Seuss. Will basically records 24 hours a day. There's a piano in the house, and Pete, who plays piano for Olivia, is playing all day.

"In Athens, everyone's always doing something. I come home from practice and Pete's playing something really interesting on the piano. I go up to my room and in the room next to me Will's recording some sort of a dream drone or a bizarre tape loop. Then I go by Julian's and he's recording some amazing saw harmony.

"It's really inspiring. In Chicago, that sort of thing was happening, too—but so spread out it could never have the same impact for me."

You can tell Neutral Milk Hotel are a band now, even though this "band" record is actually more folk-oriented, driven by Jeff's reedy choirboy voice—more in control here than on the debut—and the crisp, clear power of his acoustic guitar. Still, every accent, every note the band and friends make seems essential, and *Aeroplane* is a more cohesive record by far. On the next record I imagine there'll be still more room for the rest of the band to stretch out. I could certainly hear more instrumentals like Spillane's "The Fool," which sounds like Sweet Emma leading the Ohio State pickup ensemble

cars/Cigarettes smoking/All that they are just reeks with the sweetest belief." On *Aeroplane*, Mangum slides that belief in a spiritual direction: "I love you Jesus Christ," he declares in a high whine in "The King of Carrot Flowers Pts. Two & Three." It seems less a religious conversion than a natural extension of his worldly embrace.

And then, two lines on, Mangum utters this affirmation: "I will float until I learn how to swim/Inside my mother in a garbage bin." The underlying abortion allusion here is characteristic of the graphic physical description in these songs. Bodies come together awkwardly: hands go in mouths, tongues get torn out. Everything stinks: dresses, skin, perfume, sweat. Images are physical: "I don't wish to taste of your insides"; "The movements were beautiful/All in your ovaries." Beauty is found—even smokers "reek with the sweetest belief." But discomfort lingers.

The power of the descriptions resides in their mix of awe and disgust. This ambivalence, along with the visceral detail, supplies Mangum's love songs with the ring of experience, of truth discovered. In place of insight, he gives us a firsthand look at the process of finding it. Sensory impressions of sex, bodies, and the world outside tangle and overwhelm. The singer records them, and makes the first tentative steps toward sorting them out.

As *Aeroplane* continues, though, his steps get bigger. The record darkens. Songs circle vaguely around World War II: "Holland

1945" is about Anne Frank. Then Mangum cuts it all down to his voice and acoustic guitar on "Oh, Comely" and the two-part "Two-Headed Boy." His voice is given free rein; prettiness is sacrificed to intensity.

The first part of "Two-Headed Boy" is where this intensity peaks. The song is like a fever dream, with structure scrapped for free-form vocal improv. It's not a narrative, but a sustained moment of high, mysterious passion. It is vaguely about a "two-headed boy" listening to his radio. But as Mangum swoops, holds notes, and pushes his voice until it cracks, he makes the story a springboard for his real subject: communication at its most desperate.

"Two-Headed Boy" begins in loneliness: "I am listening to hear where you are," he sings, so loud it jumps out of the song and talks to you. The song peaks, typically, as desperation is made physical. He sings a line about the boy's radio "catching signals in the dark." Needing, suddenly, to break through that image of distance and loneliness, he free-associates, connecting the line with "In the dark we will take off our clothes." When he rolls downward on these words, the song's context shatters, and we are left with the startling, mysterious drama of the act itself.

In a sense, "Two-Headed Boy" and the other solo acoustic songs here take the uncomfortable intensity of people like Johnston, Barrett, and Roky Erickson and bring it to the sane world. This isn't to say Mangum has really been influenced by them; but the indie cults formed around those performers have made their collective style (pop structure loosened to accommodate tottering emotion; lyrics of willful innocence) into an aesthetic, a post-punk tool for expressing raw emotion.

Where those performers are tentative observers of the world, Mangum is an impassioned if somewhat dreamy participant. With his new bare-bones, freestyle approach, he's able to build his mountain of images and give it a sense of urgency. The images aren't sorted into a perspective; they become an analogous language, a surreal composition of words. Lines like "Your father made fetuses/With flesh-licking ladies" and "God is a place where you will wait for the rest of your life" say nothing specific. But when the singer twists them in his hard-edged wail, they become the sound of emotion testing its own limits, of spiritual innocence struggling to contain horrible reality.

Mangum doesn't bother to resolve this struggle. He dives into it, and comes back with thrilling, unflinchingly romantic music.

—Steve Tignor

through a turgid, mournful Eastern European folk song. But this record is stuffed with so much sound it's hard to ask for more: fuzzed-out bass, trombones, bells, something called a zanzithophone, flügelhorn, sax, a saw played perfectly in tune, a shortwave radio, tape hiss, white noise, everything.

Both *Avery* and *Aeroplane* were recorded in Denver with Robert Schneider, the head of Apples in Stereo and the E6 patriarch.

Tell me about the recording sessions.

The energy and love Robert puts into the recordings, how personally he takes it, and that there's always enough time to do exactly what you want to do, it is so amazing to work with him. I know he understands me. It's like sitting at home recording—but with a person who pushes you to new places. Robert lets you find the very best, most interesting sounds, like, inside yourself.

Do the songs change as you take them to Julian, Scott, and Jeremy?

The recording process is sort of a spontaneous thing . . .

Do Neutral Milk Hotel practice?

No, we don't really practice, we're not a practice-space band . . . A lot of the saw parts, for instance, Julian develops on tour. He'll make them up at night while we're on the road; eventually he'll have something he's happy with. The horn arrangements are done the same way.

So the song components get ironed out in playing live together?

Sort of. But there are very primitive things that flourish when we record. Julian will go, "Oh you know I play saw on this song," and I'll go, "Oh well Christ, we've been sitting here wondering what the magic key to this song was, and you've been playing saw on this song the whole time." Then he'll take what he was doing live and expand it from one saw part that was very simple, to sitting in the bathroom playing it for three hours until it's a three-part-harmony saw part that sort of sounds like Hawaiian singing or little angelic voices.

You use heavy distortion . . . it could just as easily have sounded clean . . .

All the recording sound is intentional. There's a certain way we've gotten used to things sounding, after recording on 4-track for years. There are certain sounds we love to hear. All the heavy distortion stuff is intentional. When we did *On Avery Island* and this record, we did the best-sounding record we could possibly make. We used as much old-timey equipment on *Aeroplane* as we could. I have a very limited knowledge of recording, but the miracle of being able to capture sounds on magnetic tape—of electricity and these little magnetic particles—is amazing to me. You know? ◓

CHRISTINE SIEVANEN

ROYAL TRUX

In 1998 Royal Trux had just emerged from one of the era's strangest couplings of major label and underground band. The duo's parting gift to Virgin Records—a commercially unfeasible album, even by Royal Trux standards—had been critically battered but garnished the band's reputation as uncompromising weirdos. **JAY RUTTENBERG** met Neil Hagerty and Jennifer Herrema at their home in rural Virginia as the pair readied their return to Drag City. The comeback would prove short-lived: a few years later, Royal Trux broke up as both couple and band. The pair returned in 2015 for an ill-fated reunion.

    —Man, I always knew this Royal Trux fixation would get
      you killed some day.
    —Just be careful.
    —If they get out shovels and start digging a ditch . . . run!

And so the warnings go from friends hearing of my impending pilgrimage to the sticks of Virginia to visit the home of Royal Trux front couple Jennifer Herrema and Neil Hagerty. Of course, their worries are ludicrous,

arising largely from the shortsighted press that has dogged the band: "One British guy came here to write an article, saw us sitting around the house kissing the cats, and was still freaked out," Herrema will later tell me while sitting around the house kissing the cats and freaking me out hardly at all.

    But 15 hours before the interview I cannot help feeling a pang of apprehension. I'm spending the night in, of all places, Washington, DC's Watergate complex,

275

where a friend landed a condo sublet (only to be forced into a second job when security fees skyrocketed during the Monica Lewinsky ordeal). My friend asks what the big scaredy-cat fuss is about these Royal Trux people. I tell her how I'd briefly interviewed them years before in a Boston club, how Herrema sat buried in a fur coat and cloud of nicotine, only opening her mouth to quarrel with the goonish Hagerty, who loomed over the table with a cigarette and a scowl glued to his lips. Every recent article about the pair, I explain, has mentioned the shotguns they keep inside the very pad I'm about to visit. I show her an old photograph of the Gruesome Twosome, presumably taken during their junkie days. Hagerty's perpetually glum mug is turned from the camera, his heavy-metal mane draped over the giant "55" printed on his shirt; Herrema sports patched jeans, two enormous skull rings, and a Minnesota Twins T-shirt; her nose and mouth barely protrude from a beautiful mound of blond Bam Bam–style hair that obscures her forehead, eyes, and cheeks, but not her "fuck-you-too" attitude. It's part exotic, part trailer trash: either way, the grime practically seeps out of the newsprint. My friend's still not convinced, so I opt to let the music speak for itself.

The Watergate has seen its fair share of sordid activity over the years (Bob Dole sleeps there every night, for chrissake!), yet I still feel perverse putting Royal Trux on the posh apartment's built-in player. And not just any Royal Trux record, but *Twin Infinitives*, the duo's 1990 Beefheartian epic, the one everybody talks about and nobody listens to, the seventy-minute, four-cut CD that was fueled by both a unique comprehension of rock 'n' roll's inner workings and, well, narcotics.

I press play, and the room is enveloped in a blur of chaotic noise, as if the Trux had somehow gathered the dirt from under Keith Richards's fingernails and molded it into a postmodern mud pie. Guitars belch, Herrema grunts her guts right out of her stomach and onto the acetate, Hagerty moans diabolically . . . even the synthesizer sounds viscous and scrambled. It's as if G. Gordon Liddy and James McCord had broken into the apartment and futzed with all the classic-rock tapes, inadvertently reassembling them into this brilliant, befuddled muck.

"Hmmm," my friend says as I turn down the stereo. "I'd watch myself if I were you."

Hagerty and Herrema live nearly two hours out of Washington—far enough so they only venture into the city "about once a year," associating strictly with one another and with Herrema's folks, who live an hour away. The area they've settled in is rural and picturesque—like a jigsaw puzzle sprung to life. The hills roll, the horses rollick, and Confederate flags flap gently in the breeze. It's the kind of place where the rich people name their houses and the poor people name their guns, and when I pass locals on the bending roads they wave and nod, regardless of their thoughts on my big Jewish nose.

I take a left at the Mount Lebanon Baptist Church, onto a narrow, winding road dotted with spacious houses. Herrema had warned me the addresses on their street were laid out nonsequentially—which doesn't sound legal, however appropriate it might be for Royal Trux—but I have no problem spotting their house. It's the one flying a pirate flag from the top of the staff. ("The asshole across the way has a Dixie flag, so we put up the Jolly Roger," Hagerty says later. "Our sympathies are clear.")

Theirs is also the only home without a manicured front lawn; the unruly heap of grass out front consumes everything in its path but the tip of the dirt drive and a tank of propane. I squeeze my car between their mid-'80s Jaguar (the kind with the bumpy rear lights) and "woody" Jeep Wagoneer, leaving myself a thirty-yard walk uphill to their grey country castle.

I search for a doorbell but find only stickers advertising Amnesty International and the NRA. Then the door swings open, Hagerty mumbles hello, and I follow him up a small flight of stairs and into the kitchen, where a pot of cheap coffee burps and wheezes its way to the finish line. Herrema—his partner of 13 years—is still at Walmart, and Hagerty is clearly anxious for his prettier half's return. He's also sleepy, this being 2:30 in the afternoon, a whole hour and a half before his usual wake-up time; Herrema has been "adjusting his schedule" over the last few days, he explains, in preparation for their upcoming European tour.

He is wearing baggy Lee jeans, sneakers, a T-shirt, and a large ring that covers his thumb. I'm not quite sure what his teeth look like because he never, ever laughs or smiles, even when he tells a joke ("How did Jeff Buckley die? Drowning in his own tears") or recites a routine from *Kids in the Hall* or *Larry Sanders*. I'm not sure what his eyes look like, either: he avoids eye contact at all cost. He also never stands still, pacing about his kitchen while gulping down coffee, fretting that the neighbors must hate him for his unrefined front lawn ("If they ask us to cut it we will, but we like it better this way").

He shows me the place. The couple financed it, he says, with the money they received from their deal with Virgin Records. Parts of their house were built in the 19th century: the sunroom, where well-thumbed books lie amid stacks of CDs; or the living room behind the kitchen, with an ancient, beast-like heater tucked into one of the house's five fireplaces, pictures of parents and cats, a machine Hagerty uses to monitor local police activity, and comfortable leather furniture. Other sections were added later: a room with a wraparound sofa and a television that never seems to get turned off; or the carpeted space in the right-hand wing that looks like the kind of room every high-school band practices in, except for the fancy recording equipment. ("Bought with the Virgin money," Hagerty says. "Sixty thousand dollars. But we have guns, so don't try anything.")

The second floor is less music-focused, but has an ambience of Royal Trux, or at least of artists at play. A sort of solarium houses a work space for Herrema's painting, which—to judge from RTX cover art—alternates between the cartoonish and ghoulish. Another, larger room contains a Macintosh; here Hagerty wrote *Victory Chimp* (his baffling Drag City–published novel), and here he compiles his database of "anomalous events" dug up from the *Wall Street Journal* and other "dangerously conservative" publications. Perhaps the greatest work of art, however, is the bathroom door, burdened with a rack full of Herrema's footwear. There are running shoes, cowboy boots, big shoes, small shoes, fluffy shoes, fuzzy shoes, furry boots, silver-tipped boots . . . and inside the bathroom is a walk-in closet containing the wardrobes (including a puffy Brian Jones–style—fake?—fur coat) that go with 'em.

There is a small sign under the light switch that reads: TURN OFF THE BATHROOM LIGHTS. Since visitors are a rarity in the Hagerty-Herrema household (apart from "the lady who takes care of the cats while we're on tour," the couple do not mingle locally, and even the Royal Trux sidemen sleep elsewhere when there's recording going on), I wonder who wrote the note—and who needed it. From articles I'd read about the band I'd picked up a strong sense that Jennifer plays Dr. Landy to Neil's Brian Wilson. That is, she deals with the label, the press, the concert booker, the stockbroker, and the Walmart shopping, while the reclusive Hagerty hones his guitar chops and compiles his Menckenesque database. So this seemingly outlandish knockout trades her shades for spectacles and deals with the real world, while boy genius flakes out.

Then again, maybe the note was posted for the cat sitter.

Half an hour after my arrival, the black Royal Trux van pulls into the driveway and Herrema hoists the grocery bags into the kitchen. She removes her large faux Rayban aviator glasses, revealing two thick circles of eyeliner and a doll-like face. There are slabs of metal tied around her wrists with dangling leather straps and

another chunk of cattle that tightly chokes her neck, giving the impression her head would slide right off her body if the necklace were removed.

Herrema's press kit claims she's 25. She looks all of 17, rasps like a 64-year-old Camel addict, and says she's 29, which I believe. The singer has squeezed a lot of life into her however-many years. She grew up money-eyed in DC: her father was the assistant to a Connecticut senator and later used his connections to make a killing in real estate, only to lose the farm as the Reagan age slumped to a close. Jennifer met Neil when she was a high school senior and he was lending his guitar prowess to Jon Spencer's fledgling Pussy Galore. She began making Royal Trux recordings with Hagerty, moved to New York City, dropped out of college, became a heroin addict, moved to San Francisco, became a legend of "outsider" music, stripped for money, OD'd, detoxed, OD'd, detoxed, roamed the States, guided Palace's career, settled in Virginia, stayed clean, scored a bundle of cash from a big recording label, and modeled for Calvin Klein's CK One campaign ("I'm on TV all the time")—all the while sticking with Hagerty through thick and thin.

At the moment she's just happy to see her trio of cats, who climb in and out of the brown Walmart bags searching for catnip as Hagerty helps her unload the kitty litter, prescription drugs, frozen entrees, and blank cassette tapes.

"Why'd you get ninety-minute tapes?" Hagerty groans.

"That's all they had."

"But the sixty-minute ones are better."

"That's what they had," Herrema repeats. "Neil, I've had a bad day. I was loading the groceries into the van, and when I turned around there was a guy in a pickup truck looking at me. He was jacking off."

"Fuck! Did you see his plates?"

"No. He followed me but I blew a light and lost him."

"Jesus, Jennifer, why didn't you get his plate number? How many lights did he follow you for? . . . Three? He got your plates. He's probably a fuckin' serial killer."

Hagerty walks to the front window and stares out, past the white propane tank, past the swampy lump of grass, past the van, the Jag, the Woody, and my own car. There's no killer visible, but Hagerty's not satisfied. "I should get the gun. Did you call the police? We should call the police."

"Neil, I lost him."

"You had a fuckin' killer and you let him slip out of your net. What if he goes and molests a kid?"

"I was not going to stop and take down his license-plate number."

"I'm just saying he was behind you. You could've

just looked back," Hagerty moans, stalking the room as if John Wayne Gacy is about to crawl from under the sofa cushions.

"You're paranoid," says Herrema.

For the next few hours Hagerty will sporadically pop up from his seat and peek out the window, continually returning to the subject to retread his original argument. He's a classic neurotic, belying his tough-guy exterior—as if Woody Allen were stuck inside Dee Dee Ramone's body.

Hagerty more or less agrees: "Woody Allen once said he used to watch a Knicks player go up for a dunk and all he could think about was, 'Here's this beautiful athlete, and some day he's gonna be dead.' I think that about a lot of stuff. Just neurosis. It's funny, cause rock 'n' roll is supposed to be 'cool' and totally anti-everything. But that's just not the case."

"He's totally paranoid," snorts Herrema, shaking her head with some disgust. "He won't fly, you know. We can't play Japan, 'cause he stopped flying in '95."

"No, I don't fly," Hagerty mutters. "Everybody flies, and it's so common . . . So I'm protesting it, this jet age, where you're treated like fucking cattle."

"I guess this airplane thing is a point of some contention between the two of you," I offer, in a flash of obnoxious voyeurism.

As Herrema starts to explain, they begin shouting over one another the way only well-worn couples can, their words of venom intertwining along labyrinthine paths. It's like dialogue scripted for George Costanza's parents:

—Well, you see . . .
—Well, excuse me . . .
—She's in love with this idea . . .
—No, excuse me, I had to go . . .
—She likes to go and . . .
—I had to go a month and a half ago, I HAD TO FLY . . .
—You're using the wrong . . .
—TO 11 COUNTRIES!
—You didn't have to do anything. You fuckin' wanted to . . .
—Okay, okay . . .
—AND YOU KNOW IT!
—Okay, so we have this record company in Europe. They spend a lot on us and the guy works really hard and everything . . .
—Yes, let's crunch the numbers . . .
—Shut up! Shut up, you! Look, I had to fly to 11 countries in 13 days, just to do press. And the guy's like, 'We're working this really hard, could you just do this?' And I agreed, because I feel very differently from Neil

about certain things. And you know, every morning I was on an airplane going from Germany to Italy, Ireland, Belgium, Holland—
—What about Bermuda? You left out Bermuda . . .
—It was a lot of work. But there are certain things Neil does—
—What about the Bermuda trip?
—He empties the cat litter!

"All right," I finally interject. "Why don't we go on to another question?"

Perhaps the most endearing thing Thurston Moore has uttered is, "Never trust a band that's good every night." Okay, so he most likely wasn't the first to wave the flag of fickleness—and I suspect he only did so to apologize for a crummy Sonic Youth show—but the quote establishes a crucial line separating the Bob Dylans from the Tom Pettys, the Alex Chiltons from the Rick Nielsens, and Royal Trux from just about everybody else.

Hagerty and Herrema have been releasing RTX records for a decade. They have eight LPs under their studded cowboy belts, plus enough singles to form a double-CD set (last year's *Singles, Live and Unreleased*). Each record has featured new collaborators, a fresh recording method, different rules for song structure, and new ways of examining their music altogether. If something's wrong, they fix it; if something's right, they fix it.

Seeing Royal Trux play live is an even bigger gamble. At times they are an absolutely unbeatable rock-and-roll machine; other times it's like watching your grandfather parallel park. Hagerty has been known to forsake his guitar in favor of a synthesizer, or to sit on a stool and let the audience examine his back for fifty minutes, or play astonishing Hendrix-blessed guitar lines only to bury them behind a heavy-handed keyboard player the Trux picked up from a classic-rock cover band. Herrema can sing as if possessed, swaggering faceless behind her stringy mane and good-guy cowboy hat; or she can grunt her lyrics in a grotesque monotone, seemingly wrapped up in an entirely different number than the band. Or she can ditch her post mid-show for a bathroom break.

The backup band is likewise kept in a state of perpetual flux. A bassist was recently dismissed after a pair of albums as "too skilled"; the couple replaced him with the aforementioned keyboardist, who left after *Accelerator*, when Jennifer and Neil remodeled the group as a Jefferson Airplane homage with Herrema taking female lead and Hagerty and a former drummer on male backup.

"Rock 'n' roll used to be thought of as a unique combination of individuals coming together to create a sound," Hagerty explains when asked about their rotating lineup. "That idea is total bullshit, just another myth. We fashion ourselves after jazz sessions from the '20s, which were made up of whoever was around, or in the tradition of the Brill Building, Phil Spector, or Stax/Volt, where there were anonymous session musicians. This way there's a different chemistry for each session."

This propensity for constant change makes the Royal Trux aficionado work nearly as hard as a James Joyce buff. Listeners sweated in 1990, when Hagerty and Herrema followed up their self-titled debut with *Twin Infinitives*, which challenges the nerves by nature of its layout alone (15 songs spread over four CD cuts and large gaps of silence), not to mention the sonic wasps' nest tucked inside. Further challenges came two years later, when RTX reinvented themselves on a second self-titled work (informally dubbed "Bones" after its graveyard cover art), which introduced chord structure but clung to chaos. (In part due to its low budget. The duo then received a recording allowance from Matador but "blew most of it on drugs" and never worked with the label again.)

Trux fans had to reconsider their value systems once more when the two jettisoned opiates and low fidelity for the biker blues of *Sweet Sixteen*, which juxtaposed dragging guitar sludge with the tight maverick bop of numbers like "The Spectre" and "The Flag." Hagerty attributes the style of *Cats and Dogs* (considered by many the duo's brightest hour) to its 1993 production date: "It's just a mock grunge record. That's what the Rolling Stones used to do. If the Beatles did something, then they did the exact same thing, or they did disco in the '70s, or 'Angie' when Fleetwood Mac and Elton John were big. It's a tradition: you don't hold onto some kind of aesthetic thing—you just take in all this shit, put it through the wringer, and make it rock 'n' roll."

Perhaps the biggest strain came in 1995, when Hagerty and Herrema rode the zeitgeist once again, leaving Drag City to sign with Virgin Records. Royal Trux had been Drag City's flagship act since their self-released debut caught the ear of Chicagoan Dan Koretzky, who ran out and formed the label to put out the Trux's spooky "Hero Zero" single (an early Pavement 7" soon followed). *Thank You*, the band's major-label debut, seemed to renege on their contract with the horn-rimmed underground. It was slick, benefiting from Neil Young vet David Briggs's production. And it was cold: "We started rehearsing [the *Thank You* material] six months before we recorded, so we were able to be very detached from it," Hagerty told me back in 1995. "It was like we were covering somebody else's songs."

The record got buried under a heap of critical praise—judging by its ubiquitousness in the cutout bins, you'd think Virgin gave away more than it sold. Fans missed the old disorder, new listeners got little introduction.

Coming upon Royal Trux at that point was like walking into a movie in the middle.

At the time, it seemed the Trux might have reached the logical end of the line—as if they'd bulldozed rock's walls with *Twin Infinitives*, then spent a career rebuilding them, only to discover they'd been constructing their own mausoleum. *Sweet Sixteen*, last year's follow-up to *Thank You*, only reinforced such thinking. Recorded at Hagerty and Herrema's pad sans Briggs (who had died), the album concerned itself more with techie experimentation than songs (rarely the type of record that pushes major-label units or grabs indie ears). What's more, as the middle entry in RTX's "counter-revisionist '60s, '70s, and '80s album cycle" that was mapped out for the three-album Virgin contract, *Sweet Sixteen* carried an odious 1976 tinge. No song was allowed to end before it hit the four-minute mark, and the half-baked boogie tunes all seemed to atrophy toward solo-wank platforms. Even the cover art—depicting a soiled, clogged toilet bowl—extended a taunt to all involved.

No one was surprised when the Trux were cut loose by Virgin. What is somewhat astonishing is that *Accelerator*—which marks both their return to Drag City and the '80s finale to the "decades" trilogy—ranks among their finest and most accessible albums to date. Like *Sweet Sixteen*, the new record was recorded at the Hagerty-Herrema abode and focuses on experimental guitar frequencies and other technical shenanigans. Unlike its predecessor, *Accelerator* is a tight, diverse affair, with the snappy harmonica-'n'-harmony "Yellow Kid" dropped in the middle of metallic jumbles ("I'm Ready" and "The Banana Question"), a frightening dub-like number ("New Bones"), plus a breathtaking classic rock send-off ("Stevie," reportedly about Steven Seagal). Even the opening line ("Now you know I'm ready!!!") contrasts sharply with *Sweet Sixteen*'s gambit: "Don't Try Too Hard."

Hagerty and Herrema scoff at such criticism. "'I'm Ready' and 'Don't Try Too Hard' are basically saying the same thing," explains Hagerty. "Everything we sing has a mock relationship to our situation. All of our stuff can be considered to be about us . . . Look at the two songs on the two records. *Sweet Sixteen* is so dense, it's totally misunderstood. 'now you know I'm ready' is like saying, 'We've stripped everything down, we are finally ready to connect with the audience,' which is just totally stupid."

Herrema chips in: "There's no less information on *Accelerator* than there is on *Sweet Sixteen*. It's just that *Sweet Sixteen* appears to be more obtuse . . . [with more] weight due to the bandwidth. It's the way we tracked, mixed, premastered, and mastered. If you put *Sweet*

Sixteen through a spectrum analyzer, you see that you have extreme highs and lows, and all the other information is in that wide space between. *Accelerator* was compressed at every level, so your bandwidth is condensed, and it allows the same amount of information to pass through your ear unobtrusively. The blueprint is a lot more subliminal, so it gives the illusion that it's more simple. That was the idea behind doing *Accelerator* after we did *Sweet Sixteen*."

"Do you think your audience missed the boat?" I ask.

"People's perception of all of our records is full of shit," replies Hagerty. "A lot of bands think they're communicating something, that they're reaching out to stimulate people in a certain way, which usually leads to buying the record. That's the end result, the goal—it's sort of like a vote for something.

"Now we're ready to pretend we're doing this 'accessible' record. The point of the line 'I'm ready' is all about holding paradoxes up as true, instead of resolving

things. That's the thrust of what we're trying to do: holding a paradox in your head, in your life as a true thing. And it all fits together like a Lego world. It's not one record. It's eight records. It's more records."

This philosophy nullifies the frequently made claim that Royal Trux abandoned the edge when they scribbled on the dotted line and cleansed their forearms. Screw *Twin Infinitives*—signing to Virgin was the most self-directed move they ever made. In one fell swoop they turned their backs on their fans, accumulated the dough they'd need to live autonomously, made the records they wanted to make although few wanted to hear, and crawled out of the major-label train wreck unscathed.

I don't want to talk too much about the label stuff, but . . .
NH: No, it's not that interesting. We just want to stress the fact that we got a fuckin' huge amount of money. On paper it was over a million dollars.

JH: And we got another $500,000 in publishing.

NH: In talking about the major label, we're trying to point out that it's a thing bands can do to get money, but it has to be done just right. We had creative control. We could do anything we wanted as long as it was Royal Trux. The question to be resolved in the courts is: What is Royal Trux? And I'd like to say it means that we scored some money from a company instead of getting screwed by them.

This is probably the first time I've heard about an indie band who went to a big label and left—and I ended up feeling bad for the major label. It seems like you guys rode into town and fucked them over.

NH: Well, yeah. That was our intention from the beginning. We were gonna make records our way and we asked for a large amount of money up front and said take it or leave it. We always knew what we were doing. The same way of thinking that made *Twin Infinitives* got all this money from a fuckin' major label. But we had to sell away our "credibility."

Do you really think you did that?

JH: Well, we let them believe it was tit for tat.

NH: I think that in a lot of ways—for people who give a shit about that kind of thing—the credibility's gone. Obviously, that doesn't matter. We took the credibility and the goodwill that we established with some people and sold it to the Virgin label for money. Basically, we collected on something we didn't care about in the first place, but we knew it was something they would pay money for.

You mean phony indie cred?

NH: Right. It's all phony. See, a lot of bands are already kind of popular when they get signed. That's a bad thing, 'cause then you're in a situation where you feel like with just one extra push you can make it that much further. We didn't want to be popular; we just wanted the fuckin' money.

JH: A lot of these bands do become popular, but in the process of getting to that point they spend all the money. So by the time they are popular, the only money they have got coming to them is actual sales royalties. So once they get there, they better be selling records. If they're not, then the millions of dollars that have been given to them have been spent trying to achieve this ridiculous dream. Our goal was just to get the money. Make our records, get the money.

NH: Yeah. We've always gone the opposite direction and made stuff that's difficult. You've gotta really like music to listen to our records.

Sure, you've gotta really like music to listen to Royal Trux records—because Herrema and Hagerty don't approach anything in a half-assed manner. They may be consummately art-for-art's-sake and politically left of center, but they're both greedy and savvy—and honest about it, to boot. Perhaps it's an extension of their general outlook that their music and apparel seem so deeply imbedded in 1970s America. The couple flirted with excess and returned as hardened and self-sufficient as Hunter S. Thompson or Rolling Thunder Revue–era Dylan. They are classic American nonconformists, determined to make their own mistakes, educate themselves, shed light on cultural inconsistencies and paradoxes, and never lose their skeptical edge.

"We don't work inside the American system," says Herrema. "That was the big idea when we got the Virgin money, that we weren't going to have a mortgage, and nothing on credit. We're not going to be on these payment plans where you get on and don't get off till you're dead. Nobody has any claim on us. We don't have to answer to anybody."

"We can be dissed by group A and not have to go and seek shelter from group B," says Hagerty. "We can take hits from every direction and never have it be the end of the line—it just gives us more energy."

Indeed, the pair exert more energy shaking off unwanted listeners than a mid-'90s grunge star. Royal Trux have built half their career on a heap of audience desertions, forsaking Hagerty's Pussy Galore admirers from the day they switched on the 4-track. Herrema explains: "At Pussy Galore shows, everybody looked the same, acted the same, wanted the same thing, and they all knew what they were gonna get. I was in the audience then, so I could see what the interaction was. And there were certain people who went because of Neil's guitar playing.

"When Neil quit Pussy Galore, a lot of people had specific expectations of what Royal Trux would be. We wanted nothing to do with those people. *Twin Infinitives* was a very good way of getting them off our backs. Just saying 'Look, man, we don't even want to see you at our fuckin' shows.' So we had no constraints placed upon us; none of that mattered."

Of course, the 1990 double LP that sounds so groovy when played at the Watergate complex was more than just a smack-fueled ass-in-the-air. "At the time *Twin Infinitives* came out, everybody said: 'These are incompetent, retarded drug addicts,'" Herrema continues. "After a time people actually listened to it more than once and had a very good reaction to it—once they heard it physically and emotionally. Then there was a different type of writing about it. And then at some point we interjected: Yes, we were drug addicts when we recorded it; no, we're not retarded, and neither of us has ever spent more than five days in a psych ward. When we did *Twin*

Infinitives we were pretty strung out; but the truth is, we worked diligently for a long time."

"It was nine months of actual time with long gaps in between where we couldn't do anything 'cause we were so fucked up, and also sometimes we were plotting things, or listening to tapes over and over," says Hagerty. "It has this feeling of something spun out by the insane. See, usually bands make their 'wild' record fifth or sixth—the classic example is the Beatles' "White Abum." We wanted to get that out of the way. Instead of putting out five records and then a 'masterpiece,' we wanted to do that one second, then make our own fuckin' rock 'n' roll records."

Does he consider *Twin Infinitives* a "rock" album?

"We tried to do something that would push everything out that was materially representative of rock 'n' roll—yet still be a rock 'n' roll record. Rock is absorbed by hip-hop music and vice versa—as well as the old '70s soul stuff, or minimalist music, or experimental music, or metal machine music. It's about that absorption: that's what *Twin Infinitives* is. All this crap and fuzz and craziness, and it's still rock."

But what makes it rock 'n' roll?

"It's about surviving, rebelling against authority, not copping out, not giving in to the corporate thing or becoming part of the logic and losing your individualism. It all adds up to being able to survive being a junkie. Most people fail. When people OD we laugh. It's kind of sad and cruel but we know what it's like. You have to be very careful. You always have to test shit. People get into this junkie thing and they're just stupid. They don't understand it's a fuckin' pharmaceutical, and that you need to read certain books, you need to get the pill book, you need to know your shit."

"You guys seem pretty set on making your own mistakes," I offer.

"Yeah," says Herrema. "People will tell you that you shouldn't do heroin . . ."

"And they would be right," Hagerty interrupts. "But at the same time, hey—it happened."

"Everybody will tell us one thing, but we know we've gotta push through," Herrema continues. "At the time we were making *Thank You* we became very tight with the producer, David Briggs. A lot of people were saying, 'You shouldn't be using a producer. You don't want to sign to a major.' And we were like, 'Oh yes we do!' We always came out on top, because at a certain point we realized our situation, and the kind of control we could take. You can either let something control you or you can rein it in and fucking control it."

Hagerty takes a drag from his umpteenth cigarette and slowly nods. "That's the experiment," he says. "That's what's experimental."

Which is why Royal Trux's current incarnation as a boogie band striving to appeal to townies rather than college kids (Drag City is even running ads for *Accelerator* on late-night cable) is as iconoclastic as the double record scrambled for my ears by Nixon's cronies at Watergate.

I've been at Casa de Trux for five and a half hours when the sun begins to wane and the couple enters the initial stages of kicking-out-the-guest-who-won't-leave. They split a frozen pizza, mention an impending basketball game, and say something about the neighborhood Ku Klux Klan chapter's penchant for gathering after dark. I get the point. But I have to ask them about my favorite Royal Trux song, 1994's "Shockwave Rider." Abandoned on the flip side of a forgettable gutter ballad, the number rang the curtain down on the band's first Drag City run; at the time of its release it also appeared to be setting the stage for a prosperous major-label fling.

The song is based around three samples—a Grand Funk guitar, a Bill Withers breakbeat, and some backwards Four Seasons voices—glued together by erstwhile Trux-sideman Mike Fellows. Atop this cool-as-Coolatta backdrop, Hagerty and Herrema deliver one of their finest vocal duets, Neil's muffled white-boy rap covering the verses and Jennifer taking the chorus with picture-perfect stone-cold grunts.

It's incredibly accessible: if Beck had recorded the number two years later and supported it with a Spike Jonze–directed video starring a white convertible and some Nevada desert, it would have gone triple-platinum. I mention this to the twosome and they snicker at me.

"That shit's fuckin' weak, man," says Hagerty. "Using samples is lame. It's imperialism. We just did 'Shockwave Rider' to show that 'Yeah. Yeah. Yeah, we know the whole routine, this is how it's done.' Just to check in and punch the ticket—'Look, we know how to do this and we can do it really well—but we're making these other kind of records.'

"Part of what we do is illustrate restraint," continues the proudly ascetic man who refuses to fly. "It's like: we can clone human beings now, but we don't. Until now, has man ever discovered something and said, 'Wait a minute, we don't want to go down that road'?"

"I know what you want from me and I know what you might like from me, but I'm not going to give it to you!" Herrema picks up the thread, bouncing off the sofa while Hagerty questions her caffeine intake. "That would be evil of me, just to give you what you want! I'll give you what I've got to give, and you take it on my terms, or you don't get anything. I'm not there to serve the audience and they're not there to serve me. This is a reciprocal relationship." ✪

KATHLEEN HANNA Julie Ruin

As Bikini Kill's singer, Kathleen Hanna was the most visible, often the most voluble, certainly the most volatile riot grrrl. By the late '90s, Riot Grrrl's legacy was indisputable, while its initial splendid unreasonableness had mutated into a shrewd and ambitious critique of business as usual. As Hanna's agit-pop trio Le Tigre was gestating, and long before Bikini Kill's 2019 reunion, **ELISABETH VINCENTELLI** interviewed Hanna about her solo project, Julie Ruin.

It's easy to make fun of Riot Grrrl now, just as it was when the "movement" (for lack of a better term) peaked, around 1991. Riot Grrrl invited ridicule: it was flamboyant, in your face, extreme, passionate. Most of all, it felt unreasonable to many observers—all the more so because it was often very young, very vocal girls being unreasonable. That year felt like the "school's out" bell had just rung, and the consequent sense of exhilarated freedom led to a wide range of behavior, from the most exciting (the sheer gall of it all!) to the most inane and thoughtless stunts (publicly burning a magazine because it contained a negative review).

Kathleen Hanna was at Riot Grrrl ground zero from day one. As the singer in Bikini Kill, she was the most visible member of the most visible band. As such she was quoted and misquoted, used as both a figurehead and a straw girl, praised and castigated, adored and vilified. And just about anyone who saw one of Bikini Kill's blistering live shows will agree that when they were on, the band were mindblowing, awesome.

Bikini Kill weren't comfortable being leaders, though, and their adversarial relationship with the whole concept of fame distracted them from realizing their potential as liberators. And then they just seemed to disappear from the public eye—so much so that when they announced they had broken up a few months ago, some were surprised to learn they had still been around.

Just as her band broke up, Kathleen Hanna resurfaced with a new album, and the new name of Julie Ruin. Robert Christgau ended a catty capsule review in the *Village Voice* with the words "She's 29 and she needs to move on," while Johnny Ray Huston, in these pages, found the record as frustrating as it was fascinating (see sidebar). I found myself both irritated by Julie Ruin's self-imposed limits and seduced by her barbs. At least she wasn't afraid to take a spill—something to be cherished at a time when the main options for women in rock tend to be playing temperamental divas or spiritual waifs.

Kathleen Hanna punctuates every other sentence with a "you know what I mean" that's half query, half statement. Words pour out of her in a dizzying, charismatic gush, and she answers questions in a free-associating way, dropping a topic almost as soon as she broaches it, only to return to it later. She does answer questions, but not necessarily when they're asked.

And for someone who's often been accused of being difficult, she could not be more forthcoming. She does not balk when the first thing out of my mouth is to wonder why she's still using the same damn typewriter font and the same tired cut-and-paste layout. Aesthetics obviously are a major concern (her current promo photos are very staged, Hanna posing as a foxy librarian/grad student in front of books on feminism), yet the CD design looks like an afterthought—something it almost certainly wasn't.

Right, right. [*Smiles*] But it's my style, that's how I lay things out. I wasn't even thinking about it. [*Noticing my scribbles on her bio*] Did you circle "socialism"?
Well, yes. The bio says: "There are also songs about hating cops, socialism [sic] and needing an invisible friend. Though many would like to believe it's dead, socialism is still a loaded word, especially now that it's more acceptable to question unfettered capitalism, and given the Left's current debate over whether we should focus more on gender and race or on class issues."
I was reading an essay on socialism at the time I wrote that. I feel stupid—I can't remember the woman's name. I have to look it up in my journal, where I write down stuff so later I can reference authors. Just like I take notes on books, it helps me incorporate the knowledge. A lot of my friends are college professors, so when I go to their house I look at what they read and I write it down. And then I go to libraries or used-book stores. That's where I found *Lesbian Ethics*, for instance—one of the best books I've ever read. It's about naming things that haven't been named before, about lots of problems I've seen coming up over and over in the feminist community.
Like what?
Like the way capitalism affects our relationships with each other in terms of competitiveness and jealousy. You need to have an economic analysis to go along with a gender analysis. It's not either/or.
Where do you start? Is community-building a crucial part of that process? It definitely was integral to Riot Grrrl.
Totally. I can't talk about Riot Grrrl per se because I'm not a part of that as an organization, but I try to keep

BIKINI KILL: TOBI VAIL, KATHLEEN HANNA, KATHI WILCOX (PHOTO, MICHAEL GALINSKY)

Bikini Kill were together for seven years and people would tell us we should quit! And I thought, How come the Stones can be a band forever? But then again, they suck now. It's also a totally ageist thing. More than once I've had industry-type people come up to me and say, "You know, you're not getting any younger."

That's why it was so nice to hear you quote Lesley Gore's "I'm Coolin,' No Foolin'" in "Stay Monkey." Not only does it position you on a musical continuum, but the choice of Lesley Gore is relatively provocative.

That song's chorus rules my world! Lesley Gore has a really super-sexy voice, I got kinda obsessed with her. I also listen to Holly Golightly, and almost every song starts with "Sophisticated Boom-Boom" by the Shangri-Las—not the song but the same riff.

Quoting Lesley Gore in "Stay Monkey," or the Cars on "Breakout A-Town" acknowledges the past with a wink, without being sentimentally nostalgic. There's a lot more humor and flexibility to your songwriting. Riot Grrrl could be frustrating because the politics were so progressive and yet the music was so conservative. Too often it was two-chord punk—played ineptly. Was it deliberate, to get people to pay more attention to the words?

I just like garage rock. Besides, when I first started I was just learning about music. I had been in a couple of bands, but I didn't understand much about how songs are constructed. In my head it was a medium I wanted to use to express something.

I used to be a lot—I still am—more content-oriented when it came to making art. The content predominated, so I didn't care about the technical side. Now I care about it more; I want both content and technique in order to communicate. I see how in order to express the content, I do need to care about the technical things. If I don't, it'll come out as "I Wanna Be Your Dog" over and over and over again, with feminist lyrics.

The Julie Ruin album is a bit of a stylistic departure. It sounds very new wave, or rather post-punk the way the Rough Trade bands of the early '80s were post-punk. It feels exploratory, which also explains why some of the tracks fall short: exploring means sometimes you don't find anything.

I started borrowing equipment from friends; they would show me how to use it, and I'd go home and start playing. It was liberating—I knew it would not end up sounding like Bratmobile or Bikini Kill—[*breaking off*]

up so I can give addresses to people who write to me. There's something called *Riot Grrrl Review* out of Florida, which is a review of women-run fanzines, as well as some that aren't necessarily by women but that fit with the general political agenda. Riot Grrrl Press also keeps going. A lot of the mail I get is from girls/women in high school. They talk about hanging out with their friends, listening to Bikini Kill or Sleater-Kinney. A lot of girls write about hanging out together. I'm sure it's been going on forever: people who are marginalized hang out together. A lot of the girls writing now have a consciousness level I didn't have at their age. I don't know if it has to do with Riot Grrrl.

But what happens if music becomes our only sense of community? What happens if we can get three thousand people out to see a rock show but we can't get ten people out if someone in our community gets beaten up by the cops? What if the only sense of community we have is that we consume the same products, which happen to be records? We cannot stay in this insular world and be only about consuming pop music or punk music.

It is understood in this country that if they don't talk about you, you don't exist. Hardly anyone talks about Riot Grrrl anymore, yet it still seems to exist in one form or another. How do the people who write to you hear about this stuff?

I think they read about it in *Angry Women in Rock*, the RE/Search book Andrea Juno did. And maybe some book on Nirvana mentioned Bikini Kill. I have no idea. A lot of it's probably word of mouth: "My older brother or sister told me."

Six years in music time is like a year in real life, and it's even worse for women-dominated bands. They seem to have a short shelf life.

Are you okay? [*My contact lenses have gone dry: she makes sure I have eyedrops*] So I had a really good time experimenting with the drum machine and sampler. Doing everything by myself was a bit of a reaction against being in a band and having to deal with a consensus situation—not that it was always a consensus situation!

At the same time, the experiments remain limited. This could have come out in 1981. By the way, why is it that the entire electronica scene is male, except for Neotropic?

And like, where is the female Alec Empire? I really like Atari Teenage Riot, so I started reading his interviews, and the more experimental music magazines he's in. I would never have looked at them before, but I got into ATR and thought I'd check this stuff out. And there are no women in these magazines.

Riot Grrrl felt very insular, as if the only people you could listen to were the ones sharing the exact same wavelength. And there was a generation gap with older feminists that created some misunderstandings on both sides.

I've been thinking about that—about defining yourself in opposition to something, especially if you're trying to find some kind of feminist continuum in your life. I know a lot of what I wrote in the early Bikini Kill fanzine now seems to me totally oppositional and really kinda stupid. Even though it didn't say this, part of the subtext was, "Oh, the '70s feminists were dowdy, and we're really hip and cool." Now that I look back I think, Why did I have to put down what other people have done in order to create something of my own?

But at the same time, Riot Grrrl and Bikini Kill did leave a legacy. Something as accomplished as Potential, *by 18-year-old cartoonist Ariel Schrag, probably would not have existed ten years ago. There's been a change in access (zines, the web) and mentalities. And that's where Riot Grrrl lives on, as a kind of unacknowledged mentoring.*

I don't think anything I've done would have been done without Kathy Acker. In college one time I was supposed to write an essay and I couldn't write it: I

The latest album by the artist also known as Kathleen Hanna isn't perfect, but perfection is definitely not the point. With Bikini Kill, and now solo as Julie Ruin, Hanna has always emphasized (to quote Bikini Kill's "New Radio") "the gaps in teeth, the dirty nails" of women's lives. Turning present-day struggles into songs, the anti-production on Bikini Kill's albums was designed to make them—like the ideas and emotions they contain—a challenge to consume. *Julie Ruin* applies the same approach to solo electronic music-making.

Initially, the similarities between *Julie Ruin* and Bikini Kill's recordings are more noticeable than the differences. Hanna's arsenal of vocal characters, especially, persists. She's long sabotaged what could be a purely pretty or purely powerful sound, instead adopting disobedient, conflicted, sometimes deliberately annoying tones ranging from brat(ty) girl to Valley girl. (I've long suspected some people's dislike of Bikini Kill stems from unwillingness to hear a female voice that's not friendly, that doesn't give a damn about being liked.) Julie Ruin pinpoints and emphasizes the defiant, atonal undercurrent of "sexy" '80s female new-wave singing and assorted other pop-culture voices. ("V.G.I." ends with a Fran Drescher imitation.) With its dinky digital hardcore drones and strings, "Aerobicide" is the punk Madonna that Ciccone Youth tried to imagine. "I Wanna Know What Love Is" uses another Hanna tactic: re-singing a pop sentiment (in this case the chorus of a Foreigner hit) so it's transformed from a feminine romantic fantasy into a feminist distress call.

Whereas Bikini Kill's studio sound seemed like a manifestation of the band's inner conflicts and self-destructive impulses, Ruin uses found riffs like finger paints. The resulting mess sounds like freedom, not frustration. Guitar is central to the album's electronic music-making—a playful, rule-breaking approach sure to irritate purists on both sides of the imaginary rock/electronic divide. "Radical or Pro-Parental" and "V.G.I." use sample-based arrangement techniques to add potency to rudimentary chord progressions; "On Language" loops the Kinks. With repeated listens, little vocal "mistakes" (coughs, burps), craftsy-creative instrumental decorations (patty-cake and typewriter rhythm tracks), and radio station–surfing shifts begin to function like hooks.

Lyrically, Hanna's feminism has always been more reactive than proactive, and Julie Ruin has its share of songs that respond rather than imagine. There's a virtue to this reactive approach: as the media get set to market Lilith Fair and an increasingly broad array of airbrushed pseudo-feminisms, songs grow scarce that overtly attack and reject male power structures. "A Place Called Won't Be There" does just that, to a crackling backdrop Beck would envy. And in one line, "I Wanna Know What Love Is" says more about JonBenét Ramsey than a landfill of tabloids, *New York Times* op-ed pieces, and TVs tuned to *Geraldo*. On a personal scale, this reactive approach results in the unconventionally frank kiss-off "Apartment #5," which confesses, "I'm not always truthful," then sneers, "I'm happy being me and I don't wanna be you" before dancing off to a carefree flute melody. Songs that chart a relationship in progress ("Stay Monkey"; "Breakout A-Town") have to fight for momentary pleasure; complications of connection are summarized in homilies like "Sometimes the secret is yes" and "Afraid is much better than a fake forever." When *Julie Ruin* dares to imagine, it consciously attempts to be subconscious, trying for a musical version of *l'écriture feminine*, the French feminist term for a distinct female approach to writing—one that rejects linearity and logic. The result is a muffled blur like "My Morning Is Summer"—the aural equivalent, as its title suggests, of a half-formed thought on a hot day.

An irony: though one punk parody finds Ruin railing, "Just another book about women in rock," as if the mere thought makes her wanna take up crochet, Simon Reynolds's and Joy Press's recent "women in rock" book *The Sex Revolts* also methodically applies *l'écriture feminine* to music. Amid the sonic beach-party setting of "V.G.I." Ruin declares she's not a genius but a genie, "granting girls wishes" from her "stone-cold bikini." It's a lighthearted moment, the kind that's wholly absent from Bikini Kill's albums, which practically imploded in their urgency.

For a listener, the frustration of *Julie Ruin* stems from hearing a radical artist with natural talent of pop magnitude continue to scale her work down willfully to miniaturist solitude. With slicker production, songs like "V.G.I." and "A Place Called Won't Be There" could be a radical presence on the radio. But Ruin doesn't want her revolution broadcast or televised—she'd rather whisper secrets on her own terms and hope the little girls understand. The problem is, they may not get to hear her.—*Johnny Ray Huston*

couldn't stick to one point . . . because I had political problems with sticking to one point! Then somebody gave me Acker's *Kathy Goes to Haiti*. I'd never read her before—and my writing was similar to hers. I was like, "I'm not crazy!" To me she was a real writer because she had a book with a color cover [*laughs*].

I ended up writing my final paper in fanzine form, about why I couldn't write an essay—all the reasons why—and I used weird pieces of fiction in it. Then I didn't show up for the final class, where you're supposed to turn in the essay, because I'd gotten on a Greyhound bus to Seattle. I'd heard Kathy Acker was doing a workshop there. And she told me, "Nobody goes to spoken-word events. Why don't you join a band?" So she was the reason.

*French feminists like Luce Irigaray and Hélène Cixous pop up a lot as reference. Yet their theory of biology-derived female writing (*écriture féminine*) seems to have lost some of its luster recently.*
The whole writing-from-the-body thing seems really essentialist about biological determinism, and I'm not really into that. But I think about it more in terms of sexuality—and it's probably something I got from *Cosmopolitan* or something [*laughs*]—how men experience orgasm versus how I do. Just how language or plot is structured around this slow build [*in goofy mocking voice*] to the climax. I was trying to do the song equivalent in "On Language." You can't really understand what the words are, it's supposed to be more about the sensation of something than explaining it. It is the sensation, it is the thing. Instead of writing something about experiencing the sensation, making the sensation. It's hard for me to explain. [*Laughs*]

Speculum of the Other Woman [by Irigaray] is more like that kind of writing—the propositions are supposedly wrong but they're not: you understand them in another way, not the traditional logical way. It seems to me there's a whole logic within being illogical.
I find this frustrating, because it seems to leave logic, reason, and well-balanced arguments to men. Whereas if it's fuzzy and autobiographical, it's "naturally" female. But even Hélène Cixous's recent material—particularly in her plays—is narrative-based, though one of her earlier arguments was that traditional narrative is actually a masculine trope.
I'm going in the opposite direction. I feel like what I was doing before was really . . . obvious. Or pragmatic. It was easy to grasp. The language was there to communicate in a traditional way. With the new album, I wanted to do something experimental, but to me

experimental meant . . . fucking pop music! I used to be anti–pop music—against what pop represented: total denial, a way to escape reality. But then I thought, when you're seriously suffering and you can't take a vacation, music can be a way to get out of a bad place for a few hours. It's totally valid and important.

Was this change related to collaborating with Joan Jett a few years back?

That was one of the experiences that made me want to do the Julie Ruin thing. At one point, when I was helping Joan write a song, I went into a room with this guy who wrote, like, Bryan Adams songs. He had a keyboard and in five seconds he wrote a whole song and structured it. My experience until then was, "You write songs in the basement, you tour 'em, and if they're good you record 'em." So if I'm totally underground, I'm never going to do interviews, and I'm going to write songs in this way that is "authentic"—and I have real big problems with notions of authenticity in the first place.

Seeing this guy work got me thinking. I wondered if I could take this format and make it very personal and human. So I tried to make a record using more modern technology than I'm used to. And yet you can still hear the slippages and the fuck-ups.

Is that why you chose to record as Julie Ruin? Picking a new name seems like a very pop thing to do. At the same time, you could have banked on your own name, and chosen not to do it.

I want to have a stage name now, I want to have some distance between the personal life and the music. I made most of this record while I was still in Bikini Kill, and going by the name Kathleen Hanna would have put it in opposition to Bikini Kill, which wouldn't be true.

That's another reason I'm doing interviews: I want people to know it's me, and I want them to know about this record. I'm a different person than I was five years ago. I was much more sensitive then. Now, if some guy asks me in an interview if I was sexually abused and wants me to talk about it, I can say, "It's none of your goddamn business." I can leave, and I won't look back and feel bad about myself over it. I can hold my own. I probably won't read most of the articles anyway, it freaks me out too much.

I basically created Julie Ruin as this character who's a lot stronger than me, who's more able to distance herself from these things than perhaps Kathleen was. She helped me so much, I wanted to do something nice back. So I let her make a record. ◐

THE MAGNETIC FIELDS

Stephin Merritt unleashed his magnum opus, the Magnetic Fields' three-CD *69 Love Songs*, at the end of the century. The album was an instant game changer that radically altered and elevated public appreciation of Merritt's music—suddenly, comparisons to his hero Irving Berlin didn't seem at all far-fetched. **KIAN GOH** met the songwriter in New York, and **FRANKIN BRUNO** offers an extended appreciation of an extended set of songs.

The whole idea seems at first many things: ludicrous, foolhardy, gimmicky, even pompous. Call it millennial madness, but someone had to do it—and why not the relentless perfectionist, the ardent musicologist, the sulky genius . . . For years, Stephin Merritt and the Magnetic Fields have been toying with our emotions, pulling our strings, singing to us the cloying songs we receive with equal parts affection and wonder. Having come off what most would consider a high point with their last full-length, almost four years ago—the laden and sparkling *Get Lost*—Merritt now plows into the back catalog of classic pop and emerges with a collection of sounds that is massive enough to be a magnum opus of sorts, as I'm sure it's meant to be, and one that is surprisingly manageable and full of little treasures. If he's been rather coy about these things before, Merritt calls his latest album exactly what it is: *69 Love Songs*.

We meet at an East Village café, a not surprising choice on his part. Merritt has held to a distinctly regular modus vivendi for the last five years or so, spending nights recording in his tiny apartment/studio and days writing his songs in cafés like this one, all within a couple of blocks of each other. Having spent some time myself catching Magnetic Fields live shows and bumping into both Merritt and Magnetic Fields collaborator and manager Claudia Gonson on various occasions, it seems clear he's most comfortable with a fairly small circle of close friends, and a small number of hangouts.

Now Merritt walks in, twenty minutes late and flustered, carrying a tiny dog in one hand and a dog bag in the other. Apparently, he just cabbed over in a rush after buying the bag, but the dog wouldn't get into it (the dog bag looks a bit like a duffel bag with mesh panels). Irving is a baby Chihuahua, and cute like that. They've not been together long, but Irving's already the stuff of chat and gossip in downtown circles. We settle for the interview, but not before Merritt fusses with Irving a little.

He admits what I'd suspected: the whole thing started with a title he couldn't pass up.

"The album title was the first thing that came up. I decided to write 69 love songs. I thought they would fit on two records, turned out to be three . . ."

Is it a concept album?

"Yes—well, a theme album. There used to be a distinction between concept albums and theme albums. Frank Sinatra singing songs for young lovers would be a theme album, whereas David Bowie's *Ziggy Stardust and the Spiders from Mars* would be a concept album because it followed characters . . . a concept album being more like a musical, and a theme album the same thing again and again."

It's clear that Merritt is prone to ruminations of this sort. "Now, this is so much of a theme album," he continues, "it's almost a concept album."

It does have a thread of sorts running through it, though—

"Not a narrative. The songs are in almost random order, so there can't be a narrative. I suppose if you could imagine two characters having all these experiences and there's really only one narrator and only one antagonist, then it could be a concept album, a very big concept album."

They keep falling in and out of love.

"But you could do that with any album," he finishes.

The waitress comes over. Merritt orders a BLT and white wine, just as the noise level around our table escalates.

"When you transcribe this, you're going to hear that woman's entire conversation plus a little bit of me," he predicts, echoing my thoughts. We move farther back—a difficult feat with a dog, dog bag, knapsack, newspaper, tape recorder, and notes.

There are as many kinds of love as there are pop songs, it seems, and in the course of 69 love songs Merritt has more than enough time to illustrate quite a few of them. On "I Don't Believe in the Sun," love is all emotion, forlorn and maudlin, pessimistic as the title hints, while "When My Boy Walks Down the Street" is doe-eyed, blissed-out adoration ("Maybe he should be illegal / he just makes life too complete"). On "Let's Pretend We're Bunny Rabbits" love is, well, all about being like bunny rabbits, "rapidly becoming rabid, singing little rabbit songs." The possibilities are

MUCK, BILE, AND NECTAR
A fellow songwriter ruminates on 69 Love Songs

Hospitality Room

Usually, I try to avoid mentioning my own musical activities when writing about someone else's, but bear with me this once. In the summer of 1993, Stephin Merritt and I, among others, found ourselves on a songwriters' panel at the *College Music Journal* convention, playing a couple of songs each and answering a few questions. Over bagels in the hospitality room, before we went on, Stephin commented that a song I'd sung at a *Chickfactor*-sponsored show the previous night had been stuck in his head all morning. He was even smiling. I've come to realize this was rare praise.

The panel proceeded in alphabetical order, so I began the morning's ad hoc hootenanny with my "Officer Angel," a paean to an LA policewoman/traffic-copter radio personality that rhymes "traffic" and "seraphic" (the sort of thing that makes critics cry that the rhymes preceded the song, which is both false and irrelevant). During the Q & A, I made some ill-conceived comments about my insistence on trying to "avoid clichés."

Stephin pounced: "If you're trying to avoid clichés, why do you pronounce 'angel' to rhyme with 'hell'?"

(I hadn't even noticed this, though it does fit with the song's attempt to make something of the word's connotations of mercy and vengeance.)

My sudden adversary followed up with a pithy exposition of his now well-known view that everything one can say in a pop song is always already unavoidably clichéd. I backpedaled lamely, forgot half of my next song, and this little tug-of-war between the celebration of convention and the struggle to escape it became a subtext of the remainder of the panel. (Stephin, by the way, played "When You're Old and Lonely" some time before *Get Lost* appeared. He also took Barbara Manning to task for grammatical errors.)

Replay

A year or maybe two years later, another hectic CMJ weekend. I'm in Manhattan, far from the main activities of the convention, walking to dinner with friends. Stephin materializes across the street and hails me over. He tells me, with obvious relish, that Cole Porter had rhymed 'traffic' and 'seraphic' some forty years before either of us was born. (Had I given the impression that

staggering, perhaps just as well for those of us who've been foolish enough to bemoan the death of love—or at least songs of love.

But when is it not a love song? Many—probably most—of Merritt's songs are about love, and he's been frequently held up as one of the few who can write a convincing one.

"There're not all that many topics for songs that don't seem silly or that are not clichés. There's love, there's dancing . . . there's solitude, a very common topic."

Many would say that love is the most clichéd of all—

"Probably. And dancing. You really can't say much new in a song about dancing. It's probably even worse than love . . ."

Merritt has numerous songs about dancing, on this album and on previous ones, too. But, unlike love, dancing never seems to be the focus. It's something to be done in spite of it all, a universal opiate maybe, when nothing else seems to work.

"Yeah. I recently noticed, I don't just have songs about going dancing; it's more like: let's go dancing later, or: sometimes, we go dancing . . . I suppose that's because I'm not making dance music, in the sense of music people immediately identify as something to be danced to."

These are obsessions that take up more than their share of Merritt's songwriting moments. Love, dancing . . . and then there's the moon. On *Get Lost*, there are three moon songs.

"The moon kept coming up. There're no moon songs in this one, or at least no songs with the moon in the title. People were beginning to make fun of the moon songs . . ."

We've had long albums before, but for the most part we've wished they were a bit shorter; that instead of being a decent 15-song album, if they lost the filler it would be a really good 11-song one.

"No one's going to wish there were 68 love songs . . . ," Merritt reads my mind.

I suppose it is quite ingenious. The blend of size and suggestiveness makes excuses unnecessary. How could it be 68 love songs? But one soon realizes, over several unavoidably long listening sessions, that in spite of the songs' variety, there is no filler, just different takes on a theme, other interpretations. Which doesn't mean all the songs are uniformly great.

"There are some songs no one seems to like yet, that I think are some of the best songs on the record, particularly 'Love in the Shadows,'" Merritt observes. "And I think it's because it's a bit quieter than the others, people don't notice it. But I'm very proud of the lyric, and if I'd made a whole record like that I think people would like it."

I ask if he didn't consider the shorter, quieter songs to be different from the more typical, pop-format three-minute ones.

"No, and one of the shorter songs is the loudest song. That's 'Punk Love,' one of several pieces of conceptual music on the record."

Is that one a bit of a joke?

"A lot of the songs are a bit of a joke. It would be horrible to have a three-hour album with no humor on it. "

And there's nothing if not humor on this record. Merritt is master of the simultaneously clever, clever-clever, and slightly daft lyrical pun, and this album spills over with them. One of the funniest, however, is "Yeah! Oh, Yeah!" which has been called the "I Got You Babe" of this record. Gonson plays a frustrated wife asking questions like "Do I drive you up the wall? Do you dread every phone call? Can you not stand me at all?" to Merritt's nonchalant "Yeah, oh yeah!"'s.

Another eye-opening piece of so-called conceptual music is "Experimental Music Love," which at least one acquaintance of mine cannot stand at all. If one can imagine a single line of lyric (that is, the title itself) staggered at every phrase and echoed indefinitely, that's what it sounds like.

"Is he epileptic, this Merritt? It's only twenty seconds long or something . . . it's really difficult on headphones."

Considering the scope of the effort, I was curious whether much editing was required to determine which songs might fit and which might not.

"Maybe a third of the songs that I wrote for the album are not on it. It isn't editing so much as pruning."

I noticed too that several of the songs seem to date back quite a bit.

"A few of them do, especially pieces of songs. I might have a chorus lying around for ten years. We've been playing 'I Need a New Heart' for a few years live."

I wonder, with Merritt's admission that one could imagine a thematic thread running loosely through the album—a narrator and a protagonist playing out scenes of various loves—whether any, or all, of it was at all autobiographical. Or, more pointedly, if such animated stories could be anything but autobiographical.

"Most of my songs and most love songs in general are so vague they could be either autobiographical or fictional. If I say 'You don't love me anymore,' obviously I do feel that way—there are people who

I thought I'd invented the fact that these words rhyme?) Even at the time, I was less irked by this evidence of my own unoriginality than flattered by the fact that Stephin had found room for my song in his copious memory for such things. (I could swear I've since seen this rhyme in Porter's *Complete Lyrics*. But trying to locate it again for this article, all I can find is "traffic" / "*The Graphic*"—apparently a magazine of the day—in the 1928 show *Paris*. Maybe it was Lorenz Hart?)

Triple-Set One-Upmanship

And now comes *69 Love Songs*. Beyond being a showstopping display of prowess (and megalomania) that makes me want to burn my notebooks and piano, it does help clarify what Stephin was getting at in our infrequent encounters, and confirms my suspicion that our views aren't as far apart as they seem. What makes songs dreary or intolerable, Stephin helped me realize, isn't cliché per se, but unexamined or unacknowledged cliché—the stringing together of stock images, phrases, and rhymes in the mistaken belief that the received language of popular song can be used uncritically to express the writer's "deepest feelings," about, e.g., love (feelings that often bear a marked resemblance to everyone else's). Songs can be written from the rhymes out—or under any other formal constraint one chooses—but doing so unawares can only lead to self-deception.

Take the (barely) hypothetical example of Joe Coffeehouse, working furiously on a new song in the aftermath of a breakup. "You ruined my life," he sings. And then the next line will end up being some minor variant on "This feeling cuts me, just like a knife."

This is lazy and boring; worse, the writer has let himself be led around by the nose by the convenient rhyme, while operating under the illusion that he's expressed himself sincerely. Similarly with "all by myself / left on the shelf" or, in the '30s, "charms / arms." Obviously, any of these rhymes can be revitalized with a little thought (Ira Gershwin rang a nice change on the latter in "Embraceable You"); these aren't issues of originality vs. unoriginality, but of craft and awareness of history.

Needless to say, Stephin Merritt is neither lazy nor boring, and he certainly knows his craft. When he rhymes "all over the world" with "get me back my girl" in "Acoustic Guitar," he's ribbing Joe Coffeehouse, not repeating Joe's errors. (Later, "girl" gets rhymed with "mother-of-pearl" and the unlikely but inevitable-in-context "Steve Earle.") When the rhymes are simple—not the same thing as "clichéd" in the above sense—they often comment on the very drabness of the narrator's feelings ("The only thing that I could ever feel / I can't believe it wasn't real"). And when they're Tin Pan Alley–witty, it's with full awareness of their artifice (as on disc 3's "The Night You Can't Remember" and "Queen of the Savages," which strains singability with "villages / religious," which neatly undercuts the song's back-to-nature conceit).

Two of the triple set's more pedestrian titles, "I Think I Need a New Heart" and "The Way You Say Goodnight" (the latter presumably inspired by Fields/Kern's "The Way You Look Tonight"), turn out to be the titles of fictional songs within the songs. Any number of similar observations could be made about Stephin's use of received, even venerable forms (the a-b-a-b ballad "Two Kinds of People"), chord progressions (the aptly titled "Meaningless"), tunes (I heard a direct lift from "Both Sides Now," but it might take as long to find the song as it did to find a Cole Porter rhyme), and even the vocal approach.

Of course, there's a larger sense in which an original song is impossible—once the 12 notes of the Western scale are taken as a limit, all their melodic, harmonic, and rhythmic combinations are in some sense potentially "there," waiting to be selected by the songwriter. Similarly with the English language itself.

Combine these two systems, and you get a dizzying but still finite number of possible songs. (Confine yourself to combinations that might be interpreted as "love songs," and the possibilities decrease somewhat.)

Even this is not an original observation: it's pervasive in Borges, who probably wouldn't claim it as his own. Does that make a pun like "I'm no Nino Rota, I don't know the score" (from "Reno Dakota") a cliché, simply because it waits in the language like David's already clichéd torso in a block of marble?

Metaphysics aside, *69 Love Songs* wouldn't have been possible without a thorough immersion in the stew of muck, bile, and nectar from which pop songs are distilled. But if this is "unoriginality," it has little to do with what I will charitably credit myself with having had in mind onstage six years ago.—*Franklin Bruno*

actually don't love me anymore—but so does everyone over 2 years old . . ."

But when you wrote that you probably had someone specific in mind, I counter.

"Or more than one person; but I wouldn't remember I had them in mind five minutes later, because it could apply to anybody. There are dozens of people who don't love me anymore," he chuckles. "How would I remember which one it was?"

And at some point it doesn't matter who they are—

"It immediately doesn't matter who they are. My mother used to think all my songs were about her. A lot of people thought all my songs were about them. But almost all my songs are about nobody in particular."

So it's like a collection of feelings . . .

". . . from a repertoire, yeah. In a love song you can't really write about new feelings, new emotions. There's a certain stock of emotions and there's a certain stock of situations that people are in."

A bit of a myth hangs over you, I begin—

"Yes," he says, without pause. He's probably been asked this before, and is, in any case, very aware of it.

Whether deliberately or not, Merritt has honed to perfection, both on- and offstage, the image of the difficult pop genius, quiet and sulky, tryingly soft-spoken and distant, scruffy and nicotine-fueled. Many people, admitted Magnetic Fields devotees, have said something like, "I loved the album. Then I met Stephin and he seemed really quiet—"

"And really mean. Some people think I'm really mean. They'll walk up and say, 'Hi, remember me? I met you in Florida,' and I'll say, 'Sorry, I don't recall,' and they're mortally wounded. But why would I remember?

"It's probably related to my stage persona, but I think it's mostly related to the mythmaking process of music journalism. Journalists read a press kit, form an impression of the musician, and proceed as if that were true, when it may not be."

Then there's also the part about legend. Is it true, I ask, that when Neil Hannon (of the Divine Comedy) comes to town, he plays a Magnetic Fields song to gain New York street credibility?

There's a pause before Merritt answers.

"Yeah!"

I'm sure you enjoy that.

"Yes, I enjoy that. It's funny."

Many of the 69 songs sound disturbingly familiar, often as though you'd heard them on your big sister's turntable but never found out what they were. Or

maybe an odd melodic phrase would remind you of a Stock, Aitken and Waterman album you threw away years ago. Merritt, in fact, seems most comfortable playing with our memories—both good and bad—of events which shaped our years growing up, and the unforgettable soundtracks that accompanied them. It might be devious, except that these are his favorite songs as well.

I ask him whether he even agrees.

"I do agree that I have songs that are sometimes deliberately and other times not deliberately reminiscent of other songs. Everyone has songs that seem accidentally like other songs. I have deliberate ones as well."

I've tried describing the Magnetic Fields to friends who've not heard them, and it's proven to be somewhat difficult. Invariably I end up saying something like, "It's kind of odd, pop-like, maybe Burt Bacharach meets the Pet Shop Boys . . ."

"Although nowadays," Merritt pipes up, not too insulted, "it's easy to imagine that Burt Bacharach would work with the Pet Shop Boys, and what they would come up with wouldn't sound like me."

Well, how would you describe your music?

"Before *69 Love Songs*, I suppose I would have said something like: Leonard Cohen sings the Ronettes. Now it's too varied for me to categorize."

Indeed, given Merritt's commitment to making the pop album of the century—complete with shades of everything he likes that came before—the album astounds in its breadth. The usual suspects are much in evidence—glimpses of ABBA and, yes, the Ronettes. But some of the most pleasing moments are also the most surprising ones, like "Papa Was a Rodeo," a softly sweeping country ballad that balances mock sincerity and gentle irony as only a Magnetic Fields song can.

The genre-hopping doesn't stop there. "Love Is Like Jazz" and "Punk Love" are somewhat beyond irony, the first a jazz (!) piece which, following the lyric, "Love is like jazz / you make it up as you go along," is never played the same way, and the other a three-chord romp through a total of three words. There's also a blues tune titled, confoundingly, "Xylophone Track."

Aside from Claudia Gonson, Merritt relies on the vocal talents of several friends, and many of their efforts are standouts, like the Stevie Nicks–inspired "No One Will Ever Love You," sung by Shirley Simms. I ask him if he prefers working with others.

"Well, I prefer not hearing my little, incredibly low, sad-sounding voice all the time. I like to hear the personality changing between songs.

"All my favorite bands and all the best-selling bands in history," he adds, "have had multiple songwriters and/or multiple singers: the Bee Gees, the Beatles, Fleetwood Mac, ABBA, the Kinks, the Rolling Stones even . . ."

The singer-songwriter duality harks back to the first Magnetic Fields records, on which Susan Anway was the singer, and also to the 6ths project, where every track had a different vocalist. Merritt has been working on a follow-up to the 1995 Wasps' Nests album, and this time, instead of taking the somberest of indie rock for a ride through sing-alongs, he's rumored to be assembling a dazzling array of pop divas.

But Merritt won't talk about the new 6ths album today. The waitress arrives just in time to change the subject. She says they're out of bacon for the BLT. He gets the soup of the day instead.

I ask if he'll talk about something else that intrigues me. In addition to love and dancing—essential Merritt references—there are several allusions on *69 Love Songs* to pretty girls.

"Are there?"

At least two, in rather compromising positions . . .

"'A Pretty Girl Is Like,' and then, a pretty girl in her underwear . . . you're right . . . then there's a pretty boy in the same song," he points out.

"Most of the love songs one hears have been written about supposed pretty girls, so it would be a shame to leave them out on an album of 69 love songs. But

'A Pretty Girl Is Like' is not really about pretty girls. It's about songs about pretty girls, specifically Irving Berlin's song 'A Pretty Girl Is Like a Melody.' And I'm saying if a pretty girl is like a melody, then a pretty girl is like anything you want.

"And the feminist perspective would be," he adds, "'How dare you say what a pretty girl is like!' Well, let the pretty girl say what she's like."

Right, but you're not saying that—

"I am kind of saying that. I'm saying that a pretty girl is like several ludicrous things, ludicrous and intentionally shocking things—a minstrel show, a violent crime, what's the third one?"

Something about being the dumbest in the world, I think . . .

"Really, more than being a song about other songs about pretty girls, it's a song about metaphors in general, and what they do when they're applied to people. It's a little pompous, I suppose. It wasn't before I said that, though . . ."

French onion soup arrives and Merritt ends up feeding most of it, the cheese at least, to Irving, who seems to like it very much. It's an unexpectedly cute sight.

I've heard they go for walks a lot.

"He's only 4 months old, so he doesn't really heel yet. I take him for drags. I can drag him on his leash without hurting him because he's got a harness, not a collar. It pulls on the whole dog—very holistic."

So what does someone do after attempting a triple album that sums up one's own career to date as well as the highs of the past forty years or so?

"Well, I will clearly not be doing anything I've already done," Merritt notes, fairly confidently.

"I predict that in the year 2000 it will suddenly be okay to do something different, as it hasn't been for 15 years. Music has been incredibly conservative for a long time. That's got to change at the turn of the century just because of the numbers . . . and because of the monotony."

I suggest that over five Magnetic Fields albums and side projects like Future Bible Heroes and the Gothic Archies, he's already made a career of doing things he hasn't done before.

"Yeah, well, now I have to do something nobody else has done either. And I think everybody is going to be doing the same. I'm all in favor of people trying kooky new things and failing spectacularly. As long as they do it spectacularly."

So you're looking forward to the new millennium?

"God, I'm looking forward to it. Aren't you?"

THE FLAMING LIPS

The Flaming Lips were already shape-shifting veterans by 1999, and it seemed as though mainstream success was behind them. In truth, they were just getting started, entering an experimental-pop phase that would make Wayne Coyne an unlikely celebrity. **JAY RUTTENBERG** went to Oklahoma City as the band prepared for the release of *The Soft Bulletin*.

Like Jonathan Richman, Ian MacKaye, and Wayne Coyne, I do not do drugs, which means that my life is very, very boring. It has its spurts of tamed surrealism, though, and of this shamefully tiny dollop, three wowser events have been incited by Coyne and his band, the Flaming Lips.

1) I had seen the group play a handful of times before—somnambulating at a club, playing acoustic in a record store, squinting on Lollapalooza's second stage—when they breezed into a sleazeball Boston club owned by Aerosmith and knocked my ass to the floor. This was in 1995, when the Lips were touring behind *Clouds Taste Metallic*, which wasn't nearly as good as the record that came before it (their big breakthrough, *Transmissions from the Satellite Heart*) or the one that came after it (the

already infamous *Zaireeka*, which contains four CDs designed to be played simultaneously on four separate stereos).

Aside from the Aerosmith arcade game stationed near the bar and a large sign mounted above the T-shirt stand reading something like THE FLAMING LIPS PLAY BEVERLY HILLS 90210, in salute to the Lips' recent performance on the oxy-opera, the club seemed normal enough. When the band began to play the subdued opening to "The Abandoned Hospital Ship"—also the kickoff to *Clouds*—one hardly expected the earth to tremble.

But then drummer/factotum Steven Drozd stopped playing the keyboard and sat behind his drum kit, and as he raised his arms to pound the tar out of his instrument, thousands of blinking multicolored Christmas lights (that the band had surreptitiously draped across the stage, through a rotating wheel, around a bubble machine, and over the heads of the audience) switched on, and everybody—including the four band members—couldn't help but beam Joker-style at the world's greatest homemade light show, which (along with the smiles) continued unabated for the next fifty minutes.

"Sometimes the simplest things can make it worth going out for the night," Coyne tells me later.

2) When the Lips unleashed *Zaireeka* on the world at the end of '97, they had already been toying with the concept of multiphonic sound for about a year. It had started informally with the Parking Lot Experiments, in which the band set up shop in a covered garage and distributed forty cassette tapes to their audience-musicians, who were instructed to place them in their car stereos and follow Conductor Coyne's megaphoned instructions.

Reading about these odd happenings in the Lips' native Oklahoma City, it seemed as if the band were either pulling a joke, losing their minds, or going muso. But when Warner Bros.—Warner Bros.!—dribbled *Zaireeka*'s four-CD set onto the racks, word spread quickly. It wasn't the wank-o-rama one might have suspected from the cover art's ominous warning label ("These eight compositions are to be played using as many as four compact disc players, and have synchronized start times. This recording also contains frequencies not normally heard on commercial recordings and on rare occasion has caused the listener to become disoriented." Not your everyday PMRC tocsin). Nor was *Zaireeka* the major-label pop collection that some desperate Warner exec hinted at when he bandaged the album's thick jewel box with a sticker marked: "The Flaming Lips *Zaireeka*: featuring the song 'The Big Ol' Bug Is the New Baby Now'"—as if radio stations could physically play the song on the air even if they wanted to. This *Zaireeka* thing was a different beast altogether: an accessibly arty, poppy, music-y game designed by a pack of middle-aged headbanging Okies who had been on *90210*.

And it was allegedly interesting enough to bring together four stereos and four people to play it—a veritable party in my book.

So a group of us sat on the shag carpeting of a friend's living room one Friday night, surrounded by a quartet of stereos and their eight speakers. With each cut, we'd count off and press our respective start buttons, as instructed; then everybody sat as still as possible so as not to disrupt one of the CD players and knock it out of sync with the others. This proved fruitless, which was just

as well. We listened and listened and listened, gaping at the jolt of some sounds (the ferocious dog pack roaring through "The Big Ol' Bug Is the New Baby Now"), muffling our ears at others (three of the CDs for the song "How Will We Know?" contain frequencies "that can cause a person to become disoriented, confused or nauseated"), singing along with some, and laughing hysterically at some more (at one point, in a spoken-word bit, Coyne's voice bleeds into all eight speakers as if it's about to eat the listener alive). Ridiculous smiles plastered themselves to faces around the room. We talked about how lucky our parents were to come of age in the '60s; how all their friends would gather for the weekend when a new Beatles record came out and do nothing but listen and laugh and rave about that knockout ditty Ringo does about the submarine, or the one where John sings and then an alarm clock rings and then Paul sings and then that wild sound comes in. We talked about the wild sounds we currently were hearing on the eight speakers encircling us and how peculiar and . . . well, just plain FUN!!! this was. And through that weekend I could hear the tremors of a far-flung community of agoraphobics slapping on their Chuck Taylors and creeping out of their bedroom holes in Brooklyn and Hoboken and the Mission District and Chicago and Somerville and gathering to grin at the wild sounds Wayne Coyne dreamed up in Oklahoma.

Handily the best album of 1997, *Zaireeka* was conspicuously absent from the top of the crit polls—probably because the typical Pazz & Jop voter lacks the three friends needed to hear the damn thing.

3) I am a cookie boy. That is, my current night job entails delivering $14 boxes of freshly baked cookies to the apartments and dormitories of pudgy Boston-area yuppies. It's a fairly uneventful if ludicrous job. It does let me drive around listening to music a whole lot, however, and when I get an advance copy of the Flaming Lips' new album (*The Soft Bulletin*, their ninth full-length in 15 years), I can't resist standing up my weekly hip-hop show and spinning the Lips tape instead.

From the second the album kicks in with a song called "Race for the Prize," my head—already bloated from cookies and coffee—is spinning. The roaring guitar sound the band cultivated in their early hard-rockish days, then spent a decade covering up with various studio shenanigans, is all but gone: psychotic synthesizers whine even louder than the guitars, themselves so affected they might as well be bassoons. By the time Coyne's perpetually off-key voice (most probably first used as a schoolboy trying to piss off his chorus teacher) enters the fray, the instruments have squealed to outer space and back four or five times. By the middle of the next song, he's howling over canned strings and a muffled techno beat. By the end of the next, I'm maniacally driving along with the music, for once giving the cabbies and Domino's guys a run for their money. A throbbing drum beats deeper than a college sophomore's 3 a.m. drunken discourse, a trip-hop-worthy soundscape builds around an organ and strings, Coyne whinnies about love and space . . . I ecstatically U-turn across Commonwealth Avenue, nearly colliding with a Green Line trolley. I deftly dodge the BU fraternity brothers cartoonishly hopping from bar to bar like evil bunnies as the Lips' "Gash" bursts into a grandiose freak-out replete with a melodramatically silly sing-along. My gas pedal fluctuates with the album's undulating textures as I race across the Charles River, so caught up in this crazy head music that I get lost and arrive a half hour late with the cookies to find three huffy fatsos salivating on their apartment doorstep, skim milk in hand.

I get a paltry $11 in tips for the night, but it doesn't faze me: I zoom home smiling wider than Roberto Benigni on the train to Auschwitz.

From the hotel window in Oklahoma City, I can see four parking lots, three flags (America's, Oklahoma's, and Hilton's), two chain stores, one Hooters eatery, and a whole bunch of Ford Taurus sedans. One of these Fords belongs to Wayne Coyne, who is staring out the window from the vantage of the nicest chair in the room, his feet plopped on the only footstool, and pointing toward

Steven Drozd, who is sprawled teenybop style across the bed. Drozd—who used to serve as the band's drummer but recently has branched out to piano, guitar, pedal steel, and voice—looks about ten years younger (and ten times squarer) than when I last met with him, in 1996. His hair is scoutishly trimmed, his nails are bereft of polish and his chin equally bare, while his eyes, unshielded by sunglasses, look more human than raccoon.

Conversely, Coyne looks about a decade older. The wavy mane of old is gone, in its place a sloppy workingman's tousle sandwiched between grey side-sprouts (the repercussions of coordinating *Zaireeka*?). His 38-years-old-and-beginning-to-look-it face hides behind the sloppy bristles of an upstart beard that makes the singer look a bit like Dennis Miller, but when he opens his mouth he's neither supercilious nor grandiloquent, but frank, confident, and aggressively friendly. And while this slew of modifiers may add up to "one bossy sonuva-bitch," with his Midwest charm and humble disposition, Coyne at least manages to be the sweetest of this lot.

At the moment his booming Dust Bowl drawl is taking a rare breather as he contemplates his band's transmutation from inchoate headbangers to crafty experimentalists holding musical happenings in parking garages. "Somewhere along the way, just being a standard rock band became limiting," Coyne begins. "Steven really is a great singer, guitar player, piano player, and musician in general. But in our 'rock band' format, he was just the drummer. And Michael [Ivins] was looked at as just the bass player, and I was the guitar player and the singer, and those were our respective personas. We were getting really bored with that."

Coupled with their instrumental ennui was the fact that Ronald Jones—the most accomplished in a line of second guitarists that included Mercury Rev front guy Jonathan Donahue—had quit the band following the *Clouds Taste Metallic* tours. What's more, Drozd had become temporarily incapacitated from a (metaphoric?) spider bite (alluded to on *The Soft Bulletin*: "When you got that spider bite on your hand / I thought we would have to break up the band."

But instead of breaking up, the three remaining Lips gathered their resources and entered their most interesting phase yet. Steven Drozd explains: "The way the parking lot thing happened is, one day, in the summer of '96, I came up to where Wayne lives, and he started talking about this idea. Ya know, "Wouldn't it be wild if we made a bunch of music on cassettes, parked a bunch of cars in a parking lot, and gave, say, forty people a cassette and each person put the cassette into the cassette deck in their car. And you told everyone to just hit play at the same time, and this music all came out of forty cars.' And I said something like, 'Oh, that would be pretty wild.' Sort of thinking it was a kooky idea. A couple of weeks later he actually started to work on it. By August, he had organized it, and forty or fifty people showed up with their cars.

"It was neat," the drummer-slash-many-things continues. The parking lot players were "people who go to rock shows all the time, see each other out all the time. In this particular environment it was a little weird, a little charged. No one knew what to expect. 'What are we doing here? Is this gonna work? Are we gonna laugh at this guy? Is he gonna make a fool out of himself?' People were really struck: this was something new and different. And really, there was no point. It was just to entertain ourselves, and if other people were entertained . . ."

Other people were entertained by it. Not necessarily the same people who were entertained a decade earlier by the bludgeoning *Oh My Gawd!!! . . . The Flaming Lips*. Not necessarily the same types who turned up for their Restless Records swan song, 1990's *In a Priest Driven Ambulance*. Definitely not the Jim Carrey fans who got roped in when the makers of *Batman Forever* plopped the Lips' "Bad Days" (as in "You have to sleep late when you can / And all your bad days will end") at the forefront of their movie's only watchable scene. But there were people, they were entertained, and the three musicians were inspired enough to travel to the upstate New York studio of their longtime producer, Dave Fridmann.

"With *Zaireeka* there was so much work we had no idea what we were doing and how we were going to do it," says Coyne. "Once we started to record, we found ourselves buried in work, knowing, 'Gosh, we've got this little thing that's exciting on an artistic and musical level, but there's a ton of boring, hard, technical work to make it happen.' But it was a welcome hassle to us, and to the people who are immersed in music these days—because they have to do something to hear it.

"A lot of people just buy a CD and sort of randomly listen to it," the singer continues. "It's not really a listening experience, it's just sort of something that they're putting on while they're doing the rest of their life. A normal guy who works hard all week and wants to be entertained on weekends is not going to [gather four stereos to hear *Zaireeka*]. But some people—well, you bring people over to your house to watch movies, why not bring them over to listen to a record? And lately people have gotten out of the habit of doing that, because a lot of records just aren't worth having anybody over to listen to.

"Like everybody else, we get bored with what's happening now in music. But we take responsibility and say, 'Well, we're part of this music scene. We're

complaining—but we're part of it. If it sucks, we're to blame!' So we decided to explore our ideas. If we don't pursue the things we want, who's gonna?"

Hence, *Zaireeka*—perhaps the most peculiar major-label album since Lou Reed's *Metal Machine Music*, or at least Michael Jackson's *HIStory*. And once people were entertained by the demanding 45-minute box set, the next logical step was—what else?—the Boom Box Experiment Tour. A Boom Box Symphony! I saw Experiment No. 20, according to the concert's program, which stated: "What will be happening tonight is similar to the parking-lot experiments in that what you'll be hearing are pre-recorded tapes. But, instead of being in car stereos, tonight's performance is done with hand-held boom boxes, forty of them, using volunteers from the audience to engage and manipulate each separate sound source. Me [Wayne] and Steven will be guiding the engaging and manipulation; Michael is the center monitor source."

This meant that forty audience members lined up single file, marched onstage, sat down with their designated Salvation Army boom box, and followed conductors Coyne and Drozd as they frantically waved their arms and shouted instructions. Ivins hid at the rear of the stage, anonymously tweaking knobs and dials. It felt a bit like a junior high school assembly, a bit like something you'd see on public access, a bit like a carnival attraction, a bit like a performance-art piece, and almost nothing like a typical rock show (for one thing, when somebody yelled "Freebird!" before the final song, it was kind of funny).

The Boom Box Experiments were "the leap I wanted to make," says Coyne. "Our identity is not in our instruments. It's in our ideas. And if the ideas involve using boom boxes and having the audience play them, so be it.

"At first we worried people would show up and say, 'What the fuck are you doing? We want our money back!' But the more shows we did, the more people found out about it, and the more interested they seemed to get. 'Cause there is an element that's unpredictable. To have people show up saying, 'I don't know what's gonna happen,' makes it worth it. As opposed to showing up at most rock venues and saying, 'I know what's gonna happen. I know too well what's gonna happen. Let's hope someone fuckin' kills themself during the show so we can go home and say, "Something happened!"'

"I mean, after most rock shows, if you go home and your mom says, 'What happened?' you say, 'Oh jeez, Mom, I have to tell you, the same thing happened that's been happenin' for the past fucking ten years. The show was supposed to start at 10, it didn't start till 12:30. The band was supposed to be good, they couldn't tune up their instruments. The room was too smoky, the drinks were too expensive, and the women paid no attention to me.' And she says, 'Oh, I thought you went to see a band.' And you're like, 'Well I did, but that has become not the reason why I leave the house.' The music has become the last reason for people to go to concerts, and I don't want that. I want people to come knowing, 'We're listening tonight. We're not just showing up to look at each other's fuckin' clothes.'"

I slip into the back seat of a car piloted by Michael Ivins, the bass player who once looked rock 'n' roll ferocious—with a sprawling Afro and perennial sunglasses masking his nice-as-can-be reality—but now looks a wee bit nerdish, with almost no hair at all and . . . well, the same goddamn shades. Wayne Coyne slides into the

death seat, turns to his bandmate, and says: "This is the first time I've rode in your new car." Ivins—who started Flaming Lips with Wayne and Wayne's brother Mark in 1983—says: "Yeah." Coyne says: "It's kinda sporty. You're not gonna drive fast just to impress me, are you?" And Ivins says: "Well, I drive pretty fast anyways." And when Coyne begins to cavil, the bassist says: "I'm just kidding." He hardly says anything else for the next hour.

We're driving around the northwest quarter of Oklahoma City. If it weren't for the Oklahoma license plates, we really could be anywhere, as long as it's nowhere. We pass strip mall after strip mall and fast-food joint after fast-food joint, many of them restaurants I didn't realize still existed. My Eastern-centric consternation regarding a Carl's Jr. leads to talk of the decade Coyne spent toiling for the mother of all third-tier fast-food joints. "I worked the deep fryer at Long John Silver's for 11 years," the singer explains. "And ya know what? I liked it. I'd do it again if I had to. Mindless work has its merits."

"Did you wear a uniform, like in *Fast Times at Ridgemont High*?"

"Yeah, but I really dug it. I mean, I didn't wear it when I wasn't at work or anything. But when my friends came into the restaurant I'd be like, 'Hey, look at me! I'm a pirate!' I was never embarrassed."

It's weird hearing Coyne speak of his tenure as a deep-frying pirate. I knew he was once part of the Long John team—tales of the singer's erstwhile day job have been a staple of his notoriously long-winded song introductions for years. But he seems too self-consciously savvy to get tangled up in fish sticks and fries. For 11 years.

"Any adult you run into who doesn't think about money is either independently wealthy or stupid," he says. "They may not want to talk about it, but it's always there . . . Sometimes people think of us as some sort of art project funded by Warner Bros. That would be a great way to look at us, but it simply isn't so. The reason they have us there is because they think we can make them money. They don't look at us and go, 'Ooooh, we have the Flaming Lips and that means something,' 'cause they don't care. Time Warner is a big deal, and they certainly don't need to have a little band from Oklahoma to give them a bit more credibility or power while they're fuckin' negotiating for who's gonna own this third of the world. You think it's gonna matter if they say,

'Well we've got the Flaming Lips!' 'Oh, well, fuck! Look out, now!'

"So when we approach them about something like *Zaireeka*, they don't flinch and they don't applaud. They think, 'Okay, cool. If you guys think you can do this and we can make money off it, then go and do it.' They don't really care.

"I'm 38 years old," he continues. "I want to know what's real as opposed to idealism. When bands start out, it's great to think they'll be famous and people will respect them and write about them in the future. And when you're 20 years old, that probably is more important than having a good life. We were like that. We would spend months of our lives driving around with no money, eating bread, and saying, 'This is the life for us,' just because we got to make our music. That's how important it was. But after a while you see, yes, it's important to make your music, but you have to be able to do other things. Grown men don't want to drive around in a van eating bread all their lives.

"We've made records most of the time since 1983. Our lives have been consumed with making a record, then the repercussions of it. If that's the sort of music you're gonna make, this is the type of life that you have to live because of it, ya know? The consequences of your art. If that means you've limited yourself to never having any money . . . well, why would you do that? That's dumb. But to put the pursuit of money over pursuing your ideas? Well, we don't have any money! Sometimes what we do can make money, but that isn't our thing. Our thing is making records. That's what we've spent the last 15 years doing. Our adult life has been spent in a studio, not a marketing room. But we pursue popularity—once the record's made, I'm as big of a marketing prostitute as anybody. We'd be on TV every day if they'd let us. I wouldn't sacrifice being secure for the rest of my life for any kind of 'artistic integrity.'"

The Flaming Lips' big chance to cash in came about a decade into the band's existence. It was 1994, and the window that Kurt Cobain had left open—the one that let distorted guitars and off-key singing breeze onto the FM airwaves and MTV prime-time slots—was already beginning to slide shut. The Lips' major-label debut, 1992's overbaked *Hit to Death in the Future Head*, had commercially stiffed, and its superlative follow-up, *Transmissions from the Satellite Heart*, was heading south as well. But then, nearly a year after its release, an alt-rock station in Oklahoma began spinning "She Don't Use Jelly," a goofy tune with nonsensical lyrics that just screamed novelty hit: "I know a girl who / Thinks of ghosts / She'll make you breakfast / She'll make you toast / But she don't use butter / She don't use cheese /

She don't use jelly or any of these / She uses vah-ass-uh-leeen." Soon, stations across the country jumped on board, MTV Buzz-Binned the band's self-directed video, and Wayne got the chance to "spend days and days talking to interviewers about *Beavis & Butthead* and my hair being orange in the video." The Lips headlined Lollapalooza's second stage, seducing the trench-coat mafia with searing guitars, tales of Long John Silver's employment, and a cover of "Under Pressure." They toured with Tool, Porno for Pyros, Stone Temple Pilots, and—for sixty dates—Candlebox, devising their Christmas-light show so "people would remember the opening band." They didn't tour with Counting Crows, but Counting Crows began to open their own concerts by dimming the lights and spinning "She Don't Use Jelly" just before their set. The Lips went to Japan. They went to Australia. They played on *Letterman*. And they played on *Beverly Hills 90210*, where Coyne had an epiphany.

"When they asked us to play the show, we thought, 'The only reason we'll do it is because it's so absurd,'" says Coyne. "But then we get there and we see, 'We're not deeper thinkers than the people who are watching *90210*.' It's ridiculous to pull ourselves out and say, 'Oh, they're lowbrow and we're highbrow.' 'Cause we're not. I mean, I walk around Walmart these days and I look around and I think, 'Ohhh my God.' And then I realize that I'm here at Walmart, too! I'm one of them! I'm not some elitist fool who knows more about culture than these people."

"But once you had that realization," I object, "wouldn't it spur you to tailor a more mainstream sound, rather than doing stuff like *Zaireeka*?"

"But see, that's not satisfying to us," Coyne replies. "We tried to be famous. And we don't know how to do it. We tried to be important, and we don't know how to do it. We've reached a point where we want to make music we like and present it to the world in a way that might make us money or more famous or whatever. But we know how arbitrary all that stuff is. At the end of the day, we just do what we like."

Recorded both in conjunction with and in the hulking wake of *Zaireeka*, *The Soft Bulletin* is one of those records you can tell was made by a band in full command of their tools. The album's cocksure edge comes from knowing it represents a victory lap for the threesome. "With *Zaireeka* we built up the tolerance to lay down two hundred tracks without considering it a big job," says Coyne. *The Soft Bulletin* "was like a guy who got used to running 25 miles going out and running just one."

Perhaps more crucial is the way the new album evades the missteps of the band's back catalog. While Drozd's thunderous percussion grew monotonous in the past, in recording this album he varied the sound so much he doesn't even attempt to replicate it in concert, playing guitars and keyboards and letting a backing tape take care of the drums. Whereas the band were once content to rely on familiar rock sounds, on *Bulletin* Coyne and crew "don't let the culture guide us. It felt like we were making our own music, as opposed to doing music we thought sounded cool." Unlike most psychedelic-styled recordings, this one is bold enough to hold its climactic fire until just the right moments, at which point it money-shoots effectively enough to justify the wait. Most interestingly, the album deals with empty space in ways the Lips never managed in the past: at one point Coyne duets with little more than a sparse drum thud. The Flaming Lips have learned when not to play—and according to jazzbos, that's the musician's equivalent of a black belt.

This somewhat ascetic approach carries over to the trio's newfangled live show. Not only does Drozd not play drums onstage, but Coyne mostly steers clear of his guitar, instead taking freelance percussion jobs and playing with a hand puppet while he sings. (When asked if this is a Lipian take on Miles Davis's theories of musical self-denial, Wayne laughs and says, "The truth is, I don't play very well and some of the songs are really hard.") Ivins plays bass, sings backup, and (I'm guessing) doesn't talk much between songs. In keeping with their Christmas-lights gimmick, now the group are accompanied by a carefully coordinated film showing Drozd drumming in the studio, Leonard Bernstein conducting, and the inside of Coyne's mouth. The band are also distributing sets of headphones and broadcasting the concert live on a low-frequency FM station "so the audience can hear things like stereo separation and subtle reverb effects"—a nifty idea they inadvertently stole from a 1990s concoction of Yes.

For a group who spent their formative years getting laughed at by punks who hated long hair and "Wish You Were Here" covers, it seems appropriate that the Flaming Lips have hit their hipster heyday nodding to the corniest band of rock's corniest genre of rock's corniest era. And yet the jump the band have made since the Pac-Man age is palpable. In Coyne's typical barrage of words, "If you were to listen to us in the first year we existed and listen to us now, you would not recognize us. You'd say, 'I don't even think these are the same people.' And we're not the same people. We're a lot different from how we used to be, and I think our music reflects this.

"To me it's boring that you could put on the latest Sonic Youth record and then one they did in 1980 and not necessarily know that there's been almost twenty years between. For an experimental band who've experimented for twenty years, for their first record and their latest record to sound so much alike, you've gotta wonder: 'Well what have you been experimenting with?'

"I'm sure they're happy and make a lot of money and all those other things. I'm just saying that for my own taste, I'd rather people would hear our first record and listen to what we do now and go, 'Wow! These guys have been to outer space and back four or five times!'"

A thick layer of tension hovers over Hilton room #306, and Wayne Coyne is doing little to alleviate it. In fact, if the ol' index finger of blame were to point in any direction, its tip would be aiming straight at the nicest chair, where Coyne has again perched himself.

This weekend, the hotel room belongs to some people from Los Angeles who make videos for a DVD magazine, which, I'm told, is something like a CD-ROM magazine (which, I'm told, is a little like a magazine and a little like a video). The three DVDers have traveled to Oklahoma City to shoot images of the Lips playing music and talking about *The Soft Bulletin*. They're not in the best spirits because of various American Airlines problems, subsequent lack of sleep, and the usual kvetching that follows such ordeals. To compound the crew's problems, Coyne has made the kind of about-face he's semi-famous for, refusing to allow them to film at his house/rehearsal space and instead showing up in their hotel hallway with Drozd and the Lips' manager faster than you can say "But we arranged the lighting, sound equipment, and whole fucking trip around shooting the goddamn thing at your house!"

Of course, they would never say this. Not because Coyne is a rock musician, but because he is such an outgoing and commanding personality that within seconds he holds this roomful of grouchy Angelenos (with cameras and an expense account, no less) in the palm of his hand. All eyes rest on Coyne as he sits and listens to the director's on-the-spot alternatives.

"Okay, maybe we could have one of the Hooters waitresses interview you—"

"I don't know about that."

"Or we could just do something here in the hotel room."

"See, if it was a real star that could be interesting—"

"Yeah, so—"

"But with us, it would just be some people talking in a hotel room. That would be boring."

"Okay, I was thinking of maybe having you and Steven playing separate things and then combining them, like a John Cage–type piece."

"Well, see, John Cage is great to talk about but not so great to listen to."

"Okay, maybe we can find a rehearsal space and shoot you guys playing around."

"We don't do that. We don't sit around and play like a normal band . . . If you were with us in a studio, it would probably look a lot like this. I don't think you'd ever hear a song being played on tape. You'd hear [conversations] and sounds, and then a year later you'd go, 'Oh, I remember you doing that! So that's how it turned out!'"

"This is complete chaos," somebody mutters, to which Coyne calmly twangs, "No, no. Chaos is good. We'll get happy mistakes."

A few hours later somebody finds an empty banquet room in the hotel basement. It has the kind of sliding room-divider and patched carpeting that suggest a hardware salesmen's convention, but it's spacious, bright, and Coyne is willing to give it a go. He opts for a John Cage–type thing after all, deciding to tape twenty individual minute-long bits of experimental improvisation ("Spontaneous Composition in Oklahoma Room #3, in A Minor"), which the editors will later consolidate into a two-minute mélange. Drozd sits down at his keyboard, smoking a cigarette and furiously jotting notes. Coyne searches the room for potential instruments. He finds a roll of electrical tape, some glasses of water, a dozen padded chairs, and a yellow smiley-face cookie bought for him by my mother (long story).

They begin to film the one-minute bits. Drozd plays keyboards, varying the sound for each sequence; he starts with uncluttered piano chords, digs up some Casio beats and church-organ noises, invents melodies on the spot, and by the end of the taping is playing a maudlin piano-bar medley composed of themes from *The Soft Bulletin*. His reputation as a versatile musician (who cut his teeth playing in his father's country band and a Dallas polka outfit before becoming a Flaming Lip) begins to make sense.

About halfway through the shooting Michael Ivins arrives. With little fanfare and almost no discussion, the balding bassist silently takes a seat in the back of the room, edging the chair closer to the camera with each take. His presence calls Harpo Marx to mind, with sunglasses in place of a horn.

Without a guitar, recording studio, or opportunity to sing, Coyne turns to his most natural role: the leader. He grins into the camera and rips electric tape in time to Drozd's synth beat. He runs to the back of the room, leaps onto a chair, smacks the wall, and slowly ambles back to the camera. He puts his face up against the camera's microphone, scraping a credit card across his stubble and crunching a cookie to accompany Drozd's playing. The Flaming Lips are recording, turning chaos into happy accidents.

"The band turned out to be amazing," one of the DVD women says later over a Hooters pitcher. "But musically my boss is really conservative. I don't know what she's going to make of this."

Wayne Coyne is 38-and-a-half years old. He grew up in Oklahoma and now lives on "the bad side" of Oklahoma City in a large, weird house called the Compound, which he shares with his longtime girlfriend, a number of gargoyles, four cats, and four dogs, one of which he found lying in the gutter along his jogging route.

In 1983 he started the Flaming Lips with his older brother Mark and Michael Ivins, the quiet guy who's played bass beside him ever since. Wayne sings and plays guitar, though he claims his main instrument is "the studio." His band has been around for a while and so has he. Once he had to bail a Stinson brother out of jail in time for an Oklahoma City Replacements gig.

Dinosaur Jr. were staying at Wayne's house when SST sent them the first test pressing of *You're Living All Over Me*. Along with Ivins, Coyne learned about punk rock while schlepping a PA to shows by touring bands like the Meat Puppets and Black Flag. Most of the Flaming Lips' contemporaries are now either gone, boring, or gone and boring. The Flaming Lips are as vital as ever. I think they're one of maybe three bands who currently have all their shit together. (The other two are Royal Trux and the Beastie Boys; when I say this to Coyne and Drozd they agree "that's good company to be in.")

A few years ago, some friends of mine got to tour Europe for the first time as a supporting act for Flaming Lips. They came back raving how sweet and wonderful the Lips—who "totally took us under their wing"— were, both as people and musicians. Earlier this year, Wayne got to interview Brian Wilson for an HBO show. He planned on verbally attacking the beached boy, but ended up pitying him.

I've heard stories of Wayne's assertiveness reducing people to tears. The Saturday I spent in his company, I saw him come close to doing just this—but I also saw him being very kind to people, particularly waiters and waitresses. He talks a lot, and rapidly, because he has a lot to say. At dinner he orders a girl-type drink and nurses it even more gingerly than I nurse mine. He doesn't do drugs anymore, noting that "we organize our recording ourselves, so the last thing we want to do is sacrifice our judgment." He is wearing black jeans, ugly shoes with low socks, a heart-shaped pin that someone tells me is a homage to his girlfriend, and an old button-up shirt with a loose-fitting collar that's tie-dyed all different shades of blue. ◗

ROBERT FORSTER / THE GO-BETWEENS

Two interviews with one half of the Go-Betweens' founding duo, three years apart, trace the slow-motion re-emergence of the band. When **ELISABETH VINCENTELLI** talked to Robert Forster in 1996, he and Grant McLennan were still solo artists, but had played together live once or twice under their old band name. By 1999, when **DAVID NICHOLS** caught up with him, Forster and McLennan were about to tour as the Go-Betweens (in acoustic duo format) to promote a CD of the band's long-lost early recordings. By the following year, they had signed up Sleater-Kinney to help them record a new Go-Betweens album—the first in ten years—in *Puncture*'s adopted hometown of Portland, Oregon, as **STEVE CONNELL** reported.

MICHAEL GALINSKY

Still Solo

When the Go-Betweens split up in 1989, after nearly a decade of making brilliant if commercially unsuccessful records, they left behind many teary fans and two disoriented songwriters, Grant McLennan and Robert Forster. Both got on with their lives and their solo careers, with strictly moderate success. Now Forster has come up with *Warm Nights* (Beggars Banquet), an album that, while not quite on the level of the Go-Betweens' finest work, is easily his (and one of the year's) best.

Tall, with an intense, brooding charm, Robert Forster has the kind of effortless charisma lesser artists dream of. Paying rapt attention to every word I utter (or brilliantly faking interest, it's hard to tell), he takes compliments in stride. The facade never cracks, even when I reveal that after a particularly flamboyant solo show he did two years ago, a dazzled friend told me she wanted to bear his child. Pushing 40, this master of dry wit is not just a brilliant songwriter; he's an alert and engaging conversationalist.

We met once before, in 1989, when you were promoting 16 Lovers Lane, *the last Go-Betweens album. A few things have happened since . . .*
Yes, a few.
I saw the Go-Betweens perform at Maxwell's, in New Jersey, and assumed I'd never get to see the band again. But I hear there have been some shows recently.
I've been living in Brisbane for the last four years, and Grant moved there two years ago. Last December, a

venue called the Zoo had an anniversary and they asked us if we would play a Sunday-night show. We said sure.

I'd been playing new songs from *Warm Nights* with a three-piece band in Brisbane, so Grant said, "Why don't we play with your band?" We decided to do just Go-Betweens songs. It sounded great—even longtime Go-Betweens fans were completely crying, saying it was fantastic.

Then while I was recording my album in January, Christian from [French monthly] *Les Inrockuptibles* phoned me up and said it was their tenth anniversary, and they'd like the Go-Betweens to play in Paris. So I told him the whole band wouldn't be doing it, but that last month Grant, myself, a bassist, and a drummer had played together. So we did a big show, everyone went crazy. The day before, we were on television with [tennis player] Henri Leconte, who I adore. The Go-Betweens and Henri Leconte—what a fantastic double bill.
So that was Grant, you, and your backing band. Does it count as a Go-Betweens reunion without [drummer] Lindy Morrison

and [violinist/oboist] Amanda Brown? Are you still in touch? [*Quickly, as if not wanting to linger on the topic*] Some of them I am, some of them I'm not.

I would say the shows in Paris and in Brisbane were the Go-Betweens. It was just a one-off thing in Paris: we got invited. What I like about it is that it happens in a very organic way. It's not like a manager sat down with Grant and me and said, "Okay, it's a million dollars each, there's lawyers, there's your caravan." It's nice and easy, something you can't fight against. You could sit down with promoters and say, "It's Grant and me, with a band—we don't want to be called the Go-Betweens." Promoters, booking agents, managers, will agree, then walk out the door, and it's "the Go-Betweens."

Anyway, to me the Paris show did set forth the current state of the Go-Betweens.
Will there be more of these shows?
I don't know.
You do Go-Betweens songs at your solo shows. I guess I didn't expect that.
When the Go-Betweens broke up, many things changed, but I can still do some of the songs. As far as the band of the '80s ever playing together again—that's a closed door.
You even did a new recording of "Rock'n'Roll Friend" on your new album . . .
Yes, a beautiful version. [*Forster says things like this with a completely straight face. No false modesty for him.*] I did that because it's a song I've played a lot since the band broke up—it's the last thing we recorded. I still feel close to the song: a very un-Go-Betweens-like song, a pop song that Oasis could play. I don't plan to re-record any other song, that was a particular case.
People always talk about the Go-Betweens as a classic band, but I can't think of other bands covering your songs.
There's an Australian tribute album. And a cover I really like by the Walkabouts, a song from [*Forster's solo album*] *Danger in the Past* called "The River People." They did it great justice.

But we haven't had a famous band do one of our songs. Yet. A band from Manchester did a version of "Is This What You Call Change?" Two songs from *Danger in the Past* . . . that makes me happy.
Edwyn Collins produced the new album; you've known him for 15 years—both the Go-Betweens and his band Orange Juice were on the Postcard label.
I was living in Germany when *Danger in the Past* came out; he phoned me up out of the blue and said, "I love the album." He wanted me to come over and play with him in London but I couldn't do it then. Through the early '90s he'd come to my shows whenever I played in London. Meanwhile he was also setting up a studio. He

didn't like how his recordings sounded, so he learned how to make them. He learned about sound, about microphones. We have very similar ideas about sound.

Around '93 he asked if I wanted to cut a song, but I was on tour. From about '93 to '94 I knew I wanted to make that next album in London, and that I didn't want to be the producer, I just wanted to turn up as the artist. Be involved just as an artist. By this time Ed had sold, oh, 150 million copies of "A Girl Like You." So we made my album in his studio.
Do you think a hit like "A Girl Like You" could happen to you? Edwyn Collins had been toiling in semi-obscurity for some time, then suddenly he was all over the radio.
I don't think about it. The songs are almost beyond my control. I don't try to write hits, and I don't try to write obscure art-rock. Hits, and what can happen, I leave to the gods.
Forster doesn't quite want to leave everything to the gods, though: shortly after feigning disinterest, he acknowledges being ready to promote Warm Nights *as much as possible.*
I'm in a European phase, which is good since I want to promote this album. I'll put in the time, I'll put in the effort. I want this album to be successful, I think it deserves it. I deserve to be successful.

In the Go-Betweens, band matters always came first. We drove out of town and boyfriends and girlfriends would be crying. My family didn't see me for years. I was 32 when the band broke up, and then my private life took priority. My wife's German so we have this two-countries thing. To me Germany means access to London, to Italy. I didn't want to be an idiot in his late 30s whose best friend is his tour manager. I just wanted to be at home and not tour. I met someone and this other person had a career. And I didn't want to say, "See you in six months." These have been quiet years. I didn't want to turn into some sort of idiotic rock fool.

Private living had to be done. I went back to my hometown and lived there for four years. I saw a lot of my parents. I learned how to play the piano. I learned how to speak German. Month after month of shopping, cooking, sleeping, reading. My wife went to work and I stayed home during the day. She'd come home, I cooked meals. That's what I wanted. Now we planned that all the focus would be on this record. We're going to put a lot of time into it.
The last time I saw you perform solo, you said the rumors about your writer's block were unfounded.
I've made four albums since 1988 . . . three, really, since one was all covers . . . three albums in eight years, and that's fine—people put out too many albums. But I might be saying that because it takes me two or three years to write an album. I write every day. I try to.
Do you have a huge backlog of songs?

[*Laughs*] No, no. I write them as they come. The main problem is music. It can take six months to write a piece of music, it can take a year . . . and I'm trying every day. I'm not a naturally gifted musician. Words I don't have a problem with, lyrics I can write in two or three days. So it's a long search for music; when I get that, words just come [*snaps his fingers*]. Since the album I've written one song, and that's in the last four months. It was like this in the Go-Betweens. I write two, three songs a year.

Grant is much more prolific than you are; he cranks out solo albums, and then there's Jack Frost [McLennan's occasional project with Steve Kilbey of the Church]. Were there tensions in the Go-Betweens because he wrote faster?

There were. We had an agreement that each album would have five songs from me and five songs from Grant. So a month before recording he'd have 25 songs, and I'd have three and a half. To be truthful, Grant can write 25 songs, and 15 of them are crap. I think he could do with a bit of editing. You've got to say to him: "Grant, that one's appalling!"

I can write a song and then a week later see if it's second-division: no use trying to throw it out to the group. If Grant plays one little thing, he's got to write a song and finish it. Then he brings it along and believes in it totally. I had to sit there, he'd play twenty songs, ten would be absolute crap and ten would be fantastic—and he'd play them all the same. I often wonder if he knows the crap ones are crap.

So he'd come up with ten songs, I'd have five, but my five had gone through my selection process. He'd take it badly sometimes, but he knew the way it works. He played me the demos for his new album, about ten songs. I said, "Five or six are great; you have to keep writing." He probably thought the record was done!

How would you rate your solo albums?

Danger in the Past: Absolute classic: 24-carat. Berlin, Mick Harvey, big sound.

Calling from a Country Phone: The dark star. I've come to appreciate it a lot more. It's sort of like the *Tallulah* of my solo albums.

I Had a New York Girlfriend: Madness. I don't know what I was doing. To make an album of covers you need an unlimited budget. You pick 12 songs, you go into the studio and you realize six of them aren't working. When I go in with 12 of my own songs, I've played them so much at home I know they're going to work.

Warm Nights I'm very content with. I think it's as good as *Danger in the Past*—a lot more accessible, a lot more rhythmic. I'm happy with the songwriting and production. This makes me more comfortable with the Go-Betweens: now I've proven myself, and I have a body of work made since the Go-Betweens that I'm happy with. It lightens me up so I feel more comfortable. Very basic human emotion we're talking here, almost childish.

It was weird to see you do a covers album. Hearing one of the best songwriters of his generation cover Martha & the Muffins is a bit frustrating.

People should know I'm always capable of surprises. The one huge mystery of my life is songwriting.

You've been at it for almost twenty years. Doesn't it get easier with practice?

My god, if it only did! "On a Street Corner" was my total output for 1992. "Crying Love" I wrote at the start of 1993. Then suddenly last year I wrote "I Can Do," "Warm Nights," "Snake Skin Lady," "Loneliness," and "I'll Jump," all in five months: it was the greatest burst of songwriting I've had since 1979. It's frustrating: you can set up a perfect environment—it can be a cabin somewhere with guitar, no distractions, someone bringing me food—and nothing. A week later I can go to a party, pick up the guitar, and in three minutes I get it right. I can't explain it. I think it's just luck, or where I am. I get started in odd places; then once I get a start it's all over in three days. So I can wait for months and months, then bang! Melody, chords, I'm getting it. It's done in three days. Then the search starts again.

The last time I saw you perform, you were working the crowd . . .

Right.

. . . doing these rock-star moves . . .

Right.

And you looked really confident, much more so than when I saw you with the Go-Betweens.

I enjoy performing. I didn't play acoustically until I went back to Brisbane. After the band broke up, I never played acoustically. I think it was 1992—I was 35—I did my first purely acoustic show. It's tough to see these people playing acoustic guitars, doing lots of blues riffs. When you say "acoustic guitar," you imagine people sitting on the floor cross-legged, hair cascading in their face, mumbling about pain, sorrow, hardship. They can tune the guitar while they talk to the audience. I can't do that: my guitar playing is good, it's rhythmic, but it's very straightforward. I feel comfortable doing it now. I have the songs and I know I can do it. It's natural.

I'm touring with a band soon. Bookers are coming to the show tonight, so you have to clap. People must be very enthusiastic. The bookers will go, "Boy, people love Forster, don't they? He's amazing, we've got to book him, we have to organize a US tour for this guy!"

Indeed, Forster has turned into a mesmerizing performer. Looking dashing in a canary-yellow suit the night I saw him, he played an enchanting mix of old and new material. Pared down to their basics, the songs, wrenching and unadorned, shone like rough diamonds.

I remark that his writing has an economical quality rare among modern songwriters, and ask him what he's been reading lately.

I've read *Remembrance of Things Past* . . . it took me a number of years, but I read it. I read quite a lot. I read a book by John Richardson about the first 27 years of Picasso's life. I've been book-buying all day; when I come to New York, I go to bookstores rather than record stores. Books are cheaper here, the range is overpowering. I tend to read nonfiction, biographies, history. Some are trashy; I like crass Hollywood memoirs. I quite like things that are humorous, though not comedy books. I'm not interested in childhood pain: a traumatic upbringing in the Midwest I will not read. Earnest social realism, ten people on the farm die, I'm not interested. Blood and guts, I'm not interested. Violence, I'm not interested. I like a lot of homosexual writing. I like a lot of women poets: Anne Sexton, Adrienne Rich, Sylvia Plath.

Your own songs walk a thin line: they can be very intense, but never earnest.

It's a fine line but I think I manage it. I enjoy humor done with a straight face. It's coming at you but not elbowing you in the ribs. I'm not holding a sign saying, here comes a joke. I don't think my music is very demanding. It's natural and straightforward, not white noise. It's melodic, not dirgy. To me the Cure are very demanding. I'm . . . accessible isn't the right word . . . I don't find what I do obscure, but still, if you're not obscure and you're not demanding, why aren't you in the charts? I know why I'm not in the charts [*sounding very sure of himself*], and I'm completely happy with it.

Why do you think you're not in the charts?

A certain amount of machinery is needed. I'm meeting you here [Beggars Banquet's one-room New York office]; if we were at Geffen there'd be 75 people bringing us coffee. I haven't the right producers. [*Okay, so he doesn't know why he's not in the charts.*]

Being the type of person I am, I'm always surprised that so many people get it. Some days I feel I should be selling two million records; other days I feel I'm lucky to sell two hundred.—*Elisabeth Vincentelli*

Getting Back Together

It's been nearly ten years since the Go-Betweens broke up; but Robert Forster and Grant McLennan have never quite been content to let their old band die gracefully. The only original Go-Betweens have continued to work together sporadically—usually in a live context. Their latest project, a world tour, is ostensibly to promote two "new" Go-Betweens albums: a best-of, *Bellavista Terrace*, and an album of 1978–79 recordings (eight of them previously unreleased), *The Lost Album*.

"I'm preparing myself mentally for the tour," says Forster down the phone from Bavaria, where he now lives with his wife, Karin, and their son, Louis. "I'm living day to day with . . . um, um, we now have a family, a son who's close to 11 months old, called Louis, and he's in a very boisterous stage, so the days are quite big . . . dealing with him. So I'm preparing myself for the tour and time away from Karin and from Louis, which is going to be . . . something. The tour now is quite . . . I always knew it was going to be two months, going on to two and a half months; now they want me to go to London for four days . . . it's growing."

Quite a shock for a man who's retreated, like Dakota-period Lennon, into domesticity. "Karin works a little bit, part time," he says. "But we've very much devoted our time to Louis, he's fantastic, we're totally besotted by him. You have an idea how good being a parent might be and then it exceeds that by an unbelievable amount and we can't believe how good it is.

"So I figure, I've been here 24 hours a day for virtually his first year, and now I'll spend a good two months away. That's the price I pay for all the time I spend with him."

Like their third album, *Spring Hill Fair*, the Go-Betweens' new "best-of" takes its name from their hometown of Brisbane, though this time one with much less personal resonance. "The title came from Grant," says Forster. "Grant had the idea of taking photos around Brisbane. He took some photographs with a photographer hipster by the name of Peter Fischmann. It showed up in one of the photos—Grant mentioned to me there was this street Bellavista Terrace. It was a very good idea of his."

"Bellavista" seems to have come from the often undulating Brisbane terrain, where a seemingly innocuous street may suddenly open out into a lush gully or bushy reserve. The band's music, too, always captured these elements of surprise, lucidity, and luxuriousness. However, as has often been the catch-cry of critics during the '80s and '90s, the group never translated their artistic success into commercial success.

Forster addresses this in the sleeve notes to the

album, where he claims the band were "too good for the bloody charts."

"I'm not a big fan of the '80s charts," he explains. "If you look at the '60s charts or the '50s charts you can't find a bad record. But by the 1980s it had become formulaic—regularized to such an extent there were no freaks in it. Whereas the '50s and '60s charts were full of freaks.

"I'd have liked to be in the charts. But I wasn't wringing my hands and thumping my head on the table . . . Why aren't we in the top five? Why the Thompson Twins and not us?'

"Too good for the bloody charts"—it's a line.

Unlike the previous compilation, *1978–1990*, which excluded some of the band's greatest material, *Bellavista Terrace* contains no surprises. Forster says it took twenty minutes for him and McLennan to compile it: "I've always loved the concept of best-ofs. The first Bob Dylan album I bought was *Bob Dylan's Greatest Hits*. I loved *Best of the Bee Gees*. I loved *Creedence Gold*. These are the records I was thinking of. I've always wanted a concise, clipped Best of the Go-Betweens in that tradition. So you have to run with the singles, I don't want it to be a difficult collection of album tracks. Though we did include a couple of tracks that are a step up from the singles . . . "The Wrong Road," "Jack Kerouac."

Experienced Go-Betweens fans may, however, be more excited by the new *Lost Album*, a selection of 21-year-old recordings from the band (who at that stage were Forster, McLennan, and drummer Temucin (Tim) Mustafa). The sleeve shows the trio arranged in front of a picture of Che Guevara and a poster proclaiming "The Pied Piper Follows Us." Forster recalls of this photo session, "We wanted to draw something on the wall—it was a line from Grant that I liked. Youthful bragging. Youthful *We're so good* . . . No relevance to the Che Guevara picture. No, it's a completely different statement, a statement of intent and youthful madness."

Most songwriters disown their first works after a few years. Forster, on the other hand, is inordinately proud of most of these early songs. "I'm very proud that at the age of 20 I wrote classics like 'Lee Remick' and 'Karen,'" he says. "'Karen' is my 'Roadrunner,' my 'Heroin.' My '(I'm) Stranded.' To be able to write a really good two- or three-chord classic . . . It's my 'I Saw Her Standing There.'"

Nevertheless, there was a lot of sifting for the *Lost Album* project, with many songs from the time considered and rejected. One poppy number, "Obsession with You," still causes Forster occasional worry: "I was thinking of dropping that . . . there was a little bit of 'that's on, that's off, that's off, that's on' from me here [in Germany] that was driving people in London crazy. Some lyrics in 'Obsession with You' make me wince terribly, but it was a song that fitted on, it had its place. Nothing else makes me wince."

The album also includes five of the group's six studio-recorded songs from that time, the missing track being the Monkees/Easybeats pastiche "I Want to Be Today," of which Forster says, "That can go on the Go-Betweens box set. On the 17th CD."

He may also have had cause for reflection on the past with the passing of one of his noted songwriting

ROBERT FORSTER, ROBERT VICKERS, AND GRANT McLENNAN (PHOTO, TALIN SHAHINIAN)

contemporaries, the Triffids' David McComb. "It was extremely sad," says Forster. "It was strange digesting the news miles away from anyone. It would have been good to speak to people I knew who knew David. Very sad."

In my book on the band, I relate a story from Roger Grierson, the Go-Betweens' Australian manager of the late '80s. In it, Forster is told that the Triffids are to record with Smiths producer Stephen Street. According to Grierson, Forster left the room and screamed. "The Triffids were friends and competition," Forster says now. "The Triffids came out of Perth and landed in London, with a record contract. The Go-Betweens came out of Brisbane and ended up in London with a record contract. To do that, to get out of both those towns and do those things, you have to be competitive. That's how both bands operated.

"So you know there was a competitive spirit in both bands. But the bands had a good relationship: we played on the same bills with each other, it was friendly. If it was reported that at times I had to walk out of a door and scream, I was still always aware that someone on the other side of the door was watching me scream.'"

Though the days of the Go-Betweens as chart contenders are—we must assume—well and truly gone, Forster and McLennan are considering adding to their oeuvre. "Not as the Go-Betweens," says Forster. "Not at all. But . . . it's always possible Grant and I could do something. We're just going to have to see how we get on. It's going to be a great opportunity. We've done one-off shows before, but I think when you work night after night you can get really good. I think there'll be opportunities backstage, talking, when we'll just see where it develops, where it goes. I'm completely open."

A couple of days after this interview, I discovered that former Go-Between Amanda Brown had begun legal action against Forster and McLennan to establish her "contractual rights" as a former member of the group. Perhaps this is why Forster says, "The idea of the Go-Betweens is dead. I like the idea that Grant and I go out under our own names. It gets us out of a whole minefield, and points us in a good direction." The tour involves the two of them, with acoustic guitars, and, adds Forster, "I'm pulling the harmonica out of retirement: there'll be some harmonica playing; some people compare that to Bob Dylan, others don't. No band. That feels good—like a two-guys-in-a-taxi tour, getting up and playing, getting back in the taxi, going on to the next town.

"We will be doing Go-Betweens songs, and we'll be doing new songs. We might do a couple from Grant's solo career, and from mine. I've got six or seven unrecorded songs I really like and I imagine Grant will, too. We did a show in Brisbane last year and we did two new songs: one of mine called 'He Lives My Life,' and a new song of Grant's called 'Bandages.' So if at a one-off with three days' practice we can play two new songs, on a two-month tour I would expect . . . I don't know . . . four new songs a night? That sort of thing.

"They'll probably go over better than the Go-Betweens stuff!"—*David Nichols*

A New Go-Betweens Album

When ex-Go-Betweens Robert Forster and Grant McLennan toured last summer, they promised audiences they'd get back together to record an album, And there were intriguing rumors of discussions with members of Sleater-Kinney about their possible involvement in the project.

They didn't waste much time making good on their promise. Forster and McLennan finished recording the first Go-Betweens album in more than a decade at Portland's Jackpot Studios in February. Janet Weiss played drums and various bandmates—Sam Coomes of Quasi, Sleater-Kinney's Corin Tucker and Carrie Brownstein—all helped out.

"Grant and I decided early on during the tour that we were going to make a record," says Forster. "We were talking to people about studios, getting the vibe in the different cities, seeing if the feeling was right."

Portland turned out to be right, partly because of a chance meeting with Jackpot Studios owner/engineer Larry Crane, who interviewed Forster on the Northwest leg of the tour for his magazine *Tape Op*, and partly because of a planned meeting with Sleater-Kinney in San Francisco, where the two bands' schedules intersected.

"I announced from the stage that night that Grant and I were going to make a record," Robert explains. "When we came offstage we met Sleater-Kinney for the first time and Janet immediately said, 'I'll play drums!' Well, *Dig Me Out* was such a great record—it knocked me sideways. So I knew she could do it."

Soon after their tour ended, Forster and McLennan met up in their hometown of Brisbane to demo new songs. The two unreleased songs they'd played on the tour—McLennan's "Magic in Here" and Forster's "He Lives My Life"—were givens for the record. We asked if the others were written after the tour.

"Oh god, no!" exclaims Forster. But though he's a notoriously slow writer, he had in fact accumulated several songs since his last recording in 1996. "My other songs were written after we decided to make a record," says the more prolific McLennan. "And I had some songs we didn't use, as did Robert, because we wanted to make a ten-song album, as always."

A crucial element in the project was bassist Adele Pickvance, who had recently been playing in the band FOC with McLennan in Brisbane. "She was the next ingredient," says Forster. "And it's worked out brilliantly. Adele and Janet are just *the* rhythm section."

The recording band was a basic four-piece; Sam Coomes contributed keyboards on a few tracks, while Corin Tucker and Carrie Brownstein each turn up on one song.

JANET WEISS, GRANT McLENNAN, ADELE PICKVANCE, AND ROBERT FORSTER OUTSIDE JACKPOT STUDIOS
(PHOTO, BOB JOHNSON)

The record will be mixed in May at Uphon-Tonstudio in Weilheim, Germany (where Forster now lives). Uphon is home to the musicians who record as the Notwist and Village of Savoonga, among other groupings, and Forster prizes the knob-twiddling skills of Mario Thaler. "We want to add a little European crispness to that warm organic sound" that Jackpot provides.

Meanwhile, the reunited Go-Betweens pair are quite clearly delighted with the success of their project, and with their new collaborators. "Within a day or two of rehearsing we were a band," says Grant. "All the backing tracks went down very quickly, within two days."

As indeed they had to: this was very much an indie project, quite different from the glossy big-studio production of the last Go-Betweens album, *16 Lovers Lane*. "We hadn't made a Go-Betweens record this way in a long time. *Liberty Belle* was the last one . . ."

"We could have made the album in London," muses Forster, "with someone who'd done some Oasis B-sides, someone like that, but no . . . when word filters out we've made the album here, and in this way . . . It's good, it's right. It's the place for us to re-emerge from."—*Steve Connell*

SLEATER-KINNEY

In 2000, Sleater-Kinney were smack in the middle of their astonishing initial run, demonstrating wide appeal without ever disappointing their original fan base. **ELISABETH VINCENTELLI** interviewed the trio for the cover story of what turned out to be *Puncture*'s final issue. The Portland-based band—effortlessly feminist, outwardly political, youthful punk torchbearers—marked the perfect send-off for the magazine.

The best place to start with Sleater-Kinney—maybe the only place—is on stage. We may think we have them pegged, now that they're part of a certain rock landscape. They've just released *All Hands on the Bad One*, their fifth album in five years. Their records have never been less than interesting, and have often been breathlessly, thrillingly intoxicating. Five years of glowing reviews and steadily increasing popularity. Five years of unwavering loyalty to friends and community, from the careful selection of opening acts to appearances at benefits. But having seen the band perform several times over the past few years, I realized that however we enjoy their records and admire what they stand for, we can only truly understand Sleater-Kinney when we see them live.

Take Carrie Brownstein, for instance. A tall, lanky woman in her mid-20s, she looks as if she's never as alive as when her guitar is plugged into an amp. Always in movement, she owns the stage—or rather her legs do. In François Truffaut's *The Man Who Loved Women*, the title character mused that women's legs are like a compass, measuring the Earth as they walk. Carrie Brownstein's legs, then, could measure an entire universe, sliding across the floor, launching into high kicks in a mockery of propriety and gravity. It's as if Brownstein herself has only the most tenuous control over them. But music does this to her: she'll start sashaying across the soundstage while filming a music video, forgetting that her guitar isn't plugged in. "I have a lot of energy," she needlessly comments. "I can't play guitar and stand still." She can't even watch others play and stand still, absent-mindedly playing air guitar while lurking on the balcony at a Bangs show in New York.

Brownstein's charismatic live presence arises out of her full awareness of the power inherent in rock's most conventional visual tropes. At the same time, she is completely unselfconscious. There is quite a bit of the traditional Rock God™ in her. She has Elvis Presley's rubbery legs, Mick Jagger's pout, and the young Pete Townshend's mod attitude and tight pants. She has all that, and more: she has Corin Tucker and Janet Weiss, and they in turn have her.

Tucker and Brownstein had recorded two albums with Australian drummer Lora MacFarlane before Weiss (who also plays in Quasi with ex-husband Sam Coomes) joined permanently. "I'm an experienced musician," Weiss says. "When I joined Sleater-Kinney I'd already played in a lot of bands. They're very quick writers, and ambitious, and motivated; it was a good mix because I was experienced enough to keep up with them, even push them a little." As they went along, the trio felt confident enough to start playing around with time signatures and less straightforward song structures. And nowhere has their explosive confidence been more obvious than on stage.

Live, the band's setup emphasizes a balance between individual expression and the tight cohesion of a collective effort. Usually, drummers sit in the back while guitarists and singers hog the spotlight; but Weiss's kit sits almost between Brownstein and Tucker's mike stands—not so it's in the way, but near enough to the front for the crowd to see her easily. The band deftly accomplish that alchemical feat that delivers rock's distinctive thrill: the trio are individuals with strong, distinct personalities who somehow meld. Sleater-Kinney are very good at calling up the ego that's necessary to get onstage and put on a show, while at the same time preserving balance between the parts. Brownstein was emphatic in saying, "The band is a democratic entity. I can see that in a band where ego is nurtured it would carry over into your life. But egos aren't nurtured in Sleater-Kinney. Pride is definitely encouraged, we're really proud of what we do—we're not self-deprecating. We're confident, and the new record is a confident record.

"This is also an absurd community to work in: the larger rock world is absurd, and you have to take it with a grain of salt, see the humor in it. As long as you do that, it'll keep you humbled."

Early in March, Sleater-Kinney flew to New York to perform in what may be the most absurd part of that "larger rock world": the music video. Fledgling director and fan Brett Vapnek, who has also worked on a Mary Timony video, was set to shoot the entire thing on a single soundstage and in one day. But even after ten hours miming "You're No Rock 'n' Roll Fun," the band never lost their good humor. Weiss was dispatched to goof off behind the camera when Tucker needed to laugh for a close-up; later Brownstein, glancing at a conference between Vapnek and Tucker, cracked that "Corin is getting some direction in hair shaking." The dynamics between the three women fell pretty much along expected lines: Weiss friendly and garrulous, snapping Polaroids of the crew; Tucker focused and reserved; Brownstein closely noting the goings-on and joking about the relevance of music-video clichés. But then surprisingly Weiss, expansive drummer, karaoke fiend, and no petite wallflower, was the one who needed to have the soundstage cleared for her close-ups. "It's totally emotional for me," she explained, "and I can't feel emotional when there's cameras. There's something about filming and cameras and photo shoots, and I'm really protective of what I consider to be the true essence of myself. On stage I feel so free and so powerful, really confident. I don't want to give that out to a camera . . . I save it for when I play live or on record, and that keeps me alive. You can't just throw it out, it feels cheap."

Cornered in the dressing room during some downtime, Weiss, who would win any Miss Congeniality contest, remembered that as a kid she liked "underdog members of a band: 'I don't want to like the ones everybody else likes, so I'm going to like the low-key members.' So I think now I get some of those kids, kids who want to learn how to play drums. I think maybe in certain ways I'm more accessible to the kids." Brownstein, changing in a corner, quickly interjected, "Unlike us, who are so mean!"

Weiss, laughing: "Yeah, I mean Corin can be intimidating onstage, and she's shier than we are."

Brownstein: "That's true."

Weiss: "Carrie is the favorite, so some kids might be, like, 'She's the favorite, so I'm gonna pick . . .'"

Brownstein: "That's not true."

Weiss: "I think so."

Brownstein: "I'm not the favorite. Everyone has their personal . . ."

Weiss: "I'm the drummer, the drummer is always the underdog."

Brownstein: "I don't know, I think it's between me and you."

Weiss, laughing, but also expressing heartfelt conviction: "The drummer is the underdog."

Brownstein, slyly delivering the final blow: "Corin's the underdog. She scares the kids."

Besides betraying affectionate complicity and a healthy sense of humor about their own image, the exchange emphasized the complex mechanics of identification and transference that link musician and audience. Tucker, Brownstein, and Weiss talk like people who grew up dreaming about music. Now that people dream about them and their music has become crucial to many, the three women are acutely aware of the image they project onstage. But they won't give up their position as fans. That's why Tucker and Brownstein joined a bevy of dancing girls onstage while their opening band, the Gossip, played. That's why last year Brownstein took the time to alert me via email (though we hadn't met) to the imminent release of her friend Sarah Dougher's first solo album.

When news came that all three members of Sleater-Kinney had guested on the new Go-Betweens record (Weiss drummed on the whole thing, in fact), it wasn't too surprising. "I'm a huge fan," Brownstein gushed. "We were flying to San Francisco from Japan, and we knew the Go-Betweens were also playing in San Francisco. So we got off the plane and went straight to their show. Some friends from Olympia were there and told me that in Seattle the Go-Betweens had thanked Sleater-Kinney onstage. No way! How did they even know our band? When we met them after that show, it turned out they liked *Dig Me Out* a lot; Robert [Forster] was really into my guitar playing—he didn't understand how I could play that way, which is weird because they are such great guitar players. It was one of those uncanny experiences."

Tucker concurs: "It felt like we were from the same place, musically. The way they arranged things or talked about things, we spoke the same language."

The Go-Betweens first got together in the late 1970s, almost 25 years ago. Sleater-Kinney aren't quite there yet, but they've been around for a while—long enough for us to notice their longevity. A distressingly large number of predominantly female bands have crossed the skies brightly, then faded away like shooting stars. Unlike guys, they didn't have wives holding the fort while they were on the road; and record companies didn't believe in them enough to support records and tours over the long run; and the rock lifestyle didn't accommodate motherhood; and so on. Whatever the reason, there haven't been many bands of middle-aged women roaming the continents like the Rolling Stones. (Whether having a female Rolling Stones is a good thing is debatable; still, it'd be nice to have the option.) But *All Hands on the Bad One* is Sleater-Kinney's fifth album, and perhaps their most assured one: the band now seem so comfortable with themselves and others. It tackles ye old recurring issues, like relationships, plus new ones a maturing band must eventually confront.

One is the band's position vis-à-vis their audience. "I think you get a lot of young bands feeling betrayed by the bands that have been around awhile," Brownstein said. "They wonder, 'What happened to that righteousness?'

or 'Where is your anger?' I think it goes back to differences in communication style. This kind of evolution is important, and I'm glad there are new young bands to usurp the old ones.

"I also hope there's respect for the growth and change that bands go through over time.

"There's no blueprint or template to follow anymore. A lot of people have a path that's been laid out for them historically, but for women you don't have many examples. It's kinda scary, but it's also exciting. We have to work hard at maintaining a balance and friendships in the band because it's as important as the music after a while—your connections to one another. All our records have been inspired by the connections we have among the three of us: by things that happen in our lives, by Janet writing a new drum part or Corin bringing in a song or me coming in with a new guitar part. We're not jaded. We're still impressed and excited and curious about the resources and creativity we can tap.

"But we have to keep renewing that faith. You don't really know what tomorrow will bring; it's such a fickle industry that you have to have the joy coming from the band themselves, the inspiration coming internally instead of externally."

One of the ways Sleater-Kinney have changed over time is in experimenting with narrative in the rock song. Women in rock, and especially women coming from Riot Grrrl stock, are usually assumed to speak in a confessional voice, as if the autobiographical perspective is the only one they have any control over—"as if our brains aren't big enough to put on different personalities," Tucker says, laughing. "We did two interviews where people were like, So when did you live in Paris? But in 'Milkshake 'n' Honey' I'm writing as a man!" The band had used various narrators before, but never to the extent that they do on the new album. We're not quite in Randy Newman territory, but it's obvious the "I" isn't necessarily Tucker or Brownstein. (Weiss herself doesn't write many songs, "and the ones I do write I usually end up playing with Quasi.")

Tucker explains: "A couple of things coincided when we were writing this record. One is that I'm also in [the band] Cadallaca. We wear wigs, we have different names, we make up crazy stories. It's an extreme thing—almost like theater—and I love doing it. I love feeling free from having things be so heavy and personal. It was easy for me to write in character.

"This year, on tour, we saw the musical *Hedwig and the Angry Inch*. It's incredible and it's really drag—I heard that the guy who wrote the music said one of the people he was thinking about for the voice was Corin Tucker. So I was like, Do I sound like a drag queen? Oh my god! And then I was like, Hmmm, maybe I do, and maybe that's not a bad thing. Maybe you can extend yourself through those personae and play with that."

SLEATER-KINNEY
The Hot Rock
(Kill Rock Stars)

Let's face it, the last half of the 1990s basically belongs to Sleater-Kinney. This is their third perfect album in a row, and their debut wasn't so shabby either. We're dealing with a rare band on a roll, who tap into some primal well of inspiration and repeatedly seize the times.

Sleater-Kinney's ascension brings a certain vindication for those of us who knew this Riot Grrrl thing always did matter, even as the movement became a cheap target for pundits who had no idea what was going on, while we rejoiced in Bikini Kill's sporadic brilliance and overlooked any shortcomings, knowing something vital was going on that went beyond just music. (Not that the music wasn't great, too!)

Years later, this band, emerging from that background, are so compelling that few critics would dare to pan them (other than that fool in *Time*, whose attack is tantamount to a seal of approval), for fear of revealing themselves as completely out of touch. Not that I'm trying to advance some sort of Great Woman Theory of History and elevate S-K at the expense of their peers; no, this is a band nurtured by an extraordinarily communal, collaborative scene that freely exchanges ideas and talents and supports one another. (If you've ever been in a band and experienced some of the rock world's odious competitiveness, you'll know how rare and special that is.) In fact, all three members of this trio spent a good deal of last year on other projects—and quality projects like Cadallaca, Tommy, and Quasi are not exactly Jamming with Edward. It's damn gratifying to see one of the undeniable genius bands of our time arise from a scene many people were so quick to marginalize.

Moodwise, *The Hot Rock* veers closer to the gnarled song-webs of *Call the Doctor* than the ebullient "rock anthems" of *Dig Me Out*, with the added assurance of a few more years' experience. Janet Weiss (on her second S-K album) is a revelation on drums this time around, igniting the new material with the complex scattershot accents she previously reserved for Quasi, and rendering the Sleater-Kinney sound dynamic even more wildly propulsive than before.

Meanwhile, Corin Tucker and Carrie Brownstein's voices and guitars are more deeply tangled than ever; on *The Hot Rock*, solo vocals are a rarity. Most tracks employ a two-songs-playing-at-once counterpoint that began with *Call the Doctor* and may be the band's most striking element. A year of collaborating with Lois Maffeo and Mary Timony has left its mark on Carrie's vocal style: her voice this time out is cool, relaxed, and unforced (none of the sudden screeches that were threatening to become a bit predictable), providing an unflappably calm foil for the force of nature at the other mike.

Have you ever noticed how, when Sleater-Kinney perform live, Corin is often smiling when she sings, even when she's hurling that gigantic voice of hers at some particularly angry or painful lyric? It must feel incredible to have something that powerful coming out of you. As guitarists, the pair create a mesh of angular riffs and odd chords, evoking anyone from Brix Smith to Zoot Horn Rollo, and throwing down an implicit challenge: you say the guitar is a used-up instrument? Check this out!

So what's on their minds this time? Breakups and relationships fraught with conflict are a recurring theme. (They keep getting better at this type of lyric.) And more: a high-seas epic as metaphor for the band's career so far ("The first beast that will appear will entice us with money and fame . . . tie me to the mast!"); a fairy tale of humility acquired through hard knocks; the playful "Banned from the End of the World," which pokes fun at the growing obsession with the year 2000 and the Y2K panic (Carrie: "I've no millennial fear / the future's here / it comes every year!"); the churning, grinding not-quite-math-rock of "God Is a Number" (sort of a lyrical sequel to Heavens to Betsy's "Donating My Body to Science" in its indictment of those who attempt to define life in scientific/mathematical terms—particularly roof-raising Corin vocals here); a tender Carrie-sung ballad offered to a loved one dying in a hospital; and the astonishing "Get Up," a song that dares to be cosmic in the late '90s. Life, love, rage, passion . . . all delivered with enough leaping intensity to leave you reeling after each song. Note the instructive title of one of the set's most staggering tracks (my current favorite): "Burn, Don't Freeze!"—*J Neo Marvin*

All Hands on the Bad One marks a departure from its predecessor, the oft-criticized, defensively prickly *The Hot Rock*. "We were feeling very closed off and protective then," Brownstein recalls. "It was a time to look inward, not outward. We also felt separate from one another, and so the record is like a puzzle. Corin and I are almost singing a different interpretation of the same song. It intertwines and makes something very beautiful and complex, but it's . . . not as direct. It's really a sad record. [*Short laugh, almost apologetic.*] It's the one I'm most proud of because I think it raised the bar in terms of what we can do melodically. And when we came out of that, we were like, Let's just forget it . . . forget about trying to be this brainy band. We're a rock band. Let's not worry about living up to anyone's expectations."

And so *All Hands* succeeds in reclaiming rock as something vital and exciting, a source of rambunctious joy. At a time when mainstream proponents of the genre come across as beery fratboys, Sleater-Kinney make a case for rock as life-affirming and generous. The band's first bona fide anthem, after all, was "I Wanna Be Your Joey Ramone," off 1996's *Call the Doctor*: "I wanna be your Joey Ramone / Pictures of me on your bedroom door / Invite you back after the show / I'm the queen of rock 'n' roll." On 1997's *Dig Me Out*, "Words and Guitar" added to a growing canon, which was augmented yet again on *All Hands* with the likes of "The Professional" and "You're No Rock 'n' Roll Fun." That album's "#1 Must-Have" sharply attacks commodification ("But now my inspiration rests between my beauty magazines and my credit card bills") and mainstream rock's rot ("And will there always be concerts where women are raped?"). If that were all, the song would be feisty and fun enough; but it's also a cry for self-determination: "Culture is what

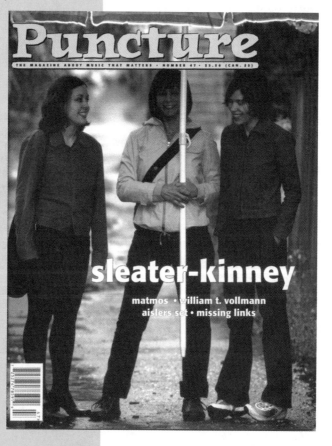

we make it / Yes it is / Now is the time / Now is the time / Now is the time to invent."

This sense of insurgency adds to the band's ever-growing appeal. Sure, they write and perform blistering songs that take you on a roller coaster of emotions. But beyond the music, one reason their fans are so devoted may be that they feel they're as necessary to the band as the band are to them. For Tucker, "The interplay is incredible at our live shows: when we're playing, we feel connected to these people." Sleater-Kinney are energized by music as they energize it—and in turn the band's impact on music and culture over the past year has been enormous.

We now live in a time when teenage boys and girls can grow up with Sleater-Kinney at their side, taking for granted the sense of power and exhilaration the band exude; seeing boys rapturously mouth the lyrics at a show is a stupendous sight. Both Tucker and Brownstein came of musical age almost ten years ago, though it feels like a world away. Both were in bands nurtured by Riot Grrrl—Tucker in Heavens to Betsy and Brownstein in Excuse 17—and both now cast an analytical (but also affectionate) eye on that time and the fruits it bore.

"This is going to sound conceited," Tucker says, "but the riot grrrls who were working at that time—Tobi Vail, Kathleen Hanna, Molly Neuman—they were all studying left-wing politics. They were cultural activists taking the tactics of the feminist movement, the civil rights movement, and rewriting them for the '90s culture. I thought that was really cool. But I think that that kind of political rhetoric is not very interesting to [today's] 19-year-old girls . . . I hope young girl activists see their work as being tied to a larger movement for change . . . and I think they do."

For Brownstein, "Riot Grrrl aimed to take feminism out of an academic context and put it into an expressive art—music—that young women could relate to. A lot of that movement was about reclaiming sexist language (i.e., 'bitch,' 'slut,' etc.) for ourselves and making the words powerful. When I see girls that grew up after Riot Grrrl, I see them embracing a non-academic style of feminism, especially in their manner of discourse. Whereas I think the women who began Riot Grrrl have incorporated a more complex theoretical approach to their politics. In some ways this must create a conflict, or at least a marked difference, in communication between the two. This kind of generational difference always impacts political movements, and it's a struggle to respect and acknowledge the differences and not lose a sense of community and cohesion."

Ah, community. From its inception (and even before, if you include Excuse 17 and Heavens to Betsy as part of a creative continuum), Sleater-Kinney have blurred the boundaries between expressions of musical, personal, and political concerns, just as they've blurred the boundaries between performer and audience. The rage in the songs found an outlet in activism on behalf of the self-defense organization Free to Fight, for instance, and over time the band have helped various causes, including Planned Parenthood. In spring and summer 2000 they were busy helping set up Ladyfest, a multi-day festival in August in Olympia. Tucker was on the band committee, Brownstein on the budget committee, with Weiss joking she'd get more involved once it started ("I'll be the muscles. I'll be hauling gear!").

"We recognize we've gotten an extraordinary amount of press, like crazy," said Tucker. "And since our community has helped us become who we are, we want to turn the spotlight back onto them when we can. We also want to show we're a part of something larger. It's important to talk about what the other people are doing; then there's a reciprocal effect on each other."

For Brownstein, "It's a struggle to get people to look at the different identities encompassed in this band—most people want to extract one identity and focus on that. To me, we are all at once a rock band, a punk band, a girl band, a feminist band, a pop band. There's no reason to compartmentalize these identities; I want to be able to toy with them, and have fun with the differences. We do look at this society through a feminist lens, and we're not afraid to incorporate that in our songs. But we want it to be part of a larger picture—part of a community, and our artistic vision."

Tucker concurs: "I want to make a difference through being a cultural activist. I want to help create culture that is not sexist and is encouraging to young women and all people."

In his 1977 book *Noise: The Political Economy of Music*, Jacques Attali wrote: "Music is prophecy: its styles and economic organization are ahead of the rest of society because it explores, much faster than material reality can, the entire range of possibilities in a given code. It makes audible the new world that will gradually become visible."

At this point in time, that prophecy still allows for a range of outcomes: a more misogynistic mayhem, for instance, or further corporate commodification. We can hope, though, that Sleater-Kinney's music, style, and even their "economic organization"—one that emphasizes a small label over a big one, friendship and support over basely capitalist exploitation—are the ones that will "gradually become visible" in society at large. It's utopian, perhaps; but if we're going to glimpse a new world, we may as well seek utopia. Perhaps we can already hear it coming. ●

ACKNOWLEDGMENTS

Thanks to Allison Dubinsky, who worked on this project—as scanner, proofreader, and copy editor—from the outset through to its completion; to Liz Pavlovic for her contributions to the layout; to Scott Nasburg for his technical expertise; and to Sleater-Kinney for letting us borrow one of their song titles for this book's title. Thanks to everyone who helped *Puncture* in so many different ways throughout its run, and above all thanks to all the writers, photographers, and artists who contributed their work to *Puncture* over the years. Take a bow, Bill Abelson, Alex Abramovich, Diana Adams, Tom Adelman, Erin Amar, Mike Appelstein, Ralph Armin, Martin Aston, Bob Bannister, Patrick Barber, Andy Barding, Jules Beckman, David Berman, Colin Berry, Rachel Blumberg, Richard Boon, Brad Bradberry, Stephen Braitman, Rob Brunner, Franklin Bruno, Bridget Burns, Tammy Rae Carland, Gregory Chance, John Chandler, Stepan Chapman, Liz Clayton, Scot Clough, Susan Compo, Jayne Cowan, John Crawford, Merri Cyr, John Darnielle, Margaret Davis, Jean Debbs, Arturo Diaz, John Dixon, Mark Dixon, Jon Dolan, Bill Donahue, Sarah Dougher, Cyndi Elliott, Uli Elser, Tim Ennis, Tom Erikson, Andrea Feldman, Bill Friskics-Warren, Michael Galinsky, Kate Garner, Carleton S. Gholz, Jon M. Gilbertson, Brian Glaser, Kian Goh, Eric Gordon, David Grad, Chrissie Haertel, Matthew Hall, Carl Hanni, Noelle Hanrahan, Gina Harp, Dave Haslam, Jeffrey Herrmann, Annie Hesse, Ed Hewitt, Amy Holberg, Ken Holt, Mark Hosler, Dana Huebler, Michael Hukin, Johnny Ray Huston, Alyssa Isenstein, Cindy Jacobson, Calvin Johnson, Rachel Jones, Jacqueline Jouret, Camden Joy, Jeffery Kennedy, Paula Keyth, Steve Kiviat, Steve Kline, Alex Kogan, Alan Korn, Donna Kossy, Krystine Kryttre, Blaine Kyllo, Stacey Levine, Heather Lewis, David Lowery, Maati Lyon, Felix Macnee, Lois Maffeo, Steven Malkmus, Sara Manaugh, Greil Marcus, Richard Martin, J Neo Marvin, Jon Matsumoto, Mike McGonigal, Bill Meyer, Jessica Meyer, Fred Mills, Joseph Mitchell, Maria Mochnacz, Colin B. Morton, Pete Moss, Scott Nasburg, Neil Nehring, David Nichols, Michael Nichols, Kim Norlen, Gail O'Hara, Will Oldham, Louise Olsen, Alan Paxton, Phil Pegg, Marty Perez, Bob Pomeroy, Mick Powers, Bert Queiroz, Diane Rhodes, Jon Roig, Jay Ruttenberg, Dan Schlatter, Curt Scholz, Brad Searles, Tom Sedlak, Talin Shahinian, Jane Shepherd, Stephanie R. Sheridan, Christine Sievanen, Tom Sinclair, Carl Snarl, James Stark, Patty Stirling, Craig Stockfleth, Dan Strachota, Terri Sutton, Judie Tallman, Michele Taylor, Jack Thompson, Steve Tignor, Jenny Toomey, Elisabeth Vincentelli, Robert Waldman, Campbell Walker, Billy Wawsaw, Cameron Weber, Marc Weingarten, Brian Willis, Diana Willis, Mike Wolf, Karen Woods, and Robert Zieger.

BIOGRAPHIES

Alex Abramovich lives and works in New York. He writes for the *London Review of Books* and other publications, and is the author of *Bullies: A Friendship* • **Tom Adelman** is **Camden Joy** is Tom Adelman is Camden Joy. In the mid-'90s, he plastered posters all over New York City. Later he started a farmers' market in Pennington, New Jersey, where he also initiated book clubs, film festivals, and environmental happenings. He currently lives in Vermont, recording music. You can hear his songs on Bandcamp • **Mike Appelstein** was the publisher of the zines *Writer's Block* and *Caught in Flux*. He currently lives in St. Louis, Missouri. See mikeappelstein.wordpress.com for archives and current projects • **Patrick Barber** was once a rock writer in Seattle, contributing to *Puncture*, the *Rocket*, and a zillion other no-longer-extant publications. Nowadays he is a dad, graphic designer, and calligrapher, living in Detroit and gardening like a madman • **David Berman** (1967–2019) led the bands the Silver Jews and Purple Mountains. He was the author of a book of poetry, *Actual Air*, and a book of cartoons, *The Portable February* • **Franklin Bruno** was the frontperson of Nothing Painted Blue and currently plays with the Human Hearts. He is the author of *Armed Forces*, in Continuum/Bloomsbury's 33⅓ series, and a book of poems, *The Accordion Repertoire* (Edge Books) • *Puncture* associate editor **John Chandler** began his career sorting through boxes of promos at Steve and Katherine's house and writing quick, cheeky summaries. He is a founding member of Giant Bug Village, America's #1 Guided By Voices tribute band and writes about horror films at horrificflicks.com • **Steve Connell** runs Verse Chorus Press, publishers of this book and others, several of them by former *Puncture* contributors. He was an editor at *Puncture* from 1985 on • **Jean Debbs** lives in splendid isolation in the Santa Lucia Mountains • **Jon Dolan** is the reviews editor for *Rolling Stone*. Previously he worked at *Spin*, *Blender*, and *City Pages*. He lives in Brooklyn • **Andrea Feldman** is a serial obsessive, armchair traveler, and music writer based in Providence, Rhode Island. She's written for the *Providence Phoenix*, the *Village Voice*, and the *Bull Tongue Review*. Twitter @visaforviolet • **Michael Galinsky** is a filmmaker, photographer, musician, and collaborator. He was inspired by, and thankful to, *Puncture* for giving him a platform for his work • **Kian Goh** is an architect and a professor of urban planning at UCLA, teaching and researching urban design, spatial politics, and climate change. Her book investigating urban climate change responses in New York, Jakarta, and Rotterdam will be published by the MIT Press • **Matthew Hall** has worked for the BBC in London and written for *Rolling Stone*, *Playboy*, the *Guardian*, and the *Sydney Morning Herald*, and many more. He is the author of three books on soccer, most recently *If I Started to Cry I Would Never Stop*.

Originally from Perth, Australia, he lives in New York City • **Gina Harp** grew up in Eugene, Oregon. She founded the HARP label in San Francisco in the early '90s, releasing records by bands such as Tribe 8 and Flophouse, as well as the influential *There's a Dyke in the Pit* EP, and worked as a music journalist there and in London. She died in 2007 • **Johnny Ray Huston** is a writer, collagist, and curator. He's acted in Gary Fembot's play *Shelter in Place* (2017–18) and movies *Mondo Bottomless* (2006) and *Scream of the Mandrake* (2015). He co-composed music, sang, and acted in Skye Thorstenson's *Tourist Trap* (2010), an award-winner at the SF International Film Festival • **Alan Korn** was a co-founding member of X-Tal, the Cat Heads, and the Ex-Cat Heads. He now practices law in the Bay Area, specializing in music- and media-related issues such as fair use, micro radio, and documentary film, and is the male member in the otherwise female band She Mob • **David Lowery** is the singer and guitarist in the bands Camper Van Beethoven and Cracker • **Lois Maffeo** is a singer-songwriter and occasional music journalist from Olympia, Washington. Her most cherished accumulation is the friendship circle she made throughout the last 35 years of participation in independent music and DIY culture • **Sara Manaugh** commutes by bike and ferry to her job at a nonprofit legal services organization. During her *Puncture* years, she was a struggling academic, a server at a moribund pizza joint, and a "knowledge engineer" at an internet startup. She lives in Brooklyn • **J Neo Marvin**, aka John Bassham, BA, BECA: SFSU 2014, *Puncture* contributor 1983–2000, has produced 27 albums and curates Ear Candle Radio at earcandleproductions.com. By day he edits articles for healthline.com, a highly trusted health website. "The most underrated songwriting genius and music producer of the 20th/21st centuries" (Davis Jones) • **Bill Meyer** lives near Chicago, Illinois, where he has written about music since 1989. He currently contributes to the *Chicago Reader*, the *Wire*, *Magnet*, *Dusted*, and *Downbeat*, and sustains a parallel career as a mental health care provider • **Fred Mills** lives with his wife, son, and feral cat in the hipster haven known as Asheville, North Carolina, though the bulk of his *Puncture*-era writing was done during his decade-long desert tenure in Tucson, Arizona, where he hopes to one day retire. His *Puncture* memories remain indelible, and "Katherine and Steve will always be in my Top 3 list of editors who (a) tolerated, and (b) guided me as an indie music journalist still figuring things out" • **Carlton B Morgan**, aka Colin B. Morton aka Clark Gwent, former collaborator on the cartoon *Great Pop Things* with Jon Langford, "Welsh vegan punk mystic" (Stewart Lee), resides in soon-to-be-independent Wales, writing science fiction based loosely on his late-capitalist existence. Extracts at soundcloud.com/larkwent. He has defeated all of his enemies • **Neil Nehring** is an English professor at the University of Texas at Austin. His publications include *Popular Music, Gender, and Postmodernism: Anger Is an Energy* and *Flowers in the Dustbin: Culture, Anarchy, and Postwar England* • **David Nichols** is

associate professor in urban planning at the University of Melbourne. His most recent books are *Dig: Australian Rock & Pop Music 1960–85*; *Urban Australia and Post-Punk: Exploring Dogs in Space*, co-edited with Sophie Perillo; and *The Alert Grey Twinkling Eyes of C J DeGaris*. He likes cats, dogs, and coffee • **Gail O'Hara** is a writer, editor, photographer, and co-founder of *chickfactor* fanzine. Her photos have appeared in many publications, books, album covers, and art shows. She is currently the editor in chief of *chickfactor*, works freelance for Bitch Media, Airship, and Jute Creative, and lives in Portland, Oregon • **Marty Perez**, secondhand-record-store clerk, Alaska fisherman, commercial diver, etc. All the while managing to have a camera nearby. Fortunate to be in the right places at the right times and be somewhat prepared. Happy to have tasted the days of analog • Toward the end of the last century, **Bob Pomeroy** covered arts and entertainment for a variety of publications, writing record and book reviews, artist profiles and features, often shadowed by a mysterious doppelgänger, "the other Bob Pomeroy," while en route to joining *Puncture*'s stable of regular contributors • **Jay Ruttenberg** began writing for *Puncture* in 1996 and later worked as its music editor. When *Puncture* closed, he moved to New York and started the comedy zine the *Lowbrow Reader*. He has contributed to the *New Yorker*, the *New York Times*, and *Time Out New York*, where he was a staff writer for many years • **Brad Searles** is an indie-rock-'n'-pop obsessive, occasional drummer, and keeper of longtime Boston-based music site Bradley's Almanac • **Christine Sievanen** is a Seattle native, a writer and photographer who loves music, vintage treasure hunting, and road trips • **Tom Sinclair** is a native New Yorker who has lived through three citywide blackouts ('65, '77, '03). He has labored at many jobs: messenger, file clerk, mail clerk, reporter, editor, PR executive, rock critic, writer at *Entertainment Weekly*, and alcoholism counselor. "Writing's cool," he says, "but I've always had a soft spot for messenger work." • **Katherine Spielmann** worked as a journalist and editor in New York and in the UK before settling in San Francisco, where she and Patty Stirling founded *Puncture*, which she edited throughout its 18-year run. She and partner Steve Connell subsequently published books under the Verse Chorus Press imprint. She died in 2016 • **Patty Stirling (pstirl)** was born in San Diego and grew up on California beaches and an Oregon homestead. After briefly attending the San Francisco Art Institute, she worked in restaurants and wrote for punk zine *Ripper*. In 1982, she met Katherine and they started publishing *Puncture*. She has traveled in Australia, Africa, Asia, and Europe, writing about music and working as a cook, and is co-editor of *Puncture: The First 6 Issues* (Tract Home Publications) • **Terri Sutton** is grateful to *Puncture* for publishing a raw enthusiast. Her work appears in *Our Neck of the Woods: Exploring Minnesota's Wild Places*; *Rock She Wrote: Women Write about Rock, Pop, and Rap*; *Trouble Girls: The Rolling Stone Book of Women in Rock*; *SPIN: Greatest Hits*; and *SPIN Alternative Record Guide* • **Steve Tignor** is a senior writer at *Tennis Magazine* and Tennis.com, and the author of *High Strung: Bjorn Borg, John McEnroe, and the Last Days of Tennis's Golden Age* • **Jenny Toomey**...DC punk rocker...co-ran Simple Machines Records...bands (Tsunami, Grenadine, Liquorice, etc.)...wrote for the *Washington Post, Tape Op, Puncture*, etc....Fascinated by the internet, she founded Future of Music Coalition, and Air Traffic Control ...Currently at the Ford Foundation, fighting inequality and injustice in the internet. Married to Brian Hartman, eats well, loves dogs and gardens. Black Lives Matter. • **Elisabeth Vincentelli** is a regular contributor to the *New York Times* and the *New Yorker*; her favorite subjects are theater, music, and skiing, but she's open to suggestions. She has written two books about ABBA. Links and more at determineddilettante.blogspot.com; thoughts and less at @EVincentelli on Twitter • **Robert Zieger** has gone from attending gnarly punk-rock shows to teaching high school history at a variety of international schools. To date, he's taught in Pakistan, Myanmar, Indonesia, the D.R. Congo, and currently Bolivia, where he and his wife are raising their 8-year-old to be an anti-fascist feminist.

IMAGE CREDITS

COVER: (*front, L–R*) Jeff Mangum (Neutral Milk Hotel) by Will Westbrook; Courtney Love (Hole) by Marty Perez; Kristin Hersh (Throwing Muses) by Andrea Feldman; Robert Pollard (Guided by Voices) and Carrie Brownstein (Sleater-Kinney) by Marty Perez; (*spine*) Mia Levin (Frightwig) by Katherine Spielmann; (*back, L–R*) PJ Harvey by Kate Garner; Beck by Marty Perez; Chan Marshall (Cat Power) by Steve Connell; Corin Tucker (Sleater-Kinney) by Marty Perez; Stephen Malkmus (Pavement) by Michael Galinsky.

INTERIOR: 8—Steve Connell. 12, 15—courtesy Ken Goes. 16, 19—Edie Winograde. 20—Steve Jennings. 23—John Ingledew. 27—Katherine Spielmann. 29—courtesy the Mekons. 30—Katherine Spielmann. 31, 33—Frances Pelzman Liscio. 34—Katherine Spielmann. 39 (*top*)—Tom Erikson; courtesy Pat Thomas. 41—courtesy Scrawl. 42, 43—Marty Perez. 45, 47—Mark Dixon. 49—Bert Queiroz. 50, 51—Darren Mock. 53—(*top*) Brad Miller, (*bottom*) Katherine Spielmann. 55, 56—Patty Stirling. 58—Katherine Spielmann. 61—courtesy K Records. 67—Steve Connell. 69—Brad Searles. 74—uncredited promo photo, courtesy Rough Trade. 76—uncredited promo photo, courtesy Beggars Banquet. 78—Ray Lego, courtesy Beggars Banquet. 81, 82, 85, 91—courtesy X-tal. 93, 96—Gina Harp. 98—Christine Sievanen. 101—Michael Galinsky. 102—courtesy K Records. 104, 105—Michael Galinsky. 109, 100, 111—courtesy the Mekons. 112—uncredited promo photo, courtesy Mute Records. 117—Katherine Spielmann. 119, 120, 121—Gina Harp. 123, 125—courtesy David Lowery. 127—Tim Overstreet. 128, 129—Michael Galinsky. 131—Francis Ford, courtesy Violent Femmes management. 134—Casliber / CC-BY-SA-3.0, https://commons.wikimedia.org/wiki/File: Violentfemmessydney90.png (cropped). 136, 138, 139—Brad Searles. 141, 143—Maria Mochnacz. 145—uncredited promo photo, courtesy Scat Records. 146—Merri Cyr. 149—Sno / CC-BY-SA-4. 0, https://commons. wikimedia. org/ wiki/File:Greil_Marcus_SRN. jpg, cropped. 150—Anne-Outram Mott; courtesy Greil Marcus. 152—Katherine Spielmann. 155—Ken Holt. 157, 159, 160— Felix Macnee. 163—Gail O'Hara. 164— Alicia Aguilera, courtesy Merge Records. 165—Gail O'Hara. 166—Kate Garner. 169, 173—Colin B. Morton and Chuck Death, from *Great Pop Things* (Verse Chorus Press). 171—Mika Väisänen / CC-SA-4.0, https://commons.wikimedia.org/wiki/File:1998-pj_harvey-01-mika.jpg (cropped). 175—Marty Perez. 176—Liz Clayton. 177—Marty Perez. 178—Dan Schlatter. 180, 181—Michael Galinsky. 183—courtesy Flying Nun. 185—Carol Tippet, courtesy Flying Nun. 187, 188—Sue P. Fox. 191, 192—courtesy Merge Records. 193—Marty Perez. 199—Joe Oldham, courtesy Drag City. 200—Dianne Bellino, courtesy Drag City. 202, 204, 205, 206—Steve Connell. 209, 211—Marty Perez. 213, 214—Michael Galinsky. 216—Andrea Feldman. 220, 223—Michael Galinsky. 224—Michael Galinsky. 229—Hilarie Sidney. 230—Tamee Ealom, courtesy SpinArt Records. 231—courtesy Flydaddy Records. 233—Will Westbrook. 234—Marty Perez. 238—Gail O'Hara. 241—Joe Oldham, courtesy Drag City. 242—Edie Vee, courtesy Drag City. 244—Joe Oldham, courtesy Drag City. 246—Marty Perez. 248, 251—Ebet Roberts. 254—Gail O'Hara. 257, 259, 260, 263—Marty Perez. 264—courtesy Jon Langford. 265—paintings by Jon Langford, reproduced from his book *Nashville Radio* (Verse Chorus Press). 266, 269, 271, 273—Will Westbrook. 275—Christine Sievanen. 276—C. Taylor Crothers, courtesy Drag City. 281—courtesy Drag City. 284—Tammy Rae Carland. 286—Michael Galinsky. 287, 289—courtesy Kathleen Hanna. 290, 295—Michael Galinsky. 297, 298, 301—courtesy Warner Bros. 305—Michael Galinsky. 309—Talin Shahinian. 311—Bob Johnson. 312, 313—Marty Perez.